W9-APQ-747

The Guns of August

By *Barbara W. Tuchman*

BIBLE AND SWORD (1956)

THE ZIMMERMANN TELEGRAM (1958)

THE GUNS OF AUGUST (1962)

THE PROUD TOWER (1966)

NOTES FROM CHINA (1972)

A DISTANT MIRROR (1978)

▶▶▶
▶▶▶
▶▶▶ *THE GUNS*

OF AUGUST

Barbara W. Tuchman

Bonanza Books
New York

Copyright © MCMLXII by Barbara W. Tuchman.
All rights reserved.

This 1982 edition is published by Bonanza Books, distributed
by Crown Publishers, Inc. by arrangement with Macmillan
Publishing Co., Inc.

Manufactured in the United States of America

Library of Congress Cataloging in Publication Data

Tuchman, Barbara Wertheim.
  The guns of August.

  Reprint. Originally published: New York: Macmillan, 1962.
  Bibliography: p.
  Includes index.
  1. World War, 1914-1918—Campaigns. I. Title.
[D530.T8   1982]   940.4′1   82-9428
ISBN 0-517-385740   AACR2

h g f e d c b a

"The human heart is the starting point of all matters pertaining to war."

MARÉCHAL DE SAXE
Reveries on the Art of War (Preface), 1732

"The terrible Ifs accumulate."

WINSTON CHURCHILL
The World Crisis, Vol. I, Chap. XI

Contents

Author's Note

This book owes a primary debt to Mr. Cecil Scott of The Macmillan Company whose advice and encouragement and knowledge of the subject were an essential element and a firm support from beginning to end. I have also been fortunate in the critical collaboration of Mr. Denning Miller who in clarifying many problems of writing and interpretation made this a better book than it would otherwise have been. For his help I am permanently grateful.

I should like to express my appreciation of the unsurpassed resources of the New York Public Library and, at the same time, a hope that somehow, someday in my native city a way will be found to make the Library's facilities for scholars match its incomparable material. My thanks go also to the New York Society Library for the continuing hospitality of its stacks and the haven of a place to write; to Mrs. Agnes F. Peterson of the Hoover Library at Stanford for the loan of the Briey *Procés-Verbaux* and for running to earth the answers to many queries; to Miss R. E. B. Coombe of the Imperial War Museum, London, for many of the illustrations; to the staff of the Bibliothèque de Documentation Internationale Contemporaine Paris, for source material and to Mr. Henry Sachs of the American

Ordnance Association for technical advice and for supplementing my inadequate German.

To the reader I must explain that the omission of Austria-Hungary, Serbia, and the Russo-Austrian and Serbo-Austrian fronts was not entirely arbitrary. The inexhaustible problem of the Balkans divides itself naturally from the rest of the war. Moreover, operations on the Austrian front during the first thirty-one days were purely preliminary and did not reach a climax, with effect on the war as a whole, until the Battle of Lemberg against the Russians and the Battle of the Drina against the Serbs. These took place between September 8 and 17, outside my chronological limits, and it seemed to me there was unity without it and the prospect of tiresome length if it were included.

After a period of total immersion in military memoirs, I had hoped to dispense with Roman-numeraled corps, but convention proved stronger than good intentions. I can do nothing about the Roman numerals which, it seems, are inseparably riveted to army corps, but I can offer the reader a helpful RULE ON LEFT AND RIGHT: rivers face downstream and armies, even when turned around and retreating, are considered to face the direction in which they started; that is, their left and right remain the same as when they were advancing.

Sources for the narrative and for all quoted remarks are given in the Notes at the end of the book. I have tried to avoid spontaneous attribution or the "he must have" style of historical writing: "As he watched the coastline of France disappear, Napoleon must have thought back over the long . . ." All conditions of weather, thoughts or feelings, and states of mind public or private, in the following pages have documentary support. Where it seems called for, the evidence appears in the Notes.

Illustrations and Maps

Following page 208

Prince Rupprecht and the Kaiser

General von François

Colonel Hoffman

German cavalry officers in Brussels

Joffre, Poincaré, King George V, Foch, and Haig

General Gallieni

General von Kluck

Maps

Maps by William A. Pieper

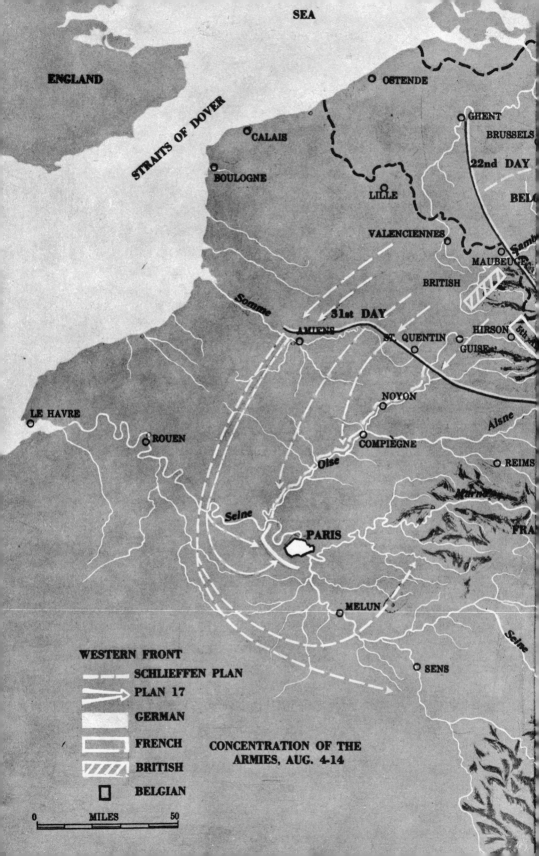

SEA

ENGLAND

OSTENDE

GHENT

BRUSSELS

22nd DAY

BEL

STRAITS OF DOVER

CALAIS

BOULOGNE

LILLE

Somme

VALENCIENNES

MAUBEUGE

Sambre

BRITISH

31st DAY

AMIENS

ST. QUENTIN

HIRSON

5th

GUISE

NOYON

Aisne

LE HAVRE

ROUEN

COMPIÈGNE

REIMS

Oise

Marne

FRA

Seine

PARIS

MELUN

Seine

WESTERN FRONT

SCHLIEFFEN PLAN

PLAN 17

GERMAN

FRENCH

BRITISH

BELGIAN

CONCENTRATION OF THE
ARMIES, AUG. 4-14

SENS

0   MILES   50

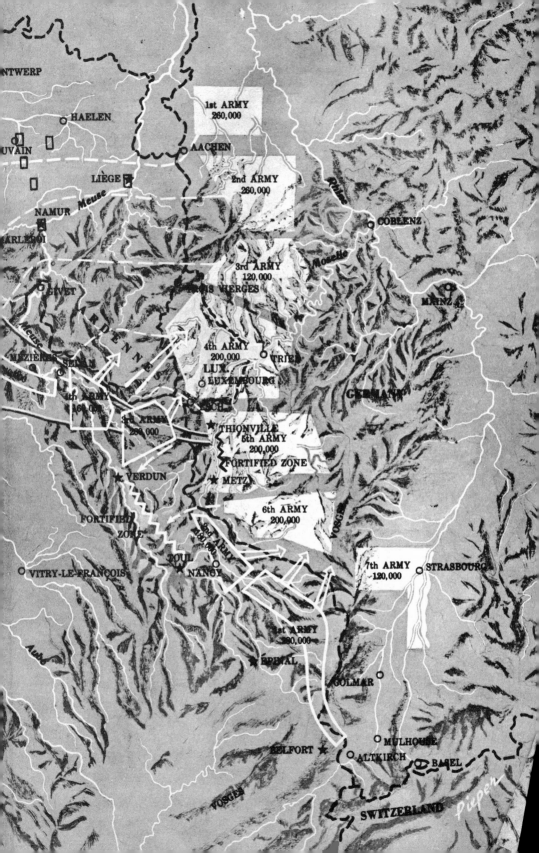

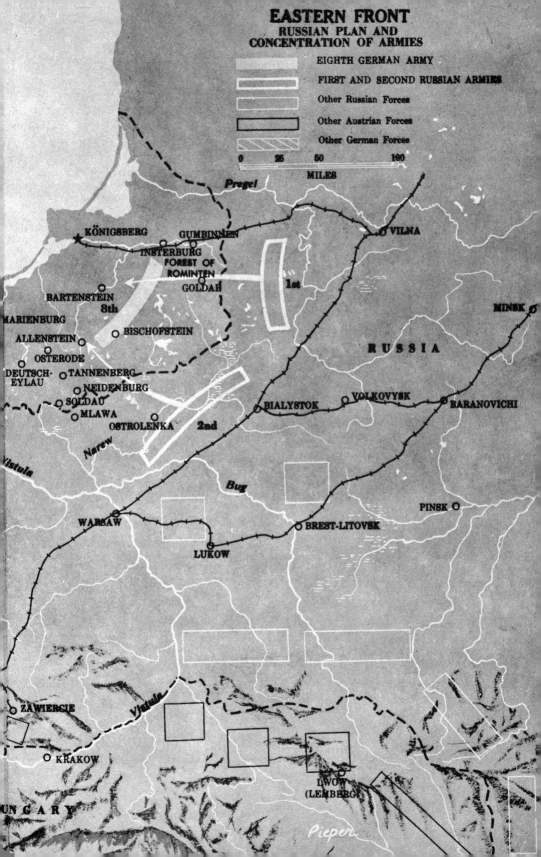

EASTERN FRONT
RUSSIAN PLAN AND
CONCENTRATION OF ARMIES

EIGHTH GERMAN ARMY

FIRST AND SECOND RUSSIAN ARMIES

Other Russian Forces

Other Austrian Forces

Other German Forces

0   25   50   100

MILES

Pregel

KÖNIGSBERG   GUMBINNEN

INSTERBURG
FOREST OF
ROMINTEN
GOLDAH

1st

VILNA

BARTENSTEIN   8th

MINSK

MARIENBURG   BISCHOFSTEIN

ALLENSTEIN

OSTERODE

DEUTSCH-
EYLAU   TANNENBERG

NEIDENBURG

SOLDAU

MLAWA

OSTROLENKA   2nd

R U S S I A

BIALYSTOK   VOLKOVYSK   BARANOVICHI

Narew

Vistula

Bug

PINSK

WARSAW

BREST-LITOVSK

LUKOW

Vistula

ZAWIERCIE

KRAKOW

LWOW
(LEMBERG)

UNGARY

Pieper

▶▶▶ *A Funeral*

So GORGEOUS WAS THE SPECTACLE ON THE MAY morning of 1910 when nine kings rode in the funeral of Edward VII of England that the crowd, waiting in hushed and black-clad awe, could not keep back gasps of admiration. In scarlet and blue and green and purple, three by three the sovereigns rode through the palace gates, with plumed helmets, gold braid, crimson sashes, and jeweled orders flashing in the sun. After them came five heirs apparent, forty more imperial or royal highnesses, seven queens—four dowager and three regnant—and a scattering of special ambassadors from uncrowned countries. Together they represented seventy nations in the greatest assemblage of royalty and rank ever gathered in one place and, of its kind, the last. The muffled tongue of Big Ben tolled nine by the clock as the cortege left the palace, but on history's clock it was sunset, and the sun of the old world was setting in a dying blaze of splendor never to be seen again.

In the center of the front row rode the new king, George V, flanked on his left by the Duke of Connaught, the late king's only surviving brother, and on his right by a personage to whom, acknowledged *The Times*, "belongs the first place among all the foreign mourners," who "even when relations are most strained has never lost his popularity amongst us"—

William II, the German Emperor. Mounted on a gray horse, wearing the scarlet uniform of a British Field Marshal, carrying the baton of that rank, the Kaiser had composed his features behind the famous upturned mustache in an expression "grave even to severity." Of the several emotions churning his susceptible breast, some hints exist in his letters. "I am proud to call this place my home and to be a member of this royal family," he wrote home after spending the night in Windsor Castle in the former apartments of his mother. Sentiment and nostalgia induced by these melancholy occasions with his English relatives jostled with pride in his supremacy among the assembled potentates and with a fierce relish in the disappearance of his uncle from the European scene. He had come to bury Edward his bane; Edward the arch plotter, as William conceived it, of Germany's encirclement; Edward his mother's brother whom he could neither bully nor impress, whose fat figure cast a shadow between Germany and the sun. "He is Satan. You cannot imagine what a Satan he is!"

This verdict, announced by the Kaiser before a dinner of three hundred guests in Berlin in 1907, was occasioned by one of Edward's continental tours undertaken with clearly diabolical designs at encirclement. He had spent a provocative week in Paris, visited for no good reason the King of Spain (who had just married his niece), and finished with a visit to the King of Italy with obvious intent to seduce him from his Triple Alliance with Germany and Austria. The Kaiser, possessor of the least inhibited tongue in Europe, had worked himself into a frenzy ending in another of those comments that had periodically over the past twenty years of his reign shattered the nerves of diplomats.

Happily the Encircler was now dead and replaced by George who, the Kaiser told Theodore Roosevelt a few days before the funeral, was "a very nice boy" (of forty-five, six years younger than the Kaiser). "He is a thorough Englishman and hates all foreigners but I do not mind that as long as he does not hate Germans more than other foreigners." Alongside George, William now rode confidently, saluting as he passed the regimental colors of the 1st Royal Dragoons of which he was honorary colonel. Once he had distributed photographs of himself wearing their uniform with the Delphic inscription written above his signature, "I bide my time." Today his time had come; he was supreme in Europe.

Behind him rode the widowed Queen Alexandra's two brothers, King Frederick of Denmark and King George of the Hellenes; her nephew, King Haakon of Norway; and three kings who were to lose their thrones: Alfonso of Spain, Manuel of Portugal and, wearing a silk turban, King Ferdinand of Bulgaria who annoyed his fellow sovereigns by calling himself Czar and kept in a chest a Byzantine Emperor's full regalia, acquired from a theatrical costumer, against the day when he should reassemble the Byzantine dominions beneath his scepter.

Dazzled by these "splendidly mounted princes," as *The Times* called them, few observers had eyes for the ninth king, the only one among them who was to achieve greatness as a man. Despite his great height and perfect horsemanship, Albert, King of the Belgians, who disliked the pomp of royal ceremony, contrived in that company to look both embarrassed and absentminded. He was then thirty-five and had been on the throne barely a year. In later years when his face became known to the world as a symbol of heroism and tragedy, it still always wore that abstracted look, as if his mind were on something else.

The future source of tragedy, tall, corpulent, and corseted, with green plumes waving from his helmet, Archduke Franz Ferdinand of Austria, heir of the old Emperor Franz Josef, rode on Albert's right, and on his left another scion who would never reach his throne, Prince Yussuf, heir of the Sultan of Turkey. After the kings came the royal highnesses: Prince Fushimi, brother of the Emperor of Japan; Grand Duke Michael, brother of the Czar of Russia; the Duke of Aosta in bright blue with green plumes, brother of the King of Italy; Prince Carl, brother of the King of Sweden; Prince Henry, consort of the Queen of Holland; and the Crown Princes of Serbia, Rumania, and Montenegro. The last named, Prince Danilo, "an amiable, extremely handsome young man of delightful manners," resembled the Merry Widow's lover in more than name, for, to the consternation of British functionaries, he had arrived the night before accompanied by a "charming young lady of great personal attractions" whom he introduced as his wife's lady in waiting with the explanation that she had come to London to do some shopping.

A regiment of minor German royalty followed: rulers of Mecklenburg-Schwerin, Mecklenburg-Strelitz, Waldeck-Pyrmont, Saxe-Coburg Gotha, of Saxony, Hesse, Württemberg, Baden, and Bavaria, of whom the last, Crown Prince Rupprecht, was soon to lead a German army in battle. There were a Prince of Siam, a Prince of Persia, five princes of the former French royal house of Orléans, a brother of the Khedive of Egypt wearing a gold-tasseled fez, Prince Tsia-tao of China in an embroidered light-blue gown whose ancient dynasty had two more years to run, and the Kaiser's brother, Prince Henry of Prussia, representing the German Navy, of which he was Commander in Chief. Amid all this magnificence were three civilian-coated gentlemen, M. Gaston-Carlin of Switzerland, M. Pichon, Foreign Minister of France, and former President Theodore Roosevelt, special envoy of the United States.

Edward, the object of this unprecedented gathering of nations, was often called the "Uncle of Europe," a title which, insofar as Europe's ruling houses were meant, could be taken literally. He was the uncle not only of Kaiser Wilhelm but also, through his wife's sister, the Dowager Empress Marie of Russia, of Czar Nicolas II. His own niece Alix was the Czarina; his daughter Maud was Queen of Norway; another niece, Ena, was Queen of Spain; a third niece, Marie, was soon to be Queen of Rumania. The Danish family of his wife, besides occupying the throne of Denmark, had mothered the Czar of Russia and supplied kings to Greece and Norway. Other relatives, the progeny at various removes of Queen Victoria's nine sons and daughters, were scattered in abundance throughout the courts of Europe.

Yet not family feeling alone nor even the suddenness and shock of Edward's death—for to public knowledge he had been ill one day and dead the next—accounted for the unexpected flood of condolences at his passing. It was in fact a tribute to Edward's great gifts as a sociable king which had proved invaluable to his country. In the nine short years of his reign England's splendid isolation had given way, under pressure, to a series of "understandings" or attachments, but not quite alliances—for England dislikes the definitive—with two old enemies, France and Russia, and one promising new power, Japan. The resulting shift in balance registered itself around the world and affected every state's relations with every other. Though Edward neither initiated nor influenced his country's policy, his personal diplomacy helped to make the change possible.

Taken as a child to visit France, he had said to Napoleon III: "You have a nice country. I would like to be your son." This preference for things French, in contrast to or perhaps in protest against his mother's for the Germanic, lasted, and after her death was put to use. When England, growing edgy over the challenge implicit in Germany's Naval Program of 1900, decided to patch up old quarrels with France, Edward's talents as *Roi Charmeur* smoothed the way. In 1903 he went to Paris, disregarding advice that an official state visit would find a cold welcome. On his arrival the crowds were sullen and silent except for a few taunting cries of "*Vivent les Boers!*" and "*Vive Fashoda!*" which the King ignored. To a worried aide who muttered, "The French don't like us," he replied, "Why should they?" and continued bowing and smiling from his carriage.

For four days he made appearances, reviewed troops at Vincennes, attended the races at Longchamps, a gala at the Opéra, a state banquet at the Elysée, a luncheon at the Quai d'Orsay and, at the theater, transformed a chill into smiles by mingling with the audience in the entr'acte and paying gallant compliments in French to a famous actress in the lobby. Everywhere he made gracious and tactful speeches about his friendship and admiration for the French, their "glorious traditions," their "beautiful city," for which he confessed an attachment "fortified by many happy memories," his "sincere pleasure" in the visit, his belief that old misunderstandings are "happily over and forgotten," that the mutual prosperity of France and England was interdependent and their friendship his "constant preoccupation." When he left, the crowds now shouted, "Vive notre roi!" "Seldom has such a complete change of attitude been seen as that which has taken place in this country. He has won the hearts of all the French," a Belgian diplomat reported. The German ambassador thought the King's visit was "a most odd affair," and supposed that an Anglo-French *rapprochement* was the result of a "general aversion to Germany." Within a year, after hard work by ministers settling disputes, the *rapprochement* became the Anglo-French Entente, signed in April, 1904.

Germany might have had an English entente for herself had not her leaders, suspecting English motives, rebuffed the overtures of the Colonial Secretary, Joseph Chamberlain, in 1899 and again in 1901. Neither the shadowy Holstein who conducted Germany's foreign affairs from behind the scenes nor the elegant and erudite Chancellor, Prince Bülow, nor the Kaiser himself was quite sure what they suspected England of but they were certain it was something perfidious. The Kaiser always wanted an agreement with England if he could get one without seeming to want it. Once, affected by English surroundings and family sentiment at the funeral of Queen Victoria, he allowed himself to confess the wish to Edward. "Not a mouse could stir in Europe without our permission," was the way he visualized an Anglo-German alliance. But as soon as the English showed signs of willingness, he and his ministers veered off, suspecting some trick. Fearing to be taken advantage of at the conference table, they preferred to stay away altogether and depend upon an ever-growing navy to frighten the English into coming to terms.

Bismarck had warned Germany to be content with land power, but his successors were neither separately nor collectively Bismarcks. He had pursued clearly seen goals unswervingly; they groped for larger horizons with no clear idea of what they wanted. Holstein was a Machiavelli without a policy who operated on only one principle: suspect everyone. Bülow had no principles; he was so slippery, lamented his colleague Admiral Tirpitz, that compared to him an eel was a leech. The flashing, inconstant, always freshly inspired Kaiser had a different goal every hour, and practiced diplomacy as an exercise in perpetual motion.

None of them believed England would ever come to terms with France, and all warnings of that event Holstein dismissed as "naïve," even a most explicit one from his envoy in London, Baron Eckhardstein. At a dinner at Marlborough House in 1902, Eckhardstein had watched Paul Cambon, the French ambassador, disappear into the billiard room with Joseph Chamberlain, where they engaged in "animated conversation" lasting twenty-eight minutes of which the only words he could overhear (the baron's memoirs do not say whether the door was open or he was listening at the keyhole) were "Egypt" and "Morocco." Later he was summoned to the King's study where Edward offered him an 1888 Uppmann cigar and told him that England was going to reach a settlement with France over all disputed colonial questions.

When the Entente became a fact, William's wrath was tremendous. Beneath it, and even more galling, rankled Edward's triumph in Paris. The *reise-Kaiser*, as he was known from the frequency of his travels, derived balm from ceremonial entries into foreign capitals, and the one above all he wished to visit was Paris, the unattainable. He had been everywhere, even to Jerusalem, where the Jaffa Gate had to be cut to permit his entry on horseback; but Paris, the center of all that was beautiful, all that was desirable, all that Berlin was not, remained closed to him. He wanted to receive the acclaim of Parisians and be awarded the Grand Cordon of the Legion of Honor, and twice let the imperial wish be known to the French. No invitation ever came. He could enter Alsace and make speeches glorifying the victory of 1870; he could lead parades through Metz in Lorraine; but it is perhaps the saddest story of the fate of kings that the Kaiser lived to be eighty-two and died without seeing Paris.

Envy of the older nations gnawed at him. He complained to Theodore Roosevelt that the English nobility on continental tours never visited Berlin but always went to Paris. He felt unappreciated. "All the long years of my reign," he told the King of Italy, "my colleagues, the Monarchs of Europe, have paid no attention to what I have to say. Soon, with my great Navy to endorse my words, they will be more respectful." The same sentiments ran through his whole nation, which suffered, like their emperor, from a terrible need for recognition. Pulsing with energy and ambition, conscious of strength, fed upon Nietzsche and Treitschke, they felt entitled to rule, and cheated that the world did not acknowledge their title. "We must," wrote Friedrich von Bernhardi, the spokesman of militarism, "secure to German nationality and German spirit throughout the globe that high esteem which is due them . . . and has hitherto been withheld from them." He frankly allowed only one method of attaining the goal; lesser Bernhardis from the Kaiser down sought to secure the esteem they craved by threats and show of power. They shook the "mailed fist," demanded their "place in the sun," and proclaimed the virtues of the sword in paeans to "blood and iron" and "shining armor." In German practice Mr. Roosevelt's current precept for getting on with your neighbors was Teutonized to, "Speak loudly and brandish a big gun." When they brandished it, when the Kaiser told his troops departing for China and the Boxer Rebellion to bear themselves as the Huns of Attila (the choice of Huns as German prototypes was his own), when Pan-German Societies and Navy Leagues multiplied and met in congresses to demand that other nations recognize their "legitimate aims" toward expansion, the other nations answered with alliances, and when they did, Germany screamed *Einkreisung!*—Encirclement! The refrain *Deutschland ganzlich einzukreisen* grated over the decade.

Edward's foreign visits continued—Rome, Vienna, Lisbon, Madrid— and not to royalty only. Every year he took the cure at Marienbad where he would exchange views with the Tiger of France, born in the same year as himself, who was premier for four of the years that Edward was king. Edward, whose two passions in life were correct clothes and unorthodox company, overlooked the former, and admired M. Clemenceau. The Tiger shared Napoleon's opinion that Prussia "was hatched from a cannon ball," and saw the cannon ball coming in his direction. He worked, he planned, he maneuvered in the shadow of one dominant idea: "the German lust for power . . . has fixed as its policy the extermination of France." He told Edward that when the time came when France needed help, England's sea power would not be enough, and reminded him that Napoleon was beaten at Waterloo, not Trafalgar.

In 1908, to the distaste of his subjects, Edward paid a state visit to the Czar aboard the imperial yacht at Reval. English imperialists regarded Russia as the ancient foe of the Crimea and more recently as the menace looming over India, while to the Liberals and Laborites Russia was the land of the knout, the pogrom, and the massacred revolutionaries of 1905, and the Czar, according to Mr. Ramsay MacDonald, "a common murderer." The distaste was reciprocated. Russia detested England's alliance with Japan and resented her as the power that frustrated Russia's historic yearning for Constantinople and the Straits. Nicholas II once combined two favorite prejudices in the simple statement, "An Englishman is a *zhid* (Jew)."

But old antagonisms were not so strong as new pressures, and under the urging of the French, who were anxious to have their two allies come to terms, an Anglo-Russian Convention was signed in 1907. A personal touch of royal friendliness was felt to be required to clear away any lingering mistrust, and Edward embarked for Reval. He had long talks with the Russian Foreign Minister, Isvolsky, and danced the Merry Widow waltz with the Czarina with such effect as to make her laugh, the first man to accomplish this feat since the unhappy woman put on the crown of the Romanovs. Nor was it such a frivolous achievement as might appear, for though it could hardly be said that the Czar governed Russia in a working sense, he ruled as an autocrat and was in turn ruled by his strong-willed if weak-witted wife. Beautiful, hysterical, and morbidly suspicious, she hated everyone but her immediate family and a series of fanatic or lunatic charlatans who offered comfort to her desperate soul. The Czar, neither well endowed mentally nor very well educated, was, in the Kaiser's opinion, "only fit to live in a country house and grow turnips."

The Kaiser regarded the Czar as his own sphere of influence and tried by clever schemes to woo him out of his French alliance which had been the consequence of William's own folly. Bismarck's maxim "Keep friends with Russia" and the Reinsurance Treaty that implemented it, William had dropped, along with Bismarck, in the first, and worst, blunder of his reign. Alexander III, the tall, stern Czar of that day, had promptly turned around in 1892 and entered into alliance with republican France, even at the cost of standing at attention to "The Marseillaise." Besides, he snubbed William, whom he considered "*un garçon mal élevé*," and would only talk to him over his shoulder. Ever since Nicholas acceded to the throne, William had been trying to repair his blunder by writing the young Czar long letters (in English) of advice, gossip, and political harangue addressed to "Dearest Nicky" and signed "Your affectionate friend, Willy." An irreligious republic stained by the blood of monarchs was no fit company for him, he told the Czar. "Nicky, take my word for it, the curse of God has stricken that people forever." Nicky's true interests, Willy told him, were with a *Drei-Kaiser Bund*, a league of the three emperors of Russia, Austria, and Germany. Yet, remembering the old Czar's snubs, he could not help patronizing his son. He would tap Nicholas on the shoulder, and say, "My advice to you is more speeches and more parades, more speeches, more parades," and he offered to send German troops to protect Nicholas from his rebellious subjects, a suggestion which infuriated the Czarina, who hated William more after every exchange of visits.

When he failed, under the circumstances, to wean Russia away from France, the Kaiser drew up an ingenious treaty engaging Russia and Germany to aid each other in case of attack, which the Czar, after signing, was to communicate to the French and invite them to join. After Russia's disasters in her war with Japan (which the Kaiser had strenuously urged her into) and the revolutionary risings that followed, when the regime was at its lowest ebb, he invited the Czar to a secret rendezvous, without attendant ministers, at Björkö in the Gulf of Finland. William knew well enough that Russia could not accede to his treaty without breaking faith with the French, but he thought that sovereigns' signatures were all that was needed to erase the difficulty. Nicholas signed.

William was in ecstasy. He had made good the fatal lapse, secured Germany's back door, and broken the encirclement. "Bright tears stood in my eyes," he wrote to Bülow, and he was sure Grandpapa (William I, who had died muttering about a war on two fronts) was looking down on him. He felt his treaty to be the master coup of German diplomacy, as indeed it was, or would have been, but for a flaw in the title. When the Czar brought the treaty home, his ministers, after one horrified look, pointed out that by engaging to join Germany in a possible war he had repudiated his alliance with France, a detail which "no doubt escaped His Majesty in the flood of the Emperor William's eloquence." The Treaty of Björkö lived its brief shimmering day, and expired.

Now came Edward hobnobbing with the Czar at Reval. Reading the German ambassador's report of the meeting which suggested that Edward really desired peace, the Kaiser scribbled furiously in the margin, "Lies. He wants war. But I have to start it so he does not have the odium."

The year closed with the most explosive faux pas of the Kaiser's career, an interview given to the *Daily Telegraph* expressing his ideas of the day on who should fight whom, which this time unnerved not only his neighbors but his countrymen. Public disapproval was so outspoken that the Kaiser took to his bed, was ill for three weeks, and remained comparatively reticent for some time thereafter.

Since then no new excitements had erupted. The last two years of the decade while Europe enjoyed a rich fat afternoon, were the quietest. Nineteen-ten was peaceful and prosperous, with the second round of

Moroccan crises and Balkan wars still to come. A new book, *The Great Illusion* by Norman Angell, had just been published, which proved that war had become vain. By impressive examples and incontrovertible argument Angell showed that in the present financial and economic interdependence of nations, the victor would suffer equally with the vanquished; therefore war had become unprofitable; therefore no nation would be so foolish as to start one. Already translated into eleven languages, *The Great Illusion* had become a cult. At the universities, in Manchester, Glasgow, and other industrial cities, more than forty study groups of true believers had formed, devoted to propagating its dogma. Angell's most earnest disciple was a man of great influence on military policy, the King's friend and adviser, Viscount Esher, chairman of the War Committee assigned to remaking the British Army after the shock of its performance in the Boer War. Lord Esher de- livered lectures on the lesson of *The Great Illusion* at Cambridge and the Sorbonne wherein he showed how "new economic factors clearly prove the inanity of aggressive wars." A twentieth century war would be on such a scale, he said, that its inevitable consequences of "commercial disaster, financial ruin and individual suffering" would be "so pregnant with restraining influences" as to make war unthinkable. He told an audience of officers at the United Service Club, with the Chief of General Staff, Sir John French, in the chair, that because of the interlacing of nations war "becomes every day more difficult and improbable."

Germany, Lord Esher felt sure, "is as receptive as Great Britain to the doctrine of Norman Angell." How receptive were the Kaiser and the Crown Prince to whom he gave, or caused to be given, copies of *The Great Illusion* is not reported. There is no evidence that he gave one to General von Bernhardi, who was engaged in 1910 in writing a book called *Germany and the Next War*, published in the following year, which was to be as influential as Angell's but from the opposite point of view. Three of its chapter titles, "The Right to Make War," "The Duty to Make War," and "World Power or Downfall" sum up its thesis.

As a twenty-one-year-old cavalry officer in 1870, Bernhardi had been the first German to ride through the Arc de Triomphe when the Germans entered Paris. Since then flags and glory interested him less than the theory, philosophy, and science of war as applied to "Germany's Historic Mission," another of his chapter titles. He had served as chief of the Military History section of the General Staff, was one of the intellectual elite of that hard-thinking, hard-working body, and author of a classic on cavalry before he assembled a lifetime's studies of Clausewitz, Treitschke, and Darwin, and poured them into the book that was to make his name a synonym for Mars.

War, he stated, "is a biological necessity"; it is the carrying out among humankind of "the natural law, upon which all the laws of Nature rest, the law of the struggle for existence." Nations, he said, must progress or decay; "there can be no standing still," and Germany must choose "world power or downfall." Among the nations Germany "is in social-political respects at the head of all progress in culture" but is "compressed into narrow, unnatural limits." She cannot attain her "great moral ends" without increased political power, an enlarged sphere of influence, and new territory. This increase in power, "befitting our importance," and "which we are entitled to claim," is a "political necessity" and "the first and foremost duty of the State." In his own italics Bernhardi announced, "What we now wish to attain must be *fought for*," and from here he galloped home to the finish line: "Conquest thus becomes a law of necessity."

Having proved the "necessity" (the favorite word of German military thinkers), Bernhardi proceeded to method. Once the duty to make war is recognized, the secondary duty, to make it successfully, follows. To be successful a state must begin war at the "most favorable moment" of its own choosing; it has "the acknowledged right . . . to secure the proud privilege of such initiative." Offensive war thus becomes another "necessity" and a second conclusion inescapable: "It is incumbent on us . . . to act on the offensive and strike the first blow." Bernhardi did not share the Kaiser's concern about the "odium" that attached to an aggressor. Nor was he reluctant to tell where the blow would fall. It was "unthinkable," he wrote, that Germany and France could ever negotiate their problems. "France must be so completely crushed that she can never cross our path again"; she "must be annihilated once and for all as a great power."

King Edward did not live to read Bernhardi. In January, 1910, he sent the Kaiser his annual birthday greetings and the gift of a walking stick before departing for Marienbad and Biarritz. A few months later he was dead.

"We have lost the mainstay of our foreign policy," said Isvolsky when he heard the news. This was hyperbole, for Edward was merely the instrument, not the architect, of the new alignments. In France the king's death created "profound emotion" and "real consternation," according to *Le Figaro*. Paris, it said, felt the loss of its "great friend" as deeply as London. Lampposts and shop windows in the Rue de la Paix wore the same black as Piccadilly; cab drivers tied crepe bows on their whips; black-draped portraits of the late king appeared even in the provincial towns as at the

death of a great French citizen. In Tokyo, in tribute to the Anglo-Japanese
alliance, houses bore the crossed flags of England and Japan with the
staves draped in black. In Germany, whatever the feelings, correct procedures were observed. All officers of the army and navy were ordered to
wear mourning for eight days, and the fleet in home waters fired a salute
and flew its flags at half-mast. The Reichstag rose to its feet to hear a
message of sympathy read by its President, and the Kaiser called in person
upon the British ambassador in a visit that lasted an hour and a half.

In London the following week the royal family was kept busy meeting
royal arrivals at Victoria Station. The Kaiser came over on his yacht the
Hohenzollern, escorted by four British destroyers. He anchored in the
Thames Estuary and came the rest of the way to London by train, arriving
at Victoria Station like the common royalty. A purple carpet was rolled
out on the platform, and purple-covered steps placed where his carriage
would stop. As his train drew in on the stroke of noon, the familiar figure
of the German emperor stepped down to be greeted by his cousin, King
George, whom he kissed on both cheeks. After lunch they went together to
Westminster Hall where the body of Edward lay in state. A thunderstorm
the night before and drenching rains all morning had not deterred the
quiet, patient line of Edward's subjects waiting to pass through the hall.
On this day, Thursday, May 19, the line stretched back for five miles. It
was the day the earth was due to pass through the tail of Halley's comet,
whose appearance called forth reminders that it was traditionally the
prophet of disaster—had it not heralded the Norman Conquest?—and
inspired journals with literary editors to print the lines from *Julius Caesar:*

> When beggars die there are no comets seen;
> The heavens themselves blaze forth the death of princes.

Inside the vast hall the bier lay in somber majesty, surmounted by
crown, orb, and scepter and guarded at its four corners by four officers,
each from different regiments of the empire, who stood in the traditional
attitude of mourning with bowed heads and white gloved hands crossed
over sword hilts. The Kaiser eyed all the customs of an imperial Lying-in-
State with professional interest. He was deeply impressed, and years later
could recall every detail of the scene in its "marvelous medieval setting."
He saw the sun's rays filtered through the narrow Gothic windows lighting
up the jewels of the crown; he watched the changing of the guards at the
bier as the four new guards marched forward with swords at the carry-up

and turned them point down as they reached their places, while the guards they relieved glided away in slow motion to disappear through some unseen exit in the shadows. Laying his wreath of purple and white flowers on the coffin, he knelt with King George in silent prayer and on rising grasped his cousin's hand in a manly and sympathetic handshake. The gesture, widely reported, caused much favorable comment.

Publicly his performance was perfect; privately he could not resist the opportunity for fresh scheming. At a dinner given by the King that night at Buckingham Palace for the seventy royal mourners and special ambassadors, he buttonholed M. Pichon of France and proposed to him that in the event Germany should find herself opposed to England in a conflict, France should side with Germany. In view of the occasion and the place, this latest imperial brainstorm caused the same fuss, that had once moved Sir Edward Grey, England's harassed Foreign Secretary, to remark wistfully, "The other sovereigns are so much *quieter*." The Kaiser later denied he had ever said anything of the kind; he had merely discussed Morocco and "some other political matters." M. Pichon could only be got to say discreetly that the Kaiser's language had been "amiable and pacific."

Next morning, in the procession, where for once he could not talk, William's behavior was exemplary. He kept his horse reined in, a head behind King George's, and, to Conan Doyle, special correspondent for the occasion, looked so "noble that England has lost something of her old kindliness if she does not take him back into her heart today." When the procession reached Westminster Hall he was the first to dismount and, as Queen Alexandra's carriage drew up, "he ran to the door with such alacrity that he reached it before the royal servants, "only to find that the Queen was about to descend on the other side. William scampered nimbly around, still ahead of the servants, reached the door first, handed out the widow, and kissed her with the affection of a bereaved nephew. Fortunately, King George came up at this moment to rescue his mother and escort her himself, for she loathed the Kaiser, both personally and for the sake of Schleswig-Holstein. Though he had been but eight years old when Germany seized the duchies from Denmark, she had never forgiven him or his country. When her son on a visit to Berlin in 1890 was made honorary colonel of a Prussian regiment, she wrote to him: "And so my Georgie boy has become a real live filthy blue-coated Pickelhaube German soldier!!! Well, I never thought to have lived to see that! But never mind, . . . it was your misfortune and not your fault."

A roll of muffled drums and the wail of bagpipes sounded as the coffin wrapped in the Royal Standard was borne from the Hall by a score of blue-jackets in straw hats. A sudden shiver of sabers glittered in the sun as the cavalry came to attention. At a signal of four sharp whistles the sailors hoisted the coffin on to the gun carriage draped in purple, red, and white. The cortege moved on between motionless lines of grenadiers like red walls that hemmed in the packed black masses of perfectly silent people. London was never so crowded, never so still. Alongside and behind the gun carriage, drawn by the Royal Horse Artillery, walked His late Majesty's sixty-three aides-de-camp, all colonels or naval captains and all peers, among them five dukes, four marquises, and thirteen earls. England's three Field Marshals, Lord Kitchener, Lord Roberts, and Sir Evelyn Wood, rode together. Six Admirals of the Fleet followed, and after them, walking all alone, Edward's great friend, Sir John Fisher, the stormy, eccentric former First Sea Lord with his queer un-English mandarin's face. Detachments from all the famous regiments, the Coldstreams, the Gordon Highlanders, the household cavalry and cavalry of the line, the Horse Guards and Lancers and Royal Fusiliers, brilliant Hussars and Dragoons of the German, Russian, Austrian, and other foreign cavalry units of which Edward had been honorary officer, admirals of the German Navy—almost, it seemed to some disapproving observers, too great a military show in the funeral of a man called the "Peacemaker."

His horse with empty saddle and boots reversed in the stirrups led by two grooms and, trotting along behind, his wire-haired terrier, Caesar, added a pang of personal sentiment. On came the pomp of England: Pour-suivants of Arms in emblazoned medieval tabards, Silver Stick in Waiting, White Staves, equerries, archers of Scotland, judges in wigs and black robes, and the Lord Chief Justice in scarlet, bishops in ecclesiastical purple, Yeomen of the Guard in black velvet hats and frilled Elizabethan collars, an escort of trumpeters, and then the parade of kings, followed by a glass coach bearing the widowed Queen and her sister, the Dowager Empress of Russia, and twelve other coaches of queens, ladies, and Oriental potentates.

Along Whitehall, the Mall, Piccadilly, and the Park to Paddington Station, where the body was to go by train to Windsor for burial, the long procession moved. The Royal Horse Guards' band played the "Dead March" from *Saul*. People felt a finality in the slow tread of the marchers and in the solemn music. Lord Esher wrote in his diary after the funeral: "There never was such a break-up. All the old buoys which have marked the channel of our lives seem to have been swept away."

▶▶▶
▶▶▶
▶▶▶ *PLANS*

▶▶▶ *2* ▶

▶▶▶ *"Let the Last Man on the Right Brush the Channel with His Sleeve"*

COUNT ALFRED VON SCHLIEFFEN, CHIEF OF THE German General Staff from 1891 to 1906 was, like all German officers, schooled in Clausewitz's precept, "The heart of France lies between Brussels and Paris." It was a frustrating axiom because the path it pointed to was forbidden by Belgian neutrality, which Germany, along with the other four major European powers, had guaranteed in perpetuity. Believing that war was a certainty and that Germany must enter it under conditions that gave her the most promise of success, Schlieffen determined not to allow the Belgian difficulty to stand in Germany's way. Of the two classes of Prussian officer, the bullnecked and the wasp-waisted, he belonged to the second. Monocled and effete in appearance, cold and distant in manner, he concentrated with such single-mindedness on his profession that when an aide, at the end of an all-night staff ride in East Prussia, pointed out to him the beauty of the river Pregel sparkling in the rising sun, the General gave a brief, hard look and replied, "An unimportant obstacle." So too, he decided, was Belgian neutrality.

A neutral and independent Belgium was the creation of England, or rather of England's ablest Foreign Minister, Lord Palmerston. Belgium's coast was England's frontier; on the plains of Belgium, Wellington had defeated the greatest threat to England since the Armada. Thereafter England was determined to make that patch of open, easily traversible territory a neutral zone and, under the post-Napoleon settlement of the Congress of Vienna, agreed with the other powers to attach it to the Kingdom of the Netherlands. Resenting union with a Protestant power, burning with the fever of the nineteenth century nationalism, the Belgians revolted in 1830, setting off an international scramble. The Dutch fought to retain their province; the French, eager to reabsorb what they had once ruled, moved in; the autocratic states—Russia, Prussia, and Austria—bent on keeping Europe clamped under the vise of Vienna, were ready to shoot at the first sign of revolt anywhere.

Lord Palmerston outmaneuvered them all. He knew that a subject province would be an eternal temptation to one neighbor or another and that only an independent nation, resolved to maintain its own integrity, could survive as a safety zone. Through nine years of nerve, of suppleness, of never swerving from his aim, of calling out the British fleet when necessary, he played off all contenders and secured an international treaty guaranteeing Belgium as an "independent and perpetually neutral state." The treaty was signed in 1839 by England, France, Russia, Prussia, and Austria.

Ever since 1892, when France and Russia had joined in military alliance, it was clear that four of the five signatories of the Belgian treaty would be automatically engaged—two against two—in the war for which Schlieffen had to plan. Europe was a heap of swords piled as delicately as jackstraws; one could not be pulled out without moving the others. Under the terms of the Austro-German alliance, Germany was obliged to support Austria in any conflict with Russia. Under the terms of the alliance between France and Russia, both parties were obliged to move against Germany if either became involved in a "defensive war" with Germany. These arrangements made it inevitable that in any war in which she engaged, Germany would have to fight on two fronts against both Russia and France.

What part England would play was uncertain; she might remain neutral; she might, if given cause, come in against Germany. That Belgium could be the cause was no secret. In the Franco-Prussian War of 1870, when Germany was still a climbing power, Bismarck had been happy enough, upon a hint from England, to reaffirm the inviolability of Belgium. Gladstone had secured a treaty from both belligerents providing that if either violated Belgian neutrality, England would cooperate with the other to the extent of defending Belgium, though without engaging in the general operations of the war. Although there was something a little impractical about the tail of this Gladstonian formula, the Germans had no reason to suppose its underlying motive any less operative in 1914 than in 1870. Nevertheless, Schlieffen decided, in the event of war, to attack France by way of Belgium.

His reason was "military necessity." In a two-front war, he wrote, "the whole of Germany must throw itself upon *one* enemy, the strongest, most powerful, most dangerous enemy, and that can only be France." Schlieffen's completed plan for 1906, the year he retired, allocated six weeks and seven-eighths of Germany's forces to smash France while one-eighth was to hold her eastern frontier against Russia until the bulk of her army could be brought back to face the second enemy. He chose France first because Russia could frustrate a quick victory by simply withdrawing within her infinite room, leaving Germany to be sucked into an endless campaign as Napoleon had been. France was both closer at hand and quicker to mobilize. The German and French armies each required two weeks to complete mobilization before a major attack could begin on the fifteenth day. Russia, according to German arithmetic, because of her vast distances, huge numbers, and meager railroads, would take six weeks before she could launch a major offensive, by which time France would be beaten.

The risk of leaving East Prussia, hearth of Junkerdom and the Hohenzollerns, to be held by only nine divisions was hard to accept, but Frederick the Great had said, "It is better to lose a province than split the forces with which one seeks victory," and nothing so comforts the military mind as the maxim of a great but dead general. Only by throwing the utmost numbers against the West could France be finished off quickly. Only by a strategy of envelopment, using Belgium as a pathway, could the German armies, in Schlieffen's opinion, attack France successfully. His reasoning, from the purely military point of view, appeared faultless.

The German Army of a million and a half that was to be used against France was now six times the size it had been in 1870, and needed room to maneuver. French fortresses constructed along the frontiers of Alsace and Lorraine after 1870 precluded the Germans from making a frontal attack across the common border. A protracted siege would provide no oppor-

tunity, as long as French lines to the rear remained open, of netting the
enemy quickly in a battle of annihilation. Only by envelopment could the
French be taken from behind and destroyed. But at either end of the
French lines lay neutral territory—Switzerland and Belgium. There was not
enough room for the huge German Army to get around the French armies
and still stay inside France. The Germans had done it in 1870 when both
armies were small, but now it was a matter of moving an army of millions
to outflank an army of millions. Space, roads, and railroads were essential.
The flat plains of Flanders had them. In Belgium there was both room for
the outflanking maneuver which was Schlieffen's formula for success as
well as a way to avoid the frontal attack which was his formula for disaster.

Clausewitz, oracle of German military thought, had ordained a quick
victory by "decisive battle" as the first object in offensive war. Occupation
of the enemy's territory and gaining control of his resources was secondary.
To speed an early decision was essential. Time counted above all else.
Anything that protracted a campaign Clausewitz condemned. "Gradual
reduction" of the enemy, or a war of attrition, he feared like the pit of
hell. He wrote in the decade of Waterloo, and his works had been accepted
as the Bible of strategy ever since.

To achieve decisive victory, Schlieffen fixed upon a strategy derived
from Hannibal and the Battle of Cannae. The dead general who mesmerized Schlieffen had been dead a very long time. Two thousand years had
passed since Hannibal's classic double envelopment of the Romans at
Cannae. Field gun and machine gun had replaced bow and arrow and
slingshot, Schlieffen wrote, "but the principles of strategy remain
unchanged. The enemy's front is not the objective. The essential thing is
to crush the enemy's flanks . . . and complete the extermination by attack
upon his rear." Under Schlieffen, envelopment became the fetish and
frontal attack the anathema of the German General Staff.

Schlieffen's first plan to include the violation of Belgium was formulated in 1899. It called for cutting across the corner of Belgium east of the
Meuse. Enlarged with each successive year, by 1905 it had expanded into
a huge enveloping right-wing sweep in which the German armies would
cross Belgium from Liège to Brussels before turning southward, where they
could take advantage of the open country of Flanders, to march against
France. Everything depended upon a quick decision against France, and
even the long way around through Flanders would be quicker than laying
siege to the fortress line across the common border.

Schlieffen did not have enough divisions for a double envelopment of

France à la Cannae. For this he substituted a heavily one-sided right wing that would spread across the whole of Belgium on both sides of the Meuse, sweep down through the country like a monstrous hayrake, cross the Franco-Belgian frontier along its entire width, and descend upon Paris along the Valley of the Oise. The German mass would come between the capital and the French armies which, drawn back to meet the menace, would be caught, away from their fortified areas, in the decisive battle of anni-hilation. Essential to the plan was a deliberately weak German left wing on the Alsace-Lorraine front which would tempt the French in that area forward into a "sack" between Metz and the Vosges. It was expected that the French, intent upon liberating their lost provinces, would attack here, and it was considered so much the better for the success of the German plan if they did, for they could be held in the sack by the German left wing while the main victory was obtained from behind. In the back of Schlieffen's mind always glimmered the hope that, as battle unfolded, a counterattack by his left wing could be mounted in order to bring about a true double envelopment—the "colossal Cannae" of his dreams. Sternly saving his greatest strength for the right wing, he did not yield to that vaulting ambition in his plan. But the lure of the left wing remained to tempt his successors.

Thus the Germans came to Belgium. Decisive battle dictated envelop-ment, and envelopment dictated the use of Belgian territory. The German General Staff pronounced it a military necessity; Kaiser and Chancellor accepted it with more or less equanimity. Whether it was advisable, whether it was even expedient in view of the probable effect on world opinion, especially on neutral opinion, was irrelevant. That it seemed neces-sary to the triumph of German arms was the only criterion. Germans had imbibed from 1870 the lesson that arms and war were the sole source of German greatness. They had been taught by Field Marshal von der Goltz, in his book *The Nation in Arms*, that "We have won our position through the sharpness of our sword, not through the sharpness of our mind." The decision to violate Belgian neutrality followed easily.

Character is fate, the Greeks believed. A hundred years of German philosophy went into the making of this decision in which the seed of self-destruction lay embedded, waiting for its hour. The voice was Schlief-fen's, but the hand was the hand of Fichte who saw the German people chosen by Providence to occupy the supreme place in the history of the universe, of Hegel who saw them leading the world to a glorious destiny of compulsory *Kultur*, of Nietzsche who told them that Supermen were above

ordinary controls, of Treitschke who set the increase of power as the highest
moral duty of the state, of the whole German people, who called their
temporal ruler the "All-Highest." What made the Schlieffen plan was not
Clausewitz and the Battle of Cannae, but the body of accumulated egoism
which suckled the German people and created a nation fed on "the desperate delusion of the will that deems itself absolute."

The goal, decisive battle, was a product of the victories over Austria
and France in 1866 and 1870. Dead battles, like dead generals, hold the
military mind in their dead grip, and Germans, no less than other peoples,
prepare for the last war. They staked everything on decisive battle in the
image of Hannibal, but even the ghost of Hannibal might have reminded
Schlieffen that though Carthage won at Cannae, Rome won the war.

Old Field Marshal Moltke in 1890 foretold that the next war might
last seven years—or thirty—because the resources of a modern state were so
great it would not know itself to be beaten after a single military defeat
and would not give up. His nephew and namesake who succeeded Schlieffen
as Chief of Staff also had moments when he saw the truth as clearly. In a
moment of heresy to Clausewitz, he said to the Kaiser in 1906, "It will be
a national war which will not be settled by a decisive battle but by a long
wearisome struggle with a country that will not be overcome until its whole
national force is broken, and a war which will utterly exhaust our own
people, even if we are victorious." It went against human nature, however
—and the nature of General Staffs—to follow through the logic of his own
prophecy. Amorphous and without limits, the concept of a long war could
not be scientifically planned for as could the orthodox, predictable, and
simple solution of decisive battle and a short war. The younger Moltke was
already Chief of Staff when he made his prophecy, but neither he nor his
Staff, nor the Staff of any other country, ever made any effort to plan for
a long war. Besides the two Moltkes, one dead and the other infirm of
purpose, some military strategists in other countries glimpsed the possibility
of prolonged war, but all preferred to believe, along with the bankers and
industrialists, that because of the dislocation of economic life a general
European war could not last longer than three or four months. One
constant among the elements of 1914—as of any era—was the disposition
of everyone on all sides not to prepare for the harder alternative, not to act
upon what they suspected to be true.

Schlieffen, having embraced the strategy of "decisive battle," pinned
Germany's fate to it. He expected France to violate Belgium as soon as
Germany's deployment at the Belgian frontier revealed her strategy, and

he therefore planned that Germany should do it first and faster. "Belgian neutrality must be broken by one side or the other," his thesis ran. "Whoever gets there first and occupies Brussels and imposes a war levy of some 1,000 million francs has the upper hand."

Indemnity, which enables a state to conduct war at the enemy's expense instead of its own, was a secondary object laid down by Clausewitz. His third was the winning of public opinion, which is accomplished by "gaining great victories and possession of the enemy's capital" and which helps to bring an end to resistance. He knew how material success could gain public opinion; he forgot how moral failure could lose it, which too can be a hazard of war.

It was a hazard the French never lost sight of, and it led them to the opposite conclusion from the one Schlieffen expected. Belgium was their pathway of attack too, through the Ardennes if not through Flanders, but their plan of campaign prohibited their armies from using it until after the Germans had violated Belgium first. To them the logic of the matter was clear: Belgium was an open path in either direction; whether Germany or France would use it depended on which of the two wanted war the more. As a French general said, "The one that willed war more than the other could not help but will the violation of Belgian neutrality."

Schlieffen and his Staff did not think Belgium would fight and add its six divisions to the French forces. When Chancellor Bülow, discussing the problem with Schlieffen in 1904, reminded him of Bismarck's warning that it would be against "plain common sense" to add another enemy to the forces against Germany, Schlieffen twisted his monocle several times in his eye, as was his habit, and said: "Of course. We haven't grown stupider since then." But Belgium would not resist by force of arms; she would be satisfied to protest, he said.

German confidence on this score was due to placing rather too high a value on the well-known avarice of Leopold II, who was King of the Belgians in Schlieffen's time. Tall and imposing with his black spade beard and his aura of wickedness composed of mistresses, money, Congo cruelties, and other scandals, Leopold was, in the opinion of Emperor Franz Josef of Austria, "a thoroughly bad man." There were few men who could be so described, the Emperor said, but the King of the Belgians was one. Because Leopold was avaricious, among other vices, the Kaiser supposed that avarice would rule over common sense, and he conceived a clever plan to tempt Leopold into alliance with an offer of French territory. Whenever the Kaiser was seized with a project he attempted instantly to execute it, usually to his astonishment and chagrin when it did not work. In 1904 he invited Leopold to visit him in Berlin, spoke to him in "the kindest way in the world" about his proud forefathers, the Dukes of Burgundy, and offered to re-create the old Duchy of Burgundy for him out of Artois, French Flanders, and the French Ardennes. Leopold gazed at him "open-mouthed," then, attempting to pass it off with a laugh, reminded the Kaiser that much had changed since the fifteenth century. In any event, he said, his Ministers and Parliament would never consider such a suggestion.

That was the wrong thing to say, for the Kaiser flew into one of his rages and scolded the King for putting respect for Parliament and Ministers above respect for the finger of God (with which William sometimes confused himself). "I told him," William reported to Chancellor von Bülow, "I could not be played with. Whoever in the case of a European war was not with me was against me." He was a soldier, he proclaimed, in the school of Napoleon and Frederick the Great who began their wars by forestalling their enemies, and "so should I, in the event of Belgium's not being on my side, be actuated by strategical considerations only."

This declared intent, the first explicit threat to tear up the treaty, dumfounded King Leopold. He drove off to the station with his helmet on back to front, looking to the aide who accompanied him "as if he had had a shock of some kind."

Although the Kaiser's scheme failed, Leopold was still expected to barter Belgium's neutrality for a purse of two million pounds sterling. When a French intelligence officer, who was told this figure by a German officer after the war, expressed surprise at its generosity, he was reminded that "the French would have had to pay for it." Even after Leopold was succeeded in 1909 by his nephew King Albert, a very different quantity, Belgium's resistance was still expected by Schlieffen's successors to be a formality. It might, for example, suggested a German diplomat in 1911, take the form of "lining up her army along the road taken by the German forces."

Schlieffen designated thirty-four divisions to take the roads through Belgium, disposing on their way of Belgium's six divisions if, as seemed to the Germans unlikely, they chose to resist. The Germans were intensely anxious that they should not, because resistance would mean destruction of railways and bridges and consequent dislocation of the schedule to which the German Staff was passionately attached. Belgian acquiescence, on the other hand, would avoid the necessity of tying up divisions in siege of the Belgian fortresses and would also tend to silence public disapproval of Germany's act. To persuade Belgium against futile resistance, Schlieffen arranged that she should be confronted, prior to invasion, by an ultimatum requiring her to yield "all fortresses, railways and troops" or face bombardment of her fortified cities. Heavy artillery was ready to transform the threat of bombardment into reality, if necessary. The heavy guns would in any case, Schlieffen wrote in 1912, be needed further on in the campaign. "The great industrial town of Lille, for example, offers an excellent target for bombardment."

Schlieffen wanted his right wing to reach as far west as Lille in order to make the envelopment of the French complete. "When you march into France," he said, "let the last man on the right brush the Channel with his sleeve." Furthermore, counting on British belligerency, he wanted a wide sweep in order to rake in a British Expeditionary Force along with the French. He placed a higher value on the blockade potential of British sea power than on the British Army, and therefore was determined to achieve a quick victory over French and British land forces and an early decision of the war before the economic consequences of British hostility could make themselves felt. To that end everything must go to swell the right wing. He had to make it powerful in numbers because the density of soldiers per mile determined the extent of territory that could be covered.

Employing the active army alone, he would not have enough divisions both to hold his eastern frontier against a Russian breakthrough and to achieve the superiority in numbers over France which he needed for a quick victory. His solution was simple if revolutionary. He decided to use reserve units in the front line. According to prevailing military doctrine, only the youngest men, fresh from the rigors and discipline of barracks and drill, were fit to fight; reserves who had finished their compulsory military service and returned to civilian life were considered soft and were not wanted in the battle line. Except for men under twenty-six who were merged with the active units, the reserves were formed into divisions of their own, intended for use as occupation troops and for other rear duty. Schlieffen changed all that. He added some twenty reserve divisions (the number varied according to the year of the plan) to the line of march of the fifty or more active divisions. With this increase in numbers his cherished envelopment became possible.

After retiring in 1906 he spent his last years still writing about Cannae, improving his plan, composing memoranda to guide his successors, and died at eighty in 1913, muttering at the end: "It must come to a fight. Only make the right wing strong."

His successor, the melancholy General von Moltke, was something of a pessimist who lacked Schlieffen's readiness to concentrate all his strength in one maneuver. If Schlieffen's motto was "Be bold, be bold," Moltke's was, "But not too bold." He worried both about the weakness of his left wing against the French and about the weakness of the forces left to defend East Prussia against the Russians. He even debated with his Staff the advisability of fighting a defensive war against France, but rejected the idea because it precluded all possibility of "engaging the enemy on his own territory." The Staff agreed that the invasion of Belgium would be "entirely just and necessary" because the war would be one for the "defense and existence of Germany." Schlieffen's plan was maintained, and Moltke consoled himself with the thought, as he said in 1913, that "We must put aside all commonplaces as to the responsibility of the aggressor. . . . Success alone justifies war." But just to be safe everywhere, each year, cutting into Schlieffen's dying request, he borrowed strength from the right wing to add to the left.

Moltke planned for a German left wing of 8 corps numbering about 320,000 men to hold the front in Alsace and Lorraine south of Metz. The German center of 11 corps numbering about 400,000 men would invade France through Luxembourg and the Ardennes. The German right wing of 16 corps numbering about 700,000 men would attack through Belgium, smash the famed gateway fortresses of Liège and Namur which held the Meuse, and fling itself across the river to reach the flat country and straight roads on the far side. Every day's schedule of march was fixed in advance. The Belgians were not expected to fight, but if they did the power of the German assault was expected to persuade them quickly to surrender. The schedule called for the roads through Liège to be open by the twelfth day of mobilization, Brussels to be taken by M-19, the French frontier crossed on M-22, a line Thionville-St. Quentin reached by M-31, Paris and decisive victory by M-39.

The plan of campaign was as rigid and complete as the blueprint for a battleship. Heeding Clausewitz's warning that military plans which leave no room for the unexpected can lead to disaster, the Germans with infinite care had attempted to provide for every contingency. Their staff officers, trained at maneuvers and at war-college desks to supply the correct solution for any given set of circumstances, were expected to cope with the unexpected. Against that elusive, that mocking and perilous quantity, every precaution had been taken except one—flexibility.

While the plan for maximum effort against France hardened, Moltke's fears of Russia gradually lessened as his General Staff evolved a credo, based on a careful count of Russian railway mileage, that Russia would not be "ready" for war until 1916. This was confirmed in German minds by their spies' reports of Russian remarks "that something was going to begin in 1916."

In 1914 two events sharpened Germany's readiness to a fine point. In April, England had begun naval talks with the Russians, and in June, Germany herself had completed the widening of the Kiel Canal, permitting her new dreadnoughts direct access from the North Sea to the Baltic. On learning of the Anglo-Russian talks, Moltke said in May during a visit to his Austrian opposite number, Franz Conrad von Hötzendorff, that from now on "any adjournment will have the effect of diminishing our chances of success." Two weeks later, on June 1st, he said to Baron Eckhardstein, "We are ready, and the sooner the better for us."

▶▶▶ *3* ▶

▶▶▶ *The Shadow of Sedan*

GENERAL DE CASTELNAU, DEPUTY CHIEF OF THE
French General Staff, was visited at the War Office one day in 1913 by the
Military Governor of Lille, General Lebas, who came to protest .the
General Staff's decision to abandon Lille as a fortified city. Situated ten
miles from the Belgian border and forty miles inland from the Channel,
Lille lay close to the path that an invading army would take if it came by
way of Flanders. In answer to General Lebas' plea for its defense, General
de Castelnau spread out a map and measured with a ruler the distance
from the German border to Lille by way of Belgium. The normal density
of troops required for a vigorous offensive, he reminded his caller, was five
or six to a meter. If the Germans extended themselves as far west as Lille,
De Castelnau pointed out, they would be stretched out two to a meter.

"We'll cut them in half!" he declared. The German active Army, he
explained, could dispose of twenty-five corps, about a million men, on the
Western Front. "Here, figure it out for yourself," he said, handing Lebas
the ruler. "If they come as far as Lille," he repeated with sardonic satisfaction, "so much the better for us."

French strategy did not ignore the threat of envelopment by a German
right wing. On the contrary, the French General Staff believed that the

stronger the Germans made their right wing, the correspondingly weaker they would leave their center and left where the French Army planned to break through. French strategy turned its back to the Belgian frontier and its face to the Rhine. While the Germans were taking the long way around to fall upon the French flank, the French planned a two-pronged offensive that would smash through the German center and left on either side of the German fortified area at Metz and by victory there, sever the German right wing from its base, rendering it harmless. It was a bold plan born of an idea—an idea inherent in the recovery of France from the humiliation of Sedan.

Under the peace terms dictated by Germany at Versailles in 1871, France had suffered amputation, indemnity, and occupation. Even a triumphal march by the German Army down the Champs Elysées was among the terms imposed. It took place along a silent, black-draped avenue empty of onlookers. At Bordeaux, when the French Assembly ratified the peace terms, the deputies of Alsace-Lorraine walked from the hall in tears, leaving behind their protest: "We proclaim forever the right of Alsatians and Lorrainers to remain members of the French nation. We swear for ourselves, our constituents, our children and our children's children to claim that right for all time, by every means, in the face of the usurper."

The annexation, though opposed by Bismarck, who said it would be the Achilles' heel of the new German Empire, was required by the elder Moltke and his Staff. They insisted, and convinced the Emperor, that the border provinces with Metz, Strasbourg, and the crest of the Vosges must be sliced off in order to put France geographically forever on the defensive. They added a crushing indemnity of five billion francs intended to hobble France for a generation, and lodged an army of occupation until it should be paid. With one enormous effort the French raised and paid off the sum within three years, and their recovery began.

The memory of Sedan remained, a stationary dark shadow on the French consciousness. *"N'en parlez jamais; pensez-y toujours"* (Never speak of it; think of it always) had counseled Gambetta. For more than forty years the thought of "Again" was the single most fundamental factor of French policy. In the early years after 1870, instinct and military weakness dictated a fortress strategy. France walled herself in behind a system of entrenched camps connected by forts. Two fortified lines, Belfort-Epinal and Toul-Verdun, guarded the eastern frontier, and one, Maubeuge-Valenciennes-Lille, guarded the western half of the Belgian frontier; the gaps between were intended to canalize the invasion forces.

Behind her wall, as Victor Hugo urged at his most vibrant: "France will
have but one thought: to reconstitute her forces, gather her energy, nourish
her sacred anger, raise her young generation to form an army of the whole
people, to work without cease, to study the methods and skills of our
enemies, to become again a great France, the France of 1792, the France
of an idea with a sword. Then one day she will be irresistible. Then she
will take back Alsace-Lorraine."

Through returning prosperity and growing empire, through the peren-
nial civil quarrels—royalism, Boulangism, clericalism, strikes, and the
culminating, devastating Dreyfus Affair—the sacred anger still glowed,
especially in the army. The one thing that held together all elements of
the army, whether old guard or republican, Jesuit or Freemason, was the
mystique d'Alsace. The eyes of all were fixed on the blue line of the Vosges.
A captain of infantry confessed in 1912 that he used to lead the men of his
company in secret patrols of two or three through the dark pines to the
mountaintops where they could gaze down on Colmar. "On our return
from those clandestine expeditions our columns reformed, choked and
dumb with emotion."

Originally neither German nor French, Alsace had been snatched back
and forth between the two until, under Louis XIV, it was confirmed to
France by the Treaty of Westphalia in 1648. After Germany annexed
Alsace and part of Lorraine in 1870 Bismarck advised giving the inhabitants
as much autonomy as possible and encouraging their particularism, for, he
said, the more Alsatian they felt, the less they would feel French. His successors did not see the necessity. They took no account of the wishes of
their new subjects, made no effort to win them over, administered the
provinces as *Reichsland*, or "Imperial territory," under German officials
on virtually the same terms as their African colonies, and succeeded only
in infuriating and alienating the population until in 1911 a constitution
was granted them. By then it was too late. German rule exploded in the
Zabern Affair in 1913 which began, after an exchange of insults between
townspeople and garrison, when a German officer struck a crippled shoemaker with his saber. It ended in the complete and public exposure of
German policy in the *Reichsland*, in a surge of anti-German feeling in
world opinion, and in the simultaneous triumph of militarism in Berlin
where the officer of Zabern became a hero, congratulated by the Crown
Prince.

For Germany 1870 was not a final settlement. The German day in
Europe which they thought had dawned when the German Empire was

proclaimed in the Hall of Mirrors at Versailles was still postponed. France was not crushed; the French Empire was actually expanding in North Africa and Indo-China; the world of art and beauty and style still worshiped at the feet of Paris. Germans were still gnawed by envy of the country they had conquered. "As well off as God in France," was a German saying. At the same time they considered France decadent in culture and enfeebled by democracy. "It is impossible for a country that has had forty-two war ministers in forty-three years to fight effectively," announced Professor Hans Delbrück, Germany's leading historian. Believing themselves superior in soul, in strength, in energy, industry, and national virtue, Germans felt they deserved the dominion of Europe. The work of Sedan must be completed.

Living in the shadow of that unfinished business, France, reviving in spirit and strength, grew weary of being eternally on guard, eternally exhorted by her leaders to defend herself. As the century turned, her spirit rebelled against thirty years of the defensive with its implied avowal of inferiority. France knew herself to be physically weaker than Germany. Her population was less, her birth rate lower. She needed some weapon that Germany lacked to give herself confidence in her survival. The "idea with a sword" fulfilled the need. Expressed by Bergson it was called *élan vital*, the all-conquering will. Belief in its power convinced France that the human spirit need not, after all, bow to the predestined forces of evolution which Schopenhauer and Hegel had declared to be irresistible. The spirit of France would be the equalizing factor. Her will to win, her *élan*, would enable France to defeat her enemy. Her genius was in her spirit, the spirit of *la gloire*, of 1792, of the incomparable "Marseillaise," the spirit of General Margueritte's heroic cavalry charge before Sedan when even Wilhelm I, watching the battle, could not forbear to cry, "*Oh, les braves gens!*"

Belief in the fervor of France, in the *furor Gallicae*, revived France's faith in herself in the generation after 1870. It was that fervor, unfurling her banners, sounding her bugles, arming her soldiers, that would lead France to victory if the day of "Again" should come.

Translated into military terms Bergson's *élan vital* became the doctrine of the offensive. In proportion as a defensive gave way to an offensive strategy, the attention paid to the Belgian frontier gradually gave way in favor of a progressive shift of gravity eastward toward the point where a French offensive could be launched to break through to the Rhine. For the Germans the roundabout road through Flanders led to Paris; for the

French it led nowhere. They could only get to Berlin by the shortest way. The more the thinking of the French General Staff approached the offensive, the greater the forces it concentrated at the attacking point and the fewer it left to defend the Belgian frontier.

The doctrine of the offensive had its fount in the Ecole Supérieure de la Guerre, or War College, the ark of the army's intellectual elite, whose director, General Ferdinand Foch, was the molder of French military theory of his time. Foch's mind, like a heart, contained two valves: one pumped spirit into strategy; the other circulated common sense. On the one hand Foch preached a *mystique* of will expressed in his famous aphorisms, "The will to conquer is the first condition of victory," or more succinctly, "*Victoire c'est la volonté*," and, "A battle won is a battle in which one will not confess oneself beaten."

In practice this was to become the famous order at the Marne to attack when the situation called for retreat. His officers of those days remember him bellowing, "Attack! Attack!" with furious, sweeping gestures while he dashed about in short rushes as if charged by an electric battery. Why, he was later asked, did he advance at the Marne when he was technically beaten? "Why? I don't know. Because of my men, because I had a will. And then—God was there."

Though a profound student of Clausewitz, Foch did not, like Clausewitz's German successors, believe in a foolproof schedule of battle worked out in advance. Rather he taught the necessity of perpetual adaptability and improvisation to fit circumstances. "Regulations," he would say, "are all very well for drill but in the hour of danger they are no more use. . . . You have to learn to think." To think meant to give room for freedom of initiative, for the imponderable to win over the material, for will to demonstrate its power over circumstance.

But the idea that morale alone could conquer, Foch warned, was an "infantile notion." From his flights of metaphysics he would descend at once, in his lectures and his prewar books *Les Principes de la Guerre* and *La Conduite de la Guerre*, to the earth of tactics, the placing of advance guards, the necessity of *sureté*, or protection, the elements of firepower, the need for obedience and discipline. The realistic half of his teaching was summed up in another aphorism he made familiar during the war, "*De quoi s'agit-il?*" (What is the essence of the problem?)

Eloquent as he was on tactics, it was Foch's *mystique* of will that captured the minds of his followers. Once in 1908 when Clemenceau was considering Foch, then a professor, for the post of Director of the War

College, a private agent whom he sent to listen to the lectures reported back in bewilderment, "This officer teaches metaphysics so abstruse as to make idiots of his pupils." Although Clemenceau appointed Foch in spite of it, there was, in one sense, truth in the report. Foch's principles, not because they were too abstruse but because they were too attractive, laid a trap for France. They were taken up with particular enthusiasm by Colonel Grandmaison, "an ardent and brilliant officer" who was Director of the Troisième Bureau, or Bureau of Military Operations, and who in 1911 delivered two lectures at the War College which had a crystallizing effect.

Colonel Grandmaison grasped only the head and not the feet of Foch's principles. Expounding their *élan* without their *sureté*, he expressed a military philosophy that electrified his audience. He waved before their dazzled eyes an "idea with a sword" which showed them how France could win. Its essence was the *offensive à outrance*, offensive to the limit. Only this could achieve Clausewitz's decisive battle which "exploited to the finish is the essential act of war" and which "once engaged, must be pushed to the end, with no second thoughts, up to the extremes of human endurance." Seizure of initiative is the *sine qua non*. Preconceived arrangements based on a dogmatic judgment of what the enemy will do are premature. Liberty of action is achieved only by imposing one's will upon the enemy. "All command decisions must be inspired by the will to seize and retain the initiative." The defensive is forgotten, abandoned, discarded; its only possible justification is an occasional "economizing of forces at certain points with a view to adding them to the attack."

The effect on the General Staff was profound, and during the next two years was embodied in new Field Regulations for the conduct of war and in a new plan of campaign called Plan 17, which was adopted in May, 1913. Within a few months of Grandmaison's lectures, the President of the Republic, M. Fallières, announced: "The offensive alone is suited to the temperament of French soldiers. . . . We are determined to march straight against the enemy without hesitation."

The new Field Regulations, enacted by the government in October, 1913, as the fundamental document for the training and conduct of the French Army, opened with a flourish of trumpets: "The French Army, returning to its traditions, henceforth admits no law but the offensive." Eight commandments followed, ringing with the clash of "decisive battle," "offensive without hesitation," "fierceness and tenacity," "breaking the will of the adversary," "ruthless and tireless pursuit." With all the ardor of orthodoxy stamping out heresy, the Regulations stamped upon and discarded the defensive. "The offensive alone," it proclaimed, "leads to positive results." Its Seventh Commandment, italicized by the authors, stated: *"Battles are beyond everything else struggles of morale. Defeat is inevitable as soon as the hope of conquering ceases to exist. Success comes not to him who has suffered the least but to him whose will is firmest and morale strongest."*

Nowhere in the eight commandments was there mention of matériel or firepower or what Foch called *sureté*. The teaching of the Regulations became epitomized in the favorite word of the French officer corps, *le cran*, nerve, or, less politely, guts. Like the youth who set out for the mountaintop under the banner marked "Excelsior!" the French Army marched to war in 1914 under a banner marked *"Cran."*

Over the years, while French military philosophy had changed, French geography had not. The geographical facts of her frontiers remained what Germany had made them in 1870. Germany's territorial demands, William I had explained to the protesting Empress Eugénie, "have no aim other than to push back the starting point from which French armies could in the future attack us." They also pushed forward the starting point from which Germany could attack France. While French history and development after the turn of the century fixed her mind upon the offensive, her geography still required a strategy of the defensive.

In 1911, the same year as Colonel Grandmaison's lectures, a last effort to commit France to a strategy of the defensive was made in the Supreme War Council by no less a personage than the Commander in Chief designate, General Michel. As Vice President of the Council, a post which carried with it the position of Commander in Chief in the event of war, General Michel was then the ranking officer in the army. In a report that precisely reflected Schlieffen's thinking, he submitted his estimate of the probable German line of attack and his proposals for countering it. Because of the natural escarpments and French fortifications along the common border with Germany, he argued, the Germans could not hope to win a prompt decisive battle in Lorraine. Nor would the passage through Luxembourg and the near corner of Belgium east of the Meuse give them sufficient room for their favored strategy of envelopment. Only by taking advantage of "the whole of Belgium," he said, could the Germans achieve that "immediate, brutal and decisive" offensive which they must launch upon France before the forces of her Allies could come into play. He pointed out that the Germans had long yearned for Belgium's great port of Antwerp, and this gave them an additional reason for an attack through Flanders. He proposed to face the Germans along a line Verdun-Namur-Antwerp with a French army of a million men whose left wing—like Schlieffen's right—should brush the Channel with its sleeve.

Not only was General Michel's plan defensive in character; it also depended upon a proposal that was anathema to his fellow officers. To match the numbers he believed the Germans would send through Belgium, General Michel proposed to double French front-line effectives by attaching a regiment of reserves to every active regiment. Had he proposed to admit Mistinguette to the Immortals of the French Academy, he could hardly have raised more clamor and disgust.

"*Les réserves, c'est zéro!*" was the classic dogma of the French officer corps. Men who had finished their compulsory training under universal service and were between the ages of twenty-three and thirty-four were classed as reserves. Upon mobilization the youngest classes filled out the regular army units to war strength; the others were formed into reserve regiments, brigades, and divisions according to their local geographical districts. These were considered fit only for rear duty or for use as fortress troops, and incapable, because of their lack of trained officers and NCOs, of being attached to the fighting regiments. The regular army's contempt for the reserves, in which it was joined by the parties of the right, was augmented by dislike of the principle of the "nation in arms." To merge the reserves with the active divisions would be to put a drag on the army's fighting thrust. Only the active army, they believed, could be depended upon to defend the country.

The left parties, on the other hand, with memories of General Boulanger on horseback, associated the army with *coups d'état* and believed in the principle of a "nation in arms" as the only safeguard of the Republic. They maintained that a few months' training would fit any citizen for war, and violently opposed the increase of military service to three years. The army demanded this reform in 1913 not only to match an increase in the German Army but also because the more men who were in training at any one time, the less reliance needed to be placed on reserve units. After angry debate, with bitterly divisive effect on the country, the Three-Year Law was enacted in August, 1913.

Disdain of the reserves was augmented by the new doctrine of the offensive which, it was felt, could only be properly inculcated in active troops. To perform the irresistible onslaught of the *attaque brusquée*, symbolized by the bayonet charge, the essential quality was *élan*, and *élan* could not be expected of men settled in civilian life with family responsibilities. Reserves mixed with active troops would create "armies of decadence," incapable of the will to conquer.

Similar sentiments were known to be held across the Rhine. The Kaiser was widely credited with the edict "No fathers of families at the front." Among the French General Staff it was an article of faith that the Germans would not mix reserve units with active units, and this led to the belief that the Germans would not have enough men in the front line to do two things at once: send a strong right wing in a wide sweep through Belgium west of the Meuse and keep sufficient forces at their center and left to stop a French breakthrough to the Rhine.

When General Michel presented his plan, the Minister of War, Messimy, treated it *"comme une insanité."* As chairman of the Supreme War Council he not only attempted to suppress it but at once consulted other members of the Council on the advisability of removing Michel.

Messimy, an exuberant, energetic, almost violent man with a thick neck, round head, bright peasant's eyes behind spectacles, and a loud voice, was a former career officer. In 1899 as a thirty-year-old captain of Chasseurs, he had resigned from the army in protest against its refusal to reopen the Dreyfus case. In that heated time the officer corps insisted as a body that to admit the possibility of Dreyfus's innocence after his conviction would be to destroy the army's prestige and infallibility. Unable to put loyalty to the army above justice, Messimy determined upon a political career with the declared goal of "reconciling the army with the nation." He swept into the War Ministry with a passion for improvement. Finding a number of generals "incapable not only of leading their troops but even of following them," he adopted Theodore Roosevelt's expedient of ordering all generals to conduct maneuvers on horseback. When this provoked protests that old so-and-so would be forced to retire from the army Messimy replied that that was indeed his object. He had been named War Minister on June 30, 1911, after a succession of four ministers in four months and the next day was met by the spring of the German gunboat *Panther* on Agadir precipitating the second Moroccan crisis. Expecting mobilization at any moment, Messimy discovered the generalissimo-designate, General Michel, to be "hesitant, indecisive and crushed by the weight of the duty that might at any moment devolve upon him." In his present post Messimy believed he represented a "national danger." Michel's "insane" proposal provided the excuse to get rid of him.

Michel, however, refused to go without first having his plan presented to the Council whose members included the foremost generals of France: Gallieni, the great colonial; Pau, the one-armed veteran of 1870; Joffre, the silent engineer; Dubail, the pattern of gallantry, who wore his kepi cocked over one eye with the *"chic exquis"* of the Second Empire. All were to hold active commands in 1914 and two were to become Marshals of France. None gave Michel's plan his support. One officer from the War Ministry who was present at the meeting said: "There is no use discussing it. General Michel is off his head."

Whether or not this verdict represented the views of all present— Michel later claimed that General Dubail, for one, had originally agreed with him—Messimy, who made no secret of his hostility, carried the Council with him. A trick of fate arranged that Messimy should be a forceful character and Michel should not. To be right and overruled is not forgiven to persons in responsible positions, and Michel duly paid for his clairvoyance. Relieved of his command, he was appointed Military Governor of Paris where in a crucial hour in the coming test he was indeed to prove "hesitant and indecisive."

Messimy having fervently stamped out Michel's heresy of the defensive, did his best, as War Minister, to equip the army to fight a successful offensive but was in his turn frustrated in his most-cherished prospect—the need to reform the French uniform. The British had adopted khaki after the Boer War, and the Germans were about to make the change from Prussian blue to field-gray. But in 1912 French soldiers still wore the same blue coats, red kepi, and red trousers they had worn in 1830 when rifle fire carried only two hundred paces and when armies, fighting at these close quarters, had no need for concealment. Visiting the Balkan front in 1912, Messimy saw the advantages gained by the dull-colored Bulgarians and came home determined to make the French soldier less visible. His project to clothe him in gray-blue or gray-green raised a howl of protest. Army pride was as intransigent about giving up its red trousers as it was about adopting heavy guns. Army prestige was once again felt to be at stake. To clothe the French soldier in some muddy, inglorious color, declared the army's champions, would be to realize the fondest hopes of Dreyfusards and Freemasons. To banish "all that is colorful, all that gives the soldier his vivid aspect," wrote the *Echo de Paris*, "is to go contrary both to French taste and military function." Messimy pointed out that the two might no longer be synonymous, but his opponents proved immovable. At a parliamentary hearing a former War Minister, M. Etienne, spoke for France.

"Eliminate the red trousers?" he cried. "Never! *Le pantalon rouge c'est la France!*"

"That blind and imbecile attachment to the most visible of all colors," wrote Messimy afterward, "was to have cruel consequences."

In the meantime, still in the midst of the Agadir crisis, he had to name a new prospective generalissimo in place of Michel. He planned to give added authority to the post by combining with it that of Chief of the General Staff and by abolishing the post of Chief of Staff to the War Ministry, currently held by General Dubail. Michel's successor would have all the reins of power concentrated in his hands.

Messimy's first choice was the austere and brilliant general in pince-nez, Gallieni, who refused it because, he explained, having been instrumental in Michel's dismissal he felt scruples about replacing him. Furthermore he had only two years to go before retirement at sixty-four, and he believed the appointment of a "colonial" would be resented by the Metropolitan Army—*"une question de bouton,"* he said, tapping his insignia. General Pau, who was next in line, made it a condition that he be allowed to name generals of his own choice to the higher commands which, as he was known for his reactionary opinions, threatened to wake the barely slumbering feud between rightist army and republican nation. Respecting him for his honesty, the government refused his condition. Messimy consulted Gallieni, who suggested his former subordinate in Madagascar, "a cool and methodical worker with a lucid and precise mind." Accordingly the post was offered to General Joseph-Jacques-Césaire Joffre, then aged fifty-nine, formerly chief of the Engineer Corps and presently Chief of the Services of the Rear.

Massive and paunchy in his baggy uniform, with a fleshy face adorned by a heavy, nearly white mustache and bushy eyebrows to match, with a clear youthful skin, calm blue eyes and a candid, tranquil gaze, Joffre looked like Santa Claus and gave an impression of benevolence and naïveté—two qualities not noticeably part of his character. He did not come of a gentleman's family, was not a graduate of St. Cyr (but of the less aristocratic if more scientific Ecole Polytechnique), had not passed through the higher training of the War College. As an officer of the Engineer Corps, which dealt with such unromantic matters as fortifications and railways, he belonged to a branch of the service not drawn upon for the higher commands. He was the eldest of the eleven children of a petit bourgeois manufacturer of wine barrels in the French Pyrénées. His military career had been marked by quiet accomplishment and efficiency in each post he filled: as company commander in Formosa and Indo-China, as a major in the Sudan and Timbuktu, as staff officer in the Railway Section of the War Ministry, as lecturer at the Artillery School, as fortifications officer under Gallieni in Madagascar from 1900 to 1905, as general of a division in 1905, of a corps in 1908, and as Director of the Rear and member of the War Council since 1910.

He had no known clerical, monarchist, or other disturbing connections; he had been out of the country during the Dreyfus Affair; his reputation as a good republican was as smooth as his well-manicured hands; he was solid and utterly phlegmatic. His outstanding characteristic was a habitual silence that in other men would have seemed self-deprecatory but, worn like an aura over Joffre's great, calm bulk, inspired confidence. He had still five years to go before retirement.

Joffre was conscious of one lack: he had had no training in the rarefied realms of staff work. On a hot July day when doors in the War Ministry on the Rue St. Dominique were left open, officers glancing out of their rooms saw General Pau holding Joffre by a button of his uniform. "Take it, *cher ami*," he was saying. "We will give you Castelnau. He knows all about staff work—everything will go of itself."

Castelnau, who was a graduate both of St. Cyr and of the War College, came, like D'Artagnan, from Gascony, which is said to produce men of hot blood and cold brain. He suffered from the disadvantage of family connections with a marquis, of associating with Jesuits, and of a personal Catholicism which he practiced so vigorously as to earn him during the war the name of *le capucin botté*, the Monk in Boots. He had, however, long experience on the General Staff. Joffre would have preferred Foch but knew Messimy to have an unexplained prejudice against him. As was his habit, he listened without comment to Pau's advice, and promptly took it.

"Aye!" complained Messimy when Joffre asked for Castelnau as his Deputy Chief. "You will rouse a storm in the parties of the left and make yourself a lot of enemies." However, with the assent of the President and Premier who "made a face" at the condition but agreed, both appointments were put through together. A fellow general, pursuing some personal intrigue, warned Joffre that Castelnau might displace him. "Get rid of me! Not Castelnau," Joffre replied, unruffled. "I need him for six months; then I'll give him a corps command." As it proved, he found Castelnau invaluable, and when war came gave him command of an army instead of a corps.

Joffre's supreme confidence in himself was expressed in the following year when his aide, Major Alexandre, asked him if he thought war was shortly to be expected.

"Certainly I think so," Joffre replied. "I have always thought so. It will come. I shall fight it and I shall win. I have always succeeded in whatever I do—as in the Sudan. It will be that way again."

"It will mean a Marshal's baton for you," his aide suggested with some awe at the vision.

"Yes." Joffre acknowledged the prospect with laconic equanimity.

Under the aegis of this unassailable figure the General Staff from 1911 on threw itself into the task of revising the Field Regulations, retraining the troops in their spirit, and making a new plan of campaign to replace the now obsolete Plan 16. The staff's guiding mind, Foch, was gone from the War College, promoted and shifted to the field and ultimately to Nancy where, as he said, the frontier of 1870 "cut like a scar across the breast of the country." There, guarding the frontier, he commanded the XXth Corps which he was soon to make famous. He had left behind, however, a "chapel," as cliques in the French Army were called, of his disciples who formed Joffre's entourage. He had also left behind a strategic plan which became the framework of Plan 17. Completed in April, 1913, it was adopted without discussion or consultation, together with the new Field Regulations by the Supreme War Council in May. The next eight months were spent reorganizing the army on the basis of the plan and preparing all the instructions and orders for mobilization, transport, services of supply, areas and schedules of deployment and concentration. By February, 1914, it was ready to be distributed in sections to each of the generals of the five armies into which the French forces were divided, only that part of it which concerned him individually going to each one.

Its motivating idea, as expressed by Foch, was, "We must get to Berlin by going through Mainz," that is, by crossing the Rhine at Mainz, 130 miles northeast of Nancy. That objective, however, was an idea only. Unlike the Schlieffen plan, Plan 17 contained no stated over-all objective and no explicit schedule of operations. It was not a plan of operations but a plan of deployment with directives for several possible lines of attack for each army, depending on circumstances, but without a given goal. Because it was in essence a plan of response, of riposte to a German attack, whose avenues the French could not be sure of in advance, it had of necessity to be, as Joffre said, "a posteriori and opportunist." Its intention was inflexible: Attack! Otherwise its arrangements were flexible.

A brief general directive of five sentences, classified as secret, was all that was shown in common to the generals who were to carry out the plan, and they were not permitted to discuss it. It offered very little for discussion. Like the Field Regulations it opened with a flourish: "Whatever the circumstance, it is the Commander in Chief's intention to advance with all forces united to the attack of the German armies." The rest of the general directive stated merely that French action would consist of two major offensives, one to the left and one to the right of the German fortified area of Metz-Thionville. The one to the right or south of Metz would attack directly eastward across the old border of Lorraine, while a secondary operation in Alsace was designed to anchor the French right on the Rhine. The offensive to the left or north of Metz would attack either to the north or, in the event the enemy violated neutral territory, to the northeast through Luxembourg and the Belgian Ardennes, but this movement would be carried out "only by order of the Commander in Chief." The general purpose, although this was nowhere stated, was to drive through to the Rhine, at the same time isolating and cutting off the invading German right wing from behind.

To this end Plan 17 deployed the five French armies along the frontier from Belfort in Alsace as far as Hirson, about a third of the way along the Franco-Belgian border. The remaining two-thirds of the Belgian frontier, from Hirson to the sea, was left undefended. It was along that stretch that General Michel had planned to defend France. Joffre found his plan in the office safe when he succeeded Michel. It concentrated the center of gravity of the French forces to this extreme left section of the line where Joffre left none. It was a plan of pure defense; it allowed for no seizing of initiative; it was, as Joffre decided after careful study, "foolishness."

The French General Staff, though receiving many indications collected by the Deuxième Bureau, or Military Intelligence, pointing to a powerful German right-wing envelopment, believed the arguments against such a maneuver more telling than the evidence for it. They did not credit the sweep through Flanders, although, in fact, they had been told about it in a dramatic manner by an officer of the German General Staff who in 1904 betrayed to them an early version of the Schlieffen plan. In a series of three rendezvous with a French intelligence officer at Brussels, Paris, and Nice, the German appeared with his head swathed in bandages, revealing only a gray mustache and a pair of piercing eyes. The documents he handed over for a considerable sum revealed that the Germans planned to come through Belgium by way of Liège, Namur, Charleroi, and invade France along the valley of the Oise, by way of Guise, Noyon and Compiègne. The route was correct for 1914, for the documents were authentic. General Pendezac, then Chief of the French General Staff, believed the information "fitted perfectly with the present tendency of German strategy which teaches the necessity of wide envelopment," but many of his colleagues were doubtful. They did not believe the Germans could mobilize enough men to maneuver on such a scale, and they suspected the information might be a feint designed to draw the French away from the area of the real attack. French planning was hampered by a variety of uncertainties, and the greatest of these was Belgium. To the logical French mind it seemed obvious that the Germans would bring England in against them if they violated Belgium and attacked Antwerp. Was it likely the Germans would deliberately do themselves this disservice? Rather, was it not "altogether likely" that, leaving Belgium unviolated, they would return to the elder Moltke's plan of attacking Russia first before the slow Russian mobilization could be completed.

Attempting to fit Plan 17 to one of several hypotheses of German strategy, Joffre and Castelnau believed that the most likely one was a major enemy offensive across the plateau of Lorraine. They expected it to violate the corner of Belgium east of the Meuse. They calculated German strength on the Western Front, without use of reserves in the front line, at twenty-six corps. For this number to be extended in strength on the far side of the Meuse was "impossible," decided Castelnau. "I was of the same opinion," agreed Joffre.

Jean Jaurès, the great socialist leader, thought differently. Leading the fight against the Three-Year Law, he insisted in his speeches and in his book *L'Armée nouvelle* that the war of the future would be one of mass armies using every citizen, that this was what the Germans were preparing, that reservists of twenty-five to thirty-three were at their peak of stamina and more committed than younger men without responsibilities, that unless France used all her reservists in the front line she would be subjected to a terrible "submersion."

Outside the chapel of Plan 17 there were still military critics who argued strongly for the defensive. Colonel Grouard, in his book *La Guerre éventuelle*, published in 1913, wrote: "It is above all the German offensive through Belgium on which we ought to fix our attention. As far as one can foresee the logical consequences of the opening of our campaign, we can say without hesitation that if we take the offensive at the outset we shall be beaten." But if France prepared a riposte against the German right wing, "all the chances are in our favor."

In 1913 the Deuxième Bureau collected enough information on the German use of reserves as active troops as to make it impossible for the French General Staff to be ignorant of this crucial factor. A critique by Moltke on German maneuvers of 1913 indicating that the reserves would be so used came into French possession. Major Melotte, Belgian military attaché in Berlin, noticed and reported the Germans calling up an unusual number of reserves in 1913 from which he concluded that they were forming a reserve corps for every active corps. But the authors of Plan 17 did not want to be convinced. They rejected evidence that argued in favor of their staying on the defensive because their hearts and hopes, as well as their training and strategy, were fixed on the offensive. They persuaded themselves that the Germans intended to use reserve units only to guard communication lines and "passive fronts" and as siege and occupation troops. They enabled themselves to reject defense of the Belgian frontier by insisting that if the Germans extended their right wing as far as Flanders, they would leave their center so thinned that the French, as Castelnau said, could "cut them in half." A strong German right wing would give the French advantage of superior numbers against the German center and left. This was the meaning of Castelnau's classic phrase, "So much the better for us!"

When General Lebas on that occasion left the Rue St. Dominique, he said to the deputy from Lille who had accompanied him, "I have two stars on my sleeve and he has three. How can I argue?"

▶▶▶ *4* ▶

▶▶▶ *"A Single*
British Soldier . . ."

BRITAIN'S JOINT MILITARY PLANS WITH FRANCE
were begotten in 1905 when Russia's far-off defeats at the hands of the
Japanese, revealing her military impotence, unhinged the equilibrium of
Europe. Suddenly and simultaneously the government of every nation
became aware that if any one of them chose that moment to precipitate a
war, France would have to fight without an ally. The German government
put the moment to an immediate test. Within three weeks of the Russian
defeat at Mukden in 1905, a challenge was flung at France in the form of
the Kaiser's sensational appearance at Tangier on March 31. To Frenchmen
it meant that Germany was probing for the moment of "Again" and
would find it, if not now, then soon. "Like everyone else I had come to
Paris at nine o'clock on that morning," wrote Charles Péguy, the poet,
editor, mystic, Socialist-against-his-party and Catholic-against-his-church,
who spoke, as nearly as one person could, for the conscience of France.
"Like everyone else I knew at half-past eleven that, in the space of those
two hours, a new period had begun in the history of my life, in the history
of this country, in the history of the world."

Of his own life Péguy was not speaking vainly. In August 1914 he was to volunteer at forty-one for military service and be killed in action at the Marne on September 7.

Britain, too, reacted to the challenge of Tangier. Her military establishment was just then being thoroughly overhauled by Lord Esher's Committee. It included, besides himself, the turbulent First Sea Lord, Sir John Fisher, who had been reforming the navy by a series of explosions, and an army officer, Sir George Clarke, known for his modern ideas on imperial strategy. The "Esher triumvirate" had created a Committee of Imperial Defence to govern policy pertaining to war, of which Esher was permanent member and Clarke was secretary, and had endowed the army with a pristine General Staff. Just at the time when the Kaiser was nervously riding a too spirited white horse through the streets of Tangier, the Staff was engaged in a theoretical war game based on the assumption that the Germans would come through Belgium in a wide flanking movement north and west of the Meuse. The map exercise proved to the Director of Military Operations, General Grierson, and to his assistant, General Robertson, that there was little chance of stopping the Germans unless British forces "arrived on the scene quickly and in strength."

At that time independent action in Belgium was what the British contemplated. Mr. Balfour, the Conservative Prime Minister, at once asked for a report on how soon a force of four divisions could be mobilized and landed in Belgium in the event of a German invasion. In the midst of the crisis, while Grierson and Robertson were over on the Continent examining the terrain along the Franco-Belgian frontier, Balfour's government lost office.

Nerves on all sides were stretched tight in the expectation that Germany might take advantage of Russia's catastrophe to precipitate war in the coming summer. No plans for common Anglo-French military action had yet been made. With Britain in the throes of a general election and ministers scattered about the country campaigning, the French were forced to make an unofficial approach. Their military attaché in London, Major Huguet, made contact with an active and eager intermediary, Colonel Repington, military correspondent of *The Times*, who, with a nod from Esher and Clarke, opened negotiations. In a memorandum submitted to the French government, Colonel Repington asked, "May we take it as a principle that France will not violate Belgian territory unless compelled to do so by previous violation by Germany?"

"Definitely, yes," the French replied.

"Do the French realise," asked the Colonel, intending to convey a warning as well as a prognosis, "that any violation of Belgian neutrality brings us into the field automatically in defense of our treaty obligations?" No British government in history ever committed itself to take action "automatically" upon an event, but the Colonel, with the bit in his teeth, was galloping far ahead of the field.

"France has always supposed so," was the somewhat dazed answer, "but has never received an official assurance."

By further leading questions, the Colonel established that France did not think highly of independent British action in Belgium and believed that unity of command—for France on land and Britain at sea—was "absolutely indispensable."

Meanwhile the Liberals had been elected. Traditionally opposed to war and foreign adventure, they were confident that good intentions could keep the peace. Their new Foreign Secretary was Sir Edward Grey, who suffered the death of his wife a month after taking office. Their new Secretary for War was a barrister with a passion for German philosophy, Richard Haldane, who, when asked by the soldiers in Council what kind of army he had in mind, replied, "A Hegelian army." "The conversation then fell off," he recorded.

Grey, warily approached by the French, indicated he had no intention of "receding" from any assurances his predecessor had given to France. Faced with a major crisis in his first week of office, he asked Haldane if arrangements existed for the British to fight alongside the French in the event of an emergency. Haldane looked in the files and found none. His inquiry disclosed that to put four divisions on the Continent would take two months.

Grey wondered if talks between the General Staffs might not now take place as a "military precaution" without committing Great Britain. Haldane consulted the Prime Minister, Sir Henry Campbell-Bannerman. Despite party affiliation, Campbell-Bannerman was personally so fond of things French that he would sometimes take the Channel steamer over and back in one day in order to lunch at Calais. He gave his assent to Staff talks, though with some misgivings about the stress laid on "joint preparations." He thought that coming, as they did, "very close to an honorable understanding," they might destroy the lovely looseness of the Entente. To avoid any such unpleasantness Haldane arranged for a letter to be signed by General Grierson and Major Huguet, stating that the talks did not commit Great Britain. With this formula safely established, he authorized the talks to begin. Thereupon he, Grey, and the Prime Minister, without informing the rest of the Cabinet, left further developments in the hands of the military as a "departmental affair."

From here the General Staffs took over. British officers, including Sir John French, a cavalry general who had made a great name in the Boer War, attended the French maneuvers that summer. Grierson and Robertson revisited the frontier in company with Major Huguet. In consultation with the French General Staff, they selected landing bases and staging areas along a front from Charleroi to Namur and into the Ardennes, predicated on a German invasion through Belgium.

The "Esher triumvirate," however, fundamentally disapproved of employing the British Army as a mere adjunct of the French and, after the tension of the Moroccan crisis relaxed, the joint planning begun in 1905 was not pushed further. General Grierson was replaced. The dominant view, represented by Lord Esher, favored action, independent of French command, in Belgium where the holding of Antwerp and the adjoining coast was a direct British interest. In the vehement opinion of Sir John Fisher, British action ought to be predominantly naval. He doubted the military capacity of the French, expected the Germans to beat them on land, and saw no purpose in ferrying the British Army over to be included in that defeat. The only land action he favored was an audacious leap onto Germany's back, and he had chosen the exact spot—a "ten-mile stretch of hard sand" along the Baltic coast of East Prussia. Here, only ninety miles from Berlin, the nearest point to the German capital that could be reached by sea, British troops landed by the navy could seize and entrench a base of operations and "keep a million Germans busy." Apart from this action the army should be "absolutely restricted to . . . sudden descents upon the coast, the recovery of Heligoland and the garrisoning of Antwerp." Its plan to fight in France was, in Fisher's opinion, "suicidal idiocy," the War Office was remarkable for its ignorance of war, and the Army should be administered as an "annex to the Navy." Early in 1910 Fisher, at sixty-nine, was simultaneously raised to the peerage and relieved of the Admiralty, but that was to be far from the end of his usefulness.

After the emergency of 1905–1906 had passed, joint military plans with the French made little progress for the next few years. In the interim two men formed a trans-Channel friendship which was to serve as the first cable for the building of a bridge.

Britain's Staff College was then commanded by Brigadier General

Henry Wilson, a tall, bony, ebullient Anglo-Irishman with a face which he thought rather resembled that of a horse. Quick and impatient, Wilson was in a constant boil of ideas, humor, passion, imagination and, above all, energy. When serving at the War Office in London, he used to trot around Hyde Park for exercise before breakfast, carrying with him the morning paper to read whenever he slowed down to a walk. Brought up by a succession of French governesses, he could speak French fluently. He was less interested in German. In January 1909 Schlieffen published an anonymous article in the *Deutsche Revue* to protest certain changes made in his plan by his successor, Moltke. The basic outline, if not the details, of the "colossal Cannae" prepared for the envelopment of the French and British armies was revealed and the identity of the author surmised. When a student at Camberley brought the article to the Commandant's attention, Wilson returned it with the casual comment, "Very interesting."

In December 1909 General Wilson took it into his head to visit his opposite number, the commandant of the Ecole Supérieure de la Guerre, General Foch. He attended four lectures and a seminar and was politely invited to tea by General Foch who, though impatient with the interruptions of distinguished visitors, felt he owed this much to his British counterpart. General Wilson, enthusiastic at what he had seen and heard, stayed for three hours' talk. When Foch was finally able to escort his visitor to the door and made what he thought were his final goodbyes, Wilson happily announced that he was returning next day to continue the conversation and see more of the curriculum. Foch could not but admire the Englishman's *cran* and be pleased by his interest. Their second talk opened their minds to each other. Within a month Wilson was back in Paris for another session. Foch accepted his invitation to come to London in the spring, and Wilson agreed to return for the French Staff tour in the summer.

In London when Foch came over, Wilson introduced him to Haldane and others at the War Office. Bursting into the room of one of his colleagues, he said: "I've got a French general outside—General Foch. Mark my words, this fellow is going to command the Allied armies when the big war comes on." Here Wilson had already accepted the principle of unity of command and picked the man for it although it was to take four years of war and the brink of defeat before events would bear him out.

During repeated visits after 1909, the two commandants became fast friends even to the extent of Wilson being admitted into the French

General Joffre with General de Castelnau (left) and General Pau.

Brown Brothers

Sir Henry Wilson talking with Foch and Colonel Huguet.
Radio Times Hulton Picture Library

General Sukhomlinov with staff officers. *The Imperial War Museum*

The Czar and Grand Duke Nicholas.   *The Imperial War Museum*

(*above*) The *Goeben*.   *The Imperial War Museum*
(*right*) Admiral Souchon.   *German Information Cent*

(*previous page*) The Kaiser and von Moltke.   *Radio Times Hulton Picture Libr*

King Albert.   *The Imperial War Museum*

family circle and invited to the wedding of Foch's daughter. With his friend "Henri," Foch spent hours in what an observer called "tremendous gossips." They used to exchange caps and walk up and down together, the short and the tall, arguing and chaffing. Wilson had been particularly impressed by the rush and dash with which studies were conducted at the War College. Officer-instructors constantly urged on officer-pupils with "*Vite, vite!*" and "*Allez, allez!*" Introduced to the classes in the Camberley Staff College, the hurry-up technique was quickly dubbed Wilson's "*allez* operations."

A question that Wilson asked of Foch during his second visit in January 1910, evoked an answer which expressed in one sentence the problem of the alliance with England, as the French saw it.

"What is the smallest British military force that would be of any practical assistance to you?" Wilson asked.

Like a rapier flash came Foch's reply, "A single British soldier—and we will see to it that he is killed."

Wilson, too, wanted to see Britain committed. Convinced that war with Germany was imminent and inevitable, he strove to infuse his own sense of urgency into his colleagues and pupils and himself became totally absorbed by it. In August 1910 came his opportunity. He was named Director of Military Operations, the post from which General Grierson had originated the Staff talks with France. When Major Huguet at once came to see the new Director to bewail the lack of progress since 1906 on the important question of Anglo-French military cooperation, Wilson replied, "Important question! But it is vital! There is no other."

Immediately the joint planning took on new impetus. Wilson could see nothing, go nowhere, but France and Belgium. On his first visit in 1909 he had spent ten days by train and bicycle touring the Franco-Belgian and Franco-German frontier from Valenciennes to Belfort. He had found that Foch's "appreciation of the German move through Belgium is exactly the same as mine, the important line being between Verdun and Namur," in other words, east of the Meuse. During the next four years he repeated his visits three and four times a year, each time making bicycle or motor tours of the old battlefields of 1870 and of anticipated future battlefields in Lorraine and the Ardennes. On each visit he conferred with Foch and after Foch's departure, with Joffre, Castelnau, Dubail, and others of the French General Staff.

Covering the whole wall of Wilson's room in the War Office was a huge map of Belgium with every road by which he thought the Germans could march marked in heavy black. When he came to the War Office, Wilson found that under the new order wrought by "Schopenhauer among the generals," as Haldane was called, the regular army had been thoroughly trained, prepared, and organized to become an expeditionary force at a moment's need, with all arrangements completed to bring it up to war strength upon mobilization day. But of plans to transport it across the Channel, billet it, feed it, move it up to concentration areas in France, align it with the French armies, there were none.

What he felt to be the lethargy of the Staff on this subject sent Wilson into periodic paroxysms of vexation, recorded in his diary: ". . . very dissatisfied . . . no rail arrangements . . . no arrangements for horse supply . . . a scandalous state of affairs! . . . no train arrangements to ports, no staff arrangements to port, no naval arrangements . . . absolutely no medical arrangements . . . horse difficulty has not been solved . . . absolutely nothing exists, which is scandalous! . . . unpreparedness disgraceful . . . horse question in disgraceful state!" Yet by March 1911 out of all this lack of arrangements—and of horses—he had brought a schedule of mobilization by which "the whole of the infantry of six divisions would embark on the 4th day, cavalry 7th day, artillery 9th day."

It was just in time. On July 1, 1911 the *Panther* came to Agadir. Through all the chancelleries of Europe ran the whispered monosyllable, "War." Wilson hurried over to Paris in the same month that the French War Council, ousting General Michel, turned its back forever on the defensive. Together with General Dubail he drew up a memorandum providing, in the event of British intervention, for an Expeditionary Force of six regular divisions and a cavalry division. Signed by Wilson and Dubail on July 20, it specified a total force of 150,000 men and 67,000 horses which were to land at Havre, Boulogne, and upriver at Rouen between the 4th and 12th days of mobilization, to proceed by rail to a concentration area in the Maubeuge region and to be ready for action on M-13.

In effect, the Dubail-Wilson agreement attached the British Army, in the event that war came and Britain entered it, to the French, placing it where it would prolong the French line and guard the French flank against envelopment. It meant, as Major Huguet gladly recorded, that the French had persuaded Wilson and the British General Staff against a "secondary theatre of operations" and in favor of common action in "the main theatre, that is to say, the French." In fact the British Navy was as much responsible as the French because its refusal to guarantee disembarkation ports above the line Dover-Calais precluded landings closer to, or within, Belgium.

Upon Wilson's return to London the question of the hour, he wrote in his diary, was whether Germany would go to war "with France and us." Consulted by Grey and Haldane over lunch, he presented an emphatic three-point program. "First we *must* join the French. Second, we *must* mobilize the same day as the French. Third, we *must* send all six divisions."

He felt "profoundly dissatisfied" with the two civilians' grasp of the situation, but he was at once given a further opportunity to instruct the government in the facts of war. On August 23 Prime Minister Asquith (Campbell-Bannerman's successor since 1908) convened a secret and special meeting of the Imperial Defence Committee to clarify British strategy in case of war. It lasted all day, with General Wilson expounding the army view in the morning and Fisher's successor, Admiral Sir Arthur Wilson, presenting the navy's view in the afternoon. Besides Asquith, Grey, and Haldane, three other Cabinet members were present: the Chancellor of the Exchequer, Lloyd George; the First Lord of the Admiralty, Mr. McKenna; and the Home Secretary, a young man of thirty-seven, impossible to ignore, who, from his inappropriate post, had pelted the Prime Minister during the crisis with ideas on naval and military strategy, all of them quite sound, had produced an astonishingly accurate prediction of the future course of the fighting, and who had no doubts whatever about what needed to be done. The Home Secretary was Winston Churchill.

Wilson, facing this group of "ignorant men," as he called them, and accompanied by his fellow officer and future chief, Sir John French, "who knows nothing at all about the subject," pinned up his great map of Belgium on the wall and lectured for two hours. He swept away many illusions when he explained how Germany, counting on Russia's slow mobilization, would send the bulk of her forces against the French, achieving superiority of numbers over them. He correctly predicated the German plan of attack upon a right-wing envelopment but, schooled in the French theories, estimated the force that would come down west of the Meuse at no more than four divisions. He stated that, if all six British divisions were sent immediately upon the outbreak of war to the extreme left of the French line, the chances of stopping the Germans would be favorable.

When the Admiral's turn came in the afternoon, the dazed civilians were astonished to discover that the navy's plan had nothing in common with the army's. He proposed to land the expeditionary force not in France, but on that "ten-mile strip of hard sand" upon the northern shores of Prussia where it would "draw off more than its weight of numbers from the German fighting line." His argument was violently combated by the generals. The absence of Lord Fisher nerved Asquith to reject it, and the Army carried the day. Fisher's growls of disgust erupted periodically thereafter. "The overwhelming supremacy of the British Navy . . . is the only thing to keep the German Army out of Paris," he wrote to a friend some months later. "Our soldiers are grotesque in their absurd ideas of war, but, happily, they are powerless. It is Antwerp we shall seize and not go fooling on the Vosges frontier." A certain inescapable logic in the Antwerp idea was to keep tugging at British military plans up to the last minute in 1914 and even afterward.

The meeting of August 1911 like that of the French War Council which had disposed of General Michel a few weeks earlier, was decisive upon British strategy and it had a decisive by-product. A shake-up in the policy-making posts of the navy being decreed, the eager Home Secretary was happily translated into First Lord of the Admiralty where, in 1914, he was to prove indispensable.

Echoes of the secret meeting of the C.I.D. angered the Cabinet members who had been left out and who belonged to the sternly pacifist wing of the party. Henry Wilson learned that he was regarded as the villain of the proceedings and that they are "calling for my head." At this time began the split in the Cabinet which was to be so critical in the ultimate days of decision. The government maintained the disingenuous position that the military "conversations" were, in Haldane's words, "just the natural and informal outcome of our close friendship with France." Natural outcome they might be; informal they were not. As Lord Esher with a certain realism said to the Prime Minister, the plans worked out jointly by the General Staffs have "certainly committed us to fight, whether the Cabinet likes it or not."

There is no record what Asquith replied or what, in his inmost mind, a region difficult to penetrate under the best of circumstances, he thought on this crucial question.

In the following year, 1912, a naval agreement was reached with France as the result of a momentous mission—not to France but to Berlin. In an effort to dissuade the Germans from passing a new Naval Law providing for increases in the fleet, Haldane was sent to talk with the Kaiser, Bethmann-Hollweg, Admiral Tirpitz, and other German leaders. It was the last Anglo-German attempt to find a common ground of understanding, and it failed. As a quid pro quo for keeping their fleet second to Britain's, the Germans demanded a promise of British neutrality in the event of war between Germany and France. This the British refused to give. Haldane returned convinced that Germany's drive for hegemony in Europe would have to be resisted sooner or later: "I thought, from my study of the German General Staff, that once the German war party had got into the saddle, it would be war not merely for the overthrow of France or Russia but for the domination of the world." Coming from Haldane this conclusion had a profound effect upon Liberal thinking and planning. The first result was a naval pact with France by which the British undertook at threat of war to safeguard the Channel and French coasts from enemy attack, leaving the French fleet free to concentrate in the Mediterranean. As this disposed the French fleet where it would not otherwise be, except by virtue of the agreement, it left a distinct obligation upon Britain.

Although the terms of the agreement were not known to the Cabinet as a whole, an uneasy sense prevailed that matters had gone too far. Not satisfied with the "no commitment" formula, the antiwar group insisted that it be put in writing. Sir Edward Grey obliged in the form of a letter to M. Cambon, the French ambassador. Drafted and approved by the Cabinet, it was a masterpiece of ellipsis. The military conversations, it said, left both parties free to decide at any future time "whether or not to assist each other by armed force." The naval agreement "was not based upon an engagement to cooperate in war." At threat of war both parties would "take into consideration" the plans of their General Staffs and "then decide what effect should be given them."

This curious document managed to satisfy everybody: the French because the whole British Cabinet Government had now officially acknowledged the existence of the joint plans, the antiwar group because it said England was not "committed," and Grey because he had evolved a formula that both saved the plans and quieted their opponents. To have substituted a definite alliance with France, as he was urged in some quarters, would "break up the Cabinet," he said.

After Agadir, as each year brought its summer crisis and the air grew heavier with approaching storm, the joint work of the General Staffs grew more intense. Sir Henry Wilson's tours abroad grew more frequent. He found the new French chief, General Joffre, "a fine, manly, imperturbable soldier with much character and determination," and Castelnau "very clever and intelligent." He continued his surveys of the Belgian frontier, cycling back and forth over the various roads and returning always to his favorite battlefield of 1870 at Mars-la-Tour near Metz where, each time he saw the statue "France," commemorating the battle, he felt a pang. On one visit, he recorded, "I laid at her feet a small bit of map I have been carrying, showing the areas of concentration of the British forces on her territory."

In 1912 he examined the new German railway constructions, all converging on Aachen and the Belgian frontier. In February of that year Anglo-French plans had reached the point where Joffre could tell the Supreme War Council that he counted on the British for six infantry divisions and one cavalry division and two mounted brigades, totaling 145,000 men. *L'Armée* "W" as, in tribute to Wilson, the force was designated by the French, would land at Boulogne, Havre, and Rouen, concentrate in the Hirson-Maubeuge region and be ready for action on the fifteenth day of mobilization. Later in 1912 Wilson attended autumn maneuvers with Joffre and Castelnau and the Grand Duke Nicholas of Russia and afterward went on to Russia for talks with the Russian General Staff. In 1913 he visited Paris every other month to confer with the French Staff chiefs and to join the maneuvers of Foch's XXth Corps guarding the frontier.

While Wilson was tightening and perfecting his arrangements with the French, Britain's new Chief of Imperial General Staff, Sir John French, made an attempt in 1912 to revert to the idea of independent action in Belgium. Discreet inquiries made by the British military attaché in Brussels put an end to this effort. The Belgians were discovered to be adamant in the strict observance of their own neutrality. When the British attaché asked about possible joint arrangements for British landings in Belgium, on the premise of a prior German violation, he was informed that the British would have to wait until their military assistance was requested. The British minister, making his own inquiries, was told that if British troops landed before a German invasion or without a formal Belgian request, the Belgians would open fire.

Belgium's rigid purity confirmed what the British never tired of repeating to the French—that everything depended upon the Germans violating Belgian neutrality first. "Never, no matter on what pretext," Lord Esher cautioned Major Huguet in 1911, "let the French commanders be led into being the first to cross the Belgian frontier!" If they did, England could never be on their side; if the Germans did, they would bring England in against them. M. Cambon, the French ambassador in London, expressed the condition the other way around; only if Germany violated Belgium, was the burden of his dispatches, could France be sure of Britain's support.

By the spring of 1914 the joint work of the French and British General Staffs was complete to the last billet of every battalion, even to the places where they were to drink their coffee. The number of French railroad cars to be allotted, the assignments of interpreters, the preparation of codes and ciphers, the forage of horses was settled or expected to be consummated by July. The fact that Wilson and his staff were in constant communication with the French had to be concealed. All the work on Plan W, as the movement of the expeditionary force was called by both Staffs, was done in utmost secrecy, confined to half a dozen officers alone, who did even the typing, filing, and clerical work. While the military prearranged the lines of battle, England's political leaders, pulling the blanket of "no commitment" over their heads, resolutely refrained from watching them.

▶▶▶ 5 ▶

▶▶▶ *The Russian*
Steam Roller

THE RUSSIAN COLOSSUS EXERCISED A SPELL UPON
Europe. On the chessboard of military planning, Russia's size and weight
of numbers represented the largest piece. Notwithstanding her shoddy
performance in the war against Japan, thought of the Russian "steam
roller" gave comfort and encouragement to France and Britain; dread of
the Slav at their backs haunted the Germans.

Although the defects of the Russian Army were notorious, although the
Russian winter, not the Russian Army, had turned Napoleon back from
Moscow, although it had been defeated on its own soil by the French and
British in the Crimea, although the Turks in 1877 had outfought it at
the siege of Plevna and only succumbed later to overwhelming numbers,
although the Japanese had outfought it in Manchuria, a myth of its
invincibility prevailed. The savage cavalry charge of yelling Cossacks was
such a fixture in European minds that newspaper artists in August, 1914,
were able to draw it in stirring detail without having been within a thousand miles of the Russian front. Cossacks and inexhaustible millions of

hardy, uncomplaining *mujiks* willing to die made up the stereotype of the Russian Army. Its numbers inspired awe: 1,423,000 in peacetime strength; an additional 3,115,000 to be called upon mobilization, and a further reserve of 2,000,000 in territorials and recruits to make a total available force of 6,500,000.

It was envisaged as a gigantic mass, initially lethargic, but once thoroughly roused into motion, rolling forward inexorably with, no matter how many losses, endless waves of manpower to fill the places of the fallen. The army's efforts to purge incompetence and corruption since the war with Japan were believed to have brought improvement. "Everyone" in French politics was "immensely impressed by the growing strength of Russia and her tremendous resources and potential power and wealth," Sir Edward Grey noticed when he was in Paris in April 1914 to negotiate a naval agreement with the Russians. He shared the impression himself. "Russian resources are so great," he told President Poincaré, "that in the long run Germany will be exhausted without our helping Russia."

To the French the success of Plan 17, the irresistible march to the Rhine, was to be the proving of their nation and one of the great moments of European history. To ensure their breakthrough of the German center, they were bent on having the Russians draw off a portion of the German forces opposing them. The problem was to get Russia to launch an offensive upon Germany's rear at the same time as the Germans and French launched theirs on the Western Front, that is, as nearly as possible to the fifteenth day of mobilization. The French knew as well as everyone else that it was physically impossible for Russia to complete mobilization and concentration of her forces in fifteen days, but they wanted her to begin battle on M-15 with whatever she had ready. They were determined that Germany must be forced to fight on two fronts from the first moment in order to reduce the German superiority in numbers against themselves.

In 1911 General Dubail, then Chief of the War Ministry Staff, was sent to Russia to indoctrinate the Russian General Staff with the need for seizing the initiative. Although half the Russian forces in a European war would be concentrated against Austria and only half of those destined to take the field against Germany would be ready by M-15, the spirit in St. Petersburg was bold and willing. Anxious to restore glory to their tarnished arms, and leaving details of planning to look after themselves, the Russians agreed, with more valor than discretion, to launch an offensive simultaneously with France. Dubail obtained a promise that as

soon as their front-line forces were in position, without waiting for concentration to be completed, the Russians would attack, crossing the
frontier of East Prussia on M-16. "It is at the very heart of Germany that
we should strike," acknowledged the Czar in a signed agreement. "The
objective for both of us ought to be Berlin."

The pact for an early Russian offensive was hardened and sharpened
in annual Staff talks that were a feature of the Franco-Russian Alliance.
In 1912 General Jilinsky, Chief of the Russian General Staff, came to
Paris; in 1913 General Joffre went to Russia. By now the Russians had succumbed to the spell of *élan*. Since Manchuria they, too, had to compensate for the humiliation of military defeat and the consciousness of military
deficiencies. Colonel Grandmaison's lectures, translated into Russian, enjoyed immense popularity. Suffused with the glittering doctrine of *offensive à outrance*, the Russian General Staff improved on its promises.
General Jilinsky undertook, in 1912, to have all of the 800,000 men destined for the German front ready by M-15, although Russia's railways
were manifestly inadequate to the task. In 1913 he advanced the date of
his offensive by two days, although Russia's armament factories were producing less than two-thirds the estimated need of artillery shells and less
than half the need of rifle cartridges.

The Allies did not seriously concern themselves with Russia's military
defects, although Ian Hamilton, Britain's military observer with the Japanese, had reported them pitilessly from Manchuria. They were: poor intelligence, disregard of cover, disregard of secrecy and swiftness, lack of dash,
lack of initiative, and lack of good generalship. Colonel Repington who
had pronounced judgment weekly on the Russo-Japanese War in *The
Times* arrived at opinions which caused him to dedicate a book of his
collected columns to the Emperor of Japan. Nevertheless the General
Staffs believed that simply to get the Russian giant in motion, regardless
of how he functioned, was all that mattered. This was difficult enough.
During mobilization the average Russian soldier had to be transported 700
miles, four times as far as the average German soldier, and Russia had
available one-tenth as many railroads per square kilometer as Germany.
As a defense against invasion these had been deliberately built on a wider
gauge than those of Germany. Heavy French loans to finance increased
railroad construction had not yet accomplished their goal. Equal speed in
mobilization was obviously impossible; but even if only half the 800,000
Russian troops promised for the German front could be put in position by
the fifteenth day for a lunge into East Prussia, however faulty their mili-

tary organization, the effect of their invasion of German territory was expected to be momentous.

To send an army into modern battle on enemy territory, especially under the disadvantage of different railway gauges, is a hazardous and complicated undertaking requiring prodigies of careful organization. Systematic attention to detail was not a notable characteristic of the Russian Army.

The officer corps was topheavy with a superabundance of aged generals whose heaviest intellectual exercise was card playing and who, to save their court perquisites and prestige, were kept on the active list regardless of activity. Officers were appointed and promoted chiefly through patronage, social or monetary, and although there were among them many brave and able soldiers the system did not tend to bring the best to the top. Their "laziness and lack of interest" in outdoor sports dismayed a British military attaché who, on visiting a frontier garrison near the Afghan border, was appalled to find "not a single tennis court." In the purges after the Japanese war large numbers had resigned or been forced out in an effort to loosen the mass clogging the top. In one year 341 generals, nearly as many as in all the French Army, and 400 colonels had been retired as inefficient. Yet despite improvements in pay and promotion there was a shortage in 1913 of 3,000 officers. Much had been done since the Japanese war to clean away the decay in the army, but the Russian regime was still the same.

"This insane regime," its ablest defender, Count Witte, the premier of 1903–06, called it; "this tangle of cowardice, blindness, craftiness, and stupidity." The regime was ruled from the top by a sovereign who had but one idea of government—to preserve intact the absolute monarchy bequeathed to him by his father—and who, lacking the intellect, energy, or training for his job, fell back on personal favorites, whim, simple mulishness, and other devices of the empty-headed autocrat. His father, Alexander III, who deliberately intended to keep his son uneducated in statecraft until the age of thirty, unfortunately miscalculated his own life expectancy, and died when Nicholas was twenty-six. The new Czar, now forty-six, had learned nothing in the interval, and the impression of imperturbability he conveyed was in reality apathy—the indifference of a mind so shallow as to be all surface. When a telegram was brought to him announcing the annihilation of the Russian fleet at Tsushima, he read it, stuffed it in his pocket, and went on playing tennis. When the premier, Kokovtsov, returning from Berlin in November 1913, gave the Czar a per-

sonal report on German preparations for war, Nicholas listened to him
with his usual intent, unwavering gaze, "looking straight into my eyes."
After a long pause, when the premier had finished, "as if waking from a
reverie, he said gravely, 'God's will be done.' " In fact, Kokovtsov concluded, he was simply bored.

At the bottom the regime was based upon an ant-heap of secret police
who penetrated every ministry, bureau, and provincial department to such
a degree that Count Witte felt obliged each year to deposit the notes and
records he was keeping for his memoirs in a bank vault in France for safe-
keeping. When another premier, Stolypin, was assassinated in 1911 the
perpetrators were discovered to be the secret police acting as *agents provo-
cateurs* to discredit the revolutionists.

Between the Czar and the secret police the mainstay of the regime were
the *Tchinovniki*, a class of bureaucrats and officials drawn from the nobility who performed the actual business of government. They were responsible to no constitutional body and subject only to arbitrary recall by the
Czar, who, bent by the winds of court intrigue and his wife's suspicions,
exercised it constantly. Under the circumstances able men did not hold
office long, and one who refused it, pleading "poor health," inspired a
colleague to comment, "In those days everyone was in poor health."

Simmering with chronic discontent, Russia in the reign of Nicholas II
was harassed by disasters, massacres, military defeats, and uprisings culminating in the revolution of 1905. When at that time the Czar was advised by Count Witte that he must either grant the constitution which
the people were demanding or restore order under military dictatorship,
he was obliged with bitter distaste to accept the first choice because his
father's cousin, the Grand Duke Nicholas, commander of the St. Petersburg Military District, refused to accept responsibility for the second. For
this default the Grand Duke was never forgiven by the hyper-Bourbons,
the Baltic barons of German blood and sympathy, the Black Hundreds—
those "anarchists of the right"—and other reactionary groups who manned
the ramparts of autocracy. They felt, as did many Germans, including the
Kaiser in alternate hours, that the common interests of autocracies, formerly linked in the *Drei-Kaiser Bund*, made Germany a more natural ally
of Russia than the democracies of the West. Regarding the liberals within
Russia as their first enemy, the Russian reactionaries preferred the Kaiser
to the Duma as the French Right of a later day were to prefer Hitler to
Léon Blum. Only the growing threat of Germany itself in the last twenty
years before the war induced Czarist Russia against her natural inclination

to make alliance with republican France. Ultimately the threat even brought her together with England, which for a century had barred her from Constantinople and of whom one of the Czar's uncles, the Grand Duke Vladimir Alexandrovich, said in 1898: "I hope to live long enough to hear England's death rattle. That is the ardent prayer I address to God each day!"

The cohorts of Vladimir dominated a court that was living out its age of Nero, whose ladies enjoyed the thrills of afternoon séances with the unwashed Rasputin. But Russia also had its Democrats and Liberals of the Duma, its Bakunin the Nihilist, its Prince Kropotkin who became an anarchist, its "intelligentsia" of whom the Czar said, "How I detest that word! I wish I could order the Academy to strike it from the Russian dictionary," its Levins who agonized endlessly over their souls, socialism, and the soil, its Uncle Vanyas without hope, its particular quality that caused a British diplomat to conclude that "everyone in Russia was a little mad" —a quality called *le charme slav*, half nonchalance, half inefficiency, a kind of *fin de siècle* fecklessness that hung like a faint mist over the city on the Neva which the world knew as St. Petersburg and did not know was the Cherry Orchard.

Insofar as readiness for war was concerned, the regime was personified by its Minister for War, General Sukhomlinov, an artful, indolent, pleasure-loving, chubby little man in his sixties of whom his colleague, Foreign Minister Sazonov, said, "It was very difficult to make him work but to get him to tell the truth was well-nigh impossible." Having won the Cross of St. George as a dashing young cavalry officer in the war of 1877 against the Turks, Sukhomlinov believed that military knowledge acquired in that campaign was permanent truth. As Minister of War he scolded a meeting of Staff College instructors for interest in such "innovations" as the factor of firepower against the saber, lance and the bayonet charge. He could not hear the phrase "modern war," he said, without a sense of annoyance. "As war was, so it has remained . . . all these things are merely vicious innovations. Look at me, for instance; I have not read a military manual for the last twenty-five years." In 1913 he dismissed five instructors of the College who persisted in preaching the vicious heresy of "fire tactics."

Sukhomlinov's native intelligence was adulterated by levity to cunning and cleverness. He was short and soft, with a catlike face, neat white whiskers and beard, and an ingratiating, almost feline manner that captivated those like the Czar whom he set himself to please. In others, like the French ambassador, Paléologue, he inspired "distrust at first sight."

Ministerial office, both appointment and dismissal, being entirely at the whim of the Czar, Sukhomlinov had won and kept himself in favor by being at once obsequious and entertaining, by funny stories and acts of buffoonery, avoidance of serious and unpleasant matters, and careful cultivation of "the Friend," Rasputin. As a result he proved immune to charges of corruption and incompetence, to a sensational divorce scandal, and to an even more resounding spy scandal.

Smitten in 1906 by the twenty-three-year-old wife of a provincial governor, Sukhomlinov contrived to get rid of the husband by divorce on framed evidence and marry the beautiful residue as his fourth wife. Naturally lazy, he now left his work more and more in the hands of subordinates while, in the words of the French ambassador, "keeping all his strength for conjugal pleasures with a wife 32 years younger than himself." Mme. Sukhomlinov delighted to order clothes in Paris, dine in expensive restaurants, and give large parties. To gratify her extravagances Sukhomlinov became an early and successful practitioner of the art of the expense account. He charged the government traveling expenses at the rate of 24 horse versts *per diem* while actually making his tours of inspection by railroad. Netting a lucrative balance, augmented by inside knowledge of trends on the stock market, he was able to bank 702,737 rubles during a six-year period in which his total salary was 270,000 rubles. In this happy exercise he was aided by an entourage who lent him money in return for military passes, invitations to maneuvers, and other forms of information. One of them, an Austrian named Altschiller who had supplied the evidence for Mme. Sukhomlinov's divorce and who was received as an intimate in the Minister's home and office where documents were left lying about, was revealed after his departure in January 1914 to have been Austria's chief agent in Russia. Another was the more notorious Colonel Myasoedev, reputed to be Mme. Sukhomlinov's lover, who though only chief of railroad police at the frontier was possessor of five German decorations and honored by the Kaiser with an invitation to lunch at Rominten, the imperial hunting lodge just over the border. Not surprisingly Colonel Myasoedev was suspected of espionage. He was arrested and tried in 1912, but as a result of Sukhomlinov's personal intervention was acquitted and enabled to continue in his former duties up to and through the first year of the war. In 1915, when his protector had finally lost office as a result of Russian reverses, he was rearrested, convicted, and hanged as a spy.

Sukhomlinov's fortunes after 1914 are significant. He escaped prosecution at the same time as Colonel Myasoedev only through the influence of the Czar and Czarina, but ultimately, in August 1917, after the Czar had abdicated and the Provisional Government was already crumbling, he too was brought to trial. In the ruin and tumult of that time he was tried less for treason, which was the nominal charge, than for all the sins of the old regime. In the prosecutor's summing up those sins came to one: that the Russian people, having been forced to fight without guns or munitions, suffered a loss of confidence in the government which had spread like a plague, with "terrible consequences." After a month of sensational testimony in which the details of his financial and amorous peculations were brought out, Sukhomlinov was acquitted of treason but found guilty of "abuse of power and inactivity." Sentenced to hard labor for life, he was liberated a few months later by the Bolsheviks and made his way to Berlin, where he lived until his death in 1926 and where in 1924 he published his memoirs which he dedicated to the deposed Kaiser. In a preface he explained that the Russian and German monarchies having been destroyed as enemies during the war, only the rapprochement of the two countries could restore them to power. This thought so impressed the Hohenzollern exile that he wrote out a dedication of his own memoirs to Sukhomlinov but was apparently dissuaded from using it in the published version.

This was the man who was Russia's Minister of War from 1908 to 1914. Embodying, as he did, the opinions and enjoying the support of the reactionaries, his preparation for war with Germany, which was the Ministry's chief task, was something less than wholehearted. He immediately halted the movement for reform of the army which had made progress since the shame of the Russo-Japanese War. The General Staff, after having been given independence in order to further its study of modern military science, was after 1908 once again subordinated to the Minister of War, who had sole access to the Czar. Shorn of initiative and power, it found no able leader or even the consistency of a single second-rate one. In the six years prior to 1914 six different Chiefs of Staff succeeded each other, with effect upon war plans that was hardly systematic.

While Sukhomlinov left work to others, he allowed no freedom of ideas. Clinging stubbornly to obsolete theories and ancient glories, he claimed that Russia's past defeats had been due to mistakes of commanding officers rather than to any inadequacy of training, preparation, or supply. With invincible belief in the bayonet's supremacy over the bullet, he made no effort to build up factories for increased production of shells, rifles, and cartridges. No country, its military critics invariably discover afterward, is ever adequately prepared in munitions. Britain's shell shortage was to become a national scandal; the French shortage of everything from heavy artillery to boots was a scandal before the war began; in Russia, Sukhomlinov did not even use up the funds the government appropriated for munitions. Russia began the war with 850 shells per gun compared to a reserve of 2,000 to 3,000 shells per gun used by the Western armies, although Sukhomlinov himself had agreed in 1912 to a compromise of 1,500 per gun. The Russian infantry division had 7 field-gun batteries compared with 14 in the German division. The whole Russian Army had 60 batteries of heavy artillery compared with 381 in the German Army. Warnings that war would be largely a duel of firepower Sukhomlinov treated with contempt.

Greater only than his aversion to "fire tactics" was Sukhomlinov's aversion to the Grand Duke Nicholas, who was eight years his junior and represented the reforming tendency within the army. Six foot six, of narrow height with handsome head, pointed beard, and boots as tall as a horse's belly, the Grand Duke was a gallant and imposing figure. After the Japanese war he had been named to reorganize the army as chief of a Council of National Defense. Its purpose was the same as that of the Esher Committee after the Boer War, but, unlike its British model, it had soon succumbed to lethargy and the mandarins. The reactionaries, who resented the Grand Duke for his share in the Constitutional Manifesto and feared his popularity, succeeded in having the Council abolished in 1908. As a career officer who had served as Inspector-General of Cavalry in the Japanese war and who knew personally almost the entire officer corps, each of whom on taking up a new post had to report to him as Commander of the St. Petersburg District, the Grand Duke was the most admired figure in the army. This was less for any specific achievement than for his commanding size and looks and manner, which inspired confidence and awe in the soldiers and either devotion or jealousy in his colleagues.

Brusque and even harsh in manner to officers and men alike, he was regarded outside court as the only "man" in the royal family. Peasant soldiers who had never seen him told stories in which he figured as a sort of legendary champion of Holy Russia against the "German clique" and palace corruption. Echoes of such sentiments did not add to his popularity at court, especially with the Czarina, who already hated "Nikolasha" because he despised Rasputin. "I have absolutely no faith in N.," she wrote to her husband. "I know him to be far from clever and having gone against a man of God his work cannot be blessed or his advice good." She continually suggested that he was plotting to force the Czar to abdicate and, relying on his popularity with the army, to place himself on the throne.

Royal suspicions had kept him from the chief command during the war with Japan and consequently from the blame that followed. In any subsequent war it would be impossible to do without him, and in the pre-war plans he had been designated to command the front against Germany, the Czar himself expecting to act as Commander in Chief with a Chief of General Staff to direct operations. In France where the Grand Duke went several times to maneuvers and where he came under the influence of Foch whose optimism he shared, he was extravagantly feted as much for his magnificent presence, which seemed a reassuring symbol of Russian might, as for his known dislike of Germany. With delight the French repeated the remarks of Prince Kotzebue, the Grand Duke's aide, who said his master believed that only if Germany were crushed once for all, and divided up again into little states each happy with its own little court, could the world expect to live in peace. No less ardent a friend of France was the Grand Duke's wife Anastasia and her sister Militza who was married to the Grand Duke's brother Peter. As daughters of King Nikita of Montenegro, their fondness for France was in direct proportion to their natural hatred of Austria. At a royal picnic in the last days of July, 1914, the "Montenegrin nightingales," as Paléologue called the two princesses, grouped themselves beside him, twittering about the crisis. "There's going to be a war . . . there will be nothing left of Austria . . . you will get back Alsace-Lorraine . . . our armies will meet in Berlin." One sister showed the ambassador a jeweled box in which she carried soil from Lorraine, while the other told how she had planted seeds of Lorraine thistles in her garden.

For the event the Russian General Staff had worked out two alternate plans of campaign, the ultimate choice depending upon what Germany would do. If Germany launched her main strength against France, Russia would launch her main strength against Austria. In this case four armies would take the field against Austria and two against Germany.

The plan for the German front provided for a two-pronged invasion of East Prussia by Russia's First and Second Armies, the First to advance north, and the Second south, of the barrier formed by the Masurian Lakes. As the First, or Vilna, Army, named for its area of concentration, had a direct railway line available, it would be ready to start first. It was to advance two days ahead of the Second, or Warsaw, Army and move against the Germans, "with the object of drawing upon itself the greatest possible enemy strength." Meanwhile the Second Army was to come around the lake barrier from the south and, moving in behind the Germans, cut off their retreat to the Vistula River. The success of the pincer movement depended upon concerted timing to prevent the Germans from engaging either Russian wing separately. The enemy was to be "attacked energetically and determinedly whenever and wherever met." Once the German Army was rounded up and destroyed, the march on Berlin, 150 miles beyond the Vistula, would follow.

The German plan did not contemplate giving up East Prussia. It was a land of rich farms and wide meadows where Holstein cattle grazed, pigs and chickens scuttled about inside stone-walled farmyards, where the famous Trakehnen stud bred remounts for the German Army and where the large estates were owned by Junkers who, to the horror of an English governness employed by one of them, shot foxes instead of hunting them properly on horseback. Further east, near Russia, was the country of "still waters, dark woods," with wide-flung lakes fringed by rushes, forests of pine and birch and many marshes and streams. Its most famous landmark was Rominten Forest, the Hohenzollern hunting preserve of 90,000 acres on the edge of Russia where the Kaiser came each year, attired in knickerbockers and feathered hat, to shoot boar and deer and an occasional Russian moose who, wandering innocently over the border, offered itself as target to the imperial gun. Although the native stock was not Teutonic but Slavic, the region had been under German rule—with some Polish interludes—for seven hundred years, ever since the Order of Teutonic Knights established themselves there in 1225. Despite defeat in 1410 by Poles and Lithuanians in a great battle at a village called Tannenberg, the Knights had remained and grown—or declined—into Junkers. In Königsberg, chief city of the region, the first Hohenzollern sovereign had been crowned King of Prussia in 1701.

With its shores washed by the Baltic, with its "King's city" where Prussia's sovereigns had been crowned, East Prussia was not a country the Germans would yield lightly. Along the river Angerapp running through the Insterburg Gap, defense positions had been carefully prepared; in the swampy eastern region roads had been built up as causeways which would confine an enemy to their narrow crests. In addition the whole of East Prussia was crisscrossed by a network of railroads giving the defending army the advantage of mobility and rapid transfer from one front to the **other to meet** the advance of either enemy wing.

When the Schlieffen plan had been first adopted, fears for East Prussia were less because it was assumed that Russia would have to keep large forces in the Far East to guard against Japan. German diplomacy, despite a certain record for clumsiness, was expected to overcome the Anglo-Japanese Treaty, an unnatural alliance as Germany regarded it, and keep Japan neutral as a constant threat to Russia's rear.

The German General Staff's specialist in Russian affairs was Lieutenant-Colonel Max Hoffmann whose task was to work out the probable Russian plan of campaign in a war with Germany. In his early forties, Hoffmann was tall and heavily built, with a large round head and a Prussian haircut shaved so close to the scalp it made him look bald. His expression was good-humored but uncompromising. He wore black-rimmed glasses and carefully trained his black eyebrows to grow in a dashing upward curve at their outer ends. He was equally careful and proud of his small, delicate hands and impeccable trouser creases. Though indolent, he was resourceful; though a poor rider, worse swordsman, and gluttonous eater and drinker, he was quick-thinking and rapid in judgment. He was amiable, lucky, astute, and respected no one. In intervals of regimental duty before the war he drank wine and consumed sausages all night at the officers' club until 7:00 A.M., when he took his company out on parade and returned for a snack of more sausages and two quarts of Moselle before breakfast.

After graduation from the Staff College in 1898, Hoffmann had served a six-months' tour of duty in Russia as interpreter and five years subsequently in the Russian section of the General Staff under Schlieffen before going as Germany's military observer to the Russo-Japanese War. When a Japanese general refused him permission to watch a battle from a nearby hill, etiquette gave way to that natural quality in Germans whose expression so often fails to endear them to others. "You are a yellow-skin; you are uncivilized if you will not let me go to that hill!" Hoffmann yelled at the general in the presence of other foreign attachés and at least one correspondent. Belonging to a race hardly second to the Germans in sense of self-importance, the general yelled back, "We Japanese are paying for this military information with our blood and we don't propose to share it with others!" Protocol for the occasion broke down altogether.

On his return to the General Staff under Moltke, Hoffmann resumed work on the Russian plan of campaign. A colonel of the Russian General Staff had sold an early version of his country's plan for a high price in 1902, but since that time, according to Hoffmann's not always wholly serious memoirs, the price had gone up beyond the stingy funds allotted to Germany's military intelligence. The terrain of East Prussia, however, made the general outlines of a Russian offensive self-evident: it would have to be a two-pronged advance around the Masurian Lakes. Hoffmann's study of the Russian Army and the factors governing its mobilization and transportation enabled the Germans to judge the timing of the offensive. The German Army, inferior in numbers, could choose either of two ways to meet a superior force advancing in two wings. They could either withdraw, or attack one wing before the other, whichever offered the best opportunity. The stern formula dictated by Schlieffen was to strike "with all available strength at the first Russian army that came within reach,"

▶▶▶
▶▶▶
▶▶▶ *OUTBREAK*

▶▶▶ *Outbreak*

"SOME DAMNED FOOLISH THING IN THE
Balkans," Bismarck had predicted, would ignite the next war. The assas-
sination of the Austrian heir apparent, Archduke Franz Ferdinand, by
Serbian nationalists on June 28, 1914, satisfied his condition. Austria-
Hungary, with the bellicose frivolity of senile empires, determined to use
the occasion to absorb Serbia as she had absorbed Bosnia and Herzegovina
in 1909. Russia on that occasion, weakened by the war with Japan, had
been forced to acquiesce by a German ultimatum followed by the Kaiser's
appearance in "shining armor," as he put it, at the side of his ally, Austria.
To avenge that humiliation and for the sake of her prestige as the major
Slav power, Russia was now prepared to put on the shining armor
herself. On July 5 Germany assured Austria that she could count on
Germany's "faithful support" if whatever punitive action she took against
Serbia brought her into conflict with Russia. This was the signal that let
loose the irresistible onrush of events. On July 23 Austria delivered an
ultimatum to Serbia, on July 26 rejected the Serbian reply (although the
Kaiser, now nervous, admitted that it "dissipates every reason for war"),
on July 28 declared war on Serbia, on July 29 bombarded Belgrade. On

that day Russia mobilized along her Austrian frontier and on July 30 both Austria and Russia ordered general mobilization. On July 31 Germany issued an ultimatum to Russia to demobilize within twelve hours and "make us a distinct declaration to that effect."

War pressed against every frontier. Suddenly dismayed, governments struggled and twisted to fend it off. It was no use. Agents at frontiers were reporting every cavalry patrol as a deployment to beat the mobilization gun. General staffs, goaded by their relentless timetables, were pounding the table for the signal to move lest their opponents gain an hour's head start. Appalled upon the brink, the chiefs of state who would be ultimately responsible for their country's fate attempted to back away but the pull of military schedules dragged them forward.

▶▶▶ *6* ▶

▶▶▶ *August 1: Berlin*

AT NOON ON SATURDAY, AUGUST 1, THE GERMAN ultimatum to Russia expired without a Russian reply. Within an hour a telegram went out to the German ambassador in St. Petersburg instructing him to declare war by five o'clock that afternoon. At five o'clock the Kaiser decreed general mobilization, some preliminaries having already got off to a head start under the declaration of *Kriegesgefahr* (Danger of War) the day before. At five-thirty Chancellor Bethmann-Hollweg, absorbed in a document he was holding in his hand and accompanied by little Jagow, the Foreign Minister, hurried down the steps of the Foreign Office, hailed an ordinary taxi, and sped off to the palace. Shortly afterward General von Moltke, the gloomy Chief of General Staff, was pulled up short as he was driving back to his office with the mobilization order signed by the Kaiser in his pocket. A messenger in another car overtook him with an urgent summons from the palace. He returned to hear a last-minute, desperate proposal from the Kaiser that reduced Moltke to tears and could have changed the history of the twentieth century.

Now that the moment had come, the Kaiser suffered at the necessary risk to East Prussia, in spite of the six weeks' leeway his Staff promised before the Russians could fully mobilize. "I hate the Slavs," he confessed to an Austrian officer. "I know it is a sin to do so. We ought not to hate anyone. But I can't help hating them." He had taken comfort, however, in the news, reminiscent of 1905, of strikes and riots in St. Petersburg, of mobs smashing windows, and "violent street fights between revolutionaries and police." Count Pourtalès, his aged ambassador, who had been seven years in Russia, concluded, and repeatedly assured his government, that Russia would not fight for fear of revolution. Captain von Eggeling, the German military attaché, kept repeating the credo about 1916, and when Russia nevertheless mobilized, he reported she planned "no tenacious offensive but a slow retreat as in 1812." In the affinity for error of German diplomats, these judgments established a record. They gave heart to the Kaiser, who as late as July 31 composed a missive for the "guidance" of his Staff, rejoicing in the "mood of a sick Tom-cat" that, on the evidence of his envoys, he said prevailed in the Russian court and army.

In Berlin on August 1, the crowds milling in the streets and massed in thousands in front of the palace were tense and heavy with anxiety. Socialism, which most of Berlin's workers professed, did not run so deep as their instinctive fear and hatred of the Slavic hordes. Although they had been told by the Kaiser, in his speech from the balcony announcing *Kriegesgefahr* the evening before, that the "sword has been forced into our hand," they still waited in the ultimate dim hope of a Russian reply. The hour of the ultimatum passed. A journalist in the crowd felt the air "electric with rumor. People told each other Russia had asked for an extension of time. The Bourse writhed in panic. The afternoon passed in almost insufferable anxiety." Bethmann-Hollweg issued a statement ending, "If the iron dice roll, may God help us." At five o'clock a policeman appeared at the palace gate and announced mobilization to the crowd, which obediently struck up the national hymn, "Now thank we all our God." Cars raced down Unter den Linden with officers standing up in them, waving handkerchiefs and shouting, "Mobilization!" Instantly converted from Marx to Mars, people cheered wildly and rushed off to vent their feelings on suspected Russian spies, several of whom were pummeled or trampled to death in the course of the next few days.

Once the mobilization button was pushed, the whole vast machinery for calling up, equipping, and transporting two million men began turning automatically. Reservists went to their designated depots, were issued uniforms, equipment, and arms, formed into companies and companies into battalions, were joined by cavalry, cyclists, artillery, medical units, cook wagons, blacksmith wagons, even postal wagons, moved according to prepared railway timetables to concentration points near the frontier where they would be formed into divisions, divisions into corps, and corps into armies ready to advance and fight. One army corps alone—out of the total of 40 in the German forces—required 170 railway cars for officers, 965 for infantry, 2,960 for cavalry, 1,915 for artillery and supply wagons, 6,010 in all, grouped in 140 trains and an equal number again for their supplies. From the moment the order was given, everything was to move at fixed times according to a schedule precise down to the number of train axles that would pass over a given bridge within a given time.

Confident in his magnificent system, Deputy Chief of Staff General Waldersee had not even returned to Berlin at the beginning of the crisis but had written to Jagow: "I shall remain here ready to jump; we are all prepared at the General Staff; in the meantime there is nothing for us to do." It was a proud tradition inherited from the elder, or "great," Moltke who on mobilization day in 1870 was found lying on a sofa reading *Lady Audley's Secret*.

His enviable calm was not present today in the palace. Face to face no longer with the specter but the reality of a two-front war, the Kaiser was as close to the "sick Tom-cat" mood as he thought the Russians were. More cosmopolitan and more timid than the archetype Prussian, he had never actually wanted a general war. He wanted greater power, greater prestige, above all more authority in the world's affairs for Germany but he preferred to obtain them by frightening rather than by fighting other nations. He wanted the gladiator's rewards without the battle, and whenever the prospect of battle came too close, as at Algeciras and Agadir, he shrank.

As the final crisis boiled, his marginalia on telegrams grew more and more agitated: "Aha! the common cheat," "Rot!" "He lies!" "Mr. Grey is a false dog," "Twaddle!" "The rascal is crazy or an idiot!" When Russia mobilized he burst into a tirade of passionate foreboding, not against the Slav traitors but against the unforgettable figure of the wicked uncle: "The world will be engulfed in the most terrible of wars, the ultimate aim of which is the ruin of Germany. England, France and Russia have conspired for our annihilation . . . that is the naked truth of the situation which was slowly but surely created by Edward VII. . . . The encirclement of Germany is at last an accomplished fact. We have run our heads into the noose. . . . The dead Edward is stronger than the living I!"

Conscious of the shadow of the dead Edward, the Kaiser would have welcomed any way out of the commitment to fight both Russia and France and, behind France, the looming figure of still-undeclared England.

At the last moment one was offered. A colleague of Bethmann's came to beg him to do anything he could to save Germany from a two-front war and suggested a means. For years a possible solution for Alsace had been discussed in terms of autonomy as a Federal State within the German Empire. If offered and accepted by the Alsatians, this solution would have deprived France of any reason to liberate the lost provinces. As recently as July 16, the French Socialist Congress had gone on record in favor of it. But the German military had always insisted that the provinces must remain garrisoned and their political rights subordinated to "military necessity." Until 1911 no constitution had ever been granted and autonomy never. Bethmann's colleague now urged him to make an immediate, public, and official offer for a conference on autonomy for Alsace. This could be allowed to drag on without result, while its moral effect would force France to refrain from attack while at least considering the offer. Time would be gained for Germany to turn her forces against Russia while remaining stationary in the West, thus keeping England out.

The author of this proposal remains anonymous, and it may be apocryphal. It does not matter. The opportunity was there, and the Chancellor could have thought of it for himself. But to seize it required boldness, and Bethmann, behind his distinguished façade of great height, somber eyes, and well-trimmed imperial, was a man, as Theodore Roosevelt said of Taft, "who means well feebly." Instead of offering France an inducement to stay neutral, the German government sent her an ultimatum at the same time as the ultimatum to Russia. They asked France to reply within eighteen hours whether she would stay neutral in a Russo-German war, and added that if she did Germany would "demand as guarantee of neutrality the handing over to us of the fortresses of Toul and Verdun which we shall occupy and restore after the war is over"—in other words, the handing over of the key to the French door.

Baron von Schoen, German ambassador in Paris, could not bring himself to pass on this "brutal" demand at a moment when, it seemed to him, French neutrality would have been such a supreme advantage to Germany that his government might well have offered to pay a price for it rather than exact a penalty. He presented the request for a statement of neutrality without the demand for the fortresses, but the French, who had intercepted and decoded his instructions, knew of it anyway. When Schoen, at

11:00 A.M. on August 1, asked for France's reply he was answered that France "would act in accordance with her interests."

In Berlin just after five o'clock a telephone rang in the Foreign Office. Under-Secretary Zimmermann, who answered it, turned to the editor of the *Berliner Tageblatt* sitting by his desk and said, "Moltke wants to know whether things can start." At that moment a telegram from London, just decoded, broke in upon the planned proceedings. It offered hope that if the movement against France could be instantly stopped Germany might safely fight a one-front war after all. Carrying it with them, Bethmann and Jagow dashed off on their taxi trip to the palace.

The telegram, from Prince Lichnowsky, ambassador in London, reported an English offer, as Lichnowsky understood it, "that in case we did not attack France, England would remain neutral and would guarantee France's neutrality."

The ambassador belonged to that class of Germans who spoke English and copied English manners, sports, and dress, in a strenuous endeavor to become the very pattern of an English gentleman. His fellow noblemen, the Prince of Pless, Prince Blücher, and Prince Münster were all married to English wives. At a dinner in Berlin in 1911, in honor of a British general, the guest of honor was astonished to find that all forty German guests, including Bethmann-Hollweg and Admiral Tirpitz, spoke English fluently. Lichnowsky differed from his class in that he was not only in manner but in heart an earnest Anglophile. He had come to London determined to make himself and his country liked. English society had been lavish with country weekends. To the ambassador no tragedy could be greater than war between the country of his birth and the country of his heart, and he was grasping at any handle to avert it.

When the Foreign Secretary, Sir Edward Grey, telephoned him that morning, in the interval of a Cabinet meeting, Lichnowsky, out of his own anxiety, interpreted what Grey said to him as an offer by England to stay neutral and to keep France neutral in a Russo-German war, if, in return, Germany would promise not to attack France.

Actually, Grey had not said quite that. What, in his elliptical way, he offered was a promise to keep France neutral if Germany would promise to stay neutral as against France *and* Russia, in other words, not go to war against either, pending the result of efforts to settle the Serbian affair. After eight years as Foreign Secretary in a period of chronic "Bosnias," as Bülow called them, Grey had perfected a manner of speaking designed to convey as little meaning as possible; his avoidance of the point-blank, said a colleague, almost amounted to method. Over the telephone, Lichnowsky, himself dazed by the coming tragedy, would have had no difficulty misunderstanding him.

The Kaiser clutched at Lichnowsky's passport to a one-front war. Minutes counted. Already mobilization was rolling inexorably toward the French frontier. The first hostile act, seizure of a railway junction in Luxembourg, whose neutrality the five Great Powers, including Germany, had guaranteed, was scheduled within an hour. It must be stopped, stopped at once. But how? Where was Moltke? Moltke had left the palace. An aide was sent off, with siren screaming, to intercept him. He was brought back.

The Kaiser was himself again, the All-Highest, the War Lord, blazing with a new idea, planning, proposing, disposing. He read Moltke the telegram and said in triumph: "Now we can go to war against Russia only. We simply march the whole of our Army to the East!"

Aghast at the thought of his marvelous machinery of mobilization wrenched into reverse, Moltke refused point-blank. For the past ten years, first as assistant to Schlieffen, then as his successor, Moltke's job had been planning for this day, The Day, *Der Tag*, for which all Germany's energies were gathered, on which the march to final mastery of Europe would begin. It weighed upon him with an oppressive, almost unbearable responsibility.

Tall, heavy, bald, and sixty-six years old, Moltke habitually wore an expression of profound distress which led the Kaiser to call him *der traurige Julius* (or what might be rendered "Gloomy Gus"; in fact, his name was Helmuth). Poor health, for which he took an annual cure at Carlsbad, and the shadow of a great uncle were perhaps cause for gloom. From his window in the red brick General Staff building on the Königsplatz where he lived as well as worked, he looked out every day on the equestrian statue of his namesake, the hero of 1870 and, together with Bismarck, the architect of the German Empire. The nephew was a poor horseman with a habit of falling off on staff rides and, worse, a follower of Christian Science with a side interest in anthroposophism and other cults. For this unbecoming weakness in a Prussian officer he was considered "soft"; what is more, he painted, played the cello, carried Goethe's *Faust* in his pocket, and had begun a translation of Maeterlinck's *Pelléas et Mélisande*.

Introspective and a doubter by nature, he had said to the Kaiser upon his appointment in 1906: "I do not know how I shall get on in the event of a campaign. I am very critical of myself." Yet he was neither personally nor politically timid. In 1911, disgusted by Germany's retreat in the Agadir crisis, he wrote to Conrad von Hotzendorff that if things got worse he would resign, propose to disband the army and "place ourselves under the protection of Japan; then we can make money undisturbed and turn into imbeciles." He did not hesitate to talk back to the Kaiser, but told him "quite brutally" in 1900 that his Peking expedition was a "crazy adventure," and when offered the appointment as Chief of Staff, asked the Kaiser if he expected "to win the big prize twice in the same lottery"—a thought that had certainly influenced William's choice. He refused to take the post unless the Kaiser stopped his habit of winning all the war games which was making nonsense of maneuvers. Surprisingly, the Kaiser meekly obeyed.

Now, on the climactic night of August 1, Moltke was in no mood for any more of the Kaiser's meddling with serious military matters, or with meddling of any kind with the fixed arrangements. To turn around the deployment of a million men from west to east at the very moment of departure would have taken a more iron nerve than Moltke disposed of. He saw a vision of the deployment crumbling apart in confusion, supplies here, soldiers there, ammunition lost in the middle, companies without officers, divisions without staffs, and those 11,000 trains, each exquisitely scheduled to click over specified tracks at specified intervals of ten minutes, tangled in a grotesque ruin of the most perfectly planned military movement in history.

"Your Majesty," Moltke said to him now, "it cannot be done. The deployment of millions cannot be improvised. If Your Majesty insists on leading the whole army to the East it will not be an army ready for battle but a disorganized mob of armed men with no arrangements for supply. Those arrangements took a whole year of intricate labor to complete"— and Moltke closed upon that rigid phrase, the basis for every major German mistake, the phrase that launched the invasion of Belgium and the submarine war against the United States, the inevitable phrase when military plans dictate policy—"and once settled, it cannot be altered."

In fact it could have been altered. The German General Staff, though committed since 1905 to a plan of attack upon France first, had in their files, revised each year until 1913, an alternative plan against Russia with all the trains running eastward.

"Build no more fortresses, build railways," ordered the elder Moltke who had laid out his strategy on a railway map and bequeathed the dogma

that railways are the key to war. In Germany the railway system was under
military control with a staff officer assigned to every line; no track could be
laid or changed without permission of the General Staff. Annual mobilization war games kept railway officials in constant practice and tested their
ability to improvise and divert traffic by telegrams reporting lines cut and
bridges destroyed. The best brains produced by the War College, it was
said, went into the railway section and ended up in lunatic asylums.

When Moltke's "It cannot be done" was revealed after the war in his
memoirs, General von Staab, Chief of the Railway Division, was so in-
censed by what he considered a reproach upon his bureau that he wrote
a book to prove it could have been done. In pages of charts and graphs
he demonstrated how, given notice on August 1, he could have deployed
four out of the seven armies to the Eastern Front by August 15, leaving
three to defend the West. Matthias Erzberger, the Reichstag deputy and
leader of the Catholic Centrist Party, has left another testimony. He says
that Moltke himself, within six months of the event, admitted to him that
the assault on France at the beginning was a mistake and instead, "the
larger part of our army ought first to have been sent East to smash the
Russian steam roller, limiting operations in the West to beating off the
enemy's attack on our frontier."

On the night of August 1, Moltke, clinging to the fixed plan, lacked the
necessary nerve. "Your uncle would have given me a different answer," the
Kaiser said to him bitterly. The reproach "wounded me deeply" Moltke
wrote afterward; "I never pretended to be the equal of the old Field
Marshal." Nevertheless he continued to refuse. "My protest that it would
be impossible to maintain peace between France and Germany while both
countries were mobilized made no impression. Everybody got more and
more excited and I was alone in my opinion."

Finally, when Moltke convinced the Kaiser that the mobilization plan
could not be changed, the group which included Bethmann and Jagow
drafted a telegram to England regretting that Germany's advance movements toward the French border "can no longer be altered," but offering
a guarantee not to cross the border before August 3 at 7:00 P.M., which
cost them nothing as no crossing was scheduled before that time. Jagow
rushed off a telegram to his ambassador in Paris, where mobilization had
already been decreed at four o'clock, instructing him helpfully to "please
keep France quiet for the time being." The Kaiser added a personal telegram to King George, telling him that for "technical reasons" mobilization
could not be countermanded at this late hour, but "If France offers me

neutrality which must be guaranteed by the British fleet and army, I shall of course refrain from attacking France and employ my troops elsewhere. I hope France will not become nervous."

It was now minutes before seven o'clock, the hour when the 16th Division was scheduled to move into Luxembourg. Bethmann excitedly insisted that Luxembourg must not be entered under any circumstances while waiting for the British answer. Instantly the Kaiser, without asking Moltke, ordered his aide-de-camp to telephone and telegraph 16th Division Headquarters at Trier to cancel the movement. Moltke saw ruin again. Luxembourg's railways were essential for the offensive through Belgium against France. "At that moment," his memoirs say, "I thought my heart would break."

Despite all his pleading, the Kaiser refused to budge. Instead, he added a closing sentence to his telegram to King George, "The troops on my frontier are in the act of being stopped by telephone and telegraph from crossing into France," a slight if vital twist of the truth, for the Kaiser could not acknowledge to England that what he had intended and what was being stopped was the violation of a neutral country. It would have implied his intention also to violate Belgium, which would have been *casus belli* in England, and England's mind was not yet made up.

"Crushed," Moltke says of himself, on what should have been the culminating day of his career, he returned to the General Staff and "burst into bitter tears of abject despair." When his aide brought him for his signature the written order canceling the Luxembourg movement, "I threw my pen down on the table and refused to sign." To have signed as the first order after mobilization one that would have annulled all the careful preparations would have been taken, he knew, as evidence of "hesitancy and irresolution." "Do what you want with this telegram," he said to his aide; "I will not sign it."

He was still brooding at eleven o'clock when another summons came from the palace. Moltke found the Kaiser in his bedroom, characteristically dressed for the occasion, with a military overcoat over his nightshirt. A telegram had come from Lichnowsky, who, in a further talk with Grey, had discovered his error and now wired sadly, "A positive proposal by England is, on the whole, not in prospect."

"Now you can do what you like," said the Kaiser, and went back to bed. Moltke, the Commander in Chief who had now to direct a campaign that would decide the fate of Germany, was left permanently shaken. "That was my first experience of the war," he wrote afterward. "I never recovered from the shock of this incident. Something in me broke and I was never the same thereafter."

Neither was the world, he might have added. The Kaiser's telephone order to Trier had not arrived in time. At seven o'clock, as scheduled, the first frontier of the war was crossed, the distinction going to an infantry company of the 69th Regiment under command of a certain Lieutenant Feldmann. Just inside the Luxembourg border, on the slopes of the Ardennes about twelve miles from Bastogne in Belgium, stood a little town known to the Germans as Ulflingen. Around it cows grazed on the hillside pastures; on its steep, cobblestone streets not a stray wisp of hay, even in August harvest time, was allowed to offend the strict laws governing municipal cleanliness in the Grand Duchy. At the foot of the town was a railroad station and telegraph office where the lines from Germany and Belgium crossed. This was the German objective which Lieutenant Feldmann's company, arriving in automobiles, duly seized.

With their relentless talent for the tactless, the Germans chose to violate Luxembourg at a place whose native and official name was Trois Vierges. The three virgins in fact represented faith, hope, and charity, but History with her apposite touch arranged for the occasion that they should stand in the public mind for Luxembourg, Belgium, and France.

At 7:30 a second detachment in automobiles arrived (presumably in response to the Kaiser's message) and ordered off the first group, saying "a mistake had been made." In the interval Luxembourg's Minister of State Eyschen had already telegraphed the news to London, Paris, and Brussels and a protest to Berlin. The three virgins had made their point. By midnight Moltke had rectified the reversal, and by the end of the next day, August 2, M–1 on the German schedule, the entire Grand Duchy was occupied.

A question has haunted the annals of history ever since: What Ifs might have followed if the Germans had gone east in 1914 while remaining on the defensive against France? General von Staab showed that to have turned against Russia was technically possible. But whether it would have been temperamentally possible for the Germans to have refrained from attacking France when *Der Tag* came is another matter.

At seven o'clock in St. Petersburg, at the same hour when the Germans entered Luxembourg, Ambassador Pourtalès, his watery blue eyes red-rimmed, his white goatee quivering, presented Germany's declaration of war with shaking hand to Sazonov, the Russian Foreign Minister.

"The curses of the nations will be upon you!" Sazonov exclaimed.

"We are defending our honor," the German ambassador replied.

"Your honor was not involved. But there is a divine justice."

"That's true," and muttering, "a divine justice, a divine justice," Pourtalès staggered to the window, leaned against it, and burst into tears. "So this is the end of my mission," he said when he could speak. Sazonov patted him on the shoulder, they embraced, and Pourtalès stumbled to the door, which he could hardly open with a trembling hand, and went out, murmuring, "Goodbye, goodbye."

This affecting scene comes down to us as recorded by Sazonov with artistic additions by the French ambassador Paléologue, presumably from what Sazonov told him. Pourtalès reported only that he asked three times for a reply to the ultimatum and after Sazonov answered negatively three times, "I handed over the note as instructed."

Why did it have to be handed over at all? Admiral von Tirpitz, the Naval Minister, had plaintively asked the night before when the declaration of war was being drafted. Speaking, he says, "more from instinct than from reason," he wanted to know why, if Germany did not plan to invade Russia, was it necessary to declare war and assume the odium of the attacking party? His question was particularly pertinent because Germany's object was to saddle Russia with war guilt in order to convince the German people that they were fighting in self-defense and especially in order to keep Italy tied to her engagements under the Triple Alliance.

Italy was obliged to join her allies only in a defensive war and, already shaky in her allegiance, was widely expected to sidle out through any loophole that opened up. Bethmann was harassed by this problem. If Austria persisted in refusing any or all Serbian concessions, he warned, "it will scarcely be possible to place the guilt of a European conflagration on Russia" and would "place us in the eyes of our own people, in an untenable position." He was hardly heard. When mobilization day came, German protocol required that war be properly declared. Jurists of the Foreign Office, according to Tirpitz, insisted it was legally the correct thing to do. "Outside Germany," he says pathetically, "there is no appreciation of such ideas."

In France appreciation was keener than he knew.

▶▶▶ 7 ▶

▶▶▶ *August 1:*

Paris and London

ONE PRIME OBJECTIVE GOVERNED FRENCH POL-
icy: to enter the war with England as an ally. To ensure that event and
enable her friends in England to overcome the inertia and reluctance
within their own Cabinet and country, France had to leave it clear beyond
question who was the attacked and who the attacker. The physical act and
moral odium of aggression must be left squarely upon Germany. Germany
was expected to do her part, but lest any overanxious French patrols or
frontier troops stepped over the border, the French government took a
daring and extraordinary step. On July 30 it ordered a ten-kilometer withdrawal along the entire frontier with Germany from Switzerland to
Luxembourg.

Premier René Viviani, an eloquent Socialist orator, formerly chiefly
concerned with welfare and labor, proposed the withdrawal. He was a
curiosity in French politics, a Premier who had never been Premier before,
and was now Acting Foreign Minister as well. He had been in office barely
six weeks and had just returned the day before, July 29, from a state visit
to Russia with President Poincaré. Austria had waited until Viviani and

Poincaré were at sea to issue her ultimatum to Serbia. On receiving this news the French President and Premier had eliminated a scheduled visit to Copenhagen and hurried home.

In Paris they were told German covering troops had taken their places a few hundred meters from the frontier. They knew nothing as yet of the Russian and Austrian mobilizations. Hopes still flourished of a negotiated settlement. Viviani was "haunted by a fear that war might burst from a clump of trees, from a meeting of two patrols, from a threatening gesture . . . a black look, a brutal word, a shot!" While there was still even the least chance of settling the crisis without war, and in order to leave the lines of aggression clear if war came, the Cabinet agreed upon the ten-kilometer withdrawal. The order, telegraphed to corps commanders, was designed, they were told, "to assure the collaboration of our English neighbors." A telegram informing England of the measure went out simultaneously. The act of withdrawal, done at the very portals of invasion, was a calculated military risk deliberately taken for its political effect. It was taking a chance "never before taken in history," said Viviani, and might have added, like Cyrano, "Ah, but what a gesture!"

Withdrawal was a bitter gesture to ask of a French Commander in Chief schooled in the doctrine of offensive and nothing but the offensive. It could have shattered General Joffre as Moltke's first experience of the war shattered him, but General Joffre's heart did not break.

From the moment of the President's and Premier's return, Joffre had been hounding the government for the order to mobilize or at least take the preliminary steps: recall of furloughs, of which many had been granted for the harvest, and deployment of covering troops to the frontier. He deluged them with intelligence reports of German premobilization measures already taken. He loomed large in authority before a new-born Cabinet, the tenth in five years, whose predecessor had lasted three days. The present one was remarkable chiefly for having most of France's strong men outside it. Briand, Clemenceau, Caillaux, all former premiers, were in opposition. Viviani, by his own evidence, was in a state of "frightful nervous tension" which, according to Messimy, who was once again War Minister, "became a permanent condition during the month of August." The Minister of Marine, Dr. Gauthier, a doctor of medicine shoved into the naval post when a political scandal removed his predecessor, was so overwhelmed by events that he "forgot" to order fleet units into the Channel and had to be replaced by the Minister of Public Instruction on the spot.

In the President, however, intelligence, experience, and strength of purpose, if not constitutional power, were combined. Poincaré was a lawyer, economist, and member of the Academy, a former Finance Minister who had served as Premier and Foreign Minister in 1912 and had been elected President of France in January, 1913. Character begets power, especially in hours of crisis, and the untried Cabinet leaned willingly on the abilities and strong will of the man who was constitutionally a cipher. Born in Lorraine, Poincaré could remember as a boy of ten the long line of spiked German helmets marching through Bar-le-Duc, his home town. He was credited by the Germans with the most bellicose intent, partly because, as Premier at the time of Agadir, he had held firm, partly because as President he had used his influence to push through the Three-Year Military Service Law in 1913 against violent Socialist opposition. This and his cold demeanor, his lack of flamboyance, his fixity, did not make for popularity at home. Elections were going against the government, the Three-Year Law was near to being thrown out, labor troubles and farmers' discontent were rife, July had been hot, wet, and oppressive with windstorms and summer thunder, and Mme. Caillaux who had shot the editor of *Figaro* was on trial for murder. Each day of the trial revealed new and unpleasant irregularities in finance, the press, the courts, the government.

One day the French woke up to find Mme. Caillaux on page two—and the sudden, awful knowledge that France faced war. In that most passionately political and quarrelsome of countries one sentiment thereupon prevailed. Poincaré and Viviani, returning from Russia, drove through Paris to the sound of one prolonged cry, repeated over and over, "*Vive la France!*"

Joffre told the government that if he was not given the order to assemble and transport the covering troops of five army corps and cavalry toward the frontier, the Germans would "enter France without firing a shot." He accepted the ten-kilometer withdrawal of troops already in position less from subservience to the civil arm—Joffre was about as subservient by nature as Julius Caesar—as from a desire to bend all the force of his argument upon the one issue of the covering troops. The government, still reluctant while diplomatic offers and counter-offers flashing over the wires might yet produce a settlement, agreed to give him a "reduced" version, that is, without calling out the reservists.

At 4:30 next day, July 31, a banking friend in Amsterdam telephoned Messimy the news of the German *Kriegesgefahr*, officially confirmed an hour later from Berlin. It was "*une forme hypocrite de la mobilisation*"

Messimy angrily told the Cabinet. His friend in Amsterdam had said war was certain and Germany was ready for it, "from the Emperor down to the last Fritz." Following hard upon this news came a telegram from Paul Cambon, French ambassador in London, reporting that England was "tepid." Cambon had devoted every day of the past sixteen years at his post to the single end of ensuring England's active support when the time came, but he had now to wire that the British government seemed to be awaiting some new development. The dispute so far was of "no interest to Great Britain."

Joffre arrived, with a new memorandum on German movements, to insist upon mobilization. He was permitted to send his full "covering order" but no more, as news had also come of a last-minute appeal from the Czar to the Kaiser. The Cabinet continued sitting, with Messimy champing in impatience at the "green baize routine" which stipulated that each minister must speak in turn.

At seven o'clock in the evening Baron von Schoen, making his eleventh visit to the French Foreign Office in seven days, presented Germany's demand to know what course France would take and said he would return next day at one o'clock for an answer. Still the Cabinet sat and argued over financial measures, recall of Parliament, declaration of a state of siege, while all Paris waited in suspense. One crazed young man cracked under the agony, held a pistol against a café window, and shot dead Jean Jaurès, whose leadership in international socialism and in the fight against the Three-Year Law had made him, in the eyes of superpatriots, a symbol of pacifism.

A white-faced aide broke in upon the Cabinet at nine o'clock with the news. Jaurès killed! The event, pregnant with possible civil strife, stunned the Cabinet. Street barricades, riot, even revolt became a prospect on the threshold of war. Ministers reopened the heated argument whether to invoke *Carnet B*, the list of known agitators, anarchists, pacifists, and sus- pected spies who were to be arrested automatically upon the day of mobilization. Both the Prefect of Police and former Premier Clemenceau had advised the Minister of Interior, M. Malvy, to enforce *Carnet B*. Viviani and others of his colleagues, hoping to preserve national unity, were opposed to it. They held firm. Some foreigners suspected of being spies were arrested, but no Frenchmen. In case of riot, troops were alerted that night, but next morning there was only deep grief and deep quiet. Of the 2,501 persons listed in *Carnet B*, 80 per cent were ultimately to volunteer for military service.

At 2:00 A.M. that night, President Poincaré was awakened in bed by the irrepressible Russian ambassador, Isvolsky, a former hyperactive foreign minister. "Very distressed and very agitated," he wanted to know, "What is France going to do?"

Isvolsky had no doubts of Poincaré's attitude, but he and other Russian statesmen were always haunted by the fear that when the time came the French Parliament, which had never been told the terms of the military alliance with Russia, would fail to ratify it. The terms specifically stated, "If Russia is attacked by Germany or by Austria supported by Germany, France will use all her available forces to attack Germany." As soon as either Germany or Austria mobilized, "France and Russia, without previous agreement being necessary, shall mobilize all their forces immediately and simultaneously and shall transport them as near the frontiers as possible. . . . These forces shall begin complete action with all speed so that Germany will have to fight at the same time in the East and in the West."

These terms appeared unequivocal but, as Isvolsky had anxiously queried Poincaré in 1912, would the French Parliament recognize the obligation? In Russia the Czar's power was absolute, so that France "may be sure of us," but "in France the Government is impotent without Parliament. Parliament does not know the text of 1892. . . . What guarantee have we that your Parliament would follow your Government's lead?"

"If Germany attacked," Poincaré had replied on that earlier occasion, Parliament would follow the Government "without a doubt."

Now, facing Isvolsky again in the middle of the night, Poincaré assured him that a Cabinet would be called within a few hours to supply the answer. At the same hour the Russian military attaché in full diplomatic dress appeared in Messimy's bedroom to pose the same question. Messimy telephoned to Premier Viviani who, though exhausted by the night's events, had not yet gone to bed. "Good God!" he exploded, "these Russians are worse insomniacs than they are drinkers," and he excitedly recommended *"Du calme, du calme et encore du calme!"*

Pressed by the Russians to declare themselves, and by Joffre to mobilize, yet held to a standstill by the need to prove to England that France would act only in self-defense, the French government found calm not easy. At 8:00 next morning, August 1, Joffre came to the War Office in the Rue St. Dominique to beg Messimy, in "a pathetic tone that contrasted with his habitual calm," to pry mobilization from the government. He named four o'clock as the last moment when the order could reach the General Post Office for dispatch by telegraph throughout France in time for mobilization to begin at midnight. He went with Messimy to the Cabinet at 9:00 A.M. and presented an ultimatum of his own: every further delay of twenty-four hours before general mobilization would mean a fifteen- to twenty-kilometer loss of territory, and he would refuse to take the responsibility as Commander. He left, and the Cabinet faced the problem. Poincaré was for action; Viviani, representing the antiwar tradition, still hoped that time would provide a solution. At 11:00 he was called to the Foreign Office to see von Schoen who in his own anxiety had arrived two hours early for the answer to Germany's question of the previous day: whether France would stay neutral in a Russo-German war. "My question is rather naïve," said the unhappy ambassador, "for we know you have a treaty of alliance."

"*Evidemment*," replied Viviani, and gave the answer prearranged between him and Poincaré. "France will act in accordance with her interests." As Schoen left, Isvolsky rushed in with news of the German ultimatum to Russia. Viviani returned to the Cabinet, which at last agreed upon mobilization. The order was signed and given to Messimy, but Viviani, still hoping for some saving development to turn up within the few remaining hours, insisted that Messimy keep it in his pocket until 3:30. At the same time the ten-kilometer withdrawal was reaffirmed. Messimy telephoned it that evening personally to corps commanders: "By order of the President of the Republic, no unit of the army, no patrol, no reconnaissance, no scout, no detail of any kind, shall go east of the line laid down. Anyone guilty of transgressing will be liable to court-martial." A particular warning was added for the benefit of the XXth Corps, commanded by General Foch, of whom it was reliably reported that a squadron of cuirassiers had been seen "nose to nose" with a squadron of Uhlans.

At 3:30, as arranged, General Ebener of Joffre's staff, accompanied by two officers, came to the War Office to call for the mobilization order. Messimy handed it over in dry-throated silence. "Conscious of the gigantic and infinite results to spread from that little piece of paper, all four of us felt our hearts tighten." He shook hands with each of the three officers, who saluted and departed to deliver the order to the Post Office.

At four o'clock the first poster appeared on the walls of Paris (at the corner of the Place de la Concorde and the Rue Royale, one still remains, preserved under glass). At Armenonville, rendezvous of the *haut-monde* in the Bois de Boulogne, tea dancing suddenly stopped when the manager stepped forward, silenced the orchestra, and announced: "Mobilization has been ordered. It begins at midnight. Play the 'Marseillaise.' " In town the streets were already emptied of vehicles requisitioned by the War Office. Groups of reservists with bundles and farewell bouquets of flowers were marching off to the Gare de l'Est, as civilians waved and cheered. One group stopped to lay its flowers at the feet of the black-draped statue of Strasbourg in the Place de la Concorde. The crowds wept and cried "*Vive l'Alsace!*" and tore off the mourning she had worn since 1870. Orchestras in restaurants played the French, Russian, and British anthems. "To think these are all being played by Hungarians," someone remarked. The playing of their anthem, as if to express a hope, made Englishmen in the crowd uncomfortable and none more so than Sir Francis Bertie, the pink and plump British ambassador who in a gray frock coat and gray top hat, holding a green parasol against the sun, was seen entering the Quai d'Orsay. Sir Francis felt "sick at heart and ashamed." He ordered the gates of his embassy closed, for, as he wrote in his diary, "though it is '*Vive l'Angleterre*' today, it may be '*Perfide Albion*' tomorrow."

In London that thought hung heavily in the room where small, white-bearded M. Cambon confronted Sir Edward Grey. When Grey said to him that some "new development" must be awaited because the dispute between Russia, Austria, and Germany concerned a matter "of no interest" to Great Britain, Cambon let a glint of anger penetrate his impeccable tact and polished dignity. Was England "going to wait until French territory was invaded before intervening?" he asked, and suggested that if so her help might be "very belated."

Grey, behind his tight mouth and Roman nose, was in equal anguish. He believed fervently that England's interests required her to support France; he was prepared, in fact, to resign if she did not; he believed events to come would force her hand, but as yet he could say nothing officially to Cambon. Nor had he the knack of expressing himself unofficially. His manner, which the English public, seeing in him the image of the strong, silent man, found comforting, his foreign colleagues found "icy." He managed only to express edgily the thought that was in everyone's mind, that "Belgian neutrality might become a factor." That was the development Grey—and not he alone—was waiting for.

Britain's predicament resulted from a split personality evident both within the Cabinet and between the parties. The Cabinet was divided, in a split that derived from the Boer War, between Liberal Imperialists represented by Asquith, Grey, Haldane, and Churchill, and "Little England-ers" represented by all the rest. Heirs of Gladstone, they, like their late leader, harbored a deep suspicion of foreign entanglements and considered the aiding of oppressed peoples to be the only proper concern of foreign affairs, which were otherwise regarded as a tiresome interference with Reform, Free Trade, Home Rule, and the Lords' Veto. They tended to regard France as the decadent and frivolous grasshopper, and would have liked to regard Germany as the industrious, respectable ant, had not the posturings and roarings of the Kaiser and the Pan-German militarists somehow discouraged this view. They would never have supported a war on behalf of France, although the injection of Belgium, a "little" country with a just call on British protection, might alter the issue.

Grey's group in the Cabinet, on the other hand, shared with the Tories a fundamental premise that Britain's national interest was bound up with the preservation of France. The reasoning was best expressed in the marvelously flat words of Grey himself: "If Germany dominated the Continent it would be disagreeable to us as well as to others, for we should be isolated." In this epic sentence is all of British policy, and from it followed the knowledge that, if the challenge were flung, England would have to fight to prevent that "disagreeable" outcome. But Grey could not say so without provoking a split in the Cabinet and in the country that would be fatal to any war effort before it began.

Alone in Europe Britain had no conscription. In war she would be dependent on voluntary enlistment. A secession from the government over the war issue would mean the formation of an antiwar party led by the dissidents with disastrous effect on recruiting. If it was the prime objective of France to enter war with Britain as an ally, it was a prime necessity for Britain to enter war with a united government.

This was the touchstone of the problem. In Cabinet meetings the group opposed to intervention proved strong. Their leader Lord Morley, Gladstone's old friend and biographer, believed he could count on "eight or nine likely to agree with us" against the solution being openly worked for by Churchill with "daemonic energy" and Grey with "strenuous simplicity." From discussions in the Cabinet it was clear to Morley that the neutrality of Belgium was "secondary to the question of our neutrality in the struggle between Germany and France." It was equally clear to Grey that only violation of Belgium's neutrality would convince the peace party of the German menace and the need to go to war in the national interest.

On August 1 the crack was visible and widening in Cabinet and Parliament. That day twelve out of eighteen Cabinet members declared themselves opposed to giving France the assurance of Britain's support in war. That afternoon in the lobby of the House of Commons a caucus of Liberal M.P.s voted 19 to 4 (though with many abstentions) for a motion that England should remain neutral "whatever happened in Belgium or elsewhere." That week *Punch* published "Lines designed to represent the views of an average British patriot":

> Why should I follow your fighting line
> For a matter that's no concern of mine? . . .
>
> I shall be asked to a general scrap
> All over the European map,
> Dragged into somebody else's war
> For that's what a double entente is for.

The average patriot had already used up his normal supply of excitement and indignation in the current Irish crisis. The "Curragh Mutiny" was England's Mme. Caillaux. As a result of the Home Rule Bill, Ulster was threatening armed rebellion against autonomy for Ireland and English troops stationed at the Curragh had refused to take up arms against Ulster loyalists. General Gough, the Curragh commander, had resigned with all his officers, whereupon Sir John French, Chief of General Staff, resigned, whereupon Colonel John Seely, Haldane's successor as Secretary of War, resigned. The army seethed, uproar and schism ruled the country, and a Palace Conference of party leaders with the King met in vain. Lloyd George talked ominously of the "gravest issue raised in this country since the days of the Stuarts," the words "civil war" and "rebellion" were mentioned, and a German arms firm hopefully ran a cargo of 40,000 rifles and a million cartridges into Ulster. In the meantime there was no Secretary of War, the office being left to Prime Minister Asquith, who had little time and less inclination for it.

Asquith had, however, a particularly active First Lord of the Admiralty. When he smelled battle afar off, Winston Churchill resembled the war horse in Job who turned not back from the sword but "paweth in the valley and saith among the trumpets, Ha, ha." He was the only British minister to have a perfectly clear conviction of what Britain should do and to act upon it without hesitation. On July 26, the day Austria rejected Serbia's reply and ten days before his own government made up its mind, Churchill issued a crucial order.

On July 26 the British fleet was completing, unconnected with the crisis, a test mobilization and maneuvers with full crews at war strength. At seven o'clock next morning the squadrons were due to disperse, some to various exercises on the high seas, some to home ports where parts of their crews would be discharged back into training schools, some to dock for repairs. That Sunday, July 26, the First Lord remembered later was "a very beautiful day." When he learned the news from Austria he made up his mind to make sure "that the diplomatic situation did not get ahead of the naval situation and that the Grand Fleet should be in its War Station before Germany could know whether or not we should be in the war *and therefore if possible before we had decided ourselves.*" The italics are his own. After consultation with the First Sea Lord, Prince Louis of Battenberg, he gave orders to the fleet not to disperse.

He then informed Grey what he had done and with Grey's assent released the Admiralty order to the newspapers in the hope that the news might have "a sobering effect" on Berlin and Vienna.

Holding the fleet together was not enough; it must be got, as Churchill expressed it in capitals, to its "War Station." The primary duty of a fleet, as Admiral Mahan, the Clausewitz of naval warfare, had decreed, was to remain "a fleet in being." In the event of war the British fleet, upon which an island nation depended for its life, had to establish and maintain mastery of the ocean trade routes; it had to protect the British Isles from invasion; it had to protect the Channel and the French coasts in fulfillment of the pact with France; it had to keep concentrated in sufficient strength to win any engagement if the German fleet sought battle; and above all it had to guard itself against that new and menacing weapon of unknown potential, the torpedo. The fear of a sudden, undeclared torpedo attack haunted the Admiralty.

On July 28 Churchill gave orders for the fleet to sail to its war base at Scapa Flow, far to the north at the tip of mist-shrouded Orkney in the North Sea. It steamed out of Portland on the 29th, and by nightfall eighteen miles of warships had passed northward through the Straits of Dover headed not so much for some rendezvous with glory as for a rendezvous with discretion. "A surprise torpedo attack" wrote the First Lord, "was at any rate one nightmare gone forever."

Having prepared the fleet for action, Churchill turned his abounding energy and sense of urgency upon preparing the country. He persuaded Asquith on July 29 to authorize the Warning Telegram which was the arranged signal sent by War Office and Admiralty to initiate the Precautionary Period. While short of the *Kriegesgefahr* or the French State of Siege which established martial law, the Precautionary Period has been described as a device "invented by a genius . . . which permitted certain measures to be taken on the *ipse dixit* of the Secretary of War without reference to the Cabinet . . . when time was the only thing that mattered."

Time pressed on the restless Churchill who, expecting the Liberal government to break apart, went off to make overtures to his old party, the Tories. Coalition was not in the least to the taste of the Prime Minister who was bent on keeping his government united. Lord Morley at seventy-six was expected by no one to stay with the government in the event of war. Not Morley but the far more vigorous Chancellor of the Exchequer, Lloyd George, was the key figure whom the government could not afford to lose, both for his proved ability in office and his influence upon the electorate. Shrewd, ambitious, and possessed of a spellbinding Welsh eloquence, Lloyd George leaned to the peace group but might jump either way. He had suffered recent setbacks in public popularity; he saw a new rival for party leadership arising in the individual whom Lord Morley called "that splendid condottierre at the Admiralty"; and he might, some of his colleagues thought, see political advantage in "playing the peace-card" against Churchill. He was altogether an uncertain and dangerous quantity.

Asquith, who had no intention of leading a divided country into war, continued to wait with exasperating patience for events which might convince the peace group. The question of the hour, he recorded in his passionless way in his diary for July 31, was, "Are we to go in or stand aside. Of course everybody longs to stand aside." In a less passive attitude, Grey, during the Cabinet of July 31 almost reached the point-blank. He said Germany's policy was that of a "European aggressor as bad as Napoleon" (a name that for England had only one meaning) and told the Cabinet that the time had come when a decision whether to support the Entente or preserve neutrality could no longer be deferred. He said that if it chose neutrality he was not the man to carry out such a policy. His implied threat to resign echoed as if it had been spoken.

"The Cabinet seemed to heave a sort of sigh," wrote one of them, and sat for several moments in "breathless silence." Its members looked at one another, suddenly realizing that their continued existence as a government was now in doubt. They adjourned without reaching a decision.

That Friday, eve of the August Bank Holiday weekend, the Stock

Exchange closed down at 10:00 A.M. in a wave of financial panic that had started in New York when Austria declared war on Serbia and which was closing Exchanges all over Europe. The City trembled, prophesying doom and the collapse of foreign exchange. Bankers and businessmen, according to Lloyd George, were "aghast" at the idea of war which would "break down the whole system of credit with London at its center." The Governor of the Bank of England called on Saturday to inform Lloyd George that the City was "totally opposed to our intervening" in a war.

That same Friday the Tory leaders were being rounded up and called back to London from country houses to confer on the crisis. Dashing from one to the other, pleading, exhorting, expounding Britain's shame if the shilly-shallying Liberals held back now, was Henry Wilson, the heart, soul, spirit, backbone, and legs of the Anglo-French military "conversations." The agreed euphemism for the joint plans of the General Staffs was "conversations." The formula of "no commitment" which Haldane had first established, which had raised misgivings in Campbell-Bannerman, which Lord Esher had rejected, and which Grey had embodied in the 1912 letter to Cambon still represented the official position, even if it did not make sense.

It made very little. If, as Clausewitz justly said, war is a continuation of national policy, so also are war plans. The Anglo-French war plans, worked out in detail over a period of nine years, were not a game, or an exercise in fantasy or a paper practice to keep military minds out of other mischief. They were a continuation of policy or they were nothing. They were no different from France's arrangements with Russia or Germany's with Austria except for the final legal fiction that they did not "commit" Britain to action. Members of the government and Parliament who disliked the policy simply shut their eyes and mesmerized themselves into believing the fiction.

M. Cambon, visiting Opposition leaders after his painful interview with Grey, now dropped diplomatic tact altogether. "All our plans are arranged in common. Our General Staffs have consulted. You have seen all our schemes and preparations. Look at our fleet! Our whole fleet is in the Mediterranean in consequence of our arrangements with you and our coasts are open to the enemy. You have laid us wide open!" He told them that if England did not come in France would never forgive her, and ended with a bitter cry, "*Et l'honneur? Est-ce-que l'Angleterre comprend ce que c'est l'honneur?*"

Honor wears different coats to different eyes, and Grey knew it would

have to wear a Belgian coat before the peace group could be persuaded to
see it. That same afternoon he dispatched two telegrams asking the French
and German governments for a formal assurance that they were prepared
to respect Belgian neutrality "so long as no other power violates it." Within
an hour of receiving the telegram in the late evening of July 31, France
replied in the affirmative. No reply was received from Germany.

Next day, August 1, the matter was put before the Cabinet. Lloyd George
traced with his finger on a map what he thought would be the German
route through Belgium, just across the near corner, on the shortest straight
line to Paris; it would only, he said, be a "little violation." When Churchill
asked for authority to mobilize the fleet, that is, call up all the naval
reserves, the Cabinet, after a "sharp discussion," refused. When Grey
asked for authority to implement the promises made to the French Navy,
Lord Morley, John Burns, Sir John Simon, and Lewis Harcourt proposed
to resign. Outside the Cabinet, rumors were swirling of the last-minute
wrestlings of Kaiser and Czar and of the German ultimatums. Grey left
the room to speak to—and be misunderstood by—Lichnowsky on the telephone, and unwittingly to be the cause of havoc in the heart of General
Moltke. He also saw Cambon, and told him "France must take her own
decision at this moment without reckoning on an assistance we are not
now in a position to give." He returned to the Cabinet while Cambon,
white and shaking, sank into a chair in the room of his old friend Sir
Arthur Nicolson, the Permanent Under-Secretary. *"Ils vont nous lâcher"*
(They are going to desert us), he said. To the editor of *The Times* who
asked him what he was going to do, he replied, "I am going to wait to
learn if the word 'honor' should be erased from the English dictionary."

In the Cabinet no one wanted to burn his bridges. Resignations were
bruited, not yet offered. Asquith continued to sit tight, say little, and await
developments as that day of crossed wires and complicated frenzy drew to
a close. That evening Moltke was refusing to go east, Lieutenant Feldmann's company was seizing Trois Vierges in Luxembourg, Messimy over
the telephone was reconfirming the ten-kilometer withdrawal, and at the
Admiralty the First Lord was entertaining friends from the Opposition,
among them the future Lords Beaverbrook and Birkenhead. To keep occupied while waiting out the tension, they played bridge after dinner.
During the game a messenger brought in a red dispatch box—it happened
to be one of the largest size. Taking a key from his pocket, Churchill
opened it, took out the single sheet of paper it contained, and read the
single line on the paper: "Germany has declared war on Russia." He

informed the company, changed out of his dinner jacket, and "went straight out like a man going to a well-accustomed job."

Churchill walked across the Horse Guards Parade to Downing Street, entered by the garden gate, and found the Prime Minister upstairs with Grey, Haldane, now Lord Chancellor, and Lord Crewe, Secretary for India. He told them he intended "instantly to mobilize the fleet notwithstanding the Cabinet decision." Asquith said nothing but appeared, Churchill thought, "quite content." Grey, accompanying Churchill on his way out, said to him, "I have just done a very important thing. I have told Cambon that we shall not allow the German fleet to come into the Channel." Or that is what Churchill, experiencing the perils of verbal intercourse with Grey, understood him to say. It meant that the fleet was now committed. Whether Grey said he had given the promise or whether he said, as scholars have since decided, that he was going to give it the next day, is not really relevant, for whichever it was it merely confirmed Churchill in a decision already taken. He returned to the Admiralty and "gave forthwith the order to mobilize."

Both his order and Grey's promise to make good the naval agreement with France were contrary to majority Cabinet sentiment. On the next day the Cabinet would have to ratify these acts or break apart, and by that time Grey expected a "development" to come out of Belgium. Like the French, he felt that he could count on Germany to provide it.

▶▶▶ *8* ▶

▶▶▶ *Ultimatum in Brussels*

LOCKED IN THE SAFE OF HERR VON BELOW-
Saleske, German Minister in Brussels, was a sealed envelope brought to him
by special courier from Berlin on July 29 with orders "not to open until you
are instructed by telegraph from here." On Sunday, August 2, Below was
advised by telegram to open the envelope at once and deliver the Note
it contained by eight o'clock that evening, taking care to give the Belgian
government "the impression that *all* the instructions relating to this affair
reached you for the first time today." He was to demand a reply from the
Belgians within twelve hours and wire it to Berlin "as quickly as possible"
and also "forward it immediately by automobile to General von Emmich
at the Union Hotel in Aachen." Aachen or Aix-la-Chapelle was the nearest
German city to Liège, the eastern gateway to Belgium.

Herr von Below, a tall, erect bachelor with pointed black mustaches
and a jade cigarette holder in constant use, had taken up his post in Belgium early in 1914. When visitors to the German Legation asked him about
a silver ash tray pierced by a bullet hole that lay on his desk, he would
laugh and reply: "I am a bird of ill omen. When I was stationed in Turkey
they had a revolution. When I was in China, it was the Boxers. One of
their shots through the window made that bullet hole." He would raise his

cigarette delicately to his lips with a wide and elegant gesture and add: "But now I am resting. Nothing ever happens in Brussels."

Since the sealed envelope arrived, he had been resting no longer. At noon on August 1 he received a visit from Baron de Bassompierre, Under-Secretary of the Belgian Foreign Office, who told him the evening papers intended to publish France's reply to Grey in which she promised to respect Belgian neutrality. Bassompierre suggested that in the absence of a comparable German reply, Herr von Below might wish to make a statement. Below was without authority from Berlin to do so. Taking refuge in diplomatic maneuver, he lay back in his chair and with his eyes fixed on the ceiling repeated back word for word through a haze of cigarette smoke everything that Bassompierre had just said to him as if playing back a record. Rising, he assured his visitor that "Belgium had nothing to fear from Germany," and closed the interview.

Next morning he repeated the assurance to M. Davignon, the Foreign Minister, who had been awakened at 6:00 A.M. by news of the German invasion of Luxembourg and had asked for an explanation. Back at the legation, Below soothed a clamoring press with a felicitous phrase that was widely quoted, "Your neighbor's roof may catch fire but your own house will be safe."

Many Belgians, official and otherwise, were disposed to believe him, some from pro-German sympathies, some from wishful thinking, and some from simple confidence in the good faith of the international guarantors of Belgium's neutrality. In seventy-five years of guaranteed independence they had known peace for the longest unbroken period in their history. The territory of Belgium had been the pathway of warriors since Caesar fought the Belgae. In Belgium, Charles the Bold of Burgundy and Louis XI of France had fought out their long and bitter rivalry; there Spain had ravaged the Low Countries; there Marlborough had fought the French at the "very murderous battle" of Malplaquet; there Napoleon had met Wellington at Waterloo; there the people had risen against every ruler—Burgundian, French, Spanish, Hapsburg, or Dutch—until the final revolt against the House of Orange in 1830. Then, under Leopold of Saxe-Coburg, maternal uncle of Queen Victoria, as King, they had made themselves a nation, grown prosperous, spent their energies in fraternal fighting between Flemings and Walloons, Catholics and Protestants, and in disputes over Socialism and French and Flemish bilingualism, in the fervent hope that their neighbors would leave them to continue undisturbed in this happy condition.

The King and Prime Minister and Chief of Staff could no longer share the general confidence, but were prevented, both by the duties of neutrality and by their belief in neutrality, from making plans to repel attack. Up until the last moment they could not bring themselves to believe an invasion by one of their guarantors would actually happen. On learning of the German *Kriegesgefahr* on July 31, they had ordered mobilization of the Belgian Army to begin at midnight. During the night and next day policemen went from house to house ringing doorbells and handing out orders while men scrambled out of bed or left their jobs, wrapped up their bundles, said their farewells, and went off to their regimental depots. Because Belgium, maintaining her strict neutrality, had not up to now settled on any plan of campaign, mobilization was not directed against a particular enemy or oriented in a particular direction. It was a call-up without deployment. Belgium was obligated, as well as her guarantors, to preserve her own neutrality and could make no overt act until one was made against her.

When, by the evening of August 1, Germany's silence in response to Grey's request had continued for twenty-four hours, King Albert determined on a final private appeal to the Kaiser. He composed it in consultation with his wife, Queen Elizabeth, a German by birth, the daughter of a Bavarian duke, who translated it sentence by sentence into German, weighing with the King the choice of words and their shades of meaning. It recognized that "political objections" might stand in the way of a public statement but hoped "the bonds of kinship and friendship" would decide the Kaiser to give King Albert his personal and private assurance of respect for Belgian neutrality. The kinship in question, which stemmed from King Albert's mother, Princess Marie of Hohenzollern-Sigmaringen, a distant and Catholic branch of the Prussian royal family, failed to move the Kaiser to reply.

Instead came the ultimatum that had been waiting in Herr von Below's safe for the last four days. It was delivered at seven on the evening of August 2 when a footman at the Foreign Office pushed his head through the door of the Under-Secretary's room and reported in an excited whisper, "The German Minister has just gone in to see M. Davignon!" Fifteen minutes later Below was seen driving back down the Rue de la Loi holding his hat in his hand, beads of perspiration on his forehead, and smoking with the rapid, jerky movements of a mechanical toy. The instant his "haughty silhouette" had been seen to leave the Foreign Office, the two Under-Secretaries rushed in to the Minister's room where they found

M. Davignon, a man until now of immutable and tranquil optimism, looking extremely pale. "Bad news, bad news," he said, handing them the German note he had just received. Baron de Gaiffier, the Political Secretary, read it aloud, translating slowly as he went, while Bassompierre, sitting at the Minister's desk took it down, discussing each ambiguous phrase to make sure of the right rendering. While they worked, M. Davignon and his Permanent Under-Secretary, Baron van der Elst, listened, sitting in two chairs on either side of the fireplace. M. Davignon's last word on any problem had always been, "I am sure it will turn out all right" while van der Elst's esteem for the Germans had led him in the past to assure his government that rising German armaments were intended only for the *Drang nach Osten* and portended no trouble for Belgium.

Baron de Broqueville, Premier and concurrently War Minister, entered the room as the work concluded, a tall, dark gentleman of elegant grooming whose resolute air was enhanced by an energetic black mustache and expressive black eyes. As the ultimatum was read to him everyone in the room listened to each word with the same intensity that the authors had put into the drafting. It had been drawn up with great care, with perhaps a subconscious sense that it was to be one of the critical documents of the century.

General Moltke had written the original version in his own hand on July 26, two days before Austria declared war on Serbia, four days before Austria and Russia mobilized, and on the same day when Germany and Austria had rejected Sir Edward Grey's proposal for a five-power conference. Moltke had sent his draft to the Foreign Office, where it was revised by Under-Secretary Zimmermann and Political Secretary Stumm, further corrected and modified by Foreign Minister Jagow and Chancellor Bethmann-Hollweg before the final draft was sent in the sealed envelope to Brussels on the 29th. The extreme pains the Germans took reflected the importance they attached to the document.

Germany had received "reliable information," the note began, of a proposed advance by the French along the route Givet-Namur, "leaving no doubt of France's intention to advance against Germany through Belgian territory." (As the Belgians had seen no evidence of French movement toward Namur, for the excellent reason that there was none, the charge failed to impress them.) Germany, the note continued, being unable to count on the Belgian Army halting the French advance, was required by "the dictate of self-preservation" to "anticipate this hostile attack." She would view it with "deepest regret" if Belgium should regard her entrance on Belgian soil as "an act of hostility against herself." If Belgium should, on the other hand, adopt "a benevolent neutrality," Germany would bind herself to "evacuate her territory as soon as peace shall have been concluded," to pay for any damages caused by German troops, and to "guarantee at the conclusion of peace the sovereign rights and independence of the kingdom." In the original the sentence had continued, "and to favor with the greatest goodwill any possible claims of Belgium for compensation at the expense of France." At the last moment Below was instructed to delete this bribe.

If Belgium opposed Germany's passage through her territory, the note concluded, she would be regarded as an enemy, and future relations with her would be left to "the decision of arms." An "unequivocal answer" was demanded within twelve hours.

"A long, tragic silence of several minutes" followed the reading, Bassompierre recalled, as each man in the room thought of the choice that faced his country. Small in size and young in independence, Belgium clung more fiercely to independence for that reason. But no one in the room needed to be told what the consequences of a decision to defend it would be. Their country would be subjected to attack, their homes to destruction, their people to reprisals by a force ten times their size with no doubt of the outcome to themselves, who were in the immediate pathway of the Germans, whatever the ultimate outcome of the war. If, on the contrary, they were to yield to the German demand, they would be making Belgium an accessory to the attack on France as well as a violator of her own neutrality, besides opening her to German occupation with small likelihood that a victorious Germany would remember to withdraw. They would be occupied either way; to yield would be to lose honor too.

"If we are to be crushed," Bassompierre recorded their sentiment, "let us be crushed gloriously." In 1914 "glory" was a word spoken without embarrassment, and honor a familiar concept that people believed in.

Van der Elst broke the silence in the room. "Well, sir, are we ready?" he asked the Premier.

"Yes, we are ready," De Broqueville answered. "Yes," he repeated, as if trying to convince himself, "except for one thing—we have not yet got our heavy artillery." Only in the last year had the government obtained increased military appropriations from a reluctant Parliament conditioned to neutrality. The order for heavy guns had been given to the German firm of Krupp, which, not surprisingly, had delayed deliveries.

One hour of the twelve had already gone by. While their colleagues began rounding up all Ministers for a Council of State to be held at nine o'clock, Bassompierre and Gaiffier started working on a draft of the reply. They had no need to ask each other what it would be. Leaving the task to them, Premier de Broqueville went to the palace to inform the King.

King Albert felt a responsibility as ruler that made his awareness of outside pressures acute. He had not been born to reign. A younger son of King Leopold's younger brother, he was left to grow up in a corner of the palace with a Swiss tutor of more than ordinary mediocrity. Coburg family life was not joyous. Leopold's own son died; in 1891 his nephew, Baudouin, Albert's older brother, died, leaving Albert heir to the throne at sixteen. The old King, embittered by the loss of his own son and of Baudouin to whom he had transferred his paternal affections, did not at first see much in Albert whom he called a "sealed envelope."

Inside the envelope were enormous physical and intellectual energies of the kind that marked two great contemporaries, Theodore Roosevelt and Winston Churchill, whom otherwise Albert resembled not at all. He was reserved where they were extroverts; yet he shared many tastes, if not temperament, with Roosevelt: his love of the outdoors, of physical exercise, of riding and climbing, his interest in natural science and conservation and his gluttony for books. Like Roosevelt, Albert consumed books at the rate of two a day on any and all subjects—literature, military science, colonialism, medicine, Judaism, aviation. He drove a motorbicycle and piloted a plane. His ultimate passion was mountaineering, which, incognito, he pursued all over Europe. As heir apparent he toured Africa to study colonial problems at firsthand; as King he studied the army or the coal mines of the Borinage or the "Red country" of the Walloons in the same way. "When he speaks the King always looks as if he wished to build something," said one of his Ministers.

In 1900 he had married Elizabeth of Wittelsbach, whose father, the Duke, practiced as an oculist in the Munich hospitals. Their obvious affection for each other, their three children, their model family life in contrast to the unseemly ways of the old regime gave Albert a head start in popular approval when, in 1909, to general relief and rejoicing, he took the place of King Leopold II upon the throne. The new King and Queen continued to ignore pomp, entertain whom they liked, exercise their curiosity and love of adventure where they liked, and remain indifferent to danger, etiquette, and criticism. They were not bourgeois, so much as bohemian royalty.

In military school Albert had been a cadet at the same time as a future Chief of Staff, Emile Galet. A shoemaker's son, Galet had been sent to the school by popular subscription of his village. Later he became an instructor in the War College, and resigned when he could no longer agree with its dauntless theories of the offensive which the Belgian Staff, regardless of the difference in circumstance, had taken over from the French. Galet had also left the Catholic Church to become a strict Evangelical. Pessimistic, hypercritical, and dedicated, he was intensely serious about his profession as about everything else—it was said he read the Bible daily and was never known to laugh. The King heard him lecture, met him at maneuvers, was impressed by his teachings: that offensive for its own sake and under all circumstances was dangerous, that an army should seek battle "only if there is prospect of important success," and that "attack calls for superiority of means." Though still a captain, though a workingman's son, though a convert to Protestantism in a Catholic country, he was chosen by King Albert as his personal military adviser, a post specially created for the purpose.

Since, according to the Belgian constitution, King Albert would become Commander in Chief only after the outbreak of war, he and Galet were unable in the meantime to impose their fears or their ideas of strategy upon the General Staff. The Staff clung to the example of 1870 when not a toe of either the Prussian or French armies had stepped over the Belgian border, although if the French had crossed into Belgian territory they would have had room enough to retreat. King Albert and Galet, however, believed that the huge growth of armies since that time made it clearer each year that if the nations marched again they would spill over onto the old pathways and meet again in the old arena.

The Kaiser had made this perfectly clear in the interview which so stunned Leopold II in 1904. After his return, Leopold's shock gradually wore off, for, as van der Elst, to whom the King reported the interview, agreed, William was such a weathercock, how could one be sure? On a return visit to Brussels in 1910, the Kaiser proved indeed to be most reassuring. Belgium had nothing to fear from Germany, he told van der Elst. "You will have no grounds of complaint against Germany. . . . I understand perfectly your country's position. . . . I shall never place her in a false position."

On the whole, Belgians believed him. They took their guarantee of neutrality seriously. Belgium had neglected her army, frontier defenses, fortresses, anything that implied lack of confidence in the protective treaty.

Socialism was the raging issue. Public apathy to what was happening abroad and a Parliament obsessed by economy allowed the army to deteriorate to a condition resembling the Turkish. Troops were ill-disciplined, slack, untidy, avoided saluting, slouched in the ranks, and refused to keep step.

The officers' corps was little better. Because the army was considered superfluous and slightly absurd, it did not attract the best minds or young men of ability and ambition. Those who did make it a career and passed through the Ecole de Guerre became infected with the French doctrine of *élan* and *offensive à outrance*. The remarkable formula they evolved was, "To ensure against our being ignored it was essential that we should attack."

However magnificent the spirit, this formula conformed ill with the realities of Belgium's position, and the doctrine of the offensive sat oddly upon an army staff committed by the duty of neutrality to plan for the defensive only. Neutrality forbade them to plan in concert with any other nation and required of them to regard the first foot put inside their territory as hostile, whether it was English, French, or German. Under the circumstances a coherent plan of campaign was not easily achieved.

The Belgian Army consisted of six divisions of infantry plus a cavalry division. These would have to face the thirty-four divisions scheduled by the Germans to march through Belgium. Equipment and training were inadequate and marksmanship inferior in view of army funds that permitted enough ammunition for only two firing practices of one round per man a week. Compulsory military service, not introduced until 1913, only served to make the army more unpopular than ever. In that year of ominous rumblings from abroad, Parliament reluctantly raised the annual contingent from 13,000 to 33,000 but agreed to appropriate funds for modernizing the defenses of Antwerp only on condition that the cost be absorbed by reducing the conscripts' period of service. No General Staff existed until 1910 when the new King insisted upon creating one.

Its effectiveness was limited by the extreme dissidence of its members. One school favored an offensive plan with the army concentrated at the frontiers upon threat of war. Another school favored the defensive with the army concentrated in the interior. A third group, consisting chiefly of King Albert and Captain Galet, favored a defensive as close as possible to the threatened frontier but without risking the lines of communication to the fortified base at Antwerp.

While the European sky was darkening, Belgium's staff officers wrangled

—and failed to complete a plan of concentration. Their difficulty was compounded by their not permitting themselves to specify who the enemy would be. A compromise plan had been agreed on but existed only in outline, without railroad timetables, supply depots, or billets.

In November 1913, King Albert was invited to Berlin as his uncle had been nine years before. The Kaiser gave him a royal dinner at a table covered with violets and set for fifty-five guests, among them Secretary of War General Falkenhayn, Secretary of the Imperial Navy Admiral Tirpitz, Chief of Staff General Moltke, and Chancellor Bethmann-Hollweg. The Belgian ambassador, Baron Beyens, who was also present, noticed that the King sat through dinner looking unusually grave. After dinner, Beyens watched him in conversation with Moltke, and saw Albert's face growing darker and more somber as he listened. On leaving he said to Beyens: "Come tomorrow at nine. I must talk to you."

In the morning he walked with Beyens through the Brandenburg Gate, past the rows of glaring white marble Hohenzollerns in heroic postures, mercifully shrouded by the morning mist, to the Tiergarten where they could talk "undisturbed." At a court ball early in his visit, Albert said, he had received his first shock when the Kaiser pointed out to him a general— it was von Kluck—as the man designated "to lead the march on Paris." Then, prior to dinner the evening before, the Kaiser, taking him aside for a personal talk, had poured forth a hysterical tirade against France. He said France never ceased provoking him. As a result of her attitude, war with France was not only inevitable; it was near at hand. The French press treated Germany with malice, the Three-Year Law was a deliberately hostile act, and all France was moved by an unquenchable thirst for *revanche*. Trying to stem the flow, Albert said he knew the French better; he visited France every year, and he could assure the Kaiser they were not aggressive but sincerely desired peace. In vain; the Kaiser kept insisting war was inevitable.

After dinner Moltke took up the refrain. War with France was coming. "This time we must make an end of it. Your Majesty cannot imagine the irresistible enthusiasm which will permeate Germany on The Day." The German Army was invincible; nothing could stand up to the *furor Teutonicus*; terrible destruction would mark its path; its victory could not be in doubt.

Troubled by what motivated these startling confidences, as much as by their content, Albert could only conclude they were intended to frighten Belgium into coming to terms. Evidently the Germans had made up their minds, and he felt that France should be warned. He instructed Beyens to repeat everything to Jules Cambon, the French ambassador in Berlin, and to charge him to report the matter to President Poincaré in the strongest terms.

Later they learned that Major Melotte, the Belgian military attaché, had been treated to an even more violent outburst by General Moltke at the same dinner. He also heard that war with France was "inevitable" and "much nearer than you think." Moltke, who usually maintained great reserve with foreign attachés, on this occasion "unbuttoned" himself. He said Germany did not want war but the General Staff was "arch-ready." He said "France must absolutely stop provoking and annoying us or we shall have to come to blows. The sooner, the better. We have had enough of these continual alerts." As examples of French provocations, Moltke cited, apart from "big things," a cold reception given in Paris to German aviators and a boycott by Paris society of Major Winterfeld, the German military attaché. The Major's mother, Countess d'Alvensleben, had complained bitterly. As for England, well, the German Navy was not built to hide in harbor. It would attack and probably be beaten. Germany would lose her ships, but England would lose mastery of the seas, which would pass to the United States, who would be the sole gainer from a European war. England knew this and, said the General, taking a sharp turn in his logic, would probably stay neutral.

He was far from finished. What would Belgium do, he asked Major Melotte, if a large foreign force invaded her territory? Melotte replied that she would defend her neutrality. In an effort to find out whether Belgium would content herself with a protest, as the Germans believed, or would fight, Moltke pressed him to be more specific. When Melotte answered, "We will oppose with all our forces whatever power violates our frontiers," Moltke pointed out smoothly that good intentions were not enough. "You must also have an army capable of fulfilling the duty which neutrality imposes."

Back in Brussels, King Albert called at once for a progress report on the mobilization plans. He found no progress had been made. On the basis of what he had heard in Berlin, he obtained De Broqueville's agreement for a plan of campaign based on the hypothesis of a German invasion. He got his own and Galet's nominee, an energetic officer named Colonel de Ryckel, appointed to carry out the work promised for April. By April it was still not ready. Meanwhile De Broqueville had appointed another officer, General de Selliers de Moranville, as Chief of Staff over De Ryckel's head. In July four separate plans of concentration were still being considered.

Discouragement did not change the King's mind. His policy was embodied in a memorandum drawn up by Captain Galet immediately after the Berlin visit. "We are resolved to declare war at once upon any power that deliberately violates our territory; to wage war with the utmost energy and with the whole of our military resources, wherever required, even beyond our frontiers, and to continue to wage war even after the invader retires, until the conclusion of a general peace."

On August 2, King Albert, presiding at the Council of State when it met at 9:00 P.M. in the palace, opened with the words: "Our answer must be 'No,' whatever the consequences. Our duty is to defend our territorial integrity. In this we must not fail." He insisted, however, that no one present should allow himself any illusions: the consequences would be grave and terrible; the enemy would be ruthless. Premier de Broqueville warned waverers not to put faith in Germany's promise to restore Belgian integrity after the war. "If Germany is victorious," he said, "Belgium, whatever her attitude, will be annexed to the German Empire."

One aged and indignant minister who had recently entertained as his house guest the Duke of Schleswig-Holstein, brother-in-law of the Kaiser, could not contain his wrath at the perfidy of the Duke's expressions of friendship and kept up an angry mumbling as chorus to the proceedings. When General de Selliers, the Chief of Staff, rose to explain the strategy of defense to be adopted, his Deputy Chief, Colonel de Ryckel, with whom his relations were, in the words of a colleague, "denuded of the amenities," kept growling between his teeth, *"Il faut piquer dedans, il faut piquer dedans"* (We must hit them where it hurts). Given the floor, he amazed his hearers with a proposal to anticipate the invader by attacking him on his own territory before he could cross the Belgian frontier.

At midnight the meeting adjourned, while a committee of the Premier, Foreign Minister, and Minister of Justice returned to the Foreign Office to draft a reply. While they were at work a motorcar drew up in the dark courtyard beneath the single row of lighted windows. A visit of the German Minister was announced to the startled Ministers. It was 1:30 A.M. What could he want at this hour?

Herr von Below's nocturnal unrest reflected his government's growing uneasiness about the effect of their ultimatum, now irrevocably committed to paper and irrevocably working upon Belgian national pride. The Ger-

mans had been telling one another for years that Belgium would not fight,
but now when the moment arrived they began to suffer an acute if
belated anxiety. A valiant and ringing "No!" from Belgium would peal
round the world with effect on the other neutral countries hardly bene-
ficial to Germany. But Germany was not so worried about the attitude
of neutral countries as she was about the delay that armed Belgian
resistance would inflict upon her timetable. A Belgian Army that chose
to fight rather than "line up along the road" would require the leaving
behind of divisions needed for the march on Paris. By destruction of
railroads and bridges it could disrupt the Germans' line of march and flow
of supplies and cause an infinity of annoyance.

Prey to second thoughts, the German government had sent Herr von
Below in the middle of the night to try to influence the Belgian reply
by further accusations against France. He informed van der Elst who
received him that French dirigibles had dropped bombs and that French
patrols had crossed the border.

"Where did these events take place?" van der Elst asked.

"In Germany," was the reply.

"In that case I fail to see the relevance of the information."

The German Minister offered to explain that the French lacked
respect for international law and could therefore be expected to violate
Belgian neutrality. This ingenious exercise in logic somehow fell short
of making its point. Van der Elst showed his visitor the door.

At 2:30 A.M., the Council reconvened in the palace to approve the
reply to Germany submitted by the Ministers. It stated that the Belgian
government "would sacrifice the honor of the nation and betray its duty
to Europe" if it accepted the German proposals. It declared itself "firmly
resolved to repel by all means in its power every attack upon its rights."

After approving the document without change, the Council fell into
dispute over the King's insistence that no appeal to the guarantor powers for assistance should be made until the Germans actually entered
Belgium. Despite vigorous disagreement he carried his point. At 4:00 A.M.
the Council broke up. The last Minister to leave turned and saw King
Albert standing with his back to the room and a copy of the reply in his
hand, staring out of the window where the dawn was beginning to light
the sky.

In Berlin, too, a late meeting was being held that night of August 2.
At the Chancellor's house, Bethmann-Hollweg, General von Moltke, and

Admiral Tirpitz were conferring about a declaration of war on France as they had conferred the night before about Russia. Tirpitz complained "again and again" that he could not understand why these declarations of war were necessary. They always had an "aggressive flavor"; an army could march "without such things." Bethmann pointed out that a declaration of war on France was necessary because Germany wanted to march through Belgium. Tirpitz repeated Ambassador Lichnowsky's warnings from London that an invasion of Belgium would bring England in; he suggested that the entry into Belgium might be delayed. Moltke, terrified by another threat to his schedule, at once declared this to be "impossible"; nothing must be allowed to interfere with the "machinery of transport."

He did not himself, he said, attach much value to declarations of war. French hostile acts during the days had already made war a fact. He was referring to the alleged reports of French bombings in the Nuremberg area which the German press had been blazing forth in extras all day with such effect that people in Berlin went about looking nervously at the sky. In fact, no bombings had taken place. Now, according to German logic, a declaration of war was found to be necessary because of the imaginary bombings.

Tirpitz still deplored it. There could be no doubt in the world, he said, that the French were "at least intellectually the aggressors"; but owing to the carelessness of German politicians in not making this clear to the world, the invasion of Belgium, which was "a pure emergency measure," would be made to appear unfairly "in the fateful light of a brutal act of violence."

In Brussels, after the Council of State broke up at 4:00 A.M. on the morning of August 3, Davignon returned to the Foreign Office and instructed his Political Secretary, Baron de Gaiffier, to deliver Belgium's reply to the German Minister. At precisely 7:00 A.M., the last moment of the twelve hours, Gaiffier rang the doorbell of the German Legation and delivered the reply to Herr von Below. On his way home he heard the cries of newsboys as the Monday morning papers announced the text of the ultimatum and the Belgian answer. He heard the sharp exclamations as people read the news and gathered in excited groups. Belgium's defiant "No!" exhilarated the public. Many expressed the belief that it would cause the Germans to skirt their territory rather than risk universal censure. "The Germans are dangerous but they are not maniacs," people assured one another.

Even in the palace and in the ministries some hope persisted; it was hard to believe that the Germans would deliberately choose to start the war by putting themselves in the wrong. The last hope vanished when the Kaiser's belated reply to King Albert's personal appeal of two days before was received on the evening of August 3. It was one more attempt to induce the Belgians to acquiesce without fighting. "Only with the most friendly intentions toward Belgium," the Kaiser telegraphed, had he made his grave demand. "As the conditions laid down make clear, the possibility of maintaining our former and present relations still lies in the hands of Your Majesty."

"What does he take me for?" King Albert exclaimed in the first show of anger he had allowed himself since the crisis began. Assuming the supreme command, he at once gave orders for the blowing up of the Meuse bridges at Liège and of the railroad tunnels and bridges at the Luxembourg frontier. He still postponed sending the appeal for military help and alliance to Britain and France. Belgian neutrality had been one collective act of the European Powers that almost succeeded. King Albert could not bring himself to sign its death certificate until the overt act of invasion had actually taken place.

▶▶▶ *9* ▶

▶▶▶ *"Home Before*

the Leaves Fall"

ON SUNDAY AFTERNOON, AUGUST 2, A FEW HOURS
before the German ultimatum was delivered in Brussels, Grey asked the
British Cabinet for authority to fulfill the naval engagement to defend
the French Channel coast. No more distressing moment can ever face a
British government than that which requires it to come to a hard and fast
and specific decision. Through the long afternoon the Cabinet squirmed
uncomfortably, unready and unwilling to grasp the handle of final commitment.

In France war came and was accepted as a kind of national fate,
however deeply a part of the people would have preferred to avoid it.
Almost in awe, a foreign observer reported the upsurge of "national
devotion" joined with an "entire absence of excitement" in a people of
whom it had so often been predicted that anarchical influences had under-
mined their patriotism and would prove fatal in the event of war. Belgium,
where there occurred one of the rare appearances of the hero in history,
was lifted above herself by the uncomplicated conscience of her King and,

faced with the choice to acquiesce or resist, took less than three hours to make her decision, knowing it might be mortal.

Britain had no Albert and no Alsace. Her weapons were ready but not her will. Over the past ten years she had studied and prepared for the war that was now upon her and had developed, since 1905, a system called the "War Book" which left nothing to the traditional British practice of muddling through. All orders to be issued in the event of war were ready for signature; envelopes were addressed; notices and proclamations were either printed or set up in type, and the King never moved from London without having with him those that required his immediate signature. The method was plain; the muddle was in the British mind.

The appearance of a German fleet in the Channel would have been no less direct a challenge to Britain than the Spanish Armada of long ago, and the Sunday Cabinet reluctantly agreed to Grey's request. The written pledge which that afternoon he handed to Cambon read, "If the German Fleet comes into the Channel or through the North Sea to undertake hostile operations against the French coasts or shipping, the British Fleet will give all protection in its power." Grey added, however, that the pledge "does not bind us to go to war with Germany unless the German fleet took the action indicated." Voicing the real fear of the Cabinet, he said that as England was uncertain of the protection of her own coasts, "it was impossible safely to send our military forces out of the country."

M. Cambon asked whether this meant Britain would never do so. Grey replied that his words "dealt only with the present moment." Cambon suggested sending two divisions for "moral effect." Grey said that to send so small a force or even four divisions "would entail the maximum risk to them and produce the minimum of effect." He added that the naval commitment must not become public until Parliament could be informed on the next day.

Half in despair but yet in hope, Cambon informed his government of the pledge in a "very secret" telegram which reached Paris at 8:30 that night. Though it was but a one-legged commitment, far less than France had counted on, he believed it would lead to full belligerency, for, as he later put it, nations do not wage war "by halves."

But the naval pledge was only wrung from the Cabinet at the cost of the break that Asquith had been trying so hard to prevent. Two ministers, Lord Morley and John Burns, resigned; the formidable Lloyd George was still "doubtful." Morley believed the dissolution of the Cabinet was "in full view that afternoon." Asquith had to confess "we are on the brink of a split."

Churchill, always ready to anticipate events, appointed himself emissary to bring his former party, the Tories, into a coalition government. As soon as the Cabinet was over he hurried off to see Balfour, the former Tory Prime Minister, who like the other leaders of his party believed that Britain must carry through the policy that had created the Entente to its logical, if bitter, end. Churchill told him he expected half the Liberal Cabinet to resign if war were declared. Balfour replied that his party would be prepared to join a coalition, although if it came to that necessity he foresaw the country rent by an antiwar movement led by the seceding Liberals.

Up to this moment the German ultimatum to Belgium was not yet known. The underlying issue in the thinking of men like Churchill and Balfour, Haldane and Grey was the threatened German hegemony of Europe if France were crushed. But the policy that required support of France had developed behind closed doors and had never been fully admitted to the country. The majority of the Liberal government did not accept it. On this issue neither government nor country would have gone to war united. To many, if not to most Englishmen, the crisis was another phase in the old quarrel between Germany and France, and none of England's affair. To make it England's affair in the eyes of the public, the violation of Belgium, child of English policy, where every step of the invaders would trample on a treaty of which England was architect and signatory, was required. Grey determined to ask the Cabinet next morning to regard such invasion as a formal *casus belli*.

That evening as he was at dinner with Haldane, a Foreign Office messenger brought over a dispatch box with a telegram which, according to Haldane's account, warned that "Germany was about to invade Belgium." What this telegram was or from whom it came is not clear, but Grey must have considered it authentic. Passing it to Haldane, Grey asked him what he thought. "Immediate mobilization," Haldane replied.

They at once left the dinner table and drove to Downing Street where they found the Prime Minister with some guests. Taking him into a private room, they showed him the telegram and asked for authority to mobilize. Asquith agreed. Haldane suggested that he be temporarily reappointed to the War Office for the emergency. The Prime Minister would be too busy next day to perform the War Minister's duties. Asquith again agreed, the more readily as he was uncomfortably conscious of the looming autocrat,

Field Marshal Lord Kitchener of Khartoum, whom he had already been urged to appoint to the empty chair.

Next morning, Bank Holiday Monday, was a clear and beautiful summer day. London was crammed with holiday crowds drawn to the capital instead of the seashore by the crisis. By midday they were so thick in Whitehall that cars could not get through, and the hum of milling people could be heard inside the Cabinet room where the ministers, meeting again in almost continuous session, were trying to make up their minds whether to fight on the issue of Belgium.

Over at the War Office Lord Haldane was already sending out the mobilization telegrams calling up Reservists and Territorials. At eleven o'clock the Cabinet received news of Belgium's decision to pit her six divisions against the German Empire. Half an hour later they received a declaration from the Conservative leaders, written before the ultimatum to Belgium was known, stating that it would be "fatal to the honor and security of the United Kingdom" to hesitate in support of France and Russia. Russia as an ally already stuck in the throats of most Liberal ministers. Two more of them—Sir John Simon and Lord Beauchamp—resigned, but the events in Belgium decided the pivotal Lloyd George to stay with the government.

At three o'clock that afternoon of August 3, Grey was due in Parliament to make the government's first official and public statement on the crisis. All Europe, as well as all England, was hanging on it. Grey's task was to bring his country into war and bring her in united. He had to carry with him his own, traditionally pacifist, party. He had to explain to the oldest and most practiced parliamentary body in the world how Britain was committed to support France by virtue of something that was not a commitment. He must present Belgium as the cause without hiding France as the basic cause; he must appeal to Britain's honor while making it clear that Britain's interest was the deciding factor; he must stand where a tradition of debate on foreign affairs had flourished for three hundred years and, without the brilliance of Burke or the force of Pitt, without Canning's mastery or Palmerston's jaunty nerve, without the rhetoric of Gladstone or the wit of Disraeli, justify the course of British foreign policy under his stewardship and the war it could not prevent. He must convince the present, measure up to the past, and speak to posterity.

He had had no time to prepare a written speech. In the last hour, as he was trying to compose his notes, the German ambassador was announced. Lichnowsky entered anxiously, asking what had the Cabinet decided? What was Grey going to tell the House? Would it be a declaration of war? Grey answered that it would not be a declaration of war but "a statement of conditions." Was the neutrality of Belgium one of the conditions? Lichnowsky asked. He "implored" Grey not to name it as one. He knew nothing of the plans of the German General Staff, but he could not suppose a "serious" violation was included in them, although German troops might traverse one small corner of Belgium. "If so," Lichnowsky said, voicing the eternal epitaph of man's surrender to events, "that could not be altered now."

They talked standing in the doorway, each oppressed by his own urgency, Grey trying to leave for some last moments of privacy in which to work on his speech, Lichnowsky trying to hold back the moment of the challenge made explicit. They parted and never saw each other officially again.

The House had gathered in total attendance for the first time since Gladstone brought in the Home Rule Bill in 1893. To accommodate all the members extra chairs were set up in the gangway. The Diplomatic Gallery was packed except for two empty seats marking the absence of the German and Austrian ambassadors. Visitors from the Lords filled the Strangers' Gallery, among them Field Marshal Lord Roberts, so long and vainly the advocate of compulsory military service. In the tense hush when, for once, no one bustled, passed notes, or leaned over benches to chat in whispers, there was a sudden clatter as the Chaplain, backing away from the Speaker, stumbled over the extra chairs in the aisle. All eyes were on the government bench where Grey in a light summer suit sat between Asquith whose bland face expressed nothing and Lloyd George whose disheveled hair and cheeks drained of all color made him look years older.

Grey, appearing "pale, haggard and worn," rose to his feet. Though he had been a member of the House for twenty-nine years and on the Government bench for the last eight, members on the whole knew little—and the country much less—of his conduct of foreign policy. Questions put to the Foreign Secretary rarely succeeded in trapping Grey into a clear or definitive answer, yet his evasiveness, which in a more adventurous statesman would have been challenged, was not regarded with suspicion. So noncosmopolitan, so English, so county, so reserved, Grey could not be regarded by anyone as a mettlesome mixer in foreign quarrels. He did not love foreign affairs or enjoy his job but deplored it as a necessary duty.

He did not run over to the Continent for weekends but disappeared into the country. He spoke no foreign language beyond a schoolboy French. A widower at fifty-two, childless, nongregarious, he seemed as unattached to ordinary passions as to his office. What passion broke through his walled personality was reserved for trout streams and bird calls.

Speaking slowly but with evident emotion, Grey asked the House to approach the crisis from the point of view of "British interests, British honor and British obligations." He told the history of the military "conversations" with France. He said that no "secret engagement" bound the House or restricted Britain's freedom to decide her own course of action. He said France was involved in the war because of her "obligation of honor" to Russia, but "we are not parties to the Franco-Russian alliance; we do not even know the terms of that alliance." He seemed to be leaning so far over backward to show England to be uncommitted that a worried Tory, Lord Derby, whispered angrily to his neighbor, "By God, they are going to desert Belgium!"

Grey then revealed the naval arrangement with France. He told the House how, as a consequence of agreement with Britain, the French fleet was concentrated in the Mediterranean, leaving the northern and western coasts of France "absolutely undefended." He said it would be his "feeling" that "if the German fleet came down the Channel and bombarded and battered the undefended coasts of France, we could not stand aside and see this going on practically within sight of our eyes, with our arms folded, looking on dispassionately, doing nothing!" Cheers burst from the Opposition benches, while the Liberals listened, "somberly acquiescent."

To explain his having already committed Britain to defend France's Channel coasts, Grey entered into an involved argument about "British interests" and British trade routes in the Mediterranean. It was a tangled skein, and he hurried on to the "more serious consideration, becoming more serious every hour," of Belgian neutrality.

To give the subject all its due, Grey, wisely not relying on his own oratory, borrowed Gladstone's thunder of 1870, "Could this country stand by and witness the direst crime that ever stained the pages of history and thus become participators in the sin?" From Gladstone too, he took a phrase to express the fundamental issue—that England must take her stand "against the unmeasured aggrandizement of any power whatsoever."

In his own words he continued: "I ask the House from the point of view of British interests to consider what may be at stake. If France is beaten to her knees . . . if Belgium fell under the same dominating influence and then Holland and then Denmark . . . if, in a crisis like this, we run away from these obligations of honor and interest as regards the Belgian Treaty . . . I do not believe for a moment that, at the end of this war, even if we stood aside, we should be able to undo what had happened, in the course of the war, to prevent the whole of the West of Europe opposite us from falling under the domination of a single power . . . and we should, I believe, sacrifice our respect and good name and reputation before the world and should not escape the most serious and grave economic consequences."

He placed before them the "issue and the choice." The House, which had listened in "painful absorption" for an hour and a quarter, broke into overwhelming applause, signifying its answer. The occasions when an individual is able to harness a nation are memorable, and Grey's speech proved to be one of those junctures by which people afterward date events. Some dissent was still vocal, for, unlike the continental parliaments, the House of Commons was not to be exhorted or persuaded into unanimity. Ramsay MacDonald, speaking for the Laborites, said Britain should have remained neutral; Keir Hardie said he would raise the working classes against the war; and afterward in the lobby, a group of unconvinced Liberals adopted a resolution stating that Grey had failed to make a case for war. But Asquith was convinced that on the whole "our extreme peace lovers are silenced though they will soon find their tongues again." The two ministers who had resigned that morning were persuaded to return that evening, and it was generally felt that Grey had carried the country.

"What happens now?" Churchill asked Grey as they left the House together. "Now," replied Grey, "we shall send them an ultimatum to stop the invasion of Belgium within 24 hours." To Cambon, a few hours later, he said, "If they refuse, there will be war." Although he was to wait almost another twenty-four hours before sending the ultimatum, Lichnowsky's fear had been fulfilled; Belgium had been made the condition.

The Germans took that chance because they expected a short war and because, despite the last-minute moans and apprehensions of their civilian leaders over what the British might do, the German General Staff had already taken British belligerency into account and discounted it as of little or no significance in a war they believed would be over in four months.

Clausewitz, a dead Prussian, and Norman Angell, a living if misunderstood professor, had combined to fasten the short-war concept upon the European mind. Quick, decisive victory was the German orthodoxy; the economic impossibility of a long war was everybody's orthodoxy.

"You will be home before the leaves have fallen from the trees," the Kaiser told departing troops in the first week of August. A diarist of German court society recorded on August 9 that Count Oppersdorf came in that afternoon and said things could not last ten weeks; Count Hochberg thought eight weeks, and after that, "You and I will be meeting again in England."

A German officer leaving for the Western Front said he expected to take breakfast at the Café de la Paix in Paris on Sedan Day (September 2). Russian officers expected to be in Berlin about the same time; six weeks was the usual allowance. One officer of the Imperial Guard asked the opinion of the Czar's physician whether he should pack at once his full-dress uniform to wear for the entry into Berlin or leave it to be brought by the next courier coming to the front. An English officer who, having served as a military attaché in Brussels, was considered *au courant*, was asked, upon joining his regiment, his opinion of the duration. He did not know, the officer replied, but he understood there were "financial reasons why the Great Powers could not continue for long." He had heard it from the Prime Minister "who told me that Lord Haldane told him so."

In St. Petersburg the question was not whether the Russians could win but whether it would take them two months or three; pessimists who suggested six months were considered defeatists. "Vasilii Fedorovitch (William, son of Frederick, that is, the Kaiser) has made a mistake; he won't be able to hold out," solemnly predicted the Russian Minister of Justice. He was not so very wrong. Germany had not planned on the need to hold out for long and upon entering the war had a stockpile of nitrates for making gunpowder sufficient for six months and no more. Only the later discovery of a method for fixing nitrogen out of the air enabled her war effort to continue. The French, gambling on a quick finish, risked no troops on what would have been a difficult defense of the Lorraine iron basin but allowed the Germans to take it on the theory that they would regain it with victory. As a result they lost 80 per cent of their iron ore for the duration and almost lost the war. The English, in their imprecise fashion, counted vaguely on victory, without specifying when, where, or how, within a matter of months.

Whether from instinct or intellect, three minds, all military, saw the dark shadow lengthening ahead into years, not months. Moltke, foretelling the "long, wearisome struggle," was one. Joffre was another. Questioned by ministers in 1912 he had said that if France won the first victory in a war, German national resistance would then commence, and vice versa. In either case other nations would be drawn in, and the result would be a war of "indefinite duration." Yet neither he nor Moltke, who were their countries' military chiefs since 1911 and 1906 respectively, made any allowance in their plans for the war of attrition which they both foresaw.

The third—and the only one to act upon his vision—was Lord Kitchener, who had no part in the original planning. Hastily recalled to become War Minister on August 4, as he was about to board a Channel steamer to take him to Egypt, he brought forth from some fathomless oracular depths of his being the prediction that the war would last three years. To an incredulous colleague he said it might last even longer, but "three years will do to begin with. A nation like Germany, after having forced the issue, will only give in after it is beaten to the ground. That will take a very long time. No one living knows how long."

Except for Kitchener who, from his first day in office insisted on preparing an army of millions for a war lasting years, no one else made plans reaching ahead for more than three or six months. In the case of the Germans, the fixed idea of a short war embraced the corollary that in a short war English belligerency would not matter.

"If only someone had told me beforehand that England would take up arms against us!" wailed the Kaiser during lunch at Headquarters one day later in the war. Someone in a small voice ventured, "Metternich," referring to the German ambassador in London who had been dismissed in 1912 because of his tiresome habit of predicting that naval increases would bring war with England no later than 1915. In 1912 Haldane had told the Kaiser that Britain could never permit German possession of the French Channel ports, and reminded him of the treaty obligation to Belgium. In 1912 Prince Henry of Prussia had asked his cousin King George point-blank "whether in the event of Germany and Austria going to war with Russia and France, England would come to the assistance of the two latter powers?" King George had replied, "Undoubtedly yes, under certain circumstances."

In spite of these warnings the Kaiser refused to believe what he knew to be true. According to the evidence of a companion, he was still "convinced" England would stay neutral when he went back to his yacht after giving Austria a free hand on July 5. His two *Corpsbrüder* from student days at Bonn, Bethmann and Jagow, whose qualification for office consisted chiefly in the Kaiser's sentimental weakness for brothers who wore the black and white ribbon of the fraternity and called each other *du*, comforted themselves at intervals, like devout Catholics fingering their beads, with mutual assurances of British neutrality.

Moltke and the General Staff did not need Grey or anyone else to spell out for them what England would do, for they already counted on her coming in as an absolute certainty. "The more English the better," Moltke said to Admiral Tirpitz, meaning the more who landed on the Continent the more would be netted in decisive defeat. Moltke's natural pessimism spared him the illusions of wishful thinking. In a memorandum he drew up in 1913 he stated the case more accurately than many Englishmen could have done. If Germany marched through Belgium without Belgian consent, he wrote, "then England will and *must* join our enemies," the more so as she had declared that intention in 1870. He did not think anyone in England would believe German promises to evacuate Belgium after defeating France, and he felt sure that in a war between Germany and France, England would fight whether Germany went through Belgium or not, "because she fears German hegemony and true to her policy of maintaining a balance of power will do all she can to check the increase of German power."

"In the years immediately preceding the war, we had no doubt whatever of the rapid arrival of the British Expeditionary Force on the French coast," testified General von Kuhl, a General Staff officer of the top echelon. The Staff calculated that the BEF would be mobilized by the tenth day, gather at embarkation ports on the eleventh, begin embarkation on the twelfth, and complete the transfer to France on the fourteenth day. This proved to be almost dead reckoning.

Nor was Germany's naval staff under any illusions. "England probably hostile in case it comes to war," the Admiralty telegraphed as early as July 11 to Admiral von Spee on board the *Scharnhorst* in the Pacific.

Two hours after Grey finished speaking in the House of Commons, that event took place which had been in the back of every mind on both sides of the Rhine since 1870 and in the front of most since 1905. Germany declared war on France. To Germans it came, said the Crown Prince, as the "military solution" of the ever-increasing tension, the end of the nightmare of encirclement. "It is a joy to be alive," rejoiced a German paper on that day in a special edition headlined "The Blessing of Arms." Germans, it said, were "exulting with happiness. . . . We have wished so much for this hour. . . . The sword which has been forced into our hand will not be sheathed until our aims are won and our territory extended as far as necessity demands." Not everyone was exulting. Deputies of the left, summoned to the Reichstag, found each other "depressed" and "nervous." One, confessing readiness to vote all war credits, muttered, "We can't let them destroy the Reich." Another kept grumbling, "This incompetent diplomacy, this incompetent diplomacy."

For France the signal came at 6:15 when Premier Viviani's telephone rang and he heard the American ambassador, Myron Herrick, tell him in a voice choked with tears that he had just received a request to take over the German Embassy and hoist the American flag on its flagpole. He had accepted the charge, Herrick said, but not the flag raising.

Knowing exactly what this meant, Viviani waited for the imminent arrival of the German ambassador, who was announced a few moments later. Von Schoen, who had a Belgian wife, entered in visible distress. He began by complaining that on the way over a lady had thrust her head through the window of his carriage and insulted "me and my Emperor." Viviani, whose own nerves were strung taut with the anguish of the last few days, asked if this complaint was the purpose of his visit. Schoen admitted he had a further duty to perform and, unfolding the document he carried, read its contents, which, as he was the "soul of honor" according to Poincaré, were the cause of his embarrassment. In consequence, it read, of French acts of "organized hostility" and of air attacks on Nuremberg and Karlsruhe and of violation of Belgian neutrality by French aviators flying over Belgian territory, "the German Empire considers itself in a state of war with France."

Viviani formally denied the charges which were included less to impress the French government, who would know they had not taken place, than to impress the German public at home that they were the victims of French aggression. He escorted von Schoen to the door and then, almost reluctant to come to the final parting, walked with him out of the building, down the steps, as far as the door of his waiting carriage. The two representatives of the "hereditary enemies" stood for a moment in mutual unhappiness, bowed wordlessly to each other, and von Schoen drove away into the dusk.

In Whitehall that evening, Sir Edward Grey, standing with a friend at the window as the street lamps below were being lit, made the remark that has since epitomized the hour: "The lamps are going out all over Europe; we shall not see them lit again in our lifetime."

At six o'clock on the morning of August 4, Herr von Below paid his last visit to the Foreign Office in Brussels. He delivered a note saying that in view of the rejection of his Government's "well intentioned proposals," Germany would be obliged to carry out measures for her own security, "if necessary by force of arms." The "if necessary" was intended to leave an opening for Belgium still to change her mind.

That afternoon the American Minister, Brand Whitlock, who had been called to take over the German Legation, found von Below and his First Secretary, von Stumm, slumped in two chairs, making no effort to pack up and seeming "nearly unstrung." Smoking with one hand and mopping his brow with the other, Below sat otherwise motionless while two aged functionaries with candles, sealing wax, and strips of paper proceeded slowly and solemnly around the room sealing the oaken cupboards which held the archives. "Oh the poor fools!" von Stumm kept repeating, half to himself, "Why don't they get out of the way of the steam roller. We don't want to hurt them but if they stand in our way they will be ground into the dirt. Oh, the poor fools!"

Only later did anyone on the German side ask himself who had been the fools on that day. It had been the day, Count Czernin, the Austrian Foreign Minister, discovered afterward, of "our greatest disaster"; the day, even the Crown Prince mournfully acknowledged long after the fact, "when we Germans lost the first great battle in the eyes of the world."

At two minutes past eight that morning the first wave of field gray broke over the Belgian frontier at Gemmerich, thirty miles from Liège. Belgian gendarmes in their sentry boxes opened fire. The force detached from the main German armies for the assault upon Liège under the command of General von Emmich consisted of six infantry brigades, each with artillery and other arms, and three cavalry divisions. By nightfall they had reached the Meuse at Visé, a name that was to become the first in a series of ruins.

Up to the moment of invasion many still believed that self-interest would divert the German armies around Belgium's borders. Why should they deliberately bring two more enemies into the field against them? As no one supposed the Germans to be stupid, the answer that suggested itself to the French mind was that the German ultimatum to Belgium was a trick. It was not intended to be followed by actual invasion but designed to "lead us into being the first to enter Belgium," as Messimy said, in an order forbidding French troops to cross the line "even by so much as a patrol or a single horseman."

Whether for this reason or some other, Grey had not yet sent England's ultimatum. King Albert had not yet appealed to the guarantor powers for military aid. He, too, feared that the ultimatum might be a "colossal feint." If he called in the French and British too soon, their presence would drag Belgium into the war in spite of herself, and at the back of his mind was a worry that once established on Belgian soil his neighbors might be in no hurry to leave. Only after the tramp of German columns marching on Liège had put an end to all doubt and left him no choice, did the King, at noon on August 4, make his appeal for "concerted and common" military action by the guarantors.

In Berlin, Moltke was still hoping that after the first shots fired for honor's sake the Belgians might be persuaded "to come to an understanding." For that reason Germany's final note had simply said "by force of arms" and for once refrained from declaring war. When Baron Beyens, the Belgian ambassador, came to demand his passports on the morning of the invasion, Jagow hurried forward asking, "Well, what have you to say to me?" as if expecting a proposal. He reiterated Germany's offer to respect Belgian independence and pay for all damages if Belgium would refrain from destroying railroads, bridges, and tunnels and let German troops pass through freely without defending Liège. When Beyens turned to go, Jagow followed him hopefully, saying, "Perhaps there will still be something for us to talk over."

In Brussels one hour after the invasion began, King Albert, in unadorned field uniform, rode to meet his Parliament. At a brisk trot the little procession came down the Rue Royale led by an open carriage in which were the Queen and her three children, followed by two more carriages and, bringing up the rear, the King alone on horseback. Houses along the way were decked with flags and flowers; an exalted people filled the streets. Strangers shook each other's hands, laughing and crying, each man feeling, as one recalled, "united to his fellow by a common bond of love and hate." Wave on wave of cheers reached out to the King as if the people in one universal emotion were trying to say he was the symbol of their country and of their will to uphold its independence. Even the Austrian Minister, who had somehow forgotten to absent himself and with other diplomats was watching the procession from the Parliament windows, was wiping tears from his eyes.

Inside the hall, after members, visitors, and the Queen and court were seated, the King came in alone, tossed his cap and gloves onto the lectern in a businesslike gesture and began to speak in a voice only faintly unsteady. When, recalling the Congress of 1830 that created an independent

Belgium, he asked, "Gentlemen, are you unalterably decided to maintain intact the sacred gift of our forefathers?" the deputies, unable to control themselves, stood up with shouts of "*Oui! Oui! Oui!*"

The American Minister, describing the scene in his diary, tells how he watched the King's twelve-year-old heir in his sailor suit, listening with an absorbed face and eyes fixed on his father, and how he wondered, "What are the thoughts in that boy's mind?" Almost as if he had been granted a glimpse into the future, Mr. Whitlock asked himself, "Will this scene ever come back to him in after years? And how? When? Under what circumstances?" The boy in the sailor suit, as Leopold III, was to surrender in 1940 to another German invasion.

In the streets, after the speech was over, enthusiasm became delirious. The army, hitherto contemned, were heroes. The people shouted, "Down with the Germans! Death to the assassins! *Vive la Belgique indépendante!*" After the King had gone, the crowds shouted for the War Minister, ordinarily, regardless of his identity, the most unpopular man in the government by virtue of his office. When M. de Broqueville appeared on the balcony, even that suave man of the world wept, overcome by the fervent emotion shared by everyone who was in Brussels on that day.

On the same day in Paris, French soldiers in red trousers and big-skirted dark blue coats, buttoned back at the corners, chanted as they marched through the streets,

> C'est l'Alsace et la Lorraine
> C'est l'Alsace qu'il nous faut,
> Oh, Oh, Oh, OH!

ending with a triumphant yell on the last "Oh!" One-armed General Pau, whose lost limb gave him an extra popularity, rode by wearing the green and black ribbon of the veterans of 1870. Cavalry regiments of cuirassiers with glistening metal breastplates and long black horsehair tails hanging down from their helmets were conscious of no anachronism. Following them came huge crates housing airplanes and wheeled platforms bearing the long narrow gray-painted field guns, the *soixante-quinzes* that were France's pride. All day the flow of men, horses, weapons and matériel poured through the huge arched portals of the Gare du Nord and the Gare de l'Est.

Down the boulevards, empty of vehicles, marched companies of volunteers with flags and banners proclaiming their purpose: "Luxembourg will never be German!" "Rumania rallies to the Mother of the Latin races," "Italy whose freedom was bought with French blood," "Spain the loving sister of France," "British volunteers for France," "Greeks who love France," "Scandinavians of Paris," "Slav peoples at the side of France," "Latin American lives for the mother of Latin American culture." Roars and cheers greeted the banner that proclaimed, "Alsatians going home."

At a joint session of the Senate and Chamber, Viviani, pale as death and looking as if he were suffering physically and mentally, surpassed his own capacity for fire and eloquence in a speech that was acclaimed, like everybody's on that day, as the greatest of his career. He carried with him in his portfolio the text of France's treaty with Russia but was not questioned about it. Ecstatic cheers greeted his announcement that Italy, "with the clarity of insight possessed by the Latin intellect," had declared her neutrality. As expected, the third member of the Triple Alliance, when the test came, had side-stepped on the ground that Austria's attack on Serbia was an act of aggression which released her from her treaty obligations. Relieving France of the need to guard her southern frontier, Italy's neutrality was worth an extra four divisions, or 80,000 men.

After Viviani had spoken, a speech by President Poincaré, who was precluded by office from attending Parliament in person, was read for him while the whole audience remained standing. France stood before the universe for Liberty, Justice, and Reason, he said, characteristically altering the traditional French trinity. Messages of sympathy and good will from every part of what he pointedly called the "civilized" world were pouring in on her. As the words were being read, General Joffre, "perfectly calm and wholly confident," came to make his farewell to the President before leaving for the front.

Rain was pouring on Berlin as the Reichstag deputies assembled to hear the Kaiser's speech from the throne. Beneath the windows of the Reichstag, where they came for a preliminary meeting with the Chancellor, they could hear the ceaseless clippety-clop of horseshoes on pavement as squadron after squadron of cavalry trotted through the glistening streets. Party leaders met Bethmann in a room adorned by a huge picture which exhibited the gratifying spectacle of Kaiser Wilhelm I trampling gloriously on the French flag. He was shown, together with Bismarck and Field Marshal Moltke, prancing upon the battlefield of Sedan while a German soldier in the foreground stretched a French flag beneath the hoofs of the Emperor's horse. Bethmann expressed concern for unity and exhorted the deputies to "be unanimous" in their decisions. "We shall be unanimous, Excellency," a spokesman for the Liberals replied obediently. The all-knowing Erzberger who, as *rapporteur* of the Military Affairs Committee and a close associate of the Chancellor, was considered to have his ear to Olympus, bustled among his fellow deputies assuring them that the Serbs would be beaten "by this time next Monday" and that everything was going well.

After services in the cathedral the deputies marched in a body to the palace where the entrances were guarded and roped off and credentials were examined at four different stages before the people's representatives were finally seated in the Weisser Saal. Entering quietly, accompanied by several generals, the Kaiser sat down on the throne. Bethmann, in the uniform of the Dragoon Guards, took his speech from the royal portfolio and handed it to the Kaiser, who stood up, looking small beside the Chancellor, and read it, his helmet on his head and one hand resting on his sword hilt. Without mentioning Belgium he declared, "We draw the sword with a clear conscience and with clean hands." The war had been provoked by Serbia with the support of Russia. Hoots and cries of "Shame!" were evoked by a discourse on Russian iniquities. After the prepared speech, the Kaiser raised his voice and proclaimed, "From this day on I recognize no parties but only Germans!" and called upon party leaders, if they agreed with these sentiments, to step forward and shake his hand. Amid "wild excitement" all did, while the rest of the assembly erupted in cheers and shouts of fervent rejoicing.

At three o'clock members reconvened in the Reichstag to hear an address by the Chancellor and to perform the remainder of their duty which consisted first of voting war credits and then adjournment. The Social Democrats agreed to make the vote unanimous, and spent their last hours of parliamentary responsibility in anxious consultation whether to join in a *"Hoch!"* for the Kaiser which they satisfactorily resolved by making it a *Hoch* for "Kaiser, People, and Country."

Everyone, as Bethmann rose to speak, waited in painful expectancy for what he had to say about Belgium. A year ago Foreign Minister Jagow had assured a secret session of the Reichstag steering committee that Germany would never violate Belgium, and General von Heeringen, then War Minister, had promised that the Supreme Command in the event of war would respect Belgium's neutrality as long as Germany's enemies did. On August 4 deputies did not know that their armies had invaded

Belgium that morning. They knew of the ultimatum but nothing of the Belgian reply because the German government, wishing to give the impression that Belgium had acquiesced and that her armed resistance was therefore illegal, never published it.

"Our troops," Bethmann informed the tense audience, "have occupied Luxembourg and perhaps"—the "perhaps" was posthumous by eight hours —"are already in Belgium." (Great commotion.) True, France had given Belgium a pledge to respect her neutrality, but "We knew that France was standing ready to invade Belgium" and "we could not wait." It was, he said inevitably, a case of military necessity, and "necessity knows no law."

So far he had his hearers, both the right which despised him and the left which mistrusted him, in thrall. His next sentence created a sensation. "Our invasion of Belgium is contrary to international law but the wrong —I speak openly—that we are committing we will make good as soon as our military goal has been reached." Admiral Tirpitz considered this the greatest blunder ever spoken by a German statesman; Conrad Haussman, a leader of the Liberal party, considered it the finest part of the speech. The act having been confessed in a public *mea culpa*, he and his fellow deputies of the left felt purged of guilt and saluted the Chancellor with a loud *"Sehr richtig!"* In a final striking phrase—and before his day of memorable maxims was over he was to add one more that would make him immortal—Bethmann said that whoever was as badly threatened as were the Germans could think only of how to "hack his way through."

A war credit of five billion marks was voted unanimously, after which the Reichstag voted itself out of session for four months or for what was generally expected to be the duration. Bethmann closed the proceedings with an assurance that carried overtones of the gladiators' salute: "Whatever our lot may be, August 4, 1914, will remain for all eternity one of Germany's greatest days!"

That evening at seven o'clock England's answer, awaited so long in such anxiety by so many, was finally made definitive. That morning the British government had finally screwed its determination to the sticking point sufficiently to deliver an ultimatum. It arrived, however, in two parts. First, Grey asked for an assurance that German demands upon Belgium would not be "proceeded with" and for an "immediate reply," but as he attached no time limit and mentioned no sanctions in case of non-reply, the message was not technically an ultimatum. He waited until after he knew the German Army had invaded Belgium before sending the second notice stating that Britain felt bound "to uphold the neutrality of Belgium and the observance of the treaty to which Germany is as much a party as ourselves." A "satisfactory reply" was demanded by midnight, failing which the British ambassador was to ask for his passports.

Why the ultimatum was not sent the night before, immediately after Parliament made plain its acceptance of Grey's speech, can only be explained by the government's irresolute state of mind. What sort of "satisfactory reply" it expected, short of the Germans meekly retreating across the frontier they had deliberately and irrevocably crossed that morning, and why England agreed to wait for so fanciful a phenomenon until midnight, can hardly be explained at all. In the Mediterranean that night the lost hours before midnight were to be crucial.

In Berlin, the British ambassador, Sir Edward Goschen, presented the ultimatum in a historic interview with the Chancellor. He found Bethmann "very agitated." According to Bethmann himself, "my blood boiled at this hypocritical harping on Belgium which was not the thing that had driven England into war." Indignation launched Bethmann into a harangue. He said that England was doing an "unthinkable" thing in making war on a "kindred nation," that "it was like striking a man from **behind while he was fighting for his life** against two assailants," that as a result of "this last terrible step" England would be responsible for all the dreadful events that might follow, and "all for just a word—'neutrality'—just for a scrap of paper. . . ."

Hardly noticing the phrase that was to resound round the world, Goschen included it in his report of the interview. He had replied that, if for strategical reasons it was a matter of life or death for Germany to advance through Belgium, it was, so to speak, a matter of life or death for Britain to keep her solemn compact. "His Excellency was so excited, so evidently overcome by the news of our action, and so little disposed to hear reason," that he refrained from further argument.

As he was leaving, two men in a press car of the *Berliner Tageblatt* drove through the streets throwing out flyers which announced—somewhat prematurely, as the ultimatum did not expire until midnight—Britain's declaration of war. Coming after Italy's defection, this last act of "treason," this latest desertion, this one further addition to their enemies infuriated the Germans, a large number of whom immediately became transformed into a howling mob which occupied itself for the next hour in stoning all the windows of the British Embassy. England became overnight the most hated enemy; *"Rassen-verrat!"* (race treason) the favorite hate slogan. The Kaiser, in one of the least profound of all comments on the war, lamented: "To think that George and Nicky should have played me false! If my grandmother had been alive she would never have allowed it."

Germans could not get over the perfidy of it. It was unbelievable that the English, having degenerated to the stage where suffragettes heckled the Prime Minister and defied the police, were going to fight. England, though wide-flung and still powerful, was getting old, and they felt for her, like the Visigoths for the later Romans, a contempt combined with the newcomer's sense of inferiority. The English think they can "treat us like Portugal," complained Admiral Tirpitz.

England's betrayal deepened their sense of friendlessness. They were conscious of being an unloved nation. How was it that Nice, annexed by France in 1860, could settle down comfortably and within a few years forget it had ever been Italian, whereas half a million Alsatians preferred to leave their homeland rather than live under German rule? "Our country is not much loved anywhere and indeed frequently hated," the Crown Prince noted on his travels.

While the crowds shrieked for vengeance in the Wilhelmstrasse, depressed deputies of the left gathered in cafés and groaned together. "The whole world is rising against us," said one. "Germanism has three enemies in the world—Latins, Slavs and Anglo-Saxons—and now they are all united against us."

"Our diplomacy has left us no friend but Austria, and it was we who had to support her," said another.

"At least one good thing is that it can't last long," a third consoled them. "We shall have peace in four months. Economically and financially we can't last longer than that."

"One hopes for the Turks and Japanese," someone else suggested.

A rumor had in fact swept the cafés the previous evening when diners heard distant hurrahs shouted in the streets. As a diarist of the time recorded it: "They came nearer. People listened, then jumped up. The hurrahs became louder; they resounded over Potsdamer Platz and reached the proportions of a storm. The guests left their food and ran out of the restaurant. I followed the stream. What has happened? 'Japan has declared war on Russia!' they roared. Hurrah! Hurrah! Uproarious rejoicing. People embraced one another. 'Long live Japan! Hurrah! Hurrah!' Endless jubilation. Then someone shouted, 'To the Japanese Embassy!' And the crowd rushed away carrying everybody with it and besieged the embassy. 'Long live Japan! Long live Japan!' people shouted impetuously until the Japanese Ambassador finally appeared and, perplexed, stammered his thanks for this unexpected and, it would seem, undeserved homage." Although by next day it was known the rumor was false, just how undeserved was the homage would not be known for another two weeks.

When Ambassador Lichnowsky and his staff subsequently left England, a friend who came to say goodbye was struck by the "sadness and bitterness" of the party at Victoria Station. They were blaming officials at home for dragging them into a war with no allies but Austria.

"What chance have we, attacked on every side? Is no one friendly to Germany?" one official asked mournfully.

"Siam is friendly, I am told," a colleague replied.

No sooner had England delivered herself of the ultimatum than fresh disputes broke out in the Cabinet over the question whether to send an Expeditionary Force to France. Having declared themselves in, they began to dispute how far in they should go. Their joint plans with the French were predicated on an Expeditionary Force of six divisions to arrive in France between M-4 and M-12 and to be ready for action on the extreme left of the French line by M-15. Already the schedule was disrupted because the British M-1 (August 5), which had been expected to be two days behind the French, was now three days behind, and further delay would follow.

Mr. Asquith's cabinet was paralyzed by fear of invasion. In 1909 the Committee of Imperial Defence after a special study of the problem had declared that as long as the home army was kept sufficiently strong to make the Germans mount an invasion force of such size that it could not evade the navy, a large-scale invasion was "impractical." Despite its assurance that the defense of the home islands was adequately guaranteed by the navy, Britain's leaders on August 4 could not summon up the courage to denude the islands of the Regular Army. Arguments were put forward for sending fewer than six divisions, for sending them later rather than sooner, even for not sending them at all. Admiral Jellicoe was told his planned escort of the Expeditionary Force across the Channel would not be required "for the present." No button at the War Office automatically put the BEF in motion because the British government could not make up its mind to push it. The War Office itself, without a minister for the last four months, was distracted for lack of a chief. Asquith had progressed as far as inviting Kitchener up to London, but could not yet nerve himself to offer him the post. The impetuous and tempestuous Sir Henry Wilson, whose uninhibited diary was to cause such anguish when published after the war, was "revolted by such a state of things." So was poor M. Cambon who went, armed with a map, to show Grey how vital it was that the French left should be extended by Britain's six divisions. Grey promised to bring the matter to the attention of the Cabinet.

General Wilson, raging at the delay which he ascribed to Grey's "sinful" hesitation, indignantly showed to his friends in the Opposition a copy of the mobilization order which instead of reading "mobilize and embark," read only "mobilize." This alone, he said, would delay the schedule by four days. Balfour undertook to spur the government. He told them, in a letter addressed to Haldane, that the whole point of the Entente and of the military arrangements which had flowed from it was the preservation of France, for if France were crushed "the whole future of Europe might be changed in a direction we should regard as disastrous." Having adopted that policy, the thing to do, he suggested, was "to strike quickly and strike with your whole strength." When Haldane came to see him to explain the nature of the Cabinet's hesitations, Balfour could not help feeling they were marked by "a certain wooliness of thought and indecision of purpose."

That afternoon of August 4, at about the time when Bethmann was addressing the Reichstag and Viviani the Chambre des Députés, Mr. Asquith announced to the House of Commons a "message from His Majesty signed by his own hand." Mr. Speaker rose from his chair and members uncovered while the Mobilization Proclamation was read. Next, from typewritten copy that trembled slightly in his hand, Asquith read the terms of the ultimatum just telegraphed to Germany. When he came to the words "a satisfactory answer by midnight," a solemn cheer rose from the benches.

All that was left was to wait for midnight (eleven o'clock, British time). At nine o'clock the government learned, through an intercepted but uncoded telegram sent out from Berlin, that Germany had considered itself at war with Britain from the moment when the British ambassador had asked for his passports. Hastily summoned, the Cabinet debated whether to declare war as of that moment or wait for the time limit set by the ultimatum to expire. They decided to wait. In silence, each encased in his private thoughts, they sat around the green table in the ill-lit Cabinet room, conscious of the shadows of those who at other fateful moments had sat there before them. Eyes watched the clock ticking away the time limit. "Boom!" Big Ben struck the first note of eleven, and each note thereafter sounded to Lloyd George, who had a Celtic ear for melodrama, like "Doom, doom, doom!"

Twenty minutes later the War Telegram, "War, Germany, act," was dispatched. Where and when the army was to act was still unsettled, the decision having been left for a War Council called for the following day. The British government went to bed a belligerent, if something less than bellicose.

Next day, with the assault on Liège, the first battle of the war began. Europe was entering, Moltke wrote that day to Conrad von Hötzendorff, upon "the struggle that will decide the course of history for the next hundred years."

▶▶▶

▶▶▶

▶▶▶ *BATTLE*

▶▶▶ *10* ▶

▶▶▶ "Goeben . . . *An Enemy*
Then Flying"

BEFORE THE LAND BATTLE BEGAN, A WIRELESS
message from the German Admiralty to the German Commander in the
Mediterranean, Admiral Wilhelm Souchon, flickered through the air in
the pre-dawn hours of August 4. It read: "Alliance with Turkey concluded
August 3. Proceed at once to Constantinople." Although its expectations
proved premature and it was almost immediately canceled, Admiral
Souchon decided to proceed as directed. His command consisted of two
fast new ships, the battle cruiser *Goeben* and the light cruiser *Breslau*. No
other single exploit of the war cast so long a shadow upon the world as
the voyage accomplished by their commander during the next seven days.

Turkey at the time of Sarajevo had many enemies and no allies because
no one considered her worth an alliance. For a hundred years the Ottoman
Empire, called the "Sick Man" of Europe, had been considered moribund
by the hovering European powers who were waiting to fall upon the
carcass. But year after year the fabulous invalid refused to die, still grasping

in decrepit hands the keys to immense possessions. Indeed, during the last six years, ever since the Young Turk Revolution overthrew the old Sultan "Abdul the Damned," in 1908, and established under his more amenable brother a government by the "Committee of Union and Progress," Turkey had begun to be rejuvenated.

The "Committee," otherwise the Young Turks, led by their "little Napoleon," Enver Bey, determined to remake the country, forge the strength necessary to hold the slipping bonds of empire, fend off the waiting eagles, and retrieve the Pan-Islamic dominion of the days of Ottoman glory. The process was watched with no relish at all by Russia, France, and England, who had rival ambitions in the area. Germany, late on the imperial scene and with Berlin-to-Bagdad dreams of her own, determined to become the Young Turks' patron. A German military mission sent in 1913 to reorganize the Turkish Army caused such furious Russian resentment that only concerted effort by the Powers to provide a face-saving device prevented the affair from becoming that "damned foolish thing in the Balkans" a year before Sarajevo.

From then on, the Turks felt creeping over them the shadow of the oncoming day when they would have to choose sides. Fearing Russia, resenting England, mistrusting Germany, they could not decide. The "Hero of the Revolution," handsome young Enver with his pink cheeks and black mustache worn in upturned points like the Kaiser's, was the only wholehearted and enthusiastic advocate of a German alliance. Like some later thinkers, he believed in the Germans as the wave of the future. Talaat Bey, political "Boss" of the "Committee," and its real ruler, a stout Levantine adventurer who could devour a pound of caviar at a sitting, washed down by two glasses of brandy and two bottles of champagne, was less sure. He believed Turkey could obtain a better price from Germany than from the Entente, and he had no faith in Turkey's chances of survival as a neutral in a war of the Great Powers. If the Entente Powers won, Ottoman possessions would crumble under their pressure; if the Central Powers won, Turkey would become a German vassal. Other groups in the Turkish government would have preferred an alliance with the Entente, if it had been obtainable, in the hope of buying off Russia, Turkey's age-old enemy. For ten centuries Russia had yearned for Constantinople, the city Russians called Czargrad that lay at the exit of the Black Sea. That narrow and famous sea passage, called the Dardanelles, fifty miles long and nowhere more than three miles wide, was Russia's only year-round egress to the rest of the world.

Turkey had one asset of inestimable value—her geographical position at the junction of the paths of empire. For that reason England had been for a hundred years Turkey's traditional protector, but the truth was that England no longer took Turkey seriously. After a century of supporting the Sultan against all comers because she preferred a weak, debilitated, and therefore malleable despot astride her road to India, England was at last beginning to tire of the fetters that bound her to what Winston Churchill amicably called "scandalous, crumbling, decrepit, penniless Turkey." The Turkish reputation for misrule, corruption, and cruelty had been a stench in the nostrils of Europe for a long time. The Liberals who had governed England since 1906 were the inheritors of Gladstone's celebrated appeal to expel the unspeakable Turk, "the one great anti-human specimen of humanity," from Europe. Their policy was shaped by an image half Sick Man, half Terrible Turk. Lord Salisbury's sporting metaphor after the Crimean War, "We have put our money on the wrong horse," acquired the status of prophecy. British influence at the Porte was allowed to lapse just at the time when it might have proved beyond price.

A request by Turkey for a permanent alliance with Great Britain was turned down in 1911 through the medium of Winston Churchill who had visited Constantinople in 1909 and established "amicable relations," as he conceived them, with Enver and other Young Turk ministers. In the imperial style used for addressing Oriental states, he suggested that although Britain could accept no alliance, Turkey would do well not to alienate British friendship by "reverting to the oppressive methods of the old regime or seeking to disturb the British status quo as it now exists." Superbly surveying the world from his Admiralty post, he reminded Turkey that British friendship would be of value so long as Britain "alone among European states . . . retains supremacy of the sea." That Turkey's friendship or even her neutrality might be of equal value to Britain was never seriously considered by him or any other minister.

In July 1914, with the two-front war looming before them, the Germans suddenly became anxious to secure the ally who could close the Black Sea exit and cut Russia off from her allies and their supplies. An earlier Turkish proposal of alliance that had been left dangling now suddenly looked desirable. The Kaiser in his alarm insisted that "the thing to do now is to get every gun in readiness in the Balkans to shoot against the Slavs." When Turkey began to haggle over terms, and made a show of leaning toward the Entente, the Kaiser in increasing panic directed his ambassador to

reply to the Turkish offer "with unmistakably plain compliance. . . .
Under no circumstances at all can we afford to turn them away."

On July 28, the day Austria declared war on Serbia, Turkey formally
asked Germany for a secret offensive and defensive alliance to become
operative in the event of either party going to war with Russia. Within
the same day, the offer was received in Berlin, accepted and a draft treaty
signed by the Chancellor telegraphed back. At the last moment the Turks
had difficulty bringing themselves to the point of tying the knot that would
tie their fate to Germany's. If only they could be sure Germany would
win . . .

While they were hesitating England helpfully gave them a push by
seizing two Turkish battleships then being built under contract in British
yards. They were first-class capital ships equal to the best of Britain's, one
of which was armed with 13.5-inch guns. The spirited First Lord "requisitioned"—to use his own word—the Turkish warships on July 28. One, the
Sultan Osman, had been completed in May and a first installment already
paid, but when the Turks wished to bring her home, the British, supplying
sinister hints about a Greek plot to attack her by submarine, had persuaded
them to leave her in Britain until her sister ship, the *Reshadieh*, was completed and the two could return together. When the *Reshadieh* was ready
early in July, further excuses for departure were offered. Speed and gunnery
trials were unaccountably delayed. On learning of Churchill's order, the
Turkish captain, who was waiting with five hundred Turkish sailors aboard
a transport in the Tyne, threatened to board his ships and hoist the Turkish
flag. Not without relish the voice at the Admiralty gave orders to resist
such an attempt "by armed force if necessary."

The ships had cost Turkey the immense sum—for that time—of
$30,000,000. The money had been raised by popular subscription after their
defeats in the Balkan Wars aroused the Turkish public to the need of
renovating the armed forces. Every Anatolian peasant had supplied his
penny. Although not yet known to the public, news of the seizure caused,
as Djemal Pasha, the Naval Minister, not excessively put it, "mental
anguish" to his government.

England took no pains to assuage it. Grey, when officially informing
the Turks of this simple piece of piracy on the Tyne, felt sure Turkey
would understand why England found it necessary to take the ships for
her "own needs in this crisis." The financial and other loss to Turkey—a
matter of "sincere regret" to His Majesty's Government—would, he
blandly said, be given "due consideration." Compensation he did not

mention. Under the cumulative effect of the "Sick Man" and "wrong horse" concepts, England had come to regard the entire Ottoman Empire as of less account than two extra warships. Grey's telegram of regrets was sent on August 3. On the same day Turkey signed the treaty of alliance with Germany.

She did not, however, declare war on Russia, as she was pledged to do, or close the Black Sea or take any action publicly compromising strict neutrality. Having obtained an alliance with a major power on her own terms, Turkey proved in no hurry to help her new ally. Her uncertain ministers preferred to wait to see which way the opening battles of the war would go. Germany was far away, whereas the Russians and British were a near and ever-present menace. The now certain entry of England in the war was causing serious second thoughts. Afraid of just such a development, the German government instructed its ambassador, Baron Wangenheim, to obtain Turkey's declaration of war on Russia "today if possible," for it was "of the greatest importance to prevent the Porte from escaping from us under the influence of England's action." The Porte, however, did not comply. All except Enver wished to delay an overt act against Russia until the progress of the war revealed some sign of its probable outcome.

In the Mediterranean gray shapes were maneuvering for coming combat. Wireless operators, tensely listening to their earphones, took down operational orders from far-away Admiralties. The immediate and primary task of the British and French fleets was to safeguard the passage from North Africa to France of the French Colonial Corps which, with its three instead of the normal two divisions, and its auxiliary arms, numbered over 80,000 men. The presence or absence of an entire army corps from its designated place in the line could be decisive upon the French plan of battle, and the war, as both sides believed, would be determined by the fate of France in the opening clash with Germany.

Both French and British Admiralties had their eyes fixed on the *Goeben* and *Breslau* as the chief menace to the French troop transports. The French had the largest fleet in the Mediterranean, with a force available for protecting their transports of 16 battleships, 6 cruisers, and 24 destroyers. The British Mediterranean fleet, based on Malta, while lacking dreadnoughts, was headed by three battle cruisers, *Inflexible*, *Indomitable*, and *Indefatigable*, each of 18,000 tons with an armament of eight 12-inch guns and a speed of 27 to 28 knots. They were designed to overtake and annihilate anything that floated except a battleship of the dreadnought class. In addition the British fleet included four armored cruisers of 14,000 tons, four light cruisers of under 5,000 tons, and 14 destroyers. The Italian fleet was neutral. The Austrian fleet, based on Pola at the head of the Adriatic, had eight active capital ships, including two new dreadnoughts with 12-inch guns and an appropriate number of other ships. A paper tiger, it was unprepared and proved inactive.

Germany, with the second largest fleet in the world, had only two warships in the Mediterranean. One was the battle cruiser *Goeben*, of 23,000 tons, as large as a dreadnought, with a recorded trial speed of 27.8 knots equal to that of the British *Inflexibles* and an approximately equal firepower. The other was the *Breslau* of 4,500 tons, a ship on a par with the British light cruisers. Because of her speed, which was greater than that of any French battleship or cruiser, the *Goeben* "would easily be able," according to the dire forecast depicted by the British First Lord, "to avoid the French battle squadrons and brushing aside or outstripping their cruisers, break in upon the transports and sink one after another of these vessels crammed with soldiers." If there was one thing characteristic of British naval thinking prior to the outbreak of war, it was the tendency to credit the German Navy with far greater audacity and willingness to take risks against odds than either the British themselves would have shown or than the Germans in fact did show when the test came.

To be ready to attack the French transports was indeed one reason why the *Goeben* and her consort had been sent to cruise the Mediterranean after their launching in 1912. At the final moment Germany discovered they had a more important function to perform. On August 3 when the Germans realized the need to bring every possible pressure upon the reluctant Turks to declare war, Admiral Tirpitz ordered Admiral Souchon to Constantinople.

Souchon, a dark, compact, and incisive sailor of fifty, had raised his flag aboard the *Goeben* in 1913. Since then he had steamed the inland seas and straits of his new command, roamed its coasts and capes, rounded its islands, visited its ports, familiarizing himself with the places and personalities with which he might have to deal in the event of war. He had been to Constantinople and met the Turks; he had exchanged courtesies with Italians, Greeks, Austrians, and French, with all but the British, who, he reported to the Kaiser, rigorously refused to allow their ships to anchor in the same ports at the same time as the Germans. Their habit was always to appear immediately afterward in order to wipe out any impression the

Germans might have made, or, as the Kaiser elegantly expressed it, "to spit in the soup."

At Haifa when he heard the news of Sarajevo, Souchon immediately felt a premonition of war and a simultaneous concern for his boilers. They had been leaking steam for some time, and the *Goeben* was in fact scheduled to be replaced by the *Moltke* in October and return to Kiel for repairs. Deciding to prepare for the worst at once, Souchon departed for Pola, after telegraphing ahead to the Admiralty to send him new boiler tubes and skilled repairmen to meet him there. Through July the work proceeded feverishly. Everyone in the crew who could wield a hammer was pressed into service. In eighteen days 4,000 damaged tubes were located and replaced. Still the repairs were not finished when Souchon received his warning telegram and left Pola lest he be bottled up in the Adriatic.

On August 1 he reached Brindisi on the heel of Italy where the Italians, making excuses about the sea being too choppy for tenders, refused him coal. Clearly Italy's anticipated betrayal of the Triple Alliance was about to become a fact, depriving Souchon of her coaling facilities. He assembled his officers to discuss what should be their course of action. Their chances of breaking through the Allied screen to the Atlantic, while inflicting what damage they could upon the French transports on their way, depended upon their speed, and this depended in turn upon the boilers.

"How many boilers leaking steam?" Souchon asked his aide.

"Two during the last four hours."

"Damn!" said the Admiral, raging at the fate which crippled his splendid ship at such an hour. He decided to make for Messina where he could rendezvous with German merchant ships from whom he could obtain coal. For the event of war Germany had divided the world's seas into a system of districts, each under a German Supply Officer, who was empowered to assign all vessels in his area to places where German warships could meet them and to commandeer the resources of German banks and business firms for the warships' needs.

All day the *Goeben*'s wireless, as she rounded the Italian boot, tapped out orders to German commercial steamers, calling them into Messina. At Taranto she was joined by the *Breslau*.

"Urgent. German ship *Goeben* at Taranto," wired the British consul on August 2. The view halloo stirred ardent hopes at the Admiralty of first blood for the British Navy; locating the enemy was half the battle. But as Britain was not yet at war, the hunt could not yet be loosed. Ever on

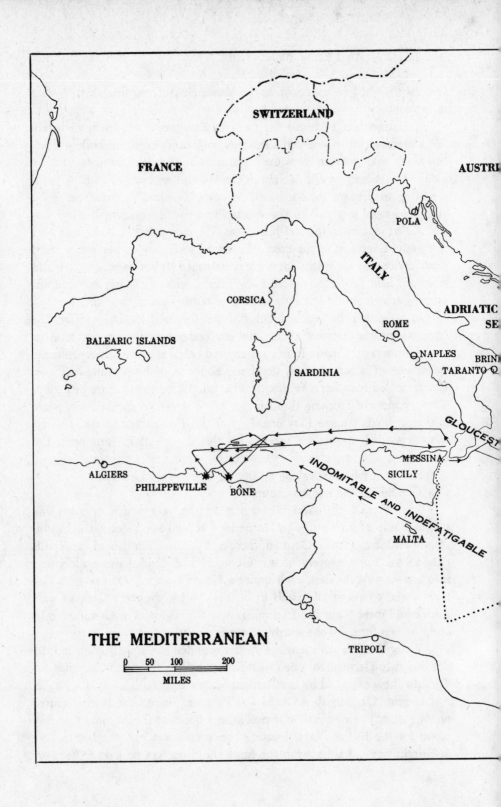

THE MEDITERRANEAN

SWITZERLAND

FRANCE

AUSTR

POLA

ITALY

CORSICA

ROME

ADRIATIC

SE

BALEARIC ISLANDS

NAPLES

BRIN

TARANTO

SARDINIA

GLOUCEST

MESSINA

SICILY

ALGIERS

PHILIPPEVILLE

BÔNE

INDOMITABLE AND INDEFATIGABLE

MALTA

TRIPOLI

0   50   100   200

MILES

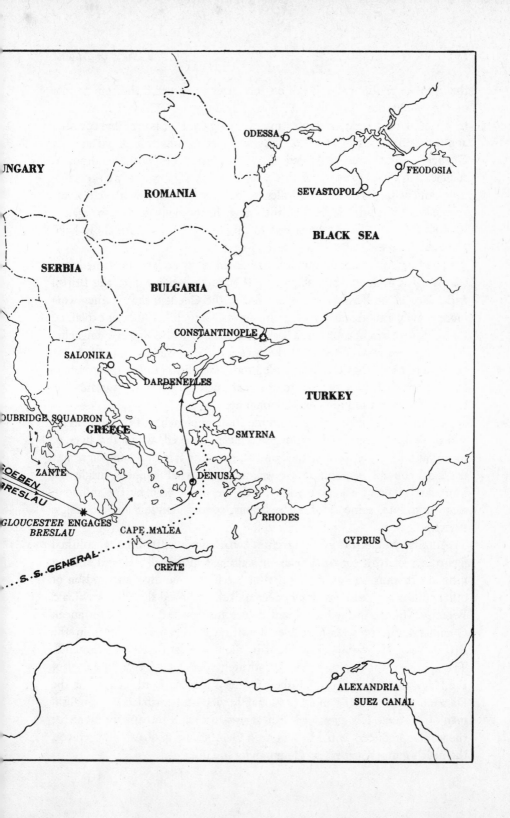

the tiptoe of readiness Churchill on July 31 had instructed the commander
of the Mediterranean Fleet, Admiral Sir Berkeley Milne, that his first
task would be to aid in protecting the French transports "by covering
and if possible bringing to action individual fast German ships, particularly
Goeben." Milne was reminded that "the speed of your Squadrons is
sufficient to enable you to choose your moment." However, at the same
time, and with a certain ambivalence, he was told "husband your force
at the outset" and "do not at this stage be brought to action against
superior forces." The last edict was to ring like a buoy's melancholy knell
through the events of the next several days.

The "superior force" Churchill had in mind, as he later explained, was
the Austrian fleet. Its battleships bore the same relationship to the British
Inflexibles as the French battleships did to the *Goeben*; that is, they were
more heavily armored and armed but slower. Churchill also later explained
that his order was not intended "as a veto upon British ships ever engaging
superior forces however needful the occasion." If it was not intended as a
veto, then it must have been intended for commanders to interpret as they
saw fit, which brings the matter to that melting point of warfare—the
temperament of the individual commander.

When the moment of live ammunition approaches, the moment to
which all his professional training has been directed, when the lives of
men under him, the issue of the combat, even the fate of a campaign may
depend upon his decision at a given moment, what happens inside the
heart and vitals of a commander? Some are made bold by the moment,
some irresolute, some carefully judicious, some paralyzed and powerless
to act.

Admiral Milne was made careful. A bachelor of fifty-nine, a polished
figure in society, a former groom in waiting to Edward VII and still an
intimate at court, son of an Admiral of the Fleet, grandson and godson of
other admirals, a keen fisherman, deer stalker, and good shot, Sir Archibald
Berkeley Milne appeared a natural choice in 1911 for the Mediterranean
Command, the most fashionable, if no longer the premier post in the
British Navy. He was appointed to it by the new First Lord, Mr. Churchill.
The appointment was promptly, if privately, denounced as a "betrayal of
the Navy" by Admiral Lord Fisher, former First Sea Lord, creator of the
Dreadnought Fleet, the most passionately vital and least laconic English-
man of his time. His cherished project was to ensure the appointment for
the war he predicted would break out in October, 1914, of Admiral Jellicoe,
the navy's gunnery expert, as Commander in Chief.

When Churchill appointed Milne to the Mediterranean, which Fisher believed put him in line for the post he wanted reserved for Jellicoe, his wrath was tremendous. He lashed out at Winston for "succumbing to court influence"; he roared and fumed and erupted in volcanic disgust for Milne as an "utterly useless commander" and "unfitted to be Senior Admiral afloat and practically Admiralissimo as you have now made him." He referred to him variously as a "backstairs cad," as a "serpent of the lowest type," and as "Sir B. Mean who buys his *Times* second hand for one penny." Everything in Fisher's letters, which always carried flaming admonitions to "Burn this!"—happily ignored by his correspondents— appears ten times life size and must be reduced proportionately if they are to be read in any reasonable relation to reality. Neither a serpent of the lowest type nor a Nelson, Admiral Milne was an average, uninspired orna- ment of the Senior Service. When Fisher discovered that he was not in fact being considered for Commander in Chief, he turned his fiery atten- tions upon other matters, leaving Sir B. Mean in untroubled enjoyment of the Mediterranean.

In June 1914 Milne, too, visited Constantinople, where he dined with the Sultan and his ministers and entertained them aboard his flagship without concerning himself, any more than did other Englishmen, about Turkey's possible place in Mediterranean strategy.

By August 1, after receiving Churchill's first warning, he had assembled at Malta his own squadron of three battle cruisers and the second squadron of armored cruisers, light cruisers, and destroyers commanded by Rear Admiral Sir Ernest Troubridge. Early on August 2 he received a second order from Churchill, saying, "*Goeben* must be shadowed by two battle cruisers" and the Adriatic "watched," presumably against the appearance of the Austrian fleet. The specific order to send two battle cruisers after the *Goeben* clearly envisaged combat, but Milne did not obey it. Instead he sent the *Indomitable* and *Indefatigable* along with Troubridge's squad- ron to watch the Adriatic. Having been informed that the *Goeben* had been seen that morning off Taranto heading southwest, he sent one light cruiser, the *Chatham*, to search the Strait of Messina where he reasoned the *Goeben* would be and where in fact she was. The *Chatham* left Malta at 5:00 P.M., ran through the Strait at seven next morning and reported back that the *Goeben* was not there. The search had missed by six hours, Admiral Souchon having already left.

He had reached Messina the previous afternoon just as Italy declared her neutrality. Again refused coal by the Italians, he was able, however, to take on two thousand tons provided by a German merchant shipping firm. He requisitioned, as a tender, a merchant steamer, the *General* of the German East Africa line, after debarking her passengers who were given the price of a railroad ticket as far as Naples. Having received no orders as yet from his Admiralty, Souchon decided to put himself in a position to taste action at the earliest moment after hostilities should begin and before superior forces could prevent him. In the darkness, at 1:00 A.M. on August 3, he left Messina, heading west toward the Algerian coast where he planned to bombard the French embarkation ports of Bone and Philippeville.

At the same hour Churchill sent a third order to Milne: "Watch on mouth of Adriatic should be maintained but *Goeben* is your objective. Follow her and shadow her wherever she goes and be ready to act upon declaration of war which appears probable and imminent." When he received this, Admiral Milne did not know where the *Goeben* was, the *Chatham* having lost her. He believed she was heading west to attack the French transports, and from a report he had received of a German collier waiting at Majorca he concluded that she would thereafter make for Gibraltar and the open sea. He now detached the *Indomitable* and *Indefatigable* from their watch on the Adriatic and sent them westward to hunt for the *Goeben*. All day of August 3 the *Goeben*, steaming westward from Messina, was followed by her hunters, a day's distance behind.

At the same time the French fleet was steaming across from Toulon to North Africa. It should have left a day earlier, but in Paris on August 2 occurred the unhappy collapse of the Naval Minister, Dr. Gauthier, after he was discovered to have forgotten to send torpedo boats into the Channel. In the uproar that followed, the orders to the Mediterranean fleet suffered. Messimy, the War Minister, became possessed by a need to hasten the arrival of the Colonial Corps. The embarrassed Dr. Gauthier, endeavoring to cover his lapse in the Channel by jumping to the opposite extreme of belligerency, proposed to attack the *Goeben* and *Breslau* before a declaration of war. "His nerves were on edge," President Poincaré thought. The Naval Minister next challenged the War Minister to a duel, but after fervent efforts by their colleagues to separate and calm the combatants, he embraced Messimy in tears and was persuaded to resign for reasons of health.

French uncertainty over the British role, which had not yet been declared, further complicated matters. At 4:00 P.M. the Cabinet managed to compose a more or less coherent telegram to the French Commander in Chief, Admiral Boué de Lapeyrère, which informed him that the *Goeben* and *Breslau* had been sighted at Brindisi, that as soon as he received the signal for the opening of hostilities he was to "stop them," and that he was to protect the transports by covering them, not by convoy.

Admiral de Lapeyrère, a forceful character largely responsible for bringing the French Navy out of its rusty obsolescence, promptly decided to form convoys anyway, since, in his view, the "doubtful" role of the British left him no choice. He started his fires at once and got under way at four o'clock next morning, a few hours after Souchon left Messina. During the next twenty-four hours the three squadrons of the French fleet steamed southward bound for Oran, Algiers, and Philippeville while the *Goeben* and *Breslau* were coming westward toward the same destination.

At 6:00 P.M., August 3, Admiral Souchon's wireless told him that war had been declared on France. He pressed forward, as did the French, but his speed was greater. At 2:00 A.M. on August 4 he was approaching his goal and the climactic moment of fire, when he received Admiral Tirpitz's order to "proceed at once to Constantinople." Unwilling to turn back without, as he wrote, "tasting that moment of fire so ardently desired by us all!" he kept on course until the Algerian coast came in view in the early morning light. He thereupon ran up the Russian flag, approached within range, and opened fire, "sowing death and panic." "Our trick succeeded brilliantly," enthused one of his crew who later published an account of the voyage. According to the *Kriegsbrauch*, or Conduct of War manual issued by the German General Staff, "The putting on of enemy uniforms and the use of enemy or neutral flags or insignia with the aim of deception are declared permissible." As the official embodiment of German thinking on these matters, the *Kriegsbrauch* was considered to supersede Germany's signature on the Hague Convention of which Article 23 prohibited the use of disguise in enemy colors.

After the shelling of Philippeville—and of Bone by the *Breslau*—Admiral Souchon turned back for Messina by the way he had come. He planned to coal there from German merchant steamers before setting course for Constantinople 1,200 miles away.

Admiral de Lapeyrère, hearing of the bombardment by wireless almost at the moment it was happening, assumed the *Goeben* would continue westward, perhaps to attack Algiers next, on her way to break out to the Atlantic. He forced his speed in the hope of intercepting the enemy "if he presented himself." He detached no ships to scout for the *Goeben* because, as he reasoned, if the enemy appeared he would be given battle;

if he did not appear he would be of no further immediate concern. Like everyone else on the Allied side, Admiral de Lapeyrère thought of the *Goeben* purely in terms of naval strategy. That she might perform a political mission, profoundly affecting and prolonging the course of the war, neither he nor anyone else ever considered. When the *Goeben* and *Breslau* did not again appear across the French path, Admiral de Lapeyrère did not seek them out. Thus on the morning of August 4 the first opportunity was lost. Another was immediately offered.

At 9:30 that morning the *Indomitable* and *Indefatigable* which had been steaming west all during the night encountered the *Goeben* and *Breslau* off Bone as the German ships were heading east back to Messina. If Grey had sent his ultimatum to Germany the night before, immediately following his speech to Parliament, Britain and Germany would then have been at war and the cruisers' guns would have spoken. As it was, the ships passed each other in silence at 8,000 yards, well within range, and had to be content with training their guns and omitting the customary exchange of salutes.

Admiral Souchon, bent on putting as much distance between himself and the British as he could before hostilities opened, sped off, straining his ship to the last ounce of speed his boilers could attain. The *Indomitable* and *Indefatigable* turned around and made after him, determined to keep in range until war should be declared. Their wireless, like a huntsman's bugle sounding a find, reported the position to Admiral Milne, who immediately informed the Admiralty, "*Indomitable* and *Indefatigable* shadowing *Goeben* and *Breslau*, 37.44 North, 7:56 East."

The Admiralty quivered in an agony of frustration. There, in the same waters that washed round Cape Trafalgar, British ships had the enemy within range—and could not fire. "Very good. Hold her. War imminent," telegraphed Churchill, and rushed off a "most urgent" minute to the Prime Minister and Grey suggesting that if the *Goeben* attacked the French transports, Milne's cruisers should be authorized "at once to engage her." Unfortunately, when reporting their position, Admiral Milne had neglected to say which way the *Goeben* and *Breslau* were going, so that Churchill assumed they were heading west with further evil intent upon the French.

"Winston with all his war paint on," as Asquith put it, "is longing for a sea fight to sink the *Goeben*." Asquith was willing to let him have it, but the Cabinet to which he unfortunately mentioned the matter, refused to authorize an act of war before the ultimatum should expire at midnight. Thus a second opportunity was lost, though it would have been lost anyway because Churchill's order was contingent upon the *Goeben* attacking the French transports, a goal she had already forsaken.

Now began a desperate chase across the calm summer surface of the sea with Admiral Souchon attempting to outdistance his pursuers and the British attempting to keep him in range until midnight. Driving his ship to its utmost, Souchon brought it up to 24 knots. Stokers who ordinarily could not work in the heat and coal dust for longer than two hours at a time were kept shoveling at an increased pace while bursting tubes scalded them with steam. Four died between morning and evening while the pace was maintained. Slowly, perceptibly, the space between prey and pursuers widened. The *Indomitable* and *Indefatigable*, also suffering from boiler trouble and understaffed furnaces, were not keeping up. In the afternoon they were joined in the long, silent chase by the light cruiser *Dublin* commanded by Captain John Kelly. As the hours wore on, the gap increased until at five o'clock the *Indomitable* and *Indefatigable* dropped out of range. Only the *Dublin* followed, keeping the *Goeben* in sight. At seven o'clock a fog descended. By nine, off the coast of Sicily, the *Goeben* and *Breslau* disappeared in the gathering gloom.

At the Admiralty all during that day Churchill and his staff "suffered the tortures of Tantalus." At 5:00 P.M. the First Sea Lord, Prince Louis of Battenberg, observed there was still time to sink the *Goeben* before dark. Restrained by the Cabinet decision, Churchill could not give the order. While the British waited for the midnight signal, the *Goeben* reached Messina and coal.

When dawn broke the British, now at war and free to fire, could not get at her. From the *Dublin's* last report before contact was lost, they judged she was at Messina, but in the meantime a new obstacle had intervened. An Admiralty order informing Milne of Italy's declaration of neutrality instructed him to "respect this rigidly and not to allow a ship to come within six miles of the Italian coast." The veto, which was designed to prevent some "petty incident" from causing trouble with Italy, was perhaps an excessive caution.

Prohibited by the six-mile limit from entering the Strait of Messina, Admiral Milne put a guard at both exits. As he was convinced that the *Goeben* would again head west, he himself on his flagship *Inflexible*, together with the *Indefatigable*, guarded the exit to the western Mediterranean while only a single light cruiser, the *Gloucester*, commanded by Captain Howard Kelly, brother of the *Dublin's* commander, was sent to patrol the exit to the eastern Mediterranean.* Also because he wanted to concentrate his strength to the west, Admiral Milne sent the *Indomitable* to coal nearby at Bizerte instead of further east at Malta. Thus none of the three *Inflexibles* was in a place where it could intercept the *Goeben* if she went east.

For two days, August 5 and 6, Milne patrolled the waters west of Sicily with the fixed idea that the *Goeben* intended to break westward. The Admiralty, which likewise could think of no other course for the *Goeben* but to break through Gibraltar or hole up at Pola, did not disapprove his arrangements.

During these two days, until the evening of August 6, Admiral Souchon was coaling against difficulties at Messina. The Italians were insisting on the laws of neutrality that required him to depart within twenty-four hours of his arrival. The coaling, which had to be done from German merchant steamers whose decks had to be ripped up and railings torn away to permit the transfer, was taking three times as long as usual. While the Admiral argued points of law with the port authorities, every man in his crew was pressed into shoveling coal. Though encouraged by extra beer rations, band music, and patriotic speeches by the officers, the men kept fainting from exertion in the August heat until blackened and sweat-soaked bodies lay all over the ship like so many corpses. By noon on August 6 when 1,500 tons had been taken on, not enough to reach the Dardanelles, no one was left capable of further effort. "With a heavy heart," Admiral Souchon ordered loading to stop, a rest for all hands, and readiness for departure at five o'clock.

Two messages had reached him at Messina which increased his peril and faced him with a critical decision. Tirpitz's order to go to Constantinople was suddenly canceled by a telegram saying, "For political reasons entry into Constantinople inadvisable at the present time." The reversal was caused by divided counsel in Turkey. Enver had given the German ambassador permission for the *Goeben* and *Breslau* to pass through the mine fields guarding the Dardanelles. Since their passage would clearly violate the neutrality that Turkey was still publicly main-

---

* The Strait of Messina runs north and south with the northern exit giving on the western Mediterranean and the southern exit on the eastern Mediterranean. For the sake of geographical clarity these are referred to as the western and eastern exits respectively.

taining, the Grand Vizier and other ministers insisted the permission must be withdrawn.

Tirpitz's second message informed Souchon that the Austrians could give no naval help to Germany in the Mediterranean, and left it up to Souchon to decide for himself where to go in the circumstances.

His boilers, Souchon knew, could not give him the speed necessary to run through the heavy enemy screen in a dash for Gibraltar. He rebelled against holing himself up in Pola, dependent on the Austrians. He decided to make for Constantinople regardless of orders to the contrary. His purpose, in his own words, was quite definite: "to force the Turks, even against their will, to spread the war to the Black Sea against their ancient enemy, Russia."

He ordered steam up for departure at five o'clock. All on board as well as on shore knew the *Goeben* and *Breslau* were preparing to run a gauntlet against heavy odds. All day excited Sicilians crowded the quays selling postcards and last souvenirs to "those about to die" and hawked extras headlined "In the Claws of Death," "Shame or Defeat," "Voyage to Death or Glory."

Expecting to be pursued, Admiral Souchon deliberately chose to leave while it was still light so that he might be seen steering northward as if for the Adriatic. When night fell he planned to change course to the southeast and elude pursuit under cover of darkness. As he lacked enough coal for the whole voyage, everything depended on his being able, unseen, to make rendezvous with a collier which had been ordered to meet him off Cape Malea at the southeast corner of Greece.

When the *Goeben* and *Breslau* came out of the eastern exit of the Strait of Messina they were immediately seen and followed by the *Gloucester*, which was patrolling outside. As the *Gloucester* was a match for the *Breslau* but could have been knocked out of the sea by the heavy guns of the *Goeben* at 18,000 yards, she could do no more than keep the enemy in sight until reinforcements came up. Captain Kelly telegraphed position and course to Admiral Milne who, with all three battle cruisers, was still patrolling west of Sicily, and followed to seaward of the *Goeben*. As darkness fell, toward eight o'clock he changed course to landward in order to keep the *Goeben* in the light of the moon as it rose on his right. The maneuver brought him within range but did not tempt the *Goeben* to fire. In the clear night the two dark shapes, dogged by a third, ran steadily northward, their smokestacks, owing to inferior coal taken on at Messina, blotching the moonlit sky with black clouds, which rendered them visible at a long distance.

Admiral Milne, on learning that the *Goeben* had left Messina by the eastern exit, stayed where he was. He reasoned that if the *Goeben* continued on her given course she would be intercepted by Admiral Troubridge's squadron which was watching the Adriatic. If, as he was inclined to believe, her course was a feint and she should turn west after all, his own battle cruiser squadron would intercept her. No other possibility occurred to him. Only one ship, the light cruiser *Dublin*, was sent east with orders to join Troubridge's squadron.

Meanwhile Souchon, unable to shake the Gloucester, could not afford to lead a false course any longer if he was to reach the Aegean on his available coal. Shadowed or not he must alter course to the east. At 10:00 P.M. he turned, at the same time jamming the *Gloucester*'s wave length in the hope of preventing his change of course from being reported. He did not succeed. Captain Kelly's wireless, signaling the change of course, reached both Milne and Troubridge about midnight. Milne then set out for Malta where he intended to coal and "continue the chase." It was now up to Troubridge, in whose direction the enemy was coming, to intercept him.

Troubridge had taken up his station at the mouth of the Adriatic under orders to "prevent the Austrians from coming out and the Germans from entering." From the *Goeben*'s course it was clear she was heading away from the Adriatic, but he saw that if he steamed south at once he might be able to head her off. Could he, however, hope to engage her on terms offering a valid hope of victory? His squadron consisted of four armored cruisers, *Defence, Black Prince, Warrior,* and *Duke of Edinburgh,* each of 14,000 tons, with 9.2-inch guns whose range was considerably less than the range of the *Goeben*'s 11-inch guns. The Admiralty's original order, forwarded to him apparently as an instruction by his superior, Admiral Milne, precluded action "against superior forces." Failing to receive any orders from Milne, Troubridge decided to try to intercept the enemy if he could do it before 6:00 A.M. when the first light of dawn in the east would give him favorable visibility and help to equalize the disadvantage of range. He set off at full speed southward shortly after midnight. Four hours later he changed his mind.

As naval attaché with the Japanese during the Russo-Japanese War, Troubridge had learned respect for the efficiency of long-range fire. Besides enjoying the correct lineage from a great-grandfather who had fought with Nelson at the Nile and a reputation as the "handsomest officer in the Navy in his younger days," he "believed in seamanship as a soldier of Cromwell believed in the Bible." Churchill valued him sufficiently to appoint him to the newly created Naval War Staff in 1912. But seamanship and excellence in staff work do not necessarily aid a commander when he faces imminent and deadly combat.

When by 4:00 A.M. Troubridge had not yet found the *Goeben*, he decided he could no longer hope to engage her under favorable circumstances. He believed that in daylight the *Goeben*, if intercepted, could stand off outside his range and sink his four cruisers one after another. While she was engaged in this feat of marksmanship and slaughter, he evidently saw little opportunity for any one of his four cruisers and eight destroyers to reach her by gunfire or torpedo. He decided she was a "superior force" which the Admiralty had said he was not to engage. He broke off the chase, so informed Milne by wireless and, after cruising off the island of Zante until 10:00 A.M., still hoping for one of Milne's battle cruisers to appear, he finally put into the port of Zante preparatory to resuming his watch for the Austrians in the Adriatic. Thus a third opportunity was lost, and the *Goeben*, carrying her tremendous cargo of fate, steamed on her way.

At 5:30 A.M. Milne, still crediting the *Goeben* with intent to turn back to the west, signaled *Gloucester* "gradually to drop astern to avoid capture." Neither he nor the Admiralty yet thought of the *Goeben* as a ship in flight, far more anxious to avoid combat than to court it, and exerting all her skills and speed to reach her distant goal. Rather, under the impression of the Philippeville raid and the years of mounting apprehensions of the German Navy, the English thought of her as a corsair ready to turn and pounce and roam the seas as a commerce raider. They expected to bring her to bay one way or another, but their chase lacked an imperative urgency because, always expecting her to turn, they did not realize she was trying to get away to the East—specifically to the Dardanelles. The failure was less naval than political. "I can recall no great sphere of policy about which the British Government was less completely informed than the Turkish," Churchill admitted ruefully long afterward. The condition was rooted in the Liberals' fundamental dislike of Turkey.

By now it was full daylight of August 7. Only the *Gloucester*, ignoring Milne's signal, was still following the *Goeben* as, rejoined by the *Breslau*, she approached the coast of Greece. Admiral Souchon, who could not afford to meet his collier within enemy view, became desperate to shake off his shadow. He ordered the *Breslau* to drop back in an attempt to ride off the *Gloucester* by passing back and forth in front of her as if laying mines and by other harassing tactics.

Captain Kelly, still expecting reinforcements, became desperate on his part to delay the *Goeben*. When the *Breslau* dropped back to intimidate him, he determined to attack her with intent to force the *Goeben* to turn around to protect her, regardless of whether she was a "superior force" or not. In true damn-the-torpedoes style he opened fire, which was returned by the *Breslau*. As expected the *Goeben* turned and fired too. No hits were scored by anyone. A small Italian passenger steamer en route from Venice to Constantinople, which happened to be passing, witnessed the action. Captain Kelly broke off action against the *Breslau* and dropped back. Admiral Souchon, who could not afford to spend precious coal on a chase, resumed course. Captain Kelly resumed his shadowing.

For three more hours he held on, keeping the *Goeben* in sight until Milne signaled imperatively, forbidding him to continue the pursuit beyond Cape Matapan at the tip of Greece. At 4:30 in the afternoon, as the *Goeben* rounded the Cape to enter the Aegean, the *Gloucester* at last gave up the chase. Free of surveillance, Admiral Souchon disappeared among the isles of Greece to meet his collier.

Some eight hours later, shortly after midnight, having coaled and made repairs, Admiral Milne with the *Inflexible*, *Indomitable*, *Indefatigable*, and the light cruiser *Weymouth* left Malta heading east. Proceeding at 12 knots, perhaps because he thought speed at this stage was a waste of coal, his pursuit was unhurried. At two o'clock next afternoon, August 8, when he was about halfway between Malta and Greece, he was brought to a sharp halt by word from the Admiralty that Austria had declared war on England. Unfortunately the word was an error by a clerk who released the prearranged code telegram for hostilities with Austria by mistake. It was enough to make Milne abandon the chase and take up a position where he could not be cut off from Malta by the possible emergence of the Austrian fleet and where he ordered Troubridge's squadron and the *Gloucester* to join him. One more opportunity was lost.

They remained concentrated there for nearly twenty-four hours until noon next day when, upon learning from an embarrassed Admiralty that Austria had not declared war after all, Admiral Milne once more resumed the hunt. By this time the *Goeben's* trail, since she was last seen entering the Aegean on the afternoon of August 7, was over forty hours old. Trying to decide in what direction to look for her, Admiral Milne, according to his own later account, considered four possible courses the *Goeben* might take. He still thought she might attempt to escape westward to the Atlantic, or might head south to attack the Suez Canal, or might seek refuge in a Greek port or even attack Salonika—two rather exotic suppositions in view of the fact that Greece was neutral. For some reason he did not credit Admiral Souchon with intent to violate Turkish neutrality; the Dardanelles as a destination did not occur to Admiral Milne any more than it did to the Admiralty at home. His strategy, as he conceived it, was to keep the *Goeben* bottled up in Aegean "to the north."

"To the north" was, of course, exactly where Souchon was going, but as the Turks had mined the entrance to the Straits he could not enter without their permission. He could go no further until he had coaled and communicated with Constantinople. His collier, the *Bogadir*, was waiting in Greek disguise at Cape Malea as ordered. Fearing to be discovered, he ordered it to make for Denusa, an island farther inside the Aegean. Unaware that the British chase had been discontinued, he lay low all during the day of August 8 and crept in to the deserted coast of Denusa only on the morning of the 9th. Here, all day, the *Goeben* and *Breslau* coaled while steam was kept up in their boilers so that they might depart on half an hour's notice. A lookout post was erected on a hilltop to keep watch for the British who were then five hundred miles away keeping watch for the Austrians.

Admiral Souchon did not dare use his wireless to communicate with Constantinople because a signal strong enough to cover the distance would have at the same time betrayed his location to the enemy. He ordered the *General*, which had followed him from Messina along a more southerly course, to go to Smyrna and from there transmit a message to the German naval attaché in Constantinople: "Indispensable military necessity requires attack upon enemy in Black Sea. Go to any lengths to arrange for me to pass through Straits at once with permission of Turkish Government if possible, without formal approval if necessary."

All day of the 9th Souchon waited for an answer. At one moment his wireless operators picked up a garbled text, but its meaning could not be deciphered. Night came without a reply. By this time Milne's squadron, having discovered the Austrian error, was advancing toward the Aegean again. Souchon decided, if no answer came, to force the Dardanelles if necessary. At 3:00 A.M. of August 10 he heard the wireless signals of the British squadron as it entered the Aegean. He could wait no longer. Just then a different series of syncopated buzzes came over the earphones. It was the *General,* at last, transmitting the Delphic message: "Enter. Demand surrender of forts. Capture pilot."

Uncertain whether this meant him to make a show of force to save Turkish face or whether he would have to force his way through, Souchon left Denusa at dawn. While all day he steamed north at 18 knots, all day Admiral Milne cruised across the exit of the Aegean to prevent him from coming out. At four that afternoon Souchon sighted Tenedos and the plains of Troy; at five he reached the entrance to the historic and impregnable passageway under the guns of the great fortress of Chanak. With his crew at battle stations and every nerve on board stretched in suspense, he slowly approached. The signal flag, "Send a pilot," fluttered up his mast.

That morning there arrived at Constantinople the small Italian passenger steamer which had witnessed the *Gloucester*'s action against the *Goeben* and *Breslau.* Among its passengers were the daughter, son-in-law, and three grandchildren of the American ambassador Mr. Henry Morgenthau. They brought an exciting tale of the boom of guns, puffs of white smoke, and the twisting and maneuvering of faraway ships. The Italian captain had told them that two of the ships were the *Goeben* and *Breslau* which had just made their notorious exit from Messina. Mr. Morgenthau, having occasion to meet Ambassador Wangenheim a few hours later, mentioned his daughter's story, in which Wangenheim displayed "an agitated interest." Immediately after lunch, accompanied by his Austrian colleague, he appeared at the American Embassy where the two ambassadors "planted themselves solemnly in chairs" in front of the American lady and "subjected her to a most minute, though very polite, cross-examination. . . . They would not permit her to leave out a single detail; they wished to know how many shots had been fired, what direction the German ships had taken, what everybody on board had said and so on. . . . They left the house in almost jubilant mood."

They had learned that the *Goeben* and *Breslau* had escaped the British fleet. It remained to obtain Turkish consent to let them through the Dardanelles. Enver Pasha, who as War Minister controlled the mine fields, was more than willing but he had to play a complicated game vis-à-vis his more nervous colleagues. A member of the German Military

Mission was with him that afternoon when another member, Lieutenant
Colonel von Kress, was urgently announced. Kress said that the commander at the Chanak reported the *Goeben* and *Breslau* requesting permission to enter the Straits and wanted immediate instructions. Enver
replied he could not decide without consulting the Grand Vizier. Kress
insisted that the fort required an answer at once. Enver sat perfectly
silent for several minutes, and then said abruptly, "They are to be allowed
to enter."

Kress and the other officer, who had unconsciously been holding their
breaths, found themselves breathing again.

"If the English warships follow them in are they to be fired on?"
Kress next asked. Again Enver refused to answer, pleading that the
Cabinet must be consulted; but Kress insisted that the fort could not
be left without definite instructions.

"Are the English to be fired on or not?" A long pause followed.
Finally Enver answered, "Yes."

At the entrance to the Straits, 150 miles away, a Turkish destroyer put
out from shore and approached the *Goeben*, watched in tense anxiety by
every eye on deck. A signal flag fluttered briefly and was recognized as
"Follow me." At nine o'clock that evening, August 10, the *Goeben* and
Breslau entered the Dardanelles, bringing, as long afterward Churchill
somberly acknowledged, "more slaughter, more misery and more ruin than
has ever before been borne within the compass of a ship."

Instantly telegraphed round the world, the news reached Malta that
night. Admiral Milne, still probing among the Aegean islands, learned
it at noon next day. So little did his superiors understand the mission of
the *Goeben* that they instructed him to establish a blockade of the
Dardanelles "in case the German ships came out."

Prime Minister Asquith's comment on the news was that it was
"interesting." But, he wrote in his diary, "as we shall insist" on the
Goeben's crew being replaced by Turks who will not be able to navigate
her, "it does not much matter." To "insist" appeared to Asquith to be
all that was necessary.

Allied ambassadors at once insisted, furiously and repeatedly. The
Turks, still hoping to hold on to neutrality as a bargaining counter,
decided to ask the Germans to disarm the *Goeben* and *Breslau* "temporarily and superficially only," but Wangenheim, invited to hear this proposal,

absolutely refused. After further agitated discussion, one minister suddenly suggested: "Could not the Germans have sold us these ships? Could not their arrival be regarded as delivery under contract?"

Everyone was delighted with this superb idea which not only solved a dilemma but dealt the British poetic justice for their seizure of the two Turkish battleships. With Germany's agreement, announcement of the sale was made to the diplomatic corps, and shortly thereafter the *Goeben* and *Breslau*, renamed the *Jawus* and *Midilli*, flying the Turkish flag and with their crews wearing Turkish fezzes, were reviewed by the Sultan amid the wild enthusiasm of his people. The sudden appearance of the two German warships, as if sent by a genie to take the place of the two of which they had been robbed, put the populace in transports of delight and invested the Germans with a halo of popularity.

Still the Turks postponed the declaration of war for which Germany was pressing. Instead, they themselves began demanding from the Allies an increasing price for their neutrality. Russia was so alarmed by the *Goeben*'s arrival at the doors of the Black Sea that she was willing to pay. Like the sinner who renounces lifelong bad habits when in extremity, she was even ready to renounce Constantinople. On August 13 Foreign Minister Sazonov proposed to France to offer Turkey a solemn guarantee of her territorial integrity and a promise of "great financial advantages at the expense of Germany" in return for her neutrality. He was actually willing to include a promise that Russia would abide by the guarantee "even if we are victorious."

The French agreed and "moved heaven and earth," in the words of President Poincaré, to keep Turkey quiet and neutral and to persuade Britain to join in a joint guarantee of Turkish territory. But the British could not bring themselves to bargain or pay for the neutrality of their onetime protégé. Churchill, at his "most bellicose" and "violently anti-Turk," proposed to the Cabinet to send a torpedo flotilla through the Dardanelles to sink the *Goeben* and *Breslau*. It was the one gesture which might have carried weight with vacillating Turks and the only gesture which could have prevented what ultimately happened. One of the keenest and boldest minds in France had already suggested it on the day the Straits were violated. "We should go right in after them," said General Gallieni; "otherwise Turkey will come in against us." In the British Cabinet Churchill's idea was vetoed by Lord Kitchener, who said England could not afford to alienate the Moslems by taking the offensive against Turkey. Turkey should be left "to strike the first blow."

For nearly three months, while the Allies alternately blustered and bargained and while German military influence at Constantinople daily increased, the groups within the Turkish government disputed and wavered. By the end of October, Germany determined that their endless procrastination must be brought to an end. Turkey's active belligerency, in order to blockade Russia from the south, had become imperative.

On October 28 the former *Goeben* and *Breslau*, under Admiral Souchon's command and accompanied by several Turkish torpedo boats, entered the Black Sea and shelled Odessa, Sevastopol, and Feodosia, causing some civilian loss of life and sinking a Russian gunboat.

Aghast at the *fait accompli* laid at their door by the German Admiral, a majority of the Turkish government wished to disavow it but was effectively prevented. The operating factor was the presence of the *Goeben* at the Golden Horn, commanded by her own officers, manned by her own crew, disdainful of restraint. As Talaat Bey pointed out, the government, the palace, the capital, they themselves, their homes, their sovereign and Caliph, were under her guns. Dismissal of the German military and naval missions which the Allies were demanding as proof of Turkey's neutrality, they were unable to perform. The act of war having been committed in the Turks' name, Russia declared war on Turkey on November 4, followed by Britain and France on November 5.

Thereafter the red edges of war spread over another half of the world. Turkey's neighbors, Bulgaria, Rumania, Italy, and Greece, were eventually drawn in. Thereafter, with her exit to the Mediterranean closed, Russia was left dependent on Archangel, icebound half the year, and on Vladivostok, 8,000 miles from the battlefront. With the Black Sea closed, her exports dropped by 98 per cent and her imports by 95 per cent. The cutting off of Russia with all its consequences, the vain and sanguinary tragedy of Gallipoli, the diversion of Allied strength in the campaigns of Mesopotamia, Suez, and Palestine, the ultimate breakup of the Ottoman Empire, the subsequent history of the Middle East, followed from the voyage of the *Goeben*.

Other sequels were as bitter if less momentous. Meeting the censure of his comrades, Admiral Troubridge demanded a Court of Inquiry which ordered his trial by court-martial in November, 1914, on the charge that "he did forbear to chase H.I.G.M.'s ship *Goeben*, being an enemy then flying." On the basic issue, whether he was justified in regarding the *Goeben* as a "superior force," the Navy, for its own sake, acquitted him. Though he performed further service in the war, he was never again, owing to feeling in the fleet, given a command at sea. Admiral Milne, recalled on August 18 in order to leave the Mediterranean under French command, came home to be retired. On August 30 the Admiralty announced that his conduct and dispositions in regard to the *Goeben* and *Breslau* had been made the subject of "careful examination" with the result that "their Lordships approved the measures taken by him in all respects." Their Lordships, who had been blind to the importance of Constantinople, did not seek a scapegoat.

▶▶▶ *11* ▶

▶▶▶ *Liège and Alsace*

WHILE CONCENTRATION OF THE ARMIES WAS proceeding, advance groups of the German and French forces moved to the attack as if through a revolving door. The Germans entered from the east and the French from the west. Each opponent's first move was to take place on his own extreme right on the rim of the revolving door's perimeter, three hundred miles apart. The Germans would proceed, regardless of what the French did, to the assault of Liège and the reduction of its ring of twelve forts in order to open the roads across Belgium to the armies of their right wing. The French, equally regardless of what the enemy did, would charge into Upper Alsace in a move, more sentimental than strategic, designed to open the war upon a wave of national enthusiasm and encourage an uprising of the local population against Germany. Strategically its purpose was to anchor the French right on the Rhine.

Liège was the portcullis guarding the gateway into Belgium from Germany. Built upon a steep slope rising 500 feet up from the left bank of the Meuse, moated by the river, here nearly 200 yards wide, surrounded by a 30-mile circumference of forts, it was popularly considered the most formidable fortified position in Europe. Ten years ago Port Arthur had withstood a siege of nine months before surrender. World opinion expected Liège certainly to equal the record of Port Arthur if not to hold out indefinitely.

Seven German armies totaling over 1,500,000 men were being assembled along the Belgian and French frontiers. They ranged in numerical order from the First Army on the German extreme right opposite Liège to the Seventh Army on the extreme left in Alsace. The Sixth and Seventh Armies composed the German left wing of 16 divisions, the Fourth and Fifth Armies the center of 20 divisions, and the First, Second, and Third Armies made up the right wing of 34 divisions which was to move through Belgium. An independent cavalry corps of three divisions was attached to the right wing. The three armies of the right wing were commanded by Generals von Kluck, von Bülow, and von Hausen, all sixty-eight years old of whom the first two were veterans of 1870. The commander of the cavalry corps was General von Marwitz.

As von Kluck's First Army had to travel the farthest, its progress was to regulate the pace of the general advance. Concentrating north of Aachen, it was to take the roads which crossed the Meuse over the five bridges of Liège whose capture was thus the vital first objective upon which all else depended. The guns of the forts of Liège dominated the gap between the Dutch frontier and the wooded and hilly Ardennes; its bridges provided the only multiple crossing of the Meuse; its junction of four railroad lines connecting Germany and Belgium with northern France was essential to the supply of the German armies on the march. Until it was taken and its forts put out of action, the German right wing could not move.

A special "Army of the Meuse" of six brigades commanded by General von Emmich was detached from the Second Army to open the way through Liège. It was expected, unless the Belgians offered serious resistance, to accomplish this while the main armies were still concentrating. In one of his prewar indiscretions, the Kaiser once said to a British officer at maneuvers, "I will go through Belgium like *that!*" cutting the air with a flip of his hand. Belgium's declared intention to fight was, the Germans believed, no more than the "rage of dreaming sheep"—in the words a Prussian statesman once applied to his domestic opponents. When Liège had been taken and the First and Second Armies were on the roads on either side of it at a point level with the city, the main advance would begin.

Henri Brialmont, the greatest fortifications engineer of his time, had

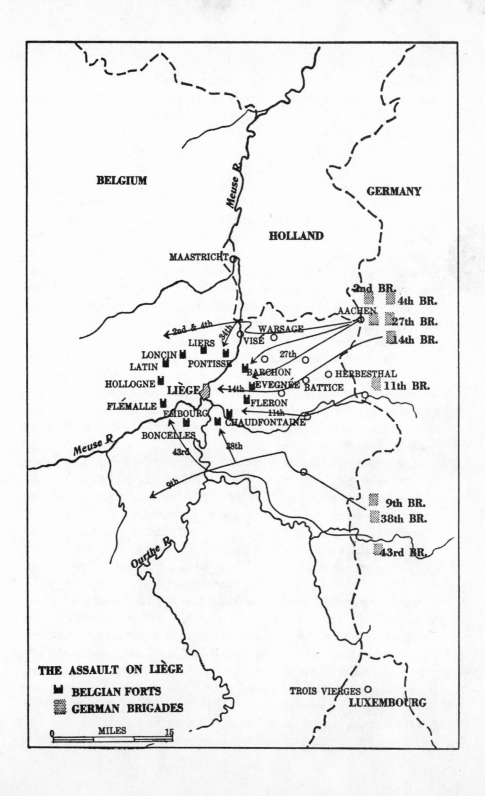

BELGIUM

GERMANY

Meuse R.

HOLLAND

MAASTRICHT

2nd BR.

4th BR.

AACHEN

27th BR.

14th BR.

2nd & 4th

24th

WARSAGE

LIERS

VISÉ

27th

LONCIN

PONTISSE

LATIN

BARCHON

HOLLOGNE

LIÈGE

EVEGNÉE

HERBESTHAL

14th

BATTICE

FLÉMALLE

FLERON

11th BR.

EMBOURG

11th

CHAUDFONTAINE

BONCELLES

Meuse R.

43rd

38th

9th

9th BR.

38th BR.

Ourthe R.

43rd BR.

THE ASSAULT ON LIÈGE

🏰 BELGIAN FORTS

▦ GERMAN BRIGADES

TROIS VIERGES

LUXEMBOURG

0 ⸻ MILES ⸻ 15

built the forts of Liège and of Namur in the 1880's at the insistence of Leopold II. Located on high ground in a circle around each city, they were designed to hold the passage of the Meuse against invaders coming from either direction. The Liège forts were situated on both banks of the river at an average distance of four to five miles from the city and two to three miles from each other. Six were on the east bank facing Germany and six on the west reaching around and behind the city. Like medieval castles sunk underground, the forts showed nothing on the surface but a triangular mound from which protruded the cupolas for the disappearing gun turrets. Everything else was subterranean. Inclined tunnels led to the chambers underground and connected the turrets with the magazines and fire control rooms. The six larger forts and the six smaller *fortins* in between had a total of 400 guns of which the largest were 8-inch (210 mm.) howitzers. In the corners of the triangles were smaller turrets for quick-firing guns and for machine guns which covered the slopes immediately below. A dry moat 30 feet deep surrounded each fort. Each had a searchlight fitted to a steel observation tower which could be lowered underground like the guns. The garrisons of each of the larger forts numbered 400, composed of two companies of artillery and one of infantry. Intended as advance posts to defend the frontier rather than as last-ditch retreats to withstand a siege, the forts depended on the Field Army to hold the spaces in between.

Overconfident in the great work of Brialmont, the Belgians had done little to keep the forts up to date, leaving them to be manned by inadequate garrisons drawn from the oldest classes of reserves with one officer per company. For fear of giving Germany the least excuse to declare Belgium's neutrality compromised, the order to construct trenches and barbed-wire barricades for defense of the intervals between the forts and to raze trees and houses in the way of the guns was not given until August 2. When the attack came these measures were barely begun.

On their part the Germans, believing the Belgians would yield to the ultimatum or at most offer a token resistance, had not brought up the surprise weapon they had in store in the form of gigantic siege cannon of such size and destructive power that it had not been thought possible such guns could be made mobile. One, built by Skoda, the Austrian munitions firm, was a 12-inch (305 mm.) mortar; the other, built by Krupp's at Essen, was a monster of 16.5 inches (420 mm.) which together with its gun carriage was 24 feet long, weighed 98 tons, fired a shell a yard long weighing 1,800 pounds at a range of 9 miles and required a crew of 200 attendants. Until then the largest guns known were Britain's 13.5-inch naval guns and the largest land guns 11-inch fixed howitzers of the coast artillery. Japan, after a six-month failure to reduce Port Arthur, had stripped her coasts of such weapons to use in the siege, but it had taken three more months under their fire before the Russian fortress surrendered.

The German schedule could allow no such period to reduce the Belgian forts. Moltke had told Conrad von Hötzendorff that he expected the decision in the West to take place by the 39th day and had promised to send German troops eastward to help Austria beginning on the 40th day. Although the Belgians were not expected to fight, nevertheless German thoroughness required that every contingency be provided for. The problem was to design the heaviest possible anti-fortification gun that could be transported overland. It had to be a mortar or short-barreled howitzer with high angle of fire capable of lobbing shells onto the tops of the forts and yet, without the rifling of a long barrel, have sufficient accuracy to hit a specific target.

Krupp's, working in iron secrecy, was ready with a model of the 420 in 1909. The sawed-off bloated giant, though fired successfully, proved excessively cumbersome to move. It had to be transported by rail in two sections each requiring a locomotive to pull it. Spur tracks had to be laid to bring the gun to its emplacement pit which, owing to the tremendous downward thrust of the recoil, had to be dug several yards deep and filled with concrete in which the gun was embedded and from which it could only be released by blasting. The emplacement process required 6 hours. For four more years Krupp's worked to construct a gun transportable by road by breaking it down into several sections. In February 1914 such a model was achieved and tested at the Kummersdorf proving ground much to the gratification of the Kaiser, who was invited for the occasion. Further tests over roads with steam and gasoline motors and even multiple horse teams as movers showed that improvements were necessary. A target date of October 1, 1914, was set.

The Austrian Skoda 305s, completed in 1910, had the advantage of superior mobility. Motor-drawn in three sections consisting of gun, mount, and portable foundation, they could travel 15 to 20 miles in a day. Instead of tires, their wheels wore continuous belts of what was then awesomely described as "iron feet." At the point of emplacement the portable steel foundation was set down, the mount bolted to it, and the gun fitted to the mount, the whole process requiring 40 minutes. Disassembly could be achieved equally quickly, which made the guns proof against capture. They could be swung right or left to an angle of 60 degrees and had a range of 7 miles. Like the 420s they fired an armor-piercing shell with a delayed-action fuse allowing the explosion to take place after penetration of the target.

When war broke out in August, several of the Austrian 305s were in Germany, loaned by Conrad von Hötzendorff until the German model should be ready. Krupp's had in existence at this time five 420s of the railroad model and two of the road model still waiting for the necessary improvements in transportation. Urgent orders to make them ready were issued on August 2. When the invasion of Belgium began, Krupp's was working desperately day and night to assemble guns, mounts, motors, equipment, horse teams for emergencies, mechanics, truck drivers, and artillery personnel who had to be given last-minute training.

Moltke still hoped to get through without needing them. If, however, the Belgians were so misguided as to fight, the Germans expected that the forts could be taken by simple assault. No detail of the assault had been left to chance. Its planning had been the study of an officer who was Schlieffen's most devoted disciple on the General Staff.

Gluttony for work and a granite character had overcome lack of a "von" to win for Captain Erich Ludendorff the right to wear the coveted red stripes of the General Staff whose ranks he entered at the age of thirty in 1895. Although his thick body, his blond mustache over a harsh down-curving mouth, his round double chin, and that bulge at the back of the neck which Emerson called the mark of the beast, characterized Ludendorff as belonging to the opposite physical type from the aristocratic Schlieffen, he modeled himself on Schlieffen's hard, shut-in personality. Deliberately friendless and forbidding, the man who within two years was to exercise greater power over the people and fate of Germany than anyone since Frederick the Great, remained little known or liked. None of the usual reminiscences of friends and family or personal stories or sayings accumulated around him; even as he grew in eminence he moved without attendant anecdotes, a man without a shadow.

Regarding Schlieffen as "one of the greatest soldiers who ever lived," Ludendorff, as a member and ultimately Chief of the Mobilization Section of the General Staff from 1904 to 1913, devoted himself to ensuring the success of his master's plan. Of its soundness, he says, the entire Staff was convinced, for "nobody believed in Belgium's neutrality." In the event of war Ludendorff expected to become Chief of Military

Operations, but in 1913, he came into conflict with the then Minister of War, General von Heeringen, and was removed from the Staff to a regimental command. In April 1914 he was promoted to general with orders, upon mobilization, to join the Second Army as Deputy Chief of Staff.* In that capacity, on August 2, he was assigned to Emmich's Army of the Meuse for the attack upon Liège, charged with liaison between the assault force and the parent command.

On August 3 King Albert became Commander in Chief of the Belgian Army—without illusions. The plan he and Galet had drawn up to meet the hypothesis of a German invasion had been frustrated. They had wanted to bring up all six Belgian divisions to take a stand along the natural barrier of the Meuse where they could reinforce the fortified positions of Liège and Namur. But the General Staff and its new chief, General Selliers de Moranville, disinclined to let the young King and the low-ranking Captain Galet dictate strategy, and itself torn between offensive and defensive ideas, had made no arrangements to bring the army up behind the Meuse. In accordance with strict neutrality the six divisions were stationed before the war to face all comers: the 1st Division at Ghent facing England, the 2nd at Antwerp, the 3rd at Liège facing Germany, the 4th and 5th at Namur, Charleroi, and Mons facing France, the 6th and the Cavalry Division in the center at Brussels. General Selliers' plan, once the enemy was identified, was to concentrate the army in the center of the country facing the invader, leaving the garrisons of Antwerp, Liège, and Namur to look after themselves. The impetus of existing plans is always stronger than the impulse to change. The Kaiser could not change Moltke's plan nor could Kitchener alter Henry Wilson's nor Lanrezac alter Joffre's. By August 3 when King Albert, becoming officially Commander in Chief, took precedence over General Selliers, it was too late to organize deployment of the whole army along the Meuse. The strategy adopted was to concentrate the Belgian Army before Louvain on the river Gette about forty miles east of Brussels where it was now decided to make a defense. The best the King could do was to insist upon the 3rd Division remaining at Liège and the 4th at Namur to reinforce the frontier garrisons instead of joining the Field Army in the center of the country.

As commander of the 3rd Division and Governor of Liège, the King had obtained the appointment in January 1914 of his own nominee,

---

* This title, which fits the functions of the post, is used in preference to the German title *Quartiermeister*, which is confusing to English-speaking readers.

General Leman, the sixty-three-year-old Commandant of the War College. A former officer of Engineers like Joffre, Leman had spent the last thirty years, except for a six-year interval on the Staff of the Engineers, at the War College where Albert had studied under him. He had had seven months to try to reorganize the defenses of the Liège forts without the support of the General Staff. When the crisis came, a conflict of orders broke over his head. On August 1 General Selliers ordered away one brigade of the 3rd Division, a third of its strength. On appeal from Leman the King countermanded the order. On August 3 General Selliers in his turn countermanded the King's order for demolition of the bridges above Liège on the ground that they were needed for movements of the Belgian Army. Again on appeal from Leman, the King supported the General against the Chief of Staff and added a personal letter charging Leman to "hold to the end the position which you have been entrusted to defend."

The will to defend the country outran the means. Of machine guns, the essential weapon for defense, the Belgian Army's proportion per man was half that of the German Army. Of heavy field artillery, needed for the defensive positions between the forts, it had none at all. The planned increase in military service which was intended to bring the Field Army up to 150,000 with 70,000 reserves and the fortress troops to 130,000 by the year 1926, had hardly got under way. In August 1914 the Field Army mustered 117,000 with no trained reserves, all the remaining reserves being used to man the forts. The Civic Guard, a gentlemanly gendarmerie in top hats and bright green uniforms were pressed into active service; many of its duties were taken over by Boy Scouts. The active army had had no practice in entrenching and hardly any tools to dig with. Transport was lacking as were tents and field kitchens; cooking utensils had to be collected from farms and villages; telephone equipment was negligible. The army marched in a chaos of improvisation.

It marched also, or was borne along, on a crest of enthusiasm, haloed by a mist of illusion. Soldiers, suddenly popular, were overwhelmed by gifts of food and kisses and beer. They soon broke ranks and strolled through the streets, showing off their uniforms and greeting friends. Parents joined their sons to see what war was like. Magnificent limousines, requisitioned as transport, sped by piled with loaves and joints of meat. Cheers roared after them. Cheers greeted the machine guns pulled, like the milk carts of Flanders, by dogs.

Early on August 4, a quiet, clear, luminous morning, seventy miles to the east of Brussels, the first invaders, units of von Marwitz's Cavalry, crossed into Belgium. Coming at a steady purposeful trot, they carried twelve-foot steel-headed lances and were otherwise hung about with an arsenal of sabers, pistols, and rifles. Harvesters looking up from the roadside fields, villagers peering from their windows, whispered "Uhlans!" The outlandish name, with its overtones of the savage Tartar horsemen from whom it derived, evoked Europe's ancestral memory of barbarian invasion. The Germans, when engaged in their historic mission of bringing *Kultur* to their neighbors, showed a preference, as in the Kaiser's use of the word "Huns," for fearful models.

As vanguard of the invasion, the cavalry's mission was to reconnoiter the position of the Belgian and French armies, to watch out for British landings, and to screen the German deployment against similar enemy reconnaissance. On the first day the duty of the advance squadrons, supported by infantry brought up in automobiles, was to seize the crossings of the Meuse before the bridges were destroyed and capture farms and villages as sources of food and forage. At Warsage, just inside the frontier, M. Fléchet, the Burgomaster of seventy-two, wearing his scarf of office, stood in the village square as the horsemen clattered over the cobblestones of the Belgian *pavé*. Riding up, the squadron's officer with a polite smile handed him a printed proclamation which expressed Germany's "regret" at being "compelled by necessity" to enter Belgium. Though wishing to avoid combat, it said, "We must have a free road. Destruction of bridges, tunnels and railroads will be regarded as hostile acts." In village squares all along the border from Holland to Luxembourg the Uhlans scattered the proclamations, hauled down the Belgian flag from the town halls, raised the black eagle of the German Empire, and moved on, confident in the assurance given them by their commanders that the Belgians would not fight.

Behind them, filling the roads that converged on Liège came the infantry of Emmich's assault force, rank after rank. Only the red regimental number painted on helmet fronts broke the monotony of field-gray. Horse-drawn field artillery followed. The new leather of boots and harness creaked. Companies of cyclists sped ahead to seize road crossings and farmhouses and lay telephone wires. Automobiles honked their way through, carrying monocled Staff officers with orderlies holding drawn pistols sitting up front and trunks strapped on behind. Every regiment had its field kitchens on wheels, said to be inspired by one the Kaiser had seen at Russian maneuvers, with fires kindled and cooks standing up stirring the stew as the wagons moved. Such was the perfection of the equipment and the precision of the marching that the invaders appeared to be on parade.

Each soldier carried sixty-five pounds: rifle and ammunition, knapsack, canteen, extra boots, entrenching tools, knife and a multiplicity of implements and kits strapped to his coat. In one bag was his "iron ration" containing two cans of meat, two of vegetables, two packages of hardtack, one of ground coffee, and a flask of whisky which was only to be opened on permission of an officer and was inspected daily to determine if its owner had cheated. Another bag held thread, needles, bandages and adhesive tape; another held matches, chocolate, and tobacco. Around the officers' necks hung binoculars and leather-bound maps covering the particular regiment's designated line of march so that no German would ever be in the predicament of the British officer who complained that battle is a process which always takes place at the junction of two maps. As they marched, the Germans sang. They sang "Deutschland über Alles," "Die Wacht am Rhein," and "Heil dir im Siegeskranz." They sang when they halted, when they billeted, when they caroused. Many who lived through the next thirty days of mounting combat, agony, and terror were to remember the sound of endless, repetitious masculine singing as the worst torment of the invasion.

General von Emmich's brigades, converging upon Liège from the north, east, and south, discovered when they reached the Meuse that the bridges above and below the city had already been destroyed. When they attempted to cross on pontoons, Belgian infantry opened fire, and the Germans to their astonishment found themselves in actual combat, hit by live ammunition, wounded and dying. They had 60,000 men to the Belgians' 25,000. By nightfall they had succeeded in crossing the river at Visé, north of the city; the brigades attacking from the south were held off; those attacking through the center where the river makes an inward bend reached the line of forts before reaching the river.

During the day as the boots and wheels and hoofs of the German ranks overran villages and trampled fields of ripe grain, the shooting increased and with it the vexation of the German troops, who had been told that the Belgians were "chocolate soldiers." Surprised and enraged by the resistance, the German soldiers in the state of heightened nerves produced by the first experience of combat were immediately susceptible to the first cry of "Snipers"! At once they imagined enraged civilians shooting at them from behind every house and hedgerow. At once they raised the cry, "*Man hat geschossen!*" that was to be the signal for every reprisal upon civilians from Visé to the gates of Paris. From the first day, the figure of the terrible *franc-tireur*, remembered from 1870, which the Germans were to conjure into gigantic proportions, began to take shape.

The spirit of resistance, soon to find its voice in the famous clandestine newspaper *Le Libre Belge*, was barely awake that first morning among the inhabitants of the frontier towns. Their own government, knowing the nature of the enemy, had already distributed notices to be posted in every community ordering civilians to deposit arms with the town authorities and warning that if caught with arms by the Germans they might be subject to the death penalty. The placards instructed the people not to fight or insult the enemy and to remain indoors behind closed windows in order to avoid "any pretext for measures of repression resulting in bloodshed or pillage or massacre of the innocent population." Thus sternly cautioned and awestruck at the sight of the invaders, the people were hardly prepared to try to halt the armored multitudes with individual rabbit guns.

Nevertheless on the first day of the invasion the Germans began the shooting not only of ordinary civilians but of Belgian priests, a more deliberate affair. On August 6, Major-General Karl Ulrich von Bülow,* brother of the ex-chancellor and commander of a cavalry division in the attack on Liège, told a brother officer that he disapproved of "the summary executions of Belgian priests which had taken place on the previous day." The pretext that Belgian priesthood was engaged in a conspiracy to encourage *franc-tireur* warfare—organized within the first twenty-four hours and in defiance of the civil government—was designed for German consumption. For Belgian consumption the executions were meant as an exercise in frightfulness according to the theory developed by the Emperor Caligula: "*Oderint dum metuant*" (Let them hate us as long as they fear us).

On the first day too the Germans shot six hostages taken at Warsage and burned the village of Battice as an example. It was "burned out, completely gutted," wrote a German officer who marched through it a few days later. "One could see through the frameless window openings into the interior of the rooms with their roasted remnants of iron bedsteads and furnishings. Broken bits of household utensils lay scattered about the street. Except for dogs and cats scavenging among the ruins, all sign of

---

* A different person from Generaloberst Karl von Bülow who commanded the Second Army.

life had been extinguished by the fire. In the market square stood the roofless, spireless church." In another place where, he was told, three German Hussars had been shot, "the whole village was in flames, cattle bellowed desperately in barns, half-burned chickens rushed about demented, two men in peasant smocks lay dead against a wall."

"Our advance in Belgium is certainly brutal," Moltke wrote to Conrad on August 5, "but we are fighting for our lives and all who get in the way must take the consequences." He did not have in mind the consequences to Germany. But the process which was to make Belgium the nemesis of Germany had begun.

On August 5 Emmich's brigades opened the attack on the four easternmost forts of Liège with a cannonade by field artillery followed by infantry assault. The light shells made no impression on the forts, and the Belgian guns poured a hail of fire on the German troops, slaughtering their front ranks. Company after company came on, making for the spaces between the forts where the Belgian entrenchments had not been completed. At some points where they broke through, the Germans stormed up the slopes where the guns could not be depressed to reach them and were mowed down by the forts' machine guns. The dead piled up in ridges a yard high. At Fort Barchon, Belgians, seeing the German lines waver, charged with the bayonet and threw them back. Again and again the Germans returned to the assault, spending lives like bullets in the knowledge of plentiful reserves to make up the losses. "They made no attempt at deploying," a Belgian officer described it later, "but came on line after line, almost shoulder to shoulder, until as we shot them down, the fallen were heaped on top of each other in an awful barricade of dead and wounded that threatened to mask our guns and cause us trouble. So high did the barricade become that we did not know whether to fire through it or to go out and clear openings with our hands. . . . But would you believe it?—this veritable wall of dead and dying enabled those wonderful Germans to creep closer, and actually to charge up the glacis. They got no farther than halfway because our machine guns and rifles swept them back. Of course we had our losses but they were slight compared to the carnage we inflicted on our enemies."

The prodigal spending of lives by all the belligerents that was to mount and mount in senseless excess to hundreds of thousands at the Somme, to over a million at Verdun began on that second day of the war at Liège. In their furious frustration at the first check, the Germans threw men recklessly against the forts in whatever numbers would be necessary to take the objective on schedule.

During the night of August 5 Emmich's brigades reassembled on their separate roads for a renewed attack, scheduled to begin at midnight. General Ludendorff, accompanying the 14th Brigade which occupied the center of the German line, found the troops gloomy and "nervous." Ahead the fortress guns loomed fearfully. Many officers doubted that infantry attack could prevail against them. Rumor reported that an entire cyclist company sent out to reconnoiter earlier in the day had been "annihilated." A column taking the wrong road in the darkness bumped up against another, tangled, and came to a confused halt. Ludendorff riding up to find the cause of the trouble discovered the orderly of General von Wussow, commander of the 14th Brigade, leading the General's horse with empty saddle. Von Wussow had been killed by machine-gun fire along the road ahead. Ludendorff with instant boldness seized opportunity by the throat. He took command of the Brigade and gave the signal for attack that was intended to pierce the interval between Fort Fleron and Fort d'Evegnée. As they advanced, men fell under fire and for the first time in his life Ludendorff heard the "peculiar thud of bullets striking human bodies."

Through some quirk in the fortunes of war, the guns of Fort Fleron less than two miles away failed to open fire. In a village where house-to-house fighting developed, Ludendorff ordered up a field howitzer which "fired right and left into the houses" and soon cleared the way through. By two o'clock on the afternoon of the 6th the Brigade had broken through the ring of forts and reached the heights on the right bank of the Meuse from where they could see Liège and its Citadel, an imposing but disused fort, directly across the river. Here they were joined by General von Emmich, but although they waited in increasing anxiety, scanning the roads to north and south, no troops of the other brigades appeared. The 14th discovered itself isolated within the circle of forts. Its field guns were trained on the Citadel and fired as a signal to the other brigades as well as "to intimidate the governor of the fortress and the inhabitants."

Angered at having to waste time and manpower fighting a people who, with ordinary common sense, should have let them pass, the Germans throughout the month of August were obsessed by the goal of "intimidating" the Belgians into giving up their stupid and futile resistance. Under a flag of truce the former German military attaché at Brussels who was personally known to General Leman had been sent the day before to persuade or, failing in that, to threaten him into surrender. Leman was told by the emissary that Zeppelins would destroy Liège if he did not let the Germans through. The parley failed of its purpose, and on August 6 the Zeppelin L-Z was duly sent from Cologne to bomb the city. The thirteen bombs it dropped, the nine civilians it killed, inaugurated a twentieth century practice.

After the bombardment Ludendorff sent another emissary under another flag of truce who also failed to persuade Leman to surrender. Ruse, too, was tried. In an effort to kidnap or kill the commander, a detachment of thirty men and six officers, disguised in unmarked uniforms resembling those of the British, drove up in automobiles to Leman's headquarters on the Rue Sainte-Foi and asked to see the General. His aide, Major Marchand, coming to the door, cried, "They are not English; they're Germans!" and was instantly shot down. He was immediately avenged by comrades who, in the spirited and unabashed reporting of 1914, "maddened at the dastardly violation of the rules of civilized warfare, spared not but slew." In the confusion, General Leman escaped to Fort Loncin, west of the city, where he continued to direct the defense.

He realized, now that a German brigade had penetrated between the forts, that he could not expect to hold the city. If the brigades attacking from the north and south also succeeded in breaking through, Liège would be encircled and the 3rd Division cut off from the rest of the army, where it could be trapped and annihilated. Leman's Intelligence had identified units of four German Army corps in the attacking force, which appeared to give Emmich the equivalent of eight divisions against Leman's one. Actually, Emmich's troops were not organized by corps but by detached brigades and now numbered, with the reinforcements hurriedly sent to him, about five divisions. The lone 3rd Division was not enough to save itself or Liège. On the morning of August 6, General Leman, knowing it was the King's fixed purpose to preserve the Field Army in being and in contact with Antwerp regardless of what happened elsewhere, ordered the 3rd Division to fall back from Liège and join the rest of the army in front of Louvain. It meant that the city, though not the forts, would fall; but even for Liège a division could not be sacrificed, for beyond Liège was the independence of Belgium. Unless the King remained in command of an army on some corner of his own soil, he would be at the mercy not only of his enemies but of his Allies.

Brussels on August 6 went mad with excitement at news of the repulse administered to the Germans the day before. *"Grande Victoire Belge!"* proclaimed newspaper extras. Happy, ardent people crowded the cafés, congratulated one another, boasted of vengeance, stayed up all night to celebrate, and next morning delightedly read to each other a Belgian communiqué which said that 125,000 Germans had "completely failed to make any impression and three army corps engaged in the attack were cut up and useless." Echoing the optimism, the Allied press reported the "German rout complete," with several regiments having surrendered, many prisoners taken, 20,000 German casualties, the defenders everywhere successful, the "invaders decisively checked," and their advance brought to a "standstill." How the withdrawal of the Belgian 3rd Division, briefly mentioned, fitted into this picture was somehow left unexplained.

At Belgian Headquarters in the old Town Hall at Louvain confidence was as high as if the Belgian Army numbered thirty-four divisions and the German six instead of the other way around. The forward group within the General Staff "hummed with wild plans for an immediate offensive."

The King vetoed it at once. He recognized in the size of the force attacking Liège, and in new reports of five German corps now identified, the outlines of the envelopment strategy of Schlieffen. There was still a chance, if he were reinforced by French and English forces in time, of halting the Germans at the river Gette midway between Antwerp and Namur. Already he had sent two urgent appeals to President Poincaré. At this stage he still expected, as did everyone in Belgium, to be joined on Belgian territory by his Allies. "Where are the French? Where are the English?" people everywhere asked one another. In one village a Belgian woman offered a bunch of flowers tied with the English colors to a soldier in a strange uniform which she thought was khaki. In some embarrassment he identified himself as German.

In France, Poincaré and Messimy who in his exuberance had instantly proposed to send five corps to help the Belgians were helpless against Joffre's silent and stubborn refusal to change his plan of deployment by so much as a brigade. Three French cavalry divisions under General Sordet would enter Belgium on August 6 to reconnoiter German strength east of the Meuse, but only the nonappearance of the English, Joffre said, would induce him to extend his left wing. Late on the night of August 5 word came from London that the War Council, after an all-day meeting, had made up its mind to send an expeditionary force, but of only four divisions, plus cavalry, instead of six. Although this was disappointing, it did not induce Joffre to shift any divisions to his left to make up the British deficiency. He was keeping everything for the French offensive through the center. All he sent to Belgium, apart from the cavalry, was a single Staff officer, Colonel Brécard, with a letter to King Albert. It suggested that the Belgian Army should postpone decisive action and retreat upon Namur where it would make contact with the French and, when the French concentration was completed, join in a common offensive. Four French divisions, Joffre said, would be sent to Namur but would not reach there until August 15.

As Joffre saw it, the Belgian Army, ignoring purely Belgian interests for the sake of a common front, should act as a wing of the French Army in conformity with French strategy. As King Albert saw it, with his clearer sense of the danger of the German right wing, if he allowed the Belgian Army to make a stand at Namur it could be cut off from its base at Antwerp by the advancing Germans and pushed out of Belgium over the French border. More intent on holding the Belgian Army on Belgian soil than upon a common strategy, King Albert was determined to keep open his line of retreat to Antwerp. Purely military considerations pointed to Namur; historical and national reasons pointed to Antwerp even at the risk of the army being bottled up there where it could exercise no direct influence upon the war as a whole.

If compelled, the Belgian Army would retreat upon Antwerp, not Namur, the King told Colonel Brécard. Bitterly disappointed Brécard informed Joffre that the Belgians could not be expected to join the French in a combined offensive.

On August 7 the French Government, which had never been consulted about Plan 17 and was now prevented by its requirements from coming to the aid of Belgium, conferred the Grand Cross of the Legion of Honor upon Liège and the Military Medal upon King Albert. The gesture, however inadequate in the circumstances, expressed something of the world's startled admiration of Belgium's fight. She is not only "defending the independence of Europe; she is the champion of honor," declared the President of the French Chamber. She has won "immortal renown" by shattering the superstition that the German armies are invincible, declared *The Times* of London.

While the tributes multiplied, the people of Liège spent the first of the countless nights that twentieth century Europeans were to spend in cellars. Following the day of terror under the Zeppelin raid, Liège was pounded all night by the exploding shells of Ludendorff's field artillery in an attempt to cow the city into surrender. The method was as fruitless as the long-range bombardment of Paris by the Big Berthas in 1918 or the Luftwaffe and V-2 bombings of London one war later.

After the preliminary softening up, Emmich and Ludendorff decided to enter the city without waiting for the other brigades to come up. Meeting no resistance, as the Belgian 3rd Division had by now been withdrawn, the 14th Brigade marched across two bridges which were still undestroyed. Ludendorff, thinking the Citadel had been taken by an advance guard sent ahead for that purpose, drove up the steep winding road in a Staff car with a single adjutant. Reaching the courtyard he found no German soldiers in possession, the advance guard having not yet arrived. He nevertheless unhesitatingly "banged on the gates" and on their being opened to him received the surrender of the Citadel from the remaining Belgian soldiers inside. He was forty-nine, twice the age of Bonaparte in 1793 and Liège was his Toulon.

Down below in the city, General Emmich, not finding Leman, arrested the burgomaster, who was told that Liège would be shelled and burned unless the forts surrendered, and was offered a safe conduct to obtain the surrender from General Leman or the King. He refused, and remained a prisoner. By evening three more German brigades had broken through the ring of forts to join the 14th inside the city.

At six that evening an officer of motor transport tore through the streets of Aachen bringing excited word to Second Army Headquarters that General Emmich was inside Liège and at that moment negotiating with the burgomaster. In the midst of shouts and *"Hochs!"* a telegram from Emmich to his wife was intercepted with the message, "Hurrah, in Liège!" At 8:00 P.M. a liaison officer brought word from Emmich that although General Leman had not been taken, the bishop and burgomaster were prisoners, the Citadel had surrendered, the city was evacuated by Belgian troops, but that he had no information about the forts.

In Berlin, where Supreme Headquarters, or *Oberste Heeresleitung* (hereafter OHL), remained until the end of the concentration period, the Kaiser was ecstatic. At the beginning, when it had appeared that the Belgians were going to fight after all, he had bitterly reproached Moltke, "Now you see you have brought the English down on me without any reason!" but at news of the fall of Liège, he called him his "dearest Julius" and, as Moltke recorded it, "I was rapturously kissed." Still the English continued to worry the Kaiser. On August 10 the American ambassador, Mr. Gerard, who came to present an offer by President Wilson to mediate, found him "despondent." Seated in the garden of the Palace at a green iron table under a sun umbrella with papers and telegraph forms scattered before him and two dachshunds lying at his feet, the Kaiser lamented, "The English change the whole situation—an obstinate people—they will keep up the war. It cannot end soon."

The bitter truth that none of the forts had been taken was learned the day after the fall of the city when Ludendorff came out of Liège to report. He insisted that the siege cannon must be brought into action at once; the Belgians still showed no disposition to surrender. Already the advance of Kluck's First Army, scheduled to be the first to start, had to be put off from the 10th to the 13th.

Meanwhile at Essen the hideous fat black siege mortars stood immobile while around them surged the frantic struggle to assemble the motor transport and trained gun crews. By August 9 the two road models were ready and that night were loaded onto freight cars to be transported as far as possible by railway to save their treads. The train left Essen on the 10th and reached Belgium by nightfall, but at Herbesthal, twenty miles east of Liège, at 11:00 P.M. came to a dead stop. The railroad tunnel, blown up by the Belgians, was blocked. Furious efforts failed to reopen it. The mammoth guns had to be unloaded and proceed by road. Though they had only eleven miles to cover to come within range of the forts, one breakdown after another thwarted their progress. Motors failed, harness broke, roads were blocked, passing troops had to be pressed into service to help haul them. All day the slow struggle with the two silent monsters went on.

While they were on their way, the German government made a last effort to persuade Belgium to yield passageway through her territory. On August 9 Mr. Gerard was asked to forward a note to his colleague in Brussels for presentation to the Belgian government. "Now that the Belgian Army has upheld its honor by heroic resistance to a very superior force," it said, the German government "beg" the King of the Belgians and his government to spare Belgium "further horrors of war." Germany was ready to make any compact with Belgium consistent with allowing her armies free passageway and would give her "solemn assurances" that she had no intention of taking Belgian territory and would evacuate the country as soon as the progress of war permitted. Both the American ministers in Brussels and at The Hague declined to be the bearer of such a proposal, but through the offices of the Dutch government it eventually reached King Albert on August 12. He refused.

His steadfastness, in view of the enormity of the threat to his country, did not seem entirely believable even to his Allies. No one had expected heroism from Belgium. "Yes," said King Albert after the war, in reply to a French statesman's praise of his conduct, "we were cornered into it." In 1914 the French had their doubts, and on August 8 sent the Under-Secretary of Foreign Affairs, M. Berthelot, to see the King on the basis of a rumor that he was going to arrange a truce with Germany. Berthelot was charged with the unhappy duty of explaining to the King that France would do everything in her power to help Belgium except interfere with her own plan of operations. Albert tried again to convey to the French his apprehension of the huge right wing that would be coming through Flanders and repeated his warning that the Belgian Army might have to withdraw to Antwerp. It would resume the offensive when, he delicately added, "the approach of the Allied armies makes itself felt."

To the outside world it seemed, as, from his pinnacle of authority, the Military Correspondent of *The Times* announced, that the German force attacking Liège "has been very handsomely beaten." For the moment this was approximately true. The vaunted German Army, which had expected to be so easily victorious over the "dreaming sheep," had failed to take the forts by assault. It came to a pause after August 9 and waited for reinforcements—though not of the human kind. It waited for the siege guns.

In France General Joffre and his staff still had their minds closed as resolutely as ever to Flanders, still focused their thoughts as ardently as ever on the Rhine. The five French armies, totaling approximately the same seventy divisions that the Germans had on the Western Front, were arranged in order from the First Army on the right to the Fifth on the left. Divided by the fortified area of Verdun-Toul, they were concentrated in two groups in much the same proportion as the German armies were grouped on either side of Metz-Thionville. The First and Second Armies, facing the German Seventh and Sixth, in Alsace and Lorraine, together formed the French right wing whose mission was by vigorous attack to throw the Germans opposite them back upon the Rhine while driving a solid wedge between the German left and center.

Farthest to the right was stationed a special assault force like Emmich's at Liège for the opening move into Alsace. Detached from the First Army and composed of the VIIth Corps and 8th Cavalry Division, it was to liberate Mulhouse and Colmar and anchor itself upon the Rhine in the corner where Germany, Alsace, and Switzerland meet.

Next to it was the First Army commanded by handsome General

Dubail. Dubail, it was said, did not recognize the impossible, combined indomitable will with unlimited energy, and for some cause hidden in the intricate defiles of French Army politics was not on the best of terms with General de Castelnau, his immediate neighbor on the left. Castelnau had left the General Staff to become commander of the Second Army which held the crucial front around Nancy.

The Third, Fourth, and Fifth Armies were gathered on the other side of Verdun for the great offensive through the German center contemplated by Plan 17. Their deployment extended from Verdun to Hirson. The Fifth Army, which held the open end, faced northeast for offense through the Ardennes, rather than north to meet the descending forces of the German right wing. The position on the Fifth Army's left, centering on the once strong but lately neglected fortress of Maubeuge, was expected to be held by the British, who, it was now learned, were not coming in the full strength originally planned. The deficiency, if it did not unduly worry Joffre and his Staff whose attention was centered elsewhere, hardly reassured the Fifth Army's commander, General Lanrezac.

As he would have to bear the impact of the German right wing, General Lanrezac was all too conscious of the danger of his position. His predecessor in command of the Fifth Army had been Gallieni who, after tours of the terrain and failure to persuade the General Staff to modernize the fortifications of Maubeuge, had not been happy with it. When Gallieni reached the age limit in February 1914, Joffre had appointed Lanrezac, a "veritable lion" whose intellectual gifts he much admired and who had been one of his three choices for Deputy Chief of Staff in 1911. Because of his "keen intelligence" Lanrezac was considered a star at the General Staff, which forgave him his caustic manner and his tendency to bad temper and impolite language for the sake of the clarity, brilliance, and logic of his lectures. At sixty-two he fitted, like Joffre, Castelnau, and Pau, the heavy-mustached, heavy-paunched pattern for French generals.

In May 1914, when each of the generals of the five armies was given the pertinent section of Plan 17 that applied to him, Lanrezac immediately pointed out the dangers to his exposed flank if the Germans came down in strength west of the Meuse. His objections were ignored on the basic General Staff theory that the stronger the German right wing, "so much the better for us." In the last days before mobilization, Lanrezac put his objections in a letter to Joffre which was to become a primary document in the mountain of criticism and controversy that after the war rose over the grave of Plan 17. Lanrezac's tone in the letter, as a fellow officer said, was less a bold challenge of a dominant plan than a professor's critique of a pupil's thesis. It pointed out that the offensive planned for the Fifth Army was based on the assumption that the Germans would come through Sedan when in fact it was more likely that they would come around farther north through Namur, Dinant, and Givet. "Clearly," expounded the professor, "once the Fifth Army is committed to an offensive in the direction of Neufchâteau [in the Ardennes] it will be unable to parry a German offensive further north."

That was in fact the crucial point, but as if to cover himself Lanrezac reduced the force of his argument by adding, "it is noted here merely as a suggestion." Joffre who received the letter on mobilization day, August 1, decided it was "entirely inopportune" and "in the midst of the important events that filled my day," did not answer it. At the same time he dismissed the fears of General Ruffey, commander of the Third Army, who came to express concern about a possible German "parade through Belgium." With characteristic economy Joffre replied "You are wrong." In his opinion it was not for a generalissimo to explain but to give orders. It was not for a general to think but to carry out orders. Once a general had received his orders he should carry them out with a mind at rest, knowing it to be his duty.

On August 3, the day Germany declared war, the generals assembled in a meeting summoned by Joffre, hoping at last to hear him explain the totality of Plan 17 and of the strategy they were to carry out. The hope was vain; Joffre waited in benign silence for remarks. At last Dubail spoke up, saying that the offensive laid out for his army required reinforcements which were not allowed for. Joffre replied with one of his cryptic phrases, "That may be your plan; it is not mine." As no one knew what this meant, Dubail, thinking he had been misunderstood, repeated his remark. Joffre, "with his customary beatific smile," replied in the same words as before, "That may be your plan; it is not mine." The truth was that to Joffre what counted in the immense chaos of war was not the plan but the energy and verve with which it was carried out. Victory he believed would come not out of the best plan but out of the strongest will and firmest confidence, and these, he had no doubt, were his.

On August 4 he established Staff headquarters, known as *Grand Quartier Général* (hereafter GQG), at Vitry-le-François on the Marne, about half way between Paris and Nancy where he would be within roughly equal distance, about eighty to ninety miles, of each of the five army headquarters. Unlike Moltke who during his brief tenure as Com-

mander in Chief never went to the front or visited field armies' headquarters, Joffre was in constant and personal contact with his commanders.
Placidly ensconced in the back seat of his car, he would be driven on his
rounds at seventy miles an hour by his appointed private chauffeur
Georges Bouillot, three times winner of the Grand Prix auto race. German
generals having been given a perfect plan to carry out were not expected
to need constant guidance. French generals were expected, as Foch said,
to think, but Joffre, always suspecting weakness of nerve or other personal
failings, liked to keep them under close supervision. After the maneuvers
in 1913 his dismissal of five generals from the active list had caused a public
sensation and a shudder in every garrison in France; nothing like it had
ever happened before. During August, under the terrible test of live ammunition, Joffre was to scatter generals like chaff at the first sign of what he
considered incompetence or insufficient élan.

Elan was high at Vitry on the banks of the tranquil tree-bordered
Marne shining green and gold in the August sun. In the school building
taken over by GQG, an unbridgeable gulf separated Operations, the
Troisième Bureau, which occupied the class rooms, from Intelligence, the
Deuxième Bureau, which was installed in the gymnasium with the
apparatus pushed against the walls and the rings tied up to the ceiling.
All day the Deuxième Bureau collected information, interrogated prisoners, deciphered documents, put together ingenious conjectures and passed
on its reports to its neighbors. Consistently these indicated German
activity west of the Meuse. All day Troisième read the reports, handed
them around, criticized, disputed, and refused to believe them if they
pointed to conclusions that would require the French to modify their plan
of offensive.

Every morning at eight o'clock Joffre presided at meetings of the
section chiefs, a majestic and immobile arbiter but never the puppet of
his entourage as outsiders, misled by his silence and his bare desk, supposed. He kept no papers on his desk and no map on his wall; he wrote
nothing and said little. Plans were prepared for him, said Foch; "he weighs
them and decides." There were few who did not tremble in his presence.
Anyone who was five minutes late at his mess was treated to a thunderous
frown and remained an outcast for the remainder of the meal. Joffre ate
in silence with a gourmet's entire devotion to the food. He complained
continuously of being kept in the dark by his staff. When an officer
referred to an article in the latest issue of *l'Illustration* which Joffre had
not seen he cried angrily, "You see, they hide everything from me!" He

used to rub his forehead, murmuring "Poor Joffre!" which his staff came to recognize as his way of refusing to do something that was being urged upon him. He was angered by anyone who tried too openly to make him change his mind. Like Talleyrand he disapproved of too much zeal. Without the probing intellect of Lanrezac or the creative intellect of Foch, he was inclined by temperament to rely on those he had chosen for his staff. But he remained the master, almost a despot, jealous of his authority, resentful of the least encroachment upon it. When it was proposed that Gallieni, having been designated by Poincaré as Joffre's successor in case of emergency, should be installed at GQG, Joffre, fearing to be in the shadow of his old commander, would have none of it. "He is difficult to place," he confided to Messimy. "I have always been under his orders. *Il m'a toujours fait mousser*" (He has always made me foam), an admission of some significance in view of the part the personal relationship between Joffre and Gallieni was to play in the fateful hours before the Marne. As a result of Joffre's refusal to have him at GQG, Gallieni was left in Paris with nothing to do.

The long-desired moment when the French flag would be raised again in Alsace had come. The covering troops, waiting among the thick, rich pines of the Vosges, trembled with readiness. These were the remembered mountains with their lakes and waterfalls and the damp delicious smell of the forests where fragrant ferns grew between the pines. Hilltop pastures, grazed by cattle, alternated with patches of forest. Ahead, the shadowed purple line of the Ballon d'Alsace, highest point in the Vosges, was hidden in mist. Patrols who ventured to the top could see down below the red-roofed villages of the lost territory, the gray church spires, and the tiny, gleaming line of the Moselle where, young and near its source, it was narrow enough to be waded. Squares of white potato blossom alternated with strips of scarlet-runner beans and gray-green-purple rows of cabbages. Haycocks like small fat pyramids dotted the fields as if arranged by a painter. The land was at its peak of fertility. The sun sparkled over all. Never had it looked so much worth fighting for. No wonder *l'Illustration* in its first issue of the war showed France in the person of a handsome *poilu* sweeping the beautiful damsel Alsace off her feet into a rapturous embrace.

A proclamation addressed to the inhabitants had already been printed by the War Ministry ready for posting on the walls of liberated towns. Airplane reconnaissance showed the area to be lightly held, almost too lightly thought General Bonneau, commander of the VIIth Corps, who feared he was "walking into a mousetrap." He sent an aide on the evening of August 6 to report to General Dubail that he considered the Mulhouse operation "delicate and hazardous" and was concerned for his right flank and rear. GQG, consulted by Dubail who had expressed similar concern at the meeting of generals on August 3, regarded all doubts as failure of the offensive spirit. Expressed at the start of an operation, a commander's doubts, however valid, too often proved a formula for retreat. In French military doctrine seizure of the initiative was more important than careful appreciation of enemy strength. Success depended upon the fighting qualities of commanders, and to permit caution and hesitation to take hold at the outset would, in the view of Joffre and his entourage, have been ruinous. GQG insisted upon the attack in Alsace being launched as soon as possible. Obeying, Dubail called General Bonneau on the telephone, asked if he was "ready," and on receiving an affirmative answer, ordered the attack for next morning.

At five o'clock on the morning of August 7, a few hours before Ludendorff led his brigade into Liège, General Bonneau's VIIth Corps spilled over the crest of the Vosges, presenting arms as they crossed the frontier, and swept down in a classic bayonet charge upon Altkirch, a town of about 4,000 on the way to Mulhouse. They took Altkirch by assault in a battle lasting six hours with 100 casualties. It was not the last bayonet charge of a war whose symbol was soon to be a mud-filled trench, but it might as well have been. Executed in the finest style and spirit of the *Règlement* of 1913, it seemed the proof of *cran*, the apotheosis of *la gloire*.

The hour, as the French communiqué reported, "was one of indescribable emotion." Frontier posts were torn from the ground and carried in triumph through the town. But General Bonneau, still uneasy, did not push on toward Mulhouse. Impatient at his lack of progress, GQG on the following morning issued an imperative order that Mulhouse be taken and the Rhine bridges destroyed that day. On August 8 the VIIth Corps entered Mulhouse without firing a shot about an hour after the last German troops, withdrawn to defend the frontier farther north, had left it.

The French cavalry in gleaming cuirasses and black horsehair plumes galloped through the streets. Almost dumfounded at the sudden apparition, the people stood at first transfixed in silence or sobbing, then gradually broke into joy. A grand review of the French troops lasting two hours was held in the main square. The bands played "The Marseillaise" and the "Sambre et Meuse." Guns were hung with flowers of red, white, and blue.

Joffre's proclamation vaunting his soldiers as "the vanguard of the great work of *revanche* . . . who carry in the folds of their flags the magic words 'Right and Liberty' " was posted on the walls. Chocolates, pastries, and pipes of tobacco were thrust upon the soldiers. From all windows flags and handkerchiefs waved and even the roofs were covered with people.

Not all were welcomers. Many of the inhabitants were Germans who had settled there since 1870. One officer riding through the crowds noticed among them "grave and impassive faces, pipe in teeth, who looked as if they were counting us,"—as indeed they were, and afterward hastened away during the night to report on the strength of the French divisions.

German reinforcements hurriedly sent from Strasbourg were deployed around the city while the French were busy occupying it. General Bonneau, who lacked faith in success from the start, had made what dispositions he could to prevent envelopment. When battle began on the morning of August 9, his left at Cernay fought fiercely and stubbornly all day, but his right, holding too long to an unthreatened sector, was not brought around in time. Finally recognizing the necessity of reinforcements which had worried Dubail from the start, GQG sent up a reserve division, but at this stage to solidify the front two would have been required. For twenty-four hours the battle swayed until 7:00 A.M. on August 10 when the French, pushed back and fearing to be enveloped, withdrew.

Humiliating as it was to the army after the glorious rhetoric of the communiqués and proclamations and the accumulated yearning of forty-four years, the loss of Mulhouse was cruelest upon the inhabitants who were now left subject to German reprisals. Those who had been most enthusiastic in welcoming the French were informed upon by their German fellow citizens with unpleasant consequences. The VIIth Corps retreated to within ten miles of Belfort. At GQG the natural and eternal enmity of Staff officers for field officers flared. Confirmed in his belief of Bonneau's lack of *cran*, Joffre began the roll of heads for which his regime was to become famous. General Bonneau became the first of the *limogés*, so-called because officers relieved of their commands reported at Limoges for rear duty. Blaming "faulty execution," Joffre within three days also dismissed the commander of the 8th Cavalry and another general of division.

Intent upon the original plan of freeing Alsace and pinning German forces to that front, and without regard for reports coming out of Belgium, Joffre took one regular and three reserve divisions and added them to the VIIth Corps to form a special Army of Alsace for renewed action on his extreme right. General Pau was called out of retirement to command it. During the four days while it was assembling, heavy pressures were building up elsewhere. On August 14, the day Pau was to move forward, thirty storks were seen flying south over Belfort, leaving Alsace two months before their usual time.

The French nation was hardly aware of what had happened. GQG's bulletins were masterpieces of the opaque. Joffre operated on the fixed principle that civilians should be told nothing. No journalists were allowed at the front; no names of generals or of casualties or of regiments were mentioned. In order to keep all useful information from the enemy, GQG adopted a principle from the Japanese, to wage war "silently and anonymously." France was divided into a Zone of the Rear and a Zone of the Armies; in the latter Joffre was absolute dictator; no civilian, not even the President, much less the despised deputies, could enter it without his permission. It was his and not the President's name that was signed to the proclamation addressed to the people of Alsace.

Ministers protested that they knew more of the movements of the German armies than of the French. Poincaré, to whom Joffre, considering himself independent of the Minister of War, reported directly, complained he was never told about reverses. On one occasion when a presidential visit to the Third Army was proposed, Joffre issued "strict orders" to its commander "not to discuss with the President any questions of strategy or foreign policy. A report of the conversation must be submitted." All his generals were cautioned against explaining military operations to members of the government. "In the reports I forward," Joffre told them, "I never make known the object of current operations or my intentions."

His system was soon to break down under rising public pressure, but in August, when frontiers fell and nations were invaded and vast armies swayed in what was still a war of movement, and the earth shook under the thud of war from Serbia to Belgium, hard news from the front was rare indeed. History while it was happening in that month, despite a thousand eager chroniclers, was not easily pinned down. General Gallieni dining in civilian clothes at a small café in Paris on August 9 overheard an editor of *Le Temps* at the next table say to a companion, "I can tell you that General Gallieni has just entered Colmar with 30,000 men." Leaning over to his friend, Gallieni said quietly, "That is how history is written."

While the Germans at Liège waited for the siege guns, while the world marveled at the continued resistance of the forts and the London *Daily*

Mail quoted a consensus of opinion that they "could never be taken," while the assembling of the armies continued, some men waited in acute anxiety for the pattern of the German offensive to reveal itself. General Gallieni was one. "What is happening behind the German front?" he worried. "What massive concentration is gathering behind Liège? With the Germans one must always expect the gigantic."

The answer to this question was what the French cavalry under General Sordet had been sent to find out. Yet so impetuous was the dash of the cuirassiers that it carried them too far too soon. They crossed into Belgium on August 6, riding along the Meuse to reconnoiter the strength and direction of the German concentration. Covering 110 miles in three days, nearly 40 miles a day, they passed Neufchâteau and reached within nine miles of Liège. As the French did not dismount or unsaddle during halts, the horses were exhausted by the forced pace. After a day's rest, the cavalry continued their reconnaissance in the Ardennes and west of the Meuse as far as Charleroi, but everywhere they were too early to find evidence that the Germans had crossed the Meuse in any great strength, and everywhere active German cavalry screened the concentration of the armies building up behind the German border. The French found themselves foiled of the thrilling cavalry charge that was the traditional way to open wars. Although farther north where they were on the offensive toward Louvain and Brussels, the German cavalry used the shock tactics of the charge, here they avoided a direct fight and kept up an impenetrable screen, supported by cyclist battalions and Jagers in motor transport who held off the French with machine-gun fire.

It was disheartening. Cavalrymen on both sides still believed in the naked sword, the *arme blanche*, despite the experience of the American Civil War when Confederate General Morgan, employing his men as mounted infantry with rifles, would cry, "Here, boys, are those fools coming again with their sabers; give it to them!" In the Russo-Japanese War an English observer, the future General Sir Ian Hamilton, reported that the only thing the cavalry could do in the face of entrenched machine guns was to cook rice for the infantry, causing the War Office to wonder if his months in the Orient had not affected his mind. When Germany's observer in the same war, the future General Max Hoffmann, reported a similar conclusion about the defensive power of entrenched machine guns, Moltke was inspired to comment, "There never was such a crazy way of making war!"

In 1914 the Germans' avoidance of cavalry encounter and their use of machine guns proved an effective screen. Sordet's reports of no large

German masses coming down on the French left confirmed GQG in its preconceived ideas. But the outlines of a German right wing envelopment were already becoming clear to King Albert and General Lanrezac who, being in its path, were more disposed to see it. Another of these was General Fournier, governor of the French fortress of Maubeuge. He informed GQG that German cavalry on August 7 had entered Huy on the Meuse and that his reports indicated they were covering an advance of five or six corps. As Huy was the site of the only bridge between Liège and Namur, this enemy force was obviously intending to cross the Meuse. Maubeuge, its governor warned, was in no condition to resist such numbers. To GQG the report of five or six corps appeared as the frightened exaggeration of a defeatist mind. Weeding out the fainthearted was for Joffre in August the most vital requirement for success and he promptly relieved General Fournier of his command. Later, after an investigation the order was rescinded. Meanwhile it was discovered that it would take at least a fortnight to put Maubeuge in any state of effective defense.

The anxiety of General Lanrezac, who had also received the report from Huy, was increasing. On August 8 he sent his Chief of Staff, General Hely d'Oissel, to impress the threat of a German right wing outflanking movement upon GQG. General Lanrezac's concern was "premature," GQG replied, because such a movement was "out of proportion to the means at the enemy's disposal." Further evidence from Belgium kept coming in, but for each report the "chapel" of Plan 17 found an explanation: the brigades seen at Huy were on "some special mission" or the sources of information were "suspicious." The attack on Liège had for its object "nothing more" than seizure of a bridgehead there. On August 10 GQG felt "confirmed in the impression that the principal German maneuver would not take place in Belgium."

Committed to its own coming offensive, the French General Staff wanted to make sure that the Belgian Army would stand fast until it could be joined by the Fifth Army and the British. Joffre sent another emissary, Colonel Adelbert, with a personal letter from Poincaré to King Albert hoping for "concerted action" by both armies. This officer, who reached Brussels on August 11, received the same answer as his predecessors: that if a German advance straight across Belgium developed as the King foresaw, he would not permit his army to risk being cut off from Antwerp. Colonel Adelbert, an ardent apostle of *élan*, could not bring himself to transmit the King's pessimism to GQG. He was saved the necessity by a battle next day from which the Belgians emerged drenched in glory.

The Uhlans, penetrating toward Louvain, were held up at the bridge at Haelen, by the massed fire of Belgian cavalry under General de Witte. Using his troops as dismounted riflemen supported by infantry, de Witte repeated General Morgan's success in Tennessee. From eight in the morning until six in the evening his steady volleys of rifle fire repelled repeated German charges with lance and saber. Slaughtered Uhlans of von Marwitz's finest squadrons covered the ground until at last a remnant turned back, leaving the field to the Belgians. The glorious victory, heralded by happy correspondents in Brussels as the decisive battle of the war, aroused the Belgian Staff and its French friends to transports of enthusiasm; they saw themselves in Berlin. Colonel Adelbert informed GQG it could regard the "retreat of the German cavalry as final and the projected attack through central Belgium as postponed or even abandoned."

The optimism seemed justified by the continuing stand of the Liège forts. Every morning Belgian newspapers published the triumphant headline, *"Les forts tiennent toujours!"* On August 12, the same day as the Battle of Haelen, the great siege guns the Germans had been waiting for to put an end to that boast, arrived.

Liège was cut off from the outside world; when the great black weapons reached the outskirts within range of the forts, only the local inhabitants saw the advent of the monsters that to one observer looked like "overfed slugs." Their squat barrels, doubled by the recoil cylinders that grew on their backs like tumors, pointed cavernous mouths upward at the sky. By late afternoon of August 12 one of them had been set up and aimed at Fort Pontisse. Its crew, wearing padding over eyes, ears, and mouth, lay flat on their stomachs ready for the firing which was done electrically at a distance of 300 yards. At 6:30 the first detonation thundered over Liège. The shell rose in an arc 4,000 feet high and took 60 seconds to reach its target. When it hit, a great conical cloud of dust, debris, and smoke rose a thousand feet in the air. Meanwhile the Skoda 305s had also been brought up, and began bombardment of other forts, "walked in" upon their targets by artillery observers stationed in church towers and balloons. Men of the Belgian garrisons heard the shells descending with a screaming whistle, felt the detonations coming each time more nearly overhead as the aiming was corrected until, as their terror mounted, the shells exploded upon them with deafening crash and the solid steel heads smashed through the concrete. Over and over the shells came, blowing men to bits, choking them with fumes released by the charge of high explosives. Ceilings fell in, galleries were blocked, fire, gas, and noise filled the underground chambers; men became "hysterical, even mad in the awful apprehension of the next shot."

Before the guns went into action only one fort had been taken by assault. Fort Pontisse withstood forty-five shells in twenty-four hours of bombardment before it was sufficiently shattered to be taken by infantry attack on August 13. Two more forts fell that day, and by the 14th all the forts east and north of the city had fallen. Their guns were destroyed; the roads north of the city were open. The advance of von Kluck's First Army began.

The siege mortars were then moved forward to be trained on the western forts. One of the 420s was dragged through the city itself to take aim on Fort Loncin. M. Célestin Demblon, deputy of Liège, was in the Place St. Pierre when he saw coming around the corner of the square "a piece of artillery so colossal that we could not believe our eyes. . . . The monster advanced in two parts, pulled by 36 horses. The pavement trembled. The crowd remained mute with consternation at the appearance of this phenomenal apparatus. Slowly it crossed the Place St. Lambert, turned into the Place du Théâtre, then along the Boulevards de la Sauveniere and d'Avroy attracting crowds of curious onlookers along its slow and heavy passage. Hannibal's elephants could not have astonished the Romans more! The soldiers who accompanied it marched stiffly with an almost religious solemnity. It was the Belial of cannons! . . . In the Parc d'Avroy it was carefully mounted and scrupulously aimed. Then came the frightful explosion; the crowd was flung back, the earth shook like an earthquake and all the window panes in the vicinity were shattered. . . ."

By August 16 eleven of the twelve forts had fallen; only Fort Loncin still held out. In the intervals of bombardment the Germans sent emissaries under flags of truce to demand General Leman's surrender. He refused. On the 16th Loncin was hit by a shell which exploded in the magazine and blew up the fort from inside. When the Germans entered through a tumble of broken cupolas and smoking concrete they found the apparently lifeless body of General Leman pinned beneath a block of masonry. "Respect the General, he is dead," said an adjutant with blackened face who stood guard over the body. Leman was, however, alive but unconscious. Revived and carried to General von Emmich, he surrendered his sword saying: "I was taken unconscious. Be sure to put that in your dispatches."

"Military honor has not been violated by your sword," replied Emmich, handing it back. "Keep it."

Later, from Germany where he was taken a prisoner, General Leman wrote to King Albert, "I would gladly have given my life, but Death would not have me." His opponents, Generals von Emmich and Ludendorff, were both awarded the blue, white, and gold cross of *Pour le Mérite*, Germany's highest military medal, to hang around their necks.

On the day after the fall of Fort Loncin the Second and Third Armies began their advance, bringing the whole mass of the German right wing into motion on its march across Belgium. As the march had not been scheduled to begin before August 15, Liège had held up the German offensive by two days, not two weeks as the world then believed. What Belgium gave the Allies was neither two days nor two weeks but a cause and an example.

▶▶▶ 12 ▶

▶▶▶ *BEF to the Continent*

DELAY IN COVERING THE EXPOSED FLANK ON
General Lanrezac's left was caused by dispute and disagreement among
the British who were to have held that end of the line. On August 5, their
first day of war, the General Staff's plan, worked out to the last detail by
Henry Wilson, instead of going into action automatically like the continental war plans, had to be approved first by the Committee of Imperial
Defence. When the Committee convened as a War Council at four o'clock
that afternoon, it included the usual civilian as well as military leaders and
one splendid colossus, taking his seat among them for the first time, who
was both.

Field Marshal Lord Kitchener was no more happy to be the new Secretary of State for War than his colleagues were to have him. The government was nervous at having in their midst the first active soldier to enter
the Cabinet since General Monk served under Charles II. The generals
were worried that he would use his position, or be used by the government,
to interfere with the sending of an Expeditionary Force to France. No
one's apprehensions were disappointed. Kitchener promptly expressed his
profound contempt for the strategy, policy, and role assigned to the British
Army by the Anglo-French plan.

What exactly was to be his authority, given his position straddling two stools, was not entirely clear. England entered the war with a vague understanding that supreme authority resided in the Prime Minister but with no precise arrangement as to whose advice he was to act on or whose advice was to be definitive. Within the army, field officers despised Staff officers as "having the brains of canaries and the manners of Potsdam," but both groups were as one in their distaste for interference by civilian ministers who were known as "the frocks." The civil arm in its turn referred to the military as "the boneheads." At the War Council of August 5, the former were represented by Asquith, Grey, Churchill, and Haldane, and the army by eleven general officers, including Field Marshal Sir John French, Commander in Chief designate of the Expeditionary Force; its two corps commanders, Sir Douglas Haig and Sir James Grierson; its Chief of Staff, Sir Archibald Murray, all lieutenant generals; and its Deputy Chief of Staff, Major General Henry Wilson, whose easy faculty for making political enemies had flourished during the Curragh crisis and lost him the higher post. In between, representing no one quite knew what, was Lord Kitchener who regarded the purpose of the Expeditionary Force with deep misgivings and its Commander in Chief without admiration. If not quite as volcanic in expressing himself as Admiral Fisher had been, Kitchener now proceeded to pour the same scorn upon the General Staff's plan to "tack on" the British Army to the tail of French strategy.

Having had no personal share in the military planning for war on the Continent, Kitchener was able to see the Expeditionary Force in its true proportions and did not believe its six divisions likely to affect the outcome in the impending clash between seventy German and seventy French divisions. Though a professional soldier—"The most able I have come across in my time," said Lord Cromer when Kitchener came out to command the Khartoum campaign—his career had lately been pursued at Olympian levels. He dealt in India, Egypt, Empire, and large concepts only. He was never seen to speak to or notice a private soldier. Like Clausewitz he saw war as an extension of policy, and took it from there. Unlike Henry Wilson and the General Staff, he was not trapped in schedules of debarkation, railroad timetables, horses, and billets. Standing at a distance he was able to view the war as a whole, in terms of the relations of the powers, and to realize the immense effort of national military expansion that would be required for the long contest about to begin.

"We must be prepared," he announced, "to put armies of millions in the field and maintain them for several years." His audience was stunned

and incredulous, but Kitchener was relentless. To fight and win a European war, Britain must have an army of seventy divisions, equal to the continental armies, and he had calculated that such an army would not reach
full strength until the third year of war, implying the staggering corollary
that the war would last that long. The Regular Army with its professional
officers and especially its NCO's, he considered to be precious and indispensable as a nucleus for training the larger force he had in mind. To
throw it away in immediate battle under what he expected to be unfavorable circumstances and where, from the long view, its presence could not
be decisive, he regarded as criminal folly. Once it was gone there were no
troops properly trained, in his opinion, to take its place.

Lack of conscription was the most striking of all differences between
the British and continental armies. The Regular Army was designed for
overseas duty rather than for defense of the homeland which was left to
the Territorials. Since the Duke of Wellington had laid down the unalter-
able dictum that recruits for foreign service "must be volunteers," Britain's
war effort consequently depended on a volunteer army which left other
nations uncertain as to how deeply Britain was, or would be, committed.
Although Lord Roberts, the senior Field Marshal, now over seventy, had
campaigned strenuously for conscription for years with one lone supporter
in the Cabinet, needless to say Winston Churchill, labor was rigorously
opposed and no government would have risked office to favor it. Britain's
military establishment in the home islands consisted of six divisions and
one cavalry division of the Regular Army, with four regular divisions totaling 60,000 men overseas, and fourteen divisions of Territorials. A Reserve
of about 300,000 was divided into two classes: the Special Reserve which
was barely enough to fill up the Regular Army to war strength and maintain it in the field through the first few weeks of fighting and the National
Reserve which was to provide replacements for the Territorials. According
to Kitchener's standards the Territorials were untrained, useless "amateurs"
whom he regarded with the same unmixed scorn—and with as little justice—as the French did their Reserves, and rated them at zero.

At the age of twenty Kitchener had fought as a volunteer with the
French Army in the war of 1870 and spoke French fluently. Whether or
not he had, as a result, an extra sympathy for France, he was no extreme
partisan of French strategy. At the time of the Agadir crisis he told the
Committee of Imperial Defence that he expected the Germans to walk
through the French "like partridges," and when invited he refused to take
part in any decision the Committee might think fit to take. He sent them

word, as Lord Esher recorded it, "that if they imagined he was going to command the Army in France he would see them damned first."

That England in 1914 gave him the War Office and thereby acquired the only man prepared to insist on organizing for a long war was not because of his opinions but because of his prestige. With no talent for the bureaucracy of administrative office and no taste for conforming to the "green baize routine" of Cabinet meetings after being accustomed to a proconsul's simple "Let it be done," Kitchener did his best to escape his fate. The government and generals, more conscious of his faults of character than of his virtues of clairvoyance, would have been glad to let him go back to Egypt but they could not do without him. He was named Secretary for War not because he was considered qualified by the holding of opinions which no one else held but because his presence was indispensable "to tranquilize public feeling."

Ever since Khartoum the country had felt an almost religious faith in Kitchener. There existed between him and the public the same mystic union that was to develop between the people of France and "Papa Joffre" or between the German people and Hindenburg. The initials "K of K" were a magic formula and his broad martial mustache a national symbol that was to England what the *pantalon rouge* was to France. Wearing its bushy magnificence with an air of power, tall and broad-shouldered, he looked like a Victorian image of Richard the Lionhearted except for something inscrutable behind the solemn blazing eyes. Beginning August 7, the mustache, the eyes and the pointing finger over the legend, "Your Country Needs YOU" were to bore into the soul of every Englishman from a famous recruiting poster. For England to have gone to war without Kitchener would have been as unthinkable as Sunday without church.

The War Council, however, put little credence in his prophecy at a moment when everyone was thinking of the immediate problem of sending the six divisions to France. "It was never disclosed," wrote Grey long afterward with perhaps needless bewilderment, "how or by what process of reasoning he made this forecast of the length of the war." Whether because Kitchener was right when everybody else was wrong or because civilians find it hard to credit soldiers with ordinary mental processes or because Kitchener was never able or never deigned to explain his reasons, all his colleagues and contemporaries assumed that he reached his conclusion, as Grey said, "by some flash of instinct rather than by reasoning."

Whatever the process, Kitchener also foretold the pattern of the coming German offensive west of the Meuse. This too he was afterward considered to have arrived at by "some gift of divination" rather than by "any knowledge of times and distances," according to one General Staff officer. In fact, like King Albert, Kitchener saw the assault on Liège casting ahead of it the shadow of Schlieffen's right-wing envelopment. He did not think Germany had violated Belgium and brought England in against her in order to make what Lloyd George had called "just a little violation" through the Ardennes. Having avoided the responsibility of the prewar planning, he could not now propose to withhold the six divisions, but he saw no reason to risk their extinction at a position as far forward as Maubeuge where he expected they would bear the full force of the invading German armies. He proposed that they concentrate instead at Amiens, seventy miles farther back.

Exasperated by this drastic change of plan with its appearance of timidity, the generals were confirmed in their worst expectations. The short, stocky, and florid Sir John French, about to take command in the field, was keyed to a pitch of valor and combativeness. His normally apoplectic expression, combined with the tight cavalryman's stock which he affected in place of collar and tie, gave him an appearance of being perpetually on the verge of choking, as indeed he often was, emotionally if not physically. When appointed Chief of the Imperial General Staff in 1912, he at once informed Henry Wilson that he intended to get the army ready for a war with Germany which he regarded as an "eventual certainty." Since then he had been nominally responsible for the joint plans with France, although in fact the French plan of campaign was practically unknown to him—as was the German. Like Joffre, he had been named head of the Staff without Staff experience or study at Staff college.

The choice, like that of Kitchener for the War Office, was less concerned with innate qualification than with rank and reputation. On the several colonial fields of battle where Britain's military reputations had been made, Sir John had shown courage and resource and what an authority called "a practical grasp of minor tactics." In the Boer War his exploits as a cavalry general, culminating in the romantic gallop through the Boer lines to the relief of Kimberley, earned him fame as a bold commander willing to take risks and a popular repute almost equal to that of Roberts and Kitchener. Since Britain's record against an untrained opponent lacking modern weapons had on the whole not been brilliant, the army was proud of and the government grateful for a hero. French's prowess, aided by social éclat, carried him far. Like Admiral Milne he moved in the Edwardian swim. As a cavalry officer he was conscious of belonging to the élite of the army. Friendship with Lord Esher was no handicap, and politically he was allied with the Liberals who came to power in 1906. In 1907 he was made Inspector General; in 1908, representing the army, he accompanied King Edward on the state visit to the Czar at Reval; in 1912 came his appointment as CIGS; in 1913 he was promoted to Field Marshal. At sixty-two he was the army's second ranking active officer after Kitchener to whom he was junior by two years although he looked older. It was generally understood that he would command the expeditionary force in the event of war.

In March 1914 when the Curragh Mutiny, crashing down upon army heads like Samson's temple, caused him to resign, he seemed to have quixotically brought his career to an abrupt end. Instead he gained added favor with the government which believed the Opposition had engineered the Mutiny. "French is a trump and I love him," wrote Grey appreciatively. Four months later when the crisis came, he was resurrected and on July 30 designated to be Commander in Chief if Britain should go to war.

Untrained to study and with a mind closed to books, at least after his early successes in action, French was less renowned for mental ability than for irritability. "I don't think he is particularly clever," King George V confided in his uncle, "and he has an awful temper." Like his vis-à-vis across the Channel, French was an unintellectual soldier with the fundamental difference that whereas Joffre's outstanding quality was solidity, French's was a peculiar responsiveness to pressures, people, and prejudices. He had, it was said, "the mercurial temperament commonly associated with Irishmen and cavalry soldiers." Joffre was imperturbable in all weathers; Sir John alternated between extremes of aggressiveness in good times and of depression in bad. Impulsive and easily swayed by gossip, he had, in the opinion of Lord Esher, "the heart of a romantic child." He once presented to his former Chief of Staff in the Boer War a gold flask inscribed as a memento of "our long and tried friendship proved in sunshine and shadow." The proved friend was the somewhat less sentimental Douglas Haig who in August 1914 wrote in his diary, "In my own heart I know that French is quite unfit for this great command at a time of crisis in our Nation's history." The knowledge in Haig's heart was not unconnected with a sense that the person best fitted for the command was himself, nor was he to rest until he obtained it.

The destination—and consequently the purpose—of the BEF having been reopened by Kitchener, the Council, who were in Henry Wilson's opinion "mostly entirely ignorant of their subjects . . . fell to discussing strategy like idiots." Sir John French suddenly "dragged in the ridiculous proposal of going to Antwerp," saying that as British mobilization was behind schedule anyway the possibility of cooperating with the Belgian Army should be considered. Haig, who like Wilson kept a diary, "trembled at the reckless way" his chief undertook to change plans. Equally upset, the new CIGS, Sir Charles Douglas, said that as everything had been arranged for landings in France and French rolling stock was set aside to transport the troops forward, any shift at the last moment would have "serious consequences."

No problem so harassed the General Staff as the unfortunate difference in capacity between French and British railroad cars. The mathematical permutations involved in transferring troops from one to the other were such as to make transport officers tremble at any threatened change of arrangements.

Happily for their peace of mind the shift to Antwerp was vetoed by Churchill who two months later was to go there himself and to conceive the bold and desperate landing of two marine brigades and a territorial division in a last-minute, vain effort to save the vital Belgian port. On August 5, however, he said the navy could not protect the troop ships over the longer route across the North Sea to the Scheldt, whereas the passage across the Strait of Dover could be guaranteed absolutely. The navy having had time to prepare for the Channel crossing, he argued that the moment was favorable and urged that all six divisions be sent at once. Haldane supported him, as did Lord Roberts. Dispute now arose over how many divisions should be sent, whether one or more should be retained until the Territorials had further time for training or until replacements could be brought home from India.

Kitchener returned to his idea of staging at Amiens, and received support from his friend and future commander of the Gallipoli campaign, Sir Ian Hamilton who, however, felt it was urgent for the BEF to reach there as soon as possible. Grierson spoke up for "decisive numbers at the decisive point." Sir John French, most forward of the forward, suggested that "we should go over at once and decide destination later." It was agreed to order transports for all six divisions immediately while leaving destination to be settled until a representative of the French General Staff, sent for hurriedly at Kitchener's insistence, could arrive for further consultation on French strategy.

Within twenty-four hours, as the result of an invasion scare that brewed up overnight, the Council changed its mind and reduced the six divisions to four. News of the discussion about the strength of the BEF had leaked out. The influential *Westminster Gazette*, organ of the Liberals, denounced the "reckless" denuding of the country. From the opposite camp Lord Northcliffe came roaring in to protest the departure of a single soldier. Although the Admiralty confirmed the conclusion of the Committee of Imperial Defence in 1909 that no serious invasion was possible, visions of hostile landings on the east coast would not vanish. To the intense disgust of Henry Wilson, Kitchener, who was now responsible for England's safety, brought home to England one division that had been scheduled to embark for France directly from Ireland and detached two brigades from other divisions which he sent to guard the east coast, thus "hopelessly messing up our plans." It was decided to send four divisions and the cavalry at once—embarkation to begin August 9—to send the 4th Division later and to keep the 6th Division in England. When the Council adjourned, Kitchener was under the impression, not shared by the generals, that Amiens had been agreed upon as the staging area.

When Colonel Huguet arrived, hastily sent over by the French General Staff, Wilson informed him of the embarkation times. Although it was hardly a matter to be kept secret from the BEF's French hosts, he incurred Kitchener's wrath and a rebuke for breach of secrecy. Wilson "answered back," having, as he wrote, "no intention of being bullied" by Kitchener, "especially when he talks such nonsense as he did today." So began, or was aggravated, a mutually cherished antipathy that was not to aid the fortunes of the BEF. Wilson, who of all the British officers had the most intimate relation with the French and the ear of Sir John French, was considered bumptious and presumptuous, and was consequently ignored by Kitchener, while in his turn Wilson professed to consider Kitchener "mad" and as "much an enemy of England as Moltke," and instilled his iniquities into the mind of the temperamentally suspicious and excitable Commander in Chief.

From August 6 to 10, while the Germans at Liège were waiting for the siege guns and the French were liberating and losing Mulhouse, 80,000 troops of the BEF with 30,000 horses, 315 field guns, and 125 machine guns were assembling at Southampton and Portsmouth. Officers' swords had been freshly sharpened in obedience to an order that prescribed sending them to the armorer's shop on the third day of mobilization, although they were never used for anything but saluting on parade. But apart from such occasional nostalgic gestures the force, in the words of its official historian, was "the best-trained, best organized and best-equipped British Army that ever went forth to war."

On August 9 embarkation began, the transports departing at intervals of ten minutes. As each left its dock every other ship in the harbor blew whistles and horns and every man on deck cheered. So deafening was the noise that it seemed to one officer that General von Kluck could not fail to hear it behind Liège. However, with the navy confident that they had sealed off the Channel from attack, there was little fear for the safety of the crossing. The transports crossed at night without escort. Waking at 4:30 in the morning, a soldier was astonished to see the whole fleet of transports with engines stopped, floating on an absolutely glassy sea without a destroyer in sight; they were waiting for transports from other embarkation ports to complete a rendezvous in mid-Channel.

When the first arrivals landed at Rouen they were received with as much rapture, said a French witness, as if they had come to conduct a service of expiation for Joan of Arc. At Boulogne others debarked at the foot of a towering column erected in honor of Napoleon on the spot from which he had planned to launch the invasion of England. Other transports came into Havre where the French garrison climbed on the roofs of their barracks and cheered wildly as their allies came down the gangplanks in the blazing heat. That evening, to the sound of far-off summer thunder, the sun went down in a blood-red glow.

In Brussels next day the British ally was at last glimpsed—though narrowly. Hugh Gibson, secretary of the American Legation, on an errand to the British military attaché, walked into his room unannounced and saw a British officer in field uniform, dirty and unshaven, writing at a desk. Hustled out by the attaché, Gibson asked irreverently if the rest of the British Army was hidden in the building. In fact the location of the British landings was so well kept from the Germans that they were not to know where or when the BEF had arrived until they ran into it at Mons.

In England antipathies among its commanders were coming to the surface. The King on a visit of inspection asked Haig, who was an intimate at court, his opinion of Sir John French as Commander in Chief. Haig felt it his duty to reply that "I had grave doubts whether either his temper was sufficiently even or his military knowledge sufficiently thorough to enable him to be an effective commander." After the King had left, Haig wrote in his diary that Sir John's military ideas during the Boer War had "often shocked me," and added his "poor opinion" of Sir Archibald Murray, an "old woman" who "weakly acquiesces" in orders which his better judgment tells him are unsound in order to avoid scenes with Sir John's temper. Neither, thought Haig, "are at all fitted for the appointments which they now hold." Sir John, he told a fellow officer, would not listen to Murray but "will rely on Wilson which is far worse." Wilson was not a soldier but "a politician," a word which, Haig explained, was "synonymous with crooked dealing and wrong values."

Unburdening himself of these sentiments, the smooth, polished, immaculate, and impeccable Haig, who had friends in all the right quarters and at fifty-three a career of unbroken success behind him, was preparing his way to further success ahead. As an officer who during the campaign in the Sudan had included "a camel laden with claret" in the personal pack train that followed him across the desert, he was accustomed to doing himself well.

On August 11, within three days of departing for France, Sir John French learned for the first time some interesting facts about the German Army. He and General Callwell, Deputy Director of Operations, visited Intelligence, whose chief began telling them about the German system of using reserves. "He kept on producing fresh batches of Reserve Divisions and Extra-Reserve Divisions," wrote Callwell, "like a conjuror producing glassfuls of goldfish out of his pocket. He seemed to be doing it on purpose—one felt quite angry with the man." These were the same facts that the Deuxième Bureau, French Intelligence, had learned in the spring of 1914, too late to impress the General Staff or change its estimate of the German right wing. They also came too late to change the British mind. For a new idea to penetrate and effect a fundamental change in strategy, as well as in all the infinite physical details of deployment, would have required time, far more time than was left.

Next day the struggle over strategy between Kitchener and the generals was fought out at a final meeting of the Council. Besides Kitchener, Sir John French, Murray, Wilson, Huguet, and two other French officers were present. Although Kitchener could not hear, unless with the mind's ear, the exploding shells of the 420s opening the roads through Liège, he asserted that the Germans would be coming through on the far side of the Meuse "in great force." With a sweep of his arm he indicated the German enveloping movement on a huge wall map. If the BEF concentrated at Maubeuge, he argued, it would be swamped before it was ready for battle and be forced into a retreat which would be disastrous for its morale in its first encounter with a European enemy since the Crimea. He insisted on a base further back at Amiens to allow freedom of action.

His six opponents, the three English and three French officers, were equally adamant on keeping to the original plan. Sir John French, coached by Wilson since his own suggestion of a shift to Antwerp, now protested that any change would "upset" the French plan of campaign, and remained determined to go forward to Maubeuge. The French officers emphasized the necessity of filling in the left end of their line. Wilson inwardly raged at the "cowardice" of concentrating at Amiens. Kitchener said the French plan of campaign was dangerous; that instead of taking the offensive, to which he was "entirely opposed," they should wait to counter a German attack. For three hours the wrangle continued until Kitchener, unconvinced, was gradually forced to give way. The plan had been in existence and he had known and fundamentally disapproved of it for five years. Now, with the troops already on the water, it had to be accepted because there was no time to make another.

In a last futile gesture—or a calculated gesture to absolve himself of responsibility—Kitchener, bringing Sir John French along with him, took the issue to the Prime Minister. "Knowing nothing at all about it," as Wilson confided to his diary, Asquith did what might be expected. Presented with Kitchener's views as against the expert and united opinion of the combined General Staffs, he accepted the latter. Reduced to four instead of six divisions, the BEF went forward as arranged. The momentum of predetermined plans had scored another victory.

Kitchener, nevertheless, unlike the French and German ministers of war, retained direction of his country's military effort, and the instructions he now issued to Sir John French for the conduct of the BEF in France reflected his desire to limit its liability in the early stages of the war. Like Churchill who, looking ahead to the vast task of the British Navy, had ordered the Mediterranean fleet both to engage the *Goeben* and avoid engaging "superior forces," Kitchener, looking ahead to the army of millions he had to build, assigned a policy and a mission to the BEF irreconcilable with each other.

"The special motive of the Force under your control," he wrote, "is to support and cooperate with the French Army . . . and to assist the French in preventing or repelling the invasion by Germany of French or Belgian territory." With a certain optimism, he added, "and eventually to restore the neutrality of Belgium"—a project comparable to restoring virginity. As the "numerical strength of the British force and its contingent reinforcement is strictly limited," and keeping this consideration "steadily in view," it will be necessary to exercise "the greatest care towards a minimum of loss and wastage." Reflecting Kitchener's disapproval of French offensive strategy, his order stated that if asked to participate in any "forward movements" in which the French were not engaged in large numbers and in which the British might be "unduly exposed to attack," Sir John was to consult his government first and must "distinctly understand that your command is an entirely independent one and that you will in no case come in any sense under the orders of any Allied general."

Nothing could be more unequivocal. At one stroke Kitchener had canceled the principle of unity of command. His motive was to preserve the British Army as a nucleus for the future; the effect, given a captain of Sir John's temperament, was practically to nullify the order to "support" and "cooperate" with the French. It was to haunt the Allied war effort long after Sir John was replaced and Kitchener himself was dead.

On August 14 Sir John French, Murray, Wilson, and a staff officer, encouragingly named Major Sir Hereward Wake, arrived at Amiens, where the British troops detrained for further advance to the concentration area around Le Cateau and Maubeuge. On that day as they began moving up, Kluck's Army began moving down from Liège. The BEF, marching cheerfully up the roads to Le Cateau and Mons, were greeted enthusiastically along the way with cries of "*Vivent les Anglais!*" The happiness of the welcome gave point to Lord Kitchener's dampening notice to his troops that they might expect to "find temptations, both in wine and women," which they must "entirely resist." The farther north the British marched, the greater was the enthusiasm. They were kissed and decked with flowers. Tables of food and drink were set out and all British offers of pay refused. A red tablecloth with bands of white sewn on it to form the St. Andrew's cross of the Union Jack was flung over a balustrade. The soldiers tossed their regimental badges, caps, and belts to smiling girls and other admirers who begged for souvenirs. Soon the British Army was marching with peasants' tweed caps on their heads and their trousers held up by string. All along the way, wrote a cavalry officer afterward, "we were feted and cheered by the people who were soon to see our backs." Looking back on it, he remembered the advance of the BEF to Mons as "roses all the way."

▶▶▶ *13* ▶

▶▶▶ *Sambre et Meuse*

ON THE WESTERN FRONT THE FIFTEENTH day brought an end to the period of concentration and preliminary attacks. The period of offensive battle began. The French right wing, opening the offensive into German-occupied Lorraine, took an old embattled path like so many in France and Belgium where, century after century, whatever the power that makes men fight brought legions tramping down the same roads, leveling the same villages. On the road east from Nancy the French passed a stone marker inscribed, "Here in the year 362 Jovinus defeated the Teutonic hordes."

While on the far right the Army of General Pau renewed the offensive in Alsace, the First and Second Armies of Generals Dubail and de Castelnau marched through two natural corridors in Lorraine which determined the French line of attack. One led toward Sarrebourg, objective of Dubail's Army; the other descending from the ring of hills around Nancy called the Grand Couronné, led via Château Salins into a valley terminating in the natural fortress of Morhange, objective of de Castelnau's Army. The Germans had prepared the region against expected French attack with barbed wire, trenches, and gun emplacements. At both Sarrebourg and Morhange they had well-fortified positions from which they could only be dislodged by an attack of irresistible *élan* or bombard-ment by heavy artillery. The French counted on the first and scorned the second.

"Thank God we don't have any!" replied a General Staff artillery officer in 1909 when questioned about 105 mm. heavy field artillery. "What gives the French Army its force is the lightness of its cannon." In 1911 the War Council proposéd to add 105s to the French Army, but the artillery men themselves, faithful to the famous French 75s, remained unalterably op-posed. They despised the heavy field cannon as drags upon the mobility of the French offensive and regarded them, like machine guns, as defensive weapons. Messimy as War Minister and General Dubail, then on the General Staff, had forced through an appropriation for several batteries of 105s, but through changes of government and the continued contempt of the artillery corps, by 1914 only a few had been incorporated into the French Army.

On the German side the Lorraine front was held by the Sixth Army of Rupprecht, Crown Prince of Bavaria, and by the Seventh Army of Gen-eral von Heeringen which on August 9 was placed under Prince Rup-precht's orders. Rupprecht's mission was to hold as many French troops on his front as possible in order to keep them away from the main front opposite the German right wing. He was to accomplish this, according to Schlieffen's strategy, by falling back and drawing the French forward into a "sack" where, having lengthened their line of communications, they could be engaged in battle while the decision took place elsewhere. The essence of the plan was to let the enemy in this sector come on as he showed every disposition to do and, while tempting him into a tactical victory, inflict upon him a strategic defeat.

Like the plan for East Prussia, this strategy involved psychological dangers. In the hour when the trumpets sounded, when his fellow com-manders were advancing to victory, it required Rupprecht to accept obedi-ently the necessity of withdrawal, not a pleasing prospect to a vigorous commander with an appetite for glory, especially not to one of semi-royal rank.

Erect and good-looking in a disciplined way, with straightforward eyes and a sensible mustache, Rupprecht had no touch about him of his capri-cious predecessors, the two King Ludwigs of Bavaria whose several and excessive passions, one for Lola Montez and the other for Richard Wagner, had caused one king to be deposed and the other to be declared mad. He came in fact from a less eccentric branch of the family which had providéd the regent for the mad king, and as a direct descendant of Henrietta, daughter of Charles I of England, was legitimist Stuart heir to the English throne. In memory of King Charles, white roses decorated the palace of Bavaria every year on the anniversary of the regicide. Rupprecht had a more current Allied connection in the person of his wife's sister Elizabeth who was married to King Albert of Belgium. The Bavarian Army, however, was thoroughly German. They were "barbarians," reported General Dubail after the first days of battle, who before evacuating a town sacked the houses in which they had been billeted, ripped up the chairs and mattresses, scattered the contents of closets, tore down curtains, smashed and trampled furniture, ornaments, and utensils. These, however, were as yet only the habits of troops sullenly retiring. Lorraine was to see worse.

For the first four days of Dubail's and Castelnau's offensive, the Germans retired slowly according to plan, fighting only rearguard action against the French. Down the broad straight roads bordered with plane trees the French came in their blue coats and red trousers. At every rise in the road they could see great distances over the checkerboard of fields, one green with alfalfa, the next gold with ripe grain, another brown, already plowed for the next crop, others dotted with haystacks in neat rows. The 75s spoke with piercing shriek over the fields as the French entered the territory that had once been theirs. In the first combats against a not too determined German resistance the French were victorious, although the German heavy artillery, when used, tore terrible gaps in their lines. General Dubail on August 15 passed carts bringing back the wounded, pale and mangled, some with limbs blown off. He saw a battlefield of the previous day still strewn with corpses. On the 17th the XXth Corps of de Castelnau's army, commanded by General Foch, took Château Salins and reached within striking distance of Morhange. On the 18th Dubail's army took Sarrebourg. Confidence soared; *offensive à outrance* appeared to have triumphed; the troops exulted and saw themselves on the Rhine. At that moment Plan 17 began to crumble, had, indeed, been crumbling for many days.

On the front opposite Belgium, General Lanrezac had all this time been hammering at GQG for permission to face north into the oncoming German right instead of northeastward for the offensive into the Ardennes against the German center. He saw himself being enveloped by the German forces coming down west of the Meuse whose true strength he suspected, and he insisted on being allowed to shift a part of his army to the left bank of the Meuse into the angle with the Sambre where it could

Field Marshal Sir John French.
The Imperial War Museum

Prince Rupprecht (*left*) and the Kaiser.　　　*The Imperial War Museum*

General von François.   *Brown Brothers*

Colonel Max Hoffmann.   *The Imperial War Museum*

German cavalry officers in Brussels.

Brown Brothers

(*above*) Joffre, Poincaré, King George V, Foch, and Haig.

The Imperial War Museum

(*left*) General Gallieni.

General von Kluck.   *The Imperial War Museum*

block the German path. Here he could hold a line along the Sambre, the river that rises in northern France and flows northeast through Belgium, edging the mining district of the Borinage, to join the Meuse at Namur. Along its banks rise cone-shaped slag heaps; coal barges ply its waters coming out of Charleroi, city of the kingly name that ever after 1914 would have for French ears a sound as mournful as Sedan.

Lanrezac bombarded GQG with reports from his own reconnaissance of German units and movements which indicated a mass pouring through on either side of Liège in hundreds of thousands, perhaps 700,000, "maybe even two million." GQG insisted the figures must be wrong. Lanrezac argued that strong German forces would come down on his flank through Namur, Dinant, and Givet just at the time the Fifth Army would be entering the Ardennes. When his Chief of Staff, Hely d'Oissel, whose normally melancholy demeanor was growing daily more somber, came to GQG to plead his case, the officer who received him cried: "What, again! Is your Lanrezac still worrying about being flanked on his left? That won't happen and"—he added, voicing GQG's basic thesis—"if it does, why so much the better."

Nevertheless, though determined to let nothing detract from the main offensive planned to start on August 15, GQG could not be entirely impervious to the mounting evidence of an enveloping maneuver by the German right wing. On August 12 Joffre permitted Lanrezac to move his left corps to Dinant. "High time," Lanrezac muttered caustically, but the move no longer sufficed, he insisted; his whole army must be shifted westward. Joffre refused, insisting the Fifth Army must remain oriented eastward to perform its appointed role in the Ardennes. Always jealous of his authority, he told Lanrezac, "The responsibility of stopping the enveloping movement is not yours." Exasperated, like all men of rapid mind at the blindness of others and accustomed to respect as a strategist, Lanrezac continued to hector GQG. Joffre grew irritated at his constant criticism and contentiousness. He conceived the whole duty of generals was to be lions in action and dogs in obedience, an ideal to which Lanrezac, with a mind of his own and an urgent sense of danger, found it impossible to conform. "My inquietude," he wrote later, "increased from hour to hour." On August 14, the last day before the opening of the offensive, he went in person to Vitry.

He found Joffre in his office buttressed by Generals Belin and Berthelot, his Chief and Assistant Chief of Staff. Belin, once known for his vivacity, was already showing the strain of overwork. Berthelot, quick and clever, like his opposite number, Henry Wilson, was an inveterate optimist who found it temperamentally difficult to anticipate trouble. He weighed 230 pounds and, having early conceded the victory of August heat over military dignity, worked in blouse and slippers. Lanrezac, whose dark Creole face was already sagging with worry, insisted the Germans would appear on his left just when he would be deep in the Ardennes where the difficult terrain made quick success unlikely and a turnabout impossible. The enemy would be left to complete his enveloping maneuver unopposed.

Speaking in what Poincaré called his "creamy tones," Joffre told Lanrezac that his fears were "premature." He added, "We have the impression the Germans have nothing ready there"—"there" meaning west of the Meuse. Belin and Berthelot repeated the assurance of "nothing ready there" and endeavored at once to soothe and encourage Lanrezac. He was urged to forget about envelopment and think only of the offensive. He left GQG, as he said, "with death in my soul."

On his return to Fifth Army headquarters at Rethel on the edge of the Ardennes he found on his desk a report from GQG Intelligence which compounded his sense of doom. It estimated an enemy force across the Meuse of eight army corps and four to six cavalry divisions—in fact an underestimate. Lanrezac instantly sent an aide with a letter to Joffre calling his attention to these reports "coming from your own headquarters" and insisting that the movement of the Fifth Army to the region between Sambre and Meuse should be "studied and prepared from this moment."

Meanwhile at Vitry another visitor arrived in deep anxiety to try to convince GQG of the danger on the left. When Joffre had refused to have Gallieni at Headquarters, Messimy had given him an office in the War Ministry where all reports were channeled to him. Although these did not include Intelligence reports from GQG which Joffre systematically refrained from sending to the government, Gallieni had gathered enough information to detect the outlines of the great flood pouring down upon France. It was the "terrible submersion" that Jaurès, foreseeing the use of reserves in the front line, had predicted. Gallieni told Messimy he must go to Vitry to make Joffre alter his plans, but Messimy who was nearly twenty years Joffre's junior and stood in awe of him said Gallieni must go himself as one to whom Joffre owed much of his career and whom he could not ignore. That was underestimating Joffre who could ignore anyone he chose. When Gallieni arrived, Joffre gave him only a few minutes and passed him on to Belin and Berthelot. They repeated the assurances they had given Lanrezac. GQG had its mind "closed to the evidence" and refused to consider the German advance west of the Meuse a serious threat, Gallieni reported to Messimy on his return.

Yet that evening, under pressure of increasing evidence, GQG began to waver. Joffre, replying to Lanrezac's last urgent message, agreed to "study" the proposed shift of the Fifth Army and to permit "preliminary arrangements" for the movement, although he still insisted that the menace to Lanrezac's flank was "far from immediate and its certainty far from absolute." By next morning, August 15, it had come much closer. GQG, with every nerve wound up for the great offensive, looked apprehensively to the left. A telephone call was put through to Lanrezac at 9:00 A.M. authorizing him to prepare the movement but not to execute it without direct order of the Commander in Chief. During the day reports reached GQG that 10,000 German cavalry had crossed the Meuse at Huy; then another report came that the enemy was attacking Dinant and had seized the citadel commanding the city from the high rock of the right bank; then a further report that they had forced a crossing but had been met by Lanrezac's Ist Corps pouring down from the left bank who had driven them back across the bridge in fierce combat (in which one of the first casualties was a twenty-four-year-old lieutenant named Charles de Gaulle). This was the corps whose movement across the river had been authorized on August 12.

The menace on the left could no longer be minimized. At 7:00 P.M. Joffre's direct order to move the Fifth Army into the angle of Sambre and Meuse was telephoned to Lanrezac, followed by his written order an hour later. GQG had succumbed—but not wholly. The order—Special Instruction No. 10—changed plans just far enough, it was felt, to meet the threat of envelopment but not so far as to give up the offensive of Plan 17. It acknowledged that the enemy "seems to be making his main effort by his right wing north of Givet"—as if Lanrezac needed to be told—and ordered the main body of the Fifth Army to move northwest "to operate together with the British and Belgian armies against the enemy forces to the north." One corps of the Fifth Army was to remain facing northeast in support of the Fourth Army to whom the chief burden of carrying the offensive into the Ardennes was now transferred. In effect the order stretched out the Fifth Army to the west over a wider front than heretofore without added men to cover it.

Order No. 10 instructed the new spearhead, General de Langle de Cary, commander of the Fourth Army, to make ready for attack "in the general direction of Neufchâteau," that is, into the heart of the Ardennes.

To strengthen the fighting quality of his army, Joffre set in motion a complicated exchange of troops between the armies of de Castelnau, Lanrezac,
and de Langle. As a result, two corps which had trained under Lanrezac
were taken from him and replaced by others new to his command. Although the new units included the two highly valued divisions from North
Africa which the *Goeben* had tried to halt, the extra movements and last-
minute changes aggravated Lanrezac's bitterness and despair.

While the rest of the French Army charged to the east, he saw himself
left to guard France's unprotected flank from the blow he believed was
designed to kill her. He saw himself given the heaviest task—though GQG
refused to recognize it as such—with the smallest means. His temper was
not improved by the prospect of operating in common with two independent armies—the British and Belgian—whose commanders outranked him
and were unknown to him. His men must execute in the August heat a
march of eighty miles requiring five days, and even if they reached the line
of the Sambre before the Germans did he feared it might be too late. By
then the Germans would have reached it in too great strength to be
stopped.

Where were the British who were supposed to be on his left? So far no
one had laid eyes on them. Though he could have learned from GQG
exactly where they were, Lanrezac no longer put any faith in GQG and
suspected darkly that France was the victim of a perfidious British trick.
Either the BEF was a myth or it was playing out a last cricket match before joining the war, and he refused to believe in its existence unless it was
seen personally by one of his own officers. Daily scouting parties which
included Lieutenant Spears, British liaison officer with the Fifth Army,
were sent out to scour the countryside but failed to find any men in khaki,
a strange functioning of liaison which Lieutenant Spears in a famous book
leaves unexplained. The failure added to Lanrezac's sense of peril. Anxieties pressed upon him. "My anguish," he wrote, "rose to its peak."

At the same time as he issued Order No. 10 Joffre asked Messimy to
transfer three Territorial divisions from coast defense to fill the space
between Maubeuge and the Channel. He was scraping the bottom of the
barrel for a makeshift defense against the German right wing rather than
subtract a single division from his cherished offensive. Not yet was he
ready to acknowledge that the enemy's will was being imposed on him.
Not all the Lanrezacs, Gallienis, and reconnaissance reports in the world
could shake GQG's central conviction that the greater the German right
wing, the more promising the prospects for the French seizure of initiative through the center.

The German march through Belgium, like the march of predator ants who periodically emerge from the South American jungle to carve a swath of death across the land, was cutting its way across field, road, village, and town, like the ants unstopped by rivers or any obstacle. Von Kluck's Army poured through north of Liège and von Bülow's south of the city, along the valley of the Meuse, toward Namur. "The Meuse is a precious necklace," King Albert had said, "and Namur is its pearl." Flowing through a broad canyon between rocky heights set back a space from the river on either side, the Meuse was a vacationland where in every other August, the traditional month of vacation, families picnicked, little boys swam, men fished from the banks under sun umbrellas, mothers sat in folding chairs knitting, little white sailboats tacked and skimmed, and the excursion boat ran from Namur to Dinant. Part of von Bülow's army was now crossing the river at Huy halfway between Liège and Namur to advance along both banks upon the second of Belgium's famed fortresses. Namur's circle of forts, constructed in the same pattern as those of Liège was the last bastion before France. With confidence in the iron fist of the siege guns which had done their work so well at Liège and were now being dragged in von Bülow's train toward their second assignment, the Germans expected to be through Namur in three days. On von Bülow's left the Third Army commanded by General von Hausen was advancing upon Dinant so that the two armies were converging upon the angle of the Sambre and Meuse just as Lanrezac's army was heading into it. While in the field Schlieffen's strategy was unrolling on schedule, behind the front a jagged crack appeared in the design.

On August 16 OHL, which had remained in Berlin until the end of the concentration period, moved to Coblenz on the Rhine some eighty miles behind the center of the German front. Here Schlieffen had envisaged a Commander in Chief who would be no Napoleon on a white horse watching the battle from a hill but a "modern Alexander" who would direct it "from a house with roomy offices where telegraph, telephone and wireless signalling apparatus are at hand, while a fleet of autos and motorcycles ready to depart, wait for orders. Here in a comfortable chair by a large table the modern commander overlooks the whole battlefield on a map. From here he telephones inspiring words and here he receives the reports from army and corps commanders and from balloons and dirigibles which observe the enemy's movements."

Reality marred this happy picture. The modern Alexander turned out to be Moltke who by his own admission had never recovered from his harrowing experience with the Kaiser on the first night of war. The "inspiring words" he was supposed to telephone to commanders were never part of his equipment and even if they had been would have been lost in transmission. Nothing caused the Germans more trouble, where they were operating in hostile territory, than communications. Belgians cut telephone and telegraph wires; the powerful Eiffel Tower wireless station jammed the air waves so that messages came through so garbled they had to be repeated three or four times before sense could be made of them. OHL's single receiving station became so clogged that messages took from eight to twelve hours to get through. This was one of the "frictions" the German General Staff, misled by the ease of communications in war games, had not planned for.

The wickedly unobliging resistance of the Belgians and visions of the Russian "steam roller" crashing through East Prussia further harassed OHL. Friction developed in the Staff. The cult of arrogance practiced by Prussian officers affected no one more painfully than themselves and their allies. General von Stein, Deputy Chief of Staff, though admittedly intelligent, conscientious, and hard-working, was described by the Austrian liaison officer at OHL as rude, tactless, disputatious, and given to the sneering, domineering manner known as the "Berlin Guards' tone." Colonel Bauer of the Operations Section hated his chief, Colonel Tappen, for his "biting tone" and "odious manner" toward subordinates. Officers complained because Moltke refused to allow champagne at mess and because fare at the Kaiser's table was so meager it had to be supplemented with private sandwiches after dinner.

From the moment the French attack began in Lorraine, Moltke's resolve to carry through Schlieffen's total reliance upon the right wing began to slip. He and his staff expected the French to bring up their main forces on their left to meet the threat of the German right wing. As anxiously as Lanrezac sent out scouts looking for the British, OHL looked for evidence of strong French movements west of the Meuse, and up to August 17 found none. That vexing problem of war presented by the refusal of the enemy to behave as expected in his own best interest beset them. They concluded from the movement in Lorraine and the lack of movement on the west that the French were concentrating their main force for an offensive through Lorraine between Metz and the Vosges. They asked themselves if this did not require a readjustment of German strategy. If this were the main French attack could not the Germans, by a shift of forces to their own left wing, bring about a decisive battle in Lorraine before the right wing could accomplish it by envelopment? Could they not in fact accomplish a true Cannae, the double envelopment that Schlieffen had held in the back of his mind? Anxious discussions of this alluring prospect and even some preliminary shifting of the weight of gravity toward the left engaged OHL from August 14 to 17. On that date they decided that the French were not massing in Lorraine to the extent believed, and reverted to the original Schlieffen plan.

But once divinity of doctrine has been questioned there is no return to perfect faith. From then on, OHL was lured by opportunity on the left wing. Mentally, Moltke had opened his mind to an alternative strategy dependent on what the enemy would do. The passionate simplicity of Schlieffen's design for total effort by one wing and rigid cleaving to plan regardless of enemy movements was broken. The plan that had appeared so faultless on paper cracked under pressure of the uncertainties, above all the emotions, of war. Having deprived himself of the comfort of a pre-arranged strategy, Moltke was thereafter tormented by indecisiveness whenever a decision was required. On August 16 Prince Rupprecht required one urgently.

He wanted permission to counterattack. His headquarters at Saint-Avold, a dreary, undistinguished town sunk in a hollow on the edge of the dingy mining district of the Saar, offered no princely amenities, no château for his lodging, not even a Grand Hotel. Westward stretched before him a land of easy rolling hills under wide open skies with no obstacles of importance before the Moselle, and, glowing on the horizon, the prize—Nancy, jewel of Lorraine.

Rupprecht argued that his given task to engage as many French troops as possible on his front could best be accomplished by attacking, a theory exactly contrary to the strategy of the "sack." For three days, from August 16 to 18, discussion raged over the telephone wire, happily all in German territory, between Rupprecht's headquarters and General Headquarters. Was the present French attack their main effort? They appeared to be doing nothing "serious" in Alsace or west of the Meuse. What did this indicate? Suppose the French refused to come forward and fall into the "sack"? Suppose Rupprecht continued to retire, would not a gap be opened up between him and the Fifth Army, his neighbor to the right, and would not the French attack through there? Might this not bring defeat to the right wing? Rupprecht and his Chief of Staff, General Krafft von Dellmensingen, contended that it would. They said their troops were impatiently awaiting the order to attack, that it was difficult to restrain them, that it would be shameful to force retreat upon troops "champing to go forward"; moreover, it was unwise to give up territory in Lorraine at the very outset of the war, even temporarily, unless absolutely forced to.

Fascinated yet frightened, OHL could not decide. A Staff major named Zollner was sent to Sixth Army Headquarters at Saint-Avold to discuss it further in person. He said OHL was considering a change in the planned retirement but could not give up the sack maneuver completely. He returned with nothing settled. Hardly had he gone when an airplane reconnaissance report was received of local French movements backward toward the Grand Couronné which were "immediately interpreted" by the Sixth Army Staff as evidence that the enemy was not coming forward into the sack after all and therefore the best thing to do was to attack him as quickly as possible.

Matters were at a crisis. More telephone conversations ensued between Rupprecht and von Krafft at one end and von Stein and Tappen at the other. Another messenger from OHL, Major Dommes, arrived—this was on August 17—with news that made a counteroffensive appear more desirable than ever. He said OHL was now sure the French were transferring troops to their western wing and were not "tied" to Lorraine; he reported the success of the siege guns at Liège which made the French fortress line look less formidable; he said OHL now believed the English had not yet landed on the Continent and, if a decisive battle could be quickly fought here in Lorraine, they might never come at all. But of course, said Major Dommes, he was obliged by Moltke's instructions to warn of all the hazards of a counteroffensive of which the chief and overwhelming one was that it would be a frontal attack—that anathema of German military doctrine—with envelopment impossible because of the mountains and the French fortresses.

Rupprecht retorted that there was less risk in attack than in further retreat, that he would take the enemy by surprise and might unbalance him, that he and his staff had considered all the risks and intended to master them. Working himself up with another eloquent ode to the offensive spirit of his gallant troops who must not be required to withdraw further, he announced he had made up his mind to attack unless he received a definite order from OHL prohibiting him. "Either let me attack," he shouted, "or issue definite orders!"

Confounded by the Prince's "forceful tone," Dommes hurried away to OHL for further instructions. At Rupprecht's headquarters "we waited, wondering if we would receive the prohibiting order." They waited all morning of the 18th, and when no word had come by afternoon von Krafft telephoned to von Stein demanding to know if an order was to be expected. Once again all the advantages and all the misgivings were thrashed over. Out of patience, von Krafft asked for a Yes or No. "Oh, no, we won't oblige you by forbidding an attack," von Stein replied with something less than the authority of a modern Alexander. "You must take the responsibility. Make your decision as your conscience tells you."

"It is already made. We attack!"

"*Na!*" answered von Stein, using a vernacular expression implying a shrug, "then strike and God be with you!"

Thus the sack maneuver was abandoned. The order was given for the Sixth and Seventh Armies to turn around and prepare for the counter-offensive.

Meanwhile the British, whom the Germans supposed not to have landed, were moving up toward their designated position on the left end of the French line. The continued rapturous greeting of the French populace sprang less from any deep love of the British, their antagonists for centuries, than from an almost hysterical thankfulness at the appearance of an ally in the struggle that was life or death for France. To the British soldiers, kissed, fed, and bedecked with flowers, it seemed like a celebration, a huge party of which they were unaccountably the heroes.

Their pugnacious Commander in Chief, Sir John French, disembarked on August 14 with Murray, Wilson, and Huguet who was now attached to the British command as liaison officer. They spent the night in Amiens and went to Paris next day to meet the President, Premier, and Minister of War. "*Vive le Général French!*" cried the delirious crowd of 20,000 who packed the square in front of the Gare du Nord and lined the streets. "'Eep, 'eep, 'ooray! *Vive l'Angleterre! Vive la France!*" All along the route to the British Embassy crowds, said to be greater than those who greeted Blériot when he flew the Channel, cheered and waved in happy welcome.

Poincaré was surprised to find his visitor a man of "quiet manner . . . not very military in appearance" with a drooping mustache whom one would take for a plodding engineer rather than the dashing cavalry commander of his reputation. He seemed slow and methodical without much *élan* and, despite his French son-in-law and a summer home in Normandy, able to speak few words of recognizable French. He proceeded to horrify Poincaré by announcing that his troops would not be ready to take the field for ten days, that is, until August 24. This was at a time when Lanrezac already feared that August 20 might be too late. "How we have been misled!" Poincaré wrote in his diary. "We thought them ready down to the last button and now they will not be at the rendezvous!"

In fact a puzzling change had come over the man whose most notable qualification for command, apart from seniority and the right friends, had been until now his military ardor. From the moment he landed in France Sir John French began to exhibit a preference for the "waiting attitude," a curious reluctance to bring the BEF to action, a draining away of the will to fight. Whether the cause was Kitchener's instructions with their emphasis on keeping the army in being and their caution against risking "losses and wastage," or whether it was a sudden realization percolating into Sir John French's consciousness that behind the BEF was no national body of trained reserves to take its place, or whether on reaching the Continent within a few miles of a formidable enemy and certain battle the weight of responsibility oppressed him, or whether all along beneath his bold words and manner the natural juices of courage had been invisibly drying up, or whether, fighting on foreign soil for someone else's homeland, it was simply a feeling of limited liability, no one who has not been in the same position can judge.

What is certain is that from the start Sir John French's meetings with his Allies left them variously disappointed, startled, or outraged. The immediate purpose for which the BEF had come to France—to prevent her being crushed by Germany—appeared to escape him, or at least he seemed to react to it with no sense of urgency. He appeared to think that his independence of command, which Kitchener had so stressed, meant he could "choose his own hours for fighting and his hours of resting," as Poincaré put it, indifferent to the possibility that the Germans might overrun France in the meantime, making any further question of fighting obsolete. As the inescapable Clausewitz had pointed out, an allied army operating under independent command is undesirable, but if unavoidable it is at least essential that its commander "should not be the most prudent and cautious but the most *enterprising*." During the next three weeks, the most critical of the war, the reason for Clausewitz's italics was to become clear.

Next day, August 16, Sir John visited GQG at Vitry where Joffre discovered him to be "firmly attached to his own ideas" and "anxious not to compromise his army." Sir John French in his turn was not impressed, owing perhaps to a British officer's sensitivity to social background. The struggle to republicanize the French Army had produced an unfortunate proportion, from the British point of view, of officers who were not "gentlemen." "*Au fond*, they are a low lot," Sir John wrote to Kitchener some months later, "and one always has to remember the class these French generals mostly come from." Indubitably the French generalissimo was the son of a tradesman.

On this occasion Joffre politely but urgently expressed his desire that the BEF should go into action on the Sambre along with Lanrezac on August 21. Contrary to what he had told Poincaré, Sir John French said he would do his best to meet this date. He requested that, as he was to hold the exposed end of the French line, Joffre should place Sordet's cavalry and two reserve divisions "directly under my orders." Joffre, needless to say, refused. Reporting the visit to Kitchener, Sir John French said he was "much impressed" by General Berthelot and the Staff, who were "deliberate, calm and confident" and exhibited a "total absence of fuss and confusion." He expressed no opinion of Joffre beyond noting that he seemed to realize the value of a "waiting attitude," a curious and self-revealing misjudgment.

The next visit was to Lanrezac. The taut temper at Fifth Army Headquarters appeared in Hely d'Oissel's first greeting to Huguet when he drove up in a car with the long-sought British officers, on the morning of August 17: "At last you're here. It's not a moment too soon. If we are beaten, we'll owe it to you."

General Lanrezac appeared on the steps to greet his visitors whose appearance in the flesh did not dispel lingering suspicions that he was being tricked by officers without divisions. Nothing said in the ensuing half-hour did much to reassure him. Speaking no English and his vis-à-vis no useful French, the two generals retired to confer alone without interpreters, a procedure of such dubious value that to explain it as done out of a mania for secrecy, as suggested by Lieutenant Spears, seems hardly adequate. They emerged shortly to join their staffs, of whom several were bilingual, in the Operations Room. Sir John French peered at the map, put on his glasses, pointed to a spot on the Meuse, and attempted to ask in French whether General Lanrezac thought the Germans would cross the river at that point which bore the virtually unpronounceable name Huy. As the bridge at Huy was the only one between Liège and Namur and as von Bülow's troops were crossing it as he spoke, Sir John French's question was correct if superfluous. He stumbled first over the phrase "cross the river" and had to be prompted by Henry Wilson who supplied "*traverser la fleuve*," but when he came to "*à Huy*," he faltered again.

"What does he say? What does he say?" Lanrezac was asking restively.

". . . *à Hoy*" Sir John French finally managed to bring out, pronouncing it as if he were hailing a ship.

It was explained to Lanrezac that the British Commander in Chief wished to know if he thought the Germans would cross the Meuse at Huy. "Tell the Marshal," replied Lanrezac, "I think the Germans have come to the Meuse to fish." His tone, which he might have applied to some particularly dim-witted question at one of his famous lectures, was not one customarily used toward the Field Marshal of a friendly army.

"What does he say? What does he say?" Sir John French, catching the tone if not the meaning, asked in his turn.

"He says they are going to cross the river, sir," Wilson answered smoothly.

In the mood engendered by this exchange, misunderstandings flourished. Billets and lines of communication, an inevitable source of friction between neighboring armies, produced the first one. There was a more serious misunderstanding about the use of cavalry, each commander wanting the use of the other's for strategic reconnaissance. Sordet's tired and half-shoeless corps which Joffre had assigned to Lanrezac had just been pulled away again on a mission to make contact with the Belgians north of the Sambre in the hope of persuading them not to retreat to Antwerp. Lanrezac was in dire need—as were the British—of information about the enemy's units and line of march. He wanted use of the fresh British cavalry division. Sir John French refused it. Having come to France with only four divisions instead of six, he wished to hold the cavalry back temporarily as reserve. Lanrezac understood him to say he intended employing it as mounted infantry in the line, a contemptible form of activity which the hero of Kimberley would as soon have used as a dry-fly fisherman would use live bait.

Most serious of all was the dispute over the date when the BEF would be ready for action. Although on the previous day he had told Joffre he would be ready by the 21st, Sir John French now reverted, either out of pure pique or from the uncertain state of his nerves, to what he had told Poincaré, that he would not be ready until the 24th. To Lanrezac it was the final affliction. Did the British General suppose the enemy would wait for him? he wondered, although not aloud. Obviously, as he had known from the start, the British were not to be relied on. The interview closed "with flushed faces." Afterward Lanrezac informed Joffre that the British would not be ready "until the 24th at the earliest," that their cavalry were to be used as mounted infantry and "cannot be counted on for any other purpose," and raised the question of possible confusion with the British along the roads, "in the event of retirement." The phrase produced a shock at GQG. Lanrezac, the "veritable lion" of admired aggressiveness, was already considering the possibility of retreat.

Sir John French also received a shock upon arriving at his headquarters, temporarily at Le Cateau, where he learned that the commander of his IInd Corps, his good friend General Grierson, had died suddenly that morning in the train near Amiens. French's request to Kitchener for a particular general to replace Grierson—"please do as I ask you in this matter," he wrote—was refused. Kitchener sent out General Sir Horace Smith-Dorrien with whom French had never got on, both being opinionated men. Like Haig, Smith-Dorrien had no great respect for the Commander in Chief and tended to act on his own initiative. Sir John French took out his resentment of Kitchener's choice in a heightened aversion to Smith-Dorrien and vented it, when all was over, in that sad and twisted document he entitled *1914* which a distinguished reviewer was to call "one of the most unfortunate books ever written."

At Belgian Army Headquarters in Louvain on August 17, the day when Sir John French was meeting Lanrezac and Rupprecht was demanding permission to counterattack, Premier de Broqueville came to discuss with King Albert the question of removing the government from Brussels to Antwerp. Detachments of all arms of von Kluck's army, outnumbering the Belgians four or five to one, were reported attacking the Belgian line at the river Gette 15 miles away; 8,000 troops of von Bülow's army were reported crossing the bridge at Huy, 30 miles away, and heading for Namur. If Liège had fallen what could Namur do? The period of concentration was over, the main German advance was on its way, and as yet the armies of Belgium's guarantors had not come. "We are alone," the King said to De Broqueville. The Germans, he concluded, would probably overrun central Belgium and occupy Brussels and "the final issue of events is still uncertain." It was true that the French cavalry was expected that day in the area of Namur. Joffre, when informing King Albert of their mission had assured him that in the best opinion of GQG the German units west of the Meuse were merely a "screen." He had promised that further French divisions would soon arrive to cooperate with the Belgians against the enemy. King Albert did not think the Germans at the Gette and at Huy were a screen. The mournful decision for the government to leave the capital was taken. On August 18 the King also ordered a general retreat of the army from the Gette to the fortified camp of Antwerp and the removal of Headquarters from Louvain fifteen miles back to Malines.

The order produced "incredulous dismay" among the forward school of the Belgian General Staff and especially in the bosom of Colonel Adelbert, President Poincaré's personal representative. Energetic and brilliantly qualified for the offensive in war, he was "less so" for diplomatic missions, ruefully admitted the French Minister to Belgium.

"You are not going to retreat before a mere cavalry screen?" exploded Colonel Adelbert. Astounded and angry, he accused the Belgians of "abandoning" the French without warning just at "the precise moment when the French cavalry corps had appeared north of the Sambre and Meuse." The military consequences, he said, would be grave, the moral success to the Germans great, and Brussels would be uncovered to "raids by German cavalry." This was his appreciation of the enemy strength that two days later was to take Brussels with over a quarter of a million men. However wrong his judgment and rude his tongue, Colonel Adelbert's anguish, from the French point of view, was understandable. Retirement to Antwerp meant that the Belgian Army would withdraw from the flank of the Allied line and break off contact with the French on the eve of the great French offensive.

During the day of August 18 the King's decision was changed several times in the agony of indecision between desire to save the Belgian Army from annihilation and reluctance to give up good positions just when French help might be arriving. Before the day was over the King's dilemma was solved for him by Joffre's Order No. 13 of that date which made it clear that the main French effort was to be made in another direction, leaving Belgium to guard the passage west of the Meuse with what assistance could be obtained from the Fifth Army and the British. King Albert hesitated no more. He reconfirmed the order for retreat to Antwerp, and that night the five Belgian divisions were disengaged from their positions on the Gette and withdrawn to the Antwerp camp, which they reached on August 20.

Joffre's Order No. 13 was the "get ready" signal for the great offensive through the German center upon which all French hopes were set. It was addressed to the Third, Fourth, and Fifth Armies and communicated to the Belgians and British. It instructed the Third and Fourth Armies of Generals Ruffey and De Langle de Cary to prepare to attack through the Ardennes and left two alternatives open to the Fifth Army, depending upon final appreciation of German strength west of the Meuse. In one case

Lanrezac was to attack northward across the Sambre "in complete liaison with the Belgian and British armies"; in the other case, supposing the enemy engaged "only a fraction of his right wing group" west of the Meuse, Lanrezac was to recross the river and support the main offensive through the Ardennes, "leaving to the Belgian and British armies the task of dealing with the German forces north of the Sambre and Meuse."

It was an impossible instruction. It required Lanrezac's army—not a unit but a heterogeneous mass of three corps and seven separate divisions stretched over an area thirty miles wide—which was then in motion on its way up to the Sambre, to face two ways and in the second alternative to return to the original deployment which Lanrezac had so painfully succeeded in turning it away from only three days ago. It could have paralyzed Lanrezac and left him stock-still, waiting for Joffre to choose one alternative or the other. Instead, the phrase "only a fraction of his right wing" sealed his loss of confidence in GQG. Ignoring the second alternative he pushed on to the Sambre. He would be in position by August 20, he informed Joffre, to counterattack any enemy forces attempting to cross the river between Namur and Charleroi and "to throw them back into the Sambre."

Moving toward that rendezvous his battalions sang the "Sambre et Meuse," a memorial of 1870 and favorite marching song of the French Army:

> The regiment of Sambre and Meuse marched to the cry of Liberty!
>> Seeking the path of glory that leads to immortality.
> The regiment of Sambre and Meuse died to the cry of Liberty!
>> Writing a page of glory that gave them immortality.

What dictated Order No. 13 was GQG's fixed determination to carry through Plan 17, the bearer of all its hopes for victory by decisive battle. In August when the war was young the idea that it could be brought to a quick finish by decisive battle still prevailed. GQG firmly believed that however strong the German right wing, a French offensive through the German center would succeed in isolating and destroying it. That night Messimy, in "anguish" about the weakly defended frontier below the Sambre, telephoned to Joffre and was told the Generalissimo was asleep. His awe greater than his anguish, Messimy agreed that he should not be awakened. Berthelot said to him comfortingly, "If the Germans commit the imprudence of an enveloping maneuver through northern Belgium, so much the better! The more men they have on their right wing, the easier it will be for us to break through their center."

On that day the German right wing was making its wheel through Belgium with von Kluck's army on the outside advancing upon Brussels, von Bülow's in the middle advancing upon Namur, and von Hausen's on the inside advancing on Dinant. Namur, held by the Belgian 4th Division and garrison troops, stood alone, still generally regarded, despite what had happened at Liège, as an impregnable fortress. Even those who took heed of Liège thought Namur would at least hold out long enough to allow Lanrezac to cross the Sambre, make contact with its defenders, and pin his forces to the rim of Namur's circle of forts. Commandant Duruy, a former military attaché in Brussels who was sent as liaison officer to Namur, gloomily reported to Lanrezac on August 19 that he did not believe the fortress could hold for long. Cut off from the rest of their army, the defenders were low in morale as well as in ammunition. Though his views were disputed by many, Duruy remained adamant in his pessimism.

On August 18 von Kluck's leading troops reached the Gette where they found themselves foiled of the Belgian Army. The destruction of that army was von Kluck's task. He had hoped to accomplish it by driving, through between the Belgians and Antwerp and rounding them up before they could reach the safety of their base. He was too late. King Albert's withdrawal saved his army and kept it in being to become a menace to von Kluck's rear when later he turned south for the march on Paris. "They always managed to escape our grasp so that their army has not been decisively beaten nor forced away from Antwerp," von Kluck was obliged to report to OHL.

He must shortly make his southward turn not only with the Belgians at his rear but with a new enemy, the British, in front of him. The Germans had worked it out that the logical place for the British to land would be at the ports nearest to the front in Belgium, and von Kluck's cavalry reconnaissance, with that marvelous human capacity to see what you expect to see even if it is not there, duly reported the British to be disembarking at Ostend, Calais, and Dunkirk on August 13. This would have brought them across von Kluck's front at almost any moment. In fact, of course, they were not there at all but were landing farther down the coast at Boulogne, Rouen, and Havre. The Ostend report, however, caused OHL to worry that as von Kluck made his southward turn his right might be attacked by the British, and if he swung his left to meet them a gap might be opened between his army and von Bülow's. To prevent such danger OHL on August 17 put von Kluck, to his extreme annoyance, under the orders of von Bülow. How it was possible for OHL to act on a report that the British were landing at Ostend and on the same day to tell Rupprecht that the British had not yet landed and might not come at all is one of the curiosities of war which can only be explained by conjecture. Perhaps the staff officers at OHL who dealt with the left wing were a different group from those who dealt with the right wing, and failed to consult each other.

The commanders of the First and Second Armies were both within two years of seventy. Von Kluck, a strange, dark, fierce-looking man, hardly looked his age, in contrast to von Bülow with his white mustache and puffy face who looked more than his. Von Kluck, who had been wounded in the war of 1870 and acquired his ennobling "von" at the age of fifty, had been chosen before the war for the leading role in the march on Paris. His was the army that was supposed to be the hammerhead of the right wing, his that was to regulate the pace of the whole, his that had been given the greatest striking power with a density of 18,000 men per mile of front (about 10 per meter) compared to 13,000 for von Bülow and 3,300 for Rupprecht. But haunted by the specter of a gap, OHL thought that von Bülow in the center of the right wing would be in the best position to keep its three armies abreast of each other. Von Kluck, bitterly resenting the arrangement, promptly disputed von Bülow's orders for each day's march, causing such havoc, what with the garbled communications, that after ten days OHL was forced to rescind the order—whereupon a gap was indeed to open up, beyond recall.

The Belgians even more than von Bülow tried von Kluck's temper. Their army by forcing the Germans to fight their way through delayed the schedule of march and by blowing up railroads and bridges disrupted the flow of ammunition, food, medicine, mail, and every other supply, causing the Germans a constant diversion of effort to keep open their lines to the rear. Civilians blocked roads and worst of all cut telephone and telegraph wires which dislocated communication not only between the German armies and OHL but also between army and army and corps and corps. This "extremely aggressive guerrilla warfare," as von Kluck called it, and especially the sniping by *franc-tireurs* at German soldiers, exasperated him and his fellow commanders. From the moment his army entered Belgium he found it necessary to take, in his own words, "severe and inexorable reprisals" such as "the shooting of individuals and the burning of homes" against the "treacherous" attacks of the civil population. Burned villages and dead hostages marked the path of the First Army. On August 19 after the Germans had crossed the Gette and found the Belgian Army withdrawn during the night, they vented their fury on Aerschot, a small town between the Gette and Brussels, the first to suffer a mass execution. In Aerschot 150 civilians were shot. The numbers were to grow larger as the process was repeated, by von Bülow's army at Ardennes and Tamines, by von Hausen's in the culminating massacre of 664 at Dinant. The method was to assemble the inhabitants in the main square, women usually on one side and men on the other, select every tenth man or every second man or all on one side, according to the whim of the individual officer, march them to a nearby field or empty lot behind the railroad station and shoot them. In Belgium there are many towns whose cemeteries today have rows and rows of memorial stones inscribed with a name, the date 1914, and the legend, repeated over and over: *"Fusillé par les Allemands"* (Shot by the Germans). In many are newer and longer rows with the same legend and the date 1944.

General von Hausen, commanding the Third Army, found, like von Kluck, that the "perfidious" conduct of the Belgians in "multiplying obstacles" in his path called for reprisals "of the utmost rigor without an instant's hesitation." These were to include "the arrest as hostages of notables such as estate-owners, mayors, and priests, the burning of houses and farms and the execution of persons caught in acts of hostility." Hausen's army were Saxons whose name in Belgium became synonymous with "savage." Hausen himself could not get over the "hostility of the Belgian people." To discover "how we are hated" was a constant amazement to him. He complained bitterly of the attitude of the D'Eggremont family in whose luxurious château of forty rooms, with greenhouses, gardens, and stable for fifty horses, he was billeted for one night. The elderly Count went around "with his fists clenched in his pockets"; the two sons absented themselves from the dinner table; the father came late to dinner and refused to talk or even respond to questions, and continued in this unpleasant attitude in spite of Hausen's gracious forbearance in ordering his military police not to confiscate the Chinese and Japanese weapons collected by Count d'Eggremont during his diplomatic service in the Orient. It was a most distressing experience.

The German campaign of reprisals was not, except individually, a spontaneous answer to Belgian provocation. It had been prepared ahead of time, with usual German care for every contingency, and was designed to save time and men by cowing the Belgians quickly. Speed was essential. It was also essential to enter France with every available battalion; Belgian resistance which required troops to be left behind interfered with this objective. Proclamations were printed in advance. As soon as the Germans entered a town its walls became whitened, as if by a biblical plague, with a rash of posters plastered on every house warning the populace against acts of "hostility." The punishment for civilians firing on soldiers was death, as it was for a variety of minor acts: "Any one approaching within 200 meters of an airplane or balloon post will be shot on the spot." Owners of houses where hidden arms were discovered would be shot. Owners of homes where Belgian soldiers were found hidden would be sent to "perpetual" hard labor in Germany. Villages where acts of "hostility" were committed against German soldiers "will be burned." If such an act took place "on the road between two villages, the same methods will be applied to the inhabitants of both."

In summary the proclamations concluded: "For all acts of hostility the following principles will be applied: all punishments will be executed without mercy, the whole community will be regarded as responsible, hostages will be taken in large numbers." This practice of the principle of collective responsibility, having been expressly outlawed by the Hague Convention, shocked the world of 1914 which had believed in human progress.

Von Kluck complained that somehow the methods employed "were slow in remedying the evil." The Belgian populace continued to show the most implacable hostility. "These evil practices on the part of the population ate into the very vitals of our Army." Reprisals grew more frequent and severe. The smoke of burning villages, the roads clogged with fleeing inhabitants, the mayors and burgomasters shot as hostages were reported to the world by the crowds of Allied, American, and other neutral correspondents who, barred from the front by Joffre and Kitchener, flocked to Belgium from the first day of war. A remarkable group of masters of vivid writing, the Americans included Richard Harding Davis for a syndicate of papers, Will Irwin for *Collier's*, Irwin Cobb for the *Saturday Evening Post*, Harry Hansen for the *Chicago Daily News*, John T. McCutcheon for the *Chicago Tribune*, and others. Securing credentials from the German Army, they followed along with it. They wrote of the debris of sacked houses, the blackened villages in which no human was left but only a silent cat on a shattered doorstep, the streets strewn with broken bottles and broken windowpanes, the agonized lowing of cows with unmilked udders, the endless files of refugees with their bundles and wagons and carts and umbrellas for sleeping on rainy nights along the roadside, of the fields of grain bending over with ripeness and no one to reap them, of the questions asked over and over: "Have you seen the French? Where are the French? Where are the British?" A rag doll lying on the road with its head squashed flat by the wheel of a gun carriage seemed to one American correspondent a symbol of Belgium's fate in the war.

On August 19 as the fusillade of shots cracked through Aerschot twenty-five miles away, Brussels was ominously quiet. The government had left the day before. Flags still decked the streets refracting the sun through their red and yellow fabric. The capital in its last hours seemed to have an extra bloom, yet to be growing quieter, almost wistful. Just before the end the first French were seen, a squadron of weary cavalry riding slowly down the Avenue de la Toison d'Or with horses' heads drooping. A few hours later four motorcars filled with officers in strange khaki uniforms drove by. People stared and raised a feeble cheer: "*Les Anglais!*" Belgium's Allies had come at last—too late to save her capital. On the 19th refugees continued to stream in from the east. The flags were being taken down; the populace had been warned; there was a menace in the air.

On August 20 Brussels was occupied. Squadrons of Uhlans moving with lances at the ready appeared suddenly in the streets. They were but the heralds of a grim parade, almost unbelievable in power and grandeur, that followed. It began at one o'clock with column after column of gray-green infantry, shaved and brushed with freshly shined boots and bayonets glinting in the sun and their ranks closed to eliminate the gaps left by the missing. The cavalry appeared in the same gray-green with black and white pennants fluttering from their lances like horsemen riding out of the Middle Ages. The phalanx of their innumerable hoofs clattering in close order seemed capable of trampling to death anything in their path. Heavy guns of the artillery thundered over the cobblestones. Drums pounded. Hoarse voices in chorus roared the victory song, "Heil dir im Siegeskranz," to the tune of "God Save the King." On and on, more and more, brigade after brigade, they came. Silent crowds watching the parade were stupefied by its immensity, its endlessness, its splendid perfection. The exhibition of equipment designed to awe the onlookers accomplished its object. Drawn by four horses, the kitchen wagons with fires lighted and chimneys smoking were no less astonishing than the trucks fitted out as cobblers' shops with cobblers standing at their benches hammering at bootsoles, and soldiers whose boots were being repaired standing on the running boards.

The parade kept to one side of the boulevards so that staff officers in motorcars and messengers on bicycles could dash up and down the line of march. Cavalry officers provided a varied show, some smoking cigarettes with careless hauteur, some wearing monocles, some with rolls of fat at the back of their necks, some carrying English riding crops, all wearing expressions of studied scorn. Hour after hour the march of the conquerors continued, all through the afternoon and evening, all that night and into the next day. For three days and three nights the 320,000 men of von Kluck's army tramped their way through Brussels. A German Governor-General took possession; the German flag was raised on the Town Hall; the clocks were put on German time; and an indemnity of 50,000,000 francs ($10,000,000) payable within ten days was imposed upon the capital and 450,000,000 francs ($90,000,000) upon the province of Brabant.

In Berlin, upon news of the fall of Brussels, bells rang out, shouts of pride and gladness were heard in the streets, the people were frantic with delight, strangers embraced, and "a fierce joy" reigned.

France on August 20 was not to be deterred from her offensive. Lanrezac had reached the Sambre, and the British were on a level with him. Sir John French after all his seesawing now assured Joffre he would be ready to go into action next day. But there was bad news from Lorraine. Rupprecht's counteroffensive had begun with tremendous impact. Castelnau's Second Army, unbalanced by the loss of the corps which Joffre had transferred to the Belgian front, was retreating, and Dubail reported being severely attacked. In Alsace, against greatly reduced German forces, General Pau had retaken Mulhouse and all the surrounding region, but now that Lanrezac's move to the Sambre had pulled away strength from the central offensive Pau's troops were needed to take their places in the line. In Joffre's sore need the decision was taken to withdraw Pau's forces: even Alsace, the greatest sacrifice, was to be laid on the altar of Plan 17. Although, like the iron mines of Briey, Alsace was expected to be regained with victory, General Pau's despair speaks through the lines of his last proclamation to the people he had just liberated. "In the north the great battle begins which will decide the fate of France and with it that of Alsace. It is there that the Commander in Chief summons all the forces of the nation for the decisive attack. For us in deep chagrin it becomes necessary to leave Alsace, momentarily, to assure her final deliverance. It is a cruel necessity to which the Army of Alsace and its Commander have had pain in submitting and to which they would never have submitted except in the last extremity." Afterward all that remained in French hands was a tiny wedge of territory around Thann where Joffre came in November and said simply, bringing tears to a silent crowd, "*Je vous apporte le baiser de la France.*" Final deliverance of the rest of Alsace was to wait four long years.

On the Sambre where Lanrezac was to take the offensive next day, "The 20th was an exciting day for the troops," in the words of Lieutenant Spears. "There was crisis in the air. Not a man but felt that a great battle was at hand. The morale of the Fifth Army was extremely high. . . . They felt certain of success." Their commander was less so. General d'Amade, commander of the group of three Territorial divisions which Joffre, as a last-minute gesture, had sent around to the left of the British, was also disquieted. In answer to a query he addressed to GQG, General Berthelot replied: "Reports on German forces in Belgium are greatly exaggerated. There is no reason to get excited. The dispositions taken at my orders are sufficient for the moment."

At three o'clock that afternoon General de Langle de Cary of the Fourth Army reported enemy movements across his front and asked Joffre if he should not begin the offensive at once. At GQG the conviction reigned firmly that the greater the movements to the German right, the thinner its center. "I understand your impatience," Joffre replied, "but in my opinion the time to attack is not yet. . . . The more the region [of the Ardennes] is depleted at the moment we pass to the offensive, the better the results to be anticipated from the advance of the Fourth Army supported by the Third. It is therefore, of the utmost importance that we allow the enemy to flow by us to the northwest without attacking him prematurely."

At nine that night he judged the time had come, and issued the order to the Fourth Army to begin the offensive at once. It was the hour of *élan*. To Messimy, Joffre reported as night fell on August 20, "There is reason to await with confidence the development of operations."

▶▶▶ *14* ▶

▶▶▶ *Debacle: Lorraine,*
Ardennes, Charleroi,
Mons

"IT IS A GLORIOUS AND AWFUL THOUGHT," WROTE Henry Wilson in his diary on August 21, "that before the week is over the greatest action the world has ever heard of will have been fought." As he wrote, the action had already begun. From August 20 to 24 the whole of the Western Front blazed with battle—in reality, four battles—known to history collectively as the Battle of the Frontiers. Beginning on the right in Lorraine where the fighting had been in progress since August 14, results were communicated all along the frontier so that the issue in Lorraine had effect on Ardennes and Ardennes on Sambre-and-Meuse (known as the Battle of Charleroi) and Charleroi on Mons.

By morning of August 20 in Lorraine the First Army of General Dubail and the Second Army of General de Castelnau had battered themselves to bruised and bloody punishment against the prepared defenses of the Germans at Sarrebourg and Morhange. *Offensive à outrance* found its limit too soon against the heavy artillery, barbed wire, and entrenched machine guns of the defense. In prescribing the tactics of assault, French Field Regulations had calculated that in a dash of 20 seconds the infantry line could cover 50 meters before the enemy infantry would have time to shoulder guns, take aim, and fire. All these "gymnastics so painfully practised at maneuvers," as a French soldier said bitterly afterward, proved grim folly on the battlefield. With machine guns the enemy needed only 8 seconds to fire, not 20. The Field Regulations had also calculated that shrapnel fired by the 75s would "neutralize" the defensive by forcing the enemy to keep his head down and "fire into the blue." Instead, as Ian Hamilton had warned from the Russo-Japanese War, an enemy under shrapnel fire if entrenched behind parapets could continue to fire through loopholes straight at the attacker.

Despite setbacks both French generals ordered an advance for August 20. Unsupported by artillery barrage their troops threw themselves against the German fortified line. Rupprecht's counterattack, which OHL had not had the nerve to deny him, opened the same morning with murderous artillery fire that tore gaping holes in the French ranks. Foch's XXth Corps of Castelnau's army formed the spearhead of the attack. The advance faltered before the defenses of Morhange. The Bavarians, whose ardor Rupprecht had been so loath to repress, attacking in their turn, plunged forward into French territory where, as soon as someone raised the cry of "*franc-tireurs!*" they engaged in a frenzy of looting, shooting, and burning. In the ancient town of Nomeny in the valley of the Moselle between Metz and Nancy, fifty civilians were shot or bayoneted on August 20, and what remained of its houses, after half had been shattered by artillery, were burned by order of Colonel von Hannapel of the 8th Bavarian Regiment.

Heavily engaged along its entire front, Castelnau's army was now strongly attacked on its left flank by a German detachment from the garrison of Metz. With his left giving way and all his reserves already thrown in, Castelnau realized all hope of advance was gone, and broke off battle. Defensive—the forbidden word, the forbidden idea—had to be recognized as the only choice. Whether he recognized, as Plan 17's most passionate critic suggests he should have, that the duty of the French Army was not to attack but to defend French soil, is doubtful. He ordered a general retreat to the defensive line of the Grand Couronné because he had to. On his right Dubail's First Army, in spite of severe casualties, was holding its ground and had even made an advance. When its right flank was uncovered by Castelnau's retreat, Joffre ordered the First Army to retire in conformity with its neighbor. Dubail's "repugnance" at having to give up territory taken after seven days of battle was strong, and his old antipathy to Castelnau was not softened by a withdrawal which he felt "the position of my army in no way required."

Although the French did not yet know it, the slaughter at Morhange snuffed out the bright flame of the doctrine of the offensive. It died on a field in Lorraine where at the end of the day nothing was visible but corpses strewn in rows and sprawled in the awkward attitudes of sudden death as if the place had been swept by a malignant hurricane. It was one of those lessons, a survivor realized afterward, "by which God teaches the law to kings." The power of the defense that was to transform the initial war of movement into a four-year war of position and eat up a generation of European lives revealed itself at Morhange. Foch, the spiritual father of Plan 17, the man who taught, "There is only one way of defending ourselves—to attack as soon as we are ready," was there to see and experience it. For four more years of relentless, merciless, useless killing the belligerents beat their heads against it. In the end it was Foch who presided over victory. By then the lesson learned proved wrong for the next war.

On August 21 General de Castelnau heard that his son had been killed in the battle. To his staff who tried to express their sympathy, he said after a moment's silence, in a phrase that was to become something of a slogan for France, "We will continue, gentlemen."

Next day the thunder of Rupprecht's heavy artillery, like the hoofs of an approaching stampede, sounded ceaselessly. Four thousand shells fell on Ste. Geneviève, near Nomeny, in a bombardment lasting seventy-five hours. Castelnau believed the situation so serious as possibly to require retreat behind the Grand Couronné, yielding Nancy. "I went to Nancy on the 21st," Foch wrote afterward; "they wanted to evacuate it. I said the enemy is five days from Nancy and the XXth Corps is there. They won't walk over the XXth without protest!" Now the metaphysics of the lecture hall became the "*Attaquez!*" of the battlefield. Foch argued that with the fortified line at their backs, the best defense was counterattack, and won his point. On August 22 he saw an opportunity. Between the French fortified zones of Toul and Epinal there was a natural gap called the Trouée de Charmes where the French had expected to canalize the German attack. Reconnaissance showed that Rupprecht by taking the offensive toward Charmes was exposing his flank to the Army of Nancy.

Rupprecht's movement had been decided in another of the fateful telephone conversations with OHL. The success of the German left-wing armies in throwing back the French from Sarrebourg and Morhange had two results: it brought Rupprecht the Iron Cross, First *and* Second Class— a relatively harmless result—and it revived OHL's vision of a decisive battle in Lorraine. Perhaps, after all, frontal attack could be mastered by German might. Perhaps Epinal and Toul would prove as vulnerable as Liège, and the Moselle no more a barrier than the Meuse. Perhaps, after all, the two armies of the left wing could succeed in breaking through the French forti- fied line and in cooperation with the right wing bring about a true Cannae —a double envelopment. As reported by Colonel Tappen, this was the prospect that shone before the eyes of OHL. Like the smile of a temptress, it overcame years of single, wedded devotion to the right wing.

While the idea was being breathlessly discussed by Moltke and his advisers, a call came through from General Krafft von Dellmensingen, Rupprecht's Chief of Staff, who wanted to know whether the attack was to continue or come to a halt. It had always been assumed that once Rupprecht's armies contained the initial French offensive and stabilized their front, they would halt, organize their defenses, and free all available forces to reinforce the right wing. An alternative known as Case 3, however, had been carefully provided which allowed for an attack across the Moselle, but only at the express order of OHL.

"We must definitely know how the operation is to continue," Krafft demanded. "I assume Case 3 is in order."

"No, no!" replied Colonel Tappen, the Chief of Operations. "Moltke hasn't decided yet. If you hold the line for five minutes I may be able to give you the orders you want." In less than five minutes he returned with a surprising answer, "Pursue direction Epinal."

Krafft was "stunned." "In those few minutes I felt that one of the most consequential decisions of the war had been made."

"Pursue direction Epinal" meant offensive through the Trouée de Charmes. It meant committing the Sixth and Seventh Armies to frontal attack upon the French fortress line instead of keeping them available for reinforcement of the right wing. Rupprecht duly attacked with vigor next day, August 23. Foch counterattacked. In the days that followed, the German Sixth and Seventh Armies locked themselves in combat against the French First and Second Armies, backed by the guns of Belfort, Epinal, and Toul. While they strained, other battles were being fought.

Failure of the offensive in Lorraine did not daunt Joffre. Rather, he saw in Rupprecht's violent counterattack deeply engaging the German left wing the right moment to unleash his own offensive against the German center. It was *after* learning of Castelnau's retreat from Morhange that Joffre on the night of August 20 gave the signal for attack in the Ardennes, the central and basic maneuver of Plan 17. At the same time as the Fourth and Third Armies entered the Ardennes, he ordered the Fifth Army to take the offensive across the Sambre against the enemy's "northern group" —GQG's term for the German right wing. He gave the order even though he had just learned from Colonel Adelbert and Sir John French that support for this offensive from the Belgians and the British would not be forthcoming as expected. The Belgian Army—except for one division at Namur—had broken off contact, and the British Army, according to its commander, would not be ready for three or four days. Besides this change in circumstances, the battle in Lorraine had revealed dangerous errors in fighting performance. These had been recognized as early as August 16 when Joffre issued instructions to all army commanders on the necessity of learning "to await artillery support" and of preventing the troops from "hastily exposing themselves to the enemy's fire."

Nevertheless France was committed to Plan 17 as her only design for decisive victory, and Plan 17 demanded the offensive—now and no later. The only alternative would have been to change at once to defense of the frontiers. In terms of the training, the planning, the thinking, the spirit of the French military organism, this was unthinkable.

Moreover GQG was convinced that the French Armies would have numerical superiority in the center. The French Staff could not release itself from the grip of the theory that had dominated all its planning— that the Germans were bound to be thinned out in the center. In that belief Joffre gave the order for the general offensive in the Ardennes and on the Sambre for August 21.

The terrain of the Ardennes is not suitable for the offensive. It is wooded, hilly, and irregular, with the slope running generally uphill from the French side and with the declivities between the hills cut by many streams. Caesar, who took ten days to march across it, described the secret, dark forest as a "place full of terrors," with muddy paths and a perpetual mist rising from the peat bogs. Much of it had since been cleared and cultivated; roads, villages, and two or three large towns had replaced Caesar's terrors, but large sections were still covered with thick leafy woods where roads were few and ambush easy. French staff officers had examined the terrain on several tours before 1914 and knew its difficulties. In spite of their warnings the Ardennes was chosen as the place of break-

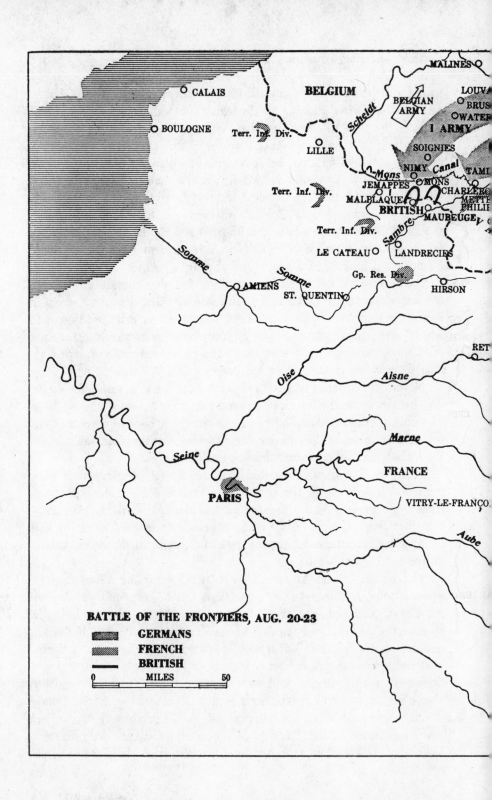

BATTLE OF THE FRONTIERS, AUG. 20-23

GERMANS

FRENCH

BRITISH

0   MILES   50

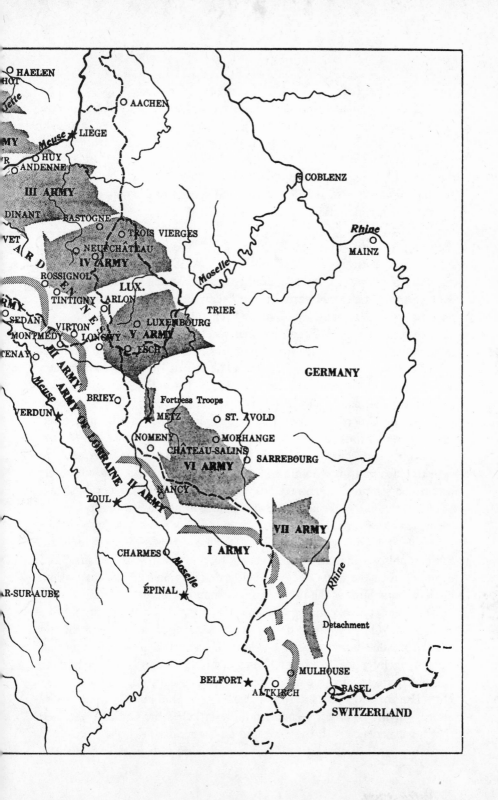

through because here, at the center, German strength was expected to be least. The French had persuaded themselves of the feasibility of the ground on the theory that its very difficulty made it, as Joffre said, "rather favorable to the side which, like ourselves, had inferiority of heavy artillery but superiority of field guns." Joffre's memoirs, despite constant use of the pronoun "I," were compiled and written by a staff of military collaborators, and represent a careful and virtually official version of the dominant thinking of the General Staff before and during 1914.

On August 20 GQG, assuming the reported enemy movements across the front to be German units heading for the Meuse, envisaged the Ardennes as relatively "depleted" of the enemy. As Joffre intended to make his attack a surprise, he forbade infantry reconnaissance which might make contact and cause skirmishes with the enemy before the main encounter. Surprise was indeed achieved—but the French took their share of it.

The bottom corner of the Ardennes meets France at the upper corner of Lorraine where the Briey iron region is located. The area had been occupied by the Prussian Army in 1870. The ore of Briey not having then been discovered, the region had not been included in that part of Lorraine annexed by Germany. The center of the iron region was Longwy on the banks of the Chiers, and the honor of taking Longwy had been reserved for the Crown Prince, commander of the German Fifth Army.

At thirty-two, the imperial scion was a narrow-chested, willowy creature with the face of a fox who did not at all resemble his five sturdy brothers whom the Empress at annual intervals had presented to her husband. William, the Crown Prince, gave an impression of physical frailty and, in the words of an American observer, "only ordinary mental calibre"—unlike his father. Like him a poseur, fond of striking attitudes, he suffered from the compulsory filial antagonism usual to the eldest sons of kings, and expressed it in the usual manner: political rivalry and private dissipation. He had made himself the patron and partisan of the most aggressive militarist opinion, and his photograph was sold in the Berlin shops carrying the inscription, "Only by relying on the sword can we gain the place in the sun that is our due but that is not voluntarily accorded to us." Despite an upbringing intended to prepare him for military command, his training had not quite reached the adequate. It included colonelcy of the Death's Head Hussars and a year's service on the General Staff but had not included either a divisional or corps command. Nevertheless the Crown Prince felt that his experience with the Staff and on Staff rides in the last few years "gave me the theoretical grounding for command of large units." His confidence would not have been shared by Schlieffen who deplored the appointment of young, inexperienced commanders. He feared they would be more interested to go dashing off on a *"wilde Jagd nach dem Pour le Mérite"*—a wild hunt after the highest honor—than to follow the strategic plan.

The role of the Crown Prince's Fifth Army, together with the Fourth Army under the Duke of Württemberg, was to be the pivot of the right wing, moving slowly forward at the center as the right wing swung out and down in its great enveloping sweep. The Fourth Army was to advance through the northern Ardennes against Neufchâteau while the Fifth Army advanced through the southern Ardennes against Virton and the two French fortress towns, Longwy and Montmédy. The Crown Prince's headquarters were at Thionville—called Diedenhofen by the Germans—where he dined on a manly soldier's fare of cabbage soup, potatoes, and boiled beef with horseradish, eked out, as concession to a prince, by wild duck, salad, fruit, wine, coffee, and cigars. Surrounded by the "grave and gloomy" faces of the native population and envying the glory won at Liège and the progress of the right wing, the Crown Prince and his staff waited feverishly for action. At last marching orders came for August 19.

Opposite the Crown Prince's Army was the French Third Army under General Ruffey. A lone apostle of heavy artillery, Ruffey was known, because of his eloquence on behalf of the big guns, as *"le poète du canon."* He had dared not only to question the omnipotence of the 75s but also to propose the use of airplanes as an offensive arm and the creation of an airforce of 3,000 planes. The idea was not admired. *"Tout ça, c'est du sport!"* exclaimed General Foch in 1910. For use by the army, he had added, *"l'avion c'est zéro!"* Next year at maneuvers General Gallieni by using airplane reconnaissance captured a colonel of the Supreme War Council with all his staff. By 1914 the French Army was using airplanes, but General Ruffey was still regarded as having "too much imagination." Besides, as he showed a disinclination to allow Staff officers to tell him what to do, he had made enemies at GQG before he ever entered the Ardennes. His headquarters were at Verdun, and his task was to throw the enemy back on Metz-Thionville and invest them there, retaking the Briey region in the course of his advance. While he folded back the enemy on the right of the German center his neighbor, the Fourth Army under General de Langle de Cary, would fold them back on the left. The two French armies would cleave their way through the middle and lop off the arm of the German right wing at the shoulder.

General de Langle, a veteran of 1870, had been retained in command despite his having reached the French age limit of sixty-four a month before the war. In appearance a sharp, alert bantam, alive with energy, he resembled Foch, and like him, always looked in photographs as if about to leap into action. General de Langle was ready, indeed aching, to leap now, and refused to be discouraged by disquieting news. His cavalry, in combat near Neufchâteau, had run into heavy opposition and had been forced to retire. A reconnaissance tour by a staff officer in an automobile had brought further warning. The officer had talked at Arlon to a worried official of the Luxembourg government who said the Germans were in the nearby forests "in strength." On the way back the officer's car was fired on but his reports to Fourth Army Headquarters were judged "pessimistic." The mood was one of valor, not discretion. The moment had come to move fast, not hesitate. It was only after the battle that General de Langle remembered that he had disapproved of Joffre's order to attack "without allowing me to take soundings first"; only afterward that he wrote, "GQG wanted surprise but it was we who were surprised."

General Ruffey was more troubled than his neighbor. He took more seriously the reports brought in by Belgian peasants of Germans lodged among the woods and cornfields. When he told GQG his estimate of enemy strength opposing him, they paid no attention to him and did not, or so he was to claim, even read his reports.

Fog was thick from the ground up everywhere in the Ardennes on the morning of August 21. The German Fourth and Fifth Armies had been moving forward on the 19th and 20th, entrenching their positions as they advanced. A French attack was expected, although they did not know when or where. In the dense fog the French cavalry patrols sent ahead to scout the ground "might as well have been blindfolded." The opposing armies, moving forward through the woods and between the hills, unable to see ahead more than a few paces, stumbled into each other before they knew what was in front of them. As soon as the first units established contact and commanders became aware that battle was erupting all around them, the Germans dug in. The French, whose officers in prewar training disdained to give the troops entrenching practice for fear of making them "sticky" and who carried as few picks and shovels as possible, threw themselves into *attaque brusquée* with the bayonet. They were mown down by machine guns. In some encounters the French 75s slaughtered German units who had likewise been taken by surprise.

On the first day the encounters were scattered and preliminary; on the

22nd the lower Ardennes was engulfed in full-scale battle. In separate combats at Virton and Tintigny and Rossignol and Neufchâteau guns roared and flared, men flung themselves at each other, the wounded fell, and the dead piled up. At Rossignol, Algerians of the French 3rd Colonial Division were surrounded by the VIth Corps of the Crown Prince's Army and fought for six hours until the survivors were but a remnant. Their divisional commander, General Raffenel, and a brigade commander, General Rondoney, were both killed. In August 1914 general officers were casualties like ordinary soldiers.

At Virton the French VIth Corps under General Sarrail took a German corps in the flank with fire from its 75s. "The battlefield afterwards was an unbelievable spectacle," reported a French officer dazed with horror. "Thousands of dead were still standing, supported as if by a flying buttress made of bodies lying in rows on top of each other in an ascending arc from the horizontal to an angle of 60°." Officers from St. Cyr went into battle wearing white-plumed shakos and white gloves; it was considered "chic" to die in white gloves. An unidentified French sergeant kept a diary: "the guns recoil at each shot. Night is falling and they look like old men sticking out their tongues and spitting fire. Heaps of corpses, French and German, are lying every which way, rifles in hand. Rain is falling, shells are screaming and bursting—shells all the time. Artillery fire is the worst. I lay all night listening to the wounded groaning—some were German. The cannonading goes on. Whenever it stops we hear the wounded crying from all over the woods. Two or three men go mad every day."

At Tintigny a German officer also kept a diary. "Nothing more terrible could be imagined," he wrote. "We advanced much too fast—a civilian fired at us—he was immediately shot—we were ordered to attack the enemy flank in a forest of beeches—we lost our direction—the men were done for—the enemy opened fire—shells came down on us like hail."

The Crown Prince, not to be outdone by Rupprecht whose victories at Sarrebourg and Morhange were now known, urged his forces to match "the prodigies of valor and sacrifice" of their comrades. He had moved his headquarters to Esch in Luxembourg just across the river from Longwy and followed the battle on huge maps pinned to the walls. The suspense was torture; telephone communications with Coblenz were awful; OHL was "much too far back"; the struggle was frightful, the losses terrible; Longwy is not yet taken, he said, but "we feel we have checked the enemy's offensive"; French units were reported retreating in disorder, not in planned retreat.

This was so. At the last moment before the battle General Ruffey was enraged to discover that three reserve divisions, altogether about 50,000 men, which formed part of his army were no longer part of it. Joffre had sequestered them, in response to the threat of Rupprecht's offensive, to form a special Army of Lorraine made up of these three divisions and four reserve divisions which he collected elsewhere. The Army of Lorraine under General Maunoury began to take form on August 21 between Verdun and Nancy to back up Castelnau's army and protect the right flank of the advance through the Ardennes. It was one of the last minute rearrangements which proved the saving flexibility of the French Army but at the moment had a negative result. It cut into Ruffey's strength and kept seven divisions immobile at a vital time. Ruffey always claimed afterward that if he had had the extra 50,000 men to whom he had already issued orders he could have won the Battle of Virton. At the time his anger proved too much for tact. When a staff officer from GQG came to his headquarters during the battle, Ruffey exploded: "You people at GQG never read the reports we send you. You are as ignorant as an oyster of all that the enemy has in his bag. . . . Tell the Generalissimo his operations are worse than 1870—he sees absolutely nothing—incapacity everywhere." This was not a message to be welcomed upon Olympus where Joffre and his attendant deities were more inclined to lay the blame on the incapacity of commanders and troops—Ruffey among them.

On the same day, August 22, General de Langle was experiencing a commander's most agonizing moments—waiting for news from the front. Chaining himself "in anguish" to his headquarters at Stenay on the Meuse, twenty miles from Sedan, he received bad reports coming hard upon each other. The instinct to rush to the scene of combat could only be checked by reminding himself that a general must not lose himself among his units but can only direct their movements at a distance. To maintain sangfroid before his staff and "that mastery of himself indispensable to a chief at critical moments" was as difficult.

As the day ended, the terrible casualties of the Colonial Corps became known. Another corps, through mishandling by its commander, as De Langle believed, was in retreat, endangering its neighbors. "Serious check at Tintigny; all troops engaged with unsatisfactory results," he had to report to Joffre, adding that losses and disorganization of his units made it impossible to carry out his orders for August 23. Joffre simply refused to believe it. With serene complacence he reported to Messimy, even after receiving De Langle's report, that the armies had been placed "where the enemy is most vulnerable and so as to assure ourselves of numerical superiority." GQG's work was done. Now it was up to the troops and their commanders "who have the advantage of that superiority." He repeated the assurance to De Langle, insisting that as he had no more than three enemy corps in front of him, he must resume the offensive.

In fact the French Armies in the Ardennes enjoyed no superiority, but the reverse. The Crown Prince's Army included, besides the three corps which the French had identified, two reserve corps with the same numerals as the active corps, as did the Duke of Württemberg's Army. Together they massed a greater number of men and guns than the French Third and Fourth Armies.

Fighting continued during August 23, but by the end of the day it was known the French arrow had broken against its target. The enemy had not been "vulnerable" in the Ardennes after all. Despite the massive strength of his right wing his center had not been weak. The French had not "cut them in half." With the cry of *"En avant!"* with waving sword, with all the ardor on which the French Army prided itself, officers led their companies to the attack—against an enemy who dug in and used his field guns. Field gray merging into the fog and shadows had beaten the too visible *pantalon rouge;* steady, solid methodical training had beaten *cran.* Both French Armies in the Ardennes were in retreat, the Third falling back on Verdun and the Fourth on Stenay and Sedan. Briey's iron ore was not regained and for four more years would serve to forge German munitions for the long war which, without that iron, Germany could not have fought.

As yet on the evening of August 23 Joffre did not realize the full extent of the defeat in the Ardennes. The offensive had been "momentarily checked," he telegraphed to Messimy, but "I will make every effort to renew the offensive."

The Crown Prince's Army on that day passed Longwy, leaving its fortress to be taken by siege troops, and was advancing with orders to head off the French Third Army from Verdun. The Prince who less than a month ago had been cautioned by his father to obey his Chief of Staff in everything and "do as he tells you" was "deeply moved" on this day of triumph to receive a telegram from "Papa William" awarding him, like Rupprecht, the Iron Cross, First *and* Second Class. The telegram was handed around among the staff to be read by all. Soon the Prince would be handing out medals himself, in a "dazzling white tunic," as an admirer describes him later in the war, walking between two lines of soldiers distributing Iron Crosses from a basket carried by an aide. By that time, an Austrian ally would report, the Iron Cross, Second Class, could only be avoided by committing suicide. Today the "hero of Longwy," as he was soon to be acclaimed, had won glory equal to Rupprecht's; and if, amid the adulation, the ghost of Schlieffen grumbled at "ordinary frontal victories" without envelopment or annihilation or muttered scornful references to a "wild hunt for medals," no one heard him.

Meanwhile on the Sambre, Lanrezac's Fifth Army had been ordered to attack across the river and, "resting on the fortress of Namur," with its left passing by Charleroi, was to take as its objective the enemy "northern group." One corps of the Fifth Army was to be held in the angle of the rivers to protect the line of the Meuse against a German attack from the east. Although Joffre had no authority to command the British, his order requested Sir John French "to cooperate in this action" by advancing "in the general direction of Soignies," that is, across the Mons Canal. The canal is an extension of the Sambre which carries navigation to the Channel by way of the Scheldt. It formed part of a continuous waterway, made by the Sambre from Namur to Charleroi and by the canal from Charleroi to the Scheldt, which lay across the path of the German right wing.

According to the German timetable, von Kluck's Army was to reach the water barrier by August 23, while Bülow's Army, which would have to reduce Namur on the way, would reach it earlier and be across it at about the same time.

According to the British timetable laid down by Sir John French's marching orders, the BEF would also reach the canal on the 23rd, the same day as the Germans. Neither army was yet aware of the coincidence. The heads of the British columns were scheduled to reach the line earlier, that is, by the night of the 22nd. On the 21st, the day Lanrezac was ordered to cross the Sambre, the BEF, which had been expected to "cooperate in the action," was a full day's march behind the French. Instead of fighting together as planned, the two armies, because of the late British start and poor liaison resulting from the unhappy relations of their commanders, were to fight two separate battles, Charleroi and Mons, while their headquarters were only thirty-five miles apart.

In General Lanrezac's heart the doctrine of the offensive was already dead. He could not see the whole picture, so clear now, of three German armies converging upon his front but he could feel their presence. Hausen's

Third Army was coming at him from the east, Bülow's Second Army from the north, and Kluck's First Army was advancing against the half-size British Army on his left. He did not know their names or numbers but he knew they were there. He knew or deduced from reconnaissance that greater numbers were coming at him than he could dispose of. Evaluation of enemy strength is not an absolute, but a matter of piecing together scraps of reconnaissance and intelligence to form a picture, if possible a picture to fit preconceived theories or to suit the demands of a particular strategy. What a staff makes out of the available evidence depends upon the degree of optimism or pessimism prevailing among them, on what they want to believe or fear to believe, and sometimes upon the sensitivity or intuition of an individual.

To Lanrezac and to GQG the same reports of German strength west of the Meuse conveyed different pictures. GQG saw a weak German center in the Ardennes. Lanrezac saw a great wave rolling down with the Fifth Army directly in its path. GQG estimated German strength west of the Meuse at 17 or 18 divisions. Opposed they counted Lanrezac's 13 divisions, a separate group of two reserve divisions, 5 British divisions, and 1 Belgian division at Namur, a total of 21 giving what they believed a comfortable superiority in numbers. Joffre's plan was for this force to hold the Germans behind the Sambre until the French Third and Fourth Armies should break through the German center in the Ardennes and then for all together to advance northward and throw the Germans out of Belgium.

The British Staff, dominated in fact if not in rank by Henry Wilson, agreed with GQG's estimate. In his diary for August 20, Wilson put down the same figure of 17 or 18 divisions for the Germans west of the Meuse, and happily concluded, "The more the better, as it will weaken their center." Back in England, far from the front, Lord Kitchener felt anxiety and foreboding. On August 19 he telegraphed Sir John French that the German sweep north and west of the Meuse, about which he had warned him, "seems definitely to be developing." He asked to be kept informed of all reports, and next day repeated the request. In truth, at that moment German strength west of the Meuse was not 17 or 18 divisions but 30: 7 active and 5 reserve corps, 5 cavalry divisions and other units. Von Hausen's Army, which at this time had not yet crossed the Meuse but which formed part of the right wing, was to add another 4 corps or 8 divisions. While for the Battle of the Frontiers as a whole, German numerical superiority was one and a half to one, the right wing's preponderance was nearer two to one.

The focus of this force was Lanrezac's Army, and he knew it. He believed the British, after his disastrous interview with their commander, to be both unready and unreliable. He knew the Belgian defense to be cracking at Namur. One of the new corps assigned to him in the recent exchange of units which was to hold his left flank west of Charleroi had not yet come into position on August 21. If he attacked across the Sambre as ordered, he believed he would be outflanked by the German forces pouring down on his left who would then have nothing between them and Paris. The guiding principle of all that he had ever taught at St. Cyr and the Ecole Supérieure, the principle that trained the French Army, was to "attack the enemy wherever met." He looked at it now, and saw the face of a skeleton.

Lanrezac hesitated. He wrote to Joffre that if he took the offensive north of the Sambre the Fifth Army "may be exposed to giving battle alone," as the British would not be ready to act in liaison with him. If both were to act in unison the Fifth Army must wait until the 23rd or 24th. Joffre replied "I leave you absolute judge of the moment to begin your offensive." The enemy was not so permissive.

Detachments of Bülow's Army whose main force was already attacking Namur plunged down upon the Sambre on August 21 and forced crossings at two points between Namur and Charleroi. Troops of the Fifth Army had been told by Lanrezac that their own offensive waited upon "neighboring armies" and that in the meantime they were to oppose any German attempts to cross the river. Defensive preparations not being in the French military vocabulary, the Xth Corps which held this sector had not dug in or laid wire or otherwise organized the defenses of the south bank, but waited to hurl themselves bodily upon the enemy. "With bugles blowing, drums beating and flags flying," but without artillery preparation, the French now dashed to the assault. After sharp combat they were driven back, and by nightfall the enemy remained in possession of Tamines and another village on the south side of the river.

Over the crack of musketry and crash of shells a deeper sound like that of a gigantic drum could be heard in the distance. The German siege guns had begun the bombardment of the forts of Namur. Dragged down from Liège, the 420s and 305s had been brought within range, cemented into emplacements, and were now pouring their two-ton shells on a second Belgian fortress. The shells came over with "a long singing scream," wrote an Englishwoman who had led a volunteer ambulance corps to Namur. They seemed to be coming directly at the listener wherever he stood and to explode within a yard of him wherever they hit. The town cowered through two days of the terrible sound as destruction thundered out of the sky upon the forts around them. The same effects as at Liège of explosive gases, of concrete crumbled like plaster, of men in the underground chambers driven mad were repeated. Cut off from the rest of the Belgian Army, the garrison troops and the 4th Division felt themselves deserted. Commandant Duruy, Lanrezac's liaison officer at Namur, returned to Fifth Army headquarters to say he did not think the forts would hold out another day without some evidence of French help. "They must see the French troops marching along with colors unfurled and a band playing. There must be a band," he pleaded. Three French battalions—one regiment of some 3,000 men—were sent off that night and joined the defense of Namur next morning. The defense numbered 37,000. The German force engaged in the assault from August 21 to 24 ranged from 107,000 to 153,000 with 400 to 500 pieces of artillery.

On the night of August 21 Sir John French reported to Kitchener that he did not think there would be serious fighting before the 24th. "I think I know the situation thoroughly and I regard it as favorable to us," he wrote. He did not know it as thoroughly as he thought. Next day, as British troops were marching up the road to Mons "in the general direction of Soignies," cavalry patrols reported a German corps marching down the Brussels-Mons road, also making for Soignies. From their position they could be expected to reach the village that night. It seemed unlikely the enemy would wait for Sir John's target date of the 24th. More alarming news was brought by a British aviator who reported another German corps marching down a road far enough to the west to outflank the British left. Envelopment. Suddenly, in startling clarity the menace loomed before British eyes—at least before the eyes of the Intelligence section. The "sweep" Kitchener eternally talked of was no longer an idea, but columns of living men. The staff commanders, under Henry Wilson's influence, discounted it. Wedded, through Wilson, to French strategy they were no more inclined than GQG to accept an alarmist view of the German right wing. "The information you have acquired and conveyed to the Commander in Chief appears to be somewhat exaggerated," they decided, and left marching orders unchanged.

They were conscious of treading on territory of past triumphs. Ten miles south of Mons they passed through Malplaquet on the border between France and Belgium and saw by the roadside the stone monument marking the spot where Marlborough had defeated the armies of Louis XIV and won immortality in a French folk song. Ahead of them between Mons and Brussels lay Waterloo. Returning to that victorious field, almost on the hundredth anniversary of the battle, they could not but feel confident.

As the heads of their columns neared Mons on the 22nd, part of a cavalry squadron scouting the road north of the canal saw a group of four horsemen riding toward them. They looked unfamiliar. At the same instant the strange riders saw the British, and halted. There was a kind of breathless pause before each realized he was looking at the enemy. The Uhlans turned to rejoin the rest of their squadron and galloped back, chased by the British, who caught up with them in the streets of Soignies. In a sharp skirmish the Uhlans were "hampered by their long lances and a good many threw them away." The British killed three or four and left the somewhat restricted field victorious. Captain Hornby, leader of the squadron, was awarded the DSO as the first British officer to kill a German with the new pattern cavalry sword. The war had opened in correct style with the most encouraging results.

First contact having been made on the road to Soignies as expected, the staff commanders were given no cause to change their estimate of the enemy's strength or position. German strength opposing the British was put by Wilson at one or possibly two corps and one cavalry division, which was inferior or at most equal to the BEF's two corps and a cavalry division. Wilson's forceful character, high spirits, and recognized familiarity with the ground and with the French carried greater persuasion than the reports of Intelligence officers—especially as Operations officers traditionally discount estimates by their brother bureau on the theory that Intelligence always assumes the worst. The death of Sir James Grierson, who among the British had been the closest student of German military theory and practice, gave Wilson's theories, which were a duplicate of GQG's, that much greater sway. Battle on the morrow was expected with confidence by the staff and corps commanders if not by Sir John French.

His mood was still murky; his hesitancy almost a replica of Lanrezac's. When General Smith-Dorrien, just arrived in France to replace Grierson, came up on the 21st he was told to "give battle on the line of the Condé Canal." When Smith-Dorrien asked if this meant offensive or defensive, he was told to "obey orders." One factor worrying Sir John French was ignorance of Lanrezac's plan of battle on his right flank and fear of a gap opening between them. He set off in a motorcar on the morning of the 22nd to confer with his unpleasing neighbor; but on being told en route that Lanrezac had gone forward to corps headquarters at Mettet where the Xth Corps was now in the heat of combat, he returned without meeting him. One piece of good news met him at Headquarters. The 4th Division, left behind in England at the start, had arrived in France and was on its way forward. The lengthening shadow of the German advance through Belgium and the withdrawal of the Belgian Army to Antwerp had decided Kitchener to send it over.

General von Kluck was more surprised than the British by the cavalry clash on the road at Soignies. Up to this moment—so effective were French and British security measures—he did not know the British were in front of him. He knew they had landed because he had read the news in a Belgian newspaper which published Kitchener's official communiqué announcing the safe arrival of the BEF "on French soil." This announcement on August 20 was the first England, the world, and the enemy knew of the landing. Kluck still thought they had landed at Ostend, Dunkirk, and Calais, chiefly because he wanted to think so, his intention being to "attack and disperse" the British along with the Belgians before meeting the French.

Now, as he moved down from Brussels, he had to worry about a Belgian sortie from Antwerp at his rear and a possible pounce upon his flank by the British, mysteriously deploying, so he thought, somewhere in Belgium to his right. He kept trying to edge his army westward in order to find and meet the British, but Bülow, in constant fear of a gap, kept issuing orders pulling him inward. Kluck protested. Bülow insisted. "Otherwise," he said, "the First Army might get too far away and not be able to support the Second Army." On discovering the British squarely in front of him at Soignies, Kluck again attempted a shift to the west in order to find the enemy flank. When again prevented by Bülow he protested furiously to OHL. OHL's notion of British whereabouts was even dimmer than the Allies' notion of the whereabouts of the German right wing. "It appears from here that no landings of great importance have taken place," said OHL, and rejected Kluck's proposal. Deprived of the opportunity to envelop the enemy and condemned to frontal attack, Kluck moved wrathfully on Mons. His orders for August 23 were to cross the canal, occupy the ground to the south, and force the enemy back into Maubeuge while cutting off his retreat from the west.

Bülow on that day, August 22, was having as much trouble with Hausen on his left as with Kluck on his right. As Kluck's tendency was to get ahead, Hausen's was to lag behind. With advance units of his army already engaged across the Sambre against Lanrezac's Xth Corps, Bülow planned a battle of annihilation in a great joint attack by his own and Hausen's Army. But on the 22nd Hausen was not ready. Bülow complained bitterly of "insufficient cooperation" from his neighbor. Hausen complained equally bitterly of "suffering" from Bülow's constant demands for help. Deciding not to wait, Bülow threw three corps into a violent attack upon the line of the Sambre.

During that day and the next Bülow's and Lanrezac's Armies grappled each other in the Battle of Charleroi, Hausen's Army joining in by the end of the first day. These were the same two days when the French Third and Fourth Armies were wrestling with disaster in the fog and forest of the Ardennes. Lanrezac was at Mettet to direct the battle, a process which consisted largely of agonized waiting for divisional and corps commanders to report back what was happening to them. They in turn found it hard enough to find out what was happening from units under heavy fire or gripped in combat in village streets or stumbling back exhausted and bleeding with hardly an officer left to make a report. Visual evidence reached Mettet before reports. A car carrying a wounded officer drove into the square where Lanrezac and his staff paced anxiously, too restless to remain indoors. The wounded man was recognized as General Boë, commander of a division of the Xth Corps. With a face the color of ashes and eyes of tragedy, he whispered slowly and painfully to Hely d'Oissel who ran to the car, "Tell him . . . tell the General . . . we held on . . . as long as we could."

On the left of the Xth Corps, the IIIrd Corps in front of Charleroi reported "terrible" losses. The sprawling industrial town lying on both sides of the river having been penetrated by the Germans during the day, the French were fighting furiously to dislodge them. When the Germans attacked in dense formation—as was their habit before they learned better —they made perfect targets for the 75s. But the 75s, which could fire 15 times a minute, were supplied with shells at a rate sufficient for only 2.25 shots per minute. At Charleroi the "Turcos" of the two Algerian divisions, recruited by voluntary enlistment, fought as valiantly as had their fathers at Sedan. One battalion charged a German gun battery, bayoneting the gunners, and returned with two men unwounded out of the battalion's complement of 1,030. Everywhere the French were enraged or demoralized, according to the circumstances in different sectors, by the shelling from batteries they usually could not see or get at. They felt helpless rage at the hawk-shaped German airplanes overhead which acted as artillery spotters and whose flight over their lines was invariably followed by a new burst of shells.

By evening Lanrezac had to report the Xth Corps "forced to fall back" having "suffered severely"; the IIIrd Corps "heavily engaged"; "heavy casualties" in officers; the XVIIIth Corps on the left intact but General Sordet's Cavalry Corps on the far left "greatly exhausted" and also forced to fall back, leaving a gap between the Fifth Army and the British. It proved to be a gap of ten miles, wide enough for an enemy corps. Lanrezac's anxiety was so acute as to move him to send word to Sir John French asking him to relieve pressure on the French by attacking Bülow's right flank. Sir John replied he could not comply, but promised to hold the line of the Mons Canal for twenty-four hours.

During the night Lanrezac's position became further imperiled when Hausen brought four fresh corps and 340 guns into action on the Meuse. He attacked during the night and gained bridgeheads across the river which were counterattacked by Franchet d'Esperey's Ist Corps whose mission was to hold the Meuse along the right side of Lanrezac's front. His was the only corps of the Fifth Army to entrench its position.

Hausen's intention, in compliance with orders from OHL, was to attack southwest toward Givet where he expected to come in upon the rear of Lanrezac's Army, which could then be caught between his and Bülow's forces, and destroyed. Bülow, however, whose units in this sector had taken as severe punishment as they had given, was determined to mount a massive and terminal attack, and ordered Hausen to attack directly westward toward Mettet upon the body of the Fifth Army instead of southwestward across its line of retreat. Hausen complied. This was an error. It engaged Hausen all during August 23 in frontal attack against the strongly held positions and vigorous generalship of Franchet d'Esperey's corps and it left Lanrezac's line of retreat open—an opening through which the opportunity for a battle of annihilation was to slip away.

Through the hot clear hours of August 23 the summer sky was spattered with the greasy black puffs of bursting shells. The French had instantly dubbed them "*marmites*" after the cast-iron soup pot that sits on every French stove. "*Il plut des marmites*" (It rained shells) was all that one tired soldier could remember of the day. In some places the French were still attacking, trying to throw the Germans back across the Sambre; in others they were holding; in still others they were retreating in crippled, broken disorder. The roads were choked with long columns of Belgian refugees, coated with dust, weighted down with babies and bundles, pushing wheelbarrows, dully, tiredly, endlessly moving toward no goal or home or refuge but only away from the awful roar of guns to the north.

The refugee columns passed through Philippeville, twenty miles from Charleroi where Lanrezac had his headquarters that day. Standing in the square, with red-trousered legs apart and hands clasped behind his back, Lanrezac watched them somberly, saying nothing. Above his black tunic his dark face looked almost pale and his fleshy cheeks sunken. He felt "prey to extreme anxiety." Enemy pressure was bending against him from all sides. No guidance came from GQG except to ask his opinion of the situation. Lanrezac felt acutely conscious of the gap made by the retreat of Sordet's cavalry. At noon came the news, foreseen yet still incredible, that the Belgian 4th Division was evacuating Namur. The city dominating the confluence of Sambre and Meuse, as well as the forts on the heights behind it, would soon be in Bülow's hands. No word came from General de Langle de Cary of the Fourth Army to whom Lanrezac had sent a message that morning asking for a maneuver to strengthen the sector where their forces joined.

Lanrezac's staff was urging him to permit a counterattack by Franchet d'Esperey who reported a glittering opportunity. A German force in pursuit of the retreating Xth Corps was presenting its flank to him. Other ardent pleaders urged a counterattack on the far left by the XVIIIth Corps to relieve pressure on the British who on this day at Mons were engaged against the full force of von Kluck's Army. To the disgust of the forward-minded, Lanrezac refused. He remained silent, gave no orders, waited. In the controversy which critics and partisans were to weave for years afterwards over the Battle of Charleroi, everyone pronounced his own version of what went on in the soul of General Lanrezac that afternoon. To some he appeared pusillanimous or paralyzed, to others as a man soberly measuring the chances in an obscure and perilous situation. Left without guidance from GQG, he had to make his own decision.

Late in the afternoon occurred the decisive incident of the day. Troops of Hausen's Army enlarged a bridgehead across the Meuse at Onhaye south of Dinant. Franchet d'Esperey at once sent a brigade under General Mangin to deal with the danger which threatened to take the Fifth Army in the rear. At the same time word at last reached Lanrezac from General de Langle. It could not have been worse. Not only was the Fourth Army not successful in the Ardennes, as an earlier communiqué from GQG had implied, but it was being forced into retreat that would leave unguarded the stretch of the Meuse between Sedan and Lanrezac's right flank. At once the presence of Hausen's Saxons at Onhaye took on added threat. Lanrezac believed—"I was bound to believe"—that this force was the van of an army that would be given liberty of action by de Langle's retreat and would be reinforced if not immediately thrown back. He did not yet know—because it had not happened yet—that General Mangin's brigade in a brilliant charge with fixed bayonets would throw the Saxons out of Onhaye.

On top of this, word came that the IIIrd Corps in front of Charleroi had been attacked, had failed to hold its ground, and was falling back. Commandant Duruy arrived with news that the Germans had taken the northern forts of Namur and entered the city. Lanrezac returned to Corps Headquarters at Chimay where he "received confirmation of the check to the Fourth Army which since morning had been retiring in such a way as to leave the Fifth Army's right completely uncovered."

To Lanrezac the danger on his right "seemed acute." The thought haunted him of that other disaster at the very place where de Langle's Army was now giving way, "where 44 years ago our army was encircled by the Germans and forced to capitulate—that abominable disaster which made our defeat irretrievable—what a memory!"

To save France from another Sedan, the Fifth Army must be saved from destruction. It was now clear to him that the French Armies were in retreat along their whole line from the Vosges to the Sambre. As long as the armies existed the defeat was not irretrievable as it had been at Sedan; the fight could go on. But if the Fifth Army were to be destroyed, the whole line would be unhinged and total defeat follow. Counterattack, however bravely pressed and urgent the need, could not save the situation as a whole.

Lanrezac finally spoke. He gave the order for a general retreat. He knew he would be taken for a "*catastrophard*" who must be got rid of—as indeed he was. His own account tells that he said to one of his officers: "We have been beaten but the evil is reparable. As long as the Fifth Army lives, France is not lost." Although the remark has the ring of memoirs written after the event, it may well have been spoken. Fateful moments tend to evoke grandeur of speech, especially in French.

Lanrezac made his decision, which he believed Joffre would disapprove, without consulting GQG. "Enemy threatens my right on the Meuse," he reported, "Onhaye occupied, Givet threatened, Namur carried." Because of this situation and "the delay of the Fourth Army," he was ordering the retirement of the Fifth Army. With that message vanished the last French hope of defeating the ancient enemy in a short war. The last of the French offensives had failed. Joffre did disapprove—but not that night. In the befogged and bitter hours of Sunday night, August 23, when the whole French plan was collapsing, when no one could be certain what was happening from sector to sector, when the specter of another Sedan haunted minds other than Lanrezac's, GQG neither questioned nor countermanded the Fifth Army's retreat. By his silence Joffre ratified the decision; he did not forgive it.

Afterward the official account of the Battle of Charleroi was to state that General Lanrezac, "thinking himself menaced on his right, ordered a retreat instead of counterattacking." That was when GQG, in need of a scapegoat for the failure of Plan 17, settled upon the commander of the Fifth Army. In the hour when he made his decision, however, no one at GQG suggested to General Lanrezac that he merely "thought" himself menaced on his right without actually being so, as the postwar phrase implied.

Far to the left, since early morning, the British and von Kluck's Army had been locked in a duel over the sixty-foot width of the Mons Canal. The August sun broke through early morning mist and rain, bringing promise of great heat later in the day. Sunday church bells were ringing as usual as the people of the mining villages went to Mass in their black Sunday clothes. The canal, bordered by railroad sidings and industrial back yards, was black with slime and reeked of chemical refuse from furnaces and factories. In among small vegetable plots, pastures, and orchards the gray pointed slag heaps like witches' hats stuck up everywhere, giving the landscape a bizarre, abnormal look. War seemed less incongruous here.

The British had taken up positions on either side of Mons. To the west the IInd Corps commanded by General Smith-Dorrien lined the fifteen-mile stretch of canal between Mons and Condé and filled in a salient formed just east of Mons where the canal makes a northward loop about two miles wide and a mile and a half deep. On the right of the IInd Corps General Haig's Ist Corps held a diagonal front between Mons and the left wing of Lanrezac's Army. The cavalry division commanded by General Allenby, future conqueror of Jerusalem, was held in reserve. Opposite Haig was the dividing line between Kluck's and Bülow's armies. Kluck was keeping as far to the west as he could, and thus Haig's corps was not attacked in the fighting of August 23 that was to become known to history and to legend as the Battle of Mons.

Sir John French's headquarters were at Le Cateau, 30 miles south of Mons. The 5 divisions he had to direct over a front of 25 miles—in contrast to Lanrezac's 13 divisions over a front of 50 miles—hardly required him to be that far back. Sir John's hesitant frame of mind may have dictated the choice. Worried by the reports of his air and cavalry reconnaissance, uncertain of his neighbor, uncomfortable about the zigzag line of the front they shared which opened multiple opportunities to the enemy, he was no more happy about undertaking an offensive than was Lanrezac.

On the night before the battle he summoned the senior staff officers of both corps and the cavalry division to Le Cateau and informed them that "owing to the retreat of the French Fifth Army," the British offensive would not take place. Except for its Xth Corps, which was not adjacent to the British, the Fifth Army was not in retreat at this time, but Sir John French had to blame someone. The same comradely spirit had moved General Lanrezac a day earlier to blame his own failure to take the offensive on the nonappearance of the British. As Lanrezac had then ordered his corps to hold the line of the Sambre instead of attacking across it, Sir John French now issued orders to hold the line of the canal. Despite Henry Wilson who was still thinking in terms of the great offensive northward that was to throw the Germans out of Belgium, the possibility of a very different kind of movement was conveyed to the commanders. Recognizing it, General Smith-Dorrien at 2:30 A.M. ordered the bridges over the canal to be prepared for demolition. It was a sensible precaution of the kind excluded by the French and, because excluded, the cause of the terrible French casualty rate of August 1914. Five minutes before the battle opened, Smith-Dorrien issued a further order directing the bridges to be destroyed on divisional order "in the event of a retirement being necessary."

At six in the morning when Sir John French gave his last instructions to corps commanders, his—or his staff's—estimate of the enemy strength they were about to meet was still the same: one or at most two army corps plus cavalry. In fact, at that moment von Kluck had four corps and three cavalry divisions—160,000 men with 600 guns—within striking distance of the BEF whose strength was 70,000 men and 300 guns. Of von Kluck's two reserve corps, one was two days' march behind and one had been left behind to mask Antwerp.

At 9:00 A.M. the first German guns opened fire on the British positions, the attack falling first upon the salient made by the loop of the canal. The bridge at Nimy at the northernmost point of the salient was the focus of the attack. Lunging at it in their dense formation, the Germans offered "the most perfect targets" to the British riflemen who, well dug in and expertly trained, delivered fire of such rapidity and accuracy that the Germans believed they faced machine guns. After repeated assault waves were struck down, they brought up more strength and changed to open formations. The British, under orders to offer "stubborn resistance," kept up their fire from the salient despite steadily growing casualties. From 10:30 on, the battle was extended along the straight section of the canal to the west as battery after battery of German guns, first of the IIIrd and then of the IVth Corps, were brought into action.

By three in the afternoon when the British regiments holding the salient had withstood shelling and infantry assault for six hours, the pressure on their dwindling numbers became too strong. After blowing up the bridge at Nimy they fell back, company by company, to a second line of defense that had been prepared two or three miles to the rear. As the yielding of the salient endangered the troops holding the straight section of the canal, these too were now ordered to withdraw, beginning about five in the evening. At Jemappes, where the loop joins the straight section, and at Mariette two miles to the west sudden peril loomed when it was found that the bridges could not be destroyed for lack of an exploder to fire the charges. A rush by the Germans across the canal in the midst of the retirement could convert orderly retreat to a rout and might even effect a breakthrough. No single Horatius could hold the bridge, but Captain Wright of the Royal Engineers swung himself hand over hand under the bridge at Mariette in an attempt to connect the charges. At Jemappes a corporal and a private worked at the same task for an hour and a half under continuous fire. They succeeded, and were awarded the V.C. and D.C.M.; but Captain Wright, though he made a second attempt in spite of being wounded, failed. He too won the V.C., and three weeks later was killed on the Aisne.

During the early evening the delicate process of disengagement was effected under sporadic fire with regiment by regiment covering the withdrawal of its neighbor until all had reached the villages and billets of the second line of defense. The Germans, who appeared to have suffered equally from the day's fighting, made no serious effort to force the undemolished bridges nor showed any appetite for pursuit. On the contrary, through the dusk the retiring British troops could hear German bugles sounding "Cease fire," then the inevitable singing, then silence across the canal.

Fortunately for the British von Kluck's more than double superiority in numbers had not been made use of. Unable, because of Bülow's hampering orders, to find the enemy flank and extend himself around it, Kluck had met the British head on with his two central corps, the IIIrd and IVth, and suffered the heavy losses consequent upon frontal attack. One German reserve captain of the IIIrd Corps found himself the only surviving officer of his company and the only surviving company commander of his battalion. "You are my sole support," wailed the major. "The battalion is a mere wreck, my proud, beautiful battalion . . ." and the regiment is "shot down, smashed up—only a handful left." The colonel of the regiment, who like everyone in war could judge the course of combat only by what was happening to his own unit, spent an anxious night, for as he said, "If the English have the slightest suspicion of our condition, and counterattack, they will simply run over us."

Neither of von Kluck's flanking corps, the IInd on his right and the IXth on his left, had been brought into the battle. Like the rest of the First Army they had marched 150 miles in 11 days and were strung out along the roads several hours' march to the rear of the two corps in the center. If all had attacked together on August 23, history might have been different. Some time during the afternoon von Kluck, realizing his mistake, ordered the two central corps to hold the British until the flanking corps could be brought up for envelopment and a battle of annihilation. Before that time a drastic change of plan forced itself upon the British.

Henry Wilson was mentally still charging forward with medieval ardor in Plan 17, unaware that it was now about as applicable to the situation as the longbow. Like Joffre who could still insist upon the offensive six hours after receiving de Langle's report of disaster in the Ardennes, Wilson, even after the line of the canal had to be given up, was eager for an offensive next day. He had made a "careful calculation" and concluded "that we had only one corps and one cavalry division (possibly two corps) opposite to us." He "persuaded" Sir John French and Murray that this was so, "with the result that I was allowed to draft orders for an attack tomorrow." At 8:00 P.M., just as his work was completed, it was nullified by a telegram from Joffre which informed the British that accumulated evidence now put the enemy force opposite them at three corps and two cavalry divisions. That was more persuasive than Wilson and at once put an end to any thought of attack. Worse news followed.

At 11:00 P.M. Lieutenant Spears arrived after a hurried drive from Fifth Army headquarters to bring the bitter word that General Lanrezac was breaking off battle and withdrawing the Fifth Army to a line in the rear of the BEF. Spears' resentment and dismay at a decision taken without consulting and without informing the British was like that of Colonel Adelbert on learning of King Albert's decision to withdraw to Antwerp. It still colors Spears' account written seventeen years later.

Lanrezac's retreat, leaving the BEF in the air, put them in instant peril. In anxious conference it was decided to draw back the troops at once as soon as orders could be drafted and delivered to the front. A delay that was to cost lives was due to the strange choice of location for Smith-Dorrien's corps headquarters. They were in a modest private country house called rather grandly the Château de la Roche at Sars-la-Bruyère, a hamlet without telegraph or telephone communication on a back country road difficult enough to find in the daytime, much more so in the middle of the night. Even Marlborough and Wellington had not disdained more convenient if less gentlemanly headquarters on the main road, one in an abbey and the other in a tavern. Smith-Dorrien's orders had to be delivered by car, and did not reach him until 3:00 A.M., whereas Haig's Ist Corps, which had not been in the battle, received its orders by telegraph an hour earlier and was able to prepare its retreat and get under way before dawn.

By that time the two German flanking corps had been brought up, the attack was renewed, and the retreat of the IInd Corps, which had been under fire all day, began under fire again. In the confusion one battalion never received its orders, and fought until it was surrounded and almost all its men were killed, wounded, or taken prisoner. Only two officers and two hundred men got away.

So ended the first day of combat for the first British soldiers to fight a European enemy since the Crimea and the first to fight on European soil since Waterloo. It was a bitter disappointment: both for the Ist Corps which had marched forward through the heat and dust and now had to turn and march back almost without having fired a shot; even more for the IInd Corps which felt proud of its showing against a famed and formidable enemy, knew nothing of his superior numbers or of the Fifth Army's withdrawal, and could not understand the order to retreat.

It was a "severe" disappointment to Henry Wilson who laid it all at the door of Kitchener and the Cabinet for having sent only four divisions instead of six. Had all six been present, he said with that marvelous incapacity to admit error that was to make him ultimately a Field Marshal, "this retreat would have been an advance and defeat would have been a victory."

Wilson's confidence and cheer began to wane, and Sir John French, mercurial at best, plunged into despondency. Though in France barely more than a week, the tensions, anxieties, and responsibility, combined with the iniquities of Lanrezac and culminating in frustration on the opening day of battle, soured him on his command. He ended his report to Kitchener next day with the ominous suggestion, indicating that he already had begun to think in terms of departure, "I think immediate attention should be directed to the defense of Havre." Havre at the mouth of the Seine was nearly a hundred miles south of the original British landing base at Boulogne.

That was the Battle of Mons. As the opening British engagement of what was to become the Great War, it became endowed in retrospect with every quality of greatness and was given a place in the British pantheon equal to the battles of Hastings and Agincourt. Legends like that of the Angels of Mons settled upon it. All its men were valorous and all its dead heroes. The deeds of every named regiment were chronicled down to the last hour and bullet of the fight until Mons came to shine mistily through a haze of such gallantry and glory as to make it seem a victory. Unquestionably, at Mons the British fought bravely and well, better than some French units but no better than many others; no better than the Belgians at Haelen or the Turcos at Charleroi or General Mangin's brigade at Onhaye or the enemy on various occasions. The battle, before the retreat began, lasted nine hours, engaged two divisions, or 35,000 British soldiers, cost a total of 1,600 British casualties, and held up the advance of von Kluck's army by one day. During the Battle of the Frontiers, of which it was a part, 70 French divisions, or about 1,250,000 men, were in combat at different times and places over a period of four days. French casualties during those four days amounted to more than 140,000, or twice the number of the whole British Expeditionary Force in France at the time.

In the wake of Charleroi and Mons, Belgium lay coated with white dust from the shattered walls of its houses and pock-marked with the debris of battles. Muddied hay used by the soldiers as beds trailed in the streets along with abandoned packs and blood-stained bandages. "And over all lay a smell," as Will Irwin wrote, "which I have never heard mentioned in any book on war—the smell of half a million unbathed men. . . . It lay for days over every town through which the Germans passed." Mingled with it was the smell of blood and medicine and horse manure and dead bodies. The human dead were supposed to be buried by their own troops before midnight, but often there were too many and there was too little time, and even less for the dead horses whose bodies, lying unburied for a longer time, became bloated and putrid. Belgian peasants trying to clear their fields of the dead after the armies passed by could be seen bending on their spades like pictures by Millet.

Derelict among the bodies lay the fragments of Plan 17 and bright broken bits of the French Field Regulations: ". . . the French Army henceforth knows no law but the offensive . . . the offensive alone leads to positive results."

Joffre, standing amid the tumbled debacle of all French hopes, with responsibility for the catastrophe resting finally upon him, with the frontiers of France breached, with every one of his armies in retreat or fighting desperately to hold a defensive line, remained magically unperturbed. By immediately casting the blame on the executors and absolving the planners, he was able to retain perfect and unblemished confidence in himself and in France—and in so doing, provide the essential and unique requirement in the calamitous days ahead.

On the morning of the 24th when, as he said, "There is no escaping the evidence of the facts," he reported to Messimy that the army was "condemned to a defensive attitude" and must hold out, resting upon its fortified lines and, while trying to wear down the enemy, wait for a favorable occasion to resume the offensive. He set about at once arranging the lines of retreat and preparing a regrouping of his armies to form a mass capable of renewing the attack from a defensive line he expected to establish on the Somme. He had been encouraged by a recent telegram from Paléologue in St. Petersburg to hope that the Germans would at any moment have to withdraw forces from the Western Front to meet the Russian threat, and on the morrow of his own disaster Joffre waited anxiously for a sound of the Russian steam roller. All that came through was a sibylline telegram reporting that "grave strategic problems" were being settled in East Prussia with promise of "further offensive operations."

Next to re-forming his lines, Joffre's most urgent task was to find the cause for failure. Without hesitancy of any kind he found it in "grave shortcomings on the part of commanders." A few had indeed crumbled under the awful responsibility of command. A general of artillery had to step into the place of the commander of the IIIrd Corps in front of Charleroi when that officer could nowhere be found during the most critical phase of the battle. In the Battle of the Ardennes a divisional general of the Vth Corps committed suicide. Human beings, like plans, prove

fallible in the presence of those ingredients that are missing in maneuvers
—danger, death, and live ammunition. But Joffre, who would admit no fal-
libility of plan, would permit none in men. Demanding the names of all
generals who had shown weakness or incapacity, he enlarged the list of the
limogés with ruthless hand.

Acknowledging, like Henry Wilson, no error of theory or strategy, he
could only ascribe the failure of the offensive, "in spite of the numerical
superiority which I thought I had secured for our armies," to a "lack of
offensive spirit." He might better have said "excess" than "lack." At Morhange in Lorraine, at Rossignol in the Ardennes, at Tamines on the
Sambre it was not too little but too much *cran* that caused the French
failure. In a "Note for All Armies" issued the very day after the debacle,
GQG amended "lack" to "false understanding" of the offensive spirit. The
Field Regulations, it said, had been "poorly understood or badly applied."
Infantry attacks were launched at too great a distance and without artillery support, thus suffering losses from machine-gun fire that might have
been avoided. Henceforth when ground was occupied, "it must be immediately organized. Entrenchments must be dug." The "capital error" had
been lack of coordination between artillery and infantry which it was an
"absolute necessity" to rectify. The 75s must fire at maximum range.
"Finally, we must copy the enemy in using airplanes to prepare artillery
attacks." Whatever else were French military faults, unwillingness to learn
from experience was not one of them—at least not in the realm of
tactics.

GQG was less quick to locate failure in its own realm of strategy, even
when on August 24 the Deuxième Bureau made a startling disclosure: it
had discovered that the enemy's active corps were followed by reserve
corps using the same corps number. This, the first evidence of reserve
units being used in the front line, revealed how the Germans had managed
to be equally strong on the right and center at once. It did not convey to
Joffre a suspicion that Plan 17 might have had a fallible basis. He continued to believe it a good plan which had failed through poor execution.
When called to testify after the war at a parliamentary inquiry into the
cause of the catastrophe that opened France to invasion, he was asked his
opinion of the prewar Staff theory that the stronger the German right
wing, the better for France.

"But I still think so," Joffre replied. "The proof is that our Battle of the
Frontiers was planned just for that and if it had succeeded our way would
have been open. . . . What is more, it would have succeeded if the

Fourth and Fifth Armies had fought well. If they had it would have meant annihilation of the whole German advance."

In the dark morning of August 1914 when the retreat began it was not the Fourth so much as the Fifth Army and its commander that he chiefly blamed. Although British malice, too, clustered about the head of General Lanrezac, an anonymous spokesman for the British Army ultimately declared that Lanrezac's decision to retreat instead of counterattacking on August 23 spared "another Sedan." Of Lanrezac's earlier insistence on shifting the Fifth Army west of the Meuse to Charleroi, the same spokesman added, "There is no doubt that this change of plan saved the BEF and probably the French Armies also from annihilation."

On August 24 all that was then clear was that the French Armies were in retreat and the enemy advancing with relentless force. The extent of the debacle was unknown to the public until August 25 when the Germans announced the capture of Namur with 5,000 prisoners. The news shocked an incredulous world. *The Times* of London had said Namur would withstand a siege of six months; it had fallen in four days. In accents of stunned understatement it was said in England that the fall of Namur "is generally recognized as a distinct disadvantage . . . and the chances of the war being brought to a speedy conclusion are considerably reduced."

How far reduced, how distant the end, no one yet knew. No one could realize that for numbers engaged and for rate and number of losses suffered over a comparable period of combat, the greatest battle of the war had already been fought. No one could yet foresee its consequences: how the ultimate occupation of all Belgium and northern France would put the Germans in possession of the industrial power of both countries, of the manufactures of Liège, the coal of the Borinage, the iron ore of Lorraine, the factories of Lille, the rivers and railroads and agriculture, and how this occupation, feeding German ambition and fastening upon France the fixed resolve to fight to the last drop of recovery and reparation, would block all later attempts at compromise peace or "peace without victory" and would prolong the war for four more years.

All this is hindsight. On August 24 the Germans felt an immense surge of confidence. They saw only beaten armies ahead; the genius of Schlieffen had been proved; decisive victory seemed within German grasp. In France, President Poincaré wrote in his diary: "We must make up our minds both to retreat and to invasion. So much for the illusions of the last fortnight. Now the future of France depends on her powers of resistance."

Elan had not been enough.

▶▶▶　*15*　▶

▶▶▶　*"The Cossacks*
Are Coming!"

ON AUGUST 5 IN ST. PETERSBURG AMBASSADOR
Paléologue of France drove past a regiment of Cossacks leaving for the
front. Its general, seeing the French flag on the ambassador's car, leaned
down from his horse to embrace him and begged permission to parade his
regiment. While Paléologue solemnly reviewed the troops from his car, the
general, between shouts of command to the ranks, addressed shouts of
encouragement to the ambassador: "We'll destroy those filthy Prussians!
. . . No more Prussia, no more Germany! . . . William to St. Helena!"
Concluding the review, he galloped off behind his men, waving his saber
and shouting his war cry, "William to St. Helena!"

The Russians, whose quarrel with Austria had precipitated the war,
were grateful to France for standing by the alliance and anxious to show
equal loyalty by support of the French design. "Our proper objective," the
Czar was dutifully made to say with more bravado than he felt, "is the
annihilation of the German army"; he assured the French that he considered operations against Austria as "secondary" and that he had ordered

the Grand Duke "at all costs to open the way to Berlin at the earliest possible moment."

The Grand Duke in the last days of the crisis had been named Commander in Chief despite the bitter rivalry of Sukhomlinov who wanted the post for himself. As between the two, even the Russian regime in the last days of the Romanovs was not mad enough to choose the German-oriented Sukhomlinov to lead a war against Germany. He remained, however, as War Minister.

From the moment the war opened, the French, uncertain that Russia really would or could perform what she had promised, began exhorting their ally to hurry. "I entreat Your Majesty," pleaded Ambassador Paléologue in audience with the Czar on August 5, "to order your armies to take an immediate offensive, otherwise there is risk of the French army being overwhelmed." Not content with seeing the Czar, Paléologue also called upon the Grand Duke who assured the ambassador that he intended a vigorous offensive to begin on August 14, in keeping with the promise of the fifteenth day of mobilization, without waiting for all his army to be concentrated. Though famous for his uncompromising, not to say sometimes unprintable habits of speech, the Grand Duke composed on the spot a message of medieval chivalry to Joffre. "Firm in the conviction of victory," he telegraphed, he would march against the enemy bearing alongside his own standard the flag of the French Republic which Joffre had given him at maneuvers in 1912.

That a gap existed between the promises given to the French and the preparations for performance was all too apparent and may have been cause for the tears the Grand Duke was reported to have shed when he was named Commander in Chief. According to a colleague, he "appeared entirely unequipped for the task and, to quote his own statement, on receipt of the imperial order spent much time crying because he did not know how to approach his duties." Regarded by a leading Russian military historian as "eminently qualified" for his task, the Grand Duke may have wept less for himself than for Russia and the world. There was an aura about 1914 that caused those who sensed it to shiver for mankind. Tears came even to the most bold and resolute. Messimy opening a Cabinet meeting on August 5 with a speech full of valor and confidence, broke off midway, buried his head in his hands, and sobbed, unable to continue. Winston Churchill wishing godspeed and victory to the BEF, when taking leave of Henry Wilson, "broke down and cried so that he could not finish the sentence." Something of the same emotion could be felt in St. Petersburg.

The Grand Duke's colleagues were not the firmest pillars of support. Chief of Staff in 1914 was General Yanushkevich, a young man of forty-four with black mustache and curly black hair who was chiefly notable for not wearing a beard and whom the War Minister referred to as "still a child." More a courtier than a soldier, he had not fought in the Japanese War although he had served in the same regiment of Guards as Nicholas II, which was as good a reason as any for rapid promotion. He was a graduate of the Staff College and later its commandant, had served on the staff of the War Ministry, and when war broke out had been Chief of Staff for barely three months. Like the German Crown Prince, he was completely under the guidance of his Deputy Chief, the stern and silent General Danilov, a 'hard worker and strict disciplinarian who was the brains of the Staff. Yanushkevich's predecessor as Chief of Staff, General Jilinsky, had preferred to be relieved of that post and had persuaded Suk-homlinov to appoint him commander of the Warsaw military district. He was now in over-all command, under the Grand Duke, of the Northwest Army Group on the front against Germany. In the Russo-Japanese War he had served with little distinction but no positive error as Chief of Staff to the Commander in Chief, General Kuropatkin, and having survived that grave of reputations had managed to remain in the upper echelons without either personal popularity or military talent.

Russia had made no preparations to meet the advanced date for attack which she had promised to the French. Improvisations had to be arranged at the last moment. A scheme of "forward mobilization" was ordered which skipped certain preliminary stages to gain several days' time. Streams of telegrams from Paris, delivered with personal eloquence by Paléologue, kept up the pressure. On August 6 the orders of the Russian General Staff said it was essential to prepare "for an energetic offensive against Germany at the earliest possible moment, in order to ease the situation of the French but, of course, only when sufficient strength has been made available." By August 10, however, the proviso for "sufficient strength" had been dropped. Orders of that date read, "Naturally it is our duty to support France in view of the great stroke prepared by Germany against her. This support must take the form of the quickest possible advance against Germany, by attacking those forces she has left behind in East Prussia." The First and Second Armies were ordered to be "in position" to advance on M–14

(August 13), although they would have to start without their services of supply, which would not be fully concentrated until M–20 (August 19).

Difficulties of organization were immense; the essence of the problem, as the Grand Duke once confessed to Poincaré, was that in an empire as vast as Russia when an order was given no one was ever sure whether it had been delivered. Shortages of telephone wire and telegraph equipment and of trained signal corpsmen made sure or quick communication impossible. Shortage of motor transport also slowed down the Russian pace. In 1914 the army had 418 motor transport vehicles, 259 passenger cars, and two motor ambulances. (It had, however, 320 airplanes.) As a result, supplies after leaving the railhead had to depend on horse transport.

Supply was hazardous at best. Testimony in trials after the Japanese war revealed bribes and graft running like a network of moles' tunnels beneath the army. When even the Governor of Moscow, General Reinbot, was convicted and imprisoned for venality in letting army contracts, he still wielded enough private influence to obtain not only a pardon but reappointment to a new post. Meeting his commissariat staff for the first time as Commander in Chief, the Grand Duke said to them, "Gentlemen, no stealing."

Vodka, another traditional companion of war, was prohibited. In the last mobilization in 1904 when soldiers came reeling in and regimental depots were a mess of drunken slumbers and broken bottles, it had taken an extra week to straighten out the confusion. Now with the French calling every day's delay a matter of life or death, Russia enacted prohibition as a temporary measure for the period of mobilization. Nothing could have given more practical or more earnest proof of loyal intention to meet French pleas for haste, but with that characteristic touch of late-Romanov rashness, the government, by ukase of August 22, extended prohibition for the duration of the war. As the sale of vodka was a state monopoly, this act at one stroke cut off a third of the government's income. It was well known, commented a bewildered member of the Duma, that governments waging war seek by a variety of taxes and levies to increase income, "but never since the dawn of history has a country in time of war renounced the principal source of its revenue."

In the last hour of the fifteenth day at 11:00 P.M. on a lovely summer evening, the Grand Duke left the capital for field headquarters at Baranovichi, a railroad junction on the Moscow-Warsaw line about midway between the German and Austrian fronts. He and his staff and their families gathered in subdued groups on the station platform in St. Petersburg waiting for the Czar to come to bid farewell to the Commander in Chief. However, the Czarina's jealousy overrode courtesy, and Nicholas did not appear. Goodbyes and prayers were spoken in low voices; the men took their places in the train in silence and departed.

Behind the front the struggle to assemble armies was still in process. Russian cavalry on reconnaissance had been probing German territory since the first day of the war. Their forays succeeded less in penetrating the German screen than in providing an excuse for screaming headlines in German newspapers and wild tales of Cossack brutalities. As early as August 4 in Frankfort on the western edge of Germany an officer heard rumors that 30,000 refugees from East Prussia were coming to be accommodated in that city. Demands to save East Prussia from the Slavic hordes began to distract the German General Staff from the task of trying to concentrate all military effort against France.

At dawn on August 12 a detachment of General Rennenkampf's First Army, consisting of a cavalry division under General Gourko supported by an infantry division, opened the invasion of East Prussia ahead of the main advance and took the town of Marggrabowa five miles inside the frontier. Shooting as they rode through the outskirts and into the empty market square, the Russians found the town undefended and evacuated by German troops. Shops were closed, but the townspeople were watching from the windows. In the countryside the inhabitants fled precipitously ahead of the advancing squadrons before there was any fighting as if by pre-arrangement. On the first morning the Russians saw columns of black smoke rising along their line of march which, on approach, were discovered to be not farms and homes burned by their fleeing owners but dumps of straw burned as signals to show the direction of the invaders. Everywhere was evidence of the German's systematic preparation. Wooden watchtowers had been built on hilltops. Bicycles were provided for local farm boys of twelve to fourteen who acted as messengers. German soldiers, posted as informers, were found dressed as peasants, even as peasant women. The latter were discovered, presumably in the course of nonmilitary action, by their government-issue underwear; but many were probably never caught, it being impossible, General Gourko regretfully admitted, to lift the skirts of every female in East Prussia.

Receiving General Gourko's reports of evacuated towns and fleeing population and concluding that the Germans were not planning a serious resistance so far east of their base on the Vistula, General Rennenkampf was the more eager to dash forward and the less concerned about his incomplete services of supply. A trim, well-set-up officer of sixty-one with a direct glance and energetic mustache turned up at the corners, he had earned a reputation for boldness, decisiveness, and tactical skill during service in the Boxer Rebellion, as commander of a cavalry division in the Russo-Japanese War, and as leader of the punitive expedition to Chita which ruthlessly exterminated the remnants of the Revolution of 1905. His military prowess was slightly shadowed by German descent and by some unexplained imbroglio which according to General Gourko "left his moral reputation considerably damaged." When in coming weeks his strange behavior caused these factors to be recalled, his colleagues nevertheless remained convinced of his loyalty to Russia.

Disregarding the cautions of General Jilinsky, commander of the Northwest Army Group, who was pessimistic from the start, and hastening the concentration of his three army corps and five and a half cavalry divisions, Rennenkampf opened his offensive on August 17. His First Army of some 200,000 men crossed the frontier along a 35-mile front split by Rominten Forest. Its objective was the Insterburg Gap, a distance of 37 miles from the frontier, or about three days' march at the Russian rate. The Gap was a stretch of open land about 30 miles wide lying between the fortified area of Königsberg to the north and the Masurian Lakes to the south. It was a country of small villages and large farms with unfenced fields and wide ranges of view from the occasional swells of high ground. Here the First Army would come through and engage the main German strength until Samsonov's Second Army, turning the lake barrier from the south, would arrive to deliver the decisive blow upon the German flank and rear. The two Russian armies were expected to join in a common front in the area of Allenstein.

General Samsonov's objective line, on a level with Allenstein, was 43 miles from the frontier, about three and a half or four days' march if all went well. Between his starting point, however, and his goal were many opportunities for the unexpected hazards—what Clausewitz called the "frictions"—of war. Owing to the lack of an east-west railway across Russian Poland to East Prussia, Samsonov's army could not cross the frontier until two days behind Rennenkampf's and would already have been on the march for a week before reaching the frontier. Its line of march was along sandy roads through a waste of undeveloped country spotted with forests and marshes and inhabited by a few poor Polish peasants. Once inside hostile territory there would be few resources of food and forage.

General Samsonov, unlike Rennenkampf, was new to the region and unfamiliar with his troops and staff. In 1877, at the age of eighteen, he had fought against the Turks; he was a general at forty-three; in the Russo-Japanese War he too had commanded a cavalry division; since 1909 he had been in semimilitary employment as governor of Turkestan. Aged fifty-five when the war broke out, he was on sick leave in the Caucasus and did not reach Warsaw and Second Army headquarters until August 12. Communication between his army and Rennenkampf's, as well as to Jilinsky's headquarters in the rear which was to coordinate the movements of both, was erratic. Precision in timing was not in any case a notable Russian virtue. Having played out the campaign in war games in April before the war with most of the same commanders and staff as were to take the field in August, the Russian General Staff was gloomily conscious of the difficulties. Although the war games, in which Sukhomlinov played the role of Commander in Chief, revealed that the First Army had started too soon, when war came the same schedule was adhered to without change. Counting two days for Rennenkampf's head start and four days for Samsonov's march, there would be a period of six days during which the German Army would have to face only one Russian army.

On August 17 General Rennenkampf's two cavalry corps, guarding his flanks on right and left, had orders not only to screen his advance but to cut both branches of the railway in order to prevent the withdrawal of German rolling stock. Having deliberately used a railroad gauge different from the German as a defense against invasion, the Russians could not bring up their own rolling stock, or use the invaluable network of railroads in East Prussia unless they captured German trains. Naturally, the Germans left little rolling stock behind to be captured. The Russian Army, moving farther and farther from its base into hostile country, began almost at once to outrun its horse-drawn and not fully organized supply train. For communication, lacking the wire to lay their own lines, the Russians were dependent on German telegraph lines and offices, and when these were found destroyed they resorted to sending messages by wireless, in clear, because their divisional staffs lacked codes and cryptographers.

Little reconnaissance or artillery spotting was accomplished by airplane, most of the Air Force having been sent to the Austrian front. At sight of an airplane, the first they had ever seen, Russian soldiers, regardless of its identity, blazed away with their rifles, convinced that such a clever invention as a flying machine could only be German. The enlisted soldier consumed quantities of black bread and tea which were said—though it is not easy to see why—to give him a characteristic odor rather like that of a

horse. He was armed with a four-edged bayonet which when mounted on
a rifle made a weapon as tall as a man and in hand-to-hand combat gave
him an advantage over the German. In firepower and fighting efficiency,
however, German preponderance in artillery made two German divisions
equal to three Russian. The Russian disadvantage was not helped by the
mutual hatred of Sukhomlinov as War Minister and the Grand Duke as
Commander in Chief, especially as liaison between front and rear was bad
enough and the problem of supply worse. Before the fighting was a month
old the shortage of shells and cartridges was already so desperate and the
indifference or lethargy of the War Ministry so discouraging that on September 8 the Grand Duke was driven to appeal directly to the Czar. On
the Austrian front, he reported, operations would have to be held up until
stocks of shells reached 100 per gun. "At present we have only 25 per gun.
I find it necessary to request Your Majesty to hasten the shipment of
shells."

The cry *"Kosaken kommen!"* (The Cossacks are coming!) echoing out
of East Prussia weakened Germany's resolve to leave the province with
only a minimum defense. The Eighth Army in East Prussia, consisting of
four and a half corps, one cavalry division, garrison troops of Königsberg
and some territorial brigades, was about equal in numbers to either one of
the two Russian armies. Its orders from Moltke were to defend East and
West Prussia but not to allow itself to be overwhelmed by superior forces
or to be driven into the fortress camp of Königsberg. If it found itself
threatened by greatly superior forces, it was to withdraw behind the Vistula, leaving East Prussia to the enemy. Such orders contained "psychological dangers for weak characters," in the opinion of Colonel Max Hoffmann who was now deputy Chief of Operations for the Eighth Army.

The weak character Hoffmann had in mind was the Eighth Army's
commander, Lieutenant-General von Prittwitz und Gaffron. As a court
favorite Prittwitz had enjoyed a career of rapid promotions because, according to a fellow officer, he "knew how to get the Kaiser's ear at table with
funny stories and salacious gossip." Now sixty-six years old and notorious
for his girth, he was a German version of Falstaff, "impressive in appearance, conscious to the highest degree of his self-importance, ruthless, even
coarse and self-indulgent." Known as *der Dicke* (Fatty), he was without
intellectual or military interests and never moved if he could help it. In
vain Moltke, who considered him unfit for his assignment, had tried for
years to remove him from the designated command of the Eighth Army;

Prittwitz's connections were proof against his efforts. The best Moltke could do was to appoint his own Deputy, Count von Waldersee, as Prittwitz' Chief of Staff. In August, Waldersee, suffering from the after effects of an operation, was in Hoffmann's opinion "not up to par," and since Prittwitz never had been, this left Hoffmann in the happy assurance that real power to direct the Eighth Army lay in the hands of the best qualified person, himself.

Anxiety for East Prussia became acute when on August 15 Japan declared for the Allies, freeing large numbers of Russian forces. In making or keeping friends, a task that forever eluded it, German diplomacy had failed again. Japan had her own ideas of her best interests in a European war, and these were well understood by their intended victim. "Japan is going to take advantage of this war to gain control of China," foretold President Yuan Shi-kai. As it proved, Japan used the opportunity of the war while the European Powers were too busy to stop her, to impose the Twenty-one Demands on China and to make the incursions into Chinese sovereignty and territory which were to twist the history of the twentieth century. To start with, the immediate effect of Japan's joining the Allies would be to release Russian forces from the Far East. Conjuring up visions of added Slavic hordes, the Germans now had new cause to be nervous about leaving East Prussia to be held by the lone Eighth Army.

From the beginning General von Prittwitz was having trouble controlling the commander of his Ist Corps, General von François, a bright-eyed officer of Huguenot ancestry, fifty-eight years old, who looked not unlike a German Foch. The Ist Corps was recruited from East Prussia, and its commander, determined that not one Slav should tread on Prussian soil, threatened to upset Eighth Army strategy by advancing too far.

Based on Hoffmann's calculations, the Eighth Army expected Rennenkampf's army to advance first, and anticipated meeting it in battle on August 19 or 20 in the area of Gumbinnen, about twenty-five miles from the Russian frontier, before it reached the Insterburg Gap. Three and a half corps, including François' Ist Corps, and a cavalry division were sent to meet it while the fourth corps was sent southeast to make contact with Samsonov's approaching army. On August 16 Eighth Army headquarters moved forward to Bartenstein, closer to the Insterburg front, where it was discovered that François had already reached and passed Gumbinnen. He believed in taking the offensive at once whereas Hoffmann's strategy was to let Rennenkampf's army come as far west as it could on its first two days' march on the theory that the farther it advanced from its base, the more vulnerable it would be. Hoffmann did not want it halted, but on the contrary allowed to reach the Gumbinnen area as soon as possible so as to give the Germans time to engage it alone before having to turn to face Samsonov.

François' advance beyond Gumbinnen where he had established his headquarters on August 16 threatened to pull the rest of the Eighth Army after him to support his flanks, thus extending itself beyond its powers. Prittwitz on the 16th peremptorily ordered him to halt. François indignantly protested by telephone that the nearer to Russia he engaged the enemy, the less risk to German territory. Prittwitz replied that a sacrifice of part of East Prussia was unavoidable, and dispatched a written order reminding François that he was "sole commander" and again prohibiting further advance. François ignored it. At 1:00 P.M on August 17, Prittwitz "to his great astonishment" received a message from François that he was already in action in Stalluponen, twenty miles beyond Gumbinnen and only five miles from the Russian frontier.

That morning when Rennenkampf's army crossed the frontier in full force, his IIIrd Corps in the center began its march, more by lack of co-ordination than by design, several hours ahead of the other two. Russian reconnaissance having located François' forces at Stalluponen, orders were given to attack. Battle was joined a few miles east of the town. General von François and his staff were watching the progress of the fight from the steeple of the Stalluponen church when, "in the midst of this nerve-wracking tension," the church bell suddenly tolled with appalling sound upon their eardrums. The steeple shook with its vibrations, the telescope trembled on its tripod, and infuriated officers let loose a hail of Teutonic oaths upon the head of the unfortunate town councilman who had felt it to be his duty to warn the people of the Russians' approach.

Equal fury raged at Eighth Army headquarters on receipt of the message from François. He was ordered by telephone and telegraph to break off action, and a major-general was rushed off in person to confirm the order. Climbing to the belfry in no less bad temper than already raged there, he shouted at General von François, "The General in Chief orders you to stop the battle instantly and retire upon Gumbinnen!" Furious at the tone and manner, François grandiloquently retorted, "Inform General von Prittwitz that General von François will break off the engagement when he has defeated the Russians!"

Meanwhile a German brigade with five batteries of artillery had been sent around from the German right flank to attack the Russians from the rear. As the early advance of the Russian IIIrd Corps, especially of its 27th Division which was now engaged at Stalluponen, had opened a gap between itself and the neighboring Russian corps on its left, it was unprotected from the German attack. The regiment upon whom the German attack fell, broke and fled, involving the whole 27th Division in retreat and leaving 3,000 prisoners to the Germans. Although the rest of Rennenkampf's army reached the objective line laid down for it that day, the 27th Division had to retire to the frontier to reform, holding up the scheduled advance for the following day. Brimming with victory, François retired that same night toward Gumbinnen, after evacuating Stalluponen, personally convinced of the virtues of disobedience.

Despite the check, Rennenkampf's Army renewed its advance. But as early as August 19 it had begun to feel the drain of incomplete services of supply. Hardly fifteen miles from their own frontier, corps commanders reported supplies not coming up and messages not getting through to each other or to army headquarters. Ahead of them roads were clogged by massive, milling droves of cattle and sheep herded by the fleeing populace. The flight of the people and the retrograde movement of François' corps caused Rennenkampf and his superior, General Jilinsky, commander of the Northwest Front, to believe that the Germans were evacuating East Prussia. This did not suit the Russians, for if the German army retired too soon it would escape destruction by the Russian pincers. Rennenkampf consequently ordered a halt for the 20th, less because of his own difficulties than to entice the enemy forward into battle and allow more time for Samsonov's Second Army to come up for the decisive blow upon the German rear.

General von François was more than willing. With battle in his nostrils once more, he telephoned General von Prittwitz at Eighth Army headquarters on the 19th and clamored for permission to counterattack instead of continuing his retreat. It was a golden opportunity, he asserted, because the Russian advance was loose and scattered. He described feelingly the flight of the inhabitants and passionately urged the shame of yielding the soil of Prussia to the horrid footprint of the Slav. Prittwitz was torn. Intending to fight behind Gumbinnen, the Eighth Army had well-prepared positions along the river Angerapp. But von François' too early advance had upset the plan and he was now some ten miles on the far side of Gumbinnen, to the east. To allow him to attack there would mean to accept battle away from the line of the Angerapp; the other two and a half corps would be pulled away with him and would be separated further from the XXth Corps sent to watch the approach of Samsonov's army from the south and which might need support at any time.

On the other hand, the spectacle of a German army retiring without serious battle, even if only for twenty miles, especially in full view of a terrified population, was distasteful. The decision was made more difficult when the Germans intercepted Rennenkampf's order to halt. The order was sent to Russian corps commanders by wireless in a simple code which a German professor of mathematics attached to the Eighth Army as cryptographer had no difficulty in solving.

This raised the question: How long would Rennenkampf halt? The time in which the Germans would be free to fight one Russian army without the other was running short; by that evening three of the six days would be gone. If the Germans waited on the Angerapp for Rennenkampf to come against them, they might be caught between both armies at once. Just at this moment, word was received from the XXth Corps that Samsonov's army had that morning crossed the frontier. The second claw of the pincer was advancing. The Germans must either fight Rennenkampf at once, giving up their prepared position on the Angerapp, or disengage and turn against Samsonov. Prittwitz and his Staff decided on the former, and told François to attack next morning, August 20. The only difficulty was that the other two and a half corps, dutifully waiting on the Angerapp, could not be activated in time to catch up with him.

Before dawn von François' heavy artillery opened fire, taking the Russians by surprise; the shelling continued for half an hour. At 4:00 A.M. his infantry moved forward over the stubbled fields in the uncertain dark until they came within rifle distance of the Russian lines. As morning broke, combat spread like a licking fire over the front. Russian field batteries poured shells on the advancing gray lines and saw the white road ahead suddenly turn gray with the bodies of the fallen. A second wave of gray charged, coming nearer. The Russians could make out the spiked helmets. Their batteries fired again, and the wave went down and another came. The Russian guns, supplied with ammunition at a rate of 244 rounds per day, were now firing at a rate of 440 per day. An airplane with black crosses flew over and bombed their artillery positions. The gray waves kept on coming. They were within 500 yards when the Russian guns stuttered and fell silent; their ammunition was used up. François' two divisions cut up the Russian 28th Division, inflicting a casualty rate of 60 per cent, virtual annihilation. François' cavalry with three batteries of horse artillery made a wide sweep around the open Russian end, unopposed by the Russian cavalry which, having no artillery, took itself off, permitting the Germans to fall upon the Russian transport in the rear. These were the fortunes of the corps on Rennenkampf's extreme right; on his center and left matters went very differently.

Here the Russians, warned by the sound of François' predawn cannon, were ready for the attack which came piecemeal over a front 35 miles wide. In the center the German XVIIth Corps did not reach the front until 8:00 A.M., four hours behind François, and on the German right the Ist Reserve Corps did not arrive till noon. The XVIIth was commanded by General August von Mackensen, another of the group of generals who had fought in 1870 and were now sixty-five or over. The Ist Reserve was commanded by General Otto von Below. They had been behind the Angerapp on the evening of the 19th when they received the unexpected order to join François in an offensive beyond Gumbinnen next morning. Hurriedly assembling his units, Mackensen crossed the river during the night to become entangled on the other side among refugees, wagons, and livestock on the roads. By the time they sorted themselves out and advanced far enough to make contact with the enemy, they had lost the advantage of surprise and the Russians opened fire first. The effect of shelling by heavy guns is devastating, whoever is on the receiving end, and in this, one of the rare cases of 1914, the receivers were Germans. The infantry was pinned to the ground lying face down, not daring to raise their heads; ammunition wagons were blown up; horses were galloping riderless. By afternoon Mackensen's 35th Division broke under the fire. A company threw away its arms and ran; another caught the panic; then a whole regiment, then those on either side of it. Soon the roads and fields were covered with battalions streaming to the rear. Staff and divisional officers and Mackensen himself tore across the front in motors, attempting to stem the rout which continued for fifteen miles before it could be halted.

On Mackensen's right von Below's Ist Reserve Corps could give no help because it had started even later and, by the time it reached its appointed sector at Goldap on the edge of Rominten Forest, was at once heavily engaged by the Russians. The rout of Mackensen's corps in the center uncovered von Below's left flank, forcing him, too, to retire, both in order to cover Mackensen's retreat and to protect himself. On von Below's right the 3rd Reserve Division, commanded by General von Morgen, which had started from the Angerapp last of all did not arrive until evening when all was over, and saw no action. Although the Germans made good their retreat and the Russians had suffered severely against François, the Battle of Gumbinnen was on the whole a Russian victory.

Prittwitz saw his whole campaign undone. A vigorous Russian pursuit through the broken German center could smash through the Insterburg Gap, splitting the Eighth Army and pushing François' corps in the north into refuge within the Königsberg fortified zone which OHL had expressly warned must not be allowed to happen. To save the Eighth Army and hold it together, Prittwitz saw retreat to the Vistula as the only solution. Moltke's last words to him had been: "Keep the army intact. Don't be driven from the Vistula, but in case of extreme need abandon the region east of the Vistula." Prittwitz felt the extreme need was now, especially after a talk over the telephone with Mackensen who vividly described the panic of his troops.

At six o'clock that evening, August 20, he called François and told him that in spite of success on his sector the army must retreat to the Vistula. Thunderstruck, François protested violently, urged reasons for Prittwitz to reconsider, contended that because of their own losses the Russians could not mount an energetic pursuit, besought him to change his mind. He hung up with an impression that Prittwitz was not entirely adamant and had agreed to think it over.

At Headquarters, through a chaos of excited comings and goings and conflicting reports, an astonishing condition began clearly to emerge: there was no pursuit. At Russian headquarters Rennenkampf had given the order to pursue between three and four o'clock that afternoon, but owing to reports of heavy German artillery fire covering Mackensen's retreat had canceled the order at 4:30. Uncertain of the extent of the German rout in the center, he waited. An exhausted staff officer who asked his permission to go to bed was told he might lie down but not undress. He slept for an hour and was wakened by Rennenkampf who stood by his bed smiling and said, "You can take off your clothes now; the Germans are retiring."

Much has been made of this remark by the military historians who swarm over a battle after it is over, especially by Hoffmann who reports it with malicious glee in a rather distorted version. They point out with some truth that when an enemy is retiring is the time to pursue, not to go to bed. Because of the momentous results of the Battle of Tannenberg of which Gumbinnen was a preliminary, the episode of Rennenkampf's halt has raised clouds of fevered explanations and accusations, not omitting references to his German ancestry and the explicit charge that he was a traitor. The more probable explanation was offered a hundred years before the event by Clausewitz. "The whole weight of all that is sensuous in an army," he wrote in discussing the problem of pursuit, "presses for rest and refreshment. It requires exceptional vigor on the part of a commander to see and feel beyond the present moment and to act at once to attain those results which at the time seem to be the mere embellishments of victory—the luxury of triumph."

Whether or not Rennenkampf perceived those ultimate results, the fact was that he could not, or felt he could not, fling himself after the fleeing enemy to pluck the final victory. His supply lines were functioning weakly; to advance further beyond his railhead would be to outrun them altogether. He would be lengthening his lines in hostile territory while the Germans, falling back toward their base, were shortening theirs. He could not use the German railways without capturing their rolling stock, and he had no railroad gangs to alter the gauge. His transport was in chaos after the German cavalry attack; his right-wing cavalry had performed miserably; he had lost most of a division. He stayed where he was.

The evening was hot. Colonel Hoffmann was standing outside the house in which German headquarters was located, debating the battle and the prospects for tomorrow with his immediate superior Major General Grünert with whom he expected to govern the weaker wills of Prittwitz and Waldersee. Just then a message was brought to them. It was from General Scholtz of the XXth Corps reporting that the southern Russian army was now across the frontier with four or five corps and advancing over a front 50 to 60 miles wide. Hoffmann in that disturbing way he had, which no one quite knew whether to take seriously, suggested "suppressing" the report in order to keep it from Prittwitz and Waldersee who in his judgment "had for the moment lost command of their nerves." No other phrase in memoirs of the war attains the universality of "He lost control of his nerves," usually applied to a colleague; in this instance it was doubtless justified. Hoffmann's brief plot was in vain, however, for at that moment Prittzwitz and Waldersee came out of the house wearing expressions showing that they too had received the report. Prittwitz called them all indoors and said: "Gentlemen, if we continue the battle against the Vilna Army, the Warsaw Army will advance on our rear and cut us off from the Vistula. We must break off the fight against the Vilna Army and retire behind the Vistula." He was no longer talking of retreat "to" but "behind" the Vistula.

Hoffmann and Grünert instantly disputed the necessity, claiming they could "finish off" battle with the Vilna Army in two or three days and

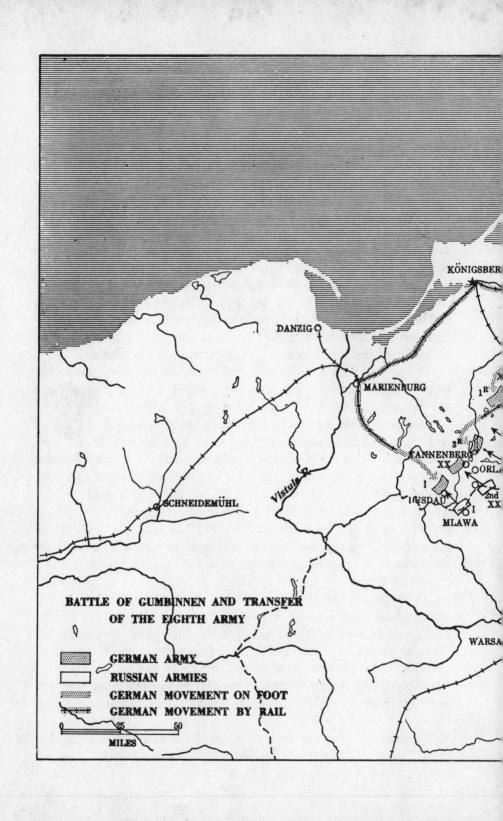

KÖNIGSBER

DANZIG O

MARIENBURG

1ᴿ

3ᴿ

TANNENBERG
XX O   O ORL

I

USDAU   I   2nd
MLAWA   XX

SCHNEIDEMÜHL

Vistula

WARSA

BATTLE OF GUMBINNEN AND TRANSFER
OF THE EIGHTH ARMY

GERMAN ARMY
RUSSIAN ARMIES
GERMAN MOVEMENT ON FOOT
GERMAN MOVEMENT BY RAIL

0   25   50

MILES

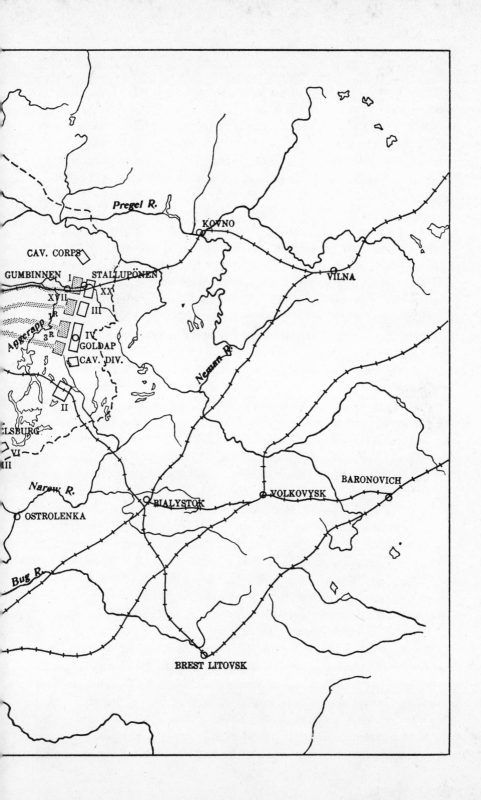

still be in time to face the danger from the south, and until then Scholtz's Corps could "manage for themselves."

Prittwitz harshly cut them off. It was up to him and Waldersee to make the decision. He insisted that the threat of the southern Russian Army was too great. Hoffmann must make the necessary arrangements for retreat behind the Vistula. Hoffmann pointed out that the left wing of the southern army was already nearer to the Vistula than the Germans were and, demonstrating with a compass, showed that the retreat had become impossible. He asked to be "instructed" how to carry it out. Prittwitz abruptly dismissed him and everyone in the room and telephoned to OHL at Coblenz announcing his intention to retreat to the Vistula if not behind it. He added that its waters in the summer heat were at low ebb and he was doubtful if he could even hold the river without reinforcements.

Moltke was aghast. This was the result of leaving that fat idiot in command of the Eighth Army, and of his own ill-considered last words to him. To yield East Prussia would be to suffer a tremendous moral defeat and lose the most valuable grain and dairy region as well. Worse, if the Russians crossed the Vistula they would threaten not only Berlin but the Austrian flank and even Vienna. Reinforcements! Where could he get reinforcements except from the Western Front where every last battalion was engaged. To withdraw troops from the Western Front now could mean loss of the campaign against France. Moltke was too shocked or too distant from the scene to think to issue a counterorder. For the moment he contented himself with ordering his staff to find out the facts in direct conversation with François, Mackensen, and the other corps commanders.

Meanwhile at Eighth Army Headquarters Hoffmann and Grünert were trying to persuade Waldersee that retreat was not the only course—was indeed an impossible course. Hoffmann now proposed a maneuver by which the Eighth Army, taking advantage of its interior lines and the use of railways, could so dispose itself as to meet the threat of both Russian armies and, if things developed as he thought they would, be in a position to throw all its weight against one of them.

He proposed, if Rennenkampf's army still did not pursue next day, and he did not think it would, to disengage François' Ist Corps and bring it the long way round by rail to reinforce Scholtz's XXth Corps on the southern front. François would take up a position on Scholtz's right opposite Samsonov's left wing, which, being nearest to the Vistula, was the most threatening. General von Morgen's division which had not been in action at Gumbinnen would also be sent to Scholtz's support by a different set of railway lines. The movement of troops with all their stores, equipment, horses, guns and munitions, the assembling of trains, the boarding at stations mobbed by refugees, the switching of trains from one line to another would be a complex matter, but Hoffmann was sure the German railroad system, on which so much brain power had been expended, would be equal to it.

While this movement was under way, the retreat of Mackensen's and von Below's corps would be directed toward the south for another two days' march so that when successfully disengaged they would be some 30 miles nearer the southern front. From here, if all went well, they would march across the short inner distance to take up a position on Scholtz's left which they should reach not long after François reached his right. Thus the whole army of four and a half corps would be in place to engage the enemy's southern army. The cavalry and Königsberg reserves would be left as a screen in front of Rennenkampf's army.

The success of this maneuver depended entirely upon a single condition—that Rennenkampf would not move. Hoffmann believed he would remain stationary for another day or more to rest and refit and make good his supply lines. His confidence was based not on any mysterious betrayal or other sinister or supernatural intelligence, but simply on his belief that Rennenkampf had come to a halt from natural causes. In any event Mackensen's and von Below's corps would not change fronts for another two or three days. By that time there should be some sign—with the help of further intercepted codes—of Rennenkampf's intentions.

Such was Hoffmann's argument, and he persuaded von Waldersee. Somehow, sometime that night Waldersee either persuaded Prittwitz or allowed Hoffmann to prepare the necessary orders without Prittwitz's approval—the record is not clear. As the Staff did not know that Prittwitz had in the meantime told OHL of his intention to retreat to the Vistula, no one bothered to inform the Supreme Command that the idea of retreat had been given up.

Next morning two of Moltke's staff, after battling the frustrations of the field telephone for some hours, succeeded in talking individually with each corps commander in the East, from whom they gathered that matters were serious but retreat too rash a solution. As Prittwitz seemed committed to retreat, Moltke decided to replace him. While he was talking it over with his deputy, von Stein, Colonel Hoffmann was enjoying the delightful sensation of being right—so far. Reconnaissance showed Rennenkampf's army quiescent; "they are not pursuing us at all." Orders were at once issued for the movement of François' Ist Corps to the south. François, according to his own account, was overcome with emotion and wept when he left Gumbinnen that afternoon. Prittwitz had apparently approved and immediately regretted it. That evening he called OHL again and told von Stein and Moltke that the proposal of his staff to advance against the Warsaw Army was "impossible—too daring." In reply to a question, he said he could not even guarantee to hold the Vistula with his "handful of men." He must have reinforcements. That sealed his dismissal.

With the Eastern Front in danger of collapse, someone bold, strong, and decisive was needed at once to take over the command. How a commander will meet the crises of real war is never certain in advance, but OHL was fortunate in knowing of a staff officer who only a week ago had proved himself in action—Ludendorff, the hero of Liège. He would do for Chief of Staff of the Eighth Army. In the German system of command exercised through a pair, the Chief of Staff was as important as the commanding officer and sometimes, depending on capacity and temperament, more so. Ludendorff was at that moment with von Bülow's Second Army on the outskirts of Namur where, following his success at Liège, he was directing the storming of Belgium's second great fortress. He was on the doorstep of France at a crucial moment—but the need of the Eastern Front was drastic. Moltke and von Stein agreed he must be called. A staff captain was instantly dispatched by motorcar with a letter which reached General Ludendorff at nine next morning, August 22.

"You may be able to save the situation in the East," wrote von Stein. "I know no other man in whom I have such absolute trust." He apologized for drawing Ludendorff away from the threshold of a decisive action "which, please God, will be conclusive," but the sacrifice was "imperative." "Of course, you will not be held responsible for what has already happened in the East but with your energy you can prevent the worst from happening."

Ludendorff left within fifteen minutes in the staff captain's car. Ten miles from Namur he drove through Wavre which "only the day before when I passed through it had been a peaceful town. Now it was in flames. Here also the populace fired on our troops."

At six that evening Ludendorff arrived at Coblenz. Within three hours he was briefed on the situation in the East, was received by Moltke, "who was looking tired," and by the Kaiser, who was "very calm" but deeply affected by the invasion of East Prussia. Ludendorff issued certain orders to the Eighth Army and departed at 9:00 P.M. by special train for the

Eastern Front. The orders he issued, besides directing Hoffmann and Grünert to meet him at Marienburg, were for François' Corps to be sent by train to support Scholtz's XXth Corps on the southern front. Macken- sen's and von Below's two corps were to complete their disengagement and rest and refit through August 23. These were the same as Hoffmann's orders, thus realizing the ideal of the German War College in which all students, given a problem, come up with the identical solution. It is also possible that Ludendorff saw a telegraphed copy of Hoffmann's orders.

During the drive through Belgium, Ludendorff was told by the staff captain that as new Commander of the Eighth Army OHL had selected a retired general but it was not yet known whether he would accept the post. His name was Paul von Beneckendorff und Hindenburg. Ludendorff did not know him. Before leaving Coblenz later that night, he learned that General von Hindenburg had been located, had accepted the post, and would board the train at Hanover next morning at 4:00 A.M.

After deciding on a Chief of Staff, OHL had turned to the problem of finding a commanding officer. Ludendorff, everybody felt, was certainly a man of undeniable ability, but to complete the pair it would be well to have a regular "von." The names of various retired corps commanders were considered. Von Stein remembered a letter he had received from a former comrade on the outbreak of war, saying, "Don't forget me if, as things develop, a commanding officer is needed anywhere," and promising that the writer was "still robust." Just the man. He came from an old Junker family established in Prussia for centuries. He had served on the General Staff under Schlieffen and risen through all the proper steps to become a corps chief of staff and subsequently a corps commander before retiring at sixty-five in 1911. He would be sixty-eight in two months but he was no older than Kluck, Bülow, and Hausen, the three generals of the right wing. What was wanted in the East, especially after Prittwitz's panic, was a man of no nerves, and Hindenburg, throughout a solid, dependable career had been known for his imperturbability. Moltke approved; the Kaiser gave his consent. A telegram was dispatched to the retired general.

Hindenburg was at home in Hanover when at 3:00 P.M. he received a telegram asking if he would accept "immediate employment." He replied, "I am ready." A second telegram instructed him to leave for the East at once to take command of the Eighth Army. OHL did not bother to invite him to Coblenz for talks. He was instructed to board the train at Hanover and informed that his Chief of Staff would be General Ludendorff who would meet him on the train en route. Hindenburg had just time to be fitted for one of the new field-gray uniforms before departing, much to his embarrassment, in the old blue uniform of a Prussian general.

When the recall of Prittwitz was made public a few days later, the invaluable diarist, Princess Blücher, noted, "A General Hindenburg, quite an old man, has taken his place." Newspaper editors hurriedly scraped together material about the new commander, which was difficult to find since he appeared under "Beneckendorff" in the Army list. They were gratified to discover that he had fought at Sedan where he received the Iron Cross, Second Class, and was also a veteran of the earlier war against Austria in 1866. His Beneckendorff ancestors were among the Teutonic Knights who had settled East Prussia; the name Hindenburg was a product of marriage connections in the eighteenth century. He was a native of Posen in West Prussia, and early in his career, as staff officer to the Ist Corps at Königsberg, had studied the military problems of the Masurian Lake district, a fact that was soon to become the germ of the legend that depicted Hindenburg planning the Battle of Tannenberg thirty years in advance. He had been brought up on his grandparents' estate in Neudeck in West Prussia and remembered having had talks as a boy with an old gardener who had once worked two weeks for Frederick the Great.

He was waiting at the station in Hanover when the train drew in at four in the morning. General Ludendorff whom he had never met "stepped briskly" to the platform to report himself. On the way east he explained the situation and the orders he had already issued. Hindenburg listened and approved. So was born, on the way to the battle that was to make them famous, the combination, the "marriage" expressed in the mystic monogram HL that was to rule imperial Germany until the end. When sometime later he was made a Field Marshal, Hindenburg earned the nickname "Marshal *Was-sagst-du*" because of his habit, whenever asked for an opinion, of turning to Ludendorff and asking, "*Was sagst du?*" (What do you say?)

Characteristically the first person OHL thought to inform of the change in the Eighth Army command was the Director of Railways on the Eastern Front, Major-General Kersten. On the afternoon of August 22, even before the special train had started on its way, this officer came into Hoffmann's office wearing "a very startled expression" and showed him a telegram announcing the arrival next day at Marienburg of an extra train bringing a new Commander and new Chief of Staff. That was how Prittwitz and Waldersee learned of their dismissal. An hour later Prittwitz received a personal telegram placing him and Waldersee on the "unattached list." "He took leave of us," says Hoffmann, "without a single word of complaint of this treatment."

Ludendorff's methods were no more tactful. Although he knew Hoffmann well, having lived in the same house with him in Berlin for four years when both were serving on the General Staff, he nevertheless telegraphed his orders to each of the corps commanders individually instead of through the Eighth Army Staff. This was not necessarily a deliberate effort to be offensive; it was normal for General Staff officers to be offensive. Hoffman and Grünert promptly felt insulted. The reception they tendered the new commanders at Marienburg was, says Ludendorff, "anything but cheerful."

The critical question on which the fate of the campaign hung now had to be faced. Should Mackensen's and von Below's corps remain where they were for defense against a further advance by Rennenkampf or should they be moved south in accordance with Hoffmann's plan to oppose Samsonov's right wing? There was no hope of defeating Samsonov's army except by the whole of the Eighth Army. François' Corps on that day, August 23, was finishing the intricate process of entrainment at five different stations between Insterberg and Königsberg and was now en route to the southern front. It would take another two days of switchings and sidings and equally intricate detrainment before it would be in position to fight. Von Morgen's division was also on its way by a different line. Mackensen's and von Below's corps were halted for the day. Cavalry reconnaissance reported continued "passivity" on the part of Rennenkampf's army. He was only separated from Mackensen and von Below by some thirty to forty miles, and if they were moved south against the other Russian army he could still—if he moved—follow and fall upon their rear. Hoffmann wanted Mackensen and von Below to start on their way at once. Ludendorff, barely thirty-six hours out of Namur and newly arrived in a situation in which a decision either way might be fatal and for which he would be responsible, was uncertain. Hindenburg, barely twenty-four hours out of retirement, was relying on Ludendorff.

On the Russian side the task of timing the pincers to close simultaneously upon the enemy tormented the higher command. So many and various, intractable and obvious were the stumbling blocks that the military chiefs were ridden with pessimism from the start. General Jilinsky, commander of the Northwest Front, whose function was to coordinate the movements of Rennenkampf's and Samsonov's armies, could think of no better way to perform it than by continued instructions to hurry. As Rennenkampf had started first and gone into action first, Jilinsky addressed all his hurry-up orders to Samsonov. At the same time Jilinsky himself was on the receiving end of a chain of ever more urgent pleas from the French. To relieve the pressure upon them in the West the French instructed their ambassador to "insist" upon the "necessity of the Russian armies prosecuting their offensive *à outrance* toward Berlin." From Joffre to Paris, from Paris to St. Petersburg, from St. Petersburg to "Stavka" (Russian General Headquarters at Baranovichi), from Stavka to Jilinsky the demands passed, and Jilinsky passed them all on to General Samsonov, struggling forward foot by foot through sand.

Since commanding a cavalry division in the Russo-Japanese War, this "simple and kindly man," as the British liaison officer with the Second Army called him, had had no experience fitting him to command an army of thirteen divisions. He was working through a staff and divisional commanders unfamiliar to him. Because the Russian Army was not organized on a regional basis, the newly reported reservists, numbering in some cases up to two-thirds of a regiment, were complete strangers to their NCOs and officers. The shortage of officers and the low, often nonexistent, level of literacy among the men did not ease the process of communicating orders down the line. Almost the worst confusion was in the signal corps. At the telegraph office in Warsaw a staff officer discovered to his horror a pile of telegrams addressed to the Second Army lying unopened and unforwarded because no communication had been established with field headquarters. The officer gathered them up and delivered them by car. Corps headquarters had only enough wire to connect with the divisional commands but not enough to connect with Army Headquarters or with neighboring corps. Hence the resort to wireless.

Because of the insistence on haste four days had been cut out of the period of concentration, leaving the organization of the rear services incomplete. One corps had to dole out its shells to another whose supply train had not come up, thus upsetting its own calculations. Bakery wagons were missing. To enable an army to live off the country in hostile territory, requisitioning parties were required to be sent ahead under cavalry escort, but no arrangements for this had been made. Single-horse power proved inadequate to pull wagons and gun carriages over the sandy roads. In some places the horses had to be unharnessed from half the wagons, hitched up in double harness to the other half, moved forward a certain distance, unhitched, brought back, harnessed up to the stranded wagons, and the process begun all over again.

"Hurry up the advance of the Second Army and hasten your operations as energetically as possible," Jilinsky wired on August 19. "The delay in the advance of the Second Army is putting the First Army in a difficult position." This was not true. Samsonov on the 19th was crossing the frontier on schedule, but Jilinsky was so sure it was going to be true that he was anticipating.

"Advancing according to timetable, without halting, covering marches of more than 12 miles over sand. I cannot go more quickly," Samsonov replied. He reported that his men were on the move for ten or twelve hours a day without halts. "I must have immediate and decisive operations," Jilinsky telegraphed three days later. "Great weariness" of his men made greater speed impossible, Samsonov answered. "The country is devastated, the horses have long been without oats, there is no bread."

On that day Samsonov's XVth Corps commanded by General Martos came up against the German XXth Corps of General Scholtz. Combat was opened. The Germans, not yet reinforced, retreated. About ten miles inside the frontier General Martos captured Soldau and Neidenburg which until a few hours before had been General Scholtz's headquarters. When Cossack patrols entering Neidenburg reported German civilians firing on them from the windows, General Martos ordered a bombardment of the town which destroyed most of the main square. A "small, gray man," he personally felt uncomfortable that night when he found himself billetted in a house whose German owners had departed, leaving behind their family photographs staring at him from the mantelpiece. It was the mayor's house, and General Martos ate a dinner prepared for the mayor and served by his maid.

On August 23, the day Ludendorff and Hindenburg arrived in the East, the Russian VIth and XIIIth corps on the right of General Martos captured more villages; General Scholtz, still alone except for some support from the Vistula garrison behind him, backed up a little farther. Ignoring Rennenkampf's inactivity in the north, Jilinsky continued to rain orders on Samsonov. The Germans on his front were hastily retreating, he told Samsonov, "leaving only insignificant forces facing you. You are therefore to execute a most energetic offensive. . . . You are to attack and intercept the enemy retiring before General Rennenkampf's army in order to cut off his retreat from the Vistula."

This was, of course, the original design, but it was predicated on Rennenkampf's holding the Germans occupied in the north. In fact, on that date Rennenkampf was no longer in contact with the enemy. He began to advance again on August 23 but in the wrong direction. Instead of moving crabwise to the south to link up with Samsonov in front of the lakes, he moved straight west to mask Königsberg, fearful that François would attack his flank if he turned south. Although it was a movement with no relevance at all to the original design, Jilinsky did nothing to alter it. Operating like Rennenkampf in a complete fog as to the German movements, he assumed they were doing what the Russians had planned on their doing—retreating to the Vistula. Accordingly, he continued to push Samsonov forward.

On the evening of August 23, General Martos' Corps, encouraged by the feel of the enemy falling back, moved on from Neidenburg and reached positions within 700 yards of the German lines. Scholtz's Corps was entrenched between the villages of Orlau and Frankenau. The Russians were under orders to take the trenches at all costs. They lay all night in position and crept forward another hundred yards before dawn. When the signal for attack came they took the last 600 yards in three rushes, throwing themselves to the ground under the fire of the German machine guns, surging forward again—and down and up again. As the wave of white-bloused figures with their glistening bayonets closed in, the Germans scrambled from the trenches, abandoned their machine guns, and fled. Elsewhere along the line German superiority in artillery punished the attackers. The Russian XIIIth Corps on Martos' right, owing to a blunder in communications or poor generalship, or both, failed to come to his support, and no great advantage was gained from the engagement. By the end of the day the Germans were in retreat but not routed. The Russians captured two field guns and some prisoners, but their own losses were high, a total of 4,000. One regiment lost 9 out of 16 company commanders. One company lost 120 out of 190 men and all its officers.

Though German losses were less, Scholtz, facing overwhelming numbers, withdrew for some ten miles, establishing his headquarters for the night in the village of Tannenberg. Still harried by Jilinsky who insisted that he must move on to the agreed line where he could cut off the enemy's "retreat," Samsonov issued orders to all his corps—the XXIIIrd on the left, the XVth and XIIIth in the center, the VIth on the right—giving their dispositions and lines of march for the following day. Beyond Neidenberg communications had become ever more feeble. One corps had run out of wire altogether and was relying on mounted orderlies. The VIth Corps did not possess the key to the cipher used by the XIIIth. Consequently, Samsonov's orders were issued by wireless in clear.

Up to this moment, some twenty-four hours since the arrival of Ludendorff and Hindenburg, the Eighth Army had not yet decided whether to bring down Mackensen's and von Below's corps to oppose Samsonov's right wing. Hindenburg and his staff came down to Tannenberg to consult Scholtz who was "grave but confident." They returned to Headquarters. That evening, Hoffmann wrote later, "was the most difficult of the whole battle." While the staff was debating, a signal corps officer brought in an intercept of Samsonov's orders for the next day, August 25. Although this assistance from the enemy did not reveal Rennenkampf's intentions which were the crucial question, it did show the Germans where they might expect to meet Samsonov's forces. That helped. The Eighth Army made up its mind to throw all its strength into battle against Samsonov. Orders went out to Mackensen and von Below to turn their backs on Rennen-kampf and march south at once.

▶▶▶ *16* ▶

▶▶▶ *Tannenberg*

Haunted by the knowledge of Rennenkampf
at his rear, Ludendorff was in a hurry to come to grips with Samsonov. He
gave orders for the first stage of the battle to begin on August 25. It was to
be an attack on Usdau by General von François Ist Corps with intent to
envelop Samsonov's left wing. François refused. His heavy artillery and
some of his infantry were still detraining from the journey that had
brought them the long way around from the Gumbinnen front and had
not yet come up. To attack without full artillery support and a full supply
of ammunition, he argued, would be to risk failure; if Samsonov's path of
retreat were left open he would escape the destruction planned for him.
He was privately upheld by Hoffmann and by General Scholtz of the
XXth Corps who, although he had been in battle against the Russians on
the previous day, assured François over the field telephone that he could
hold his ground without immediate support.

Confronted by insubordination on the second day of his new command, Ludendorff in a high temper drove down by car to François' headquarters, bringing Hindenburg and Hoffmann with him. In reply to his
insistence François said, "If the order is given, of course I shall attack but
my troops will be obliged to fight with the bayonet." To show who was in

command Ludendorff brushed aside François' reasons and reissued his orders unchanged. Hindenburg said nothing during the interview and when it was over dutifully drove off with Ludendorff. Hoffmann in another car stopped at the railroad station at Montovo, the nearest place in telephone and telegraph communication with Headquarters. Here a signal corps officer handed him two intercepted Russian wireless messages, both sent in clear, one by Rennenkampf at 5:30 that morning and one by Samsonov at 6:00 A.M. Rennenkampf's orders, giving marching distances for the First Army, revealed that his objective line for the next day would not bring him far enough to threaten the German Army from the rear. Samsonov's orders, following the previous day's battle against General Scholtz, revealed that he had misinterpreted Scholtz's backward wheel as full retreat and gave exact directions and times of movement for the pursuit of what he believed was a defeated foe.

No such boon had been granted a commander since a Greek traitor guided the Persians around the pass at Thermopylae. The very completeness of the messages made Major General Grünert, Hoffmann's immediate superior, suspicious. As Hoffmann tells it, "He kept asking me anxiously over and over if we should believe them? Why shouldn't we? . . . I myself believed every word of them on principle." Hoffmann claimed to have personal knowledge of a private quarrel between Rennenkampf and Samsonov dating from the Russo-Japanese War, in which he had been Germany's observer. He said that Samsonov's Siberian Cossacks, after a brave fight, had been obliged to yield the Yentai coal mines because Rennenkampf's cavalry division had remained inactive despite repeated orders and that Samsonov had then knocked Rennenkampf down in a heated quarrel on the platform of the Mukden railway station. Obviously, he demonstrated triumphantly, Rennenkampf would be in no hurry to come to Samsonov's aid. As it was less a question of aiding Samsonov than of winning—or losing—the campaign, it is arguable whether Hoffmann believed his own tale or only pretended to; he always remained fond of telling the story.

Grasping the intercepted messages, he and Grünert hurried to their car, sped after Hindenburg and Ludendorff, and on overtaking them within a few miles, Hoffmann ordered the chauffeur to draw level and handed over the messages while the cars were in motion. All came to a stop while the four officers studied the situation. It showed that the attack planned for next day in which Mackensen's and Below's corps were to attack Samsonov's right wing could proceed without interference from

Rennenkampf. According to differing interpretations by the disputants, it either did or did not show that François could afford to postpone his attack until all his men and material were up. Unwilling to yield an inch of authority, Ludendorff, on returning to Headquarters, reiterated his orders.

At the same time orders were given to carry out the general plan for double envelopment next day, August 26. On the German left Macken-sen's corps, supported by Below's, was to attack Samsonov's extreme right wing which had reached a position—at Bischofsburg with cavalry at Sens-burg—in front of the lakes where it could have joined fronts with Rennen-kampf if he had been there. His absence left open the flank which the Germans hoped to envelop. In the center Scholtz's XXth Corps, now supported by a Landwehr division and General von Morgen's 3rd Reserve Division, was to renew its battle of the day before. On the German right François as ordered was to open the attack that would envelop Samsonov's left wing.

All orders went out before midnight of August 25. Next morning, the opening day of general battle, Ludendorff was attacked by a fit of nerves when a reconnaissance aviator reported movements by Rennenkampf in his direction. Although Hindenburg felt assured that the Eighth Army "need not have the least hesitation" in leaving only a screen against Rennenkampf, all Ludendorff's anxiety returned. Rennenkampf's "formid-able host hung like a threatening thunder cloud to the northeast," he wrote. "He need only have closed with us and we should have been beaten." He began to feel the same fears that had assailed Prittwitz and to hesitate whether to commit all his forces against Samsonov or to abandon the offensive against the Russian Second Army and turn back against the First. The hero of Liège "seems to have lost his nerve a little," happily recorded Hoffmann, who of all military writers is the most prodigal in attributing this weakness to his colleagues. Even Hindenburg acknowledges that "grave doubts" afflicted his companion and at this moment, as he claims, it was he who stiffened his Chief of Staff. In his words, "We overcame the inward crisis."

A different crisis erupted when Headquarters discovered that François, who was still waiting for his artillery, had not begun battle as ordered. Ludendorff imperatively demanded that the attack begin at noon. Fran-çois replied that the preliminary ground which Headquarters supposed had been taken that morning had not been gained, provoking an explosion and what Hoffmann describes as a "probably unfriendly" reply from

Ludendorff. Throughout the day François managed to balk and procrastinate and wait for his own moment.

Suddenly an extraordinary telephone call all the way from OHL in Coblenz broke in upon the argument wtih François. Worried enough, without trouble from Supreme Headquarters, Ludendorff picked up the receiver and ordered Hoffmann to listen in on another receiver to "what they want." To his astonishment he heard Colonel Tappen, Chief of Operations at OHL, propose to send him reinforcements of three corps and a cavalry division. Fresh from the Western Front, Ludendorff, who had worked on the mobilization plans and knew to the last decimal the required density of manpower per mile of offensive, could hardly believe what he heard. Schlieffen's plan depended on using every last man to strengthen the right wing. What could have persuaded OHL to weaken its line by three whole corps at the height of the offensive? Appalled, he told Tappen that the reinforcements were not "positively" needed in the East and would in any event arrive too late for the battle that was already beginning. Tappen said they could be spared.

The origin of this crucial decision was the panic at OHL when the Russians launched their offensive two weeks after mobilization instead of the six weeks on which the German plan was predicated. The saving factor, as Tappen reports it, was the "great victory" on the French frontiers which "aroused in OHL the belief that the decisive battle in the West had been fought and won." Under this impression Moltke decided, on August 25, "in spite of objections put to him," to send reinforcements to save East Prussia from the Russians. The woes of the refugees, the Junker estates left to marauding Cossacks, the tearful pleas of well-born ladies to the Kaiserin to save family lands and fortunes were having their effect. In order to arouse feeling against the Russians, the German government had deliberately distributed the refugees in various cities and succeeded in frightening itself. The President of the East Prussian Bundesrat came to OHL to beg for aid to his homeland. A director of Krupp's wrote in his diary on August 25: "People said on all sides, 'Bah! the Russians will never come to the end of their mobilization. . . . We can remain on the defensive for a long time.' But today everyone thinks quite differently and the talk is all of abandoning East Prussia." The Kaiser was deeply affected. Moltke himself had always worried about the light defense in the East, for, as he wrote before the war, "all the success on the Western Front will be unavailing if the Russians arrive in Berlin."

Two of the corps he now withdrew from the Western Front had been in the fighting for Namur at the junction between the German Second and Third Armies and now, upon the fall of the Belgian fortress, were declared disposable by General von Bülow. With the 8th Cavalry Division they were detached on August 26 and marched—because of the destruction of Belgian railroads—to stations in Germany for transport "as quickly as possible" to the Eastern Front. Another corps had got as far as the railroad station in Thionville when cautionary voices at OHL persuaded Moltke to cancel its orders.

Eight hundred miles to the east General Samsonov was preparing for renewed battle on August 26. On his extreme right his VIth Corps under General Blagovestchensky had duly reached the planned rendezvous area in front of the lakes, but Samsonov had left this corps isolated and detached while he pushed the main body of his army in a more westerly direction. Although this drew it away from Rennenkampf, or from the place where Rennenkampf was supposed to be, it was the right direction, Samsonov thought, to bring him between the Vistula and the Germans supposedly retreating to the west. Samsonov's objective was the line Allenstein-Osterode where he could get astride the main German railway and from where, as he informed Jilinsky on August 23, "it would be easier to advance into the heart of Germany."

It was already apparent that his exhausted and semistarved troops who had barely managed to stumble to the frontier were hardly fit for battle much less for the heart of Germany. Rations were not coming up, the soldiers had eaten up their reserve rations, villages were deserted, hay and oats in the fields were not yet cut, and little could be scraped off the land for men or horses. All the corps commanders were calling for a halt. A General Staff officer reported to Jilinsky's Headquarters the "miserable" provisioning of the troops. "I don't know how the men bear it any longer. It is essential to organize a proper requisitioning service." At Volkovisk, 180 miles east of the battlefront as the crow flies and even farther by roundabout railway connections, Jilinsky was too remote to be disturbed by these reports. He insisted upon Samsonov continuing the offensive "to meet the enemy retreating in front of General Rennenkampf and cut off his retreat to the Vistula."

This version of what the enemy was doing was based on Rennenkampf's reports, and as Rennenkampf had kept no contact with the Germans after the Battle of Gumbinnen his reports of their movements were an amiable fantasy. By now, however, Samsonov realized from evidence of railroad movements and other bits of intelligence that he was facing not an army in full retreat but an army which had reorganized and was advancing toward him. Reports of the concentration of a new enemy force—this was François' Corps—opposite his left flank were coming in. Recognizing the danger to his left, he sent an officer to urge upon Jilinsky the necessity of shifting his army westward instead of continuing north. With a rear commander's contempt for a front commander's caution, Jilinsky took this to be a desire to go on the defensive, and "rudely" replied to the officer: "To see the enemy where he does not exist is cowardice. I will not allow General Samsonov to play the coward. I insist that he continue the offensive." His strategy, according to a colleague, seemed designed for *Poddavki*, a Russian form of checkers in which the object is to lose all one's men.

On the night of August 25 at the same time as Ludendorff was issuing his orders, Samsonov disposed his forces. In the center the XVth and XIIth Corps under General Martos and General Kliouev with one division of the XXIIIrd Corps under General Kondratovitch were to carry the main advance to the line Allenstein-Osterode. The army's left flank was to be held by General Artomonov's Ist Corps supported by the other division of the XXIIIrd Corps. Fifty miles away the isolated VIth Corps held the right flank. The reconnaissance techniques of Russian cavalry being less than competent, Samsonov did not know that Mackensen's Corps, last seen streaming in panic from the field of Gumbinnen, had reorganized and in forced marches, together with Below's Corps, had reached his front and was now advancing upon his right. At first he ordered the VIth Corps to hold its position "with the object of protecting the right flank of the army," and then changed his mind and told them to come down "with all speed" to support the advance of the center upon Allenstein. At the last minute on the morning of the 26th the order was changed to the original duty of remaining in position to protect the right flank. By that time the VIth Corps was already on the march toward the center.

Far to the rear a sense of disaster pervaded the Russian High Command. As early as August 24 Sukhomlinov, the War Minister who had not bothered to build arms factories because he did not believe in firepower, wrote General Yanushkevitch, the beardless Chief of Staff: "In God's name, issue orders for gathering up the rifles. We have sent 150,000 to the Serbs, our reserves are nearly used up and factory production is feeble." Despite the fervor of such gallant officers as the general who cantered to war shouting "William to St. Helena!" the mood of the army chiefs from the beginning was one of gloom. They entered the war without confidence and remained in it without faith. Gossip of the pessimism at Headquarters reached the inevitable ear of the French ambassador in St. Petersburg. On August 26 he was told by Sazonov that Jilinsky "considers that an offensive in East Prussia is doomed to defeat." Yanushkevitch was said to agree and to be protesting strongly against the offensive. General Danilov, Deputy Chief of the Staff, was insisting, however, that Russia could not disappoint France and would have to attack despite "indubitable risks."

Danilov was stationed with the Grand Duke at Stavka, the General Staff Headquarters at Baranovichi. A quiet place in the woods where Stavka was to remain for a year, Baranovichi was chosen because it was the junction of a north-south railway line with the main line between Moscow and Warsaw. Both fronts, the German and Austrian, were superintended from here. The Grand Duke with his personal suite, the chief officers of the General Staff, and the Allied military attachés lived and ate in the railroad cars because it was discovered that the house intended for the Commander in Chief was too far from the stationmaster's house used by the Operations and Intelligence staffs. Roofs were built over the cars to protect them from sun and rain, wooden sidewalks were laid out, and a marquee was erected in the station garden where meals were taken in summer. Pomp was absent and physical shortcomings ignored except for the low doorways against which the Grand Duke had an unfortunate tendency to bump his head. Fringes of white paper had to be fixed over all entrances to catch the Grand Duke's eye and remind him to duck.

Danilov was disquieted by Rennenkampf's obvious loss of contact with the enemy and by failing communications as a result of which Jilinsky appeared not to know where the armies were nor the armies each other. When news reached Stavka that Samsonov had engaged the enemy on August 24-25 and was about to renew the battle, anxiety about Rennenkampf's failure to bring up the other arm of the pincers became acute. On August 26 the Grand Duke visited Jilinsky's headquarters at Volkovisk to insist upon Rennenkampf being urged forward. In his leisurely pursuit begun on August 23, Rennenkampf had passed through the former German positions on the Angerapp which the Eighth Army had abandoned in its great transfer to the south. Evidences of hurried departure confirmed his picture of a beaten enemy. According to the notes of one of his Staff officers, he believed it would be a mistake to push the Germans too rapidly. They might then fall back to the Vistula before they could be cut off by Samsonov. Rennenkampf made no effort to follow closely enough to cor firm conjecture by eyesight nor did this omission appear to worry Jilinsky, who accepted Rennenkampf's version without question.

The orders Jilinsky issued to Rennenkampf on the day after the Grand Duke's visit were to pursue an enemy he still assumed to be retreating and to guard against a possible German sortie from the fortress of Königsberg upon his flank. It had been intended to mask Königsberg with six reserve divisions, but these had not yet come up. Now Jilinsky instructed Rennenkampf to blockade Königsberg with two corps until the reserve divisions arrived and with his other two corps to pursue "those enemy troops which do not take refuge in Königsberg and may be supposed to be retreating to the Vistula." "Supposing" the enemy to be retreating, he did not conceive of him threatening Samsonov and did not urge Rennenkampf to hurry to close the junction with Samsonov's right wing as originally planned. He merely told him that the "combined operations" of the First and Second Armies must aim at pressing the retreating Germans toward the sea and away from the Vistula. As the two Russian Armies were neither in contact nor moving toward each other, the word "combined" was hardly applicable.

When morning broke on August 26 Samsonov's VIth Corps began its march toward the center in obedience to orders it did not know had been canceled. One division was under way when the other division received news that enemy forces had been sighted some six miles behind it to the north. Assuming these were troops retreating from Rennenkampf, the Russian divisional commander decided to turn around and attack them. The force was in fact Mackensen's Corps, itself moving forward to attack. It fell upon the Russians, and while they were fighting to save themselves, their fellow division, which had already marched eight miles, was desperately summoned. It marched back again and after covering nineteen miles came up at the end of the day against a second enemy corps, Below's. Contact between the two Russian divisions was lost. The corps commander, General Blagovestchensky "lost his head" (in this case the formula is applied by a British military critic); the divisional commander, whose group had been in battle all day, suffering 5,000 casualties and the loss of sixteen field guns, ordered retreat on his own initiative. During the night orders and counterorders added to the confusion, units became mixed up on the roads, and by morning the VIth Corps was in a disorganized shambles and continuing to fall back. Samsonov's right wing had been turned.

While this was happening, his center of two and a half corps took the

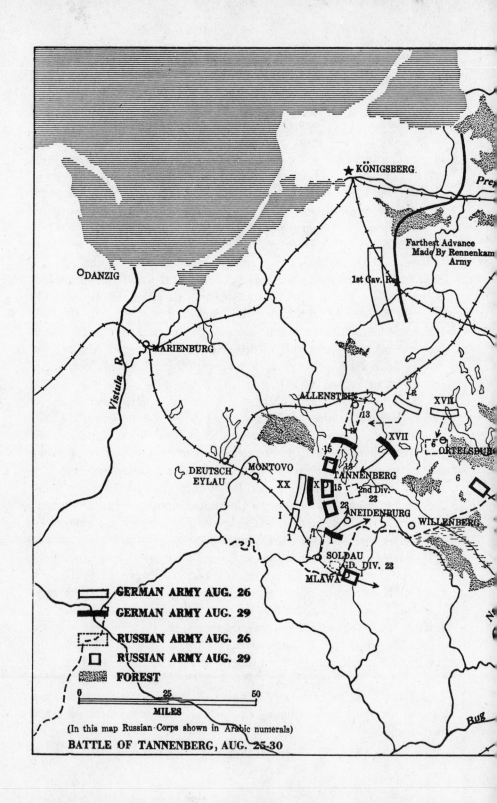

KÖNIGSBERG

Prer

DANZIG

Farthest Advance
Made By Rennenkam
Army

1st Cav. Re

MARIENBURG

Vistula R.

ALLENSTEIN

XVII

R

13

XVII

6

ORTELSBUR

15

DEUTSCH
EYLAU

MONTOVO

15

TANNENBERG

6

XX

X

15

2nd Div.
23

I

23

SNEIDENBURG

WILLENBERG

1

I

SOLDAU

GD. DIV. 23

MLAWA

Bug

GERMAN ARMY AUG. 26
GERMAN ARMY AUG. 29
RUSSIAN ARMY AUG. 26
RUSSIAN ARMY AUG. 29
FOREST

0   25   50

MILES

(In this map Russian Corps shown in Arabic numerals)

BATTLE OF TANNENBERG, AUG. 25-30

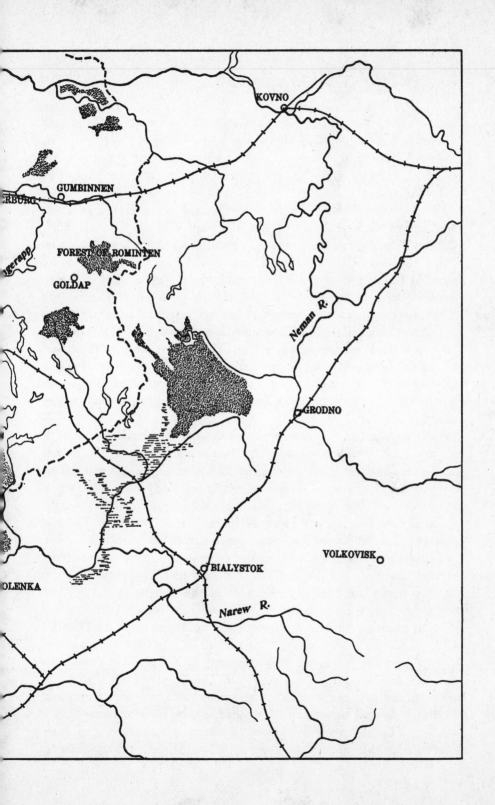

offensive. General Martos was in the middle, heavily engaged. His neighbor
on the left, a division of the XXIIIrd Corps, was repulsed and thrown
back, exposing his flank. On his right General Kliouev's XIIIth Corps took
Allenstein but learning that Martos was in trouble moved to his support,
leaving Allenstein to be occupied by the VIth Corps which Kliouev supposed to be on its way. The VIth of course never came, and a gap was
left at Allenstein.

A few miles behind the front, at Second Army Headquarters in
Neidenburg, General Samsonov was at dinner with his Chief of Staff,
General Potovsky, and the British military attaché, Major Knox, when the
beaten division of the XXIIIrd Corps poured into the streets. In the
mood of fear any sound made them think themselves pursued; an ambulance wagon clattering up raised cries of "Uhlans coming!" Hearing the
commotion Samsonov and Potovsky, a nervous individual who wore pince-
nez and was known, for some now obscure reason, as the "Mad Mullah,"
buckled on their swords and hurried out. They saw at firsthand the condition of the troops. The men were "terribly exhausted . . . they had been
three days without bread or sugar." "For two days my men received no
rations and none of the supplies came up," one regimental commander
told them.

Although he had not yet received full news of the disaster to the VIth
Corps on the right, Samsonov realized by the end of the day that it was
no longer a question of enveloping the enemy but of saving himself from
envelopment. He nevertheless decided not to break off battle but to renew
it next day with his center corps in an effort to hold the Germans until
Rennenkampf should come up to deal them the decisive blow. He sent
orders to General Artomonov, commander of the Ist Corps holding the
front opposite François on the Russians' extreme left, "to protect the flank
of the Army . . . at all costs." He felt sure that "not even a greatly
superior enemy can break the resistance of the famous Ist Corps," and
added that success of the battle depended on their holding firm.

Next morning, the 27th, the impatiently awaited moment for François'
offensive had come. His artillery had arrived. At 4:00 A.M., before it was
light, a hurricane bombardment of tremendous impact broke upon positions of the Russian Ist Corps at Usdau. The German High Command,
with Hindenburg ponderously calm, Ludendorff grim and tense, and
Hoffmann behind them, a mocking shadow, left their temporary headquarters at Löbau, twenty miles away, to take up a position on a hill from
which Ludendorff intended to "superintend on the spot" the coordination

of François' and Scholtz's corps. Before they could even reach the hill news was brought that Usdau was taken. In the midst of rejoicing the report was almost immediately followed by another denying the first. The roar of the artillery barrage continued. In the Russian trenches the men of the "famous Ist Corps," unfed like their fellows of the XXIIIrd and drained of the will to fight, fled from under the torrent of shells, leaving behind them as many dead as those who got away. By 11:00 A.M. the Russian Ist Corps had abandoned the field, the battle had been won by artillery alone, and Ludendorff, whose premature orders might have lost it, felt that the Russian Second Army was now "broken through."

But it was not beaten, and he found that "in contrast to other wars" the battle had not been won in a day. François' advance was still being held east of Usdau; the two Russian corps in the center, a formidable body of men, were still attacking; the threat of Rennenkampf still hung over his rear. Roads were clogged with refugees and livestock; whole villages were fleeing. German soldiers, too, were exhausted and they too conjured pursuit out of the clatter of hoofs and cried, "They're coming!" which, as it passed down a column, became "The Cossacks are coming!" On returning to Löbau the High Command heard with horrified disbelief a report that François' Corps was fleeing and that "relics" of its units were coming into Montovo. A frantic telephone call ascertained that retreating troops of the Ist Corps could indeed be seen in dispirited groups in front of the railroad station. If François' flank had somehow been turned the battle might be lost, and for one awful moment the prospect of a lost campaign, retreat behind the Vistula, abandonment of East Prussia, rose up as it had before Prittwitz. Then it was discovered that the troops in Montovo belonged to one battalion only that in the fighting beyond Usdau had given way.

Late that day the truth that the Germans were not after all "retreating to the Vistula" but advancing against Samsonov finally penetrated Jilinsky's Headquarters. At last he telegraphed to Rennenkampf that the Second Army was under heavy attack and he should cooperate "by moving your left flank as far forward as possible," but the objectives given were too westerly and not far enough advanced and no mention was made of haste or forced marches.

The battle was in its third day. Two armies, now totally committed, surged and gripped and broke apart and clashed again in confused and separate combats over a front of forty miles. A regiment advanced, its neighbor was thrown back, gaps appeared, the enemy thrust through or, unaccountably, did not. Artillery roared, cavalry squadrons, infantry units, heavy horse-drawn field-gun batteries moved and floundered through villages and forests, between lakes, across fields and roads. Shells smashed into farmhouses and village streets. A battalion advancing under cover of shellfire disappeared behind a curtain of smoke and mist to some unknown fate. Columns of prisoners herded to the rear blocked the advancing troops. Brigades took ground or yielded it, crossed each other's lines of communication, became tangled up with the wrong division. Field commanders lost track of their units, staff cars sped about, German scout planes flew overhead trying to gather information, army commanders struggled to find out what was happening, and issued orders which might not be received or carried out or conform to realities by the time they reached the front. Three hundred thousand men flailed at each other, marched and tiredly countermarched, fired their guns, got drunk if they were lucky enough to occupy a village or sat on the ground in the forest with a few companions while night came; and the next day the struggle went on and the great battle of the Eastern Front was fought out.

General von François opened battle at dawn on the 28th with another great artillery barrage. Ludendorff ordered him to veer left to relieve the pressure upon Scholtz's Corps, which he believed to be "greatly exhausted." Ignoring him, François held to a straight eastward advance, determined to complete envelopment of Samsonov's flank and cut off his retreat. After his successful disobedience of the day before, Ludendorff now almost pleaded with François to obey orders. The Ist Corps would "render the greatest possible service to the army by carrying out these instructions," he said. Paying no attention, François drove eastward, posting detachments along the roads as he moved to keep the enemy from breaking out.

In anxiety for the center, Ludendorff and Hindenburg waited out the battle at Scholtz's field headquarters in the village of Frögenau, about two miles from an even smaller village, Tannenberg. Orders were date-lined from Frögenau. Ludendorff was again tortured by apprehension about Rennenkampf. Worried about Scholtz's Corps, angered at François, harassed by the "very ineffective field telephone" connecting him with that insubordinate commander and by the absence of any telephone communication at all with Mackensen and Below on his left wing, he was "far from satisfied." Mackensen and Below, confused by conflicting orders to take first this direction and then that, sent a Staff officer by airplane to Headquarters to straighten matters out. He received a "far from friendly reception" because neither corps was in the location it was supposed to be Toward afternoon, however, both were moving satisfactorily, Mackensen pushing after the broken Russian right wing and Below heading for the gap at Allenstein to attack the Russian center. Now François' progress appeared more justified, and Ludendorff issued revised orders to him to pursue the direction he was already taking.

Just as the conviction of coming victory began to settle warmly over German Headquarters, news came in that Rennenkampf's army was unmistakably on the march. But the day's progress by now gave assurance that he would be too late. In fact, at that night's bivouac, Rennenkampf's nearest corps was still twenty miles from Bischofsburg where Samsonov's VIth Corps had been defeated two days before. Making slow progress in hostile territory, Rennenkampf's furthest advance by the end of the next day, August 29, was some ten miles farther west but no farther south and he had made no contact with Samsonov. None was ever to be made.

The collapse of the "famous Ist Corps" in whose resistance he had put such faith, on top of the collapse of the VIth Corps on his other wing, presaged the end to General Samsonov. Both his flanks were turned; his cavalry, the only arm in which he outnumbered the Germans, having been deployed too wide of the flanks, had played no useful part in the battle and was now isolated; supplies and communications were in complete chaos; only the steadfast XVth and XIIIth Corps were still fighting. At his headquarters in Neidenburg he could hear the sound of François' approaching guns. There seemed to him to be only one thing to do. He telegraphed Jilinsky that he was leaving for the battlefront and then, ordering baggage and wireless apparatus to be sent back to Russia, cut his communications with the rear. The reasons for his decision, it has been said, "he took with him to his grave," but they are not hard to understand. The army that had been given him to command was crumbling under him. He became again a cavalry officer and divisional general and did the thing he knew best. With seven of his Staff on horses commandeered from some Cossacks, he rode off to take personal command under fire, in the saddle where he felt at home.

Outside Neidenburg on August 28 he took farewell of Major Knox. Samsonov was sitting on the ground surrounded by his staff, studying some maps. He stood up, took Knox aside, and told him the situation was "critical." He said his own place and duty were with the army, but as Knox's duty was to report to his government he advised him to return "while there was time." He mounted, turned in the saddle and said with a wistful smile, "The enemy has luck one day, we will have luck another," as he rode away.

Later, General Martos, who was conducting the battle in his sector from a hilltop, had just ordered a column of German prisoners to be led out of the fighting line when to his astonishment the General of the Army came up on horseback with his Staff. Samsonov asked about the retiring column, and on being told they were prisoners he reined his horse close to Martos, leaned over to embrace him and said sadly, "You alone will save us." But he knew better, and that night gave the order for a general retreat of what was left of the Second Army.

The retreat during the next two days, August 29 and 30, was a mounting and inexorable disaster. The two center corps which had fought longest and best, and had advanced the farthest and retreated last, had the least chance to escape and were the most completely netted in the German envelopment. General Kliouev's Corps was still on the offensive when Below broke through the gap on his right at Allenstein and completed the cordon around the Russian center. His corps and that of General Martos thrashed about helplessly in the forests and marshes in futile marches and wrong turnings and vain attempts to regroup and make a stand as the cordon was drawn tighter. In the swampy area where the roads were causeways the Germans posted guards with machine guns at every crossing. The men of Martos' Corps in their last four days were literally starving. Kliouev's Corps covered forty-two miles in their last forty hours without rations of any kind; horses were unfed and unwatered.

On August 29 General Martos and a few of his Staff were attempting to find a way through the forest with an escort of five Cossacks. The enemy was firing all around. Major General Machagovsky, Martos' Chief of Staff, was killed by machine-gun fire. Others in the group were picked off one by one until only one Staff officer and two of his escort remained with the general. Having left his haversack with an aide who was now missing, Martos had had nothing to eat, drink, or smoke since morning. One exhausted horse lay down and died; the men dismounted and led the others. Darkness fell. They tried to guide themselves by the stars but the skies clouded over. Troops were heard approaching and were thought to be friends because the horses pulled toward them. Suddenly a German searchlight blazed through the woods and swung back and forth, searching for them. Martos tried to mount and gallop off but his horse was hit. He fell and was seized by German soldiers.

Later, in a "dirty little hotel" in Osterode where Martos was taken as a prisoner, Ludendorff came into the room and, speaking perfect Russian, taunted him with defeat and boasted that the Russian frontier was now open to German invasion. Hindenburg followed and "seeing me disturbed he held my hands for a long time begging me to calm myself." In awkward Russian with a heavy accent he promised to return Martos' sword, and took his leave with a bow saying, "I wish you happier days."

In the woods north of Neidenburg the debris of Martos' Corps were slaughtered or surrendered. Only one officer of the XVth Corps escaped to return to Russia. About ten miles east of Neidenburg the last of the XIIIth Corps, whose commander, General Kliouev, had also been captured, entrenched themselves in a circle. With four guns captured from a German battery in the woods they held off the enemy all through the night of August 30 until they had no more ammunition left and most of them were dead. The remainder were taken prisoner.

A last Russian attack was made that day, mounted with great vigor by General Sirelius, successor to General Artomonov of the Ist Corps who had been dismissed. Collecting various scattered and still fresh regiments and artillery units which had not been in battle and aggregated about a division, he launched an offensive that broke through François' lines and succeeded in retaking Neidenburg. It came too late and could not be sustained. This last act of the Russian Second Army had not been ordered by General Samsonov, for he was dead.

On the night of August 29 he too, like General Martos, was caught in the net, in a different part of the forest. Riding through the woods that fringed the railroad, he and his companions reached Willenburg, only seven miles from the Russian frontier, but the Germans had arrived there before them. The General and his group waited in the forest until nightfall and then, as it was impossible to proceed over the swampy ground in the dark on horseback, continued on foot. Matches gave out and they could no longer read their compass. Moving hand in hand to avoid losing each other in the dark, they stumbled on. Samsonov, who suffered from asthma, was visibly weakening. He kept repeating to Potovsky, his Chief of Staff: "The Czar trusted me. How can I face him after such a disaster?" After covering six miles, they stopped for a rest. It was then 1:00 A.M. Samsonov moved apart into the thicker darkness under the pines. A shot cracked the stillness of the night. Potovsky knew instantly what it meant. Earlier Samsonov had confided his intention of committing suicide but

Potovsky thought he had argued him out of it. He was now sure the
General was dead. The Staff officers tried to find the body in the darkness
but failed. They decided to wait until dawn, but as the sky began to
lighten, German troops were heard approaching. Forsaking their task, the
Russians were forced to move on toward the frontier, where they fell in
with a Cossack patrol and eventually made their way to safety. Samsonov's
body was found by the Germans, who buried it at Willenburg where in
1916, with the help of the Red Cross, his widow was able to retrieve it
and bring it back for burial in Russia.

Silence had enveloped the Second Army. At Jilinsky's Headquarters
wireless contact was dead; nothing had been heard from Samsonov for
two days. Now that it was too late, Jilinsky ordered Rennenkampf's
cavalry to break through the German lines at Allenstein and find out what
had happened to the Second Army. The mission was never to be accomplished, for already the German Eighth Army, having destroyed one arm
of the pincers that was to have crushed them, was turning to deal with the
other.

Almost with awe they realized the extent of their victory. The haul of
enemy dead and prisoners and captured guns was enormous: 92,000 prisoners were taken, and according to some claims the count was higher.
Sixty trains were required to bring them to the rear during the week after
the battle. Captured guns were counted variously between 300 and 500
out of the Second Army's total of some 600. Captured horses were driven
in herds to corrals hurriedly built to hold them. Although no agreed
casualty figure for the dead and missing exists, it was estimated at over
30,000. The XVth and XIIIth Corps by capture or death were wiped out
of existence; 50 officers and 2,100 men of these two corps were all that
escaped. Survivors of the two flank corps, the VIth and Ist, which
retreated earliest, amounted to about a division each, and of the XXIIIrd
Corps, to about a brigade.

The victors, too, suffered heavily; after the fatigue and suspense of a
six-day battle their nerves were raw. When Neidenberg, which changed
hands four times, was retaken by the Germans on August 31, a nervous
military policeman shouted "Halt!" at a car driving at high speed across
the main square. When the car, which contained General von Morgen,
ignored his order, he yelled "Stop! Russians!" and fired. Instantly a volley
of fire covered the car, killing the chauffeur and wounding an officer sitting
beside the General. The same night, after barely escaping being shot by his
own men, von Morgen was awakened by his valet who, crying "The Rus-

sians have come back!" ran off clutching the General's clothes. To his "extreme vexation" von Morgen was forced to emerge in the street strapping his revolver over his underclothes.

For all but a few officers it had been their first experience under fire, and out of the excited fancy produced by the fears and exhaustion and panic and violence of a great battle a legend grew—a legend of thousands of Russians drowning in the swamps or sinking up to their necks in bogs and quicksands, men whom the Germans were forced to slaughter with machine guns. "I will hear their cries to my dying day," one officer told an awestruck audience of friends in Germany. "The widely circulated report of Russians driven into the marshes and perishing there is a myth," Ludendorff wrote; "no marsh was to be found anywhere near."

As the extent of the enemy's defeat became clear, the German commanders began to consider that they had won, as Hoffmann wrote in his diary, "one of the great victories in history." It was decided—according to Hoffmann at his suggestion, according to Ludendorff at "my suggestion" —to name the battle Tannenberg in delayed compensation for the ancient defeat suffered there by the Teutonic Knights at the hands of the Poles and Lithuanians. In spite of this second triumph even greater than Liège, Ludendorff could not rejoice "because the strain imposed on my nerves by the uncertainty about Rennenkampf's Army had been too great." He was now able, however, to turn with greater confidence against Rennenkampf with the addition of the two new corps that Moltke was sending from the West.

His triumph owed much to others: to Hoffmann who, though right for the wrong reasons, had been firm in the conviction that Rennenkampf would not pursue and had conceived the plan and drawn up the orders for bringing the Eighth Army down to face Samsonov; to François who by defying Ludendorff's orders ensured the envelopment of Samsonov's left wing; to Hindenburg who steadied Ludendorff's nerves at a critical moment; finally and above all to a factor that never figured in the careful German planning—the Russian wireless. Ludendorff came to depend on the intercepts which his staff regularly collected during the day, decoded or translated and sent to him every night at 11:00 P.M. If by chance they were late, he would worry and appear personally in the signal corps room to inquire what was the matter. Hoffmann acknowledged the intercepts as the real victor of Tannenberg. "We had an ally," he said, "the enemy. We knew all the enemy's plans."

To the public the savior of East Prussia was the nominal commander,

Hindenburg. The elderly general dragged from retirement in his old blue
uniform was transformed into a titan by the victory. The triumph in East
Prussia, lauded and heralded even beyond its true proportions, fastened
the Hindenburg myth upon Germany. Not even Hoffmann's sly malice
could penetrate it. When, as Chief of Staff on the Eastern Front later in
the war, he would take visitors over the field of Tannenberg, Hoffmann
would tell them, "This is where the Field Marshal slept before the battle;
here is where he slept after the battle; here is where he slept during the
battle."

In Russia the disaster did not penetrate the public mind at once, being
blotted out by a great victory won at the same time over the Austrians on
the Galician front. In numbers an even greater victory than the Germans
won at Tannenberg, it had equal effect on the enemy. In a series of
engagements fought from August 26 to September 10 and culminating in
the Battle of Lemberg, the Russians inflicted 250,000 casualties, took
100,000 prisoners, forced the Austrians into a retreat lasting eighteen days
and covering 150 miles, and accomplished a mutilation of the Austro-
Hungarian Army, especially in trained officers, from which it was never to
recover. It crippled Austria but could not restore the losses or heal the
effects of Tannenberg. The Russian Second Army had ceased to exist,
General Samsonov was dead, and of his five corps commanders two were
captured and three cashiered for incompetence. General Rennenkampf in
the ensuing battle of the Masurian Lakes was chased out of East Prussia,
"lost his nerve"—in this case the customary formula was applied by
Jilinsky—deserted his army, and drove back across the frontier in a motorcar, thus completing the ruin of his reputation and bringing about his
discharge in disgrace and incidentally that of Jilinsky. In a telegram to the
Grand Duke, Jilinsky accused Rennenkampf of having decamped in panic.
This infuriated the Grand Duke, who considered the primary failure to
have been Jilinsky's. He thereupon reported to the Czar that it was
Jilinsky "who has lost his head and is incapable of controlling operations,"
with the result that another actor in the Battle of Tannenberg became a
casualty.

The inadequacy of training and materials, the incompetence of generals, the inefficiency of organization were laid bare by the battle. Alexander
Guchkov, a subsequent Minister of War, testified that he "reached the
firm conviction that the war was lost" after Tannenberg. The defeat gave
new vigor to the pro-German groups who began openly to agitate for withdrawal from the war. Count Witte was convinced the war would ruin

Russia, Rasputin that it would destroy the regime. The Ministers of Justice and of Interior drew up a Memorandum for the Czar urging peace with Germany as soon as possible on the ground that continuing alliance with democracies would be fatal. The opportunity was offered. German proposals to Russia for a separate peace began shortly afterward and continued through 1915 and 1916. Whether out of loyalty to the Allies and the Pact of London or fear of making terms with the Germans, or insensibility to the lapping tide of Revolution or simple paralysis of authority, the Russians never accepted them. In mounting chaos and dwindling ammunition their war effort went on.

At the time of the disaster General Marquis de Laguiche, the French military attaché, came to express his condolences to the Commander in Chief. "We are happy to have made such sacrifices for our Allies," the Grand Duke replied gallantly. Equanimity in the face of catastrophe was his code, and Russians, in the knowledge of inexhaustible supplies of man-power, are accustomed to accepting gigantic fatalities with comparative calm. The Russian steam roller in which the Western Allies placed such hopes, which after their debacle on the Western Front was awaited even more anxiously, had fallen apart on the road as if it had been put together with pins. In its premature start and early demise it had been, just as the Grand Duke said, a sacrifice for an ally. Whatever it cost the Russians, the sacrifice accomplished what the French wanted: withdrawal of German strength from the Western Front. The two corps that came too late for Tannenberg were to be absent from the Marne.

▶▶▶ *17* ▶

▶▶▶ *The Flames of Louvain*

IN 1915 A BOOK ABOUT THE INVASION OF HIS
country was published in exile by Emile Verhaeren, Belgium's leading
living poet whose life before 1914 had been a flaming dedication to
socialist and humanitarian ideals that were then believed to erase national
lines. He prefaced his account with this dedication: "He who writes this
book in which hate is not hidden was formerly a pacifist. . . . For him no
disillusionment was ever greater or more sudden. It struck him with such
violence that he thought himself no longer the same man. And yet, as it
seems to him that in this state of hatred his conscience becomes diminished, he dedicates these pages, with emotion, to the man he used to be."

Of all that has been written, Verhaeren's is the most poignant testimony of what war and invasion did to the mind of his time. When the
Battle of the Frontiers ended, the war had been in progress for twenty
days and during that time had created passions, attitudes, ideas, and issues,
both among belligerents and watching neutrals, which determined its
future course and the course of history since. The world that used to be
and the ideas that shaped it disappeared too, like the wraith of Verhaeren's former self, down the corridors of August and the months that
followed. Those deterrents—the brotherhood of socialists, the interlocking

of finance, commerce, and other economic factors—which had been expected to make war impossible failed to function when the time came. Nationhood, like a wild gust of wind, arose and swept them aside.

People entered the war with varying sentiments and sets of ideas. Among the belligerents some, pacifists and socialists, opposed the war in their hearts; some, like Rupert Brooke, welcomed it. "Now God be thanked who has matched us with His hour," wrote Brooke, conscious of no blasphemy, in his poem "1914." To him it seemed a time

> To turn, as swimmers into cleanness leaping
> Glad from a world grown old and cold and weary. . . .

> Honour has come back. . . .
> And Nobleness walks in our ways again,
> And we have come into our heritage.

Germans felt similar emotions. The war was to be, wrote Thomas Mann, "a purification, a liberation, an enormous hope. The victory of Germany will be a victory of soul over numbers. The German soul," he explained, "is opposed to the pacifist ideal of civilization for is not peace an element of civil corruption?" This concept, a mirror image of the essential German militarist theory that war is ennobling, was not very far from the raptures of Rupert Brooke and was widely held at the time by numbers of respectable people, among them, Theodore Roosevelt. In 1914, except for Balkan wars on the fringe, there had been no war on the European continent for more than a generation, and in the opinion of one observer the welcoming attitude toward war owed something to the "unconscious boredom of peace."

Where Brooke was embracing cleanness and nobleness, Mann saw a more positive goal. Germans being, he said, the most educated, law-abiding, peace-loving of all peoples, deserved to be the most powerful, to dominate, to establish a "German peace" out of "what is being called with every possible justification the German war." Though writing in 1917, Mann was reflecting 1914, the year that was to be the German 1789, the establishment of the German idea in history, the enthronement of *Kultur*, the fulfillment of Germany's historic mission. In August, sitting at a café in Aachen, a German scientist said to the American journalist Irwin Cobb: "We Germans are the most industrious, the most earnest, the best educated race in Europe. Russia stands for reaction, England for selfishness and perfidy, France for decadence, Germany for progress

German *Kultur* will enlighten the world and after this war there will never be another."

A German businessman sitting with them had more specific aims. Russia was to be so humbled that never again could the Slav peril threaten Europe; Great Britain was to be utterly crushed and deprived of her navy, India, and Egypt; France was to pay an indemnity from which she would never recover; Belgium was to yield her seacoast because Germany needed ports on the English Channel; Japan was to be punished in due time. An alliance of "all the Teutonic and Scandinavian races in Europe, including Bulgaria, will hold absolute dominion from the North Sea to the Black Sea. Europe will have a new map and Germany will be at the center of it."

Talk of this kind for years before the war had not increased friendliness for Germany. "We often got on the world's nerves," admitted Bethmann-Hollweg, by frequently proclaiming Germany's right to lead the world. This, he explained, was interpreted as lust for world dominion but was really a "boyish and unbalanced ebullience."

The world somehow failed to see it that way. There was a stridency in the German tone that conveyed more menace than ebullience. The world became "sore-headed and fed-up," wrote Mr. George Bernard Shaw in 1914, with Germany's clattering of the sword. "We were rasped beyond endurance by Prussian Militarism and its contempt for us and for human happiness and common sense; and we just rose at it and went for it."

Some rose at it with a clear sense of the issues, satisfying at least to them; some with only the vaguest notion of the whys and wherefores, some with none at all. Mr. H. G. Wells was one of the first kind. The enemy, he announced in the press of August 4, was German imperialism and militarism, "the monstrous vanity begotten in 1870." The victory of Germany, of "blood and iron, flagwagging Teutonic Kiplingism," would mean "the permanent enthronement of the war god over all human affairs." The defeat of Germany "may"—Mr. Wells did not say "will"— "open the way to disarmament and peace throughout the world." Less clear as to issues was a British reservist who in the train on his way to the depot explained to a fellow passenger, "I'm a'goin' to fight the bloody Belgiums, that's where I'm a'goin'." A third kind, happy to fight without any war aims at all, was Major Sir Tom Bridges, commander of the cavalry squadron which killed the first Germans on the road to Soignies. "There was no hatred of Germany," he said. "We were quite ready to fight anybody . . . and would equally readily have fought the French. Our motto was, 'We'll do it. What is it?' "

Having an old score to settle, the French had no need to explain themselves. The German at their gates was enough. Yet here too was felt the "enormous hope." Bergson believed that although the ultimate success of the Allies would require "terrible sacrifices," out of them would come, along with "the rejuvenation and enlargement of France, the moral regeneration of Europe. Then with the advent of a real peace, France and humanity can resume the march forward, only forward, toward truth and justice."

These were not the public attitudes of statesmen or the group attitudes of masses but the private attitudes of individuals. None were yet as fixed as they were to become. National hatred of Germany had not yet taken hold. Among the first and most memorable of *Punch*'s cartoons on the war was one that appeared on August 12 labeled "No Thoroughfare!" Brave little Belgium is there, a stern small boy in wooden shoes barring the way to the trespasser, Germany, pictured as a fat old bandmaster with a string of sausages hanging out of his pocket. He is ludicrous, not evil. Otherwise, in the early days, the cartoonists' pet was the Crown Prince whom they delighted to draw as an exaggerated fop with pinched waist, high tight collar, rakish cap, and an expression of fatuous vacuity. He did not last. The war becoming too serious, he was replaced by the best known German, the Supreme War Lord, whose name was signed to every order of OHL so that he seemed the author of all German acts—the Kaiser. No longer the prewar mischief-maker and saber rattler, he was now depicted as a dark, satanic tyrant, breathing cruelty and malignancy, expressing brutality in every line. The change began in August and progressed from Bridges' cool statement, "There was no hatred of Germany," to that of Stephen McKenna, who wrote in 1921, "Among those who remember, the name of a German stinks and the presence of a German is an outrage." No pseudo-heroic super-patriot but a sober, thoughtful schoolteacher whose memoirs are a social document of the time, McKenna recorded a change of sentiment that was to prevent any negotiated settlement and keep the fighting going until total victory. What wrought the change was what happened to Belgium.

The turn of events in Belgium was a product of the German theory of terror. Clausewitz had prescribed terror as the proper method to shorten war, his whole theory of war being based on the necessity of making it short, sharp, and decisive. The civil population must not be exempted from war's effects but must be made to feel its pressure and be forced by the severest measures to compel their leaders to make peace. As the object of war was to disarm the enemy, "we must place him in a situation in which continuing the war is more oppressive to him than surrender." This seemingly sound proposition fitted into the scientific theory of war which throughout the nineteenth century it had been the best intellectual endeavor of the German General Staff to construct. It had already been put into practice in 1870 when French resistance sprang up after Sedan. The ferocity of German reprisal at that time in the form of executions of prisoners and civilians on charges of *franc-tireur* warfare startled a world agape with admiration at Prussia's marvelous six-week victory. Suddenly it became aware of the beast beneath the German skin. Although 1870 proved the corollary of the theory and practice of terror, that it deepens antagonism, stimulates resistance, and ends by lengthening war, the Germans remained wedded to it. As Shaw said, they were a people with a contempt for common sense.

On August 23 placards signed by General von Bülow were posted in Liège announcing that the people of Andenne, a small town on the Meuse near Namur, having attacked his troops in the most "traitorous" manner, "with my permission the General commanding these troops has burned the town to ashes and has had 110 persons shot." The people of Liège were being informed so that they would know what fate to expect if they behaved in the same manner as their neighbors.

The burning of Andenne and the massacre—which Belgian figures put at 211—took place on August 20 and 21 during the Battle of Charleroi. Hewing to their timetable, harassed by the Belgians' blowing up of bridges and railroads, Bülow's commanders dealt out reprisals ruthlessly in the villages they entered. At Seilles, across the river from Andenne, 50 civilians were shot and the houses given over to looting and burning. At Tamines, captured on August 21, sack of the town began that evening after the battle and continued all night and next day. The usual orgy of permitted looting accompanied by drinking released inhibitions and brought the soldiers to the desired state of raw excitement which was intended to add to the fearful effect. On the second day at Tamines some 400 citizens were herded together under guard in front of the church in the main square and a firing squad began systematically shooting into the group. Those not dead when the firing ended were bayoneted. In the cemetery at Tamines there are 384 gravestones inscribed 1914: *Fusillé par les Allemands.*

When Bülow's Army took Namur, a city of 32,000, notices were posted announcing that ten hostages were being taken from every street who would be shot if any civilian fired on a German. The taking and killing of hostages was practiced as systematically as the requisitioning of food. The farther the Germans advanced, the more hostages were arrested. At first when von Kluck's Army entered a town, notices immediately went up warning the populace that the burgomaster, the leading magistrate, and the senator of the district were being held as hostages with the usual warning as to their fate. Soon three persons of prestige were not enough; a man from every street, even ten from every street were not enough. Walter Bloem, a novelist mobilized as a reserve officer in von Kluck's Army whose account of the advance to Paris is invaluable, tells how in villages where his company was billeted each night, "Major von Kleist gave orders that a man or, if no man was available, a woman, be taken from every household as a hostage." Through some peculiar failure of the system, the greater the terror, the more terror seemed to be necessary.

When sniping was reported in a town, the hostages were executed. Irwin Cobb, accompanying von Kluck's Army, watched from a window as two civilians were marched between two rows of German soldiers with fixed bayonets. They were taken behind the railroad station; there was a sound of shots, and two litters were carried out bearing still figures covered by blankets with only the rigid toes of their boots showing. Cobb watched while twice more the performance was repeated.

Visé, scene of the first fighting on the way to Liège on the first day of the invasion, was destroyed not by troops fresh from the heat of battle, but by occupation troops long after the battle had moved on. In response to a report of sniping, a German regiment was sent to Visé from Liège on August 23. That night the sound of shooting could be heard at Eysden just over the border in Holland five miles away. Next day Eysden was overwhelmed by a flood of 4,000 refugees, the entire population of Visé except for those who had been shot, and for 700 men and boys who had been deported for harvest labor to Germany. The deportations which were to have such moral effect, especially upon the United States, began in August. Afterward when Brand Whitlock, the American Minister, visited what had been Visé he saw only empty blackened houses open to the sky, "a vista of ruins that might have been Pompeii." Every inhabitant was gone. There was not a living thing, not a roof.

At Dinant on the Meuse on August 23 the Saxons of General von Hausen's Army were fighting the French in a final engagement of the Battle of Charleroi. Von Hausen personally witnessed the "perfidious" activity of Belgian civilians in hampering reconstruction of bridges, "so contrary to international law." His troops began rounding up "several hundreds" of hostages, men, women, and children. Fifty were taken from church, the day being Sunday. The General saw them "tightly crowded— standing, sitting, lying—in a group under guard of the Grenadiers, their faces displaying fear, nameless anguish, concentrated rage and desire for revenge provoked by all the calamities they had suffered." Von Hausen, who was very sensitive, felt an "indomitable hostility" emanating from them. He was the general who had been made so unhappy in the house of the Belgian gentleman who clenched his fists in his pockets and refused to speak to von Hausen at dinner. In the group at Dinant he saw a wounded French soldier with blood streaming from his head, who lay dying, mute and apathetic, refusing all medical help. Von Hausen ends his description there, too sensitive to tell the fate of Dinant's citizens. They were kept in the main square till evening, then lined up, women on one side, men opposite in two rows, one kneeling in front of the other. Two firing squads marched to the center of the square, faced either way and fired till no more of the targets stood upright. Six hundred and twelve bodies were identified and buried, including Felix Fivet, aged three weeks.

The Saxons were then let loose in a riot of pillage and arson. The medieval citadel perched like an eagle's nest on the heights of the right bank above the city it had once protected, looked down upon a repetition of the ravages of the Middle Ages. The Saxons left Dinant scorched, crumbled, hollowed out, charred, and sodden. "Profoundly moved" by this picture of desolation wrought by his troops, General von Hausen departed from the ruins of Dinant secure in the conviction that the responsibility lay with the Belgian government "which approved this perfidious street fighting contrary to international law."

The Germans were obsessively concerned about violations of inter-national law. They succeeded in overlooking the violation created by their presence in Belgium in favor of the violation committed, as they saw it, by Belgians resisting their presence. With a sigh of long-tried patience, Abbé Wetterlé, Alsatian delegate to the Reichstag, once confessed, "To a mind formed in the Latin school, the German mentality is difficult to comprehend."

The German obsession had two parts: that Belgian resistance was illegal and that it was organized from "above" by the Belgian government or by burgomasters, priests, and other persons who could be classified as "above." Together the two parts established the corollary: that German reprisals were righteous and legal, regardless of degree. The shooting of a single hostage or the massacre of 612 and the razing of a town were alike to be charged to the Belgian government—this was the refrain of every German from Hausen after Dinant to the Kaiser after Louvain. The responsibility must "fall upon those who incited the population to attack the Germans," Hausen protests constantly. There can be absolutely no doubt, he insists, that the whole population of Dinant and other regions was "animated—by whose order?—by one desire to stop the advance of the Germans." That people could be animated to stop the invader without an order from "above" was inconceivable.

The Germans saw these orders everywhere. Von Kluck claimed that the Belgian government's posters warning its citizens against hostile acts were actually "incitements to the civil population to fire on the enemy." Ludendorff accused the Belgian government of having "systematically organized civilian warfare." The Crown Prince applied the same theory to French civil resistance. He complained that the "fanatical" people of the Longwy region shot at us "treacherously and perfidiously" from doors and windows with sporting guns which had been "sent from Paris for the purpose." Had the royal travels included closer acquaintance with the French countryside where a sporting gun for shooting hare on Sundays was as normal equipment as a pair of pants, he might have known it did not require guns sent from Paris to arm the *franc-tireur*.

German accounts of their experiences in enemy territory become shrill with hysteria on the subject of guerrilla warfare. Ludendorff called it "disgusting." He whose name was soon to become a byword for trickery, violence, and cunning had taken the field, he says, "with chivalrous and humane conceptions of warfare" but *franc-tireur* methods "caused me personally bitter disillusionment." Captain Bloem was haunted by the "monstrous thought" that he might be hit or killed by a bullet fired by a civilian, although until a fortnight ago he had been a civilian himself. During an exhausting march of twenty-eight miles in one day, he reports, not one soldier fell out of line because "the thought of falling into the hands of the Walloons was worse than sore feet"—that other great agony of the march on Paris.

Fear and horror of the *franc-tireur* sprang from the German feeling that civil resistance was essentially disorderly. If there has to be a choice between injustice and disorder, said Goethe, the German prefers injustice. Schooled in a state in which the relation of the subject to the sovereign has no basis other than obedience, he is unable to understand a state organized upon any other foundation, and when he enters one is inspired by an intense uneasiness. Comfortable only in the presence of authority, he regards the civilian sniper as something particularly sinister. To the Western mind the *franc-tireur* is a hero; to the German he is a heretic who threatens the existence of the state. At Soissons there is a bronze and marble monument to three schoolteachers who raised a revolt of students and civilians against the Prussians in 1870. Gazing at it in amazement, a German officer said to an American reporter in 1914. "That's the French for you—putting up a monument to glorify *franc-tireurs*. In Germany the people would not be allowed to do such a thing. Nor is it conceivable that they would want to."

To put the German soldier in the proper frame of mind, German newspapers were filled from the first week, as Captain Bloem recorded, with stories of the Belgians' "revolting cruelties . . . of armed priests at the head of marauding bands of civilians committing every kind of atrocity . . . of treacherous ambushes on patrols, of sentries found with eyes pierced and tongues cut off." Similar "ghastly rumors" had already reached Berlin by August 11 to be recorded by Princess Blücher. A German officer whom she asked for verification told her that in Aachen at that moment there were thirty German officers lying in the hospital with their eyes put out by Belgian women and children.

Emotions aroused by such stories made it easy by a single cry of "Snipers!" to set the German soldier off on a rampage of pillage, arson, and murder, uninhibited by the officers. *Schrecklichkeit* was intended as a substitute for the occupation troops which the High Command could not afford to divert from the march on Paris.

On August 25 the burning of Louvain began. The medieval city on the road from Liège to Brussels was renowned for its University and incomparable Library, founded in 1426 when Berlin was a clump of wooden huts. Housed in the fourteenth century Clothworkers' Hall, the Library included among its 230,000 volumes a unique collection of 750 medieval manuscripts and over a thousand incunabula. The façade of the Town Hall, called a "jewel of Gothic art," was a stone tapestry of carved knights and saints and ladies, lavish even of its kind. In the church of St. Pierre were altar panels by Dierik Bouts and other Flemish masters. The burning and sack of Louvain, accompanied by the invariable shooting of civilians, lasted six days before it was called off as abruptly as it began.

Everything went smoothly when Louvain was first occupied. The shops did a rush of business. German soldiers behaved in exemplary fashion, bought postcards and souvenirs, paid for all their purchases, and stood in line with the regular customers for haircuts at the barbershop. The second day was more strained. A German soldier was shot in the leg, allegedly by snipers. The Burgomaster urgently repeated his call upon civilians to surrender arms. He and two other officials were arrested as hostages. Executions behind the railroad station became frequent. The endless tramp of von Kluck's columns continued through the city day after day.

On August 25 the Belgian Army at Malines, on the edge of the entrenched camp of Antwerp, made a sudden sharp sortie upon the rearguard of von Kluck's Army, flinging them back in disorder upon Louvain. In the turmoil of retreat a riderless horse clattering through the gates after dark frightened another horse which tried to bolt, fell in harness, and overturned the wagon. Shots rang out, setting off cries of *"Die Franzosen sind da! Die Engländer sind da!"* Later the Germans claimed they had been fired on by Belgian civilians or that civilians had fired from rooftops as signals to the Belgian Army. Belgians claimed that German soldiers had fired on one another in the dark. For weeks and months, even years, after the event that appalled the world, judicial inquiries and tribunals investigated the outbreak, and German accusations were contradicted by Belgian countercharges. Who shot whom was never established and was in any case irrelevant to what followed, for the Germans burned Louvain not as a punishment for alleged Belgian misdeeds, but as a deterrent and a warning to all their enemies—a gesture of German might before all the world.

General von Luttwitz, the new Governor of Brussels, expressed as much next morning. Visited in the course of duty by the American and Spanish Ministers, he said to them, "A dreadful thing has occurred at Louvain. Our General there has been shot by the son of the Burgomaster. The population has fired on our troops." He paused, looked at his visitors, and finished, "And now of course we have to destroy the city." Mr. Whitlock was to hear so often the story of one or another German general being shot by the son or sometimes the daughter of a burgomaster that it seemed to him the Belgians must have bred a special race of burgomasters' children like the Assassins of Syria.

Already word of the flames at Louvain had spread. Stunned and weeping refugees driven from the city told of street after street set on fire, of savage looting and continuing arrests and executions. On August 27 Richard Harding Davis, star of the American correspondents who were then in Belgium, made his way to Louvain by troop train. He was kept locked in the railroad car by the Germans, but the fire had by then reached the Boulevard Tirlemont facing the railroad station and he could see "the steady, straight columns of flames" rising from the rows of houses. The German soldiers were drunk and wild. One thrust his head through the window of the car where another correspondent, Arno Dosch, was confined and cried: "Three cities razed! Three! There will be more!"

On August 28 Hugh Gibson, First Secretary of the American Legation, accompanied by his Swedish and Mexican colleagues, went to Louvain to see for themselves. Houses with blackened walls and smoldering timbers were still burning; pavements were hot; cinders were everywhere. Dead horses and dead people lay about. One old man, a civilian with a white beard, lay on his back in the sun. Many of the bodies were swollen, evidently dead for several days. Wreckage, furniture, bottles, torn clothing, one wooden shoe were strewn among the ashes. German soldiers of the IXth Reserve Corps, some drunk, some nervous, unhappy, and bloodshot, were routing inhabitants out of the remaining houses so that, as the soldiers told Gibson, the destruction of the city could be completed. They went from house to house, battering down doors, stuffing pockets with cigars, looting valuables, then plying the torch. As the houses were chiefly of brick and stone, the fire did not spread of itself. An officer in charge in one street watched gloomily, smoking a cigar. He was rabid against the Belgians, and kept repeating to Gibson: "We shall wipe it out, not one stone will stand upon another! *Kein stein auf einander!*—not one, I tell you. We will teach them to respect Germany. For generations people will come here to see what we have done!" It was the German way of making themselves memorable.

In Brussels the Rector of the University, Monseigneur de Becker, whose rescue was arranged by the Americans, described the burning of the Library. Nothing was left of it; all was in ashes. When he came to the word "library"—*bibliothèque*—he could not say it. He stopped, tried again, uttered the first syllable, *"La bib—"* and unable to go on, bowed his head on the table, and wept.

The loss, made the subject of a public protest by the Belgian government and officially reported by the American Legation, caused an outcry in the outside world while the fire was still raging. Eyewitness accounts by refugees, reported by all the correspondents, filled the foreign press. Besides the University and Library, "all the noble public buildings," including the Town Hall and St. Pierre with all its pictures, were said to have been destroyed; only later was it found that, though damaged, the Town Hall and the church were still standing. GERMANS SACK LOUVAIN; WOMEN AND CLERGY SHOT blazed the headline in the New York *Tribune* above Davis's story. Under a subhead, "Berlin Confirms Louvain Horror," it carried a wireless statement from Berlin issued by the German Embassy in Washington that, following "perfidious" attack by Belgian civilians, "Louvain was punished by the destruction of the city." Identical with General von Luttwitz's statement, it showed that Berlin had no wish for the world to misunderstand the nature of the gesture at Louvain. Destruction of cities and deliberate, acknowledged war on noncombatants were concepts shocking to the world of 1914. In England editorials proclaimed "The March of the Hun" and "Treason to Civilization." The burning of the Library, said the *Daily Chronicle*, meant war not only on noncombatants "but on posterity to the utmost generation." Even the usually quiet and carefully neutral Dutch papers were stung to comment. Whatever the cause of the outbreak, said the Rotterdam *Courant*, "the fact of destruction remains"—a fact "so terrible that the whole world must have received the news with horror."

The reports appeared in the foreign press of August 29. On August 30 the process of destroying Louvain was terminated. On the same day an official communiqué of the German Foreign Office affirmed that "the entire responsibility for these events rests with the Belgian Government," not forgetting the usual claim that "women and girls took part in the fight and blinded our wounded, gouging their eyes out."

Why did the Germans do it? people asked all over the world. "Are you descendants of Goethe or of Attila the Hun?" protested Romain Rolland in a public letter to his former friend Gerhart Hauptmann, Germany's literary lion. King Albert in conversation with the French Minister thought the mainspring was the German sense of inferiority and jealousy: "These people are envious, unbalanced and ill-tempered. They burned the Library of Louvain simply because it was unique and universally admired" —in other words, a barbarian's gesture of anger against civilized things. Valid in part, this explanation overlooked the deliberate use of terror as prescribed by the *Kriegsbrauch*, "War cannot be conducted merely against the combatants of an enemy state but must seek to destroy the total material and intellectual (*geistig*) resources of the enemy." To the world it remained the gesture of a barbarian. The gesture that was intended by the Germans to frighten the world—to induce submission—instead convinced large numbers of people that here was an enemy with whom there could be no settlement and no compromise.

Belgium clarified issues, became to many the "supreme issue" of the war. In America, said a historian of his times looking back, Belgium was the "precipitant" of opinion and Louvain was the climax of Belgium.

Matthias Erzberger, soon to be appointed chief of propaganda when that unhappy necessity forced itself upon Germany, found that Belgium "aroused almost the entire world against Germany." The argument of his counterpropaganda, that Germany's conduct was justified by military necessity and self-defense, was, as he admitted with a certain wry regret, "insufficient."

It did the Kaiser little good to take the offensive ten days after Louvain in a telegram to President Wilson saying "my heart bleeds" for the sufferings of Belgium caused "as a result of the criminal and barbarous action of the Belgians." Their resistance, he explained, had been "openly incited" and "carefully organized" by the Belgian government, compelling his generals to take the strongest measures against the "bloodthirsty population."

It did little good for ninety-three German professors and other intellectuals to issue a Manifesto addressed "To the Civilized World" proclaiming the civilizing effects of German culture and stating, "It is not true that we have criminally violated the neutrality of Belgium. . . . It is not true that our troops have brutally destroyed Louvain." However imposing the signatories—Harnack, Sudermann, Humperdinck, Roentgen, Hauptmann—the mute ashes of the Library spoke louder. By the end of August people of the Allied nations were persuaded that they faced an enemy that had to be beaten, a regime that had to be destroyed, a war that must be fought to a finish. On September 4 the British, French, and Russian governments signed the Pact of London engaging themselves "not to conclude peace separately during the present war."

Thereafter issues hardened. The more the Allies declared their purpose to be the defeat of German militarism and the Hohenzollerns, the more Germany declared her undying oath not to lay down arms short of total victory. In reply to President Wilson's offer to mediate, Bethmann-Hollweg said the Pact of London forced Germany to fight to the limit of her endurance, and therefore Germany would make no proposals as basis for a negotiated peace. The Allies took the same stand. In this position both sides were to remain clamped throughout the war. The deeper both belligerents sank into war and the more lives and treasure they spent, the more determined they became to emerge with some compensating gain.

The gains Germany expected to win with victory were laid down within the first thirty days of battle in a Memorandum presented to the government on September 2 by Matthias Erzberger. Leader of the Catholic Centrum Party and *rapporteur* of the Military Affairs Committee, he was the Chancellor's right-hand man and closest associate in the Reichstag. A shrewd and able opportunist who represented whatever opinion was dominant, he combined energy and intelligence with a political flexibility unseen in Europe since Talleyrand's. It was said of him that he had "no convictions but only appetites." As he was one day to make himself the bearer of Germany's plea for an armistice and to serve in the first Cabinet of the Weimar Republic, so now he drew up a list of war aims that would have made the most extreme Pan-German proud. Bethmann, who relied on him, never failed to wonder where Erzberger obtained all his bright ideas when he himself never seemed to have any.

Germany, according to Erzberger, was to utilize victory to gain control of the European continent for "all time." All demands at the peace table were to be based on this premise for which three conditions were necessary: abolition of neutral states at Germany's borders, the end of England's "intolerable hegemony" in world affairs, and the breaking up of the Russian colossus. Erzberger envisioned a Confederation of European States analogous to the later Mandates system under the League of Nations. Some states would be under German "guidance"; others, such as Poland and the Baltic group annexed from Russia, would be under German sovereignty for "all time," with possible representation but no voting power in the Reichstag. Erzberger was not sure which category Belgium would fit into, but in either case Germany was to retain military control over the entire country and over the French coast from Dunkirk down to and including Boulogne and Calais. Germany would also acquire the Briey-Longwy iron basin and Belfort in Upper Alsace which she had failed to take in 1870. She would also take the French and Belgian colonies in Africa. Morocco, curiously enough, was excepted as likely to be too much of a drain on Germany's strength. No mention was made of England's colonies, which suggests that Erzberger may have been considering a negotiated settlement with England. In reparations the vanquished nations were to pay at least 10 billion marks for direct war costs, plus enough more to provide veterans' funds, public housing, gifts to generals and statesmen, and pay off Germany's entire national debt, thus obviating taxes on the German people for years to come.

Drawn up in the intoxicating days of conquest in August, these war aims on which Germany set her sights were so grandiose as to be irreducible to the level of feasible compromise. On the Allied side in August, the primary war aim was expressed by Foreign Minister Sazonov to Paléologue at a tête-à-tête luncheon in St. Petersburg on August 20. "My formula is a simple one," said Sazonov; "we must destroy German imperialism." They agreed that the war was one for existence and that its objects could be gained only by total victory. Rather rashly for a Czarist minister, Sazonov agreed that sweeping political changes must be made if Kaiserism was not to rise from its ashes. Poland must be restored, Belgium enlarged, Alsace-Lorraine returned to France, Schleswig-Holstein to Denmark, Hanover reconstituted, Bohemia set free from Austria-Hungary, and all of Germany's colonies given to France, Belgium, and England.

These were the map carvings of professional statesmen. Among private people who did not know Schleswig-Holstein from Bohemia, a deep underlying recognition had grown by the time the war was twenty days old that the world was engaged by "the largest human fact since the French Revolution." Though a tremendous catastrophe, it seemed, in August when it was still new, to contain that "enormous hope," the hope of something better afterward, the hope of an end to war, of a chance to remake the world. Mr. Britling in Wells' novel, who, though fictional, was representative, thought it might prove a "huge step forward in human life. It is the end of forty years of evil suspense. It is crisis and solution." He saw "a tremendous opportunity. . . . We can remake the map of the world. . . . The world is plastic for men to do what they will with it. This is the end and the beginning of an age. . . ."

▶▶▶ *18* ▶

▶▶▶ *Blue Water, Blockade,*
and the Great Neutral

RISK WAS THE LEAST FAVORITE CONCEPT OF THE
British Admiralty in 1914. Her fleet was Britain's most prized possession.
It was not, as Churchill had woundingly said of the Germany Navy in
1912, a "luxury fleet"; it was a vital necessity in the exact sense of the word
"vital." The British Empire could not survive naval defeat or even loss of
naval supremacy through individual ship losses. Its tasks were enormous. It
had to prevent invasion of the British Isles; it had to escort the BEF
safely to the Continent; it had to bring home troops from India to add
to the Regular Army and replace them with Territorials; above all, it had
to safeguard seaborne commerce over all the oceans of the world.

Not invasion which had been declared "impracticable" by the Committee of Imperial Defence, but "the interruption of our trade and destruction of merchant shipping" was recognized by the Admiralty as the principal
danger. Two-thirds of all Britain's food was imported. Her livelihood
depended on a foreign commerce carried in British bottoms that represented 43 per cent of the world's total merchant tonnage and carried more
than half of the world's total seaborne trade, as much as carried by all the

other nations put together. A besetting fear that fast German steamers would be converted into commerce destroyers haunted the British before the war. At least forty such vessels were expected to be let loose to supplement German cruisers in preying on the precious stream of maritime trade. British fleet units had to be spread out to protect the Suez route to Persia, India, and the Far East, the Cape route around Africa, the North Atlantic route to the United States and Canada, the Caribbean route to the West Indies, the South Atlantic and South Pacific routes to South America and Australia. The ocean crossroads where shipping lanes converged and enemy raiders were most likely to attack were the points of control.

"The whole principle of naval fighting," Fisher said in the naval equivalent of a papal bull, "is to be free to go anywhere with every damned thing the Navy possesses." Translated into practical terms this meant that the navy must be superior everywhere at once or wherever it was likely to encounter the enemy. With its vast commitments the British Navy had all it could do to muster superiority in home waters where a battle of equal strengths was at all costs to be avoided. The common expectation was of one great clash of capital ships in which maritime supremacy might be decided in a single action like the Russo-Japanese battle of Tsushima. Britain could not afford to risk loss of supremacy in such a battle, but the same was not true of the German Navy, which was expected to take chances. The rampant Germany of 1914 whose Kaiser had proclaimed "Germany's future is on the water," whose Navy Leagues had proliferated over the country and raised popular subscriptions for battleships with such slogans as "England the Foe! Perfidious Albion! The Coming War! The British Peril! England's Plan to Fall on Us in 1911!" was credited with an aggressive spirit and a readiness to dare battle at unfavorable odds that could lead to any kind of desperate adventure.

Fear of the unknown but certainly bellicose intentions of the enemy, and particularly fear of the invisible submarine, whose lethal potential loomed more alarmingly each year, made for a highly sensitive state of British naval nerves.

Almost at the farthest point to which the Grand Fleet could sail, almost the last bleak tip of British territory, a remote outpost of the British Isles, north even of the northernmost point of the mainland, Scapa Flow, a natural shelter among the Orkney Islands, was the place belatedly chosen for the fleet's wartime base. At latitude 59 opposite Norway, the Flow was at the top of the North Sea, 350 miles farther north than Heligoland, where the German fleet would come out if it chose to appear, and 550 miles north of the Portsmouth-Havre crossing of the BEF. It was farther away from the German place of sortie than the Germans were from the British transports, supposing they attempted to attack them. It was a position from which the Grand Fleet could guard its own and block Germany's lanes of seaborne commerce through the North Sea and by its presence bottle up the enemy in port or, by coming between him and his base, bring him to action if he put to sea. But it was not ready for occupancy.

Each increase in the size of ships required wider docks and harbors, and the Dreadnought program had suffered from the split personality of the Liberal government. Having allowed itself to be persuaded by the passion of Fisher and enthusiasm of Churchill to adopt the building program, the Liberals compensated for this injury to their antiwar sentiments by parsimony in paying for it. As a result, in August 1914 Scapa was not yet equipped with dry docks or fixed defenses.

The fleet, so alertly mobilized by Churchill, reached there safely by August 1 while the government was still debating whether to fight. The days after the declaration of war were, in the words of the First Lord, a period of "extreme psychological tension." As the moment approached for the crowded troop transports to depart, some action by the enemy in the form of raids on the coast to draw off the fleet or other tactics of provocation, was hourly expected, Churchill thought that "the great naval battle might begin at any moment."

His state of mind was fully shared by Admiral Sir John Jellicoe who, traveling north by train to Scapa Flow on August 4, opened a telegram marked "Secret" and discovered himself Commander in Chief of the Grand Fleet. It was not the appointment, which he had long expected, or any doubts of his own competence that weighed on Jellicoe. Since entering the navy in 1872 when he was twelve and a half years old and four and a half feet high, he had been accustomed to wide recognition of his talents. Displayed on active service and in various offices at the Admiralty, they had earned the consistent, fervent, and resonant admiration of Lord Fisher who picked Jellicoe to "be Nelson . . . when Armageddon comes along." The date had come and Fisher's candidate for Nelsonhood, from the moment he arrived, felt "the greatest anxiety constantly confronting me" over the defenseless nature of the base at Scapa. Lacking land-based guns, booms and nets and fixed mine fields, it was "open to submarine and destroyer attacks."

Jellicoe worried when German trawlers captured on August 5 were found to have carrier pigeons aboard, suspected of being informants for submarines. Fear of mines, which the Germans announced they were sowing without regard for the limits agreed upon for such devices, increased his anxiety. When one of his light cruisers rammed and sank a submarine, the U-15, on August 9 he was more disturbed than cheered, and hurriedly sent all his capital ships out of the "infected area." Once, when inside the Flow, a gun crew suddenly opened fire on a moving object reported to be a periscope and set off a flurry of shooting and a feverish hunt by destroyers, he ordered the entire fleet of three battle squadrons out to sea where it stayed all night in fear of what even the navy's official historian concedes "could have been a seal." Twice the fleet was transferred to safer bases at Loch Ewe on the west coast of Scotland and Loch Swilly on the north coast of Ireland, leaving the North Sea free to the Germans had they known it—and twice brought back. If the Germans had launched a naval offensive at this time, it might have obtained startling results.

Between bouts of nerves and sudden bolts like a horse that hears the rustle of a snake, the British Navy set about its business of laying down a blockade and patrolling the North Sea in a ceaseless watch for the appearance of the enemy. With a battle strength of 24 dreadnoughts and a knowledge that the Germans had 16 to 19, the British could count on a firm margin of superiority, and in the next class of battleships believed themselves "markedly superior to the next eight Germans." But a heavy sense of all that depended on the issue hung over them.

During the week of the passage of the transports, "the Germans have the strongest incentives to action," Churchill warned Jellicoe on August 8. Not so much as a torpedo boat was sighted. Nothing stirred. The enemy's inactivity heightened the tension. On the far-flung oceans his individual warships still at large, the *Goeben* and *Breslau* in the Mediterranean, the *Dresden* and *Karlsruhe* in the Atlantic, the *Scharnhorst*, *Gneisenau*, and *Emden* of von Spee's squadron in the Pacific were making bold raids or bolder escapes, but the High Seas Fleet, lurking motionless behind Heligoland, seemed to presage something more sinister.

"Extraordinary silence and inertia of the enemy may be prelude to serious enterprises . . . possibly a landing this week on a large scale," Churchill warned fleet commanders on August 12. He suggested that the Grand Fleet move down nearer to the "theatre of decisive action." Jellicoe, however, continued his remote patrol in the gray waste of waters between the top of Scotland and Norway, and only once, on August 16, when the transport of the BEF was at its height, ventured below latitude 56. The transports made 137 separate crossings of the Channel from August 14 to 18, while all that time the whole of the Grand Fleet, with its attendant squadrons and flotillas, patrolled in taut expectancy, watching for the white wake of a torpedo, listening for the wireless signal that would say the German fleet had come out upon the seas.

Grand Admiral von Tirpitz, the Fisher of Germany, the father and builder and soul of the German Fleet, "eternal Tirpitz" with his forked white beard like Neptune's who at sixty-five had served continuously as Secretary of the Navy since 1897, longer in one post than any minister since Bismarck, was not allowed to know the war plan for the weapon he had forged. It was "kept secret by the Naval Staff even from me." On July 30 when the operational orders were shown to him he discovered the secret: there was no plan. The navy, whose existence had been a chief factor in bringing on the war, had no active role designed for it when war came.

If the Kaiser had confined his reading to *The Golden Age*, Kenneth Grahame's dreamlike story of English boyhood in a world of cold adults, which he kept on the bed-table of his yacht, it is possible there might have been no world war. He was eclectic, however, and read an American book that appeared in 1890 with the same impact in its realm as the *Origin of Species* or *Das Kapital* in theirs. In *The Influence of Sea Power on History* Admiral Mahan demonstrated that he who controls communications by sea controls his fate; the master of the seas is master of the situation. Instantly an immense vision opened before the impressionable Wilhelm: Germany must be a major power upon the oceans as upon land. The naval building program began, and although it could not overtake England at once, pursued with German intensity it threatened to do so eventually. It challenged the maritime supremacy upon which Britain depended and knowingly created the likelihood of British enmity in war and consequently the use against Germany of Britain's chief weapon, blockade.

As a land power Germany could have fought any possible combination of continental powers without interruption of her seaborne supplies as long as Britain, the world's greatest merchant carrier, remained neutral. In that sense Germany would have been a stronger power without a navy than with one. Bismarck had disapproved of adulterating power on land by a maritime adventure that would add an enemy upon the sea. Wilhelm would not listen. He was bewitched by Mahan and tangled in the private jealousies of his love and hate for seafaring England which came to an annual peak during the yacht regattas of Cowes week. He saw the navy as his knife to cut through Encirclement. He insisted alternately that hostility to England was the last thing he had in mind and that "a larger fleet will bring the English to their senses through sheer fright." They would then "submit to the inevitable and we shall become the best friends in the world." In vain his ambassadors to England cautioned against the doubtful logic of this policy. In vain Haldane came to Berlin and Churchill warned that the fleet was an Alsace-Lorraine in Anglo-German relations. Proposals for a fixed ratio or a naval holiday were rejected.

Once the challenge had been made, British hostility could fairly be expected. There was a further cost. Built at huge expense, the navy drew money and men—enough to make two army corps—from the army. Unless it had been built to no purpose it had to perform a strategic function: either to prevent the coming of added enemy divisions against its own army or prevent blockade. As the preamble to the German Navy Law of 1900 acknowledged, "A naval war of blockade . . . even if lasting only a year would destroy Germany's trade and bring her to disaster."

As it grew in strength and efficiency, in numbers of trained men and officers, as German designers perfected its gunnery, the armor-piercing power of its shells, its optical devices and range finders, the resistant power of its armor plate, it became too precious to lose. Although ship for ship it approached a match with the British and in gunnery was superior, the Kaiser, who could hark back to no Drakes or Nelsons, could never really believe that German ships and sailors could beat the British. He could not bear to think of his "darlings," as Bülow called his battleships, shattered by gunfire, smeared with blood, or at last, wounded and rudderless, sinking beneath the waves. Tirpitz, whom once he had gratefully ennobled with a "von" but whose theory of a navy was to use it for fighting, began to appear as a danger, almost as an enemy, and was gradually frozen out of the inner councils. His high squeaky voice, like a child's or a eunuch's, that emerged as such a surprise from the giant frame and fierce demeanor was no longer heard. While he remained as administrative head, naval policy was left, under the Kaiser, to a group made up of the Chief of Naval Staff, Admiral von Pohl; the chief of the Kaiser's Marine Cabinet, Admiral von Müller; and to the Commander in Chief of the Navy, Admiral von Ingenohl. Pohl, though supporter of a fighting strategy, was a nonentity who achieved the acme of obscurity possible in Hohenzollern Germany— no mention in Bülow's encyclopedia of gossip; Müller was one of the pederasts and sycophants who decorated the court as advisers to the sovereign; Ingenohl was an officer who "took a defensive view of operations." "I need no Chief," said the Kaiser; "I can do this for myself."

When the moment of Encirclement came, the moment that had haunted his reign, the moment when the dead Edward loomed "stronger than the living I," the Kaiser's instructions read, "For the present I have ordered a defensive attitude on the part of the High Seas Fleet." The strategy adopted for the sharp-edged instrument he had at hand was to exert the influence of a "fleet in being." By staying within an impregnable fortified position, it was to act as a constant potential danger, forcing the enemy to remain on guard against a possible sortie and thereby draining the enemy's naval resources and keeping part of his forces inactive. This was a well-recognized role for the inferior of two fleets, and approved by Mahan. He, however, had later concluded that the value of a fleet-in-being "has been much overstated," for the influence of a navy that elects not to fight tends to become a diminishing quantity.

Even the Kaiser could not have imposed such a policy without good reasons and strong support. He had both. Many Germans, particularly Bethmann and the more cosmopolitan civilian groups could not bring themselves to believe at the start that England was a really serious belligerent. They cherished the thought that she could be bought off in a separate peace, especially after France had been knocked out. Erzberger's careful avoidance of a grab at England's colonies was part of this idea. The Kaiser's maternal family, the English wives of German princes, the ancient Teutonic ties created a sense of kinship. To have battle and spilled blood and deaths between them would make an arrangement between Germany and England difficult if not impossible. (Somehow in this thinking the blood to be spilled in rounding up the BEF along with the French did not count seriously.) Besides, it was hoped to keep the German fleet intact as a bargaining factor to bring the English to terms, a theory which Bethmann strongly supported and the Kaiser was happy to embrace. As time went on and victory went glimmering, the desire to carry the fleet safe and sound through the war for bargaining purposes at the peace table became even more embedded.

In August the primary enemy seemed not England but Russia, and the primary duty of the fleet was considered to be control of the Baltic—at least by those who wished to postpone the test with England. They said the fleet was needed to guard against Russian interference with seaborne supplies from the Scandinavian countries and against a possible Russian descent upon the German coast. Action against England, it was feared, might so weaken Germany's fleet as to lose command of the Baltic, allow a Russian landing, and lead to defeat on land.

Arguments can always be found to turn desire into policy. Above all else, what nullified the navy in August was confidence in decisive victory by the army and the general belief that the war would not last long enough to make blockade a matter for much concern. Tirpitz with a "right presentiment" had already on July 29, the same day that Churchill mobilized the fleet, requested the Kaiser to place control of the navy in the hands of one man. As he felt that "I have more in my little finger than Pohl in his whole anatomy" (a sentiment expressed privately to his wife, not to the Kaiser), he could only suggest that the proposed office be "entrusted to myself." His proposal was rejected. Although he contemplated resigning, he refrained on the useful grounds that the Kaiser "would not have accepted my resignation." Dragged off to Coblenz with the other ministers, he had to suffer in the triumphant aura of OHL while "the Army has all the successes and the Navy none. My position is dreadful after 20 years of effort. No one will understand."

His High Seas Fleet with its 16 dreadnoughts, 12 older battleships, 3 battle cruisers, 17 other cruisers, 140 destroyers, and 27 submarines remained in port or in the Baltic, while offensive action against England was confined to one sweep by submarines during the first week and to minelaying. The merchant navy also withdrew. On July 31 the German government ordered steamship lines to cancel all merchant sailings. By the end of August 670 German merchant steamers aggregating 2,750,000 tons, or more than half of Germany's total, were holed up in neutral ports, and the rest, except for those plying the Baltic, in home ports. Only five out of the terrible forty German armed merchant raiders materialized, and the British Admiralty, looking around in dazed surprise, was able to report on August 14: "The passage across the Atlantic is safe. British trade is running as usual." Except for the raiders *Emden* and *Königsberg* in the Indian Ocean and Admiral von Spee's squadron in the Pacific the German Navy and German merchant shipping had retired from the surface of the oceans before August was over.

Another battle, Britain's battle with the United States, the great neutral, had begun. The old issues that caused the war of 1812, the old phrases—freedom of the seas, the flag covers the goods—the old and inevitable conflict between the neutral's right of commerce and the belligerent's right of restraint was back again. In 1908, as an outgrowth of the second Hague Conference, an attempt to codify the rules had been made by a conference of all the nations who were to be belligerents in 1914 plus the United States, Holland, Italy, and Spain. Britain, as the largest carrier of seaborne trade with the greatest interest in the free flow of neutral commerce, was host nation, and Sir Edward Grey the moving spirit and sponsor, though not a delegate. Despite the vigorous presence of Admiral Mahan as chief American delegate, the resulting Declaration of London favored the neutrals' right to trade as against the belligerents' right to blockade. Even Mahan, the maritime Clausewitz, the Schlieffen of the sea, could not prevail against the suave workings of British influence. Everyone was for neutrals and business as usual, and Mahan's objections were overruled by his civilian colleagues.

Goods were divided into three categories: absolute contraband, which covered articles for military use only; conditional contraband, or articles for either military or civilian use; and a free list, which included food. Only the first could be seized by a belligerent who declared a blockade; the second could be seized only if enemy destination was proved; and the third not at all. But after the Declaration had been signed and the delegates had gone home, another British interest raised its head—sea power. Admiral Mahan's flag fluttered up the mast again. His disciples lifted their voices in horror at the betrayal of maritime supremacy, Britain's guarantee of survival. What use was it, they asked, to deny use of the seas to the enemy if neutrals were to be allowed to supply him with all his needs? They made the Declaration of London a *cause célèbre* and mounted a campaign against it in press and Parliament. It would nullify the British fleet; it was a German plot; Balfour opposed it. Although the Declaration had passed the House of Commons, the Lords in a burst of energy allowed it to fail to come to a vote, perhaps their most dynamic act of the twentieth century. By this time the government, having had second thoughts, was glad enough to let the matter lapse. The Declaration of London was never ratified.

Meanwhile new realities of naval power made Britain's traditional policy of close blockade of an enemy's ports obsolete. Up to now the Admiralty had contemplated, in war against a continental power, a close blockade by destroyer flotillas supported by cruisers and ultimately by battleships. Development of the submarine and floating mine and refinement of the rifled cannon enforced the change to a policy of distant blockade. Adopted in the Admiralty War Orders for 1912, it plunged the whole problem once more into confusion. When a ship attempts to run a close blockade, the port she is making for is obvious and the question of destination does not arise. But when ships are intercepted miles away from their destination, as at the top of the North Sea, the legality of arrest under the rules of blockade has to be shown by proof of destination or of the contraband nature of the cargo. The problem bristled like a floating mine with spikes of trouble.

When war broke, the Declaration of London was still the collected testimony of nations on the subject, and on August 6, the second day of war, the United States formally requested the belligerents to declare their adherence to it. Germany and Austria eagerly agreed on condition that the enemy would do likewise. Britain as spokesman for the Allies on naval policy composed an affirmative reply which, by reserving certain rights "essential to the efficient conduct of their naval operations," said Yes and meant No. She had as yet no fixed policy about contraband but only an empiric feeling that the terms of the Declaration of London required some stretching. A report of the Committee of Imperial Defence in 1911–12 had already proposed that ultimate destination of the goods, not the ships, should be made the criterion of conditional contraband so that leather for saddles, rubber for tires, copper, cotton, raw textiles, and paper, all convertible to military use, could not be shipped freely merely because they were consigned to a neutral receiver. If they were then to be sent overland to Germany, no blockade would be worth the expense of maintaining it. The Committee had suggested that the doctrine of continuous voyage should be "rigorously applied."

One of those phrases of mysterious power which appear and disappear in history, leaving nothing quite the same as before, "continuous voyage," was a concept invented by the British in the course of an eighteenth century war with the French. It meant that the ultimate, not the initial destination of the goods was the determining factor. Prematurely buried by the Declaration of London before it was quite dead, it was now disinterred like one of Poe's entombed cats with similar capacity for causing trouble. The War Office had been advised that foodstuffs shipped by neutrals to Holland were going to supply the German Army in Belgium. On August 20 the Cabinet issued an Order in Council declaring that henceforth Britain would regard conditional contraband as subject to capture if it was consigned to the enemy or "an agent of the enemy" or if its ultimate destination was hostile. Proof of destination was to depend not as heretofore on bills of lading but—in a phrase of matchless elasticity —on "any sufficient evidence."

Here was the doctrine of continuous voyage, alive, spitting, and sharp of claw. The practical effect, admitted Britain's ambassador in Washington, Sir Cecil Spring-Rice, was to make everything absolute contraband.

The immense train of results, the massive difficulties of implementing the decision, the halting and boarding and examining of ships, the X-ray of cargoes, the prize courts and legal complexities, the ultimate recourse to unrestricted submarine warfare which Germany would take with its ultimate effect upon the United States were not thought of then by the authors of the Order in Council. When he decided to divorce Catherine of Aragon, Henry VIII did not have in mind the Reformation. When ministers sat around the Cabinet table on August 20 they were concerned with the military necessity of stopping the flow of supplies from Rotterdam to the German Army in Belgium. The Order in Council was submitted to them on military advice and authorized after some discussion of which the only record is Asquith's airy reference in his diary to "a long Cabinet— all sorts of odds and ends about coal and contraband."

The Prime Minister was not the only person unconcerned with odds and ends of this kind. When a German official, foreseeing the change to a long war of attrition, presented Moltke with a memorandum on the need for an Economic General Staff, Moltke replied, "Don't bother me with economics—I am busy conducting a war."

By a nice coincidence the Order in Council, reviving the issue of the War of 1812, appeared exactly on the one hundredth anniversary of the burning of Washington by the British. Happily this odd chance and the Order itself were overlooked by the American public, absorbed in streaming headlines about the fall of Brussels, stranded Americans in Paris, Kaisers and Czars, fleets, Cossacks, Field Marshals, Zeppelins, Western and Eastern Fronts. The United States government, however, was shocked. The soft British preamble to the Order, which affirmed loyalty to the Declaration of London before making its delicate exceptions, failed to obscure their meaning to the lawyer's eye of Robert Lansing, Counselor to the State Department. He drew up a firm and immediate protest which precipitated a long duel extending into months and years of letters and replies, briefs and precedents, interviews between ambassadors, volumes of documents.

To the London *Daily Chronicle* on August 27 there appeared to be a "very real danger" of becoming embroiled with the United States over questions of contraband and the right of search which it understood the United States "strongly resists." This was a problem that had occurred to Sir Edward Grey, and required careful handling. In the beginning when the war was expected to be short and all that mattered was the best means of winning quickly, there seemed little likelihood of time for a serious issue with the United States to arise. After Mons and Charleroi the inescapable truth of a long war rose out of the corpse-strewn battlefields and stared the Allies in the face. In a long war they would have to draw upon the United States for food, arms, and money (no one yet thought of men) and cut Germany off from the same nourishment. Stiffening the blockade of the enemy and maintaining friendship with the great neutral became simultaneously essential—and incompatible. As every added restraint put upon the neutrals' trade with Germany raised another majestic howl from the State Department about freedom of the seas, it became uncomfortably apparent that Britain might ultimately have to decide which of two objects was the more important. For the moment, with instinctive English dislike of absolutes, Sir Edward Grey was able to pick his way from incident to incident, avoiding large principles as a helmsman avoids rocks and being careful not to allow discussion to reach a clear-cut issue that would require either side to take a position from which it could not climb down. His aim from day to day was, he said, "to secure the maximum blockade that could be enforced without a rupture with the United States."

He had a formidable opponent who was nothing if not a man of principle. Rigidly, puritanically attached to neutrality, Woodrow Wilson was driven to take and maintain a stand on traditional neutral rights less for their own sake than because they were part of the neutral's role that he grasped with fierce intensity from the beginning. He had come to office strenuously dedicated to unseating the "Interests" and dollar diplomats entrenched under the portly, protective shadow of Mr. Taft and to achieving the New Freedom in domestic and Latin-American affairs. Knowing that war stifles reform, he was bent on keeping the country out of a foreign adventure that would frustrate his program. But beyond that, he had a grander and ulterior reason. He saw in the war an opportunity for greatness on the world stage. In his first utterance on the war, spoken to a press conference on August 3, he said that he wanted to have the pride of the feeling that America "stands ready to help the rest of the world" and that he believed she could "reap a great permanent glory out of doing it." Thus early, even before the guns went off, he had formulated the role that he wanted the United States, with which he identified himself, to play; the role he clung to with increasing desperation as the hammer of events weakened his grip, that he never, even after the final involvement, abandoned in his heart.

To Wilson neutrality was the opposite of isolationism. He wanted to keep out of war in order to play a larger, not a lesser, part in world affairs. He wanted the "great permanent glory" for himself as well as for his country, and he realized he could win it only if he kept America out of the quarrel so that he could act as impartial arbiter. On August 18, in a famous statement, he commanded his countrymen to be "neutral in fact as well as in name, impartial in thought as well as in action," and explained that the ultimate purpose of neutrality was to enable the United States "to speak the counsels of peace" and "play the part of impartial mediator." In the European conflict he hoped to exercise the duty of "moral judgment," as he said in a later statement. He wanted "to serve humanity," bring to bear the force—the moral force—of the New World to save the Old World from its follies and, by applying "standards of righteousness and humanity," bring the gifts of peace through mediation under the flag that was "the flag not only of America but of humanity."

Once the British Navy had effectively gained control of the Atlantic by the end of August, the duel with the United States over contraband, however earnest, prolonged, and often bitter, remained a shadow duel. For Wilson freedom of the seas was never the overriding issue, and though once, when matters became particularly contentious, he was disturbed by the thought that he might become the second Princeton president after Madison to lead the country to war, he had no wish to push home the quarrel to the ultimate conclusion of 1812. In any case, leaping trade with the Allies, which was taking up more than the slack of lost trade with Germany, dulled the edge of national principle. As long as goods were being absorbed, the United States came gradually to acquiesce in the process begun by the Order in Council of August 20.

From that time on, through control of the high seas by the British fleet, American trade was perforce directed more and more toward the Allies. Trade with the Central Powers declined from $169 million in 1914 to $1 million in 1916, and during the same period trade with the Allies rose from $824 million to $3 billion. To supply the demand American business and industry produced the goods the Allies wanted. To enable them to pay for American supplies, financial credit for the Allies had to be arranged. Eventually, the United States became the larder, arsenal, and bank of the Allies and acquired a direct interest in Allied victory that was to bemuse the postwar apostles of economic determinism for a long time.

Economic ties develop where there is a basis of long-founded cultural ties, and economic interests where there is natural interest. American trade with England and France had always been greater than with Germany and Austria, and the effect of the blockade was to exaggerate an existing condition, not to create an artificial one. Trade follows not only a nation's flag but its natural sympathies.

"A government can be neutral," said Walter Hines Page, the American ambassador in London, "but no *man* can be." As a wholehearted adherent of the Allies, to whom the concept of neutrality was despicable, he spoke feelingly and wrote feelingly in vivid, persuasive letters to Wilson. Although Page's outspoken identification with the Allies estranged the President to the point of turning his back on the man who had been one of his earliest supporters, even Wilson could not make himself neutral in thought as he wanted other men to be. When Grey wrote him a letter of sympathy on the death of Mrs. Wilson on August 6, Wilson, who admired Grey and felt close to him as one who had lost his own wife, replied: "My hope is that you will regard me as your friend. I feel that we are bound together by common principle and purpose." There was no one in the German government to whom he could have said the same.

Wilson's cultural roots and political philosophy, like that of the majority of influential people in American life, went back to English experience and the French Revolution. He tried to repress them for the sake of his ambition to be peacemaker to the world. For three years he struggled, using every means of persuasion he could wield, to bring the belligerents to a negotiated peace, a "peace without victory." Neutrality, on which his efforts depended, was helped by a strong current of Irish or what might be called anti-George III sentiment and by the vociferous pro-German groups from Professor Hugo Münsterberg of Harvard down to the beerhalls of Milwaukee. It might have prevailed had it not been for a factor before which Wilson was helpless, which in shaping American sentiment was the greatest Allied asset—not the British fleet but German folly.

At the outbreak on August 4 the President, writing to a friend, expressed only "utter condemnation" for the conflict across the seas, and made no attempt to distinguish between the belligerents. On August 30, after a month of the war in Belgium, Colonel House recorded that the President "felt deeply the destruction of Louvain. . . . He goes even further than I in his condemnation of Germany's part in this war and almost allows his feeling to include the German people as a whole rather than the leaders alone. . . . He expressed the opinion that if Germany won it would change the course of our civilization and make the United States a military nation." A few days later Spring-Rice reported that Wilson had said to him "in the most solemn way that if the German cause succeeds in the present struggle the United States would have to give up its present ideals and devote all its energies to defense which would mean the end of its present system of government."

Holding these views, Wilson nevertheless stood to the last, a Casabianca on the burning deck of neutrality. But it was on the planks of a legal, not a felt, neutrality. He could never regard the prospect of an Allied victory as a threat to the principles on which the United States was founded, whereas the prospect of a German victory, especially after Belgium clarified the issues, could not be regarded as anything else. If Wilson, who of all his countrymen had the greatest stake in neutrality, was alienated by German actions, how much more so the average man. The sentiments aroused by Louvain muffled the resentment of Britain's blockade procedures. Each time a British search or seizure or addition to the contraband list aroused new gusts of American wrath, they would be diverted by some convenient act of German frightfulness. Just when Lansing's stiff rebuke of the Order in Council was about to ripen into major controversy, German Zeppelins on August 25 bombed the residential area of Antwerp, killing civilians and narrowly missing the Palace where the Belgian Queen had just moved with her children. As a result Lansing found himself framing a protest against "this outrage upon humanity" instead of a protest against continuous voyage.

In a moment of painful foresight Wilson confided to his brother-in-law, Dr. Axon, who remembered the date as shortly after Mrs. Wilson's funeral on August 12, "I am afraid something will happen on the high seas that will make it impossible for us to keep out of war." It was not what happened on the high seas but what did not happen that became the deciding factor. When Sherlock Holmes called Inspector Gregory's attention "to the curious incident of the dog in the night-time," the puzzled Inspector replied, "The dog did nothing in the night-time."

"That was the curious incident," remarked Holmes.

The German Navy was the dog in the night. It did not fight. Chained up by the fleet-in-being theory and by German belief in an early victory on land, it was not allowed to risk itself in the performance of a navy's function—keeping the sea lanes open to the commerce of its country. Although German industry depended on imported raw materials and German agriculture on imported fertilizer, although German dairy cattle chewed all winter on imported fodder, the Navy made no attempt to protect the flow of supplies. The only battle it fought in August was inadvertent and merely served to confirm the Kaiser's reluctance to risk his "darlings."

This was the Battle of Heligoland Bight on August 28. In a sudden challenge meant to divert German attention from the landing of marines at Ostend, submarine and destroyer flotillas of the British Channel fleet, with battle cruisers in support, steamed into the Bight, home base of the German Navy. Taken by surprise, German light cruisers were ordered out without support of heavier warships. "With all the enthusiasm of the first fight," in Tirpitz's words, they rushed about recklessly in the mist and confusion. In a tangled, dispersed, and haphazard series of combats that lasted all day, British units mistook each other for the enemy and were only saved from what Churchill delicately called "awkward embarrassments" by pure luck. The Germans, who failed to respond to the challenge by ordering the whole fleet to sea, were outnumbered and outgunned. The advantage of the day went to the British. Three German light cruisers, the *Köln*, *Mainz*, and *Ariadne*, and a destroyer were shot to pieces and sunk, three others badly damaged, and more than 1,000 men, including an Admiral and a Commodore, were killed under fire or drowned, and over 200, including Wolf Tirpitz, son of the Grand Admiral, were picked from the water and taken prisoner. The British lost no ships and suffered some 75 casualties.

Horrified at his losses and confirmed in his fear of a test with the British, the Kaiser gave orders that risks were not again to be taken, "the loss of ships was to be avoided," the initiative of the Commander of the North Sea Fleet was to be further restricted, and major movements were not to be undertaken without His Majesty's approval in advance.

Thereafter, while the British Navy built up the blockade walls around Germany, the German Navy watched passively. Straining against his chains the unhappy Tirpitz wrote in mid-September, "Our best opportunity for a successful battle was in the first two or three weeks after the declaration of war." "As time goes on," he predicted, "our chance of success will grow worse, not better." It was the English fleet that was "achieving the full effect of a 'fleet-in-being': extraordinary and increasing pressure on the neutrals, complete destruction of German sea-borne trade, the fullest practical blockade."

Eventually forced to combat the situation it had allowed to develop, German naval policy went underwater. In belated effort to break the blockade it took to the U-boats. Spawned in default of the surface navy, the U-boats ultimately fulfilled the condition on the high seas that Wilson had fearfully glimpsed during the first days of the war in August.

▶▶▶ *19* ▶

▶▶▶ *Retreat*

LIKE A SWINGING SCYTHE THE FIVE GERMAN armies of the right wing and center cut into France from Belgium after the Battle of the Frontiers. A million Germans were in the invading force whose leading columns, shooting and burning, entered French territory on August 24. No breakthrough was made on the Lorraine front where the two armies of the left wing under Prince Rupprecht continued to struggle in prolonged battle against the furious resistance of Castelnau's and Dubail's armies.

Down the long white highways of northern France, cutting a swath seventy-five miles wide, the German right wing was on the march to Paris with Kluck's Army on the extreme right seeking to envelop the Allied line. Joffre's immediate problem was to halt the retreat of his own armies while at the same time shifting weight to the left to create a force strong enough to check the enemy's enveloping movement and be "capable of resuming the offensive." In the aftermath of catastrophe, "resume the offensive" was the dominant thought at GQG. Within twenty-four hours of the debacle, without taking time to assess what was officially called the "check" to the French Armies, or to rethink strategy in terms of the possible, Joffre issued on August 25 a new General Order, the second of the war. It proposed to create in the path of the German right wing a new Sixth Army formed of forces taken from the unbroken front in Lorraine. Transported by rail to Amiens, on the left of the British, it would, together with the BEF and the Fourth and Fifth French Armies, form the mass that was to resume the offensive. While the Sixth Army was forming, the three retreating French Armies were to try to maintain a continuous front and "arrest or at least delay the advance of the enemy by short and violent counter-attacks" carried out by rearguards. As stated in General Order No. 2, Joffre expected the Sixth Army to be in position and ready to join in a renewed offensive by September 2, Sedan Day.

That date glittered too before the oncoming Germans who expected by then to accomplish Schlieffen's goal: envelopment and destruction of the French Armies in a central mass in front of Paris. Throughout the next twelve days another Sedan was in the minds of both sides. They were twelve days in which world history wavered between two courses and the Germans came so close to victory that they reached out and touched it between the Aisne and the Marne.

"Fight in retreat, fight in retreat," was the order dinned into every French regiment during these days. The necessity to hold off pursuit and gain time to regroup and reestablish a solid line gave an urgency to the fighting that had been missing from the offensive. It required rearguard actions that were almost suicidal. The Germans' need to allow the French no time to regroup pushed them on with equal intensity.

In retreat the French fought with competence and emergency-learned skills that had not always been present during the opening battles in Belgium. No longer engaged in a vast and only vaguely understood offensive in mysterious forests on alien soil, they were back on their own soil, defending France. The land they were passing through was familiar, the inhabitants were French, the fields and barns and village streets were their own, and they fought now as the First and Second Armies were fighting for the Moselle and the Grand Couronné. Though defeated in the offensive, they were not a routed army; their line, though dangerously pierced, was not yet broken. On the left in the path of the main German advance the Fifth Army, escaping from disaster at Charleroi and the Sambre, was trying to regather cohesion in retreat. In the center, with their backs to the Meuse, the Third and Fourth Armies fought savage holding actions from Sedan to Verdun against the two armies of the German center, frustrating the enemy's effort to surround them and, as the Crown Prince unhappily ad-

mitted, "recovering their freedom of movement." Despite rearguard actions the German advance was too massive to be stopped. Still fighting,
the French fell back; holding and delaying where they could but always
falling back.

At one place after crossing the Meuse, a battalion of *chasseurs à pied*
in General de Langle's Fourth Army was ordered at nightfall to hold a
bridge which dynamite charges had failed to blow up. They spent a night
of "anguish and horror" watching the Saxons of von Hausen's Army on
the opposite bank "burning the town and shooting the inhabitants under
our eyes. In the morning flames rose from the village. We could see people
running in the streets, pursued by the soldiers. There were shots. . . . At
a great distance we could see an endless movement of horsemen who
seemed to be searching out our position: far away on the plain appeared
dark masses marching." The masses approached and soon along the winding road a German infantry battalion in columns of five came "marching
steadily toward us. The road below was filled as far back as one could see
with a swarm of troops—columns of infantry preceded by officers on horseback, artillery trains, transport, cavalry—almost a division, marching in
perfect order."

"Take aim!" The order was repeated down the line of *chasseurs* in low
voices. Silently the men took their places. "Volley fire; aim at the infantry
first, each man pick his target!" Company leaders gave the range. "Open
fire!" Along the length of the river the fusillade crackled. Down among
the Germans there was a sudden stupor. Their companies whirled and
eddied; they fled. Horses struggled and reared in harness, wagons crashed.
The road was covered with hundreds of corpses. At 8:45 the French ammunition was almost gone. Suddenly from behind on their left came a burst
of rifle fire. The enemy had turned their flank. "To the rear, *à la baïon-
nette!*" Under the thrust of their bayonet charge, the Germans gave way;
the French regiment cut its way through.

Hundreds of such combats were fought by rearguards while the armies
fell back, attempting to keep a continuous front with each other and reach
a line from which the offensive could be renewed. Alongside the soldiers,
the civil population joined in the southward-moving mass, on foot and in
every kind of conveyance from families in six-horse wagons to old men
pushed in wheelbarrows and babies in perambulators. Crowding the roads,
they added to the confusion. Staff cars could not get through, officers
cursed, messages went undelivered. Jammed between marching groups,
commercial trucks and municipal buses, mobilized for army service with

their familiar markings painted over with military symbols, moved slowly, carrying the wounded men who lay in blood-soaked silence with shell-torn limbs and eyes filled with pain and the fear of death.

Each mile of the retreat was an agony of yielding further French territory to the enemy. In some places French soldiers marched past their own homes knowing the Germans would enter them next day. "We left Blombay on August 27," wrote a cavalry captain with the Fifth Army. "Ten minutes later it was occupied by the Uhlans." Units that had been in heavy combat marched in silence, out of step, without songs. Haggard men, parched and hungry, some bitter, muttered against their officers or whispered of treason. Every French position had been betrayed to the German artillery spotters, it was said in the Xth Corps of Lanrezac's Army which had lost 5,000 men on the Sambre. "The men drag themselves along, their faces marked by a terrible exhaustion," wrote an infantry captain in this corps. "They have just completed a two days' march of 62 kilometers after a sharp rearguard action." But that night they sleep, and in the morning "it is extraordinary how a few hours' sleep revives them. They are new men." They ask why they are retreating, and the captain makes a sharp speech in "a cold assured voice." He tells them they will fight again "and show the Germans we have teeth and claws."

The cavalry, once so shiny in polished boots and bright uniforms, now stained and muddy, sway in their saddles, dazed with fatigue. "The men's heads hang with weariness," writes an officer of Hussars with the 9th Cavalry Division. "They only half see where they are going; they live as if in a dream. At halts the famished and broken-down horses even before unsaddling, plunge at the hay and devour it voraciously. We no longer sleep; we march by night and face the enemy by day." They learn the Germans have crossed the Meuse behind them, are gaining ground, setting villages in flames as they pass. "Rocroi is a mass of fire and the barns burning in the neighborhood light up the trees of the nearby woods." At dawn the voice of the enemy's cannon begins; "the Germans salute the sun with their shells." Through the incessant crash and thunder the French hear the brave scream of their own 75s. They grip their positions, waiting for the artillery duel to end. A mounted orderly rides up with an order from the commander: retreat. They move on. "I contemplated the green fields and the herds of grazing sheep and I thought, 'What a fortune we are abandoning!' My men recovered their spirits. They found a system of trenches dug by the infantry which they examined with the greatest curiosity as if they were sights offered for the admiration of the tourist."

On August 25 Germans belonging to the Duke of Württemberg's Army penetrated Sedan and shelled Bazeilles, scene of the famous Battle of the Last Cartridge in 1870. The French of de Langle's Fourth Army counterattacked to keep them from crossing the Meuse. "A hot artillery duel began," wrote a German officer of the VIIIth Reserve Corps. "It was such a terrible fracas that the earth trembled. All the old bearded Territorials were crying." Later he fought in a "terrible combat on wooded slopes as steep as roofs. Four assaults with the bayonet. We had to jump over piles of our own dead. We fell back on Sedan with heavy casualties and the loss of three flags."

That night the French blew up all the railroad bridges in the area. Torn between the need to delay the enemy and the thought that tomorrow they might require bridges and railroads themselves for a return to the offensive, the French left destruction of communications to the latest possible moment, sometimes too late.

The greatest difficulty of all was the assignment of each unit, from army corps down to single regiments, each with its own supply train and auxiliaries of cavalry and artillery to its own roads and lines of communication. "Rather than yield a road to the transport wagons, the infantry mark time at the crossroads," complained a supply officer. While falling back, the units had to reform and collect again around their flags, report their losses, receive replacements of men and officers from the depots of reserves in the rear. For one corps alone, the IVth of Ruffey's Army, a total of 8,000 reserves, a quarter of its strength, were sent up to replace losses, company by company. Among the officers, devoted to the doctrine of *élan*, casualties from the rank of general down were severe. One of the causes of the debacle, in the opinion of Colonel Tanant, a staff officer with the Third Army, was that general officers would not direct operations from their proper place in the rear but led from the front; "they performed the function of corporals, not commanders."

But now from bitter experience they had learned revised tactics. Now they entrenched. One regiment, shoveling all day in its shirt sleeves under the hot sun, dug trenches deep enough to shoot from standing up. Another, ordered to entrench and organize the defense of a woods, passed the night without incident and moved on again at four in the morning, "almost sorry to go without a fight . . . for by now we are seized with anger at this continual retreat."

Yielding as little territory as possible, Joffre intended to make his stand as near as he could to the point of breakthrough. The line he laid down in General Order No. 2 was along the Somme, about fifty miles below the Mons Canal and the Sambre. Poincaré wondered whether there was not some self-deception lurking in Joffre's optimism, and there were others who would have preferred a line farther back, allowing time to solidify a front. From the day after the debacle the men in Paris already saw Paris as the front, but Joffre's mind had not traveled back to the capital and there was no one in France to question Joffre.

The government was in a frenzy; ministers, according to Poincaré, in a "state of consternation"; deputies, according to Messimy, in a "panic that painted a livid mask of fear upon their faces." Removed from direct contact with the front, lacking eyewitness evidence, uninformed as to strategy, dependent on the "laconic and sibylline" communiqués of GQG and on rumor, supposition, and conflicting reports, they were responsible to the country and the people while without authority over the military conduct of the war. Underneath the rubbed and polished sentences of Joffre's report Poincaré could make out the sharp edges of the truth—"a triple avowal of invasion, defeat and the loss of Alsace." He felt his immediate duty was to tell the country the facts and prepare the people for the "terrible trials" that lay ahead. That the need to prepare Paris for a siege was even more immediate, he did not yet realize.

Early that morning the nakedness of the capital was made known to Messimy, as Minister of War. General Hirschauer of the Engineers, in charge of the defense works and Chief of Staff to General Michel, the Military Governor of Paris, came to see him at 6:00 A.M. This was several hours before Joffre's telegram arrived, but Hirschauer had learned privately of the disaster at Charleroi and his mind took in the distance from the frontiers to the capital in a single stride. He told Messimy flatly that the defenses of the perimeter were not ready to be manned. Despite elaborate studies with every requirement foreseen, "the fortifications existed on paper but nothing had been done on the ground." Originally the date given for the defense works to be usable was August 25, but such was the faith in the French offensive that it had been put off to September 15. Because of reluctance to begin the property destruction involved in felling trees and razing houses for fields of fire and in digging trenches, no definite order for these major measures had been given. Construction of gun emplacements and infantry posts, laying of barbed wire, cutting of timber for parapets, preparation of storage shelters for ammunition were not even half finished, provisioning of the city barely begun. As Military Governor and responsible for the defenses, General Michel, perhaps permanently discouraged by the rejection of his defensive plan in 1911, had been lack-luster and ineffectual. His tenure of command which came into being with the outbreak of war had quickly floundered in anarchy and hesitancy. Confirmed in the poor opinion he had had of Michel in 1911, Messimy had called in General Hirschauer on August 13 with orders to make up the delays and complete the defenses in three weeks. Hirschauer now confessed the task was impossible.

"Palaver is the rule," he said. "Every morning I lose three hours in reports and discussions which have no results. Every decision requires an arbitration. Even as Chief of Staff to the Governor, I cannot, as a simple general of brigade, give orders to the generals of division who command the sectors."

As was his habit Messimy sent at once for Gallieni and was conferring with him when Joffre's telegram came in. Its opening phrase blaming the failure on "our troops who have not shown in the field the offensive qualities expected of them," depressed Messimy inordinately, but Gallieni looked for facts, distances, and place names.

"Briefly," he said without sentiment, "you may expect the German armies to be before the walls of Paris in twelve days. Is Paris ready to withstand a siege?"

Forced to answer No, Messimy asked Gallieni to return later, intending in the meantime to obtain authority from the government to name him Military Governor in place of Michel. At that moment he was "stupefied" to learn from another visitor, General Ebener, GQG's representative at the War Ministry, that Paris was to lose two reserve divisions, the 61st and 62nd, assigned to her defense. Joffre had ordered them north to reinforce a group of three Territorial divisions, the only French troops between the British and the sea where Kluck's right-wing corps were sweeping down. Raging, Messimy protested that, as Paris belonged to the Zone of the Interior rather than the Zone of the Armies, the 61st and 62nd were under his command, not Joffre's, and could not be removed from the Paris garrison without his permission and that of the Premier and the President of the Republic. The order was already "in execution" Ebener replied, adding in some embarrassment that he himself was to go north in command of the two divisions.

Messimy rushed off to the Elysée Palace to see Poincaré, who "exploded" on hearing the news but was equally helpless. To his question what troops were left, Messimy had to reply, one reserve cavalry division, three Territorial divisions, and no active units except a few cadres at the army depots in the area. To the two men it seemed that the government and capital of France were left without means of defense and unable to command any. Only one resource was left—Gallieni.

He was now again asked to supplant Michel as he, instead of Joffre, might have done in 1911. At the age of twenty-one, as a second lieutenant just out of St. Cyr, Gallieni had fought at Sedan and been held prisoner for some time in Germany, where he learned the language. He chose to make his further military career in the colonies where France was "growing soldiers." Although the Staff College clique professed to regard colonial service as "*le tourisme*," Gallieni's fame as the conqueror of Madagascar brought him, like Lyautey of Morocco, to the top rank of the French Army. He kept a notebook in German, English, and Italian called *Erinnerungen of my life di ragazzo*, and never ceased studying, whether it was Russian or the development of heavy artillery or the comparative administrations of the colonial powers. He wore a pince-nez and a heavy gray mustache that was rather at odds with his elegant, autocratic figure. He carried himself like an officer on parade. Tall and spare, with a distant, untouchable, faintly stern air, he resembled no other French officer of his time. Poincaré described the impression he made: "straight, slender and upright with head erect and piercing eyes behind his glasses, he appeared to us as an imposing example of powerful humanity."

At sixty-five, he was suffering from the prostatitis of which, after two · operations, he was to die within two years. Bereaved by the death of his wife within the last month, and having renounced the highest post in the French Army three years earlier, he was beyond personal ambition, a man with little time left, as irritably impatient with the politics of the army as with the rivalries of politicians. In the last months before the war when, prior to his retirement in April, the intrigues of the cliques swirled around him, some to have him named Minister of War or Commander in Chief designate in place of Joffre, others to reduce his pension or remove his friends, his diary was filled with disgust for life, for "that miserable thing, politics," for the "clan of *arrivistes*," for unreadiness and inefficiency in the army and with no great admiration for Joffre. "When I was riding I passed him in the Bois today—on foot as usual. . . . How fat and heavy he is; he will hardly last out his three years." Now in France's gravest moment since 1870 he was being asked to take over a botched job, called to defend Paris without an army. He believed it was essential to hold the capital for moral effect as well as for its railroads, supplies, and industrial capacity. He knew well enough that Paris could not be defended from the inside like a fortress, but only by an army giving battle beyond the perimeter, an army that would have to come from Joffre—who had other plans.

"They do not want to defend Paris," he said to Messimy that night when he was formally requested to become Military Governor. "In the eyes of our strategists Paris is a geographical expression—a town like any other. What do you give me to defend this immense place enclosing the heart and brain of France? A few Territorial divisions and one fine division from Africa. That is nothing but a drop in the ocean. If Paris is not to suffer the fate of Liège and Namur it must be covered for 100 kilometers around and to cover it requires an army. Give me an army of three active corps and I will agree to become Governor of Paris; on this condition, formal and explicit, you can count on me for its defense."

Messimy thanked him so effusively, "shaking my hands several times and even kissing me," that Gallieni felt assured "from the warmth of these demonstrations that the place I was succeeding to was not an enviable one."

How he was to extract one active corps, much less three, from Joffre, Messimy did not know. The only active unit he could lay his hands on was the African division mentioned by Gallieni, the 45th Infantry from Algiers, which had been formed, apart from the regular mobilization orders, at the direct instance of the Ministry of War and was just disembarking in the south. Despite repeated telephonic demands for it from GQG, Messimy determined to hang on to this "fresh and splendid" division at all costs. He still needed five more. To force Joffre to supply them in order to satisfy Gallieni's condition meant a direct clash of authority between the government and the Commander in Chief. Messimy trembled. On the solemn and unforgettable Mobilization Day he had sworn to himself "never to fall into the error committed by the War Ministry of 1870" whose interference, at the command of the Empress Eugénie, sent General MacMahon on the march to Sedan. He had carefully examined in company with Poincaré the Decrees of 1913 delimiting authority in wartime, and in all the ardor of the first day had voluntarily assured Joffre that he interpreted them as assigning the political conduct of war to the government and the military conduct to the Commander in Chief as his "absolute and exclusive domain." Further, the decrees, as he read them, gave the Commander in Chief "extended powers" in the country as a whole and "absolute" power, civil as well as military, in the Zone of the

Armies. "You are the master, we are your purveyors," he had finished. Not surprisingly Joffre "without discussion" had agreed with him. Poincaré and Viviani's neophyte Cabinet had obediently concurred.

Where was he now to find the authority he had forsworn? Searching almost until midnight back through the Decrees for a legal basis, Messimy grasped at a phrase charging the civil government "with the vital interests of the country." To prevent the capital from falling to the enemy was surely a vital interest of the country, but what form should an order to Joffre take? Through the remainder of an agonized and sleepless night the Minister of War tried to nerve himself to compose an order to the Commander in Chief. After four hours of painful labor in the lonely stretch between 2:00 and 6:00 A.M., he achieved two sentences headed "Order" which instructed Joffre that if "victory does not crown our armies and they are forced to retreat, a minimum of three active corps in good condition must be sent to the entrenched camp of Paris. The receipt of this order is to be acknowledged." Sent by telegram, it was also delivered by hand at eleven next morning, August 25, accompanied by a "personal and friendly" letter in which Messimy added, "the importance of this order will not escape you."

By this time word of the defeat at the frontiers and the extent of the retreat was spreading through Paris. Ministers and deputies were clamoring for someone to blame as "responsible"; public opinion, they said, would demand it. In the antechambers of the Elysée mutterings against Joffre were heard: ". . . an idiot . . . incapable . . . fire him on the spot." Messimy as War Minister was equally favored; "the lobbies are out for your skin," his adjutant whispered. To affirm the "sacred union" of all parties and strengthen Viviani's new and feeble ministry was a necessity in the crisis. Approaches were being made to France's leading political figures to join the government. The oldest, most feared and respected, Clemenceau, the Tiger of France, although a bitter opponent of Poincaré, was the obvious first choice. Viviani found him in a "violent temper" and without desire to join a government he expected to be out of office in two weeks.

"No, no, don't count on me," he said. "In a fortnight you will be torn to ribbons, I am not going to have anything to do with it." After this "paroxysm of passion" he burst into tears, embraced Viviani, but continued to decline to join him in office. A triumvirate made up of Briand, a former premier; Delcassé, the most distinguished and experienced Foreign Minister of the prewar period; and Millerand, a former Minister of War, was

willing to join as a group but only on condition that Delcassé and Millerand be given their old portfolios at the expense of the present holders,
Doumergue at the Foreign Office and Messimy at the War Office. With
this uncomfortable bargain, known so far only to Poincaré, hanging in
the air, the Cabinet met at ten o'clock that morning. In their minds ministers heard the sound of guns and saw broken, fleeing armies and spike-
helmeted hordes marching south, but attempting to preserve dignity and
calm, they followed the routine procedure of speaking in turn on departmental matters. As they reported on bank moratoriums, on disturbance to
the judicial process by the call-up of magistrates, on Russian aims in Constantinople, Messimy's agitation mounted. From an early pitch of enthusiasm he was nearing despair. After Hirschauer's disclosures and with
Gallieni's twelve days ringing in his ears, he felt that "hours were worth
centuries and minutes counted as years." When discussion turned upon
diplomacy in the Balkans and Poincaré brought up the subject of Albania,
he exploded.

"To hell with Albania!" he shouted, striking the table a terrible blow.
He denounced the pretense of calm as an "undignified farce," and when
begged by Poincaré to control himself, refused, saying, "I don't know about
your time but mine is too precious to waste." He flung in the face of his
colleagues Gallieni's prediction that the Germans would be outside Paris
by September 5. Everyone began talking at once, demands were made for
Joffre's removal, and Messimy was reproached for passing from "systematic
optimism to dangerous pessimism." One positive result gained was agreement to the appointment of Gallieni in place of Michel.

While Messimy returned to the Rue St. Dominique to remove Michel
a second time from office, his own removal was being exacted by Millerand,
Delcassé, and Briand. They claimed he was responsible for the false optimism of the communiqués; he was "overwrought and nervy," and besides,
his office was wanted for Millerand. A thick-set, taciturn man with an
ironic manner, Millerand was a one-time socialist of undoubted ability
and courage whose "untiring energy and sangfroid," Poincaré felt, were
badly needed. He saw Messimy becoming "gloomier and gloomier," and
since a War Minister who "foresees a great defeat" was not the most desirable colleague, the President agreed to sacrifice him. The ministerial rites
would be performed gracefully: Messimy and Doumergue would be asked
to resign and become Ministers without Portfolio; General Michel would
be offered a mission to the Czar. These soothing arrangements were not
accepted by their intended victims.

Michel stormed when asked by Messimy to resign, protested loudly and angrily and obstinately refused to go. Becoming equally excited, Messimy shouted at Michel that if he persisted in his refusal he would leave the room, not for his own office at the Invalides, but for the military prison of Cherche-Midi under guard. As their cries resounded from the room Viviani fortuitously arrived, calmed the disputants, and eventually persuaded Michel to give way.

Hardly was the official decree appointing Gallieni "Military Governor and Commandant of the Armies of Paris" signed next day when it became Messimy's turn to storm when asked for his resignation by Poincaré and Viviani. "I refuse to yield my post to Millerand, I refuse to do you the pleasure of resigning, I refuse to become a Minister without Portfolio." If they wanted to get rid of him after the "crushing labor" he had sustained in the last month, then the whole government would have to resign, and in that case, he said, "I have an officer's rank in the Army and a Mobilization order in my pocket. I shall go to the front." No persuasion availed. The government was forced to resign and was reconstituted next day. Millerand, Delcassé, Briand, Alexander Ribot, and two new socialist ministers replaced five former members, including Messimy. He departed as a major to join Dubail's army and to serve at the front until 1918, rising to general of division.

His legacy to France, Gallieni, was left "Commander of the Armies of Paris" without an army. The three active corps which were to run like a red thread through the dark and tangled confusion of the next twelve days were not forthcoming from Joffre. The Generalissimo instantly detected in Messimy's telegram "the menace of government interference in the conduct of operations." When he was busy laying hold of every brigade he could find to resume battle on the Somme, the idea of sparing three active corps "in good condition" for the capital appealed to him as little as the idea of submitting to ministerial dictation. Having no intention of doing either, he ignored the War Minister's order.

"Yes, I have the order here," admitted his deputy, General Belin, rapping his safe, when visited next day by General Hirschauer who had been sent by Gallieni to demand an answer. "The government is taking a terrible responsibility to ask for three corps to defend Paris. It might be the origin of a disaster. What does Paris matter!" Millerand, too, arrived to be told by Joffre that there could be no useful defense of Paris except by the mobile army in the field which was now needed to the last man for the maneuver and the battle that would decide the fate of the country. The distress of the government, the threat to Paris, moved him not at all. The loss of the capital, he said, would not mean the end of the struggle.

In order to dam the open space in front of the German right wing, his immediate aim was to bring the new Sixth Army into position. Its nucleus was the Army of Lorraine, hastily scraped together only a few days before and thrown into the Battle of the Frontiers under General Maunoury, called out of retirement to command it. A svelte, delicate, small-boned veteran of sixty-seven, wounded as a lieutenant in 1870, Maunoury was a former Military Governor of Paris and member of the Supreme War Council of whom Joffre had said, "This is the complete soldier." The Army of Lorraine consisted of the VIIth Corps, the same that had made the first dash into Alsace under the unfortunate General Bonneau, and the 55th and 56th reserve divisions taken from Ruffey's Army, which were displaying, as the reserves did again and again, a dependable valor that was one of the elements to sustain France. On the day they received Joffre's orders for transfer to the west, the 55th and 56th were engaged in a spirited battle to prevent passage of the Crown Prince's Army between Verdun and Toul which proved one of the great feats of the retreat. Just when their firm stand was supporting the flank of a counteroffensive by Ruffey's Army in the vital Briey basin, they were snatched from the field to shore up the failing front on the left.

They were railed to Amiens through Paris, where they were switched to the northern railways, already congested by the demands of the BEF. Although French railroad movements had not been polished by the best brains of the General Staff to the fanatic perfection of the German, the transfer was managed quickly, if not smoothly, by means of a French equivalent for German thoroughness called *le système D*, in which the "D" stands for *se débrouiller*, meaning "to muddle through" or "work it out somehow." Maunoury's troops were already detraining at Amiens on August 26, but it was not soon enough. The front was falling back faster than the new army could be got into position, and on the far end of the line von Kluck's pursuit had already caught up with the British.

If there could have been an observer in a balloon high enough to have a view of the whole French frontier from the Vosges to Lille, he would have seen a rim of red, the *pantalons rouges* of 70 French divisions and near the left end, a tiny wedge of khaki, the four British divisions. On August 24 these were joined by the newly arrived 4th Division and 19th Brigade from England, making a total of five and a half British divisions.

Now that the enveloping maneuver of the German right wing was at last clear, the British found themselves holding a place in the line more important than had been intended for them in Plan 17. They were not, however, holding the end of the line unsupported. Joffre had hurriedly sent Sordet's tired Cavalry Corps to add to a group of three French Territorial divisions under General d'Amade in the space between the British and the sea. These were reinforced by the garrison division of Lille which on August 24 was declared an open city, and evacuated. ("If they get as far as Lille," General de Castelnau had said not so long ago, "so much the better for us.") If Joffre's plan were to work, it was essential that the BEF hold the space between Lanrezac and the newly forming Sixth Army. Under General Order No. 2 Joffre intended the BEF to conform to the general pace of the retreat and, once they reached the Somme at St. Quentin, hold firm.

But that was not now the British intention. Sir John French, Murray, and even Wilson, the once enthusiastic progenitor of the plan, were horrified at the unexpected peril of their position. Not one or two but four German corps were advancing against them; Lanrezac's Army was in full retreat, uncovering their right; the whole French offensive had collapsed. Under these shocks, following immediately upon first contact with the enemy, Sir John French gave way at once to the conviction that the campaign was lost. His one idea was to save the BEF in which were nearly all Britain's trained soldiers and staff. He feared it was about to be enveloped either on his left or on his right, in the gap between him and Lanrezac. Taking justification in Kitchener's order not to risk the army, he thought no further of the purpose that had brought him to France but only of extricating his forces from the danger zone. While his troops were retreating to Le Cateau, the Commander in Chief and Headquarters Staff, on August 25, moved twenty-six miles farther back to St. Quentin on the Somme.

With bitterness the British soldiers who felt proud of their fighting at Mons found themselves caught up in continued retreat. Such was their Commander's anxiety to remove them from the danger of von Kluck's enveloping arm that he gave them no rest. Under a blazing sun the soldiers, without proper food or sleep, shuffled along, hardly awake, and when halted fell asleep instantly, standing up. Smith-Dorrien's Corps fought constant rearguard actions as the retreat from Mons began, and although Kluck's pursuit kept them under heavy artillery fire, the Germans were unable to hold the British to a standstill.

Believing the British to be peculiarly battle-wise "from their experience of small wars," German soldiers felt at a disadvantage, as if they had been Redcoats pitted against Ethan Allen's Green Mountain Men. They complained bitterly that the English "were up to all the tricks of the trade." On the second day, as at Mons, they "again vanished without leaving a trace."

Under pressure some of the British were forced onto unplanned lines of retreat. In an effort to get food to them, General "Wully" Robertson, the Quartermaster General, an unorthodox individual who had risen from private, ordered supplies to be dumped at crossroads. Some failed to be picked up, and German reports of these food dumps confirmed OHL in the impression of a foe in disorganized retreat.

When the British reached Le Cateau by the evening of August 25, the nearest corps of Lanrezac's Army had fallen back to a position on a level with, but no further south than, the BEF. Sir John, however, regarding himself as betrayed by what he called Lanrezac's "headlong" retreat, was in a mood to have nothing more to do with him. Lanrezac, rather than the enemy, seemed to him the cause of all that had gone wrong and, when reporting to Kitchener his troops' unwillingness to retreat, he said, "I shall explain to them that the operations of our Allies are the cause of this." He sent orders for the retreat to continue next day to St. Quentin and Noyon. At St. Quentin, seventy miles from the capital, the signposts begin giving the distance to Paris.

On the afternoon of August 25 when Smith-Dorrien arrived in Le Cateau a few hours ahead of his troops and went to look for the Commander in Chief, Sir John had already left, and only Sir Archibald Murray, his hard-working Chief of Staff, could be found. Usually calm, balanced, and reflective, the opposite of his Chief, Murray would have been an excellent complement for Sir John in an aggressive mood, but as he was by nature cautious and pessimistic, he acted as a stimulus to Sir John's gloom. Now worn, harassed, and overworked, he could give Smith-Dorrien no news of Haig's Corps which was expected to billet that night at Landrecies, twelve miles east of Le Cateau.

As Haig's troops were entering Landrecies, they encountered on the road a body of troops who wore French uniforms and whose officer spoke in French when challenged. Suddenly the newcomers "without the slightest warning lowered their bayonets and charged." They proved to be part of von Kluck's IVth Corps who, like the British, were scheduled to billet that night at Landrecies. In the ensuing skirmish about two regiments and a gun battery were involved on each side, but Haig, in the tension and uncertainty of darkness, thought himself under "heavy attack" and telephoned Headquarters to "send help. . . . Situation very critical."

Hearing such words from the cool Haig, Sir John French and his staff could not do otherwise than believe the Ist Corps to be in the greatest danger. Murray, who had rejoined GHQ at St. Quentin, suffered a collapse from the shock. He was sitting at a table studying a map when an aide brought him a telegram, and a moment later another officer noticed he had slumped forward in a faint. Sir John was equally affected. His uncertain temperament, wildly responsive to others, had long been influenced by that self-possessed and model officer who commanded the Ist Corps. In 1899 Haig had lent him £2,000 to meet his creditors, without which he would have had to leave the army. Now, when Haig called for help, Sir John French immediately saw envelopment, or worse—penetration by the enemy between the Ist and IInd Corps. Assuming the worst, GHQ sent orders altering Haig's line of retreat for the following day with the result that Haig's Corps was set on a line of march on the opposite side of the Oise from Smith-Dorrien's Corps; direct contact was severed and not regained for the next seven days.

Besides accomplishing the splitting of the BEF, Haig's excited and exaggerated estimate of the attack at Landrecies had an effect out of all proportion to its cause. It deepened the alarm of his old friend and impressionable Commander so that he became more intent than ever upon extricating the British Army at all hazards, and it made him that much more susceptible to the next blow. For, at this moment, as the harrowing night of August 25 paled toward dawn, he received another shock. Smith-Dorrien sent word that the IInd Corps was too closely beset by the enemy to get away and would have to make a stand and fight at Le Cateau. Appalled, the men at GHQ regarded him as as good as lost.

What had happened was that General Allenby, commander of the Cavalry Division on Smith-Dorrien's flank, had discovered during the night that the high ground and ridges he would have to occupy to cover the next day's retreat were held by the enemy. Unable to get in touch with GHQ, he went at 2:00 A.M. to consult Smith-Dorrien. Allenby warned him that the enemy was in a position to attack at the first sign of daylight and that unless the IInd Corps could move "*at once* and get away *in the dark*," it would be forced into battle before it could start the day's march. Smith-Dorrien called in his divisional commanders, who told him that some men were still coming in, many were milling around looking for their units, all were too weary to move before morning. They reported also that roads were clogged with transport and refugees and in some places washed out by the heavy storm. Silence fell in the little room. To move at once was impossible; to stay where they were and fight was a reversal of orders. As his field headquarters had no telephone communication with GHQ, the corps commander would have to decide for himself. Turning to Allenby, Smith-Dorrien asked if he would accept orders from him. Allenby said he would.

"Very well, gentlemen, we will fight," Smith-Dorrien announced, adding that he would ask General Snow of the newly arrived 4th Division to act under him as well. His message embodying the decision was sent off by motorcar to GHQ, where it caused consternation at 5:00 A.M.

Henry Wilson, like the equally ebullient Messimy, had gone in one stride from verve and fervor to defeatism. When the offensive plan, of which on the British side he was the chief architect, collapsed, he collapsed with it, at least momentarily, and with significant effect on his Chief over whose slower mind he exerted considerable influence. Although his gift of optimism, wit, and laughter could not be long repressed and was the only thing to keep Staff spirits afloat in the next days, he was now convinced of coming calamity for which he may have felt responsible.

A messenger was sent off by motorcycle to summon Smith-Dorrien to the nearest telephone. "If you stand there and fight," Wilson said to him, "there will be another Sedan." He insisted from his position twenty-six miles away that the danger could not be so great as to require a stand because "troops fighting Haig cannot fight you." Smith-Dorrien patiently explained the circumstances once more and added that in any event it was impossible to break away as the action had already begun and he could hear the guns firing as he spoke. "Good luck to you," Wilson replied; "yours is the first cheerful voice I have heard in three days."

For eleven hours on August 26 the IInd Corps and General Snow's division and a half fought at Le Cateau a rearguard action such as the French Armies were fighting on this and every other day of the retreat. Von Kluck had given orders for that day to continue "pursuit of the beaten enemy." As the most devoted disciple of Schlieffen's precept to "brush the channel with his sleeve," he was still pulling westward and, to complete the envelopment of the British, ordered his two right-wing corps to make forced marches in a southwestward direction. As a result they were never in action against the British at all on that day, but instead came up against "strong French hostile forces." These were D'Amade's Territorials and

Sordet's Cavalry whom Smith-Dorrien had informed of his predicament and who by their demonstrations barred the way around the British flank. The delay caused to the Germans, acknowledged Smith-Dorrien later, "and the brave front shown by these Territorials were of vital importance to us as otherwise it is almost certain we should have had another Corps against us on the 26th."

On von Kluck's left faulty intelligence or poor maneuvering kept another of his corps out of reach so that, although he disposed of superior numbers, he did not in fact have more than three infantry divisions in battle against Smith-Dorrien's three at Le Cateau. He had, however, assembled the artillery of five divisions which opened fire at dawn. From shallow trenches hastily and inadequately dug by French civilians, including women, the British repelled German infantry assaults with their rapid and deadly rifle fire. Nevertheless the Germans, flinging wave after wave of men against them, advanced. In one sector they surrounded a company of Argylls who kept up their rifle fire, "bringing down man after man and counting their scores aloud" while the Germans "kept sounding the British 'Cease Fire' and gesturing to persuade the men to surrender but in vain," until finally the group was rushed and overwhelmed. Other terrible holes were torn in the line. To disengage—the most difficult part of the battle—was yet to be done, and at 5:00 P.M. Smith-Dorrien judged the moment had come. It was then or never. Because of gaps and losses and infiltration by the enemy at certain points, the order to break off and retreat could not be got to all units at the same time. Some stayed in position for many hours longer, firing steadily until taken or until they got away in the dark. One unit, the Gordon Highlanders, never received its orders and, except for a few men who made their escape, ceased to exist as a battalion. Losses for that day alone in the three and a half divisions who fought at Le Cateau were over 8,000 men and 38 guns, more than twice as much as at Mons and equal to the 20 per cent casualty rate that the French suffered in August. Among the missing were some who spent the next four years in German prison camps.

Because of darkness, the fatigue of forced marches, their own heavy losses, and the confusing British habit of "slipping away unseen" in the darkness, the Germans did not immediately pursue. Kluck gave orders to halt until next day, when he expected the enveloping maneuver of his right-wing corps to take effect. For that day Smith-Dorrien's decision to turn and face a superior enemy in a pitched battle had succeeded in preventing the planned envelopment and destruction of the BEF.

On reaching St. Quentin, Smith-Dorrien found GHQ had left there at midday while the battle for the life or annihilation of the BEF was still in progress and had moved to Noyon, twenty miles farther to the rear. Troops in the town were not encouraged to see the army's chiefs depart in automobiles headed south while the guns were firing in the north. In that inevitable judgment of a countryman, "The truth is that on the 26th Lord French and his staff completely lost their heads." Sir Douglas Haig, who had by now recovered his, queried, "No news of II Corps except sound of guns from direction of Le Cateau. Can I Corps be of any assistance?" GHQ was too paralyzed to give him any answer. Failing to hear from Headquarters, Haig tried to reach Smith-Dorrien directly, saying he could hear the sound of battle but, as a consequence of the separation of the two corps, "we could form no idea of how we could assist you." By the time he sent the message the battle was over. Meanwhile GHQ had given up the IInd Corps for lost. Colonel Huguet, still attached as liaison officer, reflected their mood in a telegram he dispatched to Joffre at 8:00 P.M., "Battle lost by the English Army which appears to have lost cohesion."

At 1:00 A.M. Smith-Dorrien, having been in combat for the last four of the six days he had been in France, reached Noyon and found everyone at GHQ in bed asleep. Routed out, Sir John French appeared in his nightshirt and, seeing Smith-Dorrien turn up alive with a report that the IInd Corps was not lost but saved, rebuked him for taking too cheerful a view of the situation. Having had a bad fright, Sir John now gave way to furious anger, the more easily as he had resented Smith-Dorrien's appointment, in place of his own choice, from the beginning. The man did not even belong to the cavalry and had taken it upon himself at Le Cateau to override Staff orders. Although Sir John was forced to acknowledge in his official dispatch * that this had resulted in the "saving of the left wing," he did not soon recover from his fright. The losses of Le Cateau seemed even higher than they were until several thousand of the missing men who had merged with the trudging lines of French refugees and followed the retreat, or had made

---

* The dispatch reads, "The saving of the left wing of the army under my command on the morning of the 26th of August could never have been accomplished unless a commander of rare and unusual coolness, intrepidity and determination had been present personally to conduct the operation." Having evidently written or signed this report in one of the extreme swings of his unreliable temperament, Sir John reverted to antipathy, did not rest until he succeeded in having Smith-Dorrien recalled in 1915, and continued a malevolent vendetta against him publicly in the book he published after the war.

their way through German lines to Antwerp, thence to England, and back to France, eventually rejoined the army. Total casualties for the BEF's first five days in action proved to be just short of 15,000. They intensified the Commander in Chief's anxiety to bring his army out of the fight, out of danger, out of France.

While the Battle of Le Cateau was in progress, Joffre summoned a meeting at St. Quentin of Sir John French, Lanrezac, and their staffs to explain the instructions of General Order No. 2. When he began with a polite inquiry as to the situation of the British Army, he evoked a tirade from Sir John who said that he had been violently attacked by superior numbers, that he was threatened by envelopment on his left, that his right was uncovered by Lanrezac's headlong retreat, and that his troops were too exhausted to resume the offensive. Joffre, who believed above all in maintaining an appearance of calm before the Staff, was shocked by the Field Marshal's "excited tone." Lanrezac, after hearing Henry Wilson's somewhat softened translation of his chief's remarks, merely shrugged. Unable to issue an order, Joffre expressed the hope that the British Commander would conform to the plan contained in the new General Order of the day before.

Sir John looked blank and said he knew nothing of any such Order. Murray, suffering from his collapse of the night before, was absent. A variety of astonished and quizzical French gazes were turned on Wilson who explained that the Order had been received during the night but not yet "studied." Joffre explained its provisions but with obviously failing confidence. Discussion faltered, pauses grew longer, the embarrassment became painful, and the meeting broke up without having achieved any agreement from the British for combined action. With an impression of the "fragility" of his left wing, Joffre returned to GQG where he was met by fresh news of weakness on all fronts, discouragement in every grade of the army, including the Staff, and finally, at the end of the day, by Huguet's black telegram reporting the English Army as having "lost cohesion."

Von Kluck was under the same impression. His orders for the 27th were to "cut off the British who were in full flight westwards," and he reported to OHL that he was about to round up "all six" British divisions (only five were in France) and "if the English stand on the 27th the double envelopment may yet bring a great success." This brilliant prospect, coming the day after the fall of Namur and coinciding with Bülow's report that his opponent, the French Fifth Army, was also a "beaten enemy," confirmed OHL in the impression of imminent victory. "The German Armies have entered France from Cambrai to the Vosges after a series of continually victorious combats," announced OHL's official communiqué on August 27. "The enemy, beaten all along the line, is in full retreat . . . and is not capable of offering serious resistance to the German advance."

Amid the general enthusiasm von Kluck received his reward. When he rebelled furiously at an order of von Bülow's to invest Maubeuge, which he claimed was von Bülow's duty, and demanded to know if he was to remain subordinate, OHL on August 27 restored his independence. The attempt to keep the three armies of the right wing under one command, which had caused so much friction, was abandoned; but as the rest of the way to victory seemed easy, this did not appear important at the moment.

Von Bülow, however, was exceedingly annoyed. In the center of the right wing, he was constantly bedeviled by his neighbors' refusal to keep in step. Already, he warned OHL, Hausen's delays had caused a "regrettable gap" between the Third and Second Armies. Hausen himself, whose chief concern, second only to his reverence for titles, was a passionate attention to the amenities offered by each night's billets, was equally annoyed. On August 27, his first night in France, no château was available for himself and the Crown Prince of Saxony who accompanied him. They had to sleep in the house of a *sous-préfet* which had been left in complete disorder; "even the beds had not been made!" The following night was worse: he had to endure quarters in the house of a M. Chopin, a peasant! The dinner was meager, the lodgings "not spacious," and the staff had to accommodate itself in the nearby rectory whose curé had gone to war. His old mother, who looked like a witch, hung around and "wished us all at the devil." Red streaks in the sky showed that Rocroi, through which his troops had just passed, was in flames. Happily the following night was spent in the beautifully furnished home of a wealthy French industrialist who was "absent." Here the only discomfort suffered by Hausen was the sight of a wall covered by espaliered pear trees heavy with fruit that was "unfortunately not completely ripe." However, he enjoyed a delightful reunion with Count Münster, Major Count Kilmansegg, Prince Schoenburg-Waldenburg of the Hussars, and Prince Max, Duke of Saxe, acting as Catholic chaplain, to whom Hausen was able to convey the gratifying news that he had just received by telephone the best wishes for success of the Third Army from his sister, the Princess Mathilda.

Hausen complained that his Saxons had been on the march for ten days through hostile country, in the heat and often in battle. Supplies were not keeping up with the advance, bread and meat were lacking, troops had to live off the local livestock, horses had not had enough fodder, and yet he had managed an average march of 23 kilometers a day. In fact, this was the least required of the German armies. Kluck's Army on the rim of the wheel covered 30 kilometers or more a day and in some forced marches 40. He managed this by having the men sleep along the roadside instead of spreading out to left and right, and thus saved 6 or 7 kilometers a day. As German lines of communication stretched out and troops advanced farther from the railheads, food supplies often failed. Horses ate grain directly from unharvested fields and men marched a whole day on nothing but raw carrots and cabbages. As hot, as tired, and with feet as sore as their enemies, the Germans were increasingly hungry but on schedule.

Halfway between Brussels and Paris on August 28, von Kluck was gratified to receive a telegram from the Kaiser expressing "my imperial gratitude" for the First Army's "decisive victories" and his congratulations upon its approach to the "heart of France." That night by the light of bivouac fires regimental bands played the victory song "Heil dir im Siegeskranz" and, as one of Kluck's officers wrote in his diary, "the sound was taken up by thousands of voices. Next morning we resumed our march in the hope of celebrating the anniversary of Sedan before Paris."

On the same day a new and tempting idea presented itself to von Kluck which before the week was over was to leave its mark on history. Reconnaissance showed that the French Fifth Army, retreating in front of Bülow, was moving in a southwesterly direction which would bring it across his line of march. He saw a chance to "find the flank of this army . . . force it away from Paris and outflank it," an objective that now seemed to him of more importance than cutting the British off from the coast. He proposed to Bülow that a "wheel inwards" should be made by their two armies. Before anything could be decided, an officer from OHL arrived with a new General Order to all seven armies.

Inspired by a "universal sense of victory," according to the Crown Prince, OHL nevertheless had become aware of the transfer of French forces from Lorraine and now called for a "rapid advance to prevent assembly of fresh bodies of troops and to take from the country as much as possible of its means of continuing the struggle." Kluck's Army was to advance to the Seine southwest of Paris. Bülow's was to move directly upon Paris. Hausen, the Duke of Württemberg, and the Crown Prince were to bring their armies down to the Marne east of Paris, to Château-Thierry, Epernay, and Vitry-le-François respectively. The breakthrough of the French fortress line by the Sixth and Seventh Armies under Prince Rupprecht was left a little vague but they were expected to cross the Moselle between Toul and Epinal, "if the enemy retires." Speed was "urgently desirable" to leave France no time to regroup and organize resistance. With memories of 1870, OHL ordered "severe measures against the population to break any resistance of *franc-tireurs* as quickly as possible" and to prevent a "national rising." Strong resistance by the enemy was expected on the Aisne and then, falling back, on the Marne. Here OHL, echoing Kluck's newborn idea, concluded, "This may necessitate a wheel of the armies from a southwesterly to a southerly direction."

Apart from this suggestion the Order of August 28 followed the original war plan. However, the German Armies who were to carry it out were no longer the same. They were diminished by five corps, the equivalent of a full field army. Kluck had left behind two reserve corps to invest Antwerp and hold Brussels and other parts of Belgium. Bülow and Hausen had each lost one corps to the Russian front: brigades and divisions equal to another had been left to invest Givet and Maubeuge. In order to cover the same ground as originally planned, with the First Army passing west of Paris, the right wing would have to be stretched more thinly or allow gaps to appear between its component armies. Already this was happening: on August 28 Hausen, pulled to his left by the Duke of Württemberg's Army which was in serious combat south of Sedan and demanding "immediate assistance," could not keep up with Bülow on his right and demanded instead that Bülow cover his right flank. The two corps which should have been at the junction of these two armies were on their way to Tannenberg.

OHL began on August 28 to feel its first twinges of concern. Moltke, Stein, and Tappen discussed anxiously whether to send reinforcements from Rupprecht's armies to the right wing, but could not bring themselves to give up their attempt to smash through the French fortress line. The perfect Cannae that Schlieffen had dreamed of and renounced, the double envelopment by the left wing through Lorraine simultaneously with the right wing around Paris, now seemed possible of achievement. Rupprecht's hammer blows fell on Epinal; his armies stood at the gates of Nancy and pounded on the walls of Toul. Since the reduction of Liège, fortified places had "lost their prestige," as Colonel Tappen said, and every day seemed to be the one that would see Rupprecht break through. Destruction of the Belgian railways made a transfer of divisions impractical anyway, and OHL had convinced itself that a forcing of the Charmes Gap between Toul and Epinal was feasible and would obtain, in Tappen's words, "encirclement of the enemy armies in grand style and in the event of success, an end to the war." In consequence, the left wing under Rupprecht was retained in its full strength of twenty-six divisions, about equal to the diminished numbers of the three armies of the right wing. This was not the proportion Schlieffen had in mind when he muttered as he died, "Only make the right wing strong."

Following the drama in Belgium, the eyes of the world were fixed on the course of the war between Brussels and Paris. The public was hardly aware that all this time a fiercer, longer, more sustained battle to force the eastern doors of France raged in Lorraine. Along eighty miles of front from Epinal to Nancy two German armies swayed against the armies of Castelnau and Dubail in locked and nearly static struggle.

On August 24, having massed 400 guns with additions brought from the arsenal at Metz, Rupprecht launched a series of murderous attacks. The French, now turning all their skills to the defense, had dug themselves in and prepared a variety of improvised and ingenious shelters against shellfire. Rupprecht's attacks failed to dislodge Foch's XXth Corps in front of Nancy but farther south succeeded in flinging a salient across the Mortagne, the last river before the gap at Charmes. At once the French saw the opportunity for a flank attack, this time with artillery preparation. Field guns were brought up during the night. On the morning of the 25th Castelnau's order, *"En avant! partout! à fond!"* launched his troops on the offensive. The XXth Corps bounded down from the crest of the Grand Couronné and retook three towns and ten miles of territory. On the right Dubail's Army gained an equal advance in a day of furious combat. General Maud'huy, divisional commander of the *chasseurs alpins*, reviewing his troops before the battle, had them sing the lionhearted chorus of "La Sidi Brahim,"

> Marchons, marchons, marchons,
> Contre les ennemis de la France!

The day ended with many scattered, crippled units not knowing whether they had taken Clezentaine, their given objective. General Maud'huy, on horseback, seeing a haggard, sweat-soaked company looking for their billets, flung out his arm in a gesture pointing forward, and called to them, *"Chasseurs!* Sleep in the village you have conquered!"

For three days of bloody and relentless combat the battle for the Trouée de Charmes and the Grand Couronné continued, reaching a pitch on August 27. Joffre on that day, surrounded by gloom and dismay elsewhere and hard put to find anything to praise, saluted the "courage and tenacity" of the First and Second Armies who, since the opening battles in Lorraine, had fought for two weeks without respite and with "stubborn and unbreakable confidence in victory." They fought with every ounce of strength to hold the door closed against the enemy's battering ram, knowing that if he broke through here the war would be over. They knew nothing of Cannae but they knew Sedan and encirclement.

The need to hold the fortress line was vital, but the situation on his left was even more fragile and forced Joffre to take from his eastern armies a principal element of their energy. That element was Foch, symbol of the "will to victory," whom Joffre now needed to stiffen the failing front on the left.

A dangerous gap was widening between the Fourth and Fifth Armies and now extended to thirty miles. It was caused when General de Langle of the Fourth Army, unwilling to let the Germans cross the Meuse without a fight, gripped the high banks south of Sedan and held off the Duke of Württemberg's Army in a fierce three-day struggle from August 26 to 28. His troops' performance in the Battle of the Meuse, De Langle felt, avenged their defeat in the Ardennes. But their stand was made at the cost of losing contact with Lanrezac's Army, whose retreat was continuing with its flank on the side of the Fourth Army uncovered. It was to hold this space that Joffre sent Foch, giving him command of a special army of three corps,* drawn partly from the Fourth Army and partly from the Third Army. On the day he received the order, Foch learned that his only son, Lieutenant Germain Foch, and his son-in-law, Captain Bécourt, had both been killed on the Meuse.

Farther west, in the area filled by Lanrezac and the British, Joffre still hoped to pin the front to the Somme, but like the foundations of a sand

* Known as the Foch Detachment until September 5, when it became the Ninth Army.

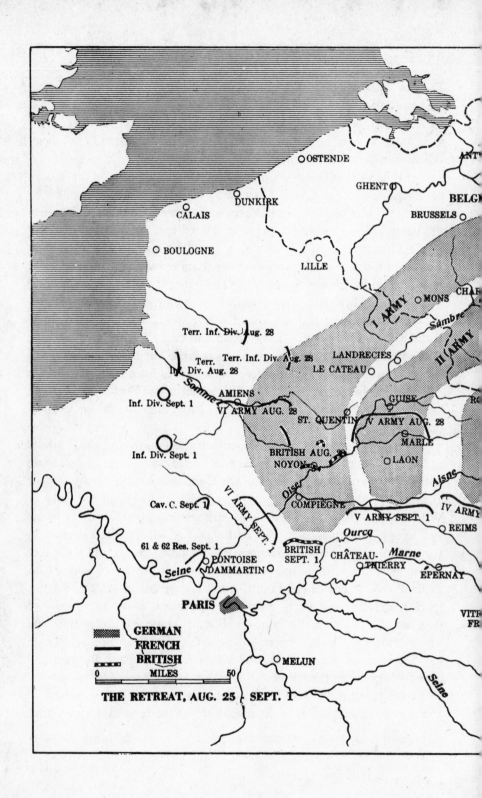

THE RETREAT, AUG. 25 – SEPT. 1

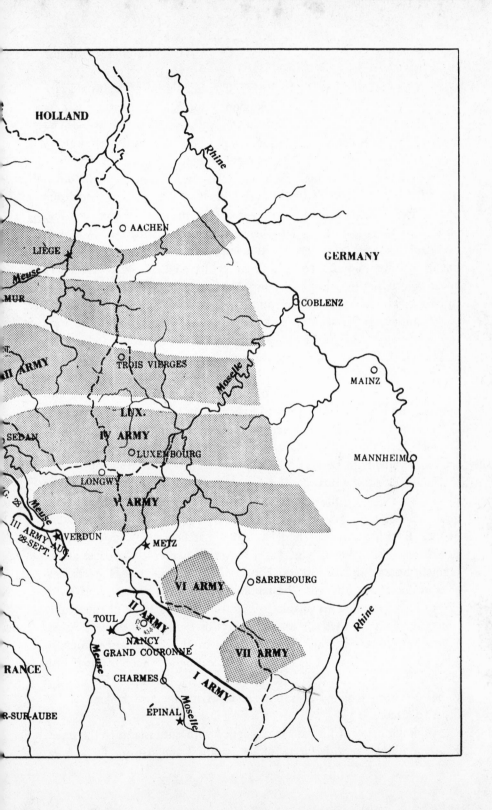

castle, it kept falling away. The British Commander in Chief would give no promise to stay in the line; his cooperation with Lanrezac was at a minimum; and Lanrezac himself, in whom Joffre was losing faith, seemed no more dependable. Although Joffre flung out generals by handfuls in August, he hesitated to dismiss one of Lanrezac's repute. His Staff was still searching out individuals on whom to blame the failure of the offensive; "I have the heads of three generals in my brief case," reported one Staff officer upon returning from a mission to the front. Lanrezac could not be disposed of so easily. Joffre believed the Fifth Army needed a more confident leader. Yet to remove its commander in the midst of retreat might endanger morale. To an aide he confessed that the problem had already given him two sleepless nights—the only occasion of the war known to have caused this grave disturbance.

Meanwhile the 61st and 62nd reserve divisions from Paris who were supposed to join the new Sixth Army had got lost; their commander, General Ebener, had been looking for them all day but nobody knew what had become of them. Fearing that the Sixth Army's detraining area was about to be overrun, Joffre, in a desperate effort to gain time for it to come into position, ordered the Fifth Army to turn and counterattack. This required an offensive in a westerly direction between St. Quentin and Guise. Colonel Alexandre, Joffre's liaison officer with the Fifth Army, conveyed the order verbally to Lanrezac's headquarters, then at Marle some twenty-five miles east of St. Quentin. At the same time, in an effort to assuage the pique and invigorate the spirit of Sir John French, Joffre sent him a telegram expressing the gratitude of the French Army for the brave assistance of their British comrades. Hardly was it dispatched when he learned the British had evacuated St. Quentin, uncovering Lanrezac's left just at the moment he was supposed to attack. According to another of Huguet's missives of doom, the BEF was "beaten and incapable of serious effort" with three of its five divisions unable to take the field again until thoroughly rested and refitted, that is, "for some days or even a few weeks." As Sir John French was reporting the same thing in almost the same words to Kitchener, Huguet cannot be blamed for reflecting the mood of the British chiefs rather than that of the troops or the facts. On top of his message came one from Colonel Alexandre saying Lanrezac was balking at the order to attack.

Although many of his officers responded with enthusiasm to the order, Lanrezac himself regarded it as "almost insane," and said so. To face the

Fifth Army west was to invite attack by the enemy on its open right flank. He believed it was necessary to disengage fully and fall further back to Laon before a firm line could be established and a counterattack made with any chance of success. An attack now in the direction ordered by Joffre required him to turn a semi-disorganized army halfway around in a complicated maneuver, dangerous in view of his position and of the menace on his right. His Chief of Operations, Commandant Schneider, attempted to explain the difficulty to Colonel Alexandre, who expressed astonishment.

"What!" said he, "why, what could be simpler? You are facing north; we ask you to face west to attack from St. Quentin." With a gesture of his hand, five fingers spread out to represent the five corps, he described a right angle turn in the air.

"Don't talk nonsense, *mon colonel!*" burst out Schneider, exasperated.

"Well, if you don't *want* to do anything . . ." Colonel Alexandre said, finishing with a contemptuous shrug which caused Lanrezac who was present to lose his temper and explain at great length and no great tact his opinion of GQG's strategy. By now his confidence in Joffre and GQG was on a par with theirs in him. Having on one wing an independent foreign general who refused to act jointly and on the other an unprotected flank (Foch's detachment did not start forming until two days later, August 29), and being now called upon for a counter-offensive, Lanrezac was under severe stress. His was not a temperament that rose to it. Given a task so fateful for France, and lacking any confidence in Joffre's judgment, he relieved his feelings in the bad temper and caustic abuse for which he had been known even in peacetime. He expounded upon his lack of respect for Joffre whom he called a "sapper," a mere engineer.

"I found General Lanrezac surrounded by a number of officers," reported a Staff officer from one of the corps who came to see him. "He seemed to be extremely displeased and expressed himself in violent language. He did not mince words in his criticism of GQG and our Allies. He was much irritated against the former and the British. The gist of what he was saying was that all he required was to be left alone, that he would retire as far as was necessary, that he would choose his own time and then he would boot the enemy back where he came from." In Lanrezac's own words, "I suffered an anxiety so awful I did not even try to dissimulate from the Staff." To show anxiety before subordinates was bad enough; to compound the sin by public criticism of GQG and the Generalissimo numbered Lanrezac's days of command.

Early next morning, August 28, Joffre himself appeared at Marle where he found Lanrezac haggard, bloodshot, and objecting with nervous gestures to the plan for a counter-offensive. When Lanrezac insisted again upon the risk of enemy attack from the right while his whole army was facing westward, Joffre suddenly fell into a violent fit of rage and shouted: "Do you wish to be relieved of your command? You must march without discussion. The fate of the campaign is in your hands." This spectacular outburst reverberated as far as Paris, taking on added thunder as it traveled, so that by the time it reached President Poincaré's diary next day it was recorded as Joffre's threat to have Lanrezac shot if he hesitated or disobeyed orders to attack.

Convinced of the error of the plan, Lanrezac refused to move without a written order. Having calmed down, Joffre assented and signed an order drawn up at his dictation by Lanrezac's Chief of Staff. In Joffre's opinion, a commander knowing his orders and his duty could have no further cause for disquiet, and he might have said to Lanrezac what he was one day to say to Pétain when giving him orders to hold Verdun under the heaviest bombardment in history, "*Eh bien, mon ami, maintenant vous êtes tranquille.*"

Something less than tranquil, Lanrezac accepted his task but insisted he could not be ready before next morning. All day while the Fifth Army was being turned sideways in a complicated and intricate transfer of corps across each other's fronts, GQG was constantly calling, telling them to "hurry" until Lanrezac in a fury ordered his staff not to answer the telephone.

On the same day the British chiefs were hurrying the BEF southward with such urgency that the soldiers were deprived of the rest they needed far more than they needed distance from the enemy. On that day, August 28, a day when von Kluck's columns gave them no trouble, Sir John French and Wilson were in such anxiety to hasten the retreat that they ordered transport wagons to "throw overboard all ammunition and other impediments not absolutely required" and carry men instead. Discarding ammunition meant abandoning further battle. As the BEF was not fighting on British soil, its Commander was prepared to pull his forces out of the line regardless of the effect of withdrawal upon his ally. The French Army had lost the opening battle and was in a serious, even desperate, situation in which every division counted to prevent defeat. But it was neither broken through nor enveloped by the enemy; it was fighting hard, and Joffre was exhibiting every intention of fighting further. Nevertheless, Sir John French, succumbing to the belief that the danger was mortal, had determined that the BEF must be preserved from being involved in a French defeat.

Field commanders did not share the pessimism of Headquarters. Receiving an order that virtually rejected any further idea of fighting, they were dismayed. Haig's Chief of Staff, General Gough, tore it up in anger. Smith-Dorrien, who regarded his situation as "excellent," with the enemy "only in small parties and those keeping at a respectful distance," countermanded the order to his own 3rd and 5th divisions. His message reached General Snow of the 4th division too late. Having received a direct order, addressed "To Snowball from Henry," to "load up your lame ducks and hustle along," he had already carried it out with "very damping effect" on the troops, who were made to think they must be in an extremity of danger and who lost their spare clothing and boots as well.

In dust, heat, and discouragement and fatigue beyond telling the British retreat continued. Trailing through St. Quentin, the tired remnants of two battalions gave up, piled up their arms in the railroad station, sat down in the Place de la Gare, and refused to go farther. They told Major Bridges whose cavalry had orders to hold off the Germans until St. Quentin was clear of troops, that their commanding officers had given the mayor a written promise to surrender in order to save the town further bombardment. Not caring to confront the battalion colonels whom he knew and who were senior to him, Bridges wished desperately for a band to rouse the two hundred or three hundred dispirited men lying about in the square. "Why not? There was a toy shop handy which provided my trumpeter and myself with a tin whistle and a drum and we marched round and round the fountain where the men were lying like the dead, playing the British Grenadiers and Tipperary and beating the drum like mad." The men sat up, began to laugh, then cheer, then one by one stood up, fell in and "eventually we moved off slowly into the night to the music of our improvised band, now reinforced with a couple of mouth organs."

Uncheered by fife or drum Sir John French, seeing only his own sector, was convinced that the Kaiser "in his rancour and hate, has really risked weakness in other parts of the field" in order to concentrate an overwhelming force "to destroy us." He demanded that Kitchener send him the Sixth Division, and when Kitchener said it could not be spared until its place in England was taken by troops from India, he considered this refusal "most disappointing and injurious." In fact for one moment after the shock of Mons, Kitchener had considered using the Sixth Division for a landing on the German flank in Belgium. The old idea, long advocated by Fisher and Esher, of using the BEF independently in Belgium instead of as an appendix to the French line, never ceased to haunt the British. Now it was tried, as it was to be again two months later at Antwerp, in miniature and in vain. Instead of the Sixth Division, three battalions of Royal Marines landed at Ostend on August 27 and 28 in an effort to draw off von Kluck's forces. They were joined by 6,000 Belgians who had followed the French retreat after the fall of Namur and were now sent up to Ostend by sea in British ships but who proved to be in no condition to fight. By this time, the retreat in France having swept the front too far away, the operation had lost its meaning, and the marines were reëmbarked on August 31.

Before that happened Sir John French on August 28 evacuated his forward base at Amiens, which was now menaced by von Kluck's westward sweep, and on the following day gave orders for moving the main British base back from Le Havre to St. Nazaire below the Normandy peninsula. In the same spirit as the order jettisoning ammunition, the move reflected the single urgent desire that now possessed him—to leave France. Partly sharing it, partly ashamed to share it, Henry Wilson, as described by a fellow officer, "walked slowly up and down the room, with that comical, whimsical expression on his face, habitual to him, clapping his hands softly together to keep time, as he chanted in a low tone, 'We shall never get there, we shall never get there.' As he passed me I said, 'Where, Henri?' And he chanted on, 'To the sea, to the sea, to the sea.'"

▶▶▶   *20*   ▶

▶▶▶   *The Front Is Paris*

THE GRANDS BOULEVARDS WERE EMPTY, SHOP fronts were shuttered, buses, trams, cars, and horse cabs had disappeared. In their place flocks of sheep were herded across the Place de la Concorde on their way to the Gare de l'Est for shipment to the front. Unmarred by traffic, squares and vistas revealed their purity of design. Most newspapers having ceased publication, the kiosks were hung meagerly with the single-page issues of the survivors. All the tourists were gone, the Ritz was uninhabited, the Meurice a hospital. For one August in its history Paris was French—and silent. The sun shone, fountains sparkled in the Rond Point, trees were green, the quiet Seine flowed by unchanging, brilliant clusters of Allied flags enhanced the pale gray beauty of the world's most beautiful city.

In the vast warren of the Invalides, Gallieni grappled with obstructionism and the hesitancy of officials to take the radical measures necessary to make the words "entrenched camp" a reality. He envisaged the camp as a base of operations, not a Troy holed up for siege. From the experience of Liège and Namur he knew that Paris could not withstand shelling by the new heavy siege guns of the enemy, but his plan was not to wait passively to be invested but to give battle—with the army he did not yet have—

beyond the outer ring of fortifications. Study of the Balkan and Man-
churian wars had convinced him that a system of deep and narrow trenches
protected by earth mounds and logs, flanked by barbed wire and "wolf
pits"—wide-mouthed holes fitted at the bottom with up-pointed stakes—
and manned by trained and determined troops armed with machine guns
would be virtually impregnable. These were what he was trying to construct in the stretches between the artillery posts, although he still did not
have the army to man them.

Every day, sometimes two and three times a day, with increasing
desperation he telephoned GQG demanding the three active corps. He
wrote to Joffre, sent emissaries, hammered at the Minister of War and the
President, repeatedly warned them Paris was unprepared. By August 29
he had received under his orders so far one naval brigade whose appearance, marching through the streets in white with high-pitched pipe, delighted the populace, if not Gallieni.

He conceived of the work to be done as tripartite: military defense,
moral defense, and provisioning. To accomplish each of these tasks it was
necessary to be frank with the public. As much as he despised politicians,
Gallieni respected the people of Paris who, he considered, could be counted
on to behave sensibly in the face of danger. He believed Poincaré and
Viviani did not want to tell the country the truth, and suspected them
of preparing a "mummery" to deceive the people. His efforts to obtain authority for demolition of buildings obstructing the forts' line of fire were
hampered by official reluctance to alarm the population. Each destruction
of property required a document signed by both the mayor of the arrondisse-
ment and the Chief of Engineers fixing the value of indemnity to the
proprietor—a process that was a source of endless harassment and delay.
Each decision was enmeshed in a further "byzantine" argument by those
who contended that Paris as the seat of government could not be a "fortified camp" to be defended militarily. The issue, as General Hirschauer
disgustedly remarked, offered a "magnificent field of controversy," and he
feared the proponents of an open city would soon succeed in proving the
post of Military Governor itself illegal. "You cannot convince the jurists
without a text," he said.

Gallieni provided one. On August 28 the Zone of the Armies was
extended to include Paris and the country on both sides down to the
Seine with the result that the municipal government of Paris was brought
under the authority of the Military Governor. At 10:00 A.M. Gallieni
assembled his military and civil cabinets in a Council of Defense which

was held with everyone standing up and was over by 10:15. Members were asked not to discuss whether Paris should be defended but simply to attest that the presence of the enemy required the institution of a "state of defense." Documents providing the legal basis were already drawn up and lying on the table. Gallieni invited each person to sign his name and immediately declared the Council adjourned. It was the first and last he held.

Ruthlessly he pursued work on the defenses, sparing no time or pity on demurrers or the irresolute, on weakness or ineptitude. Like Joffre, he liquidated incompetents, on his first day of office dismissing a general of Engineers and another general two days later. All inhabitants of the suburbs, "even the oldest and least capable," were impressed for labor with pick and shovel. An order for 10,000 spades and pickaxes to be collected within twenty-four hours was issued; by evening all had been delivered. When on the same occasion Gallieni ordered 10,000 bowie knives for use as tools his purveyor protested it was impossible because their purchase was illegal. "All the more reason," replied Gallieni, looking at him sharply over his pince-nez, and the knives were obtained.

On August 29 an area around Paris within a radius of about twenty miles, reaching to Melun on the south and Dammartin and Pontoise on the north, was brought under Gallieni's authority. Preparations were made for dynamiting bridges in the area. For those classified as "works of art" and part of the "national heritage" a system of special guards was arranged to ensure that they were not destroyed until the last extremity. All entries to the city, even the sewers, were barricaded. Bakers, butchers, market gardeners were organized and cattle brought in to graze in the Bois de Boulogne. To hasten the assembly of stocks of ammunition, Gallieni requisitioned transport "by all means available," including the taxis of Paris, so soon to become immortal. Assigned to the Artillery Staff of the entrenched camp was one already encased in history, former Captain, now Major Alfred Dreyfus, returned to active service at fifty-five.

At the front the First and Second Armies in Lorraine, under the terrible pressure of Rupprecht's guns, still held fiercely and tenaciously to the line of the Moselle. Their line wavered and bulged, in some places even was pierced by German wedges. Tightly contained by French counterattacks on their flanks, these could not be widened to major openings. The battle went on with Rupprecht's armies probing for the weakest place and Dubail and Castelnau, losing troops to Joffre's demands for the west, uncertain how long they could hold or whether they could hold. In the villages

taken by the Germans the events of Belgium were re-enacted. In Nomeny
on the outskirts of Nancy, "citizens fired on our troops," declared the German Governor of Metz in a bulletin posted on the walls. "I have therefore
ordered as a punishment that the village shall be burned to the ground.
Nomeny is thus by now destroyed."

On Castelnau's left where the front turned to the west, Ruffey's Third
Army, unbalanced by the removal of Maunoury's divisions, was falling back
behind the Meuse below Verdun. Next to it the Fourth Army, which
had rested in position on August 28 to prove the retreat was "strategic"
and not a rout, was ordered, to the disgust of General de Langle, to resume
its retreat on August 29. Further to the left where the pressure against the
French line was the greatest, General Lanrezac's Fifth Army was completing the turning maneuver preparatory for the counter-attack on St. Quentin
which Joffre had imposed upon its unwilling commander. At the extreme
end of the line, Maunoury's Sixth Army was coming into position. Between
Maunoury and Lanrezac the BEF was being pulled out by Sir John French
despite his knowledge of the battle that would be fought on the morrow.

Almost the process was interrupted by a much-needed deed of Anglo-
French cooperation when Haig sent word to Lanrezac that his troops
were "perfectly ready to attack and he wished to enter into direct communication and act in concert with the Fifth Army in its planned action
at St. Quentin." One of Lanrezac's staff immediately hastened to meet him
and found Haig standing picturesquely on a little hill, while an orderly held
his horse, beside a lance with fluttering white-cross pennon planted in the
ground. Haig said his air reconnaissance reported the enemy moving southwest of St. Quentin, "exposing his flank as he advances."

"Go quickly to your General and give him this information. . . . Let
him act. I am anxious to cooperate with him in this attack." The offer,
conveyed to Lanrezac, gave him "lively satisfaction" and moved him to
"say some nice things concerning Sir Douglas Haig." Arrangements for
joint action in the morning were confirmed, subject only to approval by
the British Commander in Chief. At 2 A.M. word came from GHQ that
Sir John French refused permission on the ground that the troops were
"very tired and must have at least one day's rest," a requirement which,
however true of the IInd Corps, was not true of the Ist Corps whose
commander himself had reported them fit and ready. Lanrezac exploded
with wrath. "*C'est une félonie!*" (It's betrayal!) he shouted, and added
what a listener described as "terrible, unpardonable things about Sir John
French and the British Army."

Nevertheless next morning, sandwiched between von Bülow who was moving down against him and Joffre who came up to superintend the offensive, Lanrezac had no choice but to attack. From papers found on a captured French officer, Bülow had learned of the coming attack and was not taken off guard. Doubting Lanrezac's mood, Joffre arrived early in the morning at Laon, now Lanrezac's headquarters, to lend him sangfroid out of his own bottomless supply. Laon is built on a high mesa from which the view extends over miles of rolling fields that rise and dip like the swells of a green ocean. Twenty miles to the north in a great semicircle the Fifth Army was drawn up facing northwest toward Guise and St. Quentin. From the tower of the cathedral at the highest point of the town the carved stone heads of cows, instead of gargoyles, gaze in bovine serenity over the landscape. Beneath them in the same silent calm, Joffre sat watching Lanrezac dictate orders and conduct the battle. He stayed for three hours without saying a word until, satisfied that Lanrezac was displaying "authority and method," he felt able to leave for a good lunch at the station restaurant before proceeding with his racing chauffeur on his next errand.

This was to find Sir John French who, he suspected, had his eyes on the Channel coast and "might be getting out of our line of battle for a long time." The place he held in the line between Lanrezac's Army and the gathering Sixth Army of Maunoury was now crucial and yet outside Joffre's power to control. He could not give orders to Field Marshal French as he did to Lanrezac or force him to fight by sitting behind him in silent surveillance. If, however, he could persuade the British to stand still, he hoped to stabilize a front on the Aisne along a line Amiens-Rheims-Verdun and resume the offensive from there. British Headquarters having taken another backward step the day before, Sir John was now established at Compiègne which was forty miles or—for tired armies—about three days' march from Paris. While its neighbor, the French Fifth Army, was fighting all during this day at Guise, lifting enemy pressure, the British Army rested. Having retreated without pursuit the day before, it now, after eight hot days of marching, digging trenches, and fighting engagements great and small, at last came to a halt. The IInd Corps made a short march during the evening hours to bring it across the Oise, but the Ist Corps enjoyed a full day's rest in the Forest of St. Gobain only five miles from where the left wing of Lanrezac's Army, which had been marching and fighting for fourteen days and was no less tired, was engaged in major battle.

When Joffre reached Compiègne he pleaded with the British Commander to stick fast until the offensive could be resumed at a favorable moment. His arguments seemed to produce no effect. He "distinctly saw" Murray tugging at the Field Marshal's tunic as if to prevent him from yielding to persuasion. It was a supererogatory effort, for Sir John French kept saying, "No, no," to Joffre and insisting that in view of his losses his army was in no condition to fight and must have two days to rest and refit. Joffre could not dismiss him on the spot as he would have a French general; he could not even throw a fit of temper to gain his ends as he had with Lanrezac at Marle. With the British backing away from the space between Lanrezac and Maunoury, neither of their armies could hold along the present line and all hope of carrying out General Order No. 2 must be abandoned. Joffre departed, by his own confession, "in very bad humor."

Sir John French's intentions were even more drastic than he admitted to Joffre. Without regard for an ally fighting on the threshhold of defeat, he now told his Inspector of Communications, Major General Robb, to plan for a "definite and prolonged retreat due south, passing Paris to the east and west." Even Kitchener's instructions could not be blamed for this. Conceived in deep disapproval of Henry Wilson's commitment to Plan 17, they were designed to restrain a too aggressive Sir John and a too Francophil Wilson from risking the British Army in some French-sponsored scheme of *offensive à outrance* that could lead to annihilation or capture. They were never intended to suggest such a degree of caution as would lead to actual desertion. But the sweat that comes from fear cannot be controlled, and Sir John was now gripped by fear of losing his army and with it his name and reputation.

His troops were not, as he pretended, a broken army unfit for further effort. By their own account they were in no mood to give up. Lieutenant Colonel Frederick Maurice of the 3rd Division Staff said that despite exhaustion, sore feet, and lack of time for cooked meals "the restorative effect of a hot meal, a good night's rest and a bath is little short of marvelous, and these were what our army chiefly needed . . . to enable it to take the field again." Captain Ernest Hamilton of the 11th Hussars said that after its day of rest on August 29 the BEF was "now in perfect trim to turn and fight at any moment." General Macready, Adjutant-General in the BEF, said "all they needed was rest and food to make them ready and eager" to show the Germans what they could do.

Nevertheless Sir John French next day sent Joffre definitive notice that the British Army would not be in condition to take its place in the line "for another ten days." Had he asked for ten days' time out when fighting with his back to London he would not have survived in command. As it was, Sir John French remained Commander in Chief for another year and a half.

That afternoon, on edge to get his men on the move and away from the vicinity of the enemy, he was anxious to have Lanrezac break off his battle and resume the retreat with him shoulder to shoulder, less out of concern for covering Lanrezac's flank than to protect his own. In an effort to obtain an order for the Fifth Army to do this, Henry Wilson called GQG and, finding that Joffre had not returned, spoke to General Berthelot who refused to assume authority but arranged to have Wilson intercept Joffre at the Hotel Lion d'Or in Rheims at 7:30 that evening. At mealtimes Joffre's whereabouts were always known. Wilson, when he found him, argued in vain. All Joffre would say was, "Lanrezac must see it out to the end," without specifying what end he had in mind. When Wilson returned with this news, Sir John decided not to wait, and gave orders for the BEF to resume the retreat next day.

Meanwhile Lanrezac's advance on St. Quentin was meeting difficulties. A regiment of the XVIIIth Corps, under orders to take a village down the road, advanced under shrapnel falling like hail. Shells "gutted the road and tore branches from the trees in huge pieces," wrote a sergeant who survived.

"It was stupid to lie down; one might as well keep moving. . . . Here and there men lay flat on their stomachs or on their backs. They were dead. One of them, under an apple tree, had all of his face missing; blood drowned his head. On the right drums sounded the bayonet charge followed by the trumpet. Our line advanced marked by the sparkle of the bayonets slanted against a blue sky. The rhythm of the drums quickened. 'Forward!' All the men cried 'Forward!' It was a superb moment. An electric shiver went through my scalp and contracted the roots of my hair. The drums beat in a rage, the hot wind carried the notes of the trumpet, the men shouted—they were transported! . . . Suddenly we were stopped. To charge a village 900 yards away against a solid defense was folly. The order came, 'Lie down, take cover.'"

The attack on St. Quentin was thrown back and, as Lanrezac had anticipated, heavy enemy pressure began to bear down upon his right. Bülow was attacking with all his forces instead of allowing the French to move forward against him so that they might be taken in the rear by the armies of Kluck and Hausen. Believing that the action was no more than the death throes of a broken army, Bülow felt "confident of the outcome." In one sector the French were driven back across the Oise, and a panic developed when the bridges and narrow roads leading off them became jammed. Displaying "the greatest quickness and comprehension," in the words of his least sympathetic observer, Lanrezac quickly ordered abandonment of the action at St. Quentin and a new concentration of effort to redeem the situation on the right at Guise.

Franchet d'Esperey, commander of the Ist Corps, the eager, sturdy little general burned by the suns of Tonkin and Morocco whom Poincaré called "a stranger to depression," was ordered to rally the IIIrd and Xth Corps on his left and right. With the aid of officers riding up and down the front on horseback and bands playing once again the quick bright chords of the "Sambre et Meuse," he reformed the line by 5:30 P.M. Preceded by a well-prepared artillery action, the French moved forward once more to the attack. The bridge at Guise was piled high with ramparts of enemy dead. On the far side resistance was desultory; the French could feel it weakening. "The Germans were running away," wrote an observer, and the French, "frantic with joy at the new and longed for sensation were carried forward in a splendid victorious wave."

At the day's end when the sergeant who had participated in the attack on St. Quentin returned to the village from which he had started that morning, he was met by a friend who had all the news. "He said it had been a great day. Our check didn't matter. The enemy was pushed back, we were the winners. The Colonel was killed by a shell; he died while they were carrying him off. Commandant Theron was wounded in the chest. Captain Gilberti was wounded and would not live. Many of the men were dead or wounded. He repeated it had been a good day because the regiment would sleep two nights in the same place."

The retirement of the Guard Corps—the élite of Bülow's Army—pulled back its neighbors and gave Lanrezac a tactical victory—at Guise, if not at St. Quentin. But he was now alone and exposed, facing north, while his neighbors on both sides, the British and the Fourth Army, each a full day's march ahead of him, were continuing their retreat and further uncovering his flanks at every step. If the Fifth Army were to be saved it must immediately break off battle and rejoin its partners. But Lanrezac could get no directive from Joffre who was not at GQG when Lanrezac telephoned.

"Is the Fifth Army to delay in the region of Guise-St. Quentin at the risk of being captured?" Lanrezac asked General Belin, Joffre's deputy.

"What do you mean, let your army be captured! That's absurd!"

"You do not understand me. I am here at the express orders of the Commander in Chief. . . . I cannot take it upon myself to withdraw to Laon. It is for the Commander in Chief to give me the order to retire." Lanrezac was not going to take the blame this time, as at Charleroi.

Refusing to assume authority, Belin said he would report the question to Joffre as soon as he returned. When Joffre did return, although he appeared still confident, still unruffled, his hopes had suffered a second crash even graver than the debacle at the frontiers because now the enemy was that much deeper into France. He had no way of knowing that Lanrezac's fight had inflicted a sharp check on Bülow's army because the results did not yet show. He could only recognize that the Fifth Army was in truth left in a dangerous position, that the BEF was backing out, and he could "no longer nourish any hope of holding our Allies on the anticipated line of battle." The Sixth Army, while still in the process of forming, was under heavy attack from Kluck's two right-wing corps; the front he had hoped to hold was dissipated; more territory would have to be yielded, perhaps as far as the Marne, perhaps even to the Seine.

During this period, the "most tragic in all French history," as its chief investigator was to call it, Joffre did not panic like Sir John French, or waver like Moltke or become momentarily unnerved like Haig or Ludendorff or succumb to pessimism like Prittwitz. What went on behind that opaque exterior he never showed. If he owed his composure to a failure of imagination, that was fortunate for France. Ordinary men, Clausewitz wrote, become depressed by a sense of danger and responsibility; if these conditions are to "lend wings to strengthen the judgment, there must be present unusual greatness of soul." If danger did not strengthen Joffre's judgment in any way, it did call forth a certain strength of soul or of character. When ruin was all around him, he maintained an even tenor, a stolid control, what Foch, who saw him on August 29, called a "wonderful calm" which held the French Army together in an hour when it most needed the cement of confidence. On one of these days Colonel Alexandre, returning from a mission to the Fifth Army, excused his expression of gloom on the ground of "the bad news I have to bring."

"What!" answered Joffre, "do you no longer believe in France? Go get some rest. You will see—everything will be all right."

That night of August 29 at 10:00 P.M. he issued the order for Lanrezac to retire and blow up the bridges of the Oise behind him. General d'Amade was ordered to blow up the bridges over the Somme at Amiens and fall back, along with Maunoury's Army On the right the Fourth

Army was ordered to retire on Rheims, and General de Langle, who demanded rest for his troops, was told that rest depended on the enemy. As his final bitter act of the night of August 29, Joffre ordered preparations made for leaving Vitry-le-François, "that headquarters of broken hopes and lost illusions." GQG was to be moved back to Bar-sur-Aube on an eastern tributary of the Seine. The news spread among the Staff, adding, as Joffre disapprovingly noted, to "the general nervousness and anxiety."

Through a Staff failure, Joffre's order to the Fifth Army did not reach Lanrezac till early next morning, causing him a long night of unnecessary agony. Fortunately von Bülow did not renew the combat or, when Lanrezac withdrew, follow after. The results of the battle were as obscure to the Germans as to the French, and Bülow's impressions seem to have been curiously mixed, for he both reported it to OHL as a success and at the same time sent a staff captain to von Kluck to say his army was "exhausted by the battle of Guise and unable to pursue." Ignorant of this, the French—Joffre as well as Lanrezac—were possessed by a single aim: to disengage the Fifth Army and bring it out of danger and into line with the other French Armies before the Germans could outflank it on the left.

Meanwhile the threat to Paris of the oncoming German right wing was evident. Joffre telegraphed Gallieni to lay charges under the bridges of the Seine immediately to the west of Paris and of the Marne immediately to the east and to post platoons of Engineers at each one to make sure that orders to blow the bridges would be carried out. Maunoury's Army, in falling back, would cover Paris and be the natural group to provide the army of three corps Gallieni was demanding. But to Joffre and GQG Paris was still a "geographical expression." To defend it for its own sake and, for that purpose, put Maunoury's Army at Gallieni's disposal and under his orders was not Joffre's intention. Paris, as he saw it, would stand or fall with the result of the battle he intended to fight with the whole field army under his own command. To the men inside Paris, however, the fate of the capital was of more direct interest.

The apparent result of the Battle of St. Quentin and Guise deepened the pall of dismay hanging over them. On the morning of the battle M. Touron, vice president of the Senate and an industrial magnate of the north, rushed into Poincaré's office "like a whirlwind," claiming that the government was "being deceived by GQG" and that our left had "been turned and the Germans are at La Fère." Poincaré repeated the stout assurances of Joffre that the left would hold and that as soon as the Sixth

Army was ready the offensive would be resumed, but in the back of his mind he feared that M. Touron might be right. Cryptic messages filtered in, indicating a great battle was in progress. Every hour he received contradictory reports. Late in the afternoon M. Touron burst in again, more excited than ever. He had just been talking over the telephone to M. Seline, a fellow Senator from the Aisne who owned a property near St. Quentin and who had been watching the battle from the roof of his house. M. Seline had seen the French troops advancing and the puffs of smoke and the black shellbursts filling the sky and then, as German reinforcements, like an army of gray ants, were brought up, had seen the French thrown back. The attack had not succeeded, the battle was lost, and M. Touron departed wailing.

The second stage of the battle—at Guise—did not come under the eyes of the Senator on the roof and was even less clear to the Government than to GQG. All that seemed clear was that Joffre's attempt to check the German right wing had failed, that Paris faced siege and might again eat rats as it had forty years before. The possibility of the fall of the capital, the question whether the government should leave, which had been lurking in ministerial minds since the Battle of the Frontiers, was now openly and urgently discussed. Colonel Penelon, liaison officer between GQG and the President, arrived early next morning, his usually smiling face for once somber, and admitted the situation was "intensely serious." Millerand as Minister of War at once advised departure to avoid being cut off from the rest of the country. Gallieni, hastily summoned for his opinion, advised telephoning Joffre. Joffre acknowledged the situation was not good; the Fifth Army had fought well but had not accomplished his hopes; the English "had not budged"; the advance of the enemy could not be slowed and Paris was "seriously menaced." He advised the government to leave so as not, by remaining, to be the means of drawing the enemy upon the capital. Joffre knew well enough that the German objective was the French Armies, not the government, but as the battlefield neared Paris, the presence of the government in the Zone of the Armies would tend to blur the lines of authority. Its withdrawal would remove a source of interference and leave GQG with enhanced power. When Gallieni on the telephone tried to convince him of the necessity of defending Paris as the material and moral hub of the war effort, and again demanded an army to attack the enemy in the field before the city could be invested, he somewhat vaguely promised to send him three corps though not at full strength and largely made up of reserve divisions. He gave

Gallieni the impression that he considered Paris expendable and was still unwilling to deplete his forces for its sake.

Then the President of the Republic, appearing "preoccupied and even dispirited," although as always "cold and reserved," asked Gallieni how long Paris could hold out and whether the government should leave. "Paris cannot hold out and you should make ready to leave as soon as possible," Gallieni replied. Desiring, no less than Joffre, to unsaddle himself of the government, he found the advice painless. Poincaré asked him to return later to explain his views to the Cabinet, which in the meantime assembled and passionately argued the question that a bare ten days ago, when the French offensive was launched, would have seemed unthinkable.

Poincaré, Ribot, and the two socialists, Guesde and Sembat, were for staying, or at least awaiting the outcome of the approaching battle. The moral effect of departure, they contended, could produce despair, even revolution. Millerand insisted upon departure. He said a company of Uhlans might penetrate below Paris and cut the railroads to the south, and the government could not take the risk of being shut up inside the capital as in 1870. This time France was fighting as part of an alliance and it was the government's duty to remain in contact with her Allies and the outside world as well as with the rest of France. Doumergue made a deep impression when he said, "It takes more courage to appear a coward and risk popular disfavor than to risk being killed." Whether the emergency required reconvening Parliament, as was demanded in excited visits by the presidents of the two chambers, provided a subject for further heated dispute.

Fretting with impatience to return to his duties, Gallieni was kept waiting outside for an hour while the ministers argued. Finally called in, he told them bluntly they were "no longer safe in the capital." His stern and soldierly appearance and manner and the "clarity and force" with which he expressed himself made a "profound effect." Explaining that without an army to fight outside the perimeter, he could not ward off assault by the enemy's siege artillery; he warned that Paris was not in a state of defense and "cannot be put in one. . . . It would be an illusion to believe that the entrenched camp could offer a serious resistance if the enemy should appear in the next few days before our line of exterior forts." The formation of an army of four or at least three corps to fight under his orders outside the city as the extreme left wing of the French line was "indispensable." The delay in preparing the defenses, before his appointment as Governor, he charged to influential groups who wanted Paris declared an open city to save it from destruction. They had been encouraged by GQG.

"That's right," Millerand interrupted. "It is the opinion at GQG that Paris should not be defended."

Guesde, the socialist, speaking his first words as minister after a lifetime of opposition, excitedly broke in. "You want to open the gates to the enemy so Paris won't be pillaged. But on the day the Germans march through our streets there will be a shot fired from every window in the working-class quarters. And then I will tell you what will happen: Paris will be burned!"

After hectic debate it was agreed that Paris must be defended and Joffre required to conform, if necessary under pain of dismissal. Gallieni argued against any rash removal of the Commander in Chief at this stage. As to whether the government should go or stay, the Cabinet remained completely at odds.

Leaving the ministers "overcome with emotion and indecision" and, as they seemed to him, "incapable of coming to a firm resolve," Gallieni returned to the Invalides, making his way through the crowds of anxious citizens besieging its doors for permits to leave the city, to take their cars, to close essential businesses, and a thousand other reasons. The buzz of anxiety was louder than usual; that afternoon for the first time a German *Taube* bombed Paris. Besides three bombs on the Quai de Valmy which killed two persons and injured others, it dropped leaflets telling Parisians that the Germans were at their gates, as in 1870, and "There is nothing you can do but surrender."

Daily thereafter one or more enemy planes returned regularly at 6:00 P.M., dropped two or three bombs, and killed an occasional passerby in an effort, presumably, to frighten the population. The fearful went south. For those who remained in Paris during this period, when no one knew if the next day might not bring the spiked helmets marching in, the flights of the *Taube*, always at the *apéritif* hour, provided excitement to compensate for the government's prohibition of absinthe. That night of its first visit Paris was blacked out for the first time. The only "little gleam of light" to pierce the general gloom, Poincaré wrote in his diary, was in the East where, according to a telegram from the French military attaché, the Russian armies were "developing their offensive toward Berlin." In fact they were being cut down and surrounded at Tannenberg, and on that night General Samsonov committed suicide in the forest.

Joffre heard a more accurate version when a German radio message, intercepted at Belfort, told of the destruction of three Russian corps, the capture of two corps commanders and 70,000 other prisoners and announced, "The Russian Second Army no longer exists." This terrible news coming when French hopes were already sinking might have dispirited even Joffre except that it was followed by other news which showed the Russian sacrifice had not been in vain. Intelligence reports revealed the transfer of at least two German corps from the Western Front to the East and were confirmed next day by reports of thirty-two troop trains passing eastward through Berlin. This was Joffre's gleam of light, this the aid for which all France's pressure on Russia had been brought to bear. Even so, it hardly counterbalanced the projected loss of the British whose commander's refusal to remain in contact with the enemy opened the way to envelopment of the Fifth Army. The Fifth was also in danger of being outflanked on its right through the space thinly filled by the Foch Detachment.

Wherever a weak sector needed reinforcement, another sector had to be dangerously depleted. On this same day, August 30, Joffre visited the front of the Third and Fourth Armies to look for forces he could assign to Foch. On the road he passed the retreating columns who had fought in the Ardennes and on the heights of the Meuse. Red trousers had faded to the color of pale brick, coats were ragged and torn, shoes caked with mud, eyes cavernous in faces dulled by exhaustion and dark with many days' growth of beard. Twenty days' campaigning seemed to have aged the soldiers as many years. They walked heavily, as if ready to drop at every step. Emaciated horses, with bones sticking out and with bleeding harness sores, sometimes dropped in the shafts, were hurriedly unharnessed by the artillerymen, and dragged off to the side of the road so as not to obstruct the way. Guns looked old and blistered with barely a few patches of their once new gray paint showing through the mud and dirt.

In contrast, other units, still vigorous, had become confident veterans in the twenty days, proud of their fighting skills and eager to halt the retreat. The ultimate compliment was earned by the 42nd Division of Ruffey's Army which, after holding the rearguard and successfully disengaging, was told by its corps commander, General Sarrail, "You have given proof of *cran*." When Joffre ordered this division transferred to Foch, General Ruffey protested violently on the ground of an anticipated attack. Unlike General de Langle of the Fourth Army whom Joffre had just found calm, confident, and "perfectly master of himself"—the one essential duty of a commander in Joffre's eyes—Ruffey appeared nervous, excitable, and "imaginative to an excessive degree." As Colonel Tanant, his Chief of Operations, said, he was very clever and full of a thousand ideas of which one was magnificent but the question was which. Like the deputies in Paris, Joffre needed a scapegoat for the failure of the offensive and Ruffey's conduct decided the selection; he was removed that day from command of the Third Army and replaced by General Sarrail. Invited to lunch next day with Joffre, Ruffey blamed his defeat in the Ardennes on the last-minute removal of the two reserve divisions that Joffre had transferred to the Army of Lorraine. If he had had those 40,000 fresh men and the 7th Cavalry Division, Ruffey said, he could have rolled up the enemy's left, and "what a success for our arms we might have won!" In one of his terse and mysterious remarks, Joffre replied, "*Chut, il ne faut pas le dire.*" His tone of voice has been lost, and it will never be known whether he meant, "You are wrong; you must not say that," or "You are right but we must not admit it."

On that Sunday, August 30, the day of Tannenberg, the day the French government was warned to leave Paris, England received a shock, since known as the "Amiens dispatch." Headed, with initial exaggeration, "Fiercest Fight in History," it appeared with awful impact in a special Sunday edition of *The Times* on the front page where, ordinarily, discreet columns of advertising screened readers from the news. Subheads proclaimed, "Heavy Losses of British Troops—Mons and Cambrai—Fight Against Severe Odds—Need for Reinforcements." This last phrase was the key; although the dispatch was to arouse an official storm, provoke a furious debate in Parliament, and earn a scolding from the Prime Minister as a "regrettable exception" to the "patriotic reticence" of the press as a whole, it was in fact published with an official purpose. Instantly seeing its qualities as recruiting propaganda, the Censor, F. E. Smith, later Lord Birkenhead, passed it and urged it upon *The Times*, which published it as a patriotic duty with an appended notice as to the "extreme gravity of the task before us." It was written by a correspondent, Arthur Moore, who had arrived at the front in the midst of the retreat from Le Cateau and the hectic despair at GHQ.

He wrote of a "retreating and a broken army" after the series of engagements "which may be called the action of Mons," of the French retreat on the flank, of the "immediate, relentless, unresting" German pursuit and its "irresistible vehemence," of British regiments "grievously injured" though with "no failure in discipline, no panic and no throwing up the sponge." In spite of everything the men were still "steady and cheerful" but "forced backwards, ever backwards." He told of "very great losses," of "bits of broken regiments," and of some divisions having "lost nearly all their officers." Evidently infected with the mood of GHQ, he wrote rather wildly of the German right wing, "so great was their estimated superiority in numbers that they could no more be stopped than the waves of the sea." Britain, he concluded, must face the fact that the "first great German effort has succeeded" and "the investment of Paris cannot be banished from the field of possibility."

When, in summarizing the need for reinforcements, he spoke of the BEF which "bore the weight of the blow," he laid the foundations of a myth. It was as if the French Army had been an adjunct somewhere in the offing. In fact the BEF was never at any time in the first month in contact with more than three German corps out of a total of over thirty, but the idea that it "bore the weight of the blow" was perpetuated in all subsequent British accounts of Mons and of the "Glorious Retreat." It succeeded in planting in the British mind the conviction that the BEF in the gallant and terrible days of its first month of battle saved France, saved Europe, saved Western civilization or, as one British writer unbashfully put it, "Mons. In that single word will be summed up the Liberation of the World."

Alone among the belligerents Britain had gone to war with no prearranged framework of national effort, no mobilization orders in every pocket. Except for the regular army, all was improvisation and, during the first weeks, before the Amiens dispatch, almost a holiday mood. Up to then the truth of the German advance was concealed by—to use Mr. Asquith's exquisite phrase—"patriotic reticence." The fighting had been presented to the British public—as to the French—as a series of German defeats in which the enemy unaccountably moved from Belgium to France and appeared each day on the map at places farther forward. All over England on August 30 as *The Times* was read at Sunday breakfast tables, people were aghast. "It was as if," thought Mr. Britling, "David had flung his pebble—and missed!"

In the sudden and dreadful realization that the enemy was winning the war, people, searching for hope, seized upon a tale that had cropped up within the last few days and turned it into a national hallucination. On August 27 a seventeen-hour delay in the Liverpool-London railway service inspired the rumor that the trouble was due to the transport of Russian troops who were said to have landed in Scotland on their way to reinforce the Western Front. From Archangel they were supposed to have crossed the Arctic Sea to Norway, thence come by ordinary steamer to Aberdeen, and from there were being carried by special troop trains to Channel ports. Anyone whose train was held up thereafter knowingly attributed the delay to "the Russians." In the gloom following the Amiens dispatch with its talk of German numbers like "the waves of the sea" and its cry for "men, men and more men," thoughts turned unconsciously toward Russia's limitless manpower, and the phantoms seen in Scotland took on body, gathering corroborative detail as the story spread.

They stamped snow off their boots on station platforms—in August; a railway porter of Edinburgh was known who had swept up the snow. "Strange uniforms" were glimpsed in passing troop trains. They were reported variously to be going via Harwich to save Antwerp or via Dover to save Paris. Ten thousand were seen after midnight in London marching along the Embankment on their way to Victoria Station. The naval battle of Heligoland was explained by the wise as a diversion to cover the transport of the Russians to Belgium. The most reliable people had seen them —or knew friends who had. An Oxford professor knew a colleague who had been summoned to interpret for them. A Scottish army officer in Edinburgh saw them in "long gaily-colored coats and big fur caps," carrying bows and arrows instead of rifles and with their own horses "just like Scottish ponies only bonier"—a description that exactly fitted the Cossacks of a hundred years ago as they appeared in early Victorian mezzotints. A resident of Aberdeen, Sir Stuart Coats, wrote to his brother-in-law in America that 125,000 Cossacks had marched across his estate in Perthshire. An English army officer assured friends that 70,000 Russians had passed through England to the Western Front in "utmost secrecy." At first said to be 500,000, then 250,000, then 125,000, the figure gradually settled at between 70,000 and 80,000—the same number as made up the departed BEF. The story spread entirely by word of mouth; owing to the official censorship nothing appeared in the papers except in the United States. Here the reports of homecoming Americans, most of whom had embarked at Liverpool, which was in a furor of excitement over the Russians, preserved the phenomenon for posterity.

Other neutrals picked up the news. Dispatches from Amsterdam reported a large force of Russians being rushed to Paris to aid in its defense. In Paris people hung about the railway stations hoping to see the arrival of the Cossacks. Passing to the Continent, the phantoms became a military factor; for the Germans, too, heard the rumors. Worry about a possible 70,000 Russians at their backs was to be as real a factor at the Marne as the absence of the 70,000 men they had transferred to the Eastern Front. It was only after the Marne, on September 15, that an official denial of the rumor appeared in the English press.

On the same Sunday as the Amiens dispatch appalled the public, Sir John French composed a report that was an even greater shock to Lord Kitchener. GHQ was then at Compiègne, forty miles north of Paris, and the British troops, relieved of pursuit the previous day, had rested while the enemy was engaged by the French. The Operation Order to the BEF that day, bearing Sir John French's signature, stated that enemy pressure "was relieved by a French advance in force on our right which met with great success in the neighborhood of Guise where the German Guard and Xth Corps were driven back into the Oise." This ready acknowledgment of the facts being totally irreconcilable with what Sir John then wrote to Kitchener, it can only be supposed that he signed it without reading it.

He informed Kitchener of Joffre's request to him to hold fast north of Compiègne, keeping in contact with the enemy, but claimed he was "absolutely unable to remain in the front line" and intended to retire "behind the Seine," keeping "at a considerable distance from the enemy." His retirement would involve an eight-day march "without fatiguing the troops" and passing west of Paris so as to be near to his base. "I do not like General Joffre's plan," Sir John continued, "and would have preferred a vigorous offensive"—a preference he had just refused to exercise at St. Quentin when he forbade Haig to cooperate with Lanrezac in the battle.

Quickly reversing himself in the next sentence, Sir John made it clear that, after ten days of campaign, he was ready to give the French up as beaten and come home. His confidence in the ability of the French "to carry the campaign to a successful conclusion is fast waning," he wrote, and "this is my real reason for moving the British forces so far back." Although "pressed very hard to remain in the front line, even in my shattered condition," he had "absolutely refused to do so" in accordance with "the letter and spirit" of Kitchener's instructions and insisted upon retaining independence of action "to retire on my base" if necessary.

Kitchener read the report, received on August 31, with astonishment mounting to consternation. Sir John French's intention to withdraw from the Allied line and separate the British from the French, with its appearance of deserting them in their most desperate hour, he regarded as "calamitous," from the political as well as the military point of view. As a violation of the spirit of the Entente, it became a question of policy, and Kitchener asked the Prime Minister to summon the Cabinet at once. Before it met he sent off a restrained telegram to Sir John expressing his "surprise" at the decision to retire behind the Seine and delicately phrasing his dismay in the form of a question: "What will be the effect of this course upon your relations with the French Army and on the general military situation? Will your retirement leave a gap in the French line or cause them discouragement of which the Germans could take advantage?" He closed with a reminder that the thirty-two troop trains moving through Berlin showed that the Germans were withdrawing forces from the Western Front.

When Kitchener, after reading Sir John's letter to the Cabinet, explained that retirement behind the Seine might mean loss of the war, the Cabinet was, as Mr. Asquith put it in his muffled way, "perturbed." Kitchener was authorized to inform Sir John of the government's anxiety at his proposed retirement and its expectation that "you will as far as possible conform with the plans of General Joffre for the conduct of the campaign." The government, he added, with care for French's *amour propre*, "have all possible confidence in your troops and yourself."

When OHL had learned of General von Prittwitz's intention to retire behind the Vistula, he was instantly dismissed; but when Sir John French proposed to give up not a province but an ally, the same solution was not applied. The reason may have been that, owing to the ravages left by the Ulster quarrel, there was no replacement upon whom government and army could agree. The government may have regarded dismissal of the Commander in Chief at such a moment as too great a shock for the public. In any event, inspired by Sir John's aura of irritability, everyone— French as well as British—continued to treat him with the utmost tact while in fact retaining very little confidence in him. "Joffre and he have never yet been within a mile of the heart of each other," wrote Sir William Robertson, the British Quartermaster General, to the King's secretary a year later. "He has never really, sincerely and honestly concerted with the French and they consider him as by no means a man of ability or a faithful friend and therefore do not confide in him." This was not a situation propitious for the Allied war effort. Kitchener, whose relations with Sir John had not been cordial since the Boer War, never regained confidence in him after August 31, but it was not until December 1915 that Sir John's own machinations against Kitchener, conducted in a manner, as Lord Birkenhead was to say, "neither decorous, fastidious nor loyal," finally nerved the British government to remove him.

While in London, Kitchener was waiting impatiently for Sir John's reply, Joffre in Paris was mobilizing the aid of the French government to try to keep the British in the front line. Joffre had by now discovered that at least half of Lanrezac's battle—the half at Guise—had been a success. Reports showing that the German Guard and Xth Corps had been "severely handled" and that Bülow's Army was not pursuing, combined with the news of the withdrawal of German troops to the East, encouraged him. He told Poincaré the government might not have to leave after all; he now felt hopeful of checking the German advance in renewed action by the Fifth and Sixth Armies. He sent a letter to the British Commander telling him the Fifth and Sixth now had orders not to yield ground except under pressure. As they could not be expected to stand if there was a gap between them, he "earnestly" requested Field Marshal French not to withdraw and "at least to leave rearguards so as not to give the enemy the clear impression of a retreat and of a gap between the Fifth and Sixth Armies."

Asked by Joffre to exert his influence as President of France to obtain a favorable reply, Poincaré called the British ambassador, who called GHQ, but all the calls and visits of liaison officers were of no avail. "I refused," as Sir John later succinctly summarized his reply, and thereby punctured Joffre's momentary, if illusory, hope.

Sir John's reply to his own government was awaited so anxiously by Kitchener that he had the decoders read it to him word by word as it came through late that night. "Of course," it said, there would be a gap in the French line caused by his retirement, but "if the French go on with their present tactics which are practically to fall back right and left of me, usually without notice, and to abandon all idea of offensive operations . . . the consequences will be borne by them. . . . I do not see why I should be called upon to run the risk of absolute disaster in order a second time to save them." This militant mistatement of the truth, after Joffre had just finished telling him the opposite, was the kind of thing that when his book *1914* was published caused his countrymen to search helplessly for a polite equivalent of "lie" and moved even Mr. Asquith to use the phrase, "a travesty of the facts." Even given Sir John's limitations of character, the mystery remains how, with Henry Wilson on the Staff with his thorough knowledge of the French language and his acquaintance with senior French officers including Joffre himself, the British Commander in Chief could have arrived at the picture he did of French defeatism.

When Kitchener finished reading the telegram at 1:00 A.M., he decided instantly there was only one thing to do and it could not wait for daybreak. He must go to France himself. As senior Field Marshal, he was head of the army and as such considered himself entitled to give orders to Sir John French on military matters as well as on matters of policy in his capacity as War Minister. Hastening to Downing Street he conferred with Asquith and a group of ministers, among them Churchill, who ordered a fast cruiser for his conveyance to be ready within two hours at Dover. He telegraphed Sir John to expect him and, lest his appearance at GHQ embarrass the sensibilities of the Commander in Chief, asked him to select a place of meeting. At 2:00 A.M. Sir Edward Grey was startled out of his sleep by the apparition of Kitchener walking into his bedroom to say he was going to France. At 2:30 he departed by special train from Charing Cross and by morning of September 1 was in Paris.

Looking "irritated, violent, his face congested, sulky and angry," Field Marshal French, accompanied by Sir Archibald Murray, arrived at the British Embassy, the meeting place he had selected. He intended it to emphasize the civilian nature of the conference for he insisted on regarding Kitchener as political head of the army only, with no status other than that of any civilian War Minister. His choler was hardly soothed to find Kitchener in uniform, which Sir John instantly took as an attempt to pull rank on him. In fact, after appearing in frock coat and silk hat on his first day at the war office, Kitchener had discarded civilian clothes for the blue undress uniform of a Field Marshal. Sir John took it as a personal affront. Clothes were a matter of the greatest importance to him and he had a tendency to use them to enhance his own dignity in ways his associates considered unorthodox. He offended King George by his habit of "wearing stars in khaki" and "covering himself with foreign baubles"; and Henry Wilson used to say of him, "He is a nice little man in his bath but when he puts his clothes on you can't trust him; you never know what he will wear."

When the meeting at the British Embassy in the presence of Sir Francis Bertie, Viviani, Millerand, and several officers representing Joffre became increasingly acrimonious, Kitchener asked Sir John to retire with him to a private room. As Sir John's version of what was said there, published after Kitchener was dead, is unreliable, only the results of their conversation are known for certain. They were expressed in a telegram from Kitchener to the government stating that "French's troops are now engaged in the fighting line where they will remain conforming to the movements of the French Army," which would mean retiring east, not west, of Paris. In a copy sent to Sir John, Kitchener said he felt sure this represented the agreement they had come to, but in any event "please consider it an instruction." By "in the fighting line," he said he meant disposing the British troops in contact with the French. In a fatal return to tact he added, "Of course you will judge as regards their position in this respect." Unmollified, the Commander in Chief retired in a sulk now deeper and more paralyzing than before.

During this and the previous day Kluck's Army, advancing by forced marches in its haste to envelop the French before they could take a firm stand, had overtaken Compiègne, crossed the Oise, pushing the Allied retreat before it, and on September 1 was in action against rearguards of the French Sixth Army and the BEF thirty miles from Paris.

In preparation for the greatest moment in Teutonic history, the Germans with admirable efficiency had already struck off, and distributed to staff officers for ultimate presentation to the troops, a bronze medal confidently inscribed *Einzug d. Deutschen Truppen in Paris* (Entry of German Troops into Paris). Beneath appeared the Eiffel Tower, the Arc de Triomphe and, combining proud memory and anticipation, the dates 1871–1914.

▶▶▶   *21* ▶

▶▶▶   *Von Kluck's Turn*

"AN AUTOMOBILE DROVE UP," WROTE M. ALBERT
Fabre, whose villa at Lassigny, twelve miles north of Compiègne, was
commandeered by the Germans on August 30. "From it descended an
officer of arrogant and impressive bearing. He stalked forward alone while
the officers standing in groups in front of the villa made way for him. He
was tall and majestic with a scarred, clean-shaven face, hard features and
a frightening glance. In his right hand he carried a soldier's rifle and his
left rested on the butt of a revolver. He turned around several times,
striking the ground with the butt end of his rifle and then halted in a
theatrical pose. No one seemed to dare to approach him and indeed he
wore a terrible air." Gazing awestruck at this be-weaponed apparition,
M. Fabre thought of Attila and learned that his visitor was "the already
too-famous von Kluck."

General von Kluck, the "last man on the right" in Schlieffen's scheme,
was at that moment considering a fateful decision. He felt himself close
to the crisis on August 30. His troops on the far right had driven back
units of Maunoury's Army with success that Kluck thought was definitive.
His pursuit in the center had not succeeded in catching up with the
British, but the jettisoned piles of coats, boots, and ammunition found

along the roadside which the British had dumped in their anxiety to bring away their men confirmed Kluck's opinion of a beaten opponent. On his left a division which he had lent to Bülow to help at the battle of Guise reported the French fleeing from that battle. Kluck was fiercely determined to allow them no time to recover.

Reports of the direction of Lanrezac's retreat indicated that the French line did not extend as far west as had been expected. Kluck believed it could be rolled up north of Paris, making a wide sweep to the west and south of the city unnecessary. The change involved a shift in the direction of his advance from due south to southeast and would have the added advantage of closing the gap between his army and Bülow's. Like everyone else he had begun the campaign assuming that reinforcements would be forthcoming from the left wing. He needed them now to replace the corps he had had to leave in front of Antwerp, the brigade in Brussels, the various units left to guard his ever-lengthening line of communications, not to mention his losses in combat. But reinforcements were not forthcoming. Moltke still had detached none from the left wing.

Moltke had many worries. True to his temperament, "Gloomy Julius" was less elated by the advance of his conquering armies than depressed by the difficulties of the advance. It was now the 30th day, and the schedule called for victory over France between the 36th and 40th days. Although his right-wing commanders continued to report the French and English as "decisively beaten" and their retreat in terms of "rout" and "flight," Moltke was uneasy. He noticed a suspicious lack of the usual signs of rout or disorganized retreat: Why were there so few prisoners? "A victory on the battlefield is of little account," his old chief Schlieffen used to say, "if it has not resulted either in breakthrough or encirclement. Though pushed back the enemy will appear again on different ground to renew the resistance he momentarily gave up. The campaign will go on. . . ."

Despite his concern Moltke did not go forward to investigate for himself but remained fretting at Headquarters, depending on delegates for reports. "It is heartbreaking," he wrote to his wife on August 29, "how little suspicions *der hohe Herr* [the Kaiser] has of the seriousness of the situation. He has already a certain shout-hurrah! mood that I hate like death."

On August 30 as the German Armies approached the climax of their campaign, OHL moved forward from Coblenz to Luxembourg City, ten miles behind the borders of France. They were now in territory emotionally if not officially hostile and which, by reason both of proximity and sentiment, was a hub of Allied rumors. Whispers circulated of the 80,000 Russians coming to help the British and French. OHL was kept busy piecing together indications of a landing somewhere on the Channel coast. The actual landing of 3,000 British marines at Ostend which, by the time the news reached Luxembourg, had swollen to serious and even Russian proportions, added apparent reality to German fears.

Besides the specter of Russians at his back, Moltke was bothered by the gaps in his battle line, especially between the armies of the right wing. There was one of twenty miles between Kluck and Bülow, another of twenty miles between Bülow and Hausen, and a third almost as wide between Hausen and the Duke of Württemberg. Moltke was uncomfortably conscious that the thinning spaces should have been filled by reinforcements drawn from the left wing which he had now committed to total involvement in the battle for the Moselle. He thought guiltily of Schlieffen's insistence that the proper course was to leave the left wing on the defensive with minimum forces and send every division that could be spared to the First and Second Armies. But the vision of a breakthrough of the French fortress line still lured OHL. Vacillating, Moltke on August 30 sent his artillery expert, Major Bauer, to make a personal survey of Rupprecht's front.

At Rupprecht's headquarters Bauer found "everything but concerted plans," and when he drove to the front lines commanders and officers gave him conflicting opinions. Some, pointing to the unmistakable withdrawal of enemy divisions from their front, were confident of imminent success. Others complained of the "difficult wooded mountains" along the Moselle, south of Toul, where the attack was running into trouble. Even if it succeeded the troops would be open to flank attack from Toul and supply lines would be lacking, since all roads and railroads led through the fortified city. Toul would have to be taken first. Back at Sixth Army Headquarters the once-aggressive enthusiasm of Prince Rupprecht had cooled to recognition that he was engaged in a "difficult and unpleasant task."

To Bauer, representing the Supreme Command, the report of French withdrawals from this front was a bad sign, for it meant that the enemy was withdrawing units to reinforce his front opposite the German right wing. He returned to OHL with the conclusion, as he told Moltke, that while the attack on Nancy-Toul and the Moselle line was "not without chances," it required an extended effort that seemed "not justifiable" at this time. Moltke agreed—and did nothing. He could not nerve himself to

call off the offensive that had already cost so much. And the Kaiser
wanted to ride in triumph through Nancy. No changed orders to the
Sixth Army went out; full-scale effort to break the Moselle line continued.

Von Kluck resented the failure to reinforce the marching wing at this
critical time. But it was not so much the need to narrow his front as the
belief that the French were already beaten and needed only to be rounded
up that decided him to make an inward wheel. Instead of brushing the
Channel with his sleeve he would brush Paris on the inside in direct
pursuit of Lanrezac's Army. That in the process he would be exposing his
flank to attack by the garrison of Paris or by Maunoury's forces falling
back upon Paris in front of him was a danger he did not ignore but did
not estimate highly. He considered the forces so far assembled under
Maunoury as negligible. The possibility of their being reinforced he considered also negligible because the French, stumbling backward in the
throes of defeat and disaster, must be too disorganized for such a
maneuver. Moreover, he assumed that all their available forces were
pinned down under the heavy pressure of the Crown Prince's Army
around Verdun and of Rupprecht's Armies along the Moselle. One of his
own corps, the laggard IVth Reserve, would be enough to leave in front
of Paris to guard the flank of his army as it slid across to the east in front
of the capital. After all, it had been proved in German war games that
garrison forces inside an entrenched camp do not venture out until
attacked, and the IVth Reserve, he believed, could contain the tatterde-
malion collection of units under Maunoury. Having learned, from a
captured letter, of Sir John French's intention to quit the line and retreat
behind the Seine, he regarded the BEF, his direct opponent up to now, as
of no further account.

Under the German system—in contrast to the French—Kluck as commander in the field was allowed the widest possible latitude for independent decision. Prepared by indoctrination, map exercises, and war games
to find the correct solution of a given military problem, a German general
was expected automatically to reach it when required. Though a deviation
from the original strategy, Kluck's plan to ignore Paris and go after the
retreating armies was the "correct" solution now that it appeared to him
possible to annihilate the French Armies in the field without enveloping
Paris. According to German military theory a fortified camp should not be
attacked until the enemy's mobile forces were overwhelmed. These once
destroyed, all the other fruits of victory followed. Although the lure of

Paris was strong, Kluck determined not to be tempted from the path of proper military procedure.

At 6:30 on the evening of August 30 a message reached him from von Bülow that made up his mind. It requested him to make the inward wheel in order to help Bülow "gain the full advantage of victory" over the French Fifth Army. Whether Bülow was in fact asking for help to exploit a victory gained at St. Quentin or to compensate for a defeat suffered at Guise, is, whatever the words he used, uncertain. His request fitted in with what Kluck wanted to do in any event, and Kluck made his decision. The objectives he gave for the next day's march were no longer due south but southeast toward Noyon and Compiègne in order to cut off the retreat of the French Fifth Army. To already protesting and footsore troops who had not rested since they had begun the advance at Liège sixteen days before, his order of August 31 read, "Again, therefore, we must call upon the troops for forced marches."

OHL, informed that the First Army would begin an inward wheel next morning, hurriedly approved. Unhappy about the gaps, Moltke saw a danger of the three armies of the right wing being unable to support each other in delivery of the final blow. Numbers had fallen below the prescribed density for an offensive, and if Kluck were to adhere to the original plan of a sweep around Paris the front would be stretched out for another fifty miles or more. Seizing upon Kluck's move as a fortunate solution, Moltke telegraphed his approval the same night.

The end was in sight: the scheduled defeat of France by the 39th day in time to turn against Russia; the proof of all German training, planning, and organization; the halfway step to winning the war and mastery of Europe. It remained only to round up the retreating French before they could regain cohesion and renew resistance. Nothing, not the gaps, nor the check to Bülow's Army at Guise nor the fatigue of the men nor any last-minute faltering or error must be allowed to check the last dash to victory. With fierce urgency Kluck drove his army forward. As officers rode up and down the roads and sergeants rasped commands, the war-stained troops wearily formed columns on the morning of August 31 to begin another day of endless foot-slogging. Knowing nothing of maps or place names, they were unaware of the change of direction. The magic word Paris drew them on. They were not told that it was no longer their destination.

Hunger added to their misery. They had outrun their supply lines, which were functioning inadequately owing to the destruction of bridges and railroad tunnels in Belgium. Repairs had not succeeded in keeping railheads up with the advance of the armies; the focal bridge at Namur, for one, was not repaired until September 30. Often the tired infantry after a long day's march found the villages where they expected to billet occupied by their own cavalry. The cavalry, who were supposed to live off the country, were always so anxious about their supply trains and horses' fodder that to secure these they "constantly installed themselves," according to the Crown Prince, a former cavalryman himself, in places meant for the infantry. In a piece of unexpected testimony coming from this source, he added, "They always halted and got in the way of the infantry the moment things in front began to look ugly."

Kluck's Army met an ugly surprise on September 1 when it ran into the heels of the British who unaccountably, since Kluck's communiqué had said they were retreating "in the most complete disorder," were able to turn upon the Germans and offer sharp and punishing combat. In a day of desperate fighting in and around the forests of Compiègne and Villers-Cotterets, the British rearguards held off the enemy while the main body of the BEF, to Kluck's disgust, again got away. Postponing a "much-needed" rest for his troops, Kluck ordered a further march next day, shifting back slightly to the west in the hope of enveloping the British. Again they succeeded in escaping him "just in time," to get across the Marne on September 3. His chance of finishing them off was now gone; having lost time, increased his casualties, and added marching distance, he resumed in no good temper his inward wheel in pursuit of the French.

"Our men are done up," wrote a German officer of Kluck's Army in his diary of September 2. "They stagger forward, their faces coated with dust, their uniforms in rags. They look like living scarecrows." After four days of marching an average of twenty-four miles a day over roads pitted with shellholes and barred by felled trees, "they march with eyes closed, singing in chorus so as not to fall asleep. . . . Only the certainty of early victory and a triumphal entry into Paris keeps them going. . . . Without this they would fall exhausted and go to sleep where they fall." The diary testified to a problem that was becoming increasingly serious in the German advance, especially further east where Bülow's and Hausen's troops were coming through Champagne. "They drink to excess but this drunkenness keeps them going. Today after inspection the General was furious. He wanted to stop this general drunkenness but we managed to dissuade him from giving severe orders. If we used too much severity the Army would not march. Abnormal stimulants are necessary to combat abnormal fatigue." "We will put all that right in Paris," the officer concluded hopefully, he, too, evidently unaware of the new direction of the march.

Through France as through Belgium the Germans left a blackened and defiled path as they passed. Villages were burned, civilians shot, homes looted and torn, horses ridden through rooms, artillery wagons dragged across gardens, latrines dug in the family burial plot of the Poincarés at Nubécourt. Kluck's IInd Corps passing through Senlis, twenty-five miles from Paris, on September 2, shot the Mayor and six other civilian hostages. A stone marker, just outside the town on the edge of a field where they are buried, bears their names:

Eugène Odène	Mayor
Emile Aubert	Tanner
Jean Barbier	Carter
Lucien Cottreau	Café waiter
Pierre Dewerdt	Chauffeur
J-B. Elysée Pommier	Baker's helper
Arthur Régant	Stonecutter

September 2 was a happy day for General von Hausen who found himself billeted in the Château of the Comte de Chabrillon at Thugny on the Aisne. Occupying the countess' bedroom, the General was delighted to discover from examination of her visiting cards that she was *née* Comtesse de Lévy-Mirepois in her own right, which caused him to sleep with that much extra pleasure in her bed. After dining on pheasant obtained by his supply officers who organized a shoot in the park of the château, Hausen counted the countess' table silver and left an inventory of it with an old man in the village.

That night Moltke, who after a second look had developed qualms about the flank that Kluck's inward wheel was exposing to Paris, issued a new General Order. As in the matter of the left wing, it showed his uncertain hand. It ratified Kluck's turn by ordering the First and Second Armies to "drive the French armies in a southeast direction away from Paris." At the same time it attempted to guard against a possible danger by ordering Kluck's army to follow "in echelon behind the Second Army" and make itself "responsible for the flank protection of the Armies."

In echelon! To Kluck the insult was worse than putting him, as OHL had done before, under Bülow's orders. The grim-visaged Attila with rifle in one hand and revolver in the other, the pace-setter of the right wing, was not going to stay behind anybody. He issued his own orders to the First Army "to continue its advance over the Marne tomorrow [September 3] in order to drive the French southeastward." He considered it sufficient for purposes of protecting the flank exposed to Paris to leave behind him his two weakest units: the IVth Reserve which was minus a brigade left back at Brussels and the 4th Cavalry Division which had suffered heavily in the fight against the British on September 1.

Captain Lepic, an officer of Sordet's Cavalry Corps, was reconnoitering northwest of Compiègne on August 31, the first morning of Kluck's turn, when he saw at a little distance an enemy cavalry column of nine squadrons, followed fifteen minutes later by an infantry column with batteries, ammunition wagons, and a company of cyclists. He noticed they were taking the road for Compiègne rather than the direct southward road for Paris. Unaware that he was the earliest witness of a historic swerve, Captain Lepic was more interested to report that the Uhlans had discarded their distinctive helmets and were wearing cloth caps and that "they ask directions of the local people in bad French, saying 'Englisch, Englisch.'" His information about their line of march did not as yet convey any great significance to GQG. The town and château of Compiègne, it was thought, might be attracting the Germans, and they could still take the road from Compiègne to Paris. Nor was Captain Lepic's view of two columns necessarily indicative of Kluck's whole Army.

The French, too, on August 31, knew the campaign was coming to a climax. Their second plan—the plan of August 25 to shift the center of gravity over to the left in an effort to halt the German right wing—had failed. The mission of the Sixth Army which, together with the British and the Fifth Army, was to have made a stand on the Somme, had failed. Now the mission of the Sixth Army, Joffre acknowledged, was "to cover Paris." The British, as he said privately, "*ne veulent pas marcher*," and the Fifth Army, with Kluck in pursuit on its flank, was still in danger of being enveloped. Indeed, alarming news was brought that a spearhead of Kluck's cavalry had already penetrated between the Fifth Army and Paris into the space left open by the British retreat. Clearly, as Colonel Pont, Joffre's Chief of Operations told him, "it seems no longer possible to oppose the right wing with sufficient forces to arrest its enveloping movement."

A new plan was necessary. Survival was the immediate aim. At GQG Joffre with his two deputies, Belin and Berthelot, and the senior officers of the Operations Bureau discussed what was to be done. Into the "chapel" of the offensive the hot wind of events had forced a new idea— "to hold out" until the French Armies could stabilize a line from which to resume the offensive. Meanwhile, it was recognized, the German advance would extend its forces along a tremendous arc from Verdun to Paris. The plan this time, rather than to oppose the marching wing of the German Army, would be to cut it off by an attack upon the German center, reverting to the strategy of Plan 17. Only, now the battlefield was in the heart of France. A French defeat this time would not be a reverse as at the frontiers, but final.

The question was, How soon should the "forward movement" be resumed? At the earliest moment, on a level with Paris, in the valley of the Marne? Or should the retreat continue to a line forty miles farther back behind the Seine? Continuing the retreat meant yielding that much more territory to the Germans, but the barrier of the Seine would provide a breathing spell for the armies to gather strength when not under direct pressure of the enemy. As the Germans' chief aim was to destroy the French armies, so "our chief aim," Belin urged, must be to "keep ourselves alive." To take the "prudent" attitude and reform behind the Seine was now both a national duty and the course best designed to frustrate the aims of the enemy. So Belin argued, eloquently supported by Berthelot. Joffre listened—and next day issued General Order No. 4.

It was September 1, eve of the anniversary of Sedan, and the outlook for France appeared as tragic as it had then. Official confirmation of the Russian defeat at Tannenberg came in from the French military attaché. General Order No. 4, in contrast to the firm tone of the Order that followed the debacle on the frontiers, reflected the shaken optimism of GQG after a week of spreading invasion. It prescribed continued retreat for the Third, Fourth, and Fifth Armies "for some time to come" and set the Seine and Aube as the limit of the movement "without necessarily implying that this limit will be reached." "As soon as the Fifth Army has escaped the menace of envelopment," the armies "will resume the offensive"; but unlike the previous Order it named no specific time or place. Yet it contained the genesis of the future battle, for it spoke of bringing reinforcements from the Armies of Nancy and Epinal to participate in the renewed offensive and said "the mobile troops of the fortified camp of Paris may also take part in the general action."

Upon this as upon every other act and order of the next four days, layers of dispute were to be heaped by the partisans of Joffre and those of

Gallieni in a long and painful controversy over the origins of the Battle of the Marne. Unquestionably Joffre had in mind *a* general battle if not *the* battle at the time and place it was actually to occur. The battle that he envisaged would take place when the five pursuing German armies would come "between the horns of Paris and Verdun," and the French Armies would be drawn up in a shallow curve or net stretched across the center of France. Joffre thought he had a week's time to make his arrangements, for he told Messimy, who came to say goodbye to him on September 1, that he expected to resume the offensive on September 8 and anticipated that it would be called "the battle of Brienne-le-Château." A town twenty-five miles behind the Marne, about halfway between that river and the Seine, Brienne had been the scene of a Napoleonic victory over Blücher. It may have seemed an appropriate omen to Joffre. Amid the general gloom of further enforced retreat, under the awful shadow of the approaching enemy, his sangfroid, his appearance of serenity and confidence, once again impressed Messimy.

It did not comfort Paris which saw itself uncovered by a retreat of the armies to the Seine. Joffre called Millerand and gave him an unsparing summary of the military situation. The "accentuated" retreat of the English had uncovered the left flank of Lanrezac's Army so that the retreat must continue until Lanrezac was disengaged. Maunoury had been ordered to fall back on Paris and place himself "in relation" to Gallieni, although Joffre said nothing about putting the Sixth Army under Gallieni's command. Enemy columns were taking a direction slightly away from Paris, which might offer some "respite"; nevertheless he considered it "urgent and essential" that the government quit Paris "without delay," either this evening or tomorrow.

Gallieni, informed of this development by a frantic government, called Joffre who managed to avoid speaking to him but was given his message: "We are in no condition to resist. . . . General Joffre must understand that if Maunoury cannot hold, Paris cannot withstand the enemy. Three active corps must be added to the forces of the fortified camp." Later that afternoon Joffre called back and informed Gallieni that he was putting Maunoury's Army under his orders. They would now become the mobile troops of the fortified camp of Paris. Such troops are traditionally commanded independently of the Field Army and could be withheld from a general battle at the will of the garrison commander. Joffre had no intention of giving them up. In a deft maneuver on the same day he requested the Minister of War to put the fortified camp of Paris and all its forces under his authority as Commander in Chief, "to enable me to use the mobile forces of the garrison in the field if the case arises." Millerand, no less under Joffre's spell than Messimy, so ordered it on September 2.

Meanwhile Gallieni had an army at last. Maunoury's forces which he could now dispose of consisted of one active division belonging to the VIIth Corps, a native Moroccan brigade, and four reserve divisions: the 61st and 62nd under General Ebener which had been taken from Paris originally, and the 55th and 56th Reserves which had fought so valiantly in Lorraine. Joffre agreed to add, since it was not under his control anyway, the first-rate 45th Division of Zouaves from Algiers which was just then de-training in Paris and one active corps from the field army. Like Kluck, he picked a damaged one, the IVth Corps of the Third Army which had suffered disastrous losses in the Ardennes. It was receiving replacements, however, and its transfer from the Third Army's front at Verdun to the Paris front was a reinforcement of which Kluck thought the French incapable. Troops of the IVth Corps, Gallieni was informed, would arrive by train in Paris on September 3 and 4.

Instantly upon receiving Joffre's verbal assignment to him of the Sixth Army, Gallieni drove north to make contact with his new command. How late was the hour was apparent when he passed refugees converging upon Paris in flight from the oncoming Germans, a look on their faces of "terror and despair." At Pontoise, just outside Paris to the northwest where the 61st and 62nd Divisions were coming in, all was disorder and dismay. The troops who had been caught in severe combat as they retreated were wearied and bloody; the local population was in panic at the sound of the guns and at reports of Uhlans in the neighborhood. After talking to General Ebener, Gallieni went on to see Maunoury at Creil on the Oise, thirty miles north of Paris. He gave Maunoury orders to blow up the Oise bridges and to try to delay the enemy's advance as he fell back on Paris and under no circumstances to allow the Germans to get between him and the capital.

Hurrying back to Paris he passed a happier sight than the refugees— the splendid Zouaves of the 45th Algerian marching through the boulevards to take their places at the forts. In their bright jackets and ballooning trousers they created a sensation and gave Parisians something to cheer once again.

But inside the ministries the mood was black. Millerand had passed on the "heart-breaking" facts to the President: "all our hopes are shattered; we are in full retreat all along the line; Maunoury's Army is falling back on Paris. . . ." As Minister of War, Millerand refused to take responsibility for the government remaining an hour longer than tomorrow evening, September 2. Poincaré faced "the saddest event of my life." It was decided that the entire administration must move to Bordeaux as a unit, leaving none behind in Paris lest the public make invidious comparisons between ministers.

Upon Gallieni's return to the city that evening, he learned from Millerand that all civil and military authority for the foremost city in Europe as it came under siege would be left in his hands. Except for the Prefect of the Seine and the Prefect of Police, "I would be alone." The Prefect of Police, upon whom he would have to depend, had been in office, he discovered, barely an hour. The former Prefect, M. Hennion, on learning that the government was leaving, flatly refused to stay behind, and upon being ordered to remain at his post, resigned "for reasons of health." For Gallieni the exit of the government at least had the advantage of silencing the advocates of an open city; their legal excuse was gone and he was free to defend Paris as a fortified camp. Although he "preferred to be without ministers," he thought that "one or two might have stayed for the sake of appearances." This was hardly fair to those who would have liked to stay, but Gallieni's contempt for politicians was all-inclusive.

Expecting the Germans at the gates in two days, he stayed up all night with his staff, making "all my dispositions to give battle north of the city from Pontoise to the Ourcq," that is, over an area forty-five miles wide. The Ourcq is a small river that feeds into the Marne east of Paris.

Late that night information reached GQG that could have spared the government the necessity of flight. During the day a bag was brought to Captain Fagalde, Intelligence Officer of the Fifth Army. It had been found on the body of a German cavalry officer attached to Kluck's Army who, while riding in an automobile, had been shot and killed by a French patrol. In the bag were papers, including a map smeared with blood which showed the lines of advance for each of Kluck's corps and the point each was to reach at the end of that day's march. The lines for the whole army pointed in a southeasterly direction from the Oise toward the Ourcq.

GQG correctly interpreted Captain Fagalde's find as showing Kluck's intention to slide by Paris between the Sixth and the Fifth Armies in an effort to roll up the left of the main French line. If they also recognized that this meant he would forego attack on Paris, they took no great pains to impress that view upon the government. When in the morning Colonel Penelon, liaison officer between GQG and the President, brought Poin-

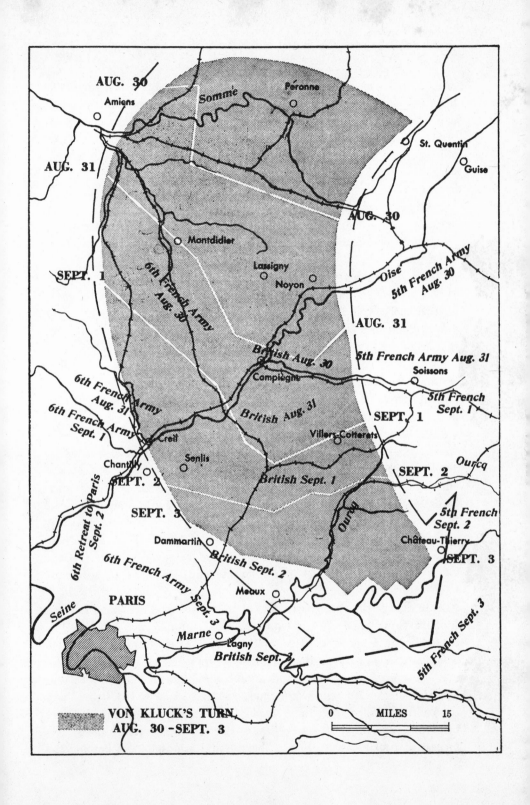

AUG. 30

Amiens

Somme   Péronne

AUG. 31   St. Quentin

                                                    Guise

                                      AUG. 30

                              Oise   5th French Army
                                              Aug. 30
Montdidier

SEPT. 1   Lassigny
                    Noyon

                                      AUG. 31

                              British Aug. 30   5th French Army Aug. 31

6th French Army   Soissons
Aug. 30
                    Compiègne
                                                          5th French
                    British Aug. 31   Sept. 1
6th French Army
Aug. 31   SEPT. 1
                                  Villers-Cotterets
6th French Army   SEPT. 2   Ourcq
Sept. 1
        Creil   SEPT. 2
Chantilly   Senlis   British Sept. 1
        SEPT. 2   5th French
                                                          Sept. 2
            SEPT. 3   Château-Thierry
                                              Ourcq   SEPT. 3
6th Retreat to Paris   Dammartin   British Sept. 2
Sept. 2
        6th French Army   Meaux   5th French Sept. 3
                    Sept. 3
Seine   PARIS
                    Marne
                    British Sept. 3   5th French Sept. 3
        Lagny
        British Sept. 3

        VON KLUCK'S TURN   0   MILES   15
        AUG. 30 - SEPT. 3

caré news of Kluck's change of direction he did not bring any suggestion from Joffre that the government need not leave. On the contrary Joffre sent word that the government must go, that Kluck's intentions could not be certain, that his columns were already at Senlis and Chantilly, twenty miles away, and Paris would be under his guns very soon. How far the significance of Kluck's turn was understood by Poincaré or Millerand is hard to say; in the midst of war and crisis nothing is as clear or as certain as it appears in hindsight. Urgency, even panic, was in the air. Once having gone through the agony of coming to a decision, the government found it hard to change. Millerand, in any event, continued adamant for departure.

It was September 2, Sedan Day, and "the hateful moment had come." When he learned that arrangements had been made for the government to leave in the middle of the night instead of by day in the sight of the public, Poincaré's "grief and humiliation" increased. The Cabinet insisted that his presence was legally required at the seat of government; even Mme. Poincaré, who begged to continue her hospital work in Paris as a public gesture, was not allowed to remain. Ambassador Myron Herrick of the United States, his face all "puckered up" came to say goodbye with tears in his eyes.

To Herrick, as to everyone inside the French capital at that moment, "the terrible onslaught of the Germans," as he wrote to his son, "seems almost beyond resistance." He had received a warning from the Germans advising him to leave for the provinces as "whole quarters" of Paris might be destroyed. He was determined to stay, however, and promised Poincaré to protect the museums and monuments of Paris under the American flag as being "in the custody of humanity at large." Already he had formed a plan, fitting the desperate and exalted mood of the hour, that "if the Germans reached the outskirts of the city and demanded its surrender, to go out and talk with their army commander and, if possible, the Kaiser." As custodian of their embassy, at their request, he could demand a hearing. In later days, when friends who had lived through the first week of September in Paris used to count themselves a select number, Gallieni would say, "Don't forget, there was also Herrick."

At seven o'clock Gallieni went to take farewell of Millerand. The War Ministry in the Rue St. Dominique was "sad, dark and deserted" and the courtyard filled with huge moving vans in which the archives were being piled for shipment to Bordeaux. The remainder were burned. The process of packing up created a "lugubrious" atmosphere. Climbing the unlit staircase, Gallieni found the Minister alone in an empty room. Now that the government was leaving, Millerand did not hesitate to allow Paris and everyone in it to come under fire. His orders to Gallieni, who hardly needed to be told, were to defend Paris "*à outrance.*"

"Do you understand, M. *le Ministre*, the significance of the words, *à outrance?*" Gallieni asked. "They mean destruction, ruins, dynamiting bridges in the center of the city."

"*À outrance*," Millerand repeated. Saying goodbye, he looked at Gallieni as at a man he was unlikely ever to see again, and Gallieni felt "pretty well persuaded, myself, that I was remaining to be killed."

Some hours later, in darkness and self-imposed secrecy that afflicted many of them with a sense of shame, ministers and members of Parliament boarded the train for Bordeaux, clothing the inglorious moment in a noble statement to the public next morning. "To hold out and fight," it said, must now become the order of the day. France would hold out and fight while on the seas England cut the enemy's communications with the rest of the world and the Russians "continue to advance and carry the decisive blow to the heart of the German empire!" (It was not considered the moment to add news of a Russian defeat.) In order to give the greatest "*élan* and effectiveness" to French resistance, the government, at the demand of the military, was moving "momentarily" to a place where it could remain in unbroken and constant contact with the whole country. "Frenchmen, let us be worthy of these tragic circumstances. We will obtain the final victory—by unfaltering will, by endurance, by tenacity—by refusing to perish."

Gallieni was content with a short sharp notice worded deliberately to dispel rumors that Paris had been declared an open city and to let the people know what to expect. His proclamation appeared on the walls of Paris in the morning:

"ARMY OF PARIS. CITIZENS OF PARIS.

The members of the Government of the Republic have left Paris to give a new impulse to the national defense. I have received a mandate to defend Paris against the invader. This mandate I shall carry out to the end.

Paris, September 3, 1914
Military Governor of Paris, Commander of the Army of Paris

Gallieni.

The shock to the public was all the greater since GQG's policy of issuing only the least explicit communiqués had left people uninformed as to the seriousness of the military situation. The government appeared to have decamped without due cause. Its nocturnal going off left a painful impression which was not dispelled by what proved to be an extended and tenacious affection for Bordeaux. Puns were made at the expense of the government, calling them *"tournedos à la Bordelaise,"* and the crowds who stormed the railway stations in their wake inspired a parody of "The Marseillaise":

> *"Aux gares, citoyens!*
> *Montez dans les wagons!"*

These were "days of anguish" for the Military Government of Paris. With the armies retreating north and east of the city, the problem of how long to hold and when to destroy the eighty bridges in the region caused increasing tension and anxiety. Commanders in each sector, as soon as they had assured passage of their own troops, were anxious to blow up the bridges behind them in order to cut off pursuit. GQG's orders were to let "no bridge fall intact into enemy hands"; at the same time the bridges would be needed for a return to the offensive. Three different commands were operating in the area: Gallieni's, Joffre's and, geographically between them, that of Sir John French whose chief concern since Kitchener's visit was to make a show of his independence of everybody. Engineers of the Paris camp guarding the bridges were beset by a conflict of orders. "A disaster is preparing," reported an officer of Engineers to General Hirschauer.

By nightfall of September 2 the British had reached the Marne and got across next day. Below Compiègne the troops discovered they were marching off their maps, and now it dawned on them that this was not after all a "strategic retreat" as they had been told by their officers. Their bases at Boulogne and Havre had by now been evacuated and all stores and personnel moved down to Saint-Nazaire at the mouth of the Loire.

About a day's march behind them the Fifth Army was still not yet out of danger of envelopment. In the continuing hot weather, retreat and pursuit went on, prey as tired as pursuers. Since the Battle of Guise the Fifth Army had been marching eighteen to twenty miles a day. Along its route groups of deserters pillaged farms and homes and spread panic among the population with tales of German terror. Executions took place.

Lanrezac thought no army ever underwent such an ordeal as his. At the same time a British officer said of the BEF, "I would never have believed that men could be so tired and so hungry and yet live." Trying to find a source of encouragement during these days, Henry Wilson said to Colonel Huguet, "The Germans are over-hasty. They urge the pursuit too fast. The whole thing is overdone. They are bound to make a big mistake and then your hour will come."

Up to this point Joffre and his advisers at GQG, although aware of Kluck's inward wheel, did not see in it an important or early opportunity for attack on his flank. Kluck's shift in pursuit of the British on September 2 left them uncertain whether he might not be turning back against Paris. In any event their minds were not on Paris but were fixed on a general battle along the Seine, not to take place until they had reestablished a solid front. After further anxious consultation at GQG, Joffre came to a decision to continue the retreat "several days' march to the rear" of where the armies then stood, which would allow time to bring up reinforcements from his right wing. Despite the risk of weakening the barely held line of the Moselle, he decided to bring over a corps each from the First and Second Armies.

His decision was embodied in secret instructions issued to the army commanders on September 2 which made the Seine and Aube definitive as the line to be reached. The object, Joffre explained, was "to extricate the armies from the enemy's pressure and enable them to reorganize," and when this had been accomplished and reinforcements from the east brought up, "at that moment to pass to the offensive." The British Army would be "asked to participate in the maneuver" and the garrison of Paris "will act in the direction of Meaux," that is, against Kluck's flank. Still omitting a date, Joffre said he would give the signal "within a few days." Commanders were ordered to take "the most draconian measures" against deserters to ensure orderly retreat. Asking each to understand the situation and extend his utmost efforts, Joffre made it clear that this would be the battle "upon which the salvation of the country depends."

Gallieni, receiving the orders in Paris, condemned Joffre's plan because it sacrificed Paris and was "divorced from reality." He believed the pace of the German pursuit would allow the French Armies no time to reach or reform upon the Seine. Scattered reports of Kluck's southeastward march were reaching him, but he had not been informed of the vital confirmation found by Captain Fagalde. On the night of September 2, expecting attack next day, he slept at his Headquarters, which were now established in the

Lycée Victor-Duruy, a girls' school across the street from the Invalides. A large building set back behind trees, it was isolated from the public and, having fewer entrances and exits than the Invalides, was easier to guard. Sentinels were posted at the doors, field telephones connected with all divisional headquarters of the fortified camp, offices set apart for the Operations and Intelligence staffs, mess and sleeping quarters arranged, and Gallieni was enabled, with great relief, to move into "a regular field Headquarters just as at the front."

The following morning, September 3, he learned definitely of Kluck's movement toward the Marne, away from Paris. Lieutenant Watteau, an aviator of the Paris garrison making a reconnaissance flight, saw the enemy columns "gliding from west to east" toward the valley of the Ourcq. Later a second airplane from the Paris camp confirmed the report.

In the staff room of Gallieni's *Deuxième Bureau* an unspoken excitement communicated itself among the officers. Colonel Girodon, an officer wounded at the front who, however, "considered himself fit to do staff work," was lying on a chaise longue with his eyes fixed on the wall map on which colored pins traced the direction of the German advance. General Clergerie, Gallieni's Chief of Staff, entered the room just as another air reconnaissance report from British aviators was brought in. As once more the pins were moved, the track of Kluck's turn appeared unmistakably on the map, and Clergerie and Girodon cried out together: "They offer us their flank! They offer us their flank!"

▶▶▶ *22* ▶

▶▶▶ *"Gentlemen, We Will*
Fight on the Marne"

GALLIENI INSTANTLY SAW THE OPPORTUNITY
offered to the Army of Paris. Without hesitating he made up his mind
to launch an attack on the flank of the German right wing at the earliest
moment and induce Joffre to support the maneuver by resuming the offensive at once, on the entire front, instead of continuing the retreat to the
Seine. Although the Army of Paris, of which Maunoury's Sixth Army was
the core, was under Gallieni's command, the camp of Paris with all its
forces had been, since the day before, under Joffre's command. To launch
the Sixth Army upon the offensive two conditions were necessary: Joffre's
consent and support of the Sixth Army's nearest neighbor, the BEF. Both
stood between Paris and Kluck's flank, Maunoury north and the British
south of the Marne.

Gallieni summoned his Chief of Staff, General Clergerie, to what
Clergerie called "one of those long conferences he holds on grave issues—
they usually last from two to five minutes." It was now 8:30 P.M. of
September 3. They agreed, if Kluck's line of march were maintained next
morning, to exert every pressure upon Joffre for an immediate combined

offensive. Aviators of the Paris camp were ordered to make early reconnaissance flights, upon which "grave decisions would depend," and to report
before 10:00 A.M.

Success of a flank attack, as General Hirschauer warned, "depends on
the spearhead penetrating," and the Sixth Army was not the strong sharp
instrument Gallieni would have liked. It had reached the positions assigned
to it in a generally exhausted condition. Some units had marched thirty-
seven miles during the day and night of September 2. Fatigue depressed
morale. Gallieni, like his colleagues, considered reserve divisions, of which
Maunoury's Army was largely composed, as of "mediocre value." The 62nd
Reserve, which had not had a day of rest or one day without combat
during the retreat, had lost two-thirds of its officers and had only reserve
lieutenants as replacements. The IVth Corps had not yet arrived. Only the
"calm and resolution" of the people of Paris—those who did not flee south
—was a source of satisfaction.

Von Kluck reached the Marne on the evening of September 3 after
Lanrezac's Army, which he was pursuing, and the British on his outer
flank, had got across earlier in the day. Between them, in the haste, weariness, and confusion of retreat, and despite, or because of, the rain of telegrams about demolitions, they left bridges intact or only partially destroyed.
Kluck held the bridgeheads and, disobeying the order to remain level with
Bülow, intended to cross in the morning, continuing his inward wheel in
pursuit of the Fifth Army. He had sent three messages to OHL announcing
his intention to cross the Marne but as wireless communication with
Luxembourg was even worse than with Coblenz, they did not get through
until the following day. Out of contact with the First Army for two days,
OHL did not know Kluck had disobeyed the order of September 2; by
the time they found out, his leading columns were across the Marne.

They had marched twenty-five to twenty-eight miles on September 3.
When the soldiers came into their billets, said a French witness, "they fell
down exhausted, muttering in a dazed way, 'forty kilometers! forty kilometers!' That was all they could say." In the coming battle many German
prisoners were taken asleep, unable to go another step. The heat of the days
was terrible. Only the expectation of reaching Paris "tomorrow or the day
after" enabled them to march at all, and the officers did not dare undeceive
them. In his fever to finish off the French, Kluck, besides wearing out his
men, outstripped not only his supply trains but also his heavy artillery.
His compatriot in East Prussia, General von François, would not budge
until he had at hand all his artillery and ammunition wagons. But François

faced battle, whereas Kluck, thinking he faced only pursuit and mopping up, ignored the precaution. He believed the French incapable, after ten days of retreat, of the morale and energy required to turn around at the sound of the bugle and fight again. Nor was he worried about his flank. "The General fears nothing from the direction of Paris," recorded an officer on September 4. "After we have destroyed the remains of the Franco-British Army he will return to Paris and give the IVth Reserve the honor of leading the entry into the French capital."

The order to remain behind as flank guard of the German advance could not be carried out, Kluck bluntly informed OHL as he pushed forward on September 4. A two-day halt, necessary to allow Bülow to catch up, would weaken the whole German offensive and give the enemy time to regain his freedom of movement. Indeed, it was only by the "bold action" of his army that the crossings of the Marne had been opened to the other armies, and "it is now to be hoped that every advantage will be taken of this success." Becoming angrier as he dictated, Kluck demanded to know how it was that "decisive victories" by the "other" armies—meaning Bülow—were always followed by "appeals for support."

Bülow was furious when his neighbor transformed "the echelon in rear of the Second Army prescribed by OHL into an echelon in advance." His troops, too, like most of the German units as they came up to the Marne, were exhausted. "We can do no more," wrote an officer of the Xth Reserve Corps. "The men fall in the ditches and lie there just to breathe. . . . The order comes to mount. I ride bent over with my head resting on the horse's mane. We are thirsty and hungry. Indifference comes over us. Such a life isn't worth much. To lose it is to lose little." Troops of Hausen's Army complained of having "no cooked food for five days in a row." In the neighboring Fourth Army an officer wrote: "We march all day in the broiling heat. With bearded faces and powdered with dust, the men look like walking sacks of flour." That the German advance was being achieved at the cost of the exhaustion and apathy of the troops did not alarm the field commanders. Like Kluck, they were convinced the French could not recoup. Bülow on September 3 reported the French Fifth Army "decisively beaten"—for the third or fourth time—and fleeing "utterly disorganized to south of the Marne."

If not "utterly disorganized," the Fifth Army was distinctly not in good shape. Lanrezac's loss of confidence in Joffre, which he took no trouble to conceal, his quarrels with liaison officers from GQG and his dispute of orders infected his staff, half of whom were at odds with the

other half. All were irritated and worried with nerves strained by the long
agony of bringing up the rear of the French retreat. General Mas de Latrie
of the XVIIIth Corps, which was nearest to the enemy, was expressing
"anguish" at the condition of his troops. But however battered, the Fifth
Army had got across the Marne with enough distance between itself and
the enemy to be considered disengaged, thus fulfilling Joffre's condition
for resuming the offensive.

Although Joffre intended to make the effort "within a few days," as he
informed the government, he was not specific, and discouragement at
GQG was deep. Every day liaison officers returned depressed from their
visits to the armies over whom, as one of them said, "blew the winds of
defeat." Arrangements were being made to move GQG back another
thirty miles to Chatillon-sur-Seine, and the move was carried out two days
later, September 5. In ten days France had lost the cities of Lille, Valenciennes, Cambrai, Arras, Amiens, Maubeuge, Mézieres, St. Quentin, Laon,
and Soissons, as well as coal and iron mines, wheat and sugarbeet areas,
and a sixth of her population. A pall descended upon everyone when
Rheims, in whose great cathedral every French king from Clovis to Louis
XVI had been crowned, was abandoned as an open city to Bülow's Army
on September 3. It was not until two weeks later, in the angry aftermath
of the Marne, that the bombardment took place which was to make the
cathedral of Rheims a symbol to the world like the Library of Louvain.

Joffre who had still shown no sign of nerves, whose appetite for three
regular meals remained steady and his ten o'clock bedtime inviolable,
faced on September 3 the one task that during this period caused him
visible discomfort. He had made up his mind that Lanrezac must go. His
stated reasons were Lanrezac's "physical and moral depression" and his
"unpleasant personal relations," by now notorious, with Sir John French.
For the sake of the coming offensive in which the role of the Fifth Army
would be crucial and participation by the British essential, he must be
replaced. Despite Lanrezac's firm conduct of the battle of Guise, Joffre
had convinced himself that since then Lanrezac had "morally gone to
pieces." Besides, he never ceased criticizing and raising objections to orders.
This was not necessarily evidence of moral depression, but it annoyed the
Generalissimo.

With few personal ideas of his own, Joffre was adept at taking advice,
and submitted more or less consciously to the reigning doctrinaires of the
Operations Bureau. They formed what a French military critic called "a
church outside which there was no salvation and which could never pardon

those who revealed the falsity of its doctrine." Lanrezac's sin was in having
been right, all too vocally. He had been right from the beginning about
the fatal underestimation of the German right wing as a result of which a
fair part of France was now under the German boot. His decision to break
off battle at Charleroi when threatened with double envelopment by
Bülow's and Hausen's armies had saved the French left wing. As General
von Hausen acknowledged after the war, this upset the whole German plan
which had counted on enveloping the French left, and ultimately caused
Kluck's inward wheel in the effort to roll up the Fifth Army. Whether
Lanrezac's withdrawal came from fear or from wisdom is immaterial, for
fear sometimes *is* wisdom and in this case had made possible the renewed
effort Joffre was now preparing. All this was to be recognized long afterward when the French government, in a belated gesture of amends, awarded
Lanrezac the Grand Cordon of the Legion of Honor. But in the bitter
failure of the first month Lanrezac's *lèse majesté* made him intolerable to
GQG. On the day he brought his army across the Marne, he was marked
for the Tarpeian Rock.

Lanrezac's mood, after all that had passed, was in reality not the most
reliable; unquestionably the mutual distrust between him and GQG,
whose so ever the fault, and between him and Sir John French made him a
risk as a commander in time of crisis. Joffre felt it necessary to take every
possible measure to avoid failure in the coming offensive. Including his
dismissals of the next two days, Joffre in the first five weeks stripped the
French Army of two army commanders, ten corps commanders and thirty-
eight, or half the total number, of divisional generals. New and mostly
better men, including three future Marshals, Foch, Pétain, and Franchet
d'Esperey, moved up to fill their places. If some injustices were committed,
the army was improved.

Joffre set out in his car for Sézanne where Fifth Army Headquarters
was located that day. At a prearranged meeting place he conferred with
Franchet d'Esperey, commander of the Ist Corps who turned up with his
head wrapped in a bath towel because of the heat.

"Do you feel yourself capable of commanding an army?" Joffre asked.

"As well as anyone else," replied Franchet d'Esperey. When Joffre
simply looked at him, he shrugged and explained: "The higher one goes,
the easier. One gets a bigger staff; there are more people to help." That
being settled, Joffre drove on.

At Sézanne he retired alone with Lanrezac and said to him: "My
friend, you are used up and undecided. You will have to give up command

of the Fifth Army. I hate to tell you this but I have to." According to Joffre, Lanrezac thought for a moment and replied, "General, you are right," and seemed like a man relieved of an overwhelming burden. According to Lanrezac's own account, he protested vigorously and demanded that Joffre cite evidence, but Joffre would only repeat "Hesitant, undecided," and complain that Lanrezac always made "observations" on orders given him. Lanrezac said this could hardly be held against him since events proved all his observations correct, which, of course, was the trouble. But Joffre was obviously not listening. He made "facial expressions indicating I had worn out his patience and his eyes refused to meet mine." Lanrezac gave up the struggle. Joffre emerged from the interview looking, according to his aide-de-camp, "very nervous," a unique occasion.

Franchet d'Esperey was now sent for. Called from his dinner at the first mouthful of soup, he stood up, swallowed off a glass of wine, put on his coat, and left for Sézanne. Held up by a transfer of military supplies taking place unhurriedly at a crossroad, he jumped from his car. So well known in the army was his compact hard figure with a head like a howitzer shell, crewcut hair, piercing dark eyes, and sharp authoritarian voice, that the men, horses, and vehicles parted as if by magic. In the coming days, as tension and his temper rose, his method of dealing with roadblocks as he dashed from corps to corps was to fire his revolver out of the window of his car. To the British soldiers he eventually became known as "Desperate Frankey." Fellow officers found him transformed from the jovial and friendly, though strict, commander they had known, to a tyrant. He became fierce, peremptory, glacial, and imposed a reign of terror upon his staff no less than upon the troops. Hardly had Lanrezac handed over to him the confidential dossier and relinquished command at Sézanne when the telephone rang and Hely d'Oissel, who answered it, was heard repeating "Yes, General. No, General," with increasing irritation.

"Who's that?" rapped out Franchet d'Esperey, and was told it was General Mas de Latrie of the XVIIIth Corps insisting he could not carry out orders for the next day because of the extreme fatigue of his troops.

"I'll take it," said the new Commander. "Hello, this is General d'Esperey. I have taken over command of the Fifth Army. There is to be no more discussion. You will march; march or drop dead." And he hung up.

September 4 opened with a sense of climax felt in widely separated places; a kind of extra-sensory awareness that great events sometimes send ahead. In Paris, Gallieni felt this was the "decisive" day. In Berlin, Princess

Blücher wrote in her diary, "Nothing is talked of but the expected entry into Paris." In Brussels the leaves had begun to fall, and a sudden wind blew them in gusts about the street. People felt the hidden chill of autumn in the air and wondered what would happen if the war were to last through the winter. At the American Legation Hugh Gibson noted a "growing nervousness" at German Headquarters where there had been no announcements of victories in four days. "I am sure there is something big in the air today."

At OHL in Luxembourg tension was at a pitch as the triumphant moment of German history approached. Stretched to the snapping point of endurance, the army was about to complete upon the Marne the work begun at Sadowa and Sedan. "It is the 35th day," said the Kaiser with triumph in his voice to a visiting minister from Berlin. "We invest Rheims, we are 30 miles from Paris. . . ."

At the front the German Armies thought of the final battle in terms of a roundup rather than a combat. "Great news," recorded an officer of the Fifth Army in his diary, "the French have offered us an armistice and are prepared to pay an indemnity of 17 billions. For the time being," he added soberly, "the armistice is being refused."

The enemy was considered beaten, and any evidence to the contrary was unwelcome. A horrid doubt entered the mind of General von Kuhl, Kluck's Chief of Staff, upon the report of a French column near Château-Thierry singing as it marched in retreat. He suppressed his doubts, "as all orders for the new movement had already been given." Apart from a few such instances there was no suspicion, or none that made itself felt upon command decisions, that the enemy was preparing a counter-offensive. Although signs were visible, German Intelligence, operating in hostile territory, failed to pick them up. An Intelligence officer from OHL came to the Crown Prince's headquarters on September 4 to say that the situation was favorable all along the front and that "We are advancing triumphantly everywhere."

One man did not think so. Moltke, unlike Joffre, may have had no confidence in his own star but neither did he have the veil that confidence can sometimes draw before the eyes, and so he saw things without illusion. In this he resembled Lanrezac. On September 4 he was "serious and depressed," and said to Helfferich, the same minister who had just talked to the Kaiser, "We have hardly a horse in the army who can go another step." After a thoughtful pause he went on: "We must not deceive ourselves. We have had success but not victory. Victory means annihilation of the enemy's power of resistance. When a million men oppose each other in battle the victor has prisoners. Where are our prisoners? Twenty thousand in Lorraine, perhaps another ten or twenty thousand altogether. And from the comparatively small number of guns captured, it seems to me the French are conducting a planned and orderly retreat." The inadmissible thought had been spoken.

On that day Kluck's message that he was about to cross the Marne finally reached OHL, too late to stop the movement. The flank Kluck thus exposed to Paris worried Moltke. Reports were coming in of heavy railroad traffic in the direction of Paris, "apparently the movement of troops." Rupprecht on that day reported the withdrawal of two French corps from his front. It was impossible any longer to avoid the evidence that the enemy's power of resistance had not come to an end.

The transfer of French troops, as Colonel Tappen pointed out, could mean "an attack from Paris upon our right flank for which we had no available reserves." This was a problem of which Moltke, as well as the field commanders, was painfully conscious. Losses sustained in the continuing combats with the French rearguards during the retreat could not be made up by reserves as the French were doing. The holes in the German lines remained and the two corps sent to East Prussia were missed. Moltke was now ready to take reinforcements from the left wing even though Rupprecht had just launched a renewed attack on the Moselle on September 3. It happened that the Kaiser was at Rupprecht's headquarters when Moltke's proposal came through. Certain that this time, at last, the defense of Nancy would be broken, the Kaiser stoutly supported Rupprecht and von Krafft in opposing any diminution of their strength. A man other than Moltke might have insisted, but Moltke did not. Since the unnerving night of August 1, the uncertainties and stresses of the campaign had weakened rather than strengthened his will. Failing reinforcements for the right wing, he decided to halt it.

The new Order, addressed to all the armies, which was drafted that night and issued early next morning, was an open admission of failure of the right wing, failure of the design for victory to which Germany had sacrificed the neutrality of Belgium. Dated September 4, a month from the day Belgium was invaded, it was an accurate appraisal of the situation. "The enemy" it said, "has evaded the enveloping attack of the First and Second Armies and a part of his forces has joined up with the forces of Paris." Enemy troops were being withdrawn from the Moselle front and moved westward "probably in order to concentrate superior forces in the region of Paris and threaten the right flank of the German Army." In consequence "the First and Second Armies must remain facing the eastern front of Paris . . . to act against any operation of the enemy from that area." The Third Army was to continue a southward advance to the Seine and the other armies to carry on under the previous order of September 2.

To halt the marching wing on the very threshhold of victory seemed stark madness to the War Minister, General von Falkenhayn, who within two weeks was to be Moltke's successor as Commander in Chief. "Only one thing is certain," he wrote in his diary for September 5. "Our General Staff has completely lost its head. Schlieffen's notes do not help any further so Moltke's wits come to an end." It was not Moltke's wits but German time that was running out. In the French troop movements Moltke correctly saw a danger developing upon his outer flank and took a proper and sensible measure to meet it. His Order had only one flaw: it was late. Even then it might have been in time had it not been for one man in a hurry—Gallieni.

Reports of the Paris aviators, at daybreak on September 4, showed him it was "vital to act quickly." The rear of Kluck's curved march to the southeast presented a clear target to Maunoury's Army and to the British if a joint attack could be launched in time. At 9:00 A.M., before obtaining Joffre's consent, he sent preliminary orders to Maunoury: "My intention is to send your army forward in liaison with the English forces against the German flank. Make your arrangements at once so that your troops will be ready to march this afternoon as the start of a general movement eastward by the forces of the Paris camp." As soon as he could Maunoury was to come to confer personally in Paris.

Gallieni then set himself to obtain an "immediate and energetic" decision from Joffre. Between them lay the remnants of an old relationship as commander and subordinate. Both were conscious of Gallieni's official designation as Commander in Chief if anything happened to Joffre. Aware that Joffre resisted and resented his influence, Gallieni counted less on persuading him than on forcing his hand. To that end he had already called Poincaré in Bordeaux to say he thought there was a "good opening" for resuming the offensive at once.

At 9:45 he put through a call to GQG, the first of a series of which he was later to say, "The real battle of the Marne was fought on the telephone." General Clergerie conducted the conversation with Colonel Pont, Chief of Operations, as Gallieni would not talk to anyone less than Joffre and Joffre would not come to the phone. He had an aversion to the instrument and used to pretend he "did not understand the mechanism." His real reason was that, like all men in high position, he had an eye on history and was afraid that things said over the telephone would be taken down without his being able to control the record.

Clergerie explained the plan to launch the Sixth Army and all available forces of the Paris camp in an attack on Kluck's flank, preferably north of the Marne, in which case contact could be made on September 6; alternatively on the south bank which would require a day's delay to allow Maunoury to cross over. In either case Clergerie asked for an order to put the Sixth Army on the march that evening. He urged Gallieni's belief that the moment had come to end the retreat and return the whole army to the offensive in combination with the Paris maneuver. GQG was left to come to a decision.

Contrary to GQG's willingness to sacrifice the capital, Gallieni from the beginning was motivated by the conviction that Paris must be defended and held. He viewed the front from the point of view of Paris and with no direct knowledge of the situation of the field armies. He was determined to seize the opportunity Kluck's swerve offered him, believing that his own move must and would precipitate a general offensive. It was a bold, even a rash, design, for without fully knowing the situation of the other armies he could not fairly judge the chances of success. Gallieni did not think there was a choice. It may be he had a great commander's instinctive feel for his moment; it is more likely he felt France would not have another.

At 11:00 A.M. Maunoury arrived for briefing; no answer had yet come from Joffre. At noon Clergerie telephoned again.

Meanwhile in the school at Bar-sur-Aube where GQG was installed, officers of the Operations staff, crowding in front of the wall map, animately discussed Gallieni's proposal for a combined offensive. The terrible trampling of French military hopes in the past month had instilled caution in the hearts of some. Others were as fervent apostles of the offensive as ever and had an answer for every counsel of caution. Joffre was present, listening to their arguments recorded by his aide-de-camp, Captain Muller. "Troops at the end of their strength? No matter, they are Frenchmen and tired of retreating. The moment they hear the order to advance they will forget their fatigue. A gap between the Armies of Foch and de Langle? It will be filled by the XXIst Corps coming from Dubail's Army. Unpreparedness of the armies to attack? Ask the field commanders; you will see how they will answer. Cooperation of the English? Ah, that's more serious.

One cannot give their Commander orders; one has to negotiate, and time is short. But the important thing is to seize the occasion, for it is fugitive. Kluck can still repair his mistake, and the movements of the Sixth Army will certainly draw his attention to the dangers to which he has exposed himself."

Without having contributed a word, Joffre went to consult Berthelot in his office and found him opposed to the plan. The Armies could not suddenly face about, he argued. They should complete the planned retreat to a strong defensive line and allow the Germans to penetrate more deeply into the net. Above all, the numerical superiority which was wanted could not be achieved until the two corps coming from the Lorraine front had time to come into position.

Silent, astride a straw-bottomed chair facing Berthelot's wall map, Joffre considered the problem. His plan for an ultimate return to the offensive had always included using the Sixth Army in an attack on the enemy's right flank. Gallieni, however, was precipitating matters. Joffre wanted the extra day for the reinforcements to come up, for the Fifth Army to prepare, and for more time in which to secure the cooperation of the British. When Clergerie's second call came through, he was told that the Commander in Chief preferred attack on the south bank of the Marne, and when Clergerie demurred about the delay he was told "the delay of a day will mean more forces available."

Joffre now faced the greater decision: whether to carry out the planned retreat to the Seine or seize the opportunity—and the risk—and face the enemy now. The heat was overpowering. Joffre went outside and sat down in the shade of a weeping ash in the school playground. By nature an arbiter, he collected the opinions of others, sorted them, weighed the personal coefficient of the speaker, adjusted the scale, and eventually announced his verdict. The decision was always his. If it succeeded his would be the glory; if it failed he would be held responsible. In the problem now before him the fate of France was at stake. During the past thirty days the French Army had failed in the great task for which it had been preparing for the past thirty years. Its last chance to save France, to prove her again the France of 1792, was now. The invader was forty miles from where Joffre sat and barely twenty from the nearest French Army. Senlis and Creil, after Kluck's Army had passed over, were in flames and the Mayor of Senlis dead. If the French turned now before the armies were ready— and failed?

The immediate requirement was to find out whether they could be made ready. As the Fifth Army was in a crucial position, Joffre sent a message to Franchet d'Esperey: "It may be advantageous to give battle tomorrow or the day after with all the forces of the Fifth Army in concert with the British and the mobile forces of Paris against the German First and Second Armies. Please advise whether your army is in a condition to do this with a chance of success. Reply immediately." A similar query was sent to Foch who stood next to Franchet d'Esperey and opposite Bülow.

Joffre continued to sit and think under the tree. For most of the afternoon the ponderous figure in black tunic, baggy red pants, and army-issue boots from which, to the despair of his aides, he had banished the affectation of spurs, remained silent and motionless.

Meanwhile Gallieni, taking Maunoury with him, left Paris at one o'clock to drive to British Headquarters at Melun on the Seine, twenty-five miles to the south. In response to his request for British support he had received a negative reply from Huguet who reported that Sir John French "adopts the counsels of prudence of his Chief of Staff," Sir Archibald Murray, and would not join an offensive unless the French guaranteed defense of the lower Seine between the British and the sea. Driving past the lines of southbound cars fleeing Paris, the two French generals reached British Headquarters at three o'clock. Kilted sentinels presented arms smartly; soldiers were busily typing indoors; but neither the Field Marshal nor his principal officers could be found, and the Staff appeared "confounded" by the situation. After a prolonged search Murray was located. Sir John French, he said, was away inspecting the troops; he could give no idea when he was expected to return.

Gallieni tried to explain his plan of attack and why British participation was "indispensable," but he could feel all the while the Englishman's "great reluctance to share our views." Murray kept repeating that the BEF was under the formal orders of its Commander in Chief to rest, reorganize, and await reinforcements, and he could do nothing until his return. After more than two hours of discussion during which Sir John French still did not appear, Gallieni succeeded in persuading Murray to write down a summary of the plan of attack and proposals for joint British action which "he did not appear to understand very well." Before leaving he secured a promise that Murray would notify him the moment his Chief returned.

At the same time another Anglo-French conference was taking place thirty-five miles up the Seine at Bray from which Sir John French was also absent. Anxious to repair the frayed relations left by Lanrezac, Franchet d'Esperey had arranged for a meeting with the Field Marshal at Bray at three o'clock. He wore for the occasion the ribbon of a Knight Commander of the Victorian Order. On reaching Bray his car was stopped by a French sentinel who reported an urgent message waiting for the General at the telegraph office. It was Joffre's query about the coming battle. Studying it, Franchet d'Esperey strode up and down the street, waiting in growing impatience for the British. After fifteen minutes a Rolls-Royce drove up with an "enormous Highlander" next to the chauffeur, but instead of the florid little Field Marshal in the back seat, "a tall devil, very ugly with an intelligent, expressive face" emerged. It was Wilson who was accompanied by the British Chief of Intelligence, Colonel Macdonogh. They had been delayed on the way when, seeing a Parisian lady in distress by the roadside Wilson gallantly took time to provide gas for her car and maps for her chauffeur.

The group retired to a room on the second floor of the Mairie with the Highlander posted as sentinel outside. Macdonogh lifted a heavy cloth to peer under the table, opened a door leading to an adjoining bedroom, looked under the bed, punched the quilt, opened the closet, and sounded the walls with his fist. Then, in answer to a question from Franchet d'Esperey about the situation of the British Army, he unfolded a map showing the exact positions, marked in blue arrows, of the enemy on his front and gave a masterly analysis of the movements of the German First and Second Armies. Franchet d'Esperey was impressed.

"You are our ally—I shall keep no secrets from you," he said, and read aloud Joffre's proposal. "I am going to answer that my army is prepared to attack," and, fixing his visitors with eyes of steel, "I hope you will not oblige us to do it alone. It is essential that you fill the space between the Fifth and Sixth Armies." He then outlined a precise plan of action which he had worked out in his head in the brief quarter-hour since receiving the telegram. It was based on the assumption, arrived at independently, of attack by Maunoury's Army north of the Marne on September 6. Wilson, concerting again with an energetic French general as he once had with Foch, readily agreed. Disposition of the two armies, the given line each was to reach by morning of September 6, and the direction of attack were decided. Wilson warned there would be difficulty in obtaining consent' from Sir John French and especially from Murray, but promised to do his best. He left for Melun while Franchet d'Esperey sent a report of their agreement to Joffre.

At Bar-sur-Aube, Joffre rose from under his shade tree. Without waiting

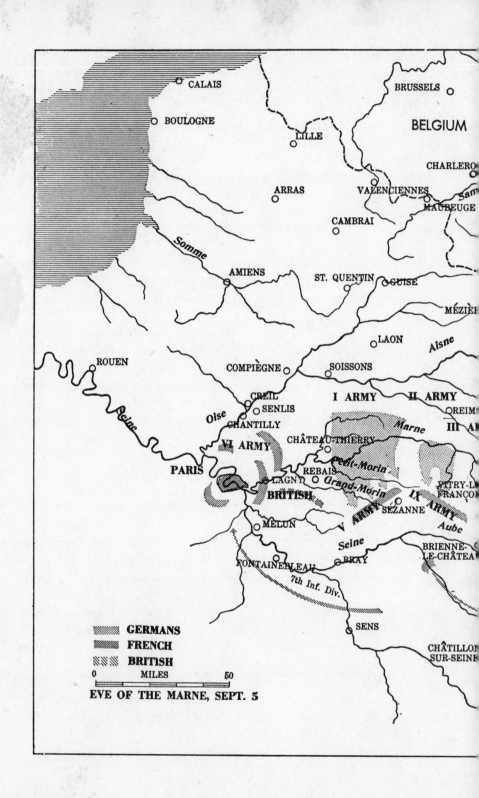

EVE OF THE MARNE, SEPT. 5

GERMANS
FRENCH
BRITISH

0   MILES   50

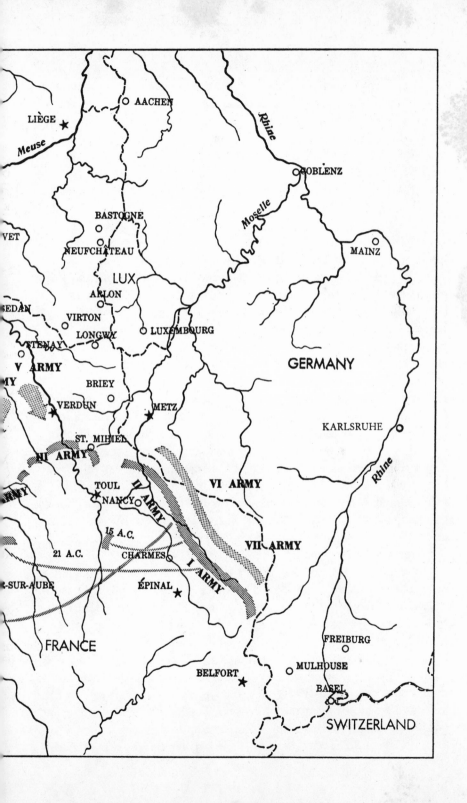

for the replies of Franchet d'Esperey and Foch, he had made up his mind. He walked into the Operations Bureau and ordered an Instruction drafted "to extend the local action envisaged by the Paris garrison to all the forces of the Allied left." Action was to begin on September 7. Instantly a great calm succeeded feverish discussion. The retreat was over. The moment to turn had come. Everyone fell to work preparing the detailed orders. To reduce the risk of leaks to the enemy it was decided not to issue the orders until the last possible moment.

It was then six o'clock, and at six-thirty Joffre went in to dinner to which he had invited two Japanese officers. While at table word was quietly whispered to him that Franchet d'Esperey had persuaded the British to join an offensive; important papers had arrived from the Fifth Army. Meals were sacred and international courtesy no less, especially as the Allies were engaged at the time in optimistic negotiations for Japanese military assistance in Europe. Joffre could not interrupt dinner but he committed the impropriety of "hurrying through" it. When he read Franchet d'Esperey's crisp answer it was like being pushed into water and forced to swim. In a tone hardly less abrupt than his "march or drop dead," D'Esperey laid down the precise times, places, and conditions of battle by the three armies, Fifth, Sixth, and British. It could open on September 6; the British Army would "execute a change of direction" on condition that its left was supported by the Sixth Army; the Sixth must reach a certain line along the Ourcq at a certain time, "if not the British will not march"; the Fifth would continue its retreat next day until south of the Grand Morin and be in position on the day after for frontal attack upon Kluck's Army while the British and Maunoury attacked his flank. "Vigorous participation" by Foch's Army against the German Second Army was a necessary condition.

"My army can fight on September 6," Franchet d'Esperey concluded, "but is not in brilliant condition." This was a bare statement of the truth. When later Franchet d'Esperey told General Hache of the IIIrd Corps that attack was set for next morning, Hache "looked as if he had been hit on the head with a club."

"It's mad!" he protested. "The troops are exhausted. They don't sleep or eat—they've been marching and fighting for two weeks! We need arms, ammunition, equipment. Everything is in terrible shape. Morale is bad. I've had to replace two generals of division. The Staff is worth nothing and good for nothing. If we had time to refit behind the Seine. . . ."

Like Gallieni, d'Esperey believed there was no choice. His immediate and bold response, like Gallieni's, proved a deciding factor and one that probably would not have been forthcoming from his predecessor. Other unreliable commanders were also weeded out. General Mas de Latrie was removed that day to be replaced by the dashing General de Maud'huy, taken from Castelnau's Army. By now the Fifth Army had undergone the replacement of its commander, 3 out of 5 corps commanders, 7 out of 13 divisional generals, and a proportionate number of generals of brigade.

Encouraged by the "intelligent audacity" of d'Esperey's reply, Joffre told the Operations Staff to make the battle orders conform to his conditions of place, although retaining September 7 as the date. He received an equally affirmative reply from Foch who announced himself simply as "ready to attack."

Henry Wilson on reaching British Headquarters found a dismaying answer. Murray, without even waiting for the return of Sir John French, had issued orders for a further retreat of ten to fifteen miles in a southwesterly direction to begin that night—"It is simply heartbreaking." Wilson also found Murray's memorandum of Gallieni's plan. He immediately sent off a wire to Paris saying, "Marshal not yet returned" and reporting the proposed retreat. He seems not to have reported it to d'Esperey, perhaps in the hope of persuading Sir John French to cancel it.

When Sir John returned, he walked into an unnerving confusion of plans and proposals. There was a letter from Joffre written prior to the day's events, proposing British action on the Seine; there was Gallieni's proposal to Murray; there was Wilson's agreement with Franchet d'Esperey; and there was Murray himself earnestly whispering retreat. Bewildered by so many calls for action, and unable to decide which took precedence over what, Sir John took refuge in no action at all. He let Murray's orders stand and informed Huguet for the benefit of all French petitioners that, "owing to the continual changes," he preferred to "restudy the situation before deciding on action." ...

At about the same hour Gallieni returned to Paris from Melun. He found Wilson's telegram and also one from Joffre sent at 12:20 P.M. confirming the preference expressed over the phone at noon that Maunoury's attack should take place south of the Marne on September 7. This was not new, but together with Wilson's message it seems to have had decisive effect on Gallieni. Time was escaping and Kluck advancing. He saw his moment slipping away, and determined to force the issue. This time he called GQG himself. Joffre tried to evade him by putting Belin on the telephone, but Gallieni insisted on speaking personally to the Generalissimo. According to a record of the conversation made by Joffre's aide-de-camp, Gallieni said, "The Sixth Army had made arrangements to attack north of the Marne and it appeared to him impossible to modify the general direction to which the army was already committed, and he insisted that the attack should be launched without any change in the conditions of time and place already laid down."

Confronted voice to voice by his former superior, Joffre may have felt again the moral authority that a man of Gallieni's commanding temperament exerted. Or, as he afterward claimed, he may have felt forced, though "unwillingly," to advance the general offensive to an earlier day for fear that Maunoury's movements, precipitated by Gallieni, would disclose the whole French maneuver to the enemy. He had assurances of readiness to fight from both Foch and Franchet d'Esperey and he thought the latter, by the spell of his magic energy, had secured a similar commitment from the British. He did not know it had become unpinned. In any event he authorized or acquiesced in attack by the Sixth Army north of the Marne and agreed to begin general action on September 6, "as Gallieni desired." Gallieni instantly, at 8:30 P.M., confirmed his marching orders to Maunoury, who was already moving. At GQG the staff revised the positions of attack to suit the advanced date. At 10:00 P.M., two hours after Moltke signed the Order halting the German right wing, Joffre signed General Order No. 6.

"The time has come," it began in full consciousness of a historic moment, "to profit by the adventurous position of the German First Army and concentrate against that army all efforts of the Allied Armies of the extreme left." Movements prescribed for the Sixth, Fifth, and British Armies were those of Franchet d'Esperey's reply. Separate orders to join the offensive were issued to the Third and Fourth Armies.

The night was not over. Hardly was the Order signed when word came from Huguet of Sir John French's refusal to ratify any plan for joint action and of his desire to "restudy" the situation. Joffre was stunned. The momentous decision had been taken; orders were on their way; in thirty-six hours the battle to save France would begin. The ally whose participation had been planned for the sake, as Foch once said, of a single dead British soldier, but who had been left by a trick of fate holding a vital place in the line, was backing out once again. Because of the time required for encoding and dispatching, the orders were not intended to reach the armies until next morning. As the only means of persuasion he could think of, Joffre sent a special copy of Order No. 6 by personal messenger to British Headquarters. When the officer reached Melun at 3:00 A.M., the three corps of the BEF had already begun the night march of retreat ordered by Murray that afternoon.

The enemy, too, at dawn of September 5 was on the march too soon. Thrusting forward in his effort to roll up the French flank, Kluck already had his army on the roads before Moltke's orders to turn and face the danger on his flank arrived by wireless at 7:00 A.M. Four corps, spread out over thirty miles of country, were headed for the Grand Morin. Kluck did not stop them. He either did not believe or did not heed the warning about a French concentration of troops on his flank. Assuming that the German Armies "were everywhere advancing victoriously along the whole front"— it was the Germans' habit to believe their own communiqués—he did not think the enemy could have forces available to threaten his flank. He, too, had begun to notice signs that the French retreat was perhaps not alto- gether disorganized and so felt it all the more urgent that no letup of pressure should give the enemy time to halt and "regain freedom of maneuver as well as offensive spirit." Disdaining Moltke's directive, Kluck advanced with his army, moving his own headquarters twenty-five miles forward to Rebais between the two Morins. By evening troops of the German First Army reached a line within ten to fifteen miles of the BEF and Franchet d'Esperey's Army, with outposts less than five miles apart. It was to be their last day of advance.

A representative from OHL with plenary powers came to Kluck's headquarters that evening. With unhappy experience both of wireless and Kluck's temperament, Moltke sent his Chief of Intelligence, Colonel Hentsch, on a 175-mile drive from Luxembourg to explain in person the reasons for the new Order and to see that it was carried out. To their "amazement," Kluck and his staff learned that Rupprecht's Armies were held up in a deadlocked battle before the French fortress line, as was the Crown Prince's Army before Verdun. Colonel Hentsch described the evidence of French troop movements which had led OHL to calculate that "very strong enemy forces" were being shifted westward in a threat to the German flank. It was under these circumstances that OHL dictated the horrid necessity of retirement. The First Army must return north of the Marne. Though it was little consolation, Colonel Hentsch said "the move- ment could be made at leisure; no special haste was necessary."

Disturbing confirmation came from the IVth Reserve Corps which had been left as flank guard north of the Marne. It reported encountering and engaging in combat an enemy force of at least two and a half divisions supported by heavy artillery. This was, of course, part of Maunoury's Army moving forward toward the Ourcq. Although the French attack was "successfully repulsed," the Commander of the IVth Reserve had ordered a retreat as soon as it was dark.

Kluck gave in. The extra distance he had dragged his army forward in the last two days since crossing the Marne had now to be retraced. Orders were drafted to begin the retirement of two corps next morning, September 6, with the others following later. After the march he had made from Liège to a level with Paris, it was a bitter moment. If he had stayed in echelon behind Bülow as ordered, if he had even halted his army that morning at seven o'clock, he would have been in position to face the threat to his flank with his whole army together. According to General Kuhl, his Chief of Staff, "Neither OHL nor the First Army Staff had the remotest idea that an immediate offensive by the whole French Army was imminent. . . . Not a sign, not a word from prisoners, not a newspaper paragraph gave warning." If Kluck did not know what lay ahead, there was one thing he could not help but know: to break off pursuit and pull back now, with four days left of the German schedule, was not a prelude to victory.

September 5 seemed a darker day to the Allies. With nothing but defeats so far, their representatives met in London that morning to sign the Pact binding each other "not to conclude any separate peace in the course of the present war."

In Paris, Maunoury asked Gallieni, "In case we should be overwhelmed, our line of retreat will be . . . ?" His eyes clouding over, Gallieni answered, "Nowhere." Preparing for possible disaster, he issued secret orders to each regional commander of the Paris camp to report all resources in his district which must be destroyed rather than fall into the hands of the enemy. Even bridges in the heart of the city like the Pont Neuf and the Pont Alexandre were to be blown up. "A void" must be left in front of the enemy in case he should break through, he told General Hirschauer.

At GQG a report from Castelnau was received which seemed to threaten disaster even before the offensive could begin. Pressure was so severe that he felt he might be forced to evacuate Nancy. Joffre ordered him to hold for another twenty-four hours before making a decision, but agreed that if it then seemed unavoidable, he approved the second line of defense suggested in Castelnau's letter.

In transferring one corps from the Third Army and two corps from the Moselle front, Joffre had taken a grave risk in order to gain this time the numerical superiority which he had not had for the opening offensive. The reinforcements were not yet in the battle line. When it came to informing the government of the decision to fight, Joffre carefully included an alibi for himself in case of failure. His telegram to the President and Premier said, "Gallieni having attacked prematurely, I have given the order to suspend the retreat and, in my turn, resume the offensive." Afterward, at a time when Joffre was systematically trying to minimize Gallieni's role at the Marne and even expunge certain things from the records, this telegram was unearthed by Briand and shown to Gallieni. "That 'prematurely' is worth gold," he said.

On the morning of September 5 Joffre's uncertainty about British intentions became "altogether agonizing." He begged Millerand by telegram to exert the government's influence. The imminent battle "can have decisive results but in case of a reverse can also have the gravest consequences for the country. . . . I count on you to call the Field Marshal's attention to the decisive importance of an offensive without *arrière-pensée*. If I could give orders to the English Army as I could to the French Army in the same position, I would pass immediately to the attack."

At three o'clock that morning Henry Wilson received Order No. 6 from Huguet who, however, did not permit Captain de Galbert, the officer who brought it, to see any of the British chiefs. At the center of every discord during this period, with a curiously malign consistency, the figure of Huguet appears. Deciding that the situation required someone of higher rank, Captain de Galbert started back at once for GQG. At 7:00 A.M. Wilson took the Order to Sir John French and during the course of the morning persuaded him to cooperate. Meanwhile De Galbert arrived back at GQG at 9:30 with no definite news but with a report that British sentiment seemed "lukewarm" toward an offensive. The Mayor of Melun had told him Sir John French's baggage was being moved back to Fontainebleau.

Joffre felt he must have the British Army in the battle line "at any price," even at the price of motoring the 115 miles to Melun. Sending a telephone message ahead to expect him, he set out with his aide and two staff officers. Despite roadblocks and the ineluctable stop for lunch, his racing chauffeur brought him to the château where Sir John French was quartered by 2:00 P.M.

The Field Marshal was standing at a table waiting for him flanked by Murray, Wilson, Huguet, "looking as usual as if he had lost his last friend," and several other members of his staff. Joffre walked over and for once took the floor at the outset. Instead of his usual laconic sentences, a passionate flood of speech poured forth punctuated by a gesture of his forearms which "seemed to throw his heart on the table." He said the "supreme moment" had arrived, his own orders were given and whatever happened the last company of the French Army would be thrown into the battle to save France. The "lives of all French people, the soil of France, the future of Europe" depended upon the offensive. "I cannot believe the British Army will refuse to do its share in this supreme crisis . . . history would severely judge your absence."

Joffre's fist crashed down on the table. "*Monsieur le Maréchal*, the honor of England is at stake!"

At these words Sir John French, who had been listening with "passionate attention," suddenly reddened. Silence fell on the company. Slowly tears came into the eyes of the British Commander in Chief and rolled down his cheeks. He struggled to say something in French and gave up. "Damn it, I can't explain. Tell him we will do all we possibly can."

Joffre looked inquiringly at Wilson who translated, "The Field Marshal says 'Yes.' " It was hardly needed, for the tears and the tone already carried conviction. Murray hurriedly put in that the British troops were now ten miles farther back than the positions called for in the Order and could start only at 9:00 A.M., not 6:00, as Joffre asked. It was a voice of caution that would continue to make itself felt. Joffre shrugged. "It cannot be helped. I have the Field Marshal's word, that is enough." Tea was then served.

The move of GQG to Chatillon-sur-Seine, planned before the offensive, had been accomplished during his absence. Joffre returned there by evening, about the time Colonel Hentsch was warning von Kluck. Entering the Operations Room to confirm a decision already taken, Joffre said to the assembled officers, "Gentlemen, we will fight on the Marne."

He signed the order that would be read to the troops when the bugles blew next morning. Ordinarily the French language, especially in public pronouncements, requires an effort if it is not to sound splendid, but this time the words were flat, almost tired; the message hard and uncompromising: "Now, as the battle is joined on which the safety of the country depends, everyone must be reminded that this is no longer the time for looking back. Every effort must be made to attack and throw back the enemy. A unit which finds it impossible to advance must, regardless of cost, hold its ground and be killed on the spot rather than fall back. In the present circumstances no failure will be tolerated."

That was all; the time for splendor was past. It did not shout "Forward!" or summon men to glory. After the first thirty days of war in 1914, there was a premonition that little glory lay ahead.

▶▶▶ *Afterward*

THE BATTLE OF THE MARNE, AS ALL THE WORLD
knows, ended in a German retreat. Between the Ourcq and the Grand
Morin, in the four days that were left of their schedule, the Germans lost
their bid for "decisive victory" and thereby their opportunity to win the
the war. For France, for the Allies, in the long run for the world, the
tragedy of the Marne was that it fell short of the victory it might have
been.

Maunoury's attack on the German flank and von Kluck's turnabout
to meet it opened a gap between the German First and Second Armies.
The issue of the battle depended on whether the Germans could succeed
in crushing the two wings—Maunoury and Foch—before Franchet d'Esperey and the British succeeded in exploiting the gap and pushing through
the German center. Maunoury, when almost defeated by Kluck, was reinforced by the IVth Corps, of whom 6,000 detraining in Paris were rushed
to the front by Gallieni in taxis, and managed to hold his ground. Foch,
pressed hard in the Marshes of St. Gond by Hausen's Army and part of
Bülow's, at a critical moment when his right was driven back and his left
ceding, gave his famous order, "Attack, whatever happens! The Germans

435

are at the extreme limit of their efforts. . . . Victory will come to the side
that outlasts the other!" Franchet d'Esperey pushed back Bülow's right;
the British entered the gap too slowly and hesitantly; Colonel Hentsch
made his historic reappearance to counsel retreat, and the German Armies
withdrew in time to avoid a piercing of their line.

So close had the Germans come to victory, so near the French to
disaster, so great, in the preceding days, had been the astonished dismay of
the world as it watched the relentless advance of the Germans and the
retreat of the Allies on Paris, that the battle that turned the tide came to
be known as the Miracle of the Marne. Henri Bergson, who had once
formulated for France the *mystique* of "will," saw in it something of a
miracle that had happened once before: "Joan of Arc won the Battle of the
Marne," was his verdict. The enemy, suddenly halted as if by a stone wall
springing up overnight, felt it too. "French *élan*, just when it is on the
point of being extinguished, flames up powerfully," wrote Moltke sorrow-
fully to his wife during the battle. The basic reason for German failure
at the Marne, "the reason that transcends all others," said Kluck afterward, was "the extraordinary and peculiar aptitude of the French soldier
to recover quickly. That men will let themselves be killed where they
stand, that is a well-known thing and counted on in every plan of battle.
But that men who have retreated for ten days, sleeping on the ground and
half dead with fatigue, should be able to take up their rifles and attack
when the bugle sounds, is a thing upon which we never counted. It was
a possibility not studied in our war academy."

Bergson notwithstanding, it was no miracle but the inherent ifs, errors,
and commitments of the first month that determined the issue at the
Marne. Kluck notwithstanding, faults of German command contributed as
much as the verve of the French soldier to the outcome. If the Germans
had not withdrawn two corps to send against the Russians, one of the two
would have been on Bülow's right and might have filled the gap between
him and Kluck; the other would have been with Hausen and might have
provided the extra strength to overwhelm Foch. Russia's loyal launching
of an unready offensive drew those troops away and was given tribute by
Colonel Dupont, French Chief of Intelligence. "Let us render to our
Allies," he said, "the homage that is their due, for one of the elements of
our victory was their debacle."

Other "ifs" accumulated. If the Germans had not committed too much
strength to the attempt at double envelopment by the left wing, if the
right wing had not outrun its supplies and exhausted its men, if Kluck

had stayed level with Bülow, if, even on the last day, he had marched back across the Marne instead of forward to the Grand Morin, the decision of the Marne might have been different and the six-week schedule for victory over France achieved—might have been, that is, except for the first and decisive "if": if the six-week schedule itself had not been based on a march through Belgium. Quite apart from the effect upon the war as a whole of bringing Britain in, and the ultimate effect on world opinion, the addition of Belgium as an enemy reduced the number of German divisions that came up to the Marne and added five British divisions to the Allied line.

At the Marne the Allies achieved the numerical superiority they had not been able to muster at any one point in the Battle of the Frontiers. The missing German divisions were partly responsible, and the balance was tipped by the added French divisions drawn from the Third Army and from the embattled and unflinching armies of Castelnau and Dubail. All during the retreat while the other armies were giving ground, these two held shut the eastern door of France. For eighteen days they fought an almost continuous battle until, finally acknowledging failure too late, Moltke called off the attack on the French fortress line on September 8. If the French First and Second Armies had given way at any point, if they had weakened under Rupprecht's final onslaught of September 3, the Germans would have won their Cannae and there would have been no opportunity for a French counter-offensive on the Marne, the Seine, or anywhere else. If there was a miracle of the Marne, it was made possible on the Moselle.

Without Joffre no Allied line would have existed to bar the German path. It was his impregnable confidence during the tragic and terrible twelve days of retreat that prevented the French Armies from disintegrating into a shattered and fragmentary mass. A more brilliant, more quick-thinking commander with ideas of his own might have avoided basic initial errors, but after the debacle the one thing France needed Joffre had. It is difficult to imagine any other man who could have brought the French Armies out of retreat, in condition and position to fight again. When the moment to turn came, alone he would have been insufficient. The stand he contemplated at the Seine might well have come too late. It was Gallieni who saw the opportunity and, with a powerful assist from Franchet d'Esperey, provoked the earlier counter-offensive. It was the broken figure of Lanrezac, allowed no share at the Marne, who in saving France from the original folly of Plan 17 made recovery possible. Ironically, both his decision at Charleroi and his replacement by Franchet d'Esperey were equally necessary to the counter-offensive. But it was Joffre, whom nothing could panic, who provided the army to fight it. "If we had not had him in 1914," said Foch, his ultimate successor, "I don't know what would have become of us."

The world remembers the battle ever since by the taxis. A hundred of them were already in the service of the Military Government of Paris. With 500 more, each carrying five soldiers and making the sixty-kilometer trip to the Ourcq twice, General Clergerie figured he could transport 6,000 troops to the hard-pressed front. The order was issued at 1:00 P.M., the hour for departure fixed for 6:00 P.M. Police passed the word to the taxis in the streets. Enthusiastically the chauffeurs emptied out their passengers, explaining proudly that they had to "go to the battle." Returning to their garages for gas, they were ordered to the place of assembly where at the given time all 600 were lined up in perfect order. Gallieni, called to inspect them, though rarely demonstrative, was enchanted. *"Eh bien, voilà au moins qui n'est pas banal!"* (Well, here at least is something out of the ordinary!) he cried. Each with its burden of soldiers, with trucks, buses, and assorted vehicles added to the train, the taxis drove off, as evening fell —the last gallantry of 1914, the last crusade of the old world.

After the incomplete victory of the Marne there followed the German retreat to the Aisne, the race to the sea for possession of the Channel ports, the fall of Antwerp, and the Battle of Ypres where officers and men of the BEF held their ground, fought literally until they died, and stopped the Germans in Flanders. Not Mons or the Marne but Ypres was the real monument to British valor, as well as the grave of four-fifths of the original BEF. After it, with the advent of winter, came the slow deadly sinking into the stalemate of trench warfare. Running from Switzerland to the Channel like a gangrenous wound across French and Belgian territory, the trenches determined the war of position and attrition, the brutal, mud-filled, murderous insanity known as the Western Front that was to last for four more years.

The Schlieffen plan had failed, but it had succeeded far enough to leave the Germans in occupation of all of Belgium and all of northern France down to the Aisne. As Clemenceau's paper was tirelessly to remind its readers, month after month, year after year, *"Messieurs les Allemands sont toujours à Noyon."* For their presence there, deep within France, the error of Plan 17 was responsible. It had allowed the enemy to penetrate too far to be dislodged by the time the French regathered their strength at the Marne. It permitted the breakthrough that could only be stemmed, and later only contained, at a cost of the terrible drain of French manhood that was to make the war of 1914–1918 the parent of 1940.* It was an error that could never be repaired. Failure of Plan 17 was as fatal as failure of the Schlieffen plan, and together they produced deadlock on the Western Front. Sucking up lives at a rate of 5,000 and sometimes 50,000 a day, absorbing munitions, energy, money, brains, and trained men, the Western Front ate up Allied war resources and predetermined the failure of back-door efforts like that of the Dardanelles which might otherwise have shortened the war. The deadlock, fixed by the failures of the first month, determined the future course of the war and, as a result, the terms of the peace, the shape of the interwar period, and the conditions of the Second Round.

Men could not sustain a war of such magnitude and pain without hope—the hope that its very enormity would ensure that it could never happen again and the hope that when somehow it had been fought through to a resolution, the foundations of a better-ordered world would have been laid. Like the shimmering vision of Paris that kept Kluck's soldiers on their feet, the mirage of a better world glimmered beyond the shell-pitted wastes and leafless stumps that had once been green fields and waving poplars. Nothing less could give dignity or sense to monstrous offensives in which thousands and hundreds of thousands were killed to gain ten yards and exchange one wet-bottomed trench for another. When every autumn

---

* In the chapel of St. Cyr (before it was destroyed during World War II) the memorial tablet to the dead of the Great War bore only a single entry for "the Class of 1914." The mortality rate is further illustrated by the experience of André Varagnac, a nephew of the cabinet minister Marcel Sembat, who came of military age in 1914 but was not mobilized in August owing to illness, and found himself, out of the twenty-seven boys in his lycée class, the only one alive by Christmas. According to *Armées Françaises*, French casualties in the month of August alone amounted to 206,515, including killed, wounded, and missing out of total effectives for the armies in the field of 1,600,000. As these figures do not include officers or garrison and Territorial divisions, the number is believed to be nearer 300,000. Most were incurred during the four days of the Battle of the Frontiers. No separate figures have been published for the Battle of the Marne, but if the estimated losses through September 11 are added to those of August, the total through the first thirty days is equivalent to a daily loss of the whole population of a town the size of Soissons or Compiègne. No exact figures can be given because in line with GQG's fixed policy against releasing any information of possible value to the enemy, casualty lists were not published. Nor is it possible to give comparable figures for the other belligerents because they tabulated losses at different intervals and on different bases. When the war was over, the known dead per capita of population were 1 to 28 for France, 1 to 32 for Germany, 1 to 57 for England and 1 to 107 for Russia.

people said it could not last through the winter, and when every spring there was still no end in sight, only the hope that out of it all some good would accrue to mankind kept men and nations fighting.

When at last it was over, the war had many diverse results and one dominant one transcending all others: disillusion. "All the great words were cancelled out for that generation," wrote D. H. Lawrence in simple summary for his contemporaries. If any of them remembered, with a twinge of pain, like Emile Verhaeren, "the man I used to be," it was because he knew the great words and beliefs of the time before 1914 could never be restored.

After the Marne the war grew and spread until it drew in the nations of both hemispheres and entangled them in a pattern of world conflict no peace treaty could dissolve. The Battle of the Marne was one of the decisive battles of the world not because it determined that Germany would ultimately lose or the Allies ultimately win the war but because it determined that the war would go on. There was no looking back, Joffre told the soldiers on the eve. Afterward there was no turning back. The nations were caught in a trap, a trap made during the first thirty days out of battles that failed to be decisive, a trap from which there was, and has been, no exit.

Sources

The following list contains only titles cited in the Notes. It is confined to primary sources, including those biographies and special studies, like Ritter's *Schlieffen Plan*, which include primary material. A short list of secondary works is given separately. All titles are given in English or French translation where these exist.

A full bibliography of the subject would fill a book. No other episode in history has been more fully documented by its participants. They seem to have known, while they lived it, that like the French Revolution, the First World War was one of the great convulsions of history, and each felt the hand of history heavily on his own shoulder. When it was over, despite courage, skill, and sacrifice, the war they had fought proved to have been, on the whole, a monument of failure, tragedy, and disillusion. It had not led to a better world. Men who had taken part at the command level, political and military, felt driven to explain their decisions and actions. Men who had fallen from high command, whether for cause or as scapegoats—and these included most of the commanders of August—wrote their private justifications. As each account appeared, inevitably shifting responsibility or blame to someone else, another was provoked. Private feuds became public; public controversies expanded. Men who would otherwise have remained mute were stung to publish, as Sir Horace Smith-Dorrien by Sir John French. Books proliferated. Whole schools of partisans, like those of Gallieni and Joffre, produced libraries of controversy.

Through this forest of special pleading the historian gropes his way, trying to recapture the truth of past events and find out "what really happened." He discovers that truth is subjective and separate, made up of little bits seen, experienced, and recorded by different people. It is like a design seen through a kaleidoscope; when the cylinder is shaken the countless colored fragments form a new picture. Yet they are the same fragments that made a different picture a moment earlier. This is the problem inherent in the records left by actors in past events. That famous goal, *"wie es wirklich war,"* is never wholly within our grasp.

Official Government Publications

CARNEGIE ENDOWMENT FOR INTERNATIONAL PEACE, *Diplomatic Documents Relating to the Outbreak of the European War*, 2 vols., ed. James Brown Scott, New York, Oxford, 1916. Contains the official publications of the various Foreign Offices which appeared at intervals after the outbreak, beginning with the hurriedly assembled and highly selective *German White Book* issued on August 4, 1914. Included are the *Austro-Hungarian Red, Belgian Grey, French Yellow, German White, British Blue I and II, Italian Green, Russian Orange I and II* and *Serbian Blue* Books.

FRANCE, Assemblée Nationale, Chambre des Deputés, Session de 1919. *Procès-Verbaux de la Commission d'Enquète sur le rôle et la situation de la metallurgie en France: defense du Bassin de Briey*, 1ʳᵉ et 2ᵐᵉ parties.
————. *Rapport de la Commission d'Enquète* par M. Fernand Engerand, deputé. 1ʳᵉ partie: "Concentration de la metallurgie française sur la frontière de l'Est." 2ᵐᵉ partie: "La perte de Briey."

These hearings (referred to in Notes as "Briey"), at which the principal chiefs of the French General Staff as well as field commanders were called to testify, are the basic source for French military policy in August, 1914. They grew out of the loss of the Briey iron ore basin which became critical as the war went on. Certain sinister underpinnings of the munitions industry with its interlocking Franco-German directorates led a deputy, M. Fernand Engerand, to pursue a persistent investigation into the circumstances of the loss of Briey and this led by natural stages to an investigation of French strategy at the outset of the war. When the war was over, M. Engerand succeeded in getting a Committee of Inquiry appointed of which he was named *rapporteur*. "As our inquiry unrolled with all its illustrious witnesses," he wrote in his Report, it was plain that the truth about the origins and failure of Plan 17 was being "obstinately hidden" from the government and the Chamber of Deputies, but "we have tried to unravel the tangled and hidden threads of this month of August, 1914, the most tragic, perhaps, in all the history of France."

FRANCE, Ministère de la Guerre; Etat-major de l'Armée, Service Historique, *Les Armées Françaises dans la grande guerre*, Tome I, Vols. 1 and 2 and *Annexes* Paris, Imprimerie Nationale 1922–1925. Referred to in Notes as AF. The first volume of the Official History, beginning with the pre-1914 war plans and the Michel incident of 1911, covers the war through the Battle of the Frontiers. The second volume covers the Retreat up to the eve of the Battle of the Marne. The real value is in the two volumes of Annexes containing the texts of orders and communications between GQG and the armies. These are the most vivid and immediate source material of all.

GERMANY, Foreign Office, *Outbreak of the World War;* German documents collected by Karl Kautsky and edited by Max Montgelas and Walther Schucking, translated by Carnegie Endowment, New York, Oxford, 1924. Referred to in Notes as "Kautsky." Assembled and published by the Weimar Government to supplement the original German White Book.

GERMANY, Generalstaab, *Kriegsbrauch im Landkriege* (Usages of War on Land), translated as *The German War Book* by J. H. Morgan, London, Murray, 1915.

GERMANY, Marine-Archiv, *Der Krieg zur See, 1914–18,* No. 5, Band 1, *Der Krieg in dem Turkische Gewassen; Die Mittelmeer Division,* Berlin, Mittler, 1928.

GERMANY, Reichsarchiv, *Der Weltkrieg 1914–18,* Band 1, *Die Militärische Operationen zu Lande; Die Grenzschlachten im Westen,* Band 3, *Von der Sambre bis zur Marne,* Berlin, Mittler, 1924.

GREAT BRITAIN, Committee of Imperial Defence, Historical Section, CORBETT, SIR JULIAN, *Naval Operations: History of the Great War Based on Official Documents,* Vol. I, New York, Longmans, 1920. Referred to in Notes as "Corbett."

———, EDMONDS, BRIGADIER-GENERAL JAMES E., *Military Operations: France and Belgium,* 1914, Vol. I and volume of maps, 3rd ed., London, Macmillan, 1933. Referred to in Notes as "Edmonds." This work of superb scholarship is particularly valuable for its selections from German and French sources, showing for a given date the actual situation of the BEF's enemies and allies and how each appeared to the other.

———, FAYLE, C. ERNEST, *Seaborne Trade,* Vol. I, London, Murray, 1920.

GREAT BRITAIN, Foreign Office. *British Documents on the Origins of the War, 1898–1914,* 11 vols., eds. G. P. Gooch and H. W. V. Temperley, London, 1927–38. Referred to in Notes as "BD."

UNITED STATES, Department of State. *Papers Relating to the Foreign Relations of the U. S. Supplements,* World War, 1914, Washington, G.P.O., 1928

Non-Official Sources

On Belgium

BASSOMPIERRE, BARON ALFRED DE, *The Night of August 2–3, 1914, at the Belgian Foreign Office,* tr. London, Hodder & Stoughton, 1916.

BEYENS, BARON, *Deux Années à Berlin, 1912–14,* 2 vols., Paris, Plon, 1931.

CAMMAERTS, EMILE, *Albert of Belgium,* tr. New York, Macmillan, 1935.

CARTON DE WIART, HENRY (Belgian Minister of Justice in 1914). *Souvenirs politiques,* Brussels, Brouwer, 1948.

Cobb, Irwin S., *Paths of Glory—Impressions of War Written at and near the Front*, New York, Dutton, 1914.

Davis, Richard Harding, *With the Allies*, New York, Scribner's, 1914.

Demblon, Celestin (deputy of Liège), *La Guerre à Liège: Pages d'un témoin*, Paris, Lib. Anglo-Française, 1915.

D'Ydewalle, Charles, *Albert and the Belgians*, tr. New York, Morrow, 1935.

Essen, Léon van der, *The Invasion and the War in Belgium from Liège to the Yser*, tr. London, Unwin, 1917.

Galet, General Emile Joseph, *Albert, King of the Belgians, in the Great War*, tr. Boston, Houghton Mifflin, 1931. This record by King Albert's personal military adviser and later Chief of Staff, is authoritative, thorough, detailed, and indispensable.

Gibson, Hugh (First Secretary of the American Legation), *A Journal from Our Legation in Belgium*, New York, Doubleday, 1917.

Klobukowski, A. (French Minister in Brussels), "Souvenirs de Belgique," *Revue de Paris*, Sept.-Oct., 1927.

———— "La Résistance belge à l'invasion allemande," *Revue d'Histoire de la Guerre*, July 1932.

Malcolm, Ian, ed., *Scraps of Paper: German Proclamations in Belgium and France*, New York, Doran, 1916.

Millard, Oscar E., *Burgomaster Max*, London, Hutchinson, 1936.

Powell, E. Alexander (correspondent of the *New York World* attached to the Belgian forces in 1914), *Fighting in Flanders*, New York, Scribner's, 1914.

Schryver, Col. A. de, *La Bataille de Liège*, Liège, Vaillant-Carmanne, 1922.

Sutherland, Millicent, Duchess of (leader of a volunteer ambulance corps of nurses to Belgium in August, 1914), *Six Weeks at the War*, Chicago, McCluny, 1915.

Verhaeren, Emile, *La Belgique sanglante*, Paris, Nouvelle Revue Française, 1915.

Whitlock, Brand, *Belgium: A Personal Narrative*, Vol. I, New York, Appleton, 1910. President Wilson's appointment as Minister to Belgium of the lawyer and former journalist who had won fame as Independent mayor of Toledo for four terms proved fortunate for history. A progressive in politics, outspoken and courageous, Whitlock was also a writer of distinction. His book, together with that of Hugh Gibson who, though a professional diplomat, wrote without wraps, constitute a remarkable record of a fatal month in the history of a nation.

On England and the BEF

Addison, Christopher (Parliamentary Secretary to Board of Education), *Four and a Half Years: A Personal Diary from June 1914 to January 1919*, London, Hutchinson, 1934.

ANGELL, NORMAN, *The Great Illusion: A Study of the Relation of Military Power to National Advantage*, 4th ed., New York, Putnam's, 1913.

ARMY QUARTERLY, London. Referred to in Notes as *AQ*. This journal's reviews of foreign books on the war, as they came out during the 1920s, provide the most inclusive and informative guide in English to the literature of the First World War.

ARTHUR, SIR GEORGE, *Life of Lord Kitchener*, Vol. III, New York, Macmillan, 1920.

——, *George V*, New York, Cape, 1930.

ASQUITH, EARL OF OXFORD AND, *Memories and Reflections*, 2 vols., London, Cassell, 1928.

ASTON, MAJOR-GENERAL SIR GEORGE, *Biography of the Late Marshal Foch*, London, Hutchinson, 1930.

BACON, ADMIRAL SIR REGINALD, *Life of Lord Fisher*, London, Hodder & Stoughton, 1929.

BEAVERBROOK, LORD, *Politicians and the War, 1914–16*, New York, Doubleday, Doran, 1928.

BERTIE, LORD, *Diary of Lord Bertie of Thame*, Vol. I, London, Hodder & Stoughton, 1924.

BIRKENHEAD, VISCOUNT, *Points of View*, Vol. I, London, Hodder & Stoughton, 1922.

BLAKE, ROBERT, ed., *Haig: Private Papers, 1914–18*, London, Eyre & Spottiswoode, 1952.

BRIDGES, LIEUT.-GENERAL SIR TOM (Officer in the 2nd Cavalry Brigade of the BEF and formerly military attaché in Brussels), *Alarms and Excursions*, London, Longmans, 1938.

CALLWELL, MAJOR-GENERAL SIR CHARLES E. (Became Director of Operations and Intelligence at the War Office in August, 1914, when Wilson and Macdonogh went to France), *Experiences of a Dug-Out, 1914–18*, London, Constable, 1920.

——, *Field Marshal Sir Henry Wilson: His Life and Diaries*, Vol. I, New York, Scribner's, 1927. All quotations in the text from Wilson's Diaries are from this book, referred to in the Notes as "Wilson."

CHAMBERLAIN, SIR AUSTEN, *Down the Years*, London, Cassell, 1935.

CHARTERIS, BRIGADIER-GENERAL JOHN, *At GHQ*, London, Cassell, 1931.

CHILDS, MAJOR-GENERAL SIR WYNDHAM, *Episodes and Reflections*, London, Cassell, 1930.

CHURCHILL, SIR WINSTON, *The World Crisis*, Vol. 1, *1911–1914*, New York, Scribner's, 1928. This is the single most important book among English sources by a person holding key office at the outbreak. Further comment in Notes to Chapter 10. All references to Churchill in the Notes are to this book unless otherwise specified.

——, *The Aftermath*, Vol. 4 of *The World Crisis*, New York, Scribner's, 1929.

——, *Great Contemporaries*, New York, Putnam's, 1937.

CORBETT-SMITH, MAJOR A. (artillery officer in Smith-Dorrien's Corps), *The Retreat from Mons*, London, Cassell, 1917.

CUST, SIR LIONEL, *King Edward and His Court: Some Reminiscences*, London, Murray, 1930.

CUSTANCE, ADMIRAL SIR REGINALD, *A Study of War*, London, Constable, 1924.

DUGDALE, BLANCHE E. C., *Arthur James Balfour*, 2 vols., New York, Putnam, 1937.

ESHER, REGINALD, VISCOUNT, *The Influence of King Edward and Other Essays*, London, Murray, 1915.

———, *The Tragedy of Lord Kitchener*, New York, Dutton, 1921.

———, *Journals and Letters*, Vol. 3, 1910–15, London, Nicolson & Watson, 1938.

FISHER, ADMIRAL OF THE FLEET, LORD, *Memories*, London, Hodder and Stoughton, 1919.

———, *Fear God and Dread Nought: Correspondence of Admiral of the Fleet Lord Fisher of Kilverstone*, 3 vols., ed. Arthur J. Marder, London, Cape, 1952–56–59.

FRENCH, FIELD MARSHAL VISCOUNT, OF YPRES, *1914*, Boston, Houghton Mifflin, 1919. The weight of animus and selective omissions in Sir John French's account makes it impossible to use this record as a reliable source for anything but the author's character.

GARDINER, A. G., *The War Lords*, London, Dent, 1915.

GREY, VISCOUNT, OF FALLODON, *Twenty-Five Years*, 2 vols., London, Hodder & Stoughton, 1925.

HALDANE, RICHARD BURDON, VISCOUNT, *An Autobiography*, New York, Doubleday, Doran, 1929. All references are to this book unless otherwise specified.

———, *Before the War*, New York, Funk & Wagnalls, 1920.

HAMILTON, CAPTAIN ERNEST W. (Captain of 11th Hussars in Allenby's Cavalry Division), *The First Seven Divisions*, New York, Dutton, 1916.

HURD, SIR ARCHIBALD, *The German Fleet*, London, Hodder & Stoughton, 1915.

———, *The British Fleet in the Great War*, London, Constable. 1919.

JELLICOE, ADMIRAL VISCOUNT, *The Grand Fleet*, 1914–16, New York, Doran, 1919.

KENWORTHY, J. M. (Lord Strabolgi), *Soldiers, Statesmen and Others*, London, Rich & Cowen, 1933.

LEE, SIR SIDNEY, *King Edward VII*, 2 vols., New York, Macmillan, 1925–27.

LLOYD GEORGE, DAVID, *War Memoirs*, Vol. I, Boston, Little, Brown, 1933.

MACREADY, GENERAL SIR NEVIL (Adjutant-General in the BEF), *Annals of an Active Life*, Vol. I., London, Hutchinson, n.d.

MACDONAGH, MICHAEL, *In London During the Great War: Diary of a Journalist*, London, Eyre & Spottiswoode, 1935.

MAGNUS, SIR PHILIP, *Kitchener*, New York, Dutton, 1959.

MAURICE, MAJOR-GENERAL SIR FREDERICK (staff officer of BEF, 3rd Division, August, 1914) *Forty Days in 1914*, New York, Doran, 1919.

MCKENNA, STEPHEN, *While I Remember*, New York, Doran, 1921.

MILNE, ADMIRAL SIR ARCHIBALD BERKELEY, *The Flight of the Goeben and the Breslau*, London, Eveleigh Nash, 1921.

MORLEY, JOHN, VISCOUNT, *Memorandum on Resignation*, New York, Macmillan, 1928.

NEWTON, THOMAS, LORD, *Lord Lansdowne*, London, Macmillan, 1929.

NICOLSON, HAROLD, *King George the Fifth*, London, Constable, 1952.

———, *Portrait of a Diplomatist: Being the Life of Sir Arthur Nicolson, First Lord Carnock*, Boston, Houghton Mifflin, 1930.

PEEL, MRS. C. S., *How We Lived Then, 1914–18*, London, John Lane, 1929.

REPINGTON, LT. COL. CHARLES À COURT, *The First World War, 1914–18*, Vol. I, Boston, Houghton Mifflin, 1920.

ROBERTSON, FIELD MARSHAL SIR WILLIAM, *From Private to Field Marshal*, Boston, Houghton Mifflin, 1921.

———, *Soldiers and Statesmen, 1914–18*, Vol. I, New York, Scribner's, 1926.

SHAW, GEORGE BERNARD, *What I Really Wrote About the War*, New York, Brentano's, 1932.

SMITH-DORRIEN, GENERAL SIR HORACE, *Memories of 48 Years' Service*, London, Murray, 1925.

SPEARS, BRIG.-GEN. EDWARD L., *Liaison, 1914: A Narrative of the Great Retreat*, New York, Doubleday, Doran, 1931. A spirited, colorful and brilliantly written memoir of war, fascinating in its richness of detail, this is by far the most interesting book in English on the opening campaign in France. When the author's personal prejudices become involved he exercises a certain freedom in manipulating the facts. See Notes to Chapters 15 and 22.

STEED, WICKHAM H. (Foreign Editor of *The Times*), *Through Thirty Years*, New York, Doubleday, Doran, 1929.

TREVELYAN, GEORGE MACAULAY, *Grey of Fallodon*, Boston, Houghton Mifflin, 1937.

WILSON, GENERAL SIR HENRY, see CALLWELL.

On France

ADAM, H. PEARL, *Paris Sees It Through: A Diary, 1914–19*, London, Hodder & Stoughton, 1919.

ALLARD, PAUL, *Les Généraux Limogés pendant la guerre*, Paris, Editions de France, 1933.

BIENAIMÉ, ADMIRAL AMADÉE, *La Guerre navale: fautes et responsabilités*, Paris, Taillander, 1920.

BRUUN, GEOFFREY, *Clemenceau*, Cambridge, Harvard, 1943.

CHARBONNEAU, COL. JEAN, *La Bataille des frontières*, Paris, Lavanzelle, 1932.

CHEVALIER, JACQUES, *Entretiens avec Bergson*, Paris, Plon, 1959.

CLERGERIE, GÉNÉRAL (Chief of Staff of GMP), *Le Rôle du Gouvernement Militaire de Paris, du 1er au 12 Septembre, 1914*, Paris, Berger-Levrault, 1920.

CORDAY, MICHEL, *The Paris Front*, tr., New York, Dutton, 1934.

DEMAZES, GÉNÉRAL, *Joffre, la victoire du caractère*, Paris, Nouvelles Editions Latines, 1955.

DUBAIL, GÉNÉRAL AUGUSTIN, *Quatres années de commandement, 1914–18: Journal de Campagne,* Tome I, 1ʳᵉ *Armée,* Paris, Fournier, 1920.

DUPONT, GÉNÉRAL CHARLES (Chief of Deuxième Bureau in 1914), *Le Haut Commandement allemand en 1914: du point de vue allemand,* Paris, Chapelot, 1922.

ENGERAND, FERNAND (deputy from Calvados and *rapporteur* of the Briey Commission of Inquiry), *La Bataille de la frontière, Aôut, 1914: Briey,* Paris, Brossard, 1920.

———, *Le Secret de la frontière, 1815–1871–1914; Charleroi,* Paris, Brossard, 1918. All references in Notes are to this book unless otherwise specified.

———, *Lanrezac,* Paris, Brossard, 1926.

FOCH, MARSHAL FERDINAND, Memoirs, tr. Col. T. Bentley Mott, New York, Doubleday, Doran, 1931.

GALLIENI, GÉNÉRAL, *Mémoires: défense du Paris, 25 Aôut- 11 Septembre, 1914,* Paris, Payot, 1920.

———, *Les Carnets de Gallieni,* eds. Gaetan Gallieni & P.-B. Gheusi, Paris, Michel, 1932.

———, *Gallieni Parle,* eds. Marius-Ary et Leblond, Paris, Michel, 1920. Gallieni died in 1916 before he had completed a finished version of his memoirs. They were supplemented by the *Notebooks,* edited by his son and a former aide, and by the *Conversations,* edited by his former secretaries.

GAULLE, GÉNÉRAL CHARLES DE, *La France et son armée,* Paris, Plon, 1938.

GIBBONS, HERBERT ADAMS, *Paris Reborn,* New York, Century, 1915.

GIRAUD, VICTOR, *Le Général de Castelnau,* Paris, Cres, 1921.

GRASSET, COLONEL A., *La Bataille des deux Morins: Franchet d'Esperey à la Marne, 6–9 Septembre, 1914,* Paris, Payot, 1934.

GROUARD, LT.-COL. AUGUSTE, *La Guerre éventuelle: France et Allemagne,* Paris, Chapelot, 1913.

———, *La Conduite de la guerre jusqu'à la bataille de la Marne,* Paris, Chapelot, 1922.

GUARD, WILLIAM J., *The Soul of Paris—Two Months in 1914 by an American Newspaperman,* New York, Sun Publishing Co., 1914.

HANOTAUX, GABRIEL, *Histoire illustrée de la guerre de 1914,* 17 vols., Paris, 1916. Especially useful for its excerpts from French and captured German officers' war diaries.

HIRSCHAUER, GÉNÉRAL, and KLÉIN, GÉNÉRAL (Chief and Deputy Chief of Engineers of Military Government of Paris in 1914), *Paris en état de défense,* Paris, Payot, 1927.

HUDDLESTON, SISLEY, *Poincaré. A Biographical Portrait,* Boston, Little, Brown, 1924.

HUGUET, GENERAL A., *Britain and the War: a French Indictment,* London, Cassell, 1928. The bitterness, which tarnishes the value of Huguet's record, is openly expressed in the title.

ISAAC, JULES, *Joffre et Lanrezac,* Paris, Chiron, 1922.

———, "L'Utilisation des reserves en 1914," *Revue d'Histoire de la Guerre,* 1924, pp. 316–337.

JOFFRE, MARSHAL JOSEPH J.-C., *Memoirs*, Vol. I, tr. Col. T. Bentley Mott, New York, Harper's, 1932. Not a book of personal memoirs, but devoted entirely to the conduct of the war, this is by far the most complete and thorough of the records of any of the major commanders—but it is not Joffre. Compared to his characteristically opaque testimony at the Briey hearings, this is lucid, precise, detailed, explanatory, and comprehensible. It shows every evidence of having been written by a devoted staff working from the official records and suffering from perhaps excessive zeal to make the Commander appear the fount and origin of all decisions. On every page he is made to say such statements as, "The conception which I caused to be set down in Col. Pont's memorandum" (228). Nevertheless, with useful sketch maps and in an admirable translation, this is an essential source, if checked against other accounts.

LANGLE DE CARY, GÉNÉRAL DE, *Souvenirs de commandement, 1914–16*, Paris, Payot, 1935.

LANREZAC, GÉNÉRAL CHARLES, *Le Plan de campagne français et le premier mois de la guerre*, Paris, Payot, 1920.

LIBERMANN, HENRI, *Ce qu'a vu en officier de chasseurs à pied. Ardennes belges-Marne-St. Gond, 2 Août-28 Septembre, 1914*, Paris, Plon, 1916.

MARCELLIN, LEOPOLD, *Politique et politiciens pendant la guerre*, Vol. I, Paris, Renaissance, 1923.

MAYER, LT.-COL. EMILE, *Nos chefs de 1914*, Paris, Stock, 1930.

MESSIMY, GÉNÉRAL ADOLPHE, *Mes Souvenirs*, Paris, Plon, 1937. There is something about everything in Messimy. As packed with information as Galet's book on Belgium, it is, in contrast, as effervescent, voluble, and uninhibited as Galet's is taciturn and disciplined. The work of a man who was Minister of War at two crucial periods, July 1911 and August 1914, it is, like Galet, Churchill, and the Kautsky documents, an essential source for material not published elsewhere.

MOTT, COL., T. BENTLEY, *Myron T. Herrick, Friend of France*, New York, Doubleday, Doran, 1929. (Chiefly excerpts from diary and letters.)

MULLER, COMMANDANT VIRGILE (aide-de-camp to Joffre), *Joffre et la Marne*, Paris, Cres, 1931.

PALAT, GÉNÉRAL BARTHÉLMY, *La Grande Guerre sur le front occidental*, Vols. I–IV, Paris, Chapelot, 1920–27.

PALÉOLOGUE, MAURICE, *Un Grand Tournant de la politique mondiale, 1904–06*, Paris, Plon, 1934.

———, "Un Prélude à l'invasion de Belgique," *Revue des Deux Mondes*, October, 1932.

PERCIN, GÉNÉRAL ALEXANDRE (Member of Supreme War Council in 1911 and Governor of Lille in 1914), *1914, Les erreurs du haut commandement*, Paris, Michel, 1920.

PIERREFEU, JEAN DE (a journalist by profession who, as an officer, was attached to GQG to prepare the communiqués for publication), *GQG. Secteur I*, Paris, Edition française Illustrée, 1920.

———, *Plutarque a menti*, Paris, Grasset, 1923.

POINCARÉ, RAYMOND, *Mémoirs*, 4 vols., tr. Sir George Arthur, New York, Doubleday, 1926–29. In fact, if not in name, Poincaré was the central figure politically as Joffre was militarily, and his record is invaluable as guide and commentary to the war, French politics, international affairs, and the civil conflict with GQG. The English edition is abridged and has a confusing habit of referring under diary entries of a certain date to events that have not yet happened.

TANANT, GÉNÉRAL (Chief of Operations in the French Third Army), *La Troisième Armée dans la bataille*, Paris, Renaissance, 1923.

VIVIANI, RENÉ, *As We See It*, tr. New York, Harper's, 1923.

WHARTON, EDITH (who was living in Paris in August, 1914), *Fighting France*, New York, Scribner's, 1915.

On Germany

BAUER, COLONEL M. (Chief of Artillery section at OHL), *Der Grosse Krieg in Feld und Heimat*, Tübingen, Osiander, 1921.

BERNHARDI, GENERAL FRIEDRICH VON, *Germany and the Next War*, tr. Allen H. Powles, London, E. Arnold, 1914.

BETHMANN-HOLLWEG, THEODOR VON, *Reflections on the World War*, tr. London, Butterworth, 1920.

BLOEM, WALTER (Reserve Captain of Brandenburg Grenadiers in IIIrd Corps of von Kluck's Army), *The Advance from Mons, 1914*, tr. G. C. Wynne, London, Davies, 1930.

BLÜCHER, EVELYN, PRINCESS, *An English Wife in Berlin*, London, Constable, 1920.

BÜLOW, BERNHARD, PRINCE VON, Memoirs, 4 vols., tr. Boston, Little, Brown, 1931–32.

BÜLOW, GENERAL KARL VON, *Mon Rapport sur la Bataille de la Marne*, tr. J. Netter, Paris, Payot, 1920.

CLAUSEWITZ, GENERAL CARL VON, *On War*, tr. Col. J. J. Graham, 3 vols., London, Kegan Paul, 1911.

CONRAD VON HÖTZENDORFF, FELDMARSCHALL FRANZ, *Aus Meiner Dienstzeit, 1906–18*, 5 vols., Vienna, 1921–25.

ECKHARDSTEIN, BARON H. VON, *Ten Years at the Court of St. James, 1895–1905*, tr., London, Butterworth, 1921.

ERZBERGER, MATTHIAS, *Souvenirs de guerre*, tr., Paris, Payot, 1921.

FOERSTER, WOLFGANG, *Le Comte Schlieffen et la Grande Guerre Mondiale*, tr. Paris, Payot, 1929.

FRANÇOIS, GENERAL HERMANN VON, *Marneschlacht und Tannenberg*, Berlin, Scherl, 1920.

FREYTAG-LORINGHOVEN, FREIHERR VON, *Menschen und Dinge wie ich sie in meinem Leben sah*, Berlin, Mittler, 1923.

GERARD, JAMES W., *My Four Years in Germany*, New York, Doran, 1917.

GRELLING, RICHARD, *J'Accuse*, tr., A. Grey, New York, Doran, 1915.

HALLAYS, ANDRÉ, *L'Opinion allemande pendant la guerre, 1914–18*, Paris, Perrin, 1919.

HANSSEN, HANS PETER (deputy of Schleswig-Holstein in the Reichstag), *Diary of a Dying Empire*, tr. O. O. Winter, Indiana University Press, 1955.

HAUSEN, GENERAL FREIHERR MAX VON, *Souvenirs de campagne de la Marne en 1914*, tr., Paris, Payot, 1922.

HAUSSMAN, CONRAD, *Journal d'un deputé au Reichstag*, tr., Paris, Payot, 1928.

HINDENBURG, FIELD MARSHAL PAUL VON, *Out of My Life*, Vol. I, tr. New York, Harper's, 1921.

HOFFMANN, GENERAL MAX, *The War of Lost Opportunities*, tr., New York, International, 1925.

———, *The Truth About Tannenberg*, included in Vol. II of his *War Diaries and Other Papers*, tr., Eric Sutton; Intro. by K. F. Nowak, London, Secker, 1929.

KLUCK, GENERAL ALEXANDER VON, *The March on Paris and Battle of the Marne, 1914*, tr., New York, Longmans, 1920.

KOPP, GEORG (a member of the crew of the *Goeben*), *Das Teufelschiff und seine kleine Schwester*, tr. as *Two Lone Ships, Goeben and Breslau*, by Arthur Chambers, London, Hutchinson, 1931.

KRAFFT VON DELLMENSINGEN, GENERAL (Chief of Staff of Rupprecht's Army), *Die Führung des Kronprinzen Rupprecht von Bayern auf dem linken Deutschen Heeresflügel bis zur Schlact im Lothringen im August, 1914*, Wissen und Wehr, Sonderheft, Berlin, Mittler, 1925.

KUHL, GENERAL HERMANN VON (Chief of Staff of Kluck's Army), *Le grand état-major allemand avant et pendant la guerre mondiale*, tr. & ed. by General Douchy, Paris, Payot, 1922.

KURENBERG, JOACHIM VON, *The Kaiser*, tr. Russell and Hagen, New York, Simon & Schuster, 1955.

LICHNOWSKY, PRINCE KARL, *Memorandum* (published in English under the title *The Guilt of Germany*) with Introduction by Viscount Bryce, New York, Putnam's, 1918.

LUDENDORFF, GENERAL ERICH, *Ludendorff's Own Story, August 1914–November 1918*, Vol. I, tr., New York, Harper's, 1919.

LUDWIG, EMIL, *Wilhelm Hohenzollern*, New York, Putnam's, 1926.

MOLTKE, GENERALOBERST HELMUTH VON, *Erinnerungen-Briefe-Dokumente, 1877–1916*, Stuttgart, Der Kommendetag, 1922.

MÜHLON, WILHELM (a director of Krupp's), *L'Europe devastée: notes prises dans les premiers mois de la guerre*, tr., Paris, Payot, 1918.

RITTER, GERARD, *The Schlieffen Plan, Critique of a Myth*, tr. (contains first published text of many of Schlieffen's papers), London, Oswald Wolff, 1958.

RUPPRECHT, CROWN PRINCE OF BAVARIA, *Mein Kriegstagebuch*, Vol. I, Munich, Deutscher National Verlag, 1929.

SANTAYANA, GEORGE, *Egotism in German Philosophy*, 2nd ed., New York, Scribner's, 1940.

SCHINDLER, OBERLEUTNANT D., *Eine 42 cm. Mörser-Batterie im Weltkrieg,*

Breslau, Hoffmann, 1934. The author served as artillery officer with the 420s at Liége and afterward. His book is the only firsthand account of the operation of the siege guns.

SCHLIEFFEN, ALFRED, FELDMARSHALL GRAF VON, *Cannae*, tr. Fort Leavenworth, Command and General Staff School Press, 1936.

SCHOEN, FREIHERR WILHELM VON, *Memoirs of an Ambassador*, tr., New York, Brentano's, 1923.

SOUCHON, ADMIRAL WILHELM, *La Percée de SMS Goeben et Breslau de Messine aux Dardanelles* in *Les marins allemands au combat*, ed. Vice-Admiral Eberhard von Mantey, Reichs Marine-Archiv, tr. Capitan R. Jouan, Paris, Payot, 1930.

STÜRGKH, GENERAL GRAF JOSEF (Austrian representative at OHL), *Im Deutschen Grossen Hauptquartier*, Leipzig, List, 1921.

TAPPEN, GENERAL GERHARD (Chief of Operations at OHL), *Jusqu'à la Marne en 1914* in *Documents allemands sur la bataille de la Marne*, tr. and ed. by Lt.-Col. L. Koeltz of the French General Staff, Paris, Payot, 1930.

TIRPITZ, GRAND ADMIRAL ALFRED VON, *My Memoirs*, 2 vols., tr., New York, Dodd, Mead, 1919.

TOPHAM, ANNE (Governess to the Kaiser's daughter), *Memories of the Kaiser's Court*, New York, Dodd, Mead, 1914. An invaluable view from the inside by an outsider.

WETTERLÉ, ABBÉ E. (deputy in the Reichstag from Alsace-Lorraine), *Behind the Scenes in the Reichstag*, tr., New York, Doran, 1918.

WILE, FREDERIC WILLIAM, *Men Around the Kaiser*, Philadelphia, Lippincott, 1913.

———, *The Assault: Germany Before—and England After—the Outbreak*, Indianapolis, Bobbs-Merrill, 1916.

WILHELM, CROWN PRINCE OF GERMANY, *My War Experiences*, tr., London, Hurst, 1922.

———, *Memoirs*, tr., New York, Scribner's, 1922.

WILHELM II, *The Kaiser's Memoirs*, New York, tr., Harper's, 1922. Reticence having unhappily overtaken the author late in life, this meagre volume by a central figure of his time is thin and disappointing.

———, *Letters from the Kaiser to the Czar*, ed. Isaac Don Levine, New York, Doubleday Page, 1920. Generally known as the Willy-Nicky Letters.

WOLFF, THEODOR (editor of the *Berliner Tageblatt*), *Eve of 1914*, tr. E. W. Dickes, New York, Knopf, 1936.

ZEDLITZ-TRUTZSCHLER, ROBERT, GRAF VON, *Twelve Years at the Imperial German Court*, tr., New York, Doran, 1924. A particularly revealing study of the Kaiser by his unhappy Court Chamberlain.

On Russia

AGOURTINE, LÉON, *Le Général Soukhomlinov*, Clichy, l'Auteur, 1951.

ALEXANDRA, EMPRESS OF RUSSIA, *Letters of the Tsaritsa to the Tsar, 1914–16*, ed. and intro. by Sir Bernard Pares, London, Duckworth, 1923.

BOTKIN, GLEB (son of the Czar's physician), *The Real Romanovs*, New York, Revell, 1931.

BUCHANAN, SIR GEORGE, *My Mission to Russia*, Boston, Little, Brown, 1923.

BRUSILOV, GENERAL A. A., *A Soldier's Notebook*, tr., London, Macmillan, 1930.

DANILOV, GENERAL YOURI, *La Russie dans la guerre mondiale*, tr., Col. A. Kaznakov, Paris, Payot, 1927.

———, *Le Premier Généralissime des armées russes: le grand-duc Nicolas*, tr., Paris, Berger-Levrault, 1932.

DOBROROLSKY, GENERAL SERGE (Chief of Mobilization Service in the Ministry of War in 1914), "La Mobilisation de l'armée russe en 1914," *Revue d' Histoire de la Guerre*, 1923, pp. 53–69 and 144–165.

GILLIARD, PIERRE (tutor to the Czar's children), *Thirteen Years at the Russian Court*, tr., New York, Doran, 1922.

GOLOVIN, LIEUT.-GENERAL NICHOLAS N., *The Russian Army in the World War*, tr., New Haven, Yale, 1931.

———, *The Russian Campaign of 1914*, tr., Captain Muntz, A.G.S. Command and General Staff School Press, Fort Leavenworth, Kansas, 1933. The first of these on the organization, and the second on the military operations, of the Russian Army are the outstanding sources on the Russian war effort in the early months.

GOURKO, GENERAL VASILII (BASIL) (Commander of a Cavalry Division in Rennenkampf's Army), *War and Revolution in Russia, 1914–17*, tr., New York, Macmillan, 1919.

GOURKO, VLADIMIR, *Features and Figures of the Past: Government and Opinion in the Reign of Nicholas II*, tr., Stanford University Press, 1939.

IRONSIDE, MAJOR-GENERAL SIR EDMUND, *Tannenberg: The First Thirty Days in East Prussia*, Edinburgh, Blackwood, 1925.

KNOX, MAJOR-GENERAL SIR ALFRED, *With the Russian Army*, London, Hutchinson, 1921.

KOKOVTSOV, COUNT V. N. (Premier, 1911–14), *Out of My Past*, tr., Stanford Univ. Press, 1935.

NIKOLAIEFF, COL. A. M., "Russian Plan of Campaign in the World War, 1914," tr., *Infantry Journal*, September-October, 1932.

PALÉOLOGUE, MAURICE, *An Ambassador's Memoirs*, tr., F. A. Holt, Vol. I, London, Hutchinson, 1923.

RADZIWILL, PRINCESS CATHERINE, *Nicholas II, Last of the Czars*, London, Cassell, 1931.

———, *Sovereigns and Statesmen of Europe*, New York, Funk & Wagnalls, 1916.

RODZIANKO, M. V. (President of the Duma), *Memoirs: Reign of Rasputin*, tr., London, Philpot, 1927.

SAZONOV, SERGEI, *Fateful Years, 1909–16*, tr., New York, Stokes, 1928.

SUKHOMLINOV, VLADIMIR, *Erinnerungen*, Berlin, Hobbing, 1924.

WITTE, COUNT SERGIUS, *Memoirs*, tr., New York, Doubleday, Page, 1921. Among the rash of memoirs inspired by the fall of the Czarist regime, this is the most solid and informative, although Witte's official career ended in 1906.

WRANGEL, BARON NICHOLAS, *Memoirs, 1847–1920*, tr., Philadelphia, Lippincott, 1927.

On Turkey

DJEMAL PASHA, *Memoirs of a Turkish Statesman, 1913–1919*, tr., New York, Doran, 1922.

EMIN, AHMED, *Turkey in the World War*, New Haven, Yale, 1930.

KANNENGIESSER, GENERAL HANS (a member of the German military mission to Turkey in 1914), *The Campaign in Gallipoli*, tr., London, Hutchinson, 1928.

MORGENTHAU, HENRY, *Ambassador Morgenthau's Story*, New York, Doubleday, Page, 1918.

NOGALES, GENERAL RAFAEL DE, *Four Years Beneath the Crescent*, New York, Scribner's, 1926.

Secondary Works

BENSON, E. F., *The Kaiser and English Relations*, London, Longmans, 1936.

BUCHAN, JOHN, *A History of the Great War*, Vol. I, London, Nelson, 1922.

CRAIG, GORDON, A., *The Politics of the Prussian Army, 1640–1945*, New York, Oxford, 1956.

CRUTTWELL, C. R. M., *A History of the Great War, 1914–18*, Oxford Univ. Press, 1936.

DE WEERD, H. A., *Great Soldiers of Two World Wars*, New York, Norton, 1941.

EARLE, EDWARD MEADE, ed., *et al.*, *Makers of Modern Stategy*, Princeton Univ. Press, 1943.

———, *Modern France*, Princeton Univ. Press, 1951.

FLORINSKY, MICHAEL T., *The End of the Russian Empire*, New Haven, Yale, 1931.

FROTHINGHAM, CAPT. THOMAS G., *The Naval History of the World War*, Vol. I, *Offensive Operations, 1914–15*, Cambridge, Harvard, 1925.

GOERLITZ, WALTER, *History of the German General Staff*, tr. Brian Battershaw, New York, Praeger, 1955.

HALÉVY, ELIE, *A History of the English People, Epilogue*, Vol. II, *1905–1915*. London, Benn, 1934.

MAUROIS, ANDRÉ, *Edwardian Era*, tr., New York, Appleton-Century, 1933.

McENTEE, COL. GIRARD L., *Military History of the World War*, New York, Scribner's, 1937.

MONTEIL, VINCENT, *Les Officiers*, Paris, Editions du Seuil, 1958.

NEAME, LT.-COL. PHILIP, *German Strategy in the Great War* (Lectures at Staff College, Camberley), London, Arnold, 1923.

PONSONBY, ARTHUR, *Falsehood in Wartime*, New York, Dutton, 1928.

RENOUVIN, PIERRE, *The Forms of War Government in France*, New Haven, Yale, 1927.

ROSINSKI, HERBERT, *The German Army*, London, Hogarth, 1939.

Notes

1. A Funeral

Accounts of the funeral, besides those in the daily press and in memoirs of the period, appear in *The Queen*, *The Sphere*, and *The Graphic* for May 21, 1910; "The Meeting of Nine Kings" by William Bayard Hale in *World's Work* for July, 1910; "An Impression of the King's Funeral" by Mary King Waddington in *Scribner's* for October, 1910; Theodore Roosevelt to David Grey, October 5, 1911, *Letters*, ed. E. E. Morison (Harvard U P., 1951–54), VII, 409–13.

PAGE

2   "Grave even to severity": *The Times*, May 21, 1910.

2   "Call this place my home": to Bülow, qtd. Ludwig, 427.

2   "He is Satan": Zedlitz-Trutschler, 177–8. The German press also represented Edward's tour as "having the sole object of forming an alliance against Germany." Lascelles to Grey, April 19, 1907, BD, VI, No. 15.

2   "A very nice boy": Roosevelt to Trevelyan, October 1, 1911, *Letters*, VII, 397.

2   "I bide my time": Lee, I, 477–8.

3   Ferdinand of Bulgaria annoyed other sovereigns: Roosevelt to Grey, *op. cit.*, 409–10. His Byzantine regalia: Sazonov, 230.

3   Prince Danilo and friend: Cust, 111, 249.

4   "You have a nice country": qtd. Maurois, 44.

4–5 Edward's visit to Paris and reports of Belgian and German envoys: Lee, II, 241–2.

5   "Not a mouse could stir": Lee, II, 11.

6   Compared to Bülow an eel was a leech: qtd. Maurois, 177.

6   Holstein called warnings "naïve": Eckhardstein, 249.

6   Eckhardstein overhears: *ibid.*, 230.

PAGE
6   Kaiser wanted to go to Paris: Paléologue, *Un Prélude*, 494–5.
6   Kaiser complained to Roosevelt: Roosevelt to Trevelyan, *Letters*, VII, 396.
6   Kaiser told King of Italy: Bülow, II, 355; Benson, 248.
7   Bernhardi, "We must secure":   Bernhardi, 81.
7   Huns of Attila: Bülow, I, 418.
7   "Legitimate aims":   Hans Delbruck, professor of history at University of Berlin and Germany's leading military historian, qtd. Wile, *Men Around the Kaiser*, 119–22.
7   *Deutschland ganzlich einzukreisen*:   *Neue Freie Presse*, April 15, 1907, qtd. Lee, II, 542.
7   Clemenceau on Germany's "lust for power":   qtd. Bruun, 116.
7   Clemenceau told Edward: Goschen to Grey, August 29, 1908, BD, VI, No. 100; Steed, I, 287.
7   Czar a "common murderer":   Lee, II, 587.
8   "An Englishman is a *zhid*":   Witte, 189.
8   Edward waltzed with Czarina: Fisher, *Memories*, 234.
8   Czar only fit "to grow turnips":   The Kaiser expressed this opinion to the British Foreign Secretary, Lord Lansdowne, at Queen Victoria's funeral, qtd. Newton, 199.
8   "*Garçon mal élevé*":   Benson, 45.
8   "Nicky, take my word for it":   October 25, 1895, *Willy-Nicky Letters*, 23.
9   "More speeches, more parades":   Botkin, 103.
9   A detail that "escaped his Majesty":   qtd. Ludwig, 263.
9   "Lies. He wants war":   qtd. Maurois, 256.
9   Kaiser took to his bed: Crown Prince, 98–100.
10 Esher's lectures on *The Great Illusion*:   "Modern War and Peace" and "La guerre et la paix" in Esher, *Essays*, 211–28 and 229–61.
10 Germany "receptive" to *The Great Illusion*:   *ibid.*, 224. Esher gave copies to the Kaiser, *ibid.*, 55.
10–11 Bernhardi the first to enter Paris in 1870:   Hindenburg, 59. Quotations for Bernhardi's book are from Chapters I, II, IV, V, IX, and X.
11–12 King Edward's death;   quotations from Isvolsky and *Le Figaro* and details of mourning in Paris, Tokyo, and Berlin are from *The Times*, May 8, 1910.
12 Kaiser's arrival at Victoria Station: *The Times*, May 20, 1910.
12 Kaiser impressed by the Lying-in-State: Kaiser's *Memoirs*, 129.
13 Kaiser's proposal to Pichon: Arthur, *George V*, 125.
13 "Other sovereigns so much quieter":   Trevelyan, 172.
13 Kaiser denies proposal to Pichon: Kaiser's *Memoirs*, 131.
13 "Amiable and pacific":   *The Times*, May 21, 1910.
13 Conan Doyle's account: *ibid.*
13 Queen Alexandra loathed Kaiser: Arthur, *George V*, 126. Her letter to George: Nicolson, *George V*, 40.
14 "There never was such a break-up":   Esher, *Journals*, III, 4.

2. *"Let the Last Man on the Right Brush the Channel with His Sleeve"*

17 "The heart of France":   qtd. Buchan, I, 118.
18 "An unimportant obstacle":   Goerlitz, 129.
19 "The whole of Germany must throw itself":   Schlieffen's Memorandum of 1912, Ritter, 172.
19 The Schlieffen plan: Schlieffen's Memoranda for 1892 and 1912 in Ritter; Schlieffen's *Cannae*, Kuhl's *Generalstab*, Förster.

PAGE

19   "It is better to lose a province": qtd. by Schlieffen, Ritter, 172.

20   "The principles of strategy remain unchanged": Schlieffen, *Cannae*, 4.

21   Von der Goltz, "We have won our position": qtd. Wile, *Men Around the Kaiser*, 222.

22   "Desperate delusion of the will": Santayana, 69.

22   Elder Moltke foretold a long war: Foerster, 21.

22   Younger Moltke, "It will be a national war": *Erinnerungen*.

23   "Belgian neutrality must be broken": General von Hahnke's notes on Schlieffen's Memorandum of 1912, Ritter, 186.

23   "Gaining great victories": Clausewitz, III, 209–10.

23   "The one that willed war more than the other": General Percin in article in *Ere Nouvelle*, January, 1925, qtd. Ponsonby, 55–6.

23   Bülow's conversation with Schlieffen: Bülow, II, 88.

23   Leopold II a "thoroughly bad man": Roosevelt to Trevelyan, October 1, 1911, *Letters*, VII, 369.

24   Kaiser's proposal to Leopold II and Leopold's reaction: Bülow, II, 82–85; Cammaerts, 108–9.

24   Two million pounds sterling: J. V. Bredt, *Die Belgische Neutralität und der Schlieffensche Feldzugsplan*, qtd. AQ, July, 1929, 289.

24   "The French would have had to pay for it": Dupont, 23.

24   "Lining up her army along the road": the diplomat was Richard von Kuhlmann, then counselor of the German Embassy in London, later, in 1917, Foreign Secretary, qtd. Cammaerts, 134.

25   "All fortresses, railways and troops": Memorandum of 1912, Ritter, 175.

25   "Lille . . . an excellent target": *ibid.*

25   "Let the last man on the right": qtd. Rosinsky, 137.

25   Schlieffen counted on British belligerency: Ritter, 161–4.

25   Use of reserves in the front line: Isaac, *Reserves*, 335; Foerster, 71.

25   "Only make the right wing strong": Foerster, 70.

26   "Engaging the enemy in his own territory": *Erinnerungen*.

26   "Entirely just and necessary": Tappen, 92.

26   "We must put aside all commonplaces": Cambon (French ambassador in Berlin) to Foreign Minister Pichon, May 6, 1913, *French Yellow Book No. 3*.

27   German spies' reports on Russia: Tirpitz, I, 343.

27   Moltke to Conrad: "Any adjournment": Conrad, III, 670

27   "We are ready and the sooner the better": Eckhardstein, *Lebenserinnerungen*, Vol. III, *Die Isolierung Deutschlands*, Leipzig, 1921, 184.

3. The Shadow of Sedan

Official sources for Plan 17 and its predecessors are AF, Tome I, Vol. I, Chaps. 1 and 2 and Joffre, 45–112. Text of the general directive and of the deployment orders to the several armies is No. 8 in Annexes to AF, I, I. The leading critics of the Plan are Engerand, General Grouard, and General Percin; the last, being blamed for the evacuation of Lille in August, 1914, had a personal ax to grind.

28   General Lebas's interview with Castelnau: Briey, session of May 23, evidence of M. Vendame, deputy of Lille, who accompanied Lebas; session of July 4, evidence of General Lebas.

28   Density of troops per meter for offensive action: Col. Grandmaison had worked it out at 6 to 8 km. per army corps. Engerand, 431.

29   "We proclaim forever the right of Alsatians": Alexandre Zevaes, *Histoire de la Troisième République*, Paris, 1926, 41.

29   Gambetta, "*N'en parlez jamais*": Huddleston, 36.

PAGE

42   General Pendezac: *ibid.*, 514.
42   "altogether likely": Joffre, 63.
42   Castelnau and Joffre on most likely path of German offensive: Giraud, 25–29.
42   Castelnau, "impossible," and Joffre, "same opinion": Joffre, 64.
43   Deuxième Bureau knew of German use of reserves: "It was known that the German plan of mobilization predicated that 'troops of the reserve will be used as active troops,' " AF, I, I, 39. The critique by Moltke is from Isaac, *Reserves*, 335, who also states that a French analysis made in May, 1914, of the German mobilization plan for that year showed the role of reserves as identical with that of the active units. This is confirmed by Joffre in his discussion of the problem, 145–7. Major Melotte's report is from Galet, 22. Joffre (61) is the authority for the belief that the Germans would use reserves only as second-line troops.
43   "I have two stars": Briey, May 23, evidence of Vendame.

4. *"A Single British Soldier . . ."*

44   Péguy, "Like everyone else": from his *Cahiers de la quinzaine*, October 22, 1905, reprinted in his *Notre Patrie*, Paris, 1915, 117–18.
45   General Staff war game of 1905: Robertson, *Private to Field Marshal*, 140; *Soldiers and Statesmen*, I, 24.
45–6   Huguet-Repington Memorandum: Repington, 6–10.
46   "A Hegelian army": Haldane, 198.
46   Grey and Haldane in crisis of 1906: Grey, I, 72–88; Haldane, 203–04; *Before the War*, 186; BD, III, 212.
46   Campbell-Bannerman, lunch at Calais: Maurois, 129.
46   Campbell-Bannerman on "honorable understanding": Grey, I, 85.
47   Haldane authorizes talks: Grey, I, 76.
47   "Departmental affair": Campbell-Bannerman's phrase, qtd. Repington, 10.
47   Plans of Grierson and Robertson: Tyler, John E., *The British Army and the Continent, 1904–14*, London, 1938, 46.
47   Esher favors action in Belgium: Esher, *Journals*, I, 375–6.
47   Fisher, landing on Prussian coast: *Letters*, III, 47; opinions of army strategy: Bacon, II, 182–3.
48   Wilson, in Hyde Park: Wilson, 51; spoke French: *ibid.*, 2.
48   Wilson's comment, "Very interesting": qtd. AQ, July, 1929, 287.
48   Wilson's visit to Foch: Wilson, 78.
48   "I've got a French general": *ibid.*, 79–80
49   "Tremendous gossips": Aston, *Foch*, 129.
49   Wilson's "allez operations": Wilson, 79.
49   "A single British soldier": *ibid.*, 78.
49   "Important question!": Huguet, 21.
49   Foch's views "same as mine": Liddell Hart, *Foch*, 51: in a letter to the British military attaché, Colonel Fairholme, Foch stated his belief that the principal front would be Epinal to Namur, BD, VI, No. 460.
50   Wilson's diary comments: Wilson, 97–8.
50   Wilson-Dubail agreement: AF, I, I, 17–18; BD, VII, No. 640.
50   "Secondary theatre . . . main theatre": Huguet, 8.
51   Wilson's talk with Grey and Haldane: Wilson, 99.
51   Secret meeting of C.I.D., August, 1911: Wilson, 99–102; Churchill, 55–9; Haldane, 226.
52   Fisher, "Overwhelming supremacy": letter of April 28, 1912, *Letters*, II, 456.
52   "Calling for my head": Wilson, 106.

PAGE

52   "Natural and informal outcome": Haldane, *Before the War*, 183.

52   "Certainly committed us": Esher, *Journals*, III, 61.

53   Haldane's mission to Berlin: 254–262, 292; *Before the War*, 72–86.

53   Naval agreement with France: Churchill, 115–16.

53   Grey's letter to Cambon: Grey, I, 97–8.

53   "Break up the Cabinet": Wilson, 113.

53–4   Wilson on Joffre and Castelnau: *ibid.*, 105; Wilson laid a piece of map: *ibid.*

54   Joffre counted on six British divisions: Joffre, 50. Haldane put the total number at 160,000: *Before the War*, 189.

54   British military talks with Belgians: BD, III, No. 217 ff.; Bridges (then military attaché in Brussels), 62–63.

54   Esher's warning to Huguet: Huguet, 18; Joffre, 54. Cambon's condition: Dupont, 25.

55   Plan W worked in secret: Wilson, 149.

5. *The Russian Steam Roller*

56   German dread of the Slav: When a German regiment in 1914 learned it was going to the western not the eastern front, there was "general rejoicing. For some indefinable reason the very thought of Russia gave one a shudder." Bloem, 20. The same thought moved a German army doctor to complain to the Duchess of Sutherland (49) how wicked it was of England to join the alliance against Germany "and leave us to those devilish Russians."

57   Numbers in the Russian Army: these and other figures about men and matériel in this chapter are from Golovin's *Army* unless otherwise noted.

57   Grey on Russian power: Grey to Sir F. Bertie, May 1, 1914, BD, X, Part 2, No. 541.

57   Franco-Russian staff talks and facts of Russian mobilization: Messimy, 179–81; Kokovtsov, 370–72; Joffre, 55–60; Golovin, *Campaign*, Chapter III, 45–73.

58   Czar, "At the heart of Germany": Joffre, 23.

58   Grandmaison popular in Russia: Golovin, *Campaign*, 61.

58   Jilinksky's promises in 1912–13: Agourtine, 25.

58   Ian Hamilton's reports: Hamilton, General Sir Ian, *A Staff Officer's Scrap Book*, London, 1907, II, 381.

59   "Not a single tennis court": Knox, xxvii.

59   "This insane regime . . . this tangle of cowardice": Witte, 270, 247.

59   Nicholas II uneducated: A few days before his 22nd birthday, on April 28, 1890, Nicholas wrote in his diary, "Today I finished definitely and forever my education." qtd. Radziwill, *Nicholas II*, 210.

60   Kokovtsov's interview with Czar: Kokovtsov, 456.

60   Stolypin assassinated by police agents: Wrangel, 208.

60   "Everyone in poor health": Witte, 319.

61   "England's death rattle": Paléologue, *Intimate Journal of the Dreyfus Case*, New York, 1957, 180.

61   "How I detest that word": Witte, 190.

61   British diplomat: Sir Arthur Nicolson, British ambassador to Russia, 1906–10. Nicolson, *Diplomatist*, 180.

61   "Difficult to make him work": Sazonov, 286.

61   Sukhomlinov on "vicious innovations": Golovin, *Campaign*, 31, 34.

61   "Distrust at first sight": Paléologue, 83; Poincaré (III, 163) had the same reaction.

PAGE

62   Sukhomlinov's wife, expenses, associations: Agourtine, 18–22; Vladimir Gurko, 552–3; Knox, 222; Sir Bernard Pares, *A History of Russia*, New York, 1953, 472–77.

63   Sukhomlinov's trial: Agourtine, 56–9.

63   "Terrible consequences": qtd. Agourtine, 59.

63   Kaiser's dedication to Sukhomlinov: a facsimile in the autograph of the Kaiser is reproduced in Ludwig, 508.

63   Sukhomlinov's responsibility for the shell shortage: Knox, obituary of Sukhomlinov in *Slavonic Review*, 1926, Vol. 5, 148; also Golovin, *Army*, 12, 32, 43.

64   Sukhomlinov hated Grand Duke; Danilov, 150; Golovin, *Campaign*, 35.

64   Grand Duke only "man" in royal family: Pares, Introduction to *Letters of Tsaritsa*, xxi.

64   "I have no faith in N.". *Letters to Tsar*, June 16, 1915, 97.

65   Foch's influence on Grand Duke: Esher, *Tragedy*, 19.

65   Prince Kotzbue's remarks: Danilov, 43.

65   "Montenegrin nightingales": Paléologue, 22–23.

65   Russia's alternate war plans: Ironside, 31–6.

66   March on Berlin: according to Danilov, Deputy Chief of Staff (130), this was the fundamental idea and goal of the Russian High Command throughout the "first period" of the war.

66   Junkers shot foxes: Ellen M. Pain. *My Impressions of East Prussia*, London, 1915.

66   Russian moose shot by the Kaiser: Topham, 254. Her Chapter XIII, "Rominten," is brilliant reporting of the Imperial habits.

67   Germany hoped to keep Japan neutral: Hoffmann, *War of Lost Opportunities*, 5.

67   Hoffmann's habits: K. F. Nowak, Introduction to Hoffmann's *War Diaries*, I, 10, 18.

67   "You are a yellow-skin", recorded by the American correspondent Frederick Palmer, qtd. De Weerd, 71.

67   Russian colonel sold war plans: Hoffmann, *War of Lost Opportunities*, 4.

68   "With all available strength": qtd. Hoffmann, *Diaries*, II, 241.

Outbreak

71   "Some damned foolish thing": recalled by Albert Ballin who quoted it to Churchill (207) in July 1914 when Ballin was sent to London by the Kaiser to persuade the British to stay neutral.

71   Kaiser's "shining armor" speech: in the Vienna Town Hall, September 21, 1910, qtd. Stanley Shaw, *William of Germany*, New York, Macmillan, 1913, 329.

71   German's "faithful support": Bethmann-Hollweg to von Tschirschky (German ambassador in Vienna), Kautsky, No. 15; Kaiser to Emperor Franz Joseph, Kautsky, No. 26.

71   "Dissipates every reason for war": Kaiser's marginal note on copy of Austria's ultimatum to Serbia, Kautsky, No. 271.

72   "Make us a distinct declaration": Bethmann-Hollweg to Pourtales, Kautsky, No. 490.

6. August 1: Berlin

The central episode in this chapter, General Moltke's traumatic experience with the Kaiser on the night of August 1, is based on Moltke's memoirs, 19–23. All quotations from the Kaiser and Moltke himself during the course of this incident are from this source. An English version was published by *Living Age*, January 20, 1923, 131–34.

PAGE

73   Ambassador instructed to declare war on Russia: Kautsky, No. 542.

73   At 5:30 Bethmann and Jagow: The American correspondent, Frederic William Wile, on his way to the Foreign Office, saw the two ministers as they came out: *Assault*, 82.

73   "I hate the Slavs": Sturgkh, 232.

74   Pourtales's and Eggeling's reports: Kautsky, Nos. 474 and 521. Eggeling's insistence up to the last moment that Russia could not fight because of artillery and transport deficiencies is reported by Kuhl, 31.

74   "Sick Tom-cat": Kautsky, No. 474.

74   A journalist in the crowd: Wile, *Assault*, 81–2; the Belgian ambassador also describes the scene: Beyens, II, 266.

74   "If the iron dice roll": Kautsky, No. 553.

74   Officers waving handkerchiefs: Wolff, 504.

74   Suspected Russian spies trampled: Hanssen, 22–23.

75   Railway transport required for one Army corps: Reichsarchiv, *Das Deutsche Feldeisenbahnwesen*, Band I, *Die Eisenbahnen zu Kriegsbeginn*, qtd. AQ, April, 1928, 96–101.

75   Elder Moltke on a sofa: Fisher, *Memories*, 230.

75   Kaiser's marginalia: Kautsky, Nos. 368 and 596.

75   "Dead Edward": Written on margin of Pourtales's dispatch, received July 30 at 7:00 A.M. reporting that Russian mobilization could not be canceled, Kautsky, No. 401, English version, Ludwig, 448.

76   Autonomy for Alsace: The alleged proposal by an anonymous "close associate" of Bethmann's is reported by Radziwill, *Sovereigns*, 70, a not too reliable source.

76   German ultimatum to France: Schoen, 192, 197; Messimy, 149.

76   French decoded it: Poincaré, III, 251.

77   "Moltke wants to know": Wolff, 504.

77   Lichnowsky's telegram: Kautsky, No. 562.

77   Dinner in Berlin, 1911: Given by Sir E. Goschen, the British ambassador, in honor of Major-General Wilson, Wilson, 94.

77   Grey's proposal to Lichnowsky: Lichnowsky, 73–74; Grey to Goschen, *British Blue Book*, No. 123; Grey, II, Appendix F, "The Suggestions of August 1, 1914."

78   "*Traurige Julius*": Sturgkh, 24.

78   Moltke's character and habits: Freytag-Loringhoven, 135–7; Bauer, 33; Goerlitz, 143; General Sir Edmund Ironside, "Two Chiefs of General Staff," *Nineteenth Century and After*, February 1926; Wile, NYT, October 6, 1914, 2:6.

79   "Very critical of myself": *Erinnerungen*, 307; "Place ourselves under Japan": qtd. Ironside, *op. cit.*, 229; "Quite brutally" about Peking: *Erinnerungen*, 308; "Win the big prize twice": *ibid.*

79   "Build railways": Neame, 2. Elder Moltke's use of railroads, Rosinski, 129.

80   Best brains ended in lunatic asylums: AQ, April, 1928, 96.

80   General von Staab: His book, *Aufmarsch nach zwei Fronten*, is analyzed by Commandant Koeltz, "La Concentration allemande et l'incident du premier Août, 1914," *Revue d'Histoire de la Guerre*, 1926, 117–130.

80   Erzberger's testimony: Erzberger's *Erlebnisse*, qtd. AQ, April, 1922, 80.

80–81   Telegrams to England: Kautsky, Nos. 578 and 579; to Paris: No. 587; to King George: No. 575.

81   Lichnowsky's second telegram: Kautsky, No. 603. King George's reply to the Kaiser saying "There must be some mistake," No. 612.

PAGE
82   Invasion of Trois Vierges: Luxembourg Minister of State Eyschen to Jagow,
      Kautsky, No. 602; Buch, German minister to Luxembourg, to Foreign Office,
      No. 619; Bethmann-Hollweg to Government of Luxembourg, No. 640.
83   Pourtalès's interview with Sazonov: Sazonov, 213; Paléologue, 48; Pourtalès's
      report, Kautsky, No. 588.
83   Tirpitz on declaration of war: Tirpitz, I, 363–5. The scene is also described
      by Bülow (III, 187) as told him by Albert Ballin who was present. Bethmann
      was pacing up and down while *Geheimrat* Kriege, a conscientious jurist
      of the Foreign Office, was searching through all the lawbooks for a model.
      "From time to time the agitated Bethmann would ask him, 'Is that
      declaration of war on Russia ready yet? I must have my declaration at once!'
      Ballin asked, 'Why such haste to declare war on Russia, Your Excellency?'
      and Bethmann answered, 'If I don't, we shan't get the Socialists to fight.' "
83   "Place guilt on Russia":   Bethmann to Tschirschky, marked "Urgent,"
      Kautsky, No. 441.

7. August 1: Paris and London

84   To leave onus of aggression on Germany: Joffre, 133.
84   10-km. withdrawal: Orders of the War Ministry for the withdrawal are
      Nos. 22, 25, 26, and 27 in *Annexes to AF*, I, I.
85   Viviani, "haunted by fear":   Viviani, 194–5.
85   "To assure collaboration":   Annexe No. 25.
85   Joffre hounding the Government: Joffre, 123–5; Messimy, 139–50.
85   "Frightful nervous tension":   Viviani, 195.
85   "Permanent condition":   Messimy, 183. The premier's nerves were also
      remarked by Bertie, 5.
85   Dr. Gauthier "forgot":   Messimy, 156.
86   Poincaré could remember as a boy: Poincaré, III, 1.
86   Prolonged cry, "*Vive la France!*":   Messimy, 138.
86   "Without firing a shot":   *ibid.*, 140.
86   "*Une forme hypocrite*":   Messimy, 144.
87   Cambon, England "tepid":   Poincaré, II, 242. "No interest to Great
      Britain":   *ibid.*, 264.
87   *Carnet B*:   Messimy, 147–8; de Gaulle, 237; Renouvin, 13, 27–8.
88   Isvolsky "very distressed":   Poincaré, II, 272.
88   Terms of Franco-Prussian Alliance: text in *Livre Jaune, l'Alliance Franco-
      Russe*, Ministère des Affaires Estrangères, Paris, 1918, 92; also in Joffre, 102.
      Over the years from 1892 to 1914 the Alliance was the subject of con-
      tinuing discussion between the contracting parties, especially as to the exact
      interpretation of its *casus foederis*, and it became gradually encrusted with
      layers of *aides-mémoires*. According to various English translations, France
      was obligated to "attack," to "oppose," or to "fight" Germany. In the
      French text the word is "*attaquer*." For Poincaré's interpretation, see
      II, 289.
88   "*Du calme, du calme*":   Messimy, 183–4.
88   Joffre in "pathetic tone":   *ibid.*, 149.
89   Schoen-Viviani talk: Poincaré, II, 265; Schoen's report of Viviani's reply,
      Kautsky, No. 571.
89   10-km. order reaffirmed, text: AF, Annexe No. 26.
89   Foch's corps "nose to nose":   Joffre, 129, n. 3.
89   General Ebener comes for mobilization order: Joffre, 128; Messimy, 150.
89–90 Scenes in Paris after mobilization: Adam, 20; Gibbons, 73; Guard, 9;
      Wharton, 14.

PAGE

90   "Played by Hungarians": Wharton, 10.
90   "Sick at heart": Bertie, I, 6–7.
90   Cambon-Grey interview: Poincaré, II, 264.
90   Grey prepared to resign: "Throughout the whole of this week I had in view the probable contingency that we should not decide at the critical moment to support France. In that event I should have to resign." Grey, II, 312.
90   Grey "icy": Lichnowsky to Jagow, April 13, 1913, qtd. Halévy, 627.
91   "If Germany dominated": Grey, I, 299.
91   Lord Morley on Cabinet divisions: Morley, 4, 5, 10.
92   Caucus of Liberal M.P.s: Addison, 32.
92   Verse from *Punch*: by Owen Seaman, *Punch*, August 5, 122.
92   Lloyd George, "gravest issue": qtd. Halévy, 547.
92   German arms to Ulster: *ibid.*, 548.
93   Churchill and Fleet: Corbett, 25–30; Churchill, 230 ff. Subsequent material on Churchill's role in the crisis and mobilization of the Fleet is from his Chapter IX, "The Crisis," and Chapter X, "Mobilization of the Navy."
94   "Invented by a genius": L. J. Maxse, "Retrospect and Reminiscence," *National Review*, Vol. LXXI, 746.
94   "Splendid condottierre" and "playing the peace-card": Morley, 24.
94   "Are we to go in": Asquith, II, 7.
94   Grey in Cabinet of July 31: Morley, 2.
94   "Cabinet seemed to heave a sigh": *ibid.*, 3.
95   Bankers "aghast" and City "totally opposed": Morley, 5; Lloyd George, 61.
95   Tory leaders: Chamberlain, 94–101; Wilson, 154.
95   Cambon, "Et l'honneur": Chamberlain, 101.
96   Grey's telegrams on Belgian neutrality and French reply: *British Blue Book*, Nos. 114, 124, 125.
96   Lloyd George, only a "little violation": Beaverbrook, 15–16.
96   Grey to Cambon, "France must take": Nicolson, *Diplomatist*, 304.
96   "*Ils vont nous lâcher*": *ibid.*, 304–5.
97   Churchill at dinner: Beaverbrook, 22–3.

8. *Ultimatum in Brussels*

98   Below-Saleske's instructions: Jagow to Below, July 29 and August 2, marked "Urgent and Secret," Kautsky, Nos. 375 and 648.
98   "I am a bird of ill omen": Whitlock, 3.
99   Bassompierre's interview with Below: Bassompierre, 15–16.
99   "Your neighbor's roof": *ibid.*
100   Queen translates appeal to Kaiser: Cammaerts, 405; text of the letter: Galet, 31.
100   Delivery of the ultimatum: Bassompierre, 17; remainder of paragraph and further account of government discussions of ultimatum are from Bassompierre unless otherwise noted.
100   Below seen driving back: Gibson, 9–10.
101   Davignon's optimism and van der Elst's esteem for Germans: Klobukowski, 34–5.
101   Moltke drafted ultimatum: Kautsky, No. 376, n. 1.
101–02 Text of ultimatum: *Belgian Grey Book*, No. 20.
103   "Sealed envelope": Cammaerts, 39.
103   "As if he wished to build something": *ibid.*, 67.
104   Galet's teachings, career, and temperament: D'Ydewalle, 94.
104   Kaiser's assurance to van der Elst: Cammaerts, 108–9, 115.

PAGE

105   "To ensure against being ignored": Galet, 8.

106   King Albert's visit to Berlin, 1913: Beyens, II, 38–43; Jules Cambon to Pichon, November 22, 1913, *French Yellow Book*, No. 6; Poincaré, II, 86; Galet, 23.

107   What Moltke said to Major Melotte: Beyens, II, 47–53.

108   Galet's memorandum: Galet, 23.

108   Council of State, August 2: Carton de Wiart, 207–9: Galet, 46–50.

108   "If Germany victorious, Belgium will be annexed": qtd. Poincaré, II, 281.

109   German anxiety about Belgian resistance: see notes on Moltke and Jagow for Chapter 9, p. 124.

109   Below's interview with van der Elst: *Belgian Grey Book*, No. 21; Cammaerts, 13.

109   King staring out the window: Carton de Wiart, 210.

110   Conference at Bethmann-Hollweg's house: Tirpitz, I, 366–70.

110   Berliners looking nervously at the sky: Hanssen, 14. More sophisticated Germans were skeptical of the reports. Conrad Haussmann (16), noting the lack of precise details, found them "not very convincing."

110   De Gaiffier delivers Belgian reply: Bassompierre, 31, 37; text of the reply, *Belgian Grey Book*, No. 22.

111   Kaiser's reply to King Albert: Galet, 58–9.

111   "What does he take me for?": Cammaerts, 19.

9. *"Home Before the Leaves Fall"*

112   Grey in Cabinet of August 2: Grey, II, 12.

112   "National devotion" in France: Report by British Consul in Dunkirk, BD, XI, 508.

113   War Book: Corbett, 20–21.

113   Grey's naval pledge to Cambon: Grey, II, Appendix D, 301.

113   Cambon-Grey conversation: Grey to Bertie, BD, XI, 487.

113   Cambon's "secret" telegram: Poincaré, II, 278.

113   Nations do not wage war "by halves": article by Cambon, *Revue de France*, July 1, 1921.

114   Dissolution of the Cabinet: Morley, 4, 17; Asquith, II, 8.

114   Churchill hurries to see Balfour: Dugdale, II, 78.

114   Haldane and Grey receive telegram from Belgium and ask Asquith to mobilize: Haldane, 294–5.

115   Conservatives urge support of France and Russia: Dugdale, II, 79–80; Chamberlain, 99–100.

115   Russia disliked as ally: Morley, 6.

116   Lichnowsky's last interview with Grey: Grey, II, 13.

116   House of Commons awaiting Grey: MacDonagh, 3; *Punch*, August 12, 153.

116   "Pale, haggard and worn": Grenfell, Field Marshall Lord, *Memoirs*, London, 1925, 204.

117   Grey's speech: full text, Grey, II, Appendix D.

117   Lord Derby's whisper: Grenfell, *op. cit.*, 204.

118   Ramsay MacDonald, Kier Hardie, and unconvinced Liberals: NYT, August 4.

118   "What happens now?": Churchill, 235.

118   "If they refuse there will be war": Poincaré, IV, 519 (French ed.).

119   "You will be home before the leaves": Blücher, 137.

119   German diarist: *ibid.*, 12, 16.

119   Breakfast in Paris on Sedan Day: Count Häseler, qtd. Grelling, 30.

PAGE

119   Russian expectations of early victory: Vladimır Gurko, 542; Botkin, 112.
119   English officer asked about duration: Bridges, 74.
119   "Vasilii Fedorovitch": Vladimir Gurko, 542.
119   German stockpile of nitrates: Erzberger, 15.
120   Joffre predicts long war: Joffre, 53.
120   Kitchener's prediction: Birkenhead, 22.
120   "If only someone had told me": qtd. Bernhard Huldermann, *Albert Ballin*, London, 1922, 212.
120   Prince Henry and King George: King George to Grey, December 8, 1912, BD, X, part 2, No. 452. On July 26, 1914, Prince Henry, who was again in England, was told by King George, "I hope we shall remain neutral. . . But if Germany declares war on Russia and France joins Russia, then ı am afraid we shall be dragged into it." Nicolson, *George V*, 245-6.
120   Kaiser "convinced" England would be neutral: Freytag-Loringhoven, qtd. AQ, April, 1924, 153.
120   *Corpsbrüder*: Wile, 212.
121   "More English, the better": Kuhl, 34.
121   Moltke's memorandum of 1913: Ritter, 68-9. Even in 1906 Schlieffen envisaged Britain as an enemy with an expeditionary force of 100,000 in Belgium, *ibid.*, 161-4.
121   "We had no doubt whatever" of the BEF: Kuhl, qtd. AQ, April, 1922, 166.
121   "England probably hostile": qtd. Frothingham, 60. The German Navy, like the Army, expected Britain to be an enemy: "There was scarcely any possible doubt that England would never countenance a military weakening of France by us," Tirpitz, I, 334.
121   Crown Prince, the "military solution": *My Waı Experiences*, 5.
121   "The Blessing of Arms": *Alldeutscher Blätter*, August 3, qtd. Hallays, 27.
122   Reichstag deputies depressed: Hanssen, 13, 19.
122   Herrick calls Viviani: Poincaré, II, 284.
122   Schoen brings declaration of war: *ibid.*, 285-8.
123   "The lamps are going out": Grey, II, 20.
123   Below's note, "if necessary": Bassompierre, 37.
123   Whitlock calls on Below: Whitlock, 64; Gibson, 22.
123   "Our greatest disaster": Czernin, *In the World War*, New York, 1920, 16.
123   "We Germans lost the first great battle": Crown Prince, *Memoirs*, 180.
123   Many suspect a trick: Galet, 51; Joffre, 135.
123   Messimy's order: Messimy, 289.
124   King Albert's appeal to guarantors: Galet, 63.
124   Moltke hopes for "an understanding": Moltke to Jagow, Kautsky, No. 788.
124   Jagow's interview with Beyens: Beyens, II, 269-72.
124   "Common bond of love and hate": Millard, 35.
124   Austrian minister's tears: Bassompierre, 41.
124-5 King Albert in Parliament: Galet, 62; Gibson, 13-19; Whitlock, 60.
125   Crowds' enthusiasm: Bassompierre, 40; Millard, 35-7.
126   Foreign volunteers in Paris: Gibbons, 27.
126   Speeches of Viviani and Poincaré: *French Yellow Book*, Nos. 158 and 159; Poincaré, II, 296-7.
126   Joffre "perfectly calm": Poincaré, *ibid.*
126   Scenes in Berlin: Hanssen, 25.
126   Picture of Wilhelm I at Sedan: Wetterlé, 29.
127   Bethmann and Erzberger meet deputies: Haussmann, 16-20.
127   Kaiser's speech in Weisser Saal: *ibid.*, 21; Hanssen, 25; text of speech is in Ralph H. Lutz, *Fall of the German Empire, Documents, 1914-18*, Stanford, 1932, Vol. I.

PAGE

127   Social Democrats debate "Hoch!": Haussmann, 23.
127   Promises of Jagow and von Heeringen: Erzberger, 231.
128   Bethmann's speech: NYT, August 5, 2:6; full text in Lutz, *op. cit.*
128-9   British ultimatum: *British Blue Book*, Nos. 153 and 159.
129   Goschen-Bethmann interview: Bethmann, 159, note; Goschen to Grey, *British Blue Book*, No. 160.
129   Stoning British Embassy: Gerard, 137; Beyens, I, 273.
130   "To think that George and Nicky": qtd. Blücher, 14.
130   "Treat us like Portugal": Tirpitz, I, 307.
130   "Not much loved": Crown Prince, *Memoirs*, 81–2.
130   Depressed deputies' comments: Haussmann, 25, 27; Hanssen, 32.
130-31 Rumor about Japan: Hanssen, 14.
131   "Siam is friendly": Blücher, 6.
132   Cambon visits Grey: Poincaré, II, 293.
132   Wilson's indignation at mobilization order: Wilson, 147, 156; Chamberlain, 103–4.
132   Balfour's letter to Haldane: Dugdale, II, 81.
132   Asquith reads ultimatum to House: *Punch*, August 12, 154; MacDonagh, 78. *Punch*'s correspondent, who was present, says Asquith's statement was received with "a deep-throated cheer . . . fierce in its intensity." *The Times* correspondent (MacDonagh) who was also present says it was received in "complete silence." This illustrates one of the perils of writing history.
133   Cabinet waits for midnight: Lloyd George, 69–71.
133   Moltke, "next 100 years": Conrad, IV, 194.

10. *"Goeben . . . an Enemy Then Flying"*

Sources for all action by, and events aboard, the *Goeben* and *Breslau*, unless otherwise noted, are Souchon, Kopp, and *Krieg zur See*, the official German naval history. Likewise, for action of the British ships, the sources are the official history, Corbett, 56–73 (with two magnificent maps, unfortunately too large to reproduce in these less expansive days), Milne, and Churchill 236–43 and 265–75. Corbett's account was published first; Milne's was written to dispute Corbett who, he felt, had done him injustice, Churchill's to compose a narrative that, while not too obviously blaming the naval commanders, would show the Admiralty to have been blameless and still claim to be history, not special pleading. This delicate feat of balancing was accomplished by placing the blame for failure to arrest the *Goeben* on accidents of fate; on "the terrible Ifs," in his words. The account is one to be read with caution not incompatible with admiration.

137   Admiralty wireless to Souchon: *Krieg zur See*, 2. Tirpitz's idea was that Souchon should be placed at the disposal of the Turkish Government "to command the Turkish fleet." Tirpitz to Jagow, Kautsky, No. 775.
138   Enver as advocate of German alliance: Emin, 68–69; Nogales, 26, Morgenthau, 30–34.
138   Talaat's appetite and views: Steed, I, 377; Morgenthau, 20–24; Nogales, 26–28.
139   Churchill on Turkey: *Aftermath*, 374.
139   Churchill's letter rejecting Turkish alliance: Churchill, 524.
139-40 Kaiser's instructions: These took the form of marginal notes on telegrams from Wangenheim, German ambassador in Constantinople, Kautsky, Nos. 141 and 149. The Kaiser was on his yacht at this time, mid-July, and his marginalia were telegraphed to the Foreign Office as instructions.
140   Turkish-German negotiations for treaty: Emin, 66–8; Djemal, 107–14;

PAGE

correspondence between Wangenheim and Jagow; Kautsky Nos. 45, 71, 117, 141, 144, 183, 285. Draft of the Treaty, signed Bethmann-Hollweg is No. 320; final text is No. 733; further discussion of terms and implementation, Nos. 398, 411, 508, 517, 726, 836.

140   British seizure of Turkish warships: Churchill, *Aftermath*, 377–8; Djemal, 96, 104, 116; Grey, II, 165–66; Grey's "regrets": *British Blue Book*, II, Nos. 1, 2, 3, and 4.

140   Turkish warships cost $30,000,000: Allen, Whitehead and Chadwick, *The Great War*, Philadelphia, 1916, II, 374.

141   Turkish ministers' second thoughts: On August 3 Wangenheim reported that Enver would like "to declare war immediately" but the other ministers were against it; Kautsky, No. 795.

143   "Spit in the soup": Souchon, 33.

143   "How many boilers leaking?": Souchon gives the conversation verbatim, 37.

143   British Consul's telegram: BD, XI, 480.

146   Churchill's July 31 instructions to Milne: Churchill, 237–8.

146   Not intended "as a veto": *ibid.*, 272.

146   "Betrayal of the Navy": Fisher, *Letters*, II, 451, April 22, 1912.

147   Fisher's wrath: *ibid.*; "succumbing to court influence," 458; "Utterly useless," *ibid.*; "unfitted," 451; "backstairs cad," 360; "serpent," 418; "Sir B. Mean," 447.

147   Churchill's Order of August 2: Churchill, 239; third order to Milne, *ibid.*

148   Gauthier challenges Messimy: Poincaré, II, 279–80.

149   Orders to Lapeyrère and his subsequent actions: Capt. Voitoux, "l'Evasion du Goeben et Breslau," *Revue Politique et Parlementaire*, March and May, 1919. The French role in the failure to arrest the *Goeben*, like the British, became a cause of extreme embarrassment to the government and was investigated in 1916 by a Parliamentary Committee of Inquiry under Admiral Amadée Bienaimé. Its report, implying blame of Admiral Lapeyrère, which he refused to answer, was never published but was analyzed in Admiral Bienaimé's book which gives the impression of making Admiral Lapeyrère the scapegoat for a general dissatisfaction with the navy. Materials collected by the Committee of Inquiry were deposited in 1919 with the Ministry of Marine.

149   "Tasting that moment of fire" and "sowing death and panic": Souchon, 40.

149   *Goeben* flew the Russian flag and "Our trick succeeded": Kopp, 23–4.

150   Milne reports position to Admiralty: Churchill, 239.

150   "Very good. Hold her": *ibid.*

150   Churchill's "urgent" message to Asquith: *ibid.*, 240.

150   "Winston with war paint": Asquith, II, 21.

151   Stokers' deaths: Kopp, 28–31, 53; Souchon, 42.

151   "Tortures of Tantalus": Churchill, 242.

151   Order to respect Italian neutrality and "petty incident": *ibid.*, 241.

152   Two messages from Tirpitz: *Krieg zur See*, 13; Souchon, 47. Turkish hesitations which caused the cancellation are reported by Wangenheim, Kautsky, Nos. 852 and 854.

153   "To force the Turks": Souchon, 47.

153   Sicilian headlines: Souchon, 45.

154   "Prevent the Austrians from coming out": Corbett, 62.

155   Troubridge, "handsomest officer" and "Believed in seamanship": Kenworthy, 32.

155   *Gloucester* ordered to "avoid capture": Milne, 104.

156   Admiralty clerk's error about Austria: Churchill, 275.

157   "Indispensable military necessity.": *Krieg zur See*, 20.

158   "Enter. Demand surrender": *ibid.*

PAGE
158 Wangenheim's "agitated interest": Morgenthau, 70–71.
159 Enver's interview with Col. Kress: Kannengiesser, 25–26.
159 "More slaughter, more misery": Churchill, 271.
159 Admiralty order to blockade Dardanelles: Corbett, 73.
159 Asquith, "We shall insist": Asquith, II, 26.
160 "Sale" of the *Goeben*: Djemal, 119–20; Morgenthau, 76–78. The "sale" and the diplomatic furor aroused by the arrival of the German warships is documented in the reports of the various ambassadors in Constantinople to their governments, especially Giers to the Russian Foreign Office and Sir Louis Mallet to the British, contained in the *Russian Orange Book, II,* and the *British Blue Book, II,* respectively.
160 Sazonov, "Even if we are victorious": Paléologue, 84–85.
160 "Most bellicose" and "violently anti-Turk": Asquith, II, 26, 28.
160 Gallieni's comment: *Gallieni parle,* 78.
160 Kitchener, "strike the first blow": *ibid.,* 26.
161 Souchon's attack in Black Sea: Emin, 75–76; Giers to Foreign Office, *Russian Orange Book, II,* No. 98; Roberts to Grey, *British Blue Book, II,* No. 178; Memorandum by Sir Louis Mallet, November 20, *ibid.*
161 "He did forbear to chase": article on Troubridge, *DNB.* On the ground that the House of Commons had the constitutional right to review courts-martial, Commander Bellairs, an M.P., made several attempts to force the Admiralty to release the report of the Court, without success. As the finding was acquittal, the Commander said he could see no reason for the Admiralty to keep the report secret, "except to prevent the public from knowing the bad arrangements they made at the outset of the war." April 15, 1919, *Parliamentary Debates,* 5th series, Vol. 114, 2863–71.
162 "Their Lordships approved": article on Milne, *DNB.*

11. Liège and Alsace

Unless otherwise noted, the operations of the Belgian Army in this chapter are based chiefly on Galet, van der Essen, and Cammaerts; of the German Army on Ludendorff's chapter "Liège," 28–46, and on Reichsarchiv, *Weltkrieg,* Vol. I, 108–20, which, rather disproportionately, gives twelve pages to the infantry assault and only one to the work of the siege guns. The assembly, transport, and operations of the guns are taken chiefly from Schindler. Operations of the Army of Alsace are from Dubail and *AF,* I, I, Chapters 4 and 5, 90–154.

163 Encourage an uprising in Alsace: Joffre, 136; Engerand, *Bataille,* 193.
164 "I will go through Belgium": qtd. J. M. Kennedy, *The Campaign Round Liège,* London, 1915.
164 "Rage of dreaming sheep": a remark applied by Baron von Stein to the Tugenbund, qtd. Buchan, 129.
167 Moltke on the 39th day: In correspondence with Conrad in 1909 Moltke at first said he expected to be able to transfer troops to help Austria, after defeating France, "between the 36th and 40th day of mobilization." Conrad, I, 369. Later he thought he could defeat France by the 21st day if she took the offensive and by the 28th day if she fought behind her frontiers. *Ibid.,* 374. Five years later, on May 12, 1914, when Conrad visited Moltke at Karlsbad, Moltke said, "We hope to be finished with France in six weeks from the start of operations or at least to be so far forward that we can turn our main forces to the East." *Ibid.,* III, 669. On this occasion, he specified achieving a decision in the west "on the 39th or 40th day after mobilization." Karl Friedrich Nowak, *Les Dessous de la défait,* Paris, Payot, 1925, 53.
167–8 Siege guns: In addition to Schindler, whose account is largely concerned with

PAGE

the transport and actual operation of the guns, the technical facts are taken from Army War College, *Study on Development of Large Calibre Mobile Artillery in the European War*, Washington, GPO, 1916, p. 8; *U.S. Field Artillery Journal*, October 1914, p. 591 and January 1915, p. 35; "Austria's Famous 'Skoda' Mortars," *Scientific American*, July 3, 1915.

168   Emerson, mark of the beast: qtd. Whitlock, 126.
168   "One of the greatest soldiers": Ludendorff, 28.
168   "Nobody believed in Belgium's neutrality": *ibid.*, 29.
170   "Hold to the end": Galet, 56.
171   M. Flechet, Burgomaster of Warsage: Hanotaux, III, 84.
171   German proclamations: van der Essen, 52.
172   "Chocolate soldiers": Schryver, qtd. AQ, October, 1922, 157.
173   Belgian Government proclamations: Gibson, 31; Cobb, 90.
173   "Summary executions of priests": Bülow, III, 160. General von Bülow was killed the same day. According to rumor at the time, he committed suicide; according to an investigation conducted by Prince Bülow, he was shot by a *franc-tireur*.

173   Six hostages of Warsage shot: Hanotaux, III, 125.
173   Battice "burnt out . . . gutted": Bloem, 27, 29.
174   "Our advance is certainly brutal": Conrad, IV, 193.
174   Belgian officer's account: qtd. *Times History of the War*, I, 336.
175   "To intimidate the governor": Ludendorff, 41.
176   Ultimatum to Leman to surrender: Schryver, 103.
176   Zeppelin attack: *Weltkrieg*, I, 115.
176   Attempt to kidnap Leman: van der Essen, 62.
176   "Spared not but slew": Martin H. Donohue in NYT, August 10.
177   "Hummed with wild plans": Cammaerts, 147.
177   Woman offers flowers by mistake to German: Bloem, 48.
177   Joffre's refusal to divert troops to Belgium: Poincaré, III, 7.
178   Joffre's letter to King Albert and King's reply: Galet, 83–4.
178   Belgium "defending the independence of Europe": M. Deschanel, qtd. *Times*, August 7. So great was the moral effect of Belgium's resistance that even the Irish Nationalist leader, John Redmond, said there was no sacrifice he would not make on behalf of Belgium, *Times History of the War*, I, 357.
179   "Hurrah in Liège!": Bülow, 22.
179   Kaiser reproaches, then kisses Moltke: Moltke, *Erinnerungen*, 24.
179   Kaiser "despondent": Gerard, 198, 206.
180   German Note of August 9: Gibson, 44.
181   "We were cornered into it": Cammaerts, 20.
181   Berthelot's mission and King's reply: Galet, 93–5.
182   Dubail: Engerand, 456–7.
182   Lanrezac "a veritable lion": Spears, 345. One of Joffre's choices: Joffre, 12, 236.
183   Lanrezac's letter criticizing strategy: AF, I, I, Annexe 19, 59–60; Lanrezac, 54–56; Engerand, 412–15.
183   Joffre ignored it: Joffre, 130–31.
183   Joffre's reply to Ruffey: Briey, April 15, 1919, evidence of Ruffey.
183   "That may be your plan": *ibid.*, also Dubail, 12, and Lanrezac, 60–61.
184   Chauffeur, Georges Bouillot: NYT, September 20, IV, 3.
184–5 Joffre's habits and characteristics: Mayer, 40; Pierrefeu, GQG, 96–99.
185   "*Il m'a toujours fait mousser*": *Gallieni parle*, 69.
186   Bonneau's fears: Dubail, 14–20.
186–7 Entry into Altkirch and parade in Mulhouse: Hanotaux, III, 179, 185–92.
187   "Faulty execution": qtd. Mayer, 35; Joffre, 152, 156.
188   Storks leave Alsace: Poincaré, III, 51.

PAGE
188   "Silently and anonymously" and Joffre's orders to generals not to discuss strategy: Gallieni, *Mémoires*, 172; Corday, 138; Poincaré, III, 92. Messimy, 243–52, gives a heart-rending account of the Government's "anguish" at being kept uninformed by GQG of events at the front and of its persistent efforts to force Joffre out of his "obstinate mutism." Although his exasperation nerved Messimy at one point to inform his liaison officer with GQG that "this intolerable and even ridiculous situation" could not continue, and to appoint André Tardieu as his own representative at GQG, Joffre calmly continued in his "systematic defiance" of the Government and managed to "seduce" Tardieu to his views.

188   Joffre orders generals not to discuss strategy: Gallieni, *Mémoires*, 172; Corday, 138.

188   "That is how history is written": Gallieni, *Carnets*, 33, n. 1.

189   Gallieni worries: *ibid.*, 32, n. 2.

189   French cavalry's advance: Maurice, 30; Spears, 100. The French cavalry's habits were severely disapproved by British cavalrymen. "They never got off," says Major Bridges, 81.

189   Ian Hamilton, Hoffmann and Moltke's "crazy way": qtd. De Weerd, 72.

190   Fournier's report and dismissal: Poincaré, III, 19; Engerand, 422.

190   Lanrezac's anxiety "premature": Joffre, 159.

190   GQG's arguments disposing of German threat: Joffre, 141, 147–8, 150.

190   Col. Adelbert's mission: Galet, 96.

191   Saw themselves in Berlin and German retreat "final": *ibid.*, 100.

191   Siege guns begin bombardment: Schindler, 119; Muhlon, 92; Essen, 77–79; Sutherland, 34, 83, who was in Namur when the same guns shelled those forts ten days later.

192   Demblon describes gun dragged through streets: Demblon, 110–11.

192   Capture of General Leman: Hanotaux, III, 254.

193   "Death would not have me": Cammaerts, 151.

12. *BEF to the Continent*

Unless otherwise noted, facts about the BEF are from Edmonds and all quotations from Sir Henry Wilson and Haig are from their diaries edited by Callwell and Blake respectively.

195   "Brains of canaries": Philip Gibbs, *Now It Can Be Told*.

195   "Frocks" and "Boneheads": Childs, 134.

195   Kitchener scorns plan to "tack on" BEF: qtd. F. Maurice, *Life of General Rawlinson*, 95.

195   "We must be prepared": qtd. Magnus, 284. On Kitchener's views, see also Esher, *Tragedy*, 31, 38–9.

196   Duke of Wellington: qtd. Hurd, *British Fleet*, 29.

196   "Like partridges": qtd. Magnus, 279.

197   "See them damned first": Esher, *Journals*, III, 58.

197   "Tranquilize public feeling": Arthur, 13.

197   "It was never disclosed . . . by some flash of instinct": Grey, II, 69.

198   War with Germany an "eventual certainty": Wilson, 112.

198   "practical grasp of minor tactics": article on French, *DNB*.

199   "French is a trump": qtd. Trevelyan, 198.

199   "I don't think he is clever": to the Duke of Connaught, May 23, 1915, qtd. Nicolson, *George V*, 266.

199   "Mercurial temperament": qtd. Cruttwell, 23.

199   "Heart of a romantic child": Esher, *Tragedy*, 43.

PAGE
200   Proceedings of War Council of August 5: Churchill, 248–55; Haldane, 296; Wilson, 158–9; Blake, 68–9; Esher, *Tragedy*, 24.
201   "As much an enemy as Moltke": qtd. Magnus, 302.
201   Officers' swords sharpened: *Memoirs of Field Marshal Montgomery of Alamein*, New York, 1958, 30.
202   "Best-trained . . . best-equipped": Edmonds, 11.
202   It seemed to an officer that Kluck could hear: Childs, 115.
202   A French witness at Rouen: qtd. Poincaré, III, 31.
202   Thunder and blood-red sunset: Childs, 117.
203   Haig told a fellow officer: Charteris, 11.
203   Sir John French and Callwell visit Intelligence: Callwell, *Dug-Out*, 17.
203–4   Proceedings of War Council of August 12: Huguet, 41–2; Wilson, 162–3; Arthur, *Kitchener*, 22.
204–5   Kitchener's instructions to C. in C.: Edmonds, Appendix 8.
205   "Temptations in wine and women": text in Spears, Appendix XIII.
205   French greetings along the way: Corbett-Smith, 32.
205   "Roses all the way": Bridges, 75.

13. *Sambre et Meuse*

Spears' narrative, Chapters IV through VIII, is the most vivid and valuable in English for the Sambre and Meuse front if its strong anti-Lanrezac bias and other prejudices are skirted and Lanrezac, Engerand, and other French accounts are read to balance it. All French orders cited are in the *Annexes to AF*, I, I.

207   "Thank God we don't have any!": qtd. Monteil, 34; also on the artillery, Dubail, 44; Messimy, 86–87.
207   "Sack" strategy of Rupprecht's Army: Rupprecht, 12, 15.
208   White roses for King Charles: NYT, Obituary of Rupprecht, August 9, 1955.
208   "Barbarians": Dubail, 39.
209   Lanrezac's fears and efforts to shift the Fifth Army to the left: Lanrezac, 67–77.
209   "Maybe even two million": Percin, 105.
209   "What, again!": Lanrezac, 73.
209   "The responsibility is not yours": Pierrefeu, *Plutarque*, 69.
210   "The Germans have nothing ready there": Lanrezac, 78.
210   "Death in my soul": *ibid.*
210   Lanrezac's letter to Joffre on Intelligence report: *ibid.*, 79; Annexe No. 283; Joffre, 159.
210   Gallieni goes to Vitry: Joffre, 158; Messimy, "Comment j'ai nommé Gallieni," *Revue de Paris*, September 15, 1921, 247–61.
211   Joffre agrees to "preliminary arrangements": Annexe No. 270.
211   Special Instruction No. 10: Annexe No. 307.
212   Complicated exchange of troops: Joffre, 164; Engerand, 523–4.
212   Lanrezac suspects a British trick: Spears, 89.
213   "Modern Alexander": Schlieffen's *Cannae*, qtd. Earle, *Modern Strategy*, 194.
214   German wireless garbled and channels clogged: Bauer, 47; Kuhl, qtd. AQ, January, 1921, 346.
214   Von Stein, rude, tactless, Berlin Guards' tone: Sturgkh, 24.
214   Tappen's "odious manner": Bauer, 34.
214   Moltke forbade champagne and Kaiser's meager fare: *ibid.*, 46.
214–15 OHL weighs shift of strategy to left wing: Tappen, 103–4.
215–17 Arguments of Rupprecht and Krafft in favor of attack: Rupprecht, 13–21; these and the following account of events at Sixth Army Hq., visits of Zoll-

ner and Dommes, conversations with them and OHL are from Krafft, 12–22.

217   Greetings to Sir John French and Poincaré's reactions: Guard, 23; Poincaré, III, 51.

218   "Waiting attitude": French, 39.

218   "Choose his own hours for fighting": Poincaré, III, 225.

218   Clausewitz, "the most enterprising": qtd. Poincaré, III, 169.

218   Sir John's visit to Joffre: Joffre, 161; French, 34–5.

219   "*Au fond* they are a low lot": qtd. Magnus, 302.

219   Sir John "favorably impressed": to Kitchener, August 17, French, 39–40.

219   "At last you're here": Huguet, 51.

219–20   Meeting of Sir John French and Lanrezac and the conversation about Huy: Besides the accounts of the two principals which are of little interest, there are four eyewitness reports of this encounter: Wilson's in Callwell, 164; Spears, 72–82; Huguet, 51, and a postwar speech by Captain Fagalde, Intelligence officer of Lanrezac's staff, to the Forum Club, London, qtd. AQ, April, 1925, 35.

220   Misunderstandings about cavalry and date and Lanrezac's report to Joffre: Spears, 80–81; Annexe No. 430.

221   "Please do as I ask you in this matter": French, 40.

221   French and Smith-Dorrien never got on: Bridges, 80.

221   "One of the most unfortunate books": J. W. Fortescue, *Quarterly Review*, October 1919, 363.

221   King Albert's talk with De Broqueville: Galet, 103, 116–19.

221   Germans west of the Meuse a "screen": Galet, 106.

222   "Incredulous dismay": Galet, 122.

222   Col. Adelbert's outburst: Klobukowski, *Résistance belge*; D'Ydyewalle, 109; Galet, 122.

222   Special Instruction No. 13: Annexe No. 430.

223   "Throw them back into the Sambre": Spears, 92.

224   Bethelot to Messimy, "So much the better": Briey, March 28, evidence of Messimy.

224   Commandant Duruy: Spears, 87–8, 94.

224   "They always managed to escape": Kluck, 32.

224   Kluck's cavalry report British at Ostend: Kluck, 18.

225   Kluck's extreme annoyance: Kluck, 22; Bülow, 37.

225   Density figures for German armies: Edmonds, 44.

225   Kluck disputed Bülow's orders: Kluck, 29–30.

225   "Severe and inexorable reprisals": *ibid.*, 25–6.

226   Aerschot, 150 killed: Whitlock, 209; Dinant: Gibson, 326–29. Method of procedure: Gibson, 151; Whitlock, Cobb, *et al.*, see Notes to Chap. 16.

226   Quotations from Hausen: Hausen, 25, 135, 141, 152–3.

227   German proclamations quoted: Whitlock, 70–71; 162.

227   "Slow in remedying the evil": Kluck, 26.

228   Rag doll seemed a symbol: Cobb, 79.

228–9   German entry into Brussels: Gibson, 115; Whitlock, 113, 124–6, 138.

229   A "fierce joy" in Berlin: Blücher, 20.

230   General Pau's farewell: *La France héroïque et ses alliés*, Paris, Larousse, 1916, I, 44. Joffre's speech at Thann: Hinzelen, Emile, *Notre Joffre*, Paris, Delagrave, 1919, 39.

230   Berthelot, "No reason to get excited": Annexe No. 587.

230   "I understand your impatience": Annexe No. 589.

230   "There is reason to await with confidence": Annexe No. 585.

14. *Debacle: Lorraine, Ardennes, Charleroi, Mons*

PAGE

231   "It is a glorious and awful thought": Wilson, 165.

232   Field Regulations and "gymnastics so painfully practised": qtd. Lt.-Col. Fliecx, *Les Quatre Batailles de la France*, Paris, 1958, 12–13.

232   Plan 17's most passionate critic: Engerand, 473.

233   Dubail's "repugnance": Dubail, 57. Battles of Morhange-Sarrebourg: AF, I, I, 176–265, *passim*.

233   Nothing visible but corpses and "God teaches the law to kings": Engerand, 473.

233   "To attack as soon as we are ready": qtd. Edmonds, 507.

233   "We will continue, gentlemen": Giraud, 535.

233   "I went to Nancy on the 21st": Aston, *Foch*, 115.

234   OHL lured by the left wing: Tappen, 15 (German ed.).

234   Case 3 and Krafft's call to Tappen: Rupprecht, 37, n.; Krafft, 47.

235   Joffre's order for attack in Ardennes: Annexes Nos. 592 and 593. Battle of Ardennes: AF, I, I, 351–432, *passim*.

235   "Await artillery support": Annexe No. 352.

238   Ardennes favorable to side lacking heavy artillery: Joffre, 66.

238   Joffre's memoirs: Messimy (88) says they were written by "a group of faithful and devoted officers."

238   "Only ordinary mental calibre": Wile, *Men Around the Kaiser*, 69.

238   "Only by relying on the sword": Grelling, 46.

238   "Gave me theoretical grounding": Crown Prince, *War Experiences*, 3.

239   "*Wilde jagd nach dem Pour le Mérite*": qtd. Goerlitz, 158.

239   "Grave and gloomy faces": Crown Prince, *War Experiences*, 12.

239   *Poète du canon* and "too much imagination": Engerand, 483, 488–9.

239   "*Tout ça c'est du sport*": qtd. Monteil, 34.

240   Fourth Army reconnaissance officer is judged "pessimistic": Engerand, 491.

240   "We who were surprised": Langle, 137.

240   GQG ignored Ruffey's reports: Briey, April 15, evidence of Ruffey.

240   "Might as well have been blindfolded": Commandant A. Grasset, *Un Combat de rencontre, Neufchâteau, 22 Août, 1914*, qtd. AQ, January, 1924, 390.

241   "Battlefield unbelievable spectacle": qtd. Engerand, 499, 504.

241   French sergeant's diary: qtd. W. E. Grey, *With the French Eastern Army*, London, 1915, 49.

241   German officer's diary: Charbonneau, 54.

241   "prodigies of valor" and remainder of paragraph: Crown Prince, *War Experiences*, 26, 29–37.

242   Ruffey loses three divisions: Joffre, 166; Briey, April 15, evidence of Ruffey.

242   "You people at GQG . . . ignorant as an oyster": Briey, *ibid*.

242   Langle's "anguish": Langle, 137. "Serious check at Tintigny": Annexe No. 1098.

243   "Advantage of numerical superiority": Annexe No. 1044.

243   Germany could not have fought without Briey ore: A memorandum addressed to the German Supreme Command by Dr. Reichert of the Iron and Steel Association in December 1917 supported a plea for annexation of Briey with the argument that without the ores of this region "the continuation of the war would have been impossible. If we had not possessed Briey we would have been defeated long ago." *Wirtschaftzeitung der Zentralmaechte*, December 17, 1917, qtd. Engerand, 486. The subject is fully discussed in Engerand's *Rapport* on Briey, *première partie*.

243   "Every effort to renew the offensive": qtd. Isaac, *Joffre at Lanrezac*, 87.

243   "Do as he tells you": qtd. AQ, April, 1923, 37.

243   Telegram from Papa William: Crown Prince, *War Experiences*, 37.

243   "Dazzling white tunic": Sven Hedin, qtd. Gardiner, 223.

244   Iron Cross could only be avoided by suicide: Sturgkh.

244   Joffre orders Lanrezac to attack and BEF to "cooperate": Annexe No. 695. Battle of Charleroi: AF, I, I, 433–480, *passim.*

245   Kitchener's telegram of August 19: Arthur, 29.

246   "Give battle alone": Spears, 127. "I leave you absolute judge": Annexe No. 705.

246   No trenches or fixed defenses: Spears, 105; Engerand, 530–31.

246   "With bugles blowing": Spears, 132.

246   "Long singing scream": Sutherland, 36–9.

247   "There must be a band": Spears, 128.

247   "I know the situation thoroughly": Arthur, 30.

247   "Information . . . exaggerated": Spears, 137, n.

248   Cavalry encounter at Soignies: Bridges, 77.

248   Orders to Smith-Dorrien: Edmonds, preface to Bloem, viii.

249   Kluck intended to "attack and disperse": Kluck, 33.

249   Kluck protests, Bülow insists: Kluck 37–8, 41–2.

249   "No landings of importance": Bülow, 50.

250   Bülow's and Hausen's complaints: Bülow, 58; Hausen, 165–6, 191–3.

250   General Boë: Spears, 144.

250   IIIrd Corps "terrible" losses: Annexe No. 894.

250   2.25 shots per minute: Lanrezac, 135.

251   "Forced to fall back . . . suffered severely" *et seq.*: Annexe No. 876.

251   Lanrezac's request to Sir John French and his reply: Spears, 149–50; Edmonds, 92, n. 2.

251   *"Il plut des marmites"*: Engerand, 537.

252–53   "Prey to extreme anxiety" and all quotations on these pages: Lanrezac, 181, 183–4, 196. General Spears has stated (173) that the retreat of the Fourth Army "was not the reason" for Lanrezac's decision because, according to Spears, Lanrezac did not know of it until next morning, a direct contradiction of Lanrezac's own statement that he had "received confirmation" of it before he made his decision. Writing after Lanrezac was dead, Spears states (173 n.), "There is not the least trace of such a communication." In view of the fact that, as Messimy testified at the Briey hearings, the archives contained 45,000 to 50,000 files of 500 to 1,000 documents each, a probable total of 25 to 30 million pieces, Spears' negative is hardly susceptible of proof. His verdict was conditioned less by the evidence than by his feeling that Lanrezac's retreat "left the British in the lurch" (176).

254   "Thinking himself menaced on his right": Lanrezac, 185; Pierrefeu, *Plutarque*, 74.

255   "Owing to the retreat of the Fifth Army": Edmonds, 68, 72. For the battle of Mons, see also Maurice, 58–76.

255   Smith-Dorrien's orders on bridges: Edmonds, 72, n. 1.

256   "Most perfect targets": Smith-Dorrien, 386.

256   "Stubborn resistance": Edmonds, 77.

256   Efforts to blow the bridges: Hamilton, 28; Edmonds, 86.

257   "You are my sole support" *et seq.*: Bloem, 72–73.

257   Wilson made a "careful calculation" and "persuaded": Wilson, 165.

257   Telegram from Joffre: French, 64; Wilson, 167.

258   Sar-la-Bruyère difficult to find: Smith-Dorrien, 388; and experience of the author in 1959.

258   Wilson blames lack of six divisions: Wilson, 167.

259   "Defense of Havre": Arthur, 36.

PAGE
259   "Over all lay a smell":   qtd. Mark Sullivan, *Our Times*, V, 26.
260–61   Joffre blames executors and all quotations from following three paragraphs:
         Joffre, 178, 181, 183–5, 187.
261   Deuxième Bureau discovery about reserves: Joffre, 187.
261–62   Joffre's postwar testimony: Briey, July 4, evidence of Joffre.
262   Anonymous British spokesman: editor of *Army Quarterly*, April, 1925, 35.
262   Fall of Namur a "distinct disadvantage":   NYT from London, August 26, 1:3.
262   "We must make up our minds":   Poincaré, III, 88.

15. *"The Cossacks Are Coming!"*

Chief sources for military operations in this chapter are Golovin (all references are to his *Campaign of 1914*), Gourko who was with Rennenkampf's Army, Knox who was with Samsonov's Army, Hoffmann and François who were with the Eighth Army, Danilov and Bauer who were at Russian and German Headquarters, respectively, and finally, Ironside who assembled material from both sides. (Hoffmann's two books are referred to in the Notes as *WLO* and *TaT*.)

263   "William to St. Helena!":   Paléologue, 65.
263   Czar, "Our proper objective":   Golovin, 89.
264   "I entreat Your Majesty":   Paléologue, 61.
264   Grand Duke's message to Joffre: Joffre, 140.
264   Grand Duke's tears: The colleague who reported them was General Poliva-
         nov, War Minister in 1915–16, qtd. Florinsky, *Russia*, New York, 1958, II,
         1320.
264   Tears of Messimy and Churchill: Poincaré, III, 3 and Wilson, 163.
265   Russian mobilization orders: Ironside, 39–50.
266   General Reinbot: Gardiner, 132.
266   "Gentlemen, no stealing":   *ibid.*, 133.
266   "Never since the dawn of history":   qtd. Florinsky, *End of the Empire*, 38.
267   Rumors in Frankfort of 30,000 refugees: Bloem, 13.
269   Faulty schedule of war games repeated in war: Golovin, 38–9.
269   Russians used wireless in clear: Danilov, 203; Hoffmann, *TaT*, 265.
269   Characteristic odor of a horse: Julius West, *Soldiers of the Tsar*, London,
         1915, 8.
270   Two German divisions equal to three Russian: McEntee, 90.
270   "Only 25 shells per gun":   Golovin, *Army*, 144.
270   "*Kosaken kommen!*":   Gourko, 33.
270   "Psychological dangers":   Hoffmann, *WLO*, 17.
270   "How to get the Kaiser's ear":   Lt.-Gen. Kabisch, *Streitfragen des Welt-
         krieges*, qtd. AQ, July, 1925, 414.
271   "Japan is going to take advantage":   qtd. Stephen King-Hall, *Western
         Civilization and the Far East*, London, 1924, 160.
272   Prittwitz's orders and François's protest: François, 156; Hoffmann, *WLO*, 17.
272   Scene in the steeple: François, 170–76.
273   Rennenkampf's halt and his reasons: Danilov, 192–3; Golovin, 155.
274   German professor of mathematics: François, 276.
276   Moltke's last words to Prittwitz: François, *Tannenberg, Das Cannae des
         Weltkrieges*, qtd. AQ, January, 1927, 411–13.
276   Prittwitz orders François to retreat to Vistula: François, 190.
276   "You can take your clothes off now":   Knox, 88.
277   "The whole weight of all that is sensuous":   Clausewitz, I, 224.
277   "Lost command of their nerves":   Hoffmann, *WLO*, 20–22.
280   Prittwitz and Hoffmann dispute retreat to Vistula: Hoffman, *TaT*, 248.

PAGE

280   Prittwitz telephones OHL: from Prittwitz's papers, found after his death and published in *Militär Wochenblatt*, April 22 and May 7, 1921, qtd. AQ, October, 1921, 88–92.

280   Moltke aghast and his orders: Bauer, 45.

280–1   Hoffmann proposes maneuver to meet Samsonov: Hoffmann, WLO, 23.

281   "They are not pursuing us at all": Hoffmann, *TaT*, 250.

282   "Impossible—too daring": Lt.-Gen. Kabisch, qtd. AQ, July, 1925, 416.

282   Circumstances of Ludendorff's appointment: Ludendorff, 49–55.

283–4   Circumstances of Hindenburg's appointment: Hindenburg, 100–03; John Wheeler-Bennett, *Wooden Titan*, New York, 1936, 14–16; Ludwig, *Hindenburg*, Philadelphia, 1935, 83.

284   Gardener who worked for Frederick the Great: Hindenburg, 8.

284   Hindenburg and Ludendorff meet: Ludendorff, 55; Hindenburg, 103.

284   Marshall *Was sagst du*: Capt. Henri Carré, *The Real Master of Germany*, qtd. NYT, May 19, 1918.

284   "A very startled expression": Hoffmann, *TaT*, 253.

286   French "insist" upon offensive upon Berlin: Paléologue, 102.

286   "Simple and kindly man": Knox, 60.

286   Horses hitched in double harness: Golovin, 183.

287   Jilinsky's orders and Samsonov's protests: Ironside, 126–9.

287   "A small, gray man," Knox, 62.

287   Martos eats the mayor's dinner: Martos Ms. qtd. Golovin, 188.

287   Further orders of Jilinsky to Samsonov: Ironside, 134–5.

288   VII and XIII Corps did not have the same cipher: Golovin, 171

289   Scholtz "grave but confident": Hoffmann, *TaT*, 261.

289   Intercept of Samsonov's orders: *ibid.*, 265; Ludendorff, 59.

16. *Tannenberg*

290   François refuses to attack without artillery: Hoffmann, 273–5; (all references in this chapter to Hoffmann are to his *Truth About Tannenberg*).

290   "If the order is given": François, 228.

291   Two intercepted Russian messages: Ludendorff, 59; Hoffmann, 265-68. "He kept asking me anxiously": qtd. Nowak, Introduction to Hoffmann's *Diaries*, I, 18. Hoffmann's account of Rennenkampf-Samsonov quarrel, 314; his handing over the messages while cars in motion, 268.

292   Ludendorff's fit of nerves: Ludendorff, 58; Hindenburg, 115, 118; Hoffmann, 282.

293   Tappen's call from OHL: Hoffmann, 315–16. OHL's reasons: Tappen, 16–19, 110–111. President of the Prussian Bundesrat: Ludwig, 456. Director of Krupp: Muhlon, 113. Kaiser deeply affected: François, 51. Moltke quoted: Memorandum of 1913, Ritter, 68–9.

294   Three corps withdrawn from Belgium: Bülow, 64–5; Hansen, 179.

294   "Advance into the heart of Germany": Ironside, 133.

294   "I don't know how the men bear it": *ibid.*, 130.

294   Jilinsky's orders "to meet the enemy retreating from Rennenkampf": *ibid.*, 134.

295   "To see the enemy where he does not exist": Golovin, 205; *Poddavki*: *ibid.*, 217.

295   Samsonov's orders to VIth Corps: Ironside, 155-7.

295   "In God's name": Agourtine, 34.

296   Army chiefs' pessimism quoted by Sazonov: Paléologue, 104.

296   Description of Stavka: Danilov, 44–46.

296   Notes of Rennenkampf's Staff officer: Ironside, 198.

PAGE
297   "May be supposed to be retreating to the Vistula": *ibid.*, 200.
297   Blagovestchensky "lost his head": *ibid.*, 157.
300   Samsonov and Potovsky see retreat at first hand: Knox, 68–9; "Terribly exhausted": Ironside, 176.
300   Samsonov's orders to General Artomonov: *ibid.*, 164.
300–01 Battle of Usdau: Ludendorff, 62–3; Hoffmann, 285–89.
301   Report that François' Corps beaten: Ludendorff, 62.
301   Jilinsky's order, "by moving your left flank": Ironside, 207.
302   Ludendorff begs François to "render greatest possible service": Hoffmann, 305.
302   Ludendorff "far from satisfied": Ludendorff, 64.
302   Mackensen's messenger receives "far from friendly welcome": Hoffmann, 310.
303   "He took with him to his grave": Golovin, 254.
303   Samsonov's farewell to Knox: Knox, 73–4.
304   "You alone will save us": Martos Ms., qtd. Golovin, 263.
304   Martos' and Kliouev's corps starving: Kliouev, 245; Knox, 80.
305   Capture of Martos and meeting with Hindenburg and Ludendorff: Martos Ms., qtd. Golovin, 294, 327.
305   "The Czar trusted me" and Samsonov's death: Potovsky Ms., qtd. Golovin, 301; Knox, 82, 88.
306   Prisoners and casualties: François, 243–45.
306   General von Morgen at Neidenberg: François, 240.
307   "I will hear their cries": Blücher, 37.
307   Marshes a myth: Ludendorff, 68; François (245) also calls it a "legend."
307   "One of the great victories": Hoffmann, *Diaries*, I, 41. Naming the battle Tannenberg: Hoffman, 312; Ludendorff, 68. "Strain on my nerves": *ibid.*
307   Ludendorff would go personally to inquire for intercepts: Dupont, 9.
307   "We had an ally": Hoffmann, *Diaries*, I, 41. Tappen (108) also acknowledges that the detailed knowledge of Russian movements obtained from the intercepts "greatly facilitated" German command decisions in East Prussia.
308   "This is where the Field Marshall slept": qtd. De Weerd, 80. Hoffmann remained on the Eastern Front throughout the war, eventually succeeding Ludendorff as Chief of Staff on that front and conducting the German side of the negotiations at Brest-Litovsk. He appears as General Wilhelm Clauss, the central character of Arnold Zweig's novel *The Crowning of a King*, N.Y., 1938.
308   Disgrace of Rennenkampf and Jilinsky: Gurko, 83; Golovin, 386.
308   "Firm conviction that the war was lost": Golovin, *Army*, 24.
309   Ministers' Memorandum urging peace: Richard Charques, *The Twilight of Imperial Russia*, New York, 1959, 216.
309   "We are happy to have made such sacrifices": Knox, 90; Paléologue, 106.

17. *The Flames of Louvain*

310–13 The quotations on these pages, with three exceptions, are taken from the books by the persons quoted, listed under Sources, as follows: Verhaeren, *Dedicace*, unpaged; Cobb, 176–7; Bethmann-Hollweg, 95; Shaw, 37; Bridges, 73; Bergson (Chevalier), 24; McKenna, 158; Clausewitz, I, 5. The statement by Thomas Mann is from his "Reflections of a Nonpolitical Man," 1917, qtd. Hans Kohn, *The Mind of Germany*, New York, 1960, 253–5. H. G. Wells is quoted from NYT, August 5, 3:1. "I'm a'goin' to fight the bloody Belgiums" is from Peel, 21.
314   Placards signed by Bülow: facsimile in Gibson, 324.

PAGE

314   Massacre at Andenne, Seilles, Tamines: Apart from Belgian sources, the most complete firsthand record of these events is that of the American Minister, Mr. Whitlock, in his chapters xxx, "Dinant"; xxxi, "Namur, Andenne and Elsewhere"; xxxii, "Tamines"; and xxxiii, "*Man Hat Gechossen.*" For estimated total of civilians shot in August, see *Encyc. Brit.*, 14th ed., article "Belgium."

314   10 hostages from each street in Namur: Sutherland, 45.

315   Bloem on hostages: 34.

315   Cobb watched from a window: 104.

315   Visé: NYT from Maestricht, August 25, 2:2; Whitlock, 198.

316   Hausen on Dinant: 167–70. 612 dead: Gibson, 329. For description of Dinant after the destruction, Cobb, 409–10.

317–18 Quotations on these pages are from the works of the persons cited, as follows: Wetterlé, 231; Kluck, 29; Ludendorff, 37; Crown Prince, *War Experiences,* 41–2, 50; Bloem, 28, 32, 20, Blücher, 16, 26.

317   Goethe: qtd. Arnold Zweig, *Crowning of a King,* N.Y., 1938, 306.

318   "That's the French for you": Cobb, 269.

319   Riderless horse sets off panic at Louvain: Whitlock, 152.

319   Luttwitz, "A dreadful thing has occurred": *ibid.*

320   Richard Harding Davis: qtd. Mark Sullivan, *Our Times,* V, 29; Arno Dosch in *World's Work,* Oct. and Nov., 1914.

320   Gibson at Louvain: 154–172.

320   Monseigneur de Becker: Whitlock, 160.

321   *Rotterdam Courant* and other papers quoted: NYT, August 30.

321   German Foreign Office quoted: *ibid.,* August 31.

321   King Albert quoted: Poincaré, III, 166.

321   *Kriegsbrauch* quoted: 52.

321   Belgium "supreme issue": Wile, *Assault,* 115. "Precipitant": Mark Sullivan, *loc. cit.*

322   Erzberger quoted: 23.

322   Kaiser's telegram: NYT, Sept. 11.

322   Manifesto of the 93 intellectuals: text in *Literary Digest,* Oct. 24, 1914.

322   Bethmann's reply to Wilson: NYT, September 18, 1:4.

323   "No convictions but only appetites": Wetterlé, 144.

323   Bethmann on Erzberger's bright ideas: Bülow, III, 235.

323   Erzberger's Memorandum: Among others to whom Erzberger sent it was Grand Admiral von Tirpitz, who published it after the war in his *Politische Dokumente,* Hamburg, 1926, III, 68–73. See also Karl Epstein, *Matthias Erzberger,* Princeton, 1959, chap. v.

324   "Largest human fact since the French Revolution": Frank H. Simonds in "1914—the End of an Era," *New Republic,* Jan. 2, 1915.

18. Blue Water, Blockade, and the Great Neutral

Sources used for this chapter only:

Baker, Ray Stannard, *Woodrow Wilson, Life and Letters,* Vol. V, N.Y., Doubleday, Doran, 1935

Consett, Rear-Admiral Montagu, *The Triumph of the Unarmed Forces, 1914–18,* London, Williams and Norgate, 1923

Guichard, Lieut. Louis, *The Naval Blockade, 1914–18,* tr. N.Y., Appleton, 1930

House, Edward M., *The Intimate Papers,* ed. Charles Seymour, Vol. I, Boston, Houghton Mifflin, 1926

Page, Walter Hines, *Life and Letters,* Vol. I, ed. Burton J. Hendrick, London, Heinemann, 1923

Parmelee, Maurice, *Blockade and Sea Power*, N.Y., Crowell, 1924
Puleston, Captain William (USN), *High Command in the World War*, N.Y., Scribner's, 1934
Salter, J. A., *Allied Shipping Control*, Oxford U.P., 1921
Siney, Marion C., *The Allied Blockade of Germany*, 1914–16, Univ. of Michigan Press, 1957
Spring-Rice, Sir Cecil, *Letters and Friendships*, ed. Stephen Gwynn, Boston, Houghton Mifflin, 1929.

PAGE
325   "Luxury Fleet": Churchill, 103.
325   Invasion "impracticable": Fisher, *Letters*, II, 504. Report of the "Invasion Committee" of the CID in 1912: Churchill, 158.
325   "Interruption of our trade": qtd. Custance, 104. Trade and tonnage figures: Fayle, 6, 15.
326   "Whole principle of naval fighting": Fisher, *Memories*, 197.
326   "Germany's future is on the water": Kurenberg, 129.
326   Navy League slogans: Wile, *Men Around the Kaiser*, 145–6.
327   "Extreme psychological tension" *et seq.*: Churchill, 276.
327   Jellicoe opened telegram marked "Secret": *DNB*, Jellicoe.
327   Jellicoe "to be Nelson": Fisher, *Letters*, II, 416; III, 33.
327   "Greatest anxiety confronting me": Jellicoe, 92. His chaps. IV and V; "Declaration of War" and "Submarine and Mine Menace in the North Sea" describe this anxiety feelingly on every page.
328   "Infected area": Corbett, 79.
328   "Could have been a seal": *ibid.*, 67.
328   "Markedly superior": Churchill, 261.
328   "Strongest incentives to action": *ibid.*, 276.
328   "Extraordinary silence": *ibid.*, 278.
329   "Kept secret even from me": Tirpitz, II, 87.
329   *Golden Age* on Kaiser's bed-table: Peter Green, *Kenneth Grahame*, N.Y., 1959, 291.
329   Kaiser read Mahan: Kurenberg, 126.
330   "Bring the English to their senses" *et seq.*: Ludwig, 423.
330   Navy Law of 1900 quoted: Hurd, *German Fleet*, 183–4.
330   Kaiser's "darlings": Bülow, I, 198.
330   Tirpitz's squeaky voice: Wetterlé, 218. Müller's characteristics: Ludwig, 465.
331   Ingenohl took a "defensive view": Tirpitz, II, 91. "I need no Chief": Ludwig, 466.
331   "I have ordered a defensive attitude": Ludwig, 465.
332   Tirpitz's request for control, reason for not resigning, and "My position is dreadful": Tirpitz, II, 118–20, 219–20, 223.
332   "Passage of the Atlantic is safe": Corbett, 54.
333   London Conference, Mahan, Declaration: Halévy, 223; Puleston, 130; Siney, 11; Salter, 98–99.
334   U.S. requested adherence and British reply: Secretary Bryan to Ambassador Page, *U.S. For. Rel.*, 1914, 215–16, 218–20.
334   CID proposed continuous voyage be "rigorously applied": Siney, 12.
334   Order in Council of August 20: *ibid.*, ff.; Parmelee, 37; Guichard, 17.
335   Spring-Rice quoted: *U.S. For Rel.*, 1914, 234.
335   "All sorts of odds and ends": Asquith, II, 33.
335   "Don't bother me with economics": qtd. L. Farago, ed. *Axis Grand Strategy*, N.Y., 1942, 499.
336   "To secure the maximum blockade": Grey, II, 103.
337   America "stands ready to help" and "permanent glory": Baker, 2–3.

PAGE

337   "Neutral in fact" and further quotations in this paragraph: *ibid.*, 18, 24-5, 73.

337   U.S. trade figures: Arthur S. Link, *American Epoch*, N.Y., 1955, 177. Foot-note on hidden trade: Consett, *passim*, and figures in *Encyc. Brit.*, 14th ed., article "Blockade."

338   "A government can be neutral": Page, 361.

338   Wilson to Grey: Baker, 55-6.

338   "Utter condemnation": *ibid.*, 62; "Felt deeply the destruction of Louvain": House, 293; "In the most solemn way": Spring-Rice, 223.

339   "This outrage upon humanity": *Lansing Papers*, I, 29-30.

339   "I am afraid something will happen": Baker, 74.

340   "Enthusiasm of the first fight": Tirpitz, II, 91. "Awkward embarrassments": Churchill, 331-35.

340   Kaiser's orders after the battle: Tirpitz, II, 93. What Tirpitz wrote after-ward: to Admiral von Pohl, Sept. 16 and Oct. 1, Tirpitz, II, 95-7.

19. Retreat

342   General Order No. 2: AF, I, II, 21; Joffre, 189-90.

343   A night of "anguish and horror": Libermann, 37-50.

344-45 "We left Blombay" and further incidents of French retreat quoted from soldiers' diaries: Hanotaux, V, 221-22; VII, 212, 268; VIII, 76-8.

345   "Corporals, not commanders": Tanant.

345   "Sorry to go without a fight": Hanotaux, VIII, 76.

346-53 Ministers in "consternation" and "panic": Poincaré, III, 92; Messimy, 364. Events and discussions in Paris during August 25-27 and all direct quotations, unless otherwise noted, are from the following sources: Poincaré, III, 89-99 and 118; Gallieni's *Mémoires*, 20-21, supplemented by his *Carnets*, 17-22, 39-46, Hirschauer, 59-63, and above all from Messimy's helpfully outspoken if confusingly arranged *Souvenirs*, Part Three, Chap. IV, "Nomination de Gallieni comme Gouverneur Militaire de Paris," 206-228; Chap. V, "Le Gouvernement et le G.Q.G.," 229-265 and the last part of Chap. VII, "Le Ministère de la Guerre en Août 1914," the paragraphs entitled, "La panique parlementaire," "la journée du 25 Août" and "la journée du 26 Août," pp. 364-375.

348   "Growing soldiers": Hanotaux, IX, 41. "Le tourisme": Monteil, 37.

350   "You are the master": qtd. Renouvin, 83.

352   Joffre detects "menace of government interference": Joffre, 193.

355   "All the tricks of the trade" *et seq.*: qtd. Edmonds, 115.

355   Robertson's food dumps and German reaction: Spears, 221.

355   Lanrezac's "headlong" retreat and report to Kitchener: French, 84; Arthur, 38.

355   Incident at Landrecies: Maurice, 101-02; Hamilton, 52-3; "Without the slightest warning": Edmonds, 134.

356   "Send help . . . very critical": Edmonds, 135.

356   Murray's faint: Childs, 124; MacReady, 206; Wilson, 169.

356   Haig's loan of £2,000: Blake, 37.

356-57 Allenby's warning and decision to fight at Le Cateau: Smith-Dorrien, 400-01.

357   Wilson on telephone to Smith-Dorrien: *ibid.*, 405; Wilson, 168-9.

357   Kluck orders pursuit of "beaten enemy": qtd. Edmonds, 169-70.

357   "Strong French forces": *ibid.*, 211.

358   "Brave front of these Territorials": Smith-Dorrien, 409.

358   Battle of Le Cateau: Edmonds' account, which occupies three chapters

484 Notes to Chapter 19

PAGE

and sixty pages, 152–211, has all the relevant information but is too detailed to give a very clear impression. Smith-Dorrien, 400–410, Hamilton, 59–79, and Maurice, 113–14, are more readable. Casualties: Edmonds, 238.

359 "Lord French and staff lost their heads": J. W. Fortescue, *Quarterly Review*, Oct. 1919, 356.

359 Haig offers help to Ist Corps: Edmonds, 291, n. 2.

359 Huguet's telegram: Joffre, 197.

359 Sir John French in his nightshirt: Smith-Dorrien, 411.

359 "Saving of the left wing": *ibid.*, 412.

360 Conference at St. Quentin: Joffre, 195–97; Lanrezac, 209; Huguet, 67; Spears, 233–37.

361 Kluck and Bülow report enemy beaten: Bülow, 64.

361 OHL communiqué: qtd. Edmonds, 204.

361 Friction between German commanders: Bülow, 68–9, 78; Kluck, 51, 63.

361–62 Hausen's lodgings and complaints: 182, 197–99, 204–5, 215.

362 Kluck's troops slept along roadside: Briey, evidence of Messimy, March 28.

362 Kaiser's telegram: Kluck, 75.

362 "In the hope of celebrating Sedan": qtd. Maurice, 126–7.

362 Kluck proposes "wheel inwards": Kluck, 76.

362 "Sense of victory": Crown Prince, *War Experiences*, 59. OHL General Order of August 28: qtd. Edmonds, 235.

364 OHL deliberations and "an end to the war": Tappen, 105.

364 Battle of the Mortagne: Giraud, 538; AF, I, II, 305 ff.

365 General de Maud'huy: Hanotaux, VI, 274.

365 "Courage and tenacity": Joffre, 203.

365 De Langle's battle on the Meuse: De Langle, 20–21, 139; AF, I, II, 184–201.

365 Formation of the Foch Detachment: Foch, 41–47.

368 "I have the heads of three generals": Percin, 131.

368 Joffre confessed to sleepless nights: Mayer, 194.

368 61st and 62nd divisions lost: Joffre, 209, 212; Spears, 270, n.

368 Huguet reports BEF "beaten and incapable": Joffre, 203–4.

368 "Almost insane": Spears, 256.

369 Schneider and Alexandre: Lanrezac, 218–19; Spears, 256–7.

369 Lanrezac called Joffre a sapper: Mayer, 176.

369 "I suffered an anxiety": Lanrezac, 282.

370 Joffre's rage at Marle: Lanrezac, 225–6; Joffre, 207.

370 Order to Pétain at Verdun: qtd. Pierrefeu, GQG, 132.

371 Order to "throw overboard ammunition": text, Edmonds, Appendix 17; Wilson's version: Spears, 254; Gough tore it up: Charteris, 21; Smith-Dorrien countermanded it: Smith-Dorrien, 416–17; "Very damping effect": *ibid.*

371 Toy whistle and drum: Bridges, 87–8.

371 Sir John French on Kaiser: Arthur, 37, 43. On Kitchener's refusal: *ibid.*, 39.

372 Ostend operation: Corbett, 99–100, Churchill, 334–35. Asquith in his diary for August 26 (II, 28–9) records a discussion with Kitchener, Churchill, and Grey about "an idea of Hankey's" (Sir Maurice Hankey, Secretary of the CID) to send 3,000 marines to Ostend which would "please the Belgians and annoy and harass the Germans who would certainly take it to be the pioneer of a larger force." Winston was "full of ardour" about the plan. It was conceived in response to the shock of the news from Mons and the Allied debacle which Churchill received at 7:00 A.M. on August 24 when Kitchener appeared in his bedroom looking "distorted and discolored" as if his face "had been punched with a fist." Saying "Bad

news" in a hoarse voice, he handed Churchill Sir John French's telegram
reporting the debacle and ending with the ominous proposal to defend
Havre. It was hoped by the Ostend operation to draw back some of Kluck's
forces to the coast, a move in which it only partially succeeded; but German
nervousness about this threat, combined with rumors of Russian landings,
contributed to the German decision to retreat at the Marne.

372   "To the sea, to the sea": MacReady, 206.

20. *The Front Is Paris*

373   Sheep in the Place de la Concorde: Guard, 17.
374   Gallieni's plans for defense of Paris: *Carnets*, 46; *Gallieni parle*, 36–42;
Hirschauer, 59–63, 93–4, 101, 129. "Byzantine" arguments: *ibid.*, 176.
374   Paris included in Zone of Armies: *AF*, I, II, 585.
375   Gallieni's 15-minute Council of Defense: Hirschauer, 98–99.
375   Work on the defenses, bridges, barricades, taxis, etc.: Gallieni, *Mémoires*,
33–36 and *Gallieni parle*, 52; Hirschauer, *passim*.
375   Reappearance of Dreyfus: Paléologue, *Intimate Journal of the Dreyfus
Case*, 309.
376   "Nomeny is thus destroyed": qtd. Poincaré, III, 108.
376   Haig's offer to Lanrezac and Sir John French's refusal: Lanrezac, 229–31;
Spears, 264–67. "Terrible, unpardonable" things: *ibid.*, 266. "C'est une
félonie!": qtd. Lyon, Laurence, *The Pomp of Power*, N.Y., 1922, 37,
n. 22.
377   Joffre at Laon superintends Lanrezac: Joffre, 212; Lanrezac, 239. Battle
of St. Quentin-Guise: AG, I, II, 67–81.
377   Fears Sir John "might be getting out": Joffre, 213. Conference at Compiègne: *ibid.*, 214; Edmonds, 241.
378   "Definite and prolonged retreat": Edmonds, 241. Maurice quoted, 129;
Hamilton quoted, 82–3; MacReady quoted, 105. "Another ten days": Edmonds, 245, Joffre, 217.
379   Wilson sees Joffre at Rheims: Huguet, 75; Wilson, 172.
379–80 Battle of St. Quentin; French sergeant's account: Sergeant André Vienot,
qtd. Hanotaux, VIII, 111–12; Bülow "felt confident": Bülow, 85; captured
French orders: McEntee, 65. Lanrezac showed "greatest quickness and
comprehension": Spears, 276; Germans were "running away": *ibid.*, 279;
Lanrezac-Belin conversation: Lanrezac, 241; Spears, 281–2.
381   "No longer nourish any hope": Joffre, 217.
381   "Most tragic in all French history": Engerand, Briey, *Rapport*. Clausewitz
quoted: III, 89. "Wonderful calm": Foch, 42. What Joffre said to Alexandre: Demazes, 65.
382   Preparations to leave Vitry: Joffre, 217. "Broken hopes": Muller, 27.
382   Bülow's mixed report: qtd. Edmonds, 251, n. 4; Kühl, qtd. AQ, April, 1927,
157.
382   Defense of Paris not Joffre's intention: According to a lecture given at the
Sorbonne in 1927 by Commandant Demazes, a member of Joffre's staff and his
biographer, qtd. Messimy, 264.
383   M. Touron: Poincaré, III, 111–12.
383–84 Cabinet discussions about leaving Paris, visit of Col. Penelon, Joffre's advice,
his talk with Gallieni on telephone, Gallieni's talk with Poincaré, Millerand,
Doumergue, and Gallieni's advice to Cabinet: Poincaré, III, 115–122; Joffre,
122; Gallieni, *Mémoires*, 37–39; *Carnets*, 48–49.
385   Guesde's outburst: interview with Briand, *Revue de Paris*, Oct. 1, 1930, qtd.
Carnets, 128, n. 1.

PAGE

385   Threat to dismiss Joffre: *ibid.* The phrase used by Briand was, "*de lui fendre l'oreille.*"

385   Ministers "incapable of firm resolve": Gallieni, *Carnets,* 49.

385   Taube raids: Poincaré, III, 120; Gallieni, *Mémoires,* 40, and *Carnets,* 50; Gibbons, 159. Text of the German proclamation: AF, I, II, Annexe No. 1634.

386   German report of Tannenberg and reports of 32 troop trains: Joffre, 222.

386   "You have given proof of *cran*": Hanotaux, VII, 250.

387   Joffre finds De Langle calm, Ruffey nervous: Joffre, 216, 221. Col. Tanant quoted: 22; Ruffey's conversation with Joffre: Engerand, *Bataille,* xv.

387–8   Amiens dispatch: *The History of the Times,* New York, Macmillan, 1952, IV, Part 1, 222–27. "Patriotic reticence": in Parliament, August 31, qtd. *Times,* Sept. 1, p. 10. "Liberation of the world": Corbett-Smith, 237.

389–90   The Russian phantoms: D. C. Somervell, *Reign of George* V, London, 1935, 106, 117–18, and R. H. Gretton, *A Modern History of the English People,* 1880–1922, New York, 1930, 924–25, contain many of the stories current at the time. Other references in MacDonagh, 24, Gardiner, 99, Carton de Wiart, 226. Stories told by returning Americans: NYT, Sept. 4, (front page), 5 and 6. Sir Stuart Coats' letter: NYT, Sept. 20, II, 6:3.

390   Operation Order to BEF: Edmonds, Appendix 20.

390   Sir John French's letter to Kitchener: Arthur, 46–7.

390–91   Kitchener's consternation and telegram to French: *ibid.,* 50; Edmonds, 249.

391   Cabinet "perturbed": Asquith, II, 30. "You will conform": Arthur, 51–52. Robertson's letter: to Lord Stamfordham, June 23, 1915, Nicolson, *George* V, 266. This was at a time when Sir John French was supplying Northcliffe with information for a campaign to blame Kitchener for the munitions shortage. King George went to France to talk to army commanders whom he found, as he wrote to Stamfordham, Oct. 25, 1915, to have "entirely lost confidence" in Sir John French and who assured him the feeling "was universal that he must go." *ibid.,* 267.

391   Kitchener never regained confidence: Magnus, 292. Birkenhead quoted: 29.

392   Joffre tells Poincaré he has hope, "earnestly" requests BEF to hold, Poincaré exerts influence, Sir John French—"I refused": Joffre, 223; Poincaré, III, 121–22; Edmonds, 249; French, 97.

392   Sir John French's reply to Kitchener: Arthur, 52–4. "A travesty of the facts": Asquith qtd. in *Living Age,* July 12, 1919, 67.

393   Kitchener considered himself entitled to give orders to French: Blake, 34.

393   Kitchener confers at Downing St., wakes Grey: Arthur, 54; Asquith, II, 30.

393   "Irritated, violent": Huguet, 84.

393   Sir John French resents Kitchener's uniform: French, 101. Kitchener wore it customarily: Esher, *Tragedy,* 66; Magnus, 281–2.

393   "Wearing stars in khaki" and "Nice little man in his bath": Sir Frederick Ponsonby, *Recollections of Three Reigns,* New York, 1952, 443–4.

393   Meeting at Embassy: Huguet, 84; French, 101–02.

394   Kitchener's telegram to Government and copy to French: Edmonds, 264. One of these medals, found by a French infantry officer in the captured luggage of a German staff officer at the Marne, is now in the possession of the author through the courtesy of the nephew of the finder.

21. Von Kluck's Turn

395   M. Fabre describes von Kluck: Hanotaux, VIII, 158.

396   Kluck's reasons for turn to southeast: Kluck, 77, 82–84.

396   Moltke uneasy: Bauer, 52.

396   Schlieffen, "A victory on the battlefield": qtd. Hanotaux, VII, 197.

396   "He has a shout-Hurrah! mood": Moltke, *Erinnerungen,* 382.

PAGE

397   Rumors in Luxembourg of Ostend landings and of Russians: Tappen, 115.
397   Moltke worries about gaps in right wing: Tappen, 106.
397   Bauer's visit to Rupprecht's front: Bauer, 53 ff.; Rupprecht, 77–79.
398   Kluck's estimate of enemy strength: Kluck, 91; captured British letter: Edmonds, 244.
399   Bülow's request: Kluck, 83; Kluck's order of August 31 for forced march: Bloem, 112; Moltke's approval of inward wheel: Kluck, 83–4; Hausen, 195.
400   Cavalry "always halted": Crown Prince, *War Experiences*, 64.
400   "Much needed" rest and British got away "just in time": Kluck, 90.
400   "Our men are done up": qtd. Maurice, 150–51. General Maurice adds (152) that after the Battle of the Marne when the Germans were in retreat to the Aisne, "Whole parties of officers were captured because they were too intoxicated to move."
401   Latrines dug in Poincaré's burial plot: Poincaré, III, 204.
401   Mayor of Senlis and six others shot: *ibid.*; Gallieni, *Mémoires*, 120. Names on the memorial stone were copied by the author on the site.
401   Hausen's happy night: Hausen, 208–10.
401   Moltke's General Order of Sept. 2: Kluck, 94.
402   Kluck orders advance across Marne: Kluck, 100.
402   Captain Lepic's report: AF, I, II, Annexe No. 1772.
402   Sixth Army to "cover Paris": *ibid.*, Annexe No. 1783; Joffre, 225.
402   Sixth Army *"ne veulent pas marcher"*: Gallieni, *Mémoires*, 52.
402   Col. Pont, "It seems no longer possible": Joffre, 218–19.
403   Discussion of new plan at GQG with Belin and Berthelot: *ibid.*, 230–33.
403   General Order No. 4: AF, I, II, Annexe No. 1792.
404   "The battle of Brienne-le-Château": Messimy, 379.
404   Joffre's call to Millerand, "urgent and essential": Poincaré, III, 126; Joffre, 232.
404   Gallieni's call to Joffre: Gallieni, *Carnets*, 53.
404–05   Maunoury put under Gallieni and Paris put under Joffre: Because these events were taking place at a time of great tension and also because of later efforts during the quarrel over credit for the Marne, to obscure the question of who was under whose orders, this issue is still not entirely clear. The relevant sources are Joffre, 226, 234–5, 239–42; Gallieni, *Mémoires*, 43, and *Carnets*, 53; Joffre's request to have Paris put under his command is Annexe No. 1785; the order putting Maunoury under Gallieni is Annexe No. 1806; Millerand's order complying with Joffre's request is Annexe No. 1958.
405   Composition of the Army of Paris: AF, I, II, 772–4. The 55th and 56th Reserve Divisions who were now to fight for the capital had been withdrawn from Lorraine on August 25, causing General Ruffey, whose flank they were supporting in a counteroffensive in the Briey basin, to break off action. Briey, as Ruffey said in his postwar testimony, was thus "the ransom of Paris." Fighting as a reserve officer with one of these divisions, the 55th, Charles Péguy was killed on September 7.
405   Gallieni visits Ebener and Maunoury: *Mémoires*, 42, 48–9.
405   Millerand reports "heart-breaking" facts; decision of Government to leave: Poincaré, III, 125–27.
406   Gallieni and Prefect of Police: *Mémoires*, 51–52; "preferred to be without ministers": *Parle*, 38; "Made all my dispositions": *Mémoires*, 57.
406   Captain Fagalde's find: Spears, 331–32; his report: AF, I, II, Annexe No 1848.
408   Joffre still urges Government to leave: Poincaré, III, 131.
408   "Hateful moment had come": *ibid.*, 134.
408   Herrick's visit and his plans: *ibid.*, 131; Mott, 155–7, 160–63; *Carnets*, 61
409   Gallieni's farewell to Millerand: *Mémoires*, 59–64; *Parle*, 49.
409   Proclamations of Government and Gallieni: Hanotaux, IX, 39; *Carnets*, 55.

PAGE

410   Puns and parody of "Marseillaise": Marcellin, 41.
410   "Days of anguish": Hirschauer, 142.
410   Fifth Army desertions and executions: Lanrezac, 254–56.
411   "I never would have believed": qtd. Edmonds, 283; Germans are "over-
       hasty": Huguet, 70.
411   Joffre's secret instructions of Sept. 2: AF, I, II, 829 and Annexes Nos. 1967
       and 1993. Order for reinforcements to be taken from Ist and IInd Armies is
       Annexe No. 1975.
411   Gallieni believes it "divorced from reality": *Mémoires*, 79; *Parle*, 50.
412   Moves to Lycée Victor-Duruy: *Mémoires*, 60–61.
412   Lieutenant Watteau's report: Pierrefeu, *Plutarque*, 102–3.
412   "They offer us their flank!": Hirschauer, 180.

22. *"Gentlemen, We Will Fight on the Marne"*

413   Gallieni decides instantly to attack: *Mémoires*, 95–96; Clergerie, 6–7.
413   "One of those long conferences": Clergerie, 127.
414   Sixth Army of "mediocre value"; "calm and resolution" of people of Paris:
       Mémoires, 75, 76.
414   "Forty kilometers!": qtd. Hanotaux, VIII, 222; German prisoners taken
       asleep: Briey, March 28, evidence of Messimy; "tomorrow or the day after":
       qtd. Maurice, 152.
415   "The General fears nothing from Paris": *ibid.*, 153.
415   Kluck's insubordinate letter to OHL of Sept. 4: Kluck, 102.
415   Bülow furious at "echelon in advance": Bülow, 103.
415   "We can do no more": qtd. Hanotaux, VIII, 223; "No cooked food":
       ibid., 276; "Broiling heat": *ibid.*, 279.
415   "Decisively beaten" and "utterly disorganized": Kuhl, 29; Kluck, 102.
416   Joffre plans offensive "within a few days": Annexe No. 2152.
416   "Blew the winds of defeat": Muller, 80.
416   Lanrezac's "physical and moral depression" and further comments: Joffre,
       236–7.
416   "A church outside which": Grouard, 114. As Hausen acknowledged: in
       Revue Militaire Suisse, Nov. 11, 1919, qtd. Engerand, *Bataille*, xxi.
417   Joffre's dismissals in first five weeks: Allard, 15.
417   The meeting with Franchet d'Esperey on the road: Grasset, 44; Joffre, 237.
418   The meeting with Lanrezac at Sezanne: Lanrezac, 276–7; Joffre, 237-8;
       Muller, 104–5; Spears, 377–78. In his lively account Spears says the conver-
       sation between the two generals took place outdoors as they walked "up and
       down the courtyard whilst I watched with fascinated interest." Although this
       obliging arrangement allowed Spears to write as an eyewitness, it does not fit
       with the probabilities, for Joffre would hardly have chosen to conduct what
       was to him the most distressing operation of the war so far, in full view of
       spectators. In fact he did not. "Lanrezac was in his office. I went in there
       and remained alone with him," he says specifically.
418   Franchet d'Esperey: Grasset, *passim*; Spears, 398.
418   "March or drop dead": Grasset, 45. The phrase he used was *"Marcher ou
       crever."*
419   Sept. 4, a sense of climax: *Gallieni Parle*, 53; Blücher, 23; in Brussels people
       felt a chill: Gibson, 191.
419   Kaiser, "It is the 35th day": Helfferich, *Der Weltkrieg*, Berlin, 1919, Vol. II,
       279.
419   French "have offered us an armistice": qtd. Hanotaux, VIII, 279.
419   General Kuhl's doubts: Kuhl, 19.

PAGE

419   "We are advancing triumphantly everywhere": Crown Prince, *War Experiences*, 69.

420   Moltke to Helfferich: Helfferich, *op. cit.*, 17–18.

420   Reports reach OHL of French troop movements: Tappen, 115.

420   "An attack from Paris": *ibid.*

420   Moltke's order of Sept. 4: full text, Edmonds, 290–91.

421   Falkenhayn quoted: from Zwehl's life of Falkenhayn, qtd. AQ, April, 1926, 148.

421   Gallieni's order to Maunoury of Sept. 4: *Mémoires*, 112.

421   "Immediate and energetic decision": *ibid.*, 107.

421   Gallieni tells Poincaré there is a "good opening": The fact of this call was disclosed by Poincaré after the war in an interview with *Le Matin*, Sept. 6, 1920.

421   The real battle "fought on the telephone": *Gallieni Parle*, 53.

422   Joffre's aversion to telephone: Muller. "I have always disliked using the telephone myself," Joffre, 250.

422   Clergerie's conversation with Col. Pont: *Mémoires*, 119; Joffre, 245.

422   Discussions at GQG: Muller, 85–6; Joffre, 243–4; Mayer, 41.

423   Joffre under the weeping ash: Muller, 87.

424   Joffre's messages to Franchet d'Esperey and Foch: *ibid.*, 91–2; AF, I, II, Annexe No. 2327.

424   Gallieni's visit to British Hq.: *Mémoires*, 121–4; *Parle*, 55; Clergerie, 16.

425   Franchet d'Esperey's meeting with Wilson: Grasset, 51–53; Spears, 400–01; Wilson, 174.

428   Joffre at dinner with the Japanese: Joffre, 249.

428   Franchet d'Esperey's reply: full text in Edmonds, 279.

428   General Hache's protest: Grasset, 74.

429   "Intelligent audacity" and Foch's reply: Joffre, 250.

429   Murray's orders "simply heartbreaking": Wilson, 174.

429   "Marshal not yet returned": Gallieni, *Mémoires*, 128.

429   Sir John French decides to "re-study the situation": Joffre, 252.

430   Gallieni's conversation with Joffre: *Mémoires*, 130; Joffre agreed "unwillingly" and "as Gallieni desired": Joffre, 251.

430   General Order No. 6: AF, I, II, Annexe No. 2332.

430   Joffre receives Huguet's message: Joffre, 252.

431   Kluck assumes Germans "everywhere advancing victoriously": Kluck, 106. "Regain freedom of maneuver": *ibid.*

431   Col. Hentsch's visit to Kluck's Hq.: Kluck, 107; report of Commander of IVth Reserve: *ibid.*, 108; Kuhl, "Neither OHL nor the First Army": qtd. Edmonds, 292, n. 2.

432   Gallieni replied "Nowhere": *Gallieni Parle*, 57, n. 1. His orders for destruction: AF, I, II, Annexe No. 2494; "A void": Hirschauer, 228.

433   "Gallieni having attacked prematurely": *Gallieni Parle*, 64; "That is worth gold": *Carnets*, 78, n. 3. (To the present author it seems unnecessary to ascribe all credit for the Marne either to Gallieni as, for example, Captain Liddell-Hart does in *Reputations Ten Years After*, at the cost of making Joffre out a fool, or to Joffre as General Spears does at the cost of making Gallieni out a liar. As Poincaré said long ago, there was credit enough for both.)

433   Joffre's uncertainty "altogether agonizing": Joffre, 252; his telegram to Millerand: AF, I, II, Annexe No. 2468.

433   Wilson transmits Order No. 6 to Sir John French: Wilson, 174. Huguet, de Galbert and British "lukewarm": Joffre, 253; Mayor of Melun: Hirschauer, 179.

433   "At any price": Joffre, 252.

PAGE

433–34   The meeting at Melun: Joffre, 254; Muller, 106; Wilson, 174; Spears, 415–18. The phrase "Threw his heart on the table" is Muller's, as is the description of Huguet which reads in the original, *"qui semble, à son habitude, porter le diable en terre."* (Unfamiliar to most French friends queried, this phrase was variously translated for me as meaning that Huguet looked satanic, bored, or gloomy. I have adopted the last as proposed by the only person who seemed certain.)

    Spears, in his vivid and dramatic account of the meeting, performs another historical sleight of hand. Unwilling to give the reader an impression of British reluctance to fight, he claims that Joffre made the trip to Melun—a six-to-seven-hour round trip by car just before the crucial battle—in order to "thank" Sir John French for his cooperation. Inexplicably, Spears then quotes Joffre as saying, "with an appeal so intense as to be irresistible, *'Monsieur le Maréchal, c'est la France qui vous supplie.'"* This does not sound compatible with thanks.

434   "Gentlemen, we will fight on the Marne":   Poincaré, III, 136.
434   Order to the troops for Sept. 6:   AF, I, II, Annexe No. 2641.

Afterward

436   Foch's order: Aston, *Foch*, 124.
436   Joan of Arc won the battle: Bergson said this on several occasions; Chevalier, 25, 135, 191, 249.
436   Moltke to his wife: *Erinnerungen*, 385–6.
436   Kluck's explanation: Interview given to a Swedish journalist in 1918, qtd. Hanotaux, IX, 103.
436   Col. Dupont's tribute to the Russians: Danilov, *Grand Duke*, 57; Dupont, 2.
437   Numerical superiority: In five Armies present at the Marne, the Germans had about 900,000 men in 44 infantry and 7 cavalry divisions. In six armies the Allies had about 1,082,000 men in 56 infantry and 9 cavalry divisions. AF, I, III, 17–19.
438   "If we had not had him in 1914":   Aston, *Foch*, 125.
438   The taxis: Clergerie, 134–45; *Gallieni parle*, 56.
439   Footnote: experience of André Varagnac from private information; casualty figures from AF, I, II, 825; AQ, October 1927, 58–63; Samuel Dumas and K. D. Vedel-Petersen, *Losses of Life Caused by War*, Oxford, 1923, Chap. 1.
440   "All the great words cancelled":   in *Lady Chatterley*.

Index